SOLANO COMMUNITY COLLEGE

3 7045 00010 4499

D0121808

SOLANO COLLEGE
100 Whitney Avenue
Vallejo, California 94590

HOUGHTON MIFFLIN COMPANY
EDITORIAL ADVISORY COMMITTEE
IN EDUCATION

Herold C. Hunt, *Harvard University*

C. Gilbert Wrenn, *Arizona State University*

Van Cleve Morris, *University of Illinois at Chicago Circle*

Samuel A. Kirk, *University of Illinois*

William Van Til, *New York University*

Paul R. Hanna, *Stanford University*

THE DISADVANTAGED CHILD

Issues and Innovations

EDITED BY

Joe L. Frost, *University of Texas*

Glenn R. Hawkes, *University of California, Davis*

HOUGHTON MIFFLIN COMPANY · BOSTON

New York · Atlanta · Geneva, Ill.
Dallas · Palo Alto

COPYRIGHT © 1966

by Joe L. Frost and Glenn R. Hawkes

All rights reserved. The selections in this book are used by permission of and special arrangement with the proprietors of their respective copyrights.

PRINTED IN THE U.S.A.

9/18/68
Houghton + 9.57 1.18 Bernt mund 12/30/18

LC
4091
F7
28929

WE DEDICATE this book
to the children of the poor
in the hope that it will
in some small measure help
to alter their destiny
in the schools.

✧ CONTENTS

Poverty, delinquency, unemployment, illiteracy, school dropouts, and the necessity for public assistance are not new to American society. What is new is the vigorous national effort to abolish these social pathologies. Especially since 1963, the Congress has launched attacks on many of these social ills in the form of legislation and financial assistance to educational agencies. The profusion of bills that have been passed include the Elementary and Secondary Education Act of 1965, the Civil Rights Act of 1964, the National Defense Education Act of 1964, the Economic Opportunity Act of 1964, the Vocational Education Act of 1963, the Mental Retardation Facilities Act of 1963, and many others.

In 1966, more than three billion dollars will flow from the federal treasury through the U.S. Office of Education to schools, colleges, teachers, students, libraries, and librarians. Over a billion dollars more will be allotted through the Office of Economic Opportunity for what has been termed the War on Poverty — the Job Corps, work training, Volunteer Services (VISTA), community action programs, and Headstart.

One may ask, why is such great emphasis being put on anti-poverty programs at this particular time, when the problems caused by poverty have been with us for so long? There are three main answers to this question:

1. In the first place, the problem of social inequities is not an easy one to solve. For centuries it has been recognized but no solution found. Plato postulated changes. The Russian Revolution was fought to abolish social inequities. Even our own American Revolution sought to remove inequalities in society. But it is not easy to equate varying goals and values — to retain individual rights and group demands, to provide both political freedom and economic freedom, and at the same time to meet the diverse needs of various groups and individuals.

2. The increased urbanization and mechanization of our life today are putting a strain on our traditional American concepts of the individual rights and dignity of man. The proximity of living is greater today than ever before. Overpopulation and the ever-increasing preference of Americans to live in large cities or in the suburbs of large cities rather than in small villages and towns have brought people closer together, where the irritation of contiguous living often creates disintegration and incoherent behavior.

Automation has intensified some of our social problems. It is an example of the uneven progress made by our society. As progress is made in one area, other areas become disjointed, and new ways must be found to rectify the evils which are sometimes a natural consequence of progress. Thus society seems to go two steps ahead and one step backward.

In the face of these difficulties — or perhaps because of them — we are renewing our efforts to find a solution to the problems of delinquency, destitution, unemployment, and illiteracy.

3. We are becoming more and more aware of an ominous schism within our American society. The rich are getting richer and the poor are getting poorer. Unfortunately, some of our programs are promoting the schism. For example, the poorer neighborhoods in urban society usually have the poorer schools. Inexperienced teachers must often serve an apprenticeship there, then ask for a transfer to a "better" neighborhood if they show they are good teachers. Yet the areas having high rates of unemployment, delinquency, and public assistance are the areas where good schools and experienced, effective personnel are most needed. Similarly, children from these areas need preschool experiences most because their out-of-school experiences are limited. Yet traditionally nursery schools have been available only to economically advantaged children, since they are privately operated on a tuition basis.

The present trend toward giving the most to those whose need is the least threatens to broaden the gap between two subcultures of our society, and if it continues, one-half or two-thirds of our population will soon be supporting the other half or third through public assistance or in institutions.

One method of attacking the social ills poverty causes is to establish rehabilitation programs for adults — and this is being attempted through basic education programs for illiterate adults, job training for the unemployed, and programs to combat delinquency. But from a long-term point of view prevention is a sounder approach, and the prescription for prevention is undoubtedly education — and specifically early childhood education. This means the initiation of preschool educational programs for disadvantaged children aged three, four, and five. The Headstart program and the forthcoming program of support under the Elementary and Secondary Education Act of 1965 represent an effort in this direction. These programs are aimed at providing children from what we have termed "disadvantaged" homes with a cultural model which will counteract their disorganized home life and the model of dependency which would otherwise be their social inheritance.

Great emphasis has also been placed on improving schools in the economically underdeveloped and disadvantaged areas of our urban communities. This does not mean that other schools should not also be developed to their fullest. It is not a question of sharing poverty but one of sharing wealth. It is a swing of the pendulum in the direction of the most crying need — an attempt to compensate for the mistakes of the past and to provide a transitional period which can lead to better education for *all* children.

In time, as our society becomes more committed to the improvement of the education of the disadvantaged, the need for rehabilitating adults may diminish because these new adults will have grown up through schools which are better equipped and have teachers who are more supportive and capable of providing the knowledge and skills needed to develop greater personal satisfaction and economic self-sufficiency. This should promote less disruptive home lives for the following generation.

The initial coagulation of this societal commitment has caught many schools and communities off guard. Community programs for two-, three-, and four-year-olds were virtually nonexistent. Teachers were not available. Space was not available. Curricula were not available. With the introduction of the Headstart programs a sudden shift was necessary, and measures of expediency, though admirably reflecting society's new commitment, often left much lacking in the way of quality. It became necessary to recruit and train a large group of teachers. Short-course training programs were developed throughout the country. Literature on the subject was new and scattered throughout many journals and periodicals. Duplicated materials, when available, were eagerly sought.

In *The Disadvantaged Child* we have for the first time an organized compilation of representative literature relating to the characteristics and education of children from disadvantaged or culturally deprived homes. These articles have been gathered from many sources and carefully analyzed. The teacher, the teacher-educator, the school administrator, and others will find here between the covers of one book the best current thinking on this topic.

Samuel A. Kirk

✧ PREFACE

More than a million children starting to school each fall are disadvantaged — victims of too little, too late. The impoverishment of their lives is so severe that failure is a natural consequence. For those caught up in this most vicious of cycles, compensatory education is desperately needed to preclude tragedy. For it is tragic when even one child is denied the opportunity to make maximum use of his potential.

If we are to break this cycle and achieve the lofty and heady aims of a democratic society, the educational processes within our affluent society must be reorganized. Although this is a task that obviously cannot be accomplished quickly or easily, we have at least made a beginning. Curricula are undergoing careful examination and experimental programs are being developed. The year 1965 saw the inception of "Operation Headstart," a nationwide program of community involvement in the preschool education of disadvantaged children. This widespread public involvement offers hope for sustained support in the future.

This book of readings is offered to provide a needed reference for a wide segment of the population. It should help teachers, students, and other interested citizens to understand what is involved in the creation of a desirable environment for disadvantaged children and to discover ways in which they can help to foster healthy and beneficial programs for these young people. We have tried to bring together the best literature on the subject from a variety of sources. Both research reports and opinion articles are included to aid the reader in his development of sound educational programs and practices. We have not hesitated to include controversial material, for it is through controversy that many wise decisions are made. And it is through exploration on the frontiers of knowledge that significant innovations come into being. We have also included an extensive bibliography to aid the reader who wishes to pursue the subject in greater detail.

We wish to acknowledge the excellent cooperation of the authors and publishers who have so graciously allowed us to include their works in this volume. We also wish to thank our many students who have contributed suggestions for the selection of articles. And finally, our warmest thanks to Betty Frost and Barbara Pahre for their help in the preparation of the material. They were always there when needed.

Joe L. Frost
Glenn R. Hawkes

THE DISADVANTAGED CHILD

Issues and Innovations

✧ INTRODUCTION

The Disadvantaged Child

OVERVIEW AND RECOMMENDATIONS

Numerous labels are commonly used to identify the children of the poor: culturally deprived, low socioeconomic group, economically restricted, and disadvantaged. In an educational context, "disadvantaged" refers to children with a particular set of educationally associated problems arising from and residing extensively within the culture of the poor. This is not to say that other cultural groups within society escape similar problems, but that the ills restricting the intellectual, social, and physical growth of children tend to be concentrated here. We may change the name but the problems remain, passing from generation to generation and sustained by discrimination, lack of opportunity, and an exploding population.

The Problem of Poverty

The problem of poverty is universal, existing in every geographical area of this country. The poor are concentrated in the slums of cities, certain rural areas, migrant labor camps, and Indian reservations.

CHILDREN OF THE SLUMS. Within the doughnut shaped arena encircling the central complex of major cities reside the slum dwellers. Many are newcomers, fleeing from the frustrations of life in the deep South and Appalachia to the bewilderment of the city slum, searching for elusive advantages which never come to pass. Tomorrow, they say, they will return to the farm; history says they are here to stay. "Some are attempting to build their second or third set of hopes; to others, time has taught the futility of dreams, aspirations, and initiative." (32)

The retreat of whites from the decaying inner cities to the suburbs has reached alarming proportions. The annual exodus from New York numbers fifty thousand; from Chicago, fifteen thousand; and from Cleveland, three thousand. (20) While the middle-class white is fleeing, the Negro continues to move into the cities. Negro population density in major Northern cities is four times that of whites. (34) Almost half of the country's 18,871,831 Negroes now live outside the original Confederate states.

In 1950, approximately one child in ten residing in our largest cities was disadvantaged. This ratio is now about one in three, and by 1970, one-half of the children residing in large cities will be disadvantaged unless the cur-

1

rently developing programs of compensatory education are successful. (25) A school principal in a west-side Chicago slum area recently told a group of Iowa State University students, "We have 5,000 school-age children in this sixteen-square-block area; every conceivable human misery and ill exists here."

The effects of crowded living forced by poverty, ignorance, and discrimination create a society of chronic dependence. One study showed that 6 per cent of the families in St. Paul, Minnesota, absorbed more than half of the community's welfare services. (29) Other metropolitan areas have reported similar conditions. Obviously, the monetary consequences of poverty are more costly than the cure. The cost in human potentiality is infinite.

THE RURAL POOR. The disadvantaged rural children are concentrated in the Appalachian Mountains, where several thousand one- or two-room schools are still in operation and pot-bellied stoves and outdoor privies are standard pieces of equipment. There is little in Appalachia to attract and hold well-trained teachers who may earn less than three thousand dollars annually or who may suffer personal injustices merely for backing the wrong faction in an election. "When a grade-school teacher recently asked her pupils what they wanted to do when they grew up, several answered, 'to get on the welfare.' " Of those who started first grade in Perry County, Kentucky, in 1948, about 12 per cent graduated in 1960. (28)

MIGRANT CHILDREN. "Each year 150,000 children move with their parents across the croplands of the country, harvesting as they go. They are burdened by poverty and disease, deprived of education and legislation which could alleviate their condition. These are the migrants — rejected by communities and unwelcomed in schools. Temporary residence status makes them ineligible for public assistance and other legal benefits. Many are illiterate; most are educationally retarded. With an annual income of about $800 per family, migrants are among the poorest people in America.

"Child labor and school attendance laws are inadequate and often ignored as children (at times as young as four years of age) work in the fields beside their parents. Deprived of cultural experiences which contribute much to success in schools, these children are frequently destined for failure in school and become misfits in adult living. Thus the vicious cycle proliferates." (12)

INDIAN CHILDREN. The Indians comprise less than 2 per cent of the American poor, yet they illustrate the effects of rapid change and the increasing obsolescence of the uneducated. Impoverishment is characteristic of the half million Indians in the United States. For example, the per capita income of the Papagos of Arizona "is $440 a year, one-fifth that of the average American, and they suffer from disease and dietary deficiency." (1)

Contrary to general belief, the Indian population is growing rapidly. By 1975 there may be 750,000 or three quarters of a million Indians. "Ten thousand teachers with no special training are teaching the Indians who need to be taught by persons understanding the Indian value system." (5)

The Consequences of Poverty

Four common consequences of impoverished living are school dropout, delinquency, mental retardation, and educational retardation.

THE SCHOOL DROPOUT. The disadvantaged child is more likely than other children to drop out of school. Nationwide statistics show that for sixteen-year-old boys, one of three whose family income is under three thousand dollars and whose parents failed to complete high school, has dropped out of school. Only one of seventeen boys whose parents were high-school graduates with incomes of seven thousand dollars or more has dropped out.

THE DELINQUENT. The majority (85 per cent) of our delinquent population (those violating legal norms) comes from the lower class. The search for thrill and stimulation is a major concern of the lower-class child, particularly the slum child. Feats of toughness and endurance are constant conversation pieces in street-corner society. The street-corner boy will say, "Man, I ain't been home or ain't slept for two nights. I've been on the prowl." Or, "They grilled me and beat me with a hose but I didn't admit nothin'." Or, "My old man and me had one helluva fight. Man, he beat me up good." (21)

THE MENTALLY RETARDED. Many disadvantaged children are placed in special classes for the mentally retarded. Most of these children suffer no apparent neurological defects but rather are mentally restricted by the impoverishment of their educational and cultural experiences.

A study by Wakefield (35) has revealed that a large proportion of the educable mentally retarded children in the public schools come from families of low intelligence, poor schooling, and inferior economic status, and concluded that a very large population of retarded individuals *might* owe their retardation to environmental factors.

In an investigation of the effect of stimulation on mentally retarded children by Skeels (30), thirteen mentally retarded children (experimental group) were transferred at an early age to an institution which provided a personal relationship with adult mentally retarded women. Later, eleven of these children were transferred to adoptive homes. A control group of twelve children, initially at a higher level of intelligence, remained in a relatively unstimulating environment for a prolonged period. In the initial study the children in the experimental group showed a decided increase in rate of mental growth, while the control group showed progressive mental retardation.

In a follow-up study conducted after the children had reached adulthood, all subjects in the experimental group were found to be self-supporting, and none was a ward of any institution. Eleven of the thirteen were married, and nine had children. The median grade in school completed was the twelfth, and one girl who had an initial I.Q. of 35 had graduated from high school and taken one semester of college work. Of the twelve children in the control group, one died in adolescence following continued residence in a state institution for the mentally retarded, and four were still wards of institutions — one in a mental hospital and three in institutions for the mentally retarded. Only two of the group had married, and one of these was divorced. Two of the four females were sterilized in late adolescence. The cost to the state for this group had totaled about $100,000. The median school grade completed was the third.

As this study and others show, environmental stimulation in a variety of forms ranging from mothering to playing with manipulative play materials is essential for development during the pre-school years.

THE EDUCATIONALLY RETARDED. Upon entry to school the disadvantaged child is retarded in the skills prerequisite to successful school achievement. The ordinary school environment fails to compensate for this initial retardation, resulting in cumulative deficiencies through time. (9, 10, 11) A study comparing the effects of an enriched elementary-school environment, individualized instruction, child-study by teachers, special services, provision for food and health, and home involvement resulted in significant differences in achievement (reading, language, and arithmetic), personality test scores, and mental maturity in favor of the enriched program. Although the direction of growth in these areas showed positive acceleration across grade levels, none of the disadvantaged children reached the national norm in any measured area. (9)

The results of this study and other similar studies suggest that curricular adjustment for disadvantaged children after they have entered the public schools helps but does not compensate for environmental restriction in infancy and early childhood.

The Effects of Early Deprivation

EVIDENCE FROM ANIMAL RESEARCH. Sensory deprivation in animals in infancy appears to produce striking modifications in adult behavior.

Animal research into problems closely paralleling those of cultural deprivation in humans was conducted by Melzack and Scott (22), who studied dogs reared in isolation from birth. Confined in small cages with no objects to explore and no chance to acquire pain expectancies, the dogs were unable to learn to avoid pain when released at maturity. The results of a similar study by Melzack and Thompson (23) showed that dogs reared in isolation were unable to acquire normal social interactions when released at maturity.

In another study, Riesen (24) compared chimpanzees reared in darkness with a normal control group. The normal animals quickly learned to avoid objects associated with a painful electric shock, while the animals reared in darkness required many weeks of repetition of cues before becoming capable of utilizing the visual cue to avoid pain.

Thompson and Heron (33) investigated the effects of modifications of the environment on later problem-solving ability in dogs. Twenty-six Scottish terrier puppies were selected from several litters. Half were given an opportunity for enriched learning experiences by being placed in homes as pets. The remaining animals were subjected to varying degrees of isolation from the time of weaning to eighteen months of age. Following this period, the performance of the home-reared animals was markedly superior on fifteen of eighteen problem-solving tasks.

EVIDENCE FROM STUDIES WITH HUMANS. Bugelski (4), Hebb (15), and Hunt (18) have reported numerous studies which support the theory of perception as learned behavior, which is in direct opposition to the widely held Gestalt theory of perception as innate and structurally determined. Here we have the ever-present controversy regarding the relative importance of heredity and environment in structuring the individual. A clear answer to this controversy has been given by Byron Hughes:

> No evidence indicates heredity to be more important than nurture and environment; emphatically, no evidence indicates it to be less important. It is a major intellectual blunder . . . to minimize the significance of the one to demonstrate the importance of the other. Heredity and nurture always operate together; one without the other is devoid of meaning. When we talk about heredity we imply nurture to be present to maintain it. When one or the other is absent there is no life. Each has implications for the other, and these implications are as varied and as numerous as are the variations in nurture and in heredity. Education is a form of nurture and is provided by the environment in which a person lives. Heredity comes from parentage. (16)

Ethical considerations preclude rigorously controlled studies of sensory deprivation in children, and, of course, children are never totally deprived of sensory experiences in actual living. Society, however, has ruthlessly provided observable deprivation in its own way. Poverty, war, and parental neglect have supplied cases on every hand. (31)

Goldfarb (13) compared two groups of adolescents. The children in one group had been placed in institutions as infants, while those in the other had been institutionalized much later. The early-institutionalized group showed marked symptoms of emotional deprivation; they were relatively apathetic and immature during the adolescent years. It appears likely that once attitudes are firmly established, later experiences will have little effect toward their alteration.

In a Teheran orphanage, where changes in on-going stimulation were minimal, 60 per cent of the two-year-olds could not sit alone and 85 per cent of the four-year-olds could not walk alone. This dramatizes the great effect preverbal experiences can have on even the rate of locomotor development. (6)

Changing Theories of Intellectual Development

Hunt has asserted, with extensive supporting evidence (17, 19), that the concepts of fixed intelligence and predetermined intelligence are no longer tenable. Psychologists have attempted to explain learning in terms of stimulus-response bonds, using the telephone as a mechanical model of the brain's operation. Thus they have envisioned the brain as a static switchboard through which each stimulus could be connected with a variety of responses, which in turn could become the stimuli for still other responses.

But some kind of active process goes on between the ears. The programming of electronic computers clarifies the general nature of the requirements for solving logical problems. Three major components of these requirements have been described: (1) memories or information coded and stored, (2) operations of a logical sort which can act upon the memories; and (3) hierarchically arranged programs of these operations for various purposes.

A likely place for the brain's equivalents of such components lies within the intrinsic portions of the cerebrum which have no direct connections with either the incoming fibers from the receptors of experience or the outgoing fibers to the muscles and glands. The intrinsic portion of the brain is very small in animals; consequently the belief in predetermined development has appeared tenable. The increasing proportion of the intrinsic portion of the brain in higher animals suggests an anatomic basis for the increased emphasis on the role of infantile experience in development.

Experience may be regarded as programming the intrinsic portions of the cerebrum for learning and problem-solving, and intellectual capacity at any given time may be thought of as a function of the nature and quality of the programming. (17, 19) Consequently, the I.Q. score may vary as much as 20 to 40 points as a result of environmental stimulation or lack of environmental stimulation.

Hunt (18) views intelligence as a ". . . problem-solving capacity based on hierarchical organization of symbolic representations and information processing strategies derived to a considerable degree from past experiences." This concept has emerged from several sources, including Jean Piaget's observations on the development of children, which show what these concepts of vertically ordered information-processing operations and a continuous interaction between the child and his environment mean in terms of human development.

Piaget has observed that children pass through four general periods of development from birth to adulthood: the Sensorimotor Period (birth to two years), the Preconceptual Period (ages two to seven) including the phase of Intuitive Thought (ages four to seven), the Period of Concrete Operations (ages seven to eleven), and the period of Formal Operations (ages eleven to fifteen).

The age ranges are approximate for children in our culture. Ages at which the various periods are reached varies markedly from child to child and from culture to culture, but the sequence of development is invariant.

Piaget sees constant interaction between the child and his environment as a part of the developmental process. The mechanism whereby the child passes through the developmental periods includes organization and adaptation or, in Piaget's terms, assimilation and accomodation.

Assimilation is the incorporation of objects into the child's patterns of behavior, the changing of the signals the child receives from his environment to fit the structure he already has. . . . Accommodation is the modification of existing ways of doing things to new variations in environment and the changing of mental structure to fit the signals received from the environment. (27)

Thus there exists a continuous reorganization of the structures of the mind contingent upon continuous creative interaction between the child and his environment. Early stimulating experiences are crucial.

From observations of Piaget's work come a number of principles relevant to the educative process. First, the persistence of action sequences which form a cognitive structure (schemata) for the child depends upon opportunity for use. Second, there is continuous development through use and stimulation. Third, accomodation by the child depends upon a proper match between existing mental structure (schemata) and objects encountered. Fourth, the greater the variety of situations to which the child must accomodate his behavioral structures, the more differentiated and mobile they become, the more rapid is his rate of intellectual development, and the greater is his range of interest in new ideas and experiences. Fifth, gradual change occurs in mental structures as a result of the continuous interaction of the child and his environment. Finally, the rate of development appears to be the result of a variety of stimulations during infancy and early childhood. (18)

Work with disadvantaged children indicates that a restrictive environment leads to the learning of responses that are foreign to the expectations of the school. The disadvantaged are frequently lagging behind their peers in the attainment of tasks characteristic of a particular age-range and seem too bound to immediate perceptions and needs to deal effectively with complex relationships and long-range goals. The additional factors of fear and anxiety, rooted in the culture of the home and then reinforced by inappropriate school expectations, prevent the attainment of a more mature level of cognitive development.

Summary

The major points of the above presentation are as follows: (1) The problem of poverty is universal. (2) Children of the poor suffer numerous cultural disadvantages which affect their intellectual development and impose serious social consequences. (3) The disadvantaged child is retarded before his entry into school. (4) An enriched environment can positively affect achievement. (5) The pre-school years are critical periods for development. (6) Early sensory stimulation appears essential for adequate programming of the brain. (7) Lack of early environmental stimulation results in retardation of cognitive, locomotor, and social development. (8) The child moves through an invariant sequence of development at a highly variant rate. (9) Intellectual development and, consequently, school progress are dependent upon the developmental level of the child and upon the attainment of a proper match between objects in and expectations arising from the environment. The development of intelligent behavior is cumulative. Early experiences of a stimulating nature lay the groundwork for school achievement. When these early experiences are lacking the child can be expected to develop a pattern of failure which is reinforced with the passage of time.

Implications for the Educative Process

We do not know nearly as much as we need to know about coordinating methods, materials, and the developmental levels of children, and we are highly insecure about the role of the teacher in intervention. We do know that most middle-class children learn amazingly well in some schools that are generally recognized as mediocre. And we know that a high degree of retardation in achievement is often found among the gifted, although most people are not aware of this fact, since the gifted regularly score well above average on tests of achievement. Conversely, the disadvantaged child experiences failure from the start. If his I.Q. isn't low enough in the first or second grade for special classroom placement the chances are good that it will be by the time he reaches the fourth grade. For the disadvantaged child, only the best we have to offer — teachers, programs, and services — can significantly alter the course of failure.

Many of our current educational practices reflect a greater concern for what is taught than for the process of learning. Similarly, many schools are organized as though it would be easier for the child to change his needs than for the school to modify its demands. This is evidenced by a strict adherence to grade-level standards without regard for individual differences, the assignment of instructional material without consideration for the child's level of development, a failure to recognize and provide for the basic needs of disadvantaged children, the use of instructional materials inconsistent with the child's ability, and an enforced estrangement between the school and the parents of the poor.

The schools should initiate active programs of compensatory education for disadvantaged children, consistent with current knowledge from various disciplines, with the expectation that these programs will come closer to meeting the needs of *all* children than do existing programs. In situations in which citizens have been aroused, programs have been developed which clearly demonstrate that something *can* be done.

Such programs include the following points:

1. As much time should be allowed for the active study of children as is now allowed for curricular study in workshops and inservice programs. Such study should emphasize techniques for evaluation of the child's social, emotional, physical, and intellectual development, with subsequent practical implementation in the classroom. Evidence of levels of development, achievement motivation, experiental background, and special strengths and weaknesses, compiled from careful observation of the child in varied situations should be used in assessment. Teaching should then proceed on the basis of *diagnosis* of individual and group needs.

2. The basic needs of food, clothing, health, and affection must be satisfied if school experiences are to have real meaning. If these needs are not met by the family, they must be met by the school in ways that allow the child to preserve his dignity. We know enough about human behavior to be very sure that schools can do little, if anything, until these needs are attended to.

Attention to these needs will probably make as much difference in educational achievement as any curricular revision we are likely to make. This has been recognized by administrators of the federal government's "Operation Headstart." At the inception of this program, Washington estimated that of the 560,000 children involved during the summer of 1965, 110,000 would be found to need glasses, 50,000 would be found to be partially deaf, 75,000 would need basic shots, and 25,000 would be suffering from severe malnutrition.(7)[1] Yet these children represent only a limited age group and a small proportion of the children in need. The schools must provide supplementary health services, food, and compassionate teachers for *all* disadvantaged children.

3. No recommendation has greater support from research and the professions than that for the provision of preschool programs as an antidote for cultural restriction. The need is clearly established, the machinery is in operation, and it is to be hoped that universal, public preschool education will soon be reality. It will be some time before optimum age ranges for maximum educational compensation are clearly defined. The optimum age to preclude the effects of a disadvantaged environment is probably younger than we are now willing to accept.

4. The pupil-teacher ratio must be reduced. It is inconsistent with our current knowledge of children and the learning process to assume that one teacher can satisfactorily meet the needs of twenty-five to thirty children. Furthermore, the classroom teacher cannot actively and creatively provide intellectual stimulation for so large a group.

5. The teaching staff should be provided with special inservice training. Teachers should be selected for qualities of excellence, including a desire and enthusiasm for working with disadvantaged children.

6. The classroom organization should support many experiences which will provide children with opportunities for success in school, however insignificant these experiences may seem to be. Fear of failure should be eliminated. A true nongraded structure and individualized teaching will allow a close match between the materials of instruction and the variations in children's abilities to learn.

7. Materials of instruction should include many reading materials, including easy-to-read books. The construction of stories using the language of children can provide valuable reading materials for children with restricted vocabularies, including those who use expressive language not

---

[1] These predictions proved to be amazingly accurate, according to Sargent Shriver's report to President Johnson of August 31, 1965, following the termination of the 1965 summer Headstart program.

commonly found in books. Printed literature may be rephrased into the words of the disadvantaged child. An eleven-year-old slum child paraphrased the Twenty-Third Psalm in this fashion:

> The Lord is like my probation officer.
> He will help me.
> He tries to help me make it every day.
> He makes me play it cool. (2)

Materials should also be developed which appeal to the physical orientations of boys. Because of the effeminate content of many basal readers, some boys give up any aspirations they may have for literacy in order to preserve their masculinity.

8. The schools should fully utilize available equipment. For example, school buses should be used for frequent trips designed to facilitate language and conceptual development.

9. The schools must involve parents who know little about fostering their children's aspirations. These parents must be involved with the school in ways that will help them develop an understanding of the importance of education so they can provide support and reinforcement for the learning tasks of the school. They deserve and have the right to expect involvement. Effective school programs should strengthen family life. The child cannot reconcile differences between the home and school world if the divergence is great.

Gearing the school program to the problems and needs of disadvantaged children means shifting from narrow emphases to a divergent view of the educative process, soliciting the services of workers from many disciplines, applying the operations of science to the study of learning problems, and finally, placing increased emphasis upon *teaching as an art*.

Rich, stimulating living in the school can provide the "long pull" for those deprived of the "headstart" ordinarily gained in the home or in nursery schools and kindergartens. The contributions of enriched living inherent in an effective program of compensatory education, though comparatively small, can make the difference between dropout and retention, illiteracy and lifelong habits of reading, delinquency and positive social contributions, and institutional and family living. Americans are assured the right to equal educational opportunity. The school has promises to keep.

REFERENCES

1. Bagdikian, Ben H. *In the Midst of Plenty: A New Report on the Poor in America.* New York: The New American Library, 1964.

2. Burke, Rev. Carl F. "Rephrasing Makes Bible Meaningful to Children from Urban Slums," *Today's Child,* May, 1965.

3. Bloom, Benjamin S., and others. *Compensatory Education for Cultural Deprivation.* New York: Holt, Rinehart & Winston, Inc., 1965.

4. Bugelski, B. R. *The Psychology of Learning.* New York: Henry Holt & Co., Inc., 1965.

5. Clark, Erma. "A Nursery School on the Ute Indian Reservation," *Childhood Education*, 40:407–410; April, 1965.

6. Dennis, W. "Causes of Retardation Among Institutional Children," *Journal of Genetic Psychology*, 96:47–59; 1960.

7. "Fast Start for Head Start," *Time*, July 2, 1965.

8. Frost, Joe L. "Disadvantaged Children and Early Childhood Education," *Child Development: Focus on Home Economics*, 1:5–6, Iowa State University, Ames, Iowa, January, 1965.

9. ————. "School Environment and Disadvantaged Children," *Collected Papers* of the Inter-Institutional Seminar in Child Development, The Edison Institute, June, 1965.

10. ————. "Welfare Recipiency Status and School Achievement of Rural Elementary School Children," *Association for Research in Growth Relationships Journal*, 6:13–22; November, 1964.

11. ————, and King, O. Ray. "Educating Disadvantaged Children," *Arkansas Education Association Journal*, 37:6, 28; September, 1964.

12. ————. "School and the Migrant Child," *Childhood Education*, 41:129–132; November, 1964.

13. Goldfarb, W. "The Effects of Early Institutional Care on Adolescent Personality," *Journal of Experimental Education*, 12:106–129; 1953.

14. Hebb, D. O. "The Effects of Early Experience on Problem-Solving at Maturity," *American Psychologist*, 2:306–307; 1947.

15. ————. *The Organization of Behavior*. New York: John Wiley & Sons, Inc., 1949.

16. Hughes, Bryon O. "Implications of Heredity for Education," University of Michigan School of Education *Bulletin*, 18:41–44; 1946.

17. Hunt, J. McV. "How Children Develop Intellectually," *Children*, 11:83–91; May, 1964.

18. ————. *Intelligence and Experience*. New York: The Ronald Press Company, 1961.

19. ————. "The Psychological Basis for Using Preschool Enrichment as an Antidote for Cultural Deprivation," Report of the Arden House Conference on Preschool Enrichment of Socially Disadvantaged Children, December 16, 1962, *Merrill-Palmer Quarterly*, July, 1964.

20. Knoll, Erwin. "The Truth About Desegregation in Washington, D.C., Public Schools," *The Journal of Negro Education*, 28:92–113; Spring, 1959.

21. Kvaraceus, William C.; Miller, Walter B.; and others. *Delinquent Behavior: Culture and the Individual*. Washington: National Education Association, 1959.

22. Melzack, Ronald, and Scott, T. H. "The Effects of Early Experience on the Response to Pain," *Journal of Comparative and Physiological Psychology*, 50: 155–161; 1957.

23. Melzack, Ronald, and Thompson, William R. "Effects of Early Experience on Social Behavior," *Canadian Journal of Psychology*, 10:82–90; 1956.

24. Riesen, Austin H. "The Development of Visual Perception in Man and Chimpanzee," *Science*, 106:107–108; 1947.

25. Riessman, Frank. *The Culturally Deprived Child*. New York: Harper & Brothers, 1962.

26. Roberts, G., Jr. "Negro Education for What?" *Time*, November 19, 1961.

27. Rosenbloom, Paul. "Implications of Psychological Research," in *A Methods Manual for Teaching Science in the Elementary School*. Minneapolis: University of Minnesota School Mathematics and Science Teaching Project, 1964.

28. Schrag, Peter. "The Schools of Appalachia," *Saturday Review*, May 15, 1965.
29. Shorr, Alvin L. *Slums and Social Insecurity*. Washington: Government Printing Office, 1963.
30. Skeels, Harold M. "Effects of Adoption on Children from Institutions," *Children*, 12:33–34; January-February, 1965.
31. Stagner, Ross. *Psychology of Personality*. New York: McGraw-Hill Book Co., Inc., 1961.
32. Strom, Robert D. *Teaching in the Slum School*. Columbus, Ohio: Charles E. Merrill Books, Inc., 1965.
33. Thompson, W. R., and Heron, W. "The Effects of Restricting Early Experience on the Problem-Solving Capacity of Dogs," *Canadian Journal of Psychology*, 8:17–31; 1954.
34. Vontress, Clemmont E. "Our Demoralizing Slum Schools," *Phi Delta Kappan*, 45:77–81; November, 1963.
35. Wakefield, Robert A. "An Investigation of the Family Backgrounds of Educable Mentally Retarded Children in Special Classes," *Exceptional Children*, 31:143; November, 1964.

Who Are the Disadvantaged?

During recent years the term "disadvantaged" has gained common usage as a label for those children of the very poor who suffer various social, intellectual, emotional, and physical restrictions. The scope of the problem is described in Part One and further elaborated upon throughout this book. As indicated in the introduction, the ills and problems restricting growth and development of children tend to be concentrated in the culture of the poor, particularly among those residing in the major pockets of poverty in this nation — the city slums and certain rural areas.

Disadvantaged children are defined or described by Robert J. Havighurst in terms of family characteristics, and in terms of social group characteristics of families. He places the number of socially disadvantaged children at about 15 per cent of the child population. In recent discussions of education for the disadvantaged some have proposed the development of school programs that allow the child to profit from certain "positive" qualities. Havighurst calls this "sentimental talk" and adds, "There is substantial doubt that the socially disadvantaged children in our big cities have *any* positive qualities of potential value in urban society in which they are systematically better than the children of families who participate fully in the mass culture." Certainly the disadvantaged can be identified early, and they need special attention in the schools and special help for overcoming the disadvantages conferred on them by conditions of family living.

Helen L. Witmer, in presenting facts about poverty that are of potential use to those planning action programs, considers three main points, citing statistics for each:

1. What is meant by poverty and to what extent does the over-all amount of poverty depend on the sort of measuring rod that is used?
2. How many and what proportion of the nation's children and youth are growing up in poverty?
3. Where, geographically and socially, are these children of the poor to be found?

Margaret I. Liston also raises some very pertinent questions that require answers before action groups can proceed. For example, "What are the who, what, where, why, and how of serious poverty? What groups or subcultures are impoverished and what is the relative seriousness of that impoverishment? . . . Is it temporary and transitional, or inherited and relatively permanent, flowing from generation to generation? . . . What phases are amenable to preventative action? And what kinds of action are most appropriate?" According to Liston, "Poverty is a persistent gap between 'what is' and 'what ought to be' as viewed subjectively by the individual himself, objectively by science, or according to the standards of society." Poverty means not only a low-level life maintenance but also a lack of human growth toward self-actualization. It is humanistic as well as economic.

From the final selection in Part One, an editorial from the *New Republic,* some insight into the world scope of poverty and its effects upon human living may be gained. We who live in the most affluent of nations may grasp remotely the relative significance of this nation's poverty and disadvantageness in a world context of disadvantaged millions. But a single mind fails to understand world significance and scope just as it fails to understand the number "million." The statistics *sound* like this: Two billion people live in the "developing" countries of the world. In a country like Libya one child in five reaches the age of fifteen, and in Vietnam, 40 per cent do not live to be four. Seven of every ten preschool Vietnamese children suffer from malnutrition; by the time the survivors are twelve years old they have the physical development of a normal eight-year-old. In East Pakistan alone, fifty thousand infants every year become blind for life because of a deficiency of Vitamin A. All these problems are further complicated by the population explosion. India annually increases its population by an equivalent to the size of Greater New York.

Thus we see in concrete fashion the consequences of not enough know-how and not enough material resources. As pointed out in the introduction to this book, we need not deliberately subject children to conditions of deprivation for experimental purposes. Poverty, abuse, and neglect have produced cases on every hand — in every geographical area of this country and in every country of the world.

❖ ❖ 1 ❖ ❖

Who Are the Socially Disadvantaged?

ROBERT J. HAVIGHURST

In all of our big cities, and in many smaller cities and rural counties, educators are trying to find better ways of teaching a group of children and youth who are variously called "culturally deprived," "intellectually deprived," or "socially disadvantaged." This is a major movement, which enlists a large amount of money and time of skilled teachers, and also a considerable amount of research effort.

There is consensus that this group of children and their families present a great social problem, perhaps the greatest of our domestic social problems. It is important that the problem be seen clearly.

Different writers and different workers in this area have defined the target group somewhat differently. The group is sometimes (and frequently enough to cause confusion in the minds of readers) described as all children of manual workers. But few if any educators care to call this large working-class group, some two-thirds of the child population, "socially disadvantaged."

A more useful definition of the "socially disadvantaged" can be arrived at in the way that is demonstrated in this chapter. Children with social disadvantages have always been present in any society, but probably the numbers are unusually large in the present American society, due to the urbanism of this society and to changes in the labor force which make it difficult for youth aged sixteen to twenty to find employment.

The question which gives title to this chapter may be answered in various ways. One way is to illustrate by describing some cases of social disadvantage.

Suppose we observe two mothers riding with their four-year-old children on a bus. The mothers want to teach their children to sit properly on a bus seat, while the bus starts and stops suddenly.

CASE A

Mother: Hold on tight to your seat.
Child: Why?

❖ From *The Journal of Negro Education*, Summer, 1964, pp. 210–217. Used by permission of the author and the publisher. Robert J. Havighurst is Professor of Education, University of Chicago.

Mother:	Hold on tight.
Child:	Why?
Mother:	You'll fall.
Child:	Why?
Mother:	I told you to hold on tight, didn't I?

CASE B

Mother:	Hold on tightly, darling.
Child:	Why?
Mother:	If you don't you will be thrown forward and then you'll fall.
Child:	Why?
Mother:	Because if the bus stops suddenly you'll jerk forward and bump against the seat in front.
Child:	Why?
Mother:	Now hold on tightly, darling, and don't make such a fuss.

The first thing that strikes the observer of these two cases is that the mother in case A does not try to explain to the child. Thus the child does not have an opportunity to learn the "why" of things, and if this kind of situation occurs again and again, the child may lose the habit of asking *why?* The next thing is that the vocabulary in case A is more restricted than in case B. Thus the child does not get practice in extending his vocabulary. Perhaps the next thing that will be noticed is that there is a difference in the *relation* between child and mother in the two situations. In case A the mother asserts her authority through categorical statements. She does not really try to explain why the child should hold on tight, but *orders* the child to do so. The mother's authority is invoked almost at once, with the result that the natural curiosity of the child is pushed back, and the child is learning *not* to think for himself. In case B the mother attempts to satisfy the child's curiosity with explanations. Although she finally resorts to her authority, she has first given the child a chance to learn about the world in a relationhip which permits him to challenge authority with his questions.

The child who experiences language and social relations of case A during his early years is likely to develop a different kind of mind than the child who experiences language and social relations of case B. The child in Case A is socially disadvantaged when compared with the child in Case B.

Disadvantaged for What?

Disadvantage is a relative term. When we speak of a child as being *socially disadvantaged* we mean that he has a disadvantage relative to some other child for some kind of social life. As the term is used in this book, it means diadvantaged for living competently in an urban, industrial, and democratic society. The socially disadvantaged child is one who is handicapped in the task of growing up to lead a competent and satisfying life in the American society.

Consider, for example, Michael, who is a ten-year-old boy living in an ordinary town. His father is a truck driver and makes a good income, though he must be away from home frequently for days at a time. Michael's mother stays at home and does her best to give her three children a good start in life. She looks after the children faithfully, and wishes they had enough money to rent a house in a "better" part of town where the neighbors had nicer children and there were not so many Saturday night fights and Monday morning hangovers.

When Michael was seven years old he was put into an experimental second grade class consisting of eighteen children who had failed the first grade by not learning to read at the proper grade level. Instead of making them repeat the first grade, the principal put them all in one class with a teacher who volunteered to work with them, and with a social worker who spent a day a week visiting the homes of the children. Michael had an I.Q. of 97. He began to read by Thanksgiving of the second year, and soon was reading at a second grade level. He liked especially the trips his group took to the public library, where the children's librarian read to them and encouraged them to borrow books and take them home. Michael read about twenty children's books by the spring of the year. But he forgot to return his books on time, and one day his mother received a post card telling her that there was a sixteen cent fine for overdue books. She sent Michael to the library with the money, but told him, "Don't you ever go near that library again. They didn't have a right to fine you."

To Michael' mother, a fine was a bad thing. She associated it with the punishment some of her neighbors suffered when they got drunk and had a fight at a nearby tavern and were arrested and fined "for being drunk and disorderly." She was raising her children to avoid this kind of life, and she did not think Michael was guilty of a crime by keeping the library books too long.

Michael got along fairly well in school; his grades were average, and he was a good boy. One day, when he was in the fifth grade, he was playing after school and he spied the social worker who used to visit his home when he was in the experimental second grade. He greeted her, and said, "Miss Jansen, please come to my house and see my books." He took her into his home and showed her a set of Britannica Junior books. "These are all mine," he said. "My dad pays five dollars a month for them." The social worker said, "That's wonderful, Michael, and do your folks read to you from these books?" "Oh, no," said Michael, "they don't like to read much, and, besides, they said that these are my books, for me to read. Of course, I can't understand everything, but I've been reading about the animals of the world."

Just then, Michael's mother came in and greeted the social worker warmly. "We'll never forget how much you helped us when Michael was in the second grade," she said, "and don't you think these books are wonderful?"

This was a case of social disadvantage, and illustrates the fact that parents may take very good care of their children in an emotional sense, but still deprive them of a good intellectual start in life. This mother and father simply did not *know* how to help their children do well in school. In spite of their good intentions, they deprived Michael of the use of the library, which might have been a major intellectual resource for him, and then they splurged by getting him a children's encyclopedia but they did not set an example of reading, and they did not read to him or help him learn to read.

Who Are the Socially Disadvantaged?

The socially disadvantaged children may be defined and described in three ways; in terms of certain family characteristics relating directly to the child; in terms of their personal characteristics; or in terms of the social group characteristics of their families.

FAMILY CHARACTERISTICS. Compared with other children whose families give them average or better advantages for getting started in modern urban life, the socially disadvantaged child lacks several of the following:

A *family conversation which:* answers his questions and encourages him to ask questions; extends his vocabulary with words and with adjectives and adverbs; gives him a right and a need to stand up for and to explain his point of view on the world.

A *family environment which:* sets an example of reading; provides a variety of toys and play materials with colors, sizes and objects that challenge his ingenuity with his hands and his mind.

Two parents who: read a good deal; read to him; show him that they believe in the value of education; reward him for good school achievement.

Bernstein (1) has studied the language behavior of families that relate to the intellectual development of their children. He distinguishes between two forms or *types* of language. (These language types are statistically related to social class, as will be pointed out later.) One form of language is called *restricted* and the other form is called *elaborated*. A family which employs restricted language gives a child a language environment characterized by:

1. Short, grammatically simple, often unfinished sentences with a poor syntactical form stressing the active voice.
2. Simple and repetitive use of conjunctions (so, then, because).
3. Little use of subordinate clauses to break down the initial categories of the dominant subject.
4. Inability to hold a formal subject through a speech sequence; thus a dislocated informational content is facilitated.
5. Rigid and limited use of adjectives and adverbs.
6. Constraint on the self-reference pronoun; frequent use of personal pronoun.
7. Frequent use of statements where the reason and conclusion are confounded to produce a categoric statement.
8. A large number of statements/phrases which signal a requirement for the previous speech sequence to be reinforced: "Wouldn't it? You see? You know?" etc. This process is termed "sympathetic circularity."

9. Individual selection from a group of idiomatic phrases or sequences will frequently occur.
10. The individual qualification is implicit in the sentence organization; it is a language of implicit meaning.

On the other hand, a family which employs an *elaborated* language gives the child a language environment characterized by:

1. Accurate grammatical order and syntax regulate what is said.
2. Logical modifications and stress are mediated through a grammatically complex sentence construction, especially through the use of a range of conjunctions and subordinate clauses.
3. Frequent use of prepositions which indicate logical relationships as well as prepositions which indicate temporal and spatial contiguity.
4. Frequent use of the personal pronoun "I."
5. A discriminative selection from a range of adjectives and adverbs.
6. Individual qualification is verbally mediated through the structure and relationships within and between sentences.
7. Expressive symbolism discriminates between meanings within speech sequences rather than reinforcing dominant words or phrases, or accompanying the sequence in a diffuse, generalized manner.
8. A language use which points to the possibilities inherent in a complex conceptual hierarchy for the organizing of experience.

A child who has learned a *restricted* language at home is likely to have difficulty in school, where an *elaborate* language is used and taught by the teacher; and the difficulty of the child is likely to increase as he goes further in school, unless he learns the elaborate language that is expected in the school. On the other hand, the child who has had experience with an elaborate language from his earliest years has a relatively easy time in school, because he must simply go on developing the kind of language and related thinking which he has already started.

PERSONAL CHARACTERISTICS. The family environment with the characteristics just cited tends to produce children with certain personal deficits. Martin Deutsch (2) has studied such children with techniques of the experimental psychologists, and he finds them to have inferior auditory discrimination, inferior visual discrimination, inferior judgment concerning time, number, and other basic concepts. He finds that this inferiority is not due to physical defects of eyes and ears and brain, but is due to inferior *habits* of hearing and seeing and thinking. Presumably, the family environment of these children did not teach them to "pay attention" to what was being said around them, or to the visual scene. Then, when they came to school, their school performance suffered because they had not learned to "listen" to the teacher and other important people or to "see" the things they were shown.

SOCIAL GROUP CHARACTERISTICS. We introduce the social group characteristics of socially disadvantaged children last so as to avoid giving the impression that there is a hard-and-fast relation between socioeconomic status, or some other group characteristic, and social disadvantage for the child. While there are statistical relations and very important ones between socioeconomic status and social disadvantages of children, there are so many individual exceptions to the statistical generalizations that any educational policy aimed at identifying socially disadvantaged children should avoid reliance upon general socioeconomic characteristics as the decisive criteria.

Above all, it is important to avoid the error of saying that all children of working class families are socially disadvantaged. Approximately 65 per cent of the children of this country are living in working-class homes. That is, their fathers or mothers do manual work for a living. The great majority of these families give their children a fairly good start for life in an urban industrial democratic society. Their children are adequately fed and clothed. They are loved and protected by their parents. They learn to respect teachers and to like school. They do fairly well or better than that in school.

While working-class children as a group are somewhat different from the children of white-collar workers, it would not be reasonable to say that the working-class children are socially disadvantaged or culturally deprived. Working-class children as a group score slightly below children of white-collar families in intelligence tests; they fall slightly below on tests of school achievement; they attain somewhat less formal education. But the differences are relatively small, and become even smaller when the socially disadvantaged children are removed and the majority of working-class youth who remain are compared with white-collar children.

Most working-class families participate fully in the American mass or core culture. This is certainly not a culture of deprivation. While the differences between the upper working-class and the middle-class are real and they are interesting, these differences should not be described in terms of social advantage or social disadvantage. The great amount of movement of people across the boundary between these two classes as they grow up is evidence that the differences between these two classes are not fundamental ones.

Who, then, are the socially disadvantaged when we attempt to describe them in terms of observable social groups? They are groups with the following characteristics:

1. They are at the bottom of the American society in terms of income.
2. They have a rural background.
3. They suffer from social and economic discrimination at the hands of the majority of the society.
4. They are widely distributed in the United States. While they are most visible in the big cities, they are present in all except the very high income communities. There are many of them in rural areas.

In racial and ethnic terms, these groups are about evenly divided between whites and nonwhites. They consist mainly of the following:

1. Negroes from the rural South who have migrated recently to the Northern industrial cities.
2. Whites from the rural South and the Southern mountains who have migrated recently to the Northern industrial cities.
3. Puerto Ricans who have migrated to a few Northern industrial cities.
4. Mexicans with a rural background who have migrated into the West and Middle West.
5. European immigrants with a rural background, from East and Southern Europe.

Altogether, these groups make up about 15 per cent of the United States population. Since they tend to have large families, their children make up as much as 20 per cent of the child population. Not all socially disadvantaged children come from these groups, but the great majority do. Not all children in these groups are socially disadvantaged, but the great majority are.

How Many Are Socially Disadvantaged?

There is an infinite graduation of social advantage-disadvantage, and therefore any quantitative estimate of the number of socially disadvantaged children and youth must be a personal rather than a scientific statement.

The writer would place the number of socially disadvantaged children at about 15 per cent of the child population. One basis for this estimate is the proportion of unemployed, out-of-school youth between the ages of sixteen and twenty. These young people have been relatively unsuccessful in school and in the labor market. The great majority of them come from the social groups listed above. There are about 11 per cent of boys and 17 per cent of girls in this group. The boys are clearly maladjusted to society. Some of the girls are not; they are simply doing what girls have done for a long time, helping out at home while waiting to get married. But these figures place a minimum on the numbers of socially disadvantaged youth. There are a few others who have jobs which are below their capacity or are disadvantaged in other ways — enough to bring the total up to about 15 per cent.

Since these children and their families tend to concentrate in the large cities, while upper-income people tend to move out from the cities to the suburbs, the socially disadvantaged children are in big cities in larger proportions than 15 per cent. Probably *30 per cent of the children* in such cities as New York, Chicago, Philadelphia, Washington, Detroit, Cleveland, and Baltimore fall into the socially disadvantaged category.

Do the Socially Disadvantaged Have Special Advantages?

In discussions of education for the socially disadvantaged there is a good deal of sentimental talk about the "valuable" or the "positive" characteristics of the cultures from which these children come, and about the desirability of developing school programs that allow the child to profit from these positive qualities.

It is said that this kind of child is "physically oriented" — that he likes action rather than words. It is said that he has nonlanguage skills that can serve him for learning. It is said that he can perceive (see, hear, and smell) in superior fashion. It is said that he has more of certain kinds of creativity. It is said that he has a different "mental style" from that of children who do well in the ordinary school.

This set of propositions is conceivably correct. The child growing up in a rural culture certainly gains some skills that are likely to be more highly developed than they would be if he grew up in a city. Every culture has characteristics that are positive in its own situation. For example, in a study of Hopi Indian children of the American Southwest, it was found that their drawings were superior in many ways to the drawings of American white children. A university art teacher made systematic comparisons of the drawings and found that, according to his own criteria of good children's art, the Hopi drawings were superior to those of Midwest white children of the middle-class. Yet the same Hopi children were inferior to Midwest children on a verbal test of intelligence. Thus one might make use of this positive quality of the Hopi children in developing schools to fit them for participation in the surrounding American culture.

However, there is substantial doubt that the socially disadvantaged children in our big cities have *any* positive qualities of potential value in urban society in which they are systematically better than the children of families who participate fully in the mass culture. (The writer does not know any comparative study which shows American lower-lower class children to be superior in any positive respect to American upper working-class or middle-class children.) As a group they are inferior in tests of spatial perception, for example, as well as in tests of vocabulary and arithmetic. It is true that the difference between the socially disadvantaged and the mass culture majority is less on tests of certain nonverbal skills than on tests of more verbal and abstract abilities. This fact might suggest that the socially disadvantaged could learn more rapidly and efficiently if they had more concrete experience on which to base their vocabulary and their reasoning skills. This is probably true, but it does not argue for a difference in "mental style" and therefore a difference in school curriculum. It argues for more building of "readiness" for reading and arithmetic in the pre-school and primary grades.

Conclusion

The *socially disadvantaged* children can be defined and discovered at an early age. While social disadvantage and social advantage are concepts which shade into each other, it is possible to make working distinctions which are a basis for identification of some 30 per cent of the children of the big cities as socially disadvantaged. These are not necessarily working-class, or lower-class children. The majority of children of working-class families are not socially disadvantaged as the term is used in this discussion.

The socially disadvantaged children tend to come from families that are poor, and that are recent immigrants to the big cities. They are a group that need special attention in the schools and special help to assist them to overcome the disadvantages conferred on them by their families.

REFERENCES

1. Bernstein, Basil. "Language and Social Class," *British Journal of Sociology*, 11:271–276, 1960.

————. "Social Class and Linguistic Development: A Theory of Social Learning," pp. 288ff. in A. H. Halsey, J. Floud, and C. A. Anderson (eds.), *Economy, Education and Society*. New York: The Free Press of Glencoe, 1961.

————. "Social Class, Linguistic Codes and Grammatical Elements," *Language and Speech*. 5:221–240; October-December 1962; "Elaborated and Restricted Codes: Their Origins and Some Consequences," *American Anthropologist*, 1964.

2. Deutsch, Martin P. "The Disadvantaged Child and the Learning Process," in A. Harry Passow (ed.), *Education in Depressed Areas*. New York: Bureau of Publications, Teachers College, Columbia University, 1963.

Children and Poverty

HELEN L. WITMER

The purpose of this brief report is to present some facts about poverty as it affects children and youth in the United States today, in the particular hope that this information may be of use to those who are involved in planning community programs. Three main points will be considered:

1. What is meant by poverty and to what extent does the over-all amount of poverty depend on the sort of measuring rod that is used?

2. How many and what proportion of the Nation's children and youth are growing up in poverty?

3. Where, geographically and socially, are these children of the poor to be found?

✧ From *Children*, November-December, 1964, pp. 207–213. Used by permission of the author and the publisher, the Children's Bureau, U.S. Department of Health, Education and Welfare. Helen L. Witmer is Director, Division of Research, Children's Bureau.

The third point is of especial importance, for by this information the nature of present-day poverty as it affects American children is suggested and some clues are given as to where an attack on poverty can be made.

How Poor Is "Poor"?

Poverty is currently defined by reference to cost-of-living budgets, attempts being made to identify annual income figures that mark the minimum required to meet basic needs at an "economy" level.

The figure most frequently cited as marking the poverty line in the United States today is an annual income of $3000 for a family. This is the figure used in the 1964 "Economic Report of the President," prepared by the Council of Economic Advisers (2), and in most of the subsequent publicity on the subject. The figure refers to annual money income before taxes are paid, expressed in terms of 1962 prices. It amounts to an income of less than $60 a week.

In seeking a cutoff point for poverty, the Council reviewed a number of studies of the cost of maintaining families at various levels of living, citing specifically one made recently by the Social Security Administration. The figure that was chosen was close to that study's estimate ($3195) of the cost of an "economy-plan" budget for a nonfarm family of four. This budget assumes that such a famliy would have to spend a third of its income on food — $5 a person a week. · If rent cost $800 a year (about $65 a month), the family would have $25 a week left for clothing, medical care, recreation, and all other purposes.

Objections to this definition are easy to make. Many families consist of more than four persons, and many consist of less. Some families live on farms and others live in small towns in which costs may be lower than this budget assumes. "Money income" is not all the income. some families receive; some get income in kind and in other nonmoney forms. The Council was well aware of these deficiencies but found the use of a single figure necessary for its purpose of "assessing the dimensions of the task of eliminating poverty, setting broad goals of policy, and measuring our past and future progress toward its accomplishment." (2)

Several other ways of determining the line that separates "the poor" from the rest of the population have been suggested in studies published in recent years. One of these meets the objection that nonmoney income should be included. Another takes account not only of that objection but also of the one relating to size and composition of families. A third uses federal income tax standards as the basis of estimate. Each — not unexpectedly — arrives at a different income figure for defining poverty.

The first of these studies in the one made by the Conference on Economic Progress (1). Here the poverty line was drawn at $4000 in "disposable income" for families and $2000 for unattached individuals. (The President's Council considered $1500 the cutoff point for unattached individuals.)

These figures refer not only to money income but also to nonmoney income, such as the money value of food and fuel produced by farm families, wages received in kind, and the rental value of owner-occupied homes.

The writers of the Conference report based their selection of the $4000 level on studies of workers' family budgets conducted in 1959 by the Bureau of Labor Statistics in twenty American cities. These studies showed that, in 1960 dollars, a "modest but adequate budget" cost a three-person family from about $4500 to $6300 a year, while for a six-person family the cost varied from $6100 to $9400. Assuming that $6000 would be the average cost of this sort of budget, the investigators decided that it was reasonable to reduce that figure by a third, apply it to all families, and call the resulting $4000 figure the poverty line. Such a figure, they pointed out, makes generous allowances for variations in cost from place to place and for variations in family size.

The second study — one that takes account both of nonmoney income and of size and composition of family — was made by a team of social economists headed by James N. Morgan of the University of Michigan's Institute for Social Research (5). The investigators started from the minimum family budget figures worked out by the Community Council of Greater New York in 1959. This is a scheme that takes account of age and sex of family members in relation to their need for food, clothing, and other items.

Using these budgets as a standard, the Michigan investigators called those families poor whose "disposable" income (money and nonmoney) covered less than 90 per cent of their minimum budget requirements and who had less than $5000 in liquid assets. According to this way of calculating, a family consisting of an employed father, a mother, and two children aged eight and eleven needed an income of at least $4330 a year for minimum maintenance in New York City. Other families required proportionately more or less. In cities other than New York the poverty line might be set at as much as 20 per cent lower, the study reports.

A third way of determining the poverty line is reported in a recent publication of the Social Security Administration (3). It employs, as a very conservative definition of poverty, the lower limit for federal income taxation used by the law that was in force in 1963. Such a definition calls a two-person family poor that has less than $1325 in money income, while a family that consists of six persons would be poor if its income were less than $4000.

By these various calculations, then, the poverty level for families has been set at a $3000 annual money income, a $4000 annual money and nonmoney income, and an income of varying size depending on the number of family members. What is the effect of these different ways of counting the poor on the over-all estimate of the size of the poverty problem in the United States today? Perhaps surprisingly, the answer is "very little," as the following figures show.

■ TABLE 1 *Families with Own Children, 1960, by Various Categories; Proportion of Each Classified as Poor[a] (in thousands)*

All Families With Own Children			
Total 25,661		Poor 4278 (17%)	

White Families			
Total 23,263		Poor 3154 (14%)	

Male head

Total 21,869
Poor 2364 (11%)

Urban		Rural	
Total 15,043		Total 6826	
Poor 953 (6%)		Poor 1411 (21%)	

South	Non-South	South	Non-South
Total 3571	Total 11,472	Total 2509	Total 4317
Poor 370	Poor 583	Poor 741	Poor 670
(10%)	(5%)	(30%)	(16%)

Female head

Total 1394
Poor 790 (57%)

Urban		Rural	
Total 1085		Total 309	
Poor 580 (53%)		Poor 210 (68%)	

South	Non-South	South	Non-South
Total 278	Total 807	Total 134	Total 175
Poor 163	Poor 417	Poor 100	Poor 110
(59%)	(52%)	(75%)	(63%)

How Many Are Poor?

When the $3000 money-income figure is used as the cutoff point, Bureau of the Census reports show that about 9.3 of the 47 million families in the United States were living in poverty in 1962 — 20 per cent of the total. The corresponding proportions in the 3 preceding years were 21 or 22 per cent.

When the level is raised to $4000 and both money and nonmoney income are counted, the figures of the Office of Business Economics, U.S. Department of Commerce (used in the study made by the Conference on Economic Progress) show the proportion of poor ranging from 20 per cent in 1959 to 17 per cent in 1962. When allowance is made for variation in size and composition of the family, the estimate based on the University of Michigan's survey in 1959 showed one-fifth of American families living in poverty. Approximately the same proportion was found by the Social Security Administration's investigator who used income tax levels as the basis of her estimates for 1959. Apparently, then, no matter which of these vari-

TABLE 1   (*Continued*)

Nonwhite Families

Total 2,398		Poor 1,124 (47%)	

Male head

Total 1901
Poor 723 (38%)

Urban		Rural	
Total 1388		Total 513	
Poor 374 (27%)		Poor 349 (68%)	

South	Non-South	South	Non-South
Total 589	Total 799	Total 433	Total 80
Poor 240	Poor 134	Poor 319	Poor 30
(41%)	(17%)	(74%)	(38%)

Female head

Total 497
Poor 401 (81%)

Urban		Rural	
Total 413		Total 84	
Poor 326 (79%)		Poor 75 (89%)	

South	Non-South	South	Non-South
Total 182	Total 231	Total 73	Total 11
Poor 156	Poor 170	Poor 66	Poor 9
(86%)	(74%)	(90%)	(82%)

[a] U.S. Census: 1960, PC(1)D. U.S. volume, Table 225; State volume, Table 140. "Poor" is defined as less than $3000 in money income in 1959.

ous methods is used, the often cited statement that in the early sixties about 20 per cent of American families were living in poverty is correct.

This similarity in proportions is attributable to the canceling-out effect of the differences in the criteria used. An example will show how this can come about [see Table 1]. Take a family with $2500 in money income. This family would be classified as poor according to the $3000 definition whether or not it also had nonmoney income. However, when the poverty line is drawn at $4000 and nonmoney income is included, this family would not be counted as poor if it had an additional $1500 income from nonmoney sources. At the same time, a family with a money income of $3999 and no nonmoney income would be called poor by the latter way of reckoning, although it would not be poor by the $3000 money-income standard.

Similarly, when account is taken of size of family, some large families are counted as poor whose money income is over $3000 and some very small ones are considered not poor whose income is under that figure. In other words, each method of determining who is poor includes more of some kinds of families and fewer of other kinds as compared with the other methods. Thus the over-all proportion of poor families can be about the same no matter which method is used.

This finding justifies the use of the $3000 cutoff point for over-all purposes — for determining the national total of poor families, for instance, and for noting changes in that number from year to year, the value of money being held constant. The $3000 cutoff point is not adequate for all purposes, however. For instance, in local planning, when choices have to be made as to what kind and amount of services are to be provided and which families and individuals are to be served, this criterion may be an inadequate guide. More important for our present purpose, the $3000 figure is quite inadequate for determining the total number of children who are growing up in poverty.

To settle, however, for any particular income figure as providing an indication of the living standard of the American poor today is to dull one's conception of the severity of the poverty problem. This is because the figure is apt to be taken to imply that most families classified as poor have an income close to the specified amount. The true situation is much worse than any of these poverty-line figures suggest.

No matter at which of these income levels the line is drawn, many families have incomes far below it. For instance, many more families had less than $2000 in money income in 1962 than had up to $1000 or more. Even worse, a fifth of the families below the $3000 level had less than $1000 a year in cash to live on. Far from $3000 or $4000 being close to the usual income of families that are called poor, considerably over half of them did not come within $1000 of these figures. And within that proportion, a third to a half of the families were another $1000 below the poverty line.

The answer, then, to the question "How poor is poor?" is "Very poor indeed." In the statements about the income of the poor — under $3000, under $4000, etc. — the emphasis should be on *under*. Many families and individuals are very much under the poverty line.

Clearly, in this era of affluence and rapid technological change, with jobs for the poor growing scarcer and scarcer, poverty is a major national problem. It is especially a problem for and with respect to the children of the poor. Change for the better, for all the Nation, depends particularly on the poor children's lot in life being greatly improved. Accordingly, it is to an analysis of these numbers and of certain characteristics of the children and their families that the rest of this report is devoted.

Children of the Poor

To say that about 20 per cent of all American families are poor gives no indication of how many children are growing up in the handicapping condition that poverty implies. This is not only because not all families contain children and because poor families are apt to have more children than the average; it is also because the $3000 poverty-line figure is itself a sort of average and one that does injustice to large families. To discover how many children are being reared in poverty we must therefore consider not only the census figures but also the calculation of the poverty line itself. In doing so, we shall rely on the analysis made by Mollie Orshansky (6) of the situation in 1961. She is now in the process of making a more refined analysis, based on 1963 income figures (7).

Not all families with incomes under $3000 contain children. Of the 46.3 million families in the United States at the time 1961 income was ascertained, 18.7 million contained no children under eighteen related to the adults; 27.6 million contained such children. In 26.2 million of the latter, the children were the families' own; in 1.4 million families, the children were related to the adults but were not their own. In other words, 60 per cent of all families contained children who were related to them; 57 per cent contained children who were their own. In much of the following discussion we shall confine our remarks to families with their own children, for the economic situation of children who are members of subfamilies (those who live with one or both parents in families headed by other relatives) and those who are parentless and wholly supported by relatives is more difficult to determine.

Now, how many of these families with children had less than $3000 in money income? Twenty-one per cent of all families had incomes under $3000 in 1961. Families with own children fared somewhat better — among them the proportion with incomes under $3000 was 16 per cent. Families with related but not own children were much worse off, 36 per cent of them having incomes under $3000.

In numbers, this means that 4.2 million families with own children were living in poverty. In addition, there were about 500,000 families with related but not own children in that situation, making a total of 4.7 million families who had insufficient income to provide adequately for their children's needs. Such families constituted slightly less than half of all families that were poor in 1961.

How many children does this involve, and what proportion of the total child population? This might seem a simple question to answer, since the Bureau of the Census reports show the proportion of families with various numbers of related children having various amounts of money income. In fact, using this information, the President's Council of Economic Advisers reported that the children of the poor numbered about eleven million in 1962 — one-sixth of the population under eighteen years of age. Consideration of the method by which this disturbingly large figure was arrived at suggests that it considerably underestimates the size of the problem. That this is so was stated by Walter Heller, the author of the Council's report, in recent testimony before a congressional committee (4). To explain why this is so we must go back to the question of how the $3000 poverty-line figure was arrived at.

It will be recalled that $3000 was chosen to mark the poverty line because various studies showed this to be about the cost of a minimum budget for an average urban American family, consisting of husband, wife, and two children. This use of what amounts to an average income figure yields a satisfactory answer so far as families are concerned, because the greater budgetary needs of large families are counterbalanced by the smaller requirements of one-child families. When *children* rather than families are the unit of count, however, this averaging-out no longer works. This is because the $3000 ceiling excludes some large families whose minimum needs come to more than $3000 and includes some very small ones whose minimum needs are a bit below that figure.

The extent of the error is seen when the estimate of the number of poor children based on the $3000 standard is compared with the estimate made by Orshansky (6) who devised a poverty line that rose as the size of the family increased. The minimum budget figure for a family of four that she used ($3195) is the one cited in the report of the President's Council of Economic Advisers in justifying the $3000 figure.

In calculating minimum budgets, Orshansky started from the proposition that the proportion of income that must be spent on food is a good indicator of standard of living. To this she joined the finding of recent studies that, on the average, both farm and urban families in the United States spend about a third of their income on food. Then, taking the U.S. Department of Agriculture low-cost food plan as a guide, she estimated the cost of food for families of each size, taking into account their composition with respect to adults and children. Food costs for farm families were assumed to be 60 per cent of those of nonfarm families, this judgment being based on recent studies made by the U.S. Department of Agriculture. The resulting figures were then reduced 20 per cent to represent the cost of an "economy" rather than a "low-cost" food budget. For calculating total minimum budgets, these food-cost budgets were tripled.

By such calculations, Orshansky found that 18 per cent of all families with own children under 18 were living in poverty — 4.8 million families in all. This is sufficiently close to the number of such families that had incomes of less than $3000 (4.6 million) to justify the claim that essentially the same degree of poverty was being measured by the two methods.

Counting the number of own children in these poor families, Orshansky found that they numbered about 15,859,000. To these she added an estimate of the number of children who lived in families headed by relatives who were not their parents and who were equally poor. The resulting total for children living in poverty was about seventeen million — a figure more than half again as high as the eleven million estimate commonly cited.

This is a crude count, to be sure, but on the basis of this estimate it appears that in 1961 about a fourth of all American children were growing up in families whose incomes were clearly inadequate to meet their basic needs. Three million of these seventeen million children belonged to families whose income was under $1000 a year. Today the number and proportion of poor children may be somewhat smaller, for the most recent sample survey of the Bureau of the Census shows that the over-all proportion of poor *families* has dropped nearly three percentage points since 1961 and is now 18.5 per cent. Even so, there is little doubt eleven million is still much too low a figure.

Who the Poor Children Are

With poverty handicapping the development of so many children, it becomes most important to know who these children are and where they live. Detailed information on these points may suggest where some of the major attacks on poverty as it affects children had best be made.

Unfortunately, up-to-date figures about families and children, broken down into all the useful groups, are not available. For the most part, the best we can do in tracing the children is to use the figures from the 1960 census that deal with the income and certain related traits of families with own children.

The family characteristics on which the 1960 census volumes report in relation to income are race, type of family, and residence — both geographical and urban-rural. In combination with income, family figures based on these traits show rather well where poverty among children was — and doubtless still is — concentrated.

The figures on these points are shown in the table on pages 26 and 27. It should be noted that, of necessity, the under-$3000 standard for poverty was used, instead of the standard more adequate for our purpose that was developed by Orshansky. Then, too, since the chart refers to *families* rather than to children, the percentages shown in it are not strictly applicable to the child population. However, the percentages are probably sufficiently accurate to indicate the relative size of the poverty problem among groups of children in our society.

A table as detailed as this one can be read in many more ways than can be pointed out in the space of this article. Of major importance, however, is the fact that each of these main family characteristics sharply differentiates one group of families in the population from that with which it is contrasted.

First, in respect to race, in 1960 the proportion of nonwhite families that were poor (47 per cent) was more than three times as great as the proportion of white families that were poor (14 per cent). Since nonwhite families are apt to have more children per family, the difference between those proportions would be even greater if children instead of families had been counted. The difference is reversed, however, when actual numbers are considered, because of the fact that in the whole population there were 10 times as many white as nonwhite families. Thus, white families that were poor were almost three times as numerous as poor nonwhite families.

Second, in respect to type of family, the financial disadvantage to children in families headed by women is extreme. Sixty-three per cent of these families were poor as compared with 13 per cent of those headed by men. But, again, in actual numbers the situation is reversed, with three million families headed by men being poor as contrasted with slightly over one million families headed by women.

Third, rural residence considerably increases the chance of a family's being poor: 26 per cent of the rural families were poor as compared with 11 per cent of those living in urban areas. However, the actual number of poor families was about the same regardless of place of residence, being about two million in each case.

Fourth, living in the South also increases the likelihood of poverty. Thirty per cent of Southern families were poor as contrasted with 11 per cent in the rest of the country. In this case the actual number of poor families was about the same in the two groups, about two million in each case.

As would be expected, a piling-up of disadvantages increases the likelihood of poverty — so much so, indeed, that in the most disadvantaged group in 1960, 90 per cent of the families were poor as contrasted with 5 per cent of the most advantaged group. In detail, the situation was as follows. When to a family's disadvantage of belonging to a nonwhite race was added the disadvantage of having the chief wage earner a woman, the likelihood of poverty rose from 47 per cent to 81 per cent. The likelihood of poverty was further increased by rural residence (89 per cent of such families were poor) and even more (raising the proportion to 90 per cent) by rural residence in the South.

When advantages rather than disadvantages pile up the opposite is true. Fourteen per cent of all white families with own children were poor in 1960. When these families had a male head the proportion of poor dropped to 11 per cent. When, in addition, such families lived in an urban area, only 6 per cent were poor. And when the urban area was one that was outside the South, the proportion of poor families dropped to 5 per cent.

Many more comparisons could be drawn from the table, especially if combinations in addition to the particular ones shown there were made, but the comparison cited here may be sufficient to highlight three points:

1. The frequently quoted figure, 20 per cent, which indicates the over-all amount of poverty in the United States, is an average that is of rather little use for specific local planning purposes.

2. There are easily identifiable categories of children in which large proportions are growing up in poverty.

3. There are other categories in which the proportion of children living in poverty is low but in which the total number of poor children is nevertheless great.

Implications for Planning

Planning for the reduction of poverty should take both the proportions and the absolute numbers of the poor into account. In pinpointing the reasons for the existence of poverty, the proportions provide the best leads. After these leads are followed, the importance of the absolute numbers comes into play.

When the proportion of poor families in a category is large, it is evident that there is something about the category itself that predisposes to low income. What this is may be fairly well known — for instance, in the category, nonwhite, and the category, female head. The disadvantages of families belonging to these categories are additionally confirmed by the Bureau of the Census reports which show that most families in these categories who are not below the poverty line are nevertheless very near to it.

When the proportion of poverty-stricken families in a category is relatively small, clues to what causes the poverty in which the children live probably are not to be found in conditions relevant to the whole category but must be sought in other factors that differentiate the poor families in the category from the great majority who are at least reasonably well off. This would be the case with the large category, white race, especially in the also large subcategory, white race and male family head, in which in 1960 only 5 per cent of the 11.5 million families were poor. In these categories the process of analysis should be carried further, until subcategories containing large proportions of poor families are found. In these significant subcategories, then, clues to what needs to be altered in the families' situations would probably be found.

After the categories and subcategories of families that have a high incidence of poverty are identified, it is obviously worthwhile to know how many poor families there are in each of them. In addition, the actual income distribution within these identified categories would be a most useful item of information for planning, for this would indicate how poor the poor families really are, how much worse off they are than others in the category, and how many families only slightly above the poverty line should be reached lest they soon be added to the number of the poor.

REFERENCES

1. Conference on Economic Progress. *Poverty and Deprivation in the United States.* Washington: 1962.

2. Council of Economic Advisers. *Economic Report of the President Together with the Annual Report of the Council of Economic Advisers.* Washington: 1964.

3. Epstein, Lenore. "Unmet Need in a Land of Abundance," *Social Security Bulletin,* May, 1963.

4. House of Representatives. "Part I: Economic Opportunity Act of 1964." Hearings before the Subcommittee on the War on Poverty Program of the Committee on Education and Labor. Washington: 1964.

5. Morgan, James N., et al. *Income and Welfare in the United States.* New York: McGraw-Hill Book Co., 1962.

6. Orshansky, Mollie. "Children of the Poor," *Social Security Bulletin,* July, 1963.

7. ———. "Counting the Poor: Another Look at the Poverty Profile," *Social Security Bulletin,* January, 1965.

Profiles of Poverty

MARGARET I. LISTON

Poverty seems to flow on and on from time to time and place to place. It appears in different forms, arises from different causes, and commands different degrees of attention. In our nation of relative economic abundance, poverty has recently come into particular focus, even to being identified by some as a "subculture" of our society.

The spotlight is on the educationally underprivileged, the aged, the under- and unemployed, the farmers, and certain minorities. Politicians argue; social scientists analyze and calculate consequences. Government officials and welfare workers do what they can to help. The press and other media play up poverty 'midst plenty. The public tries to understand what it is all about. All the while the impoverished themselves tend toward apathy or aggression.

Confusion arises from several circumstances, among them the variety of ways in which poverty may be conceived, defined, and dealt with. Literature abounds in pictures of pauperism. The Bible tells of the beggars at the temple. Dickens offered images of poverty. Children are introduced to poverty via Old Mother Hubbard.

Poverty has many profiles. These differ from nation to nation and subculture to subculture and among families and individuals.

What are the who, what, where, why, and how of serious poverty? What groups or subcultures are impoverished and what is the relative seriousness of that impoverishment? Where are they? Are they isolated cases, or island neighborhoods in a prosperous community? Are they more extensive areas or regions, such as Appalachia?

And what of the duration of impoverishment? Is it temporary and transitional, or inherited and relatively permanent, flowing from generation to generation? What are the direct and indirect circumstances which have created the situation, that is, what are the causes as well as the symptoms? What phases are amenable to preventive action? And what kinds of action are most appropriate?

✧ Reprinted from the *AAUW Journal*, October, 1964, pp. 12–14, by permission of the author and the publisher. Margaret I. Liston is Professor and Head of the Department of Home Management, Iowa State University.

Poverty Is Relative

Poverty is a state of being in serious need. It is relative. Whether or not it exists depends on the nature and extent of the gap between the observer's view of the situation and his concept of necessary requirements.

Poverty may be considered a chronic circumstance which falls short of its potential for measuring up to someone's standard of what ought to be. This may be the personal judgment of an individual for himself, i.e., *felt* poverty, the declaration of scientists based on objective criteria, or the consensus of a society as to the level below which its members should not be permitted to remain for any extended time.

One criterion currently used by our government is three thousand dollars as a minimum level for family income. Another is the requirements recommended by the National Research Council for nutrients essential in human diets at minimum levels of adequacy and cost. Still another is the minimum budgets used by welfare agencies to determine amounts of aid to be provided.

Maintenance First, Growth Second

But in our society of abundant resources there may also be poverty of growth. A central value of our culture is to get ahead, progress, grow, develop. An individual or a family able to reach only a minimum level of well-being and go no higher may still be impoverished.

When underdevelopment or inadequate growth is apparent, three questions should be asked. Can the available resources accomplish the standard sought; will they meet minimum needs even when used most judiciously? If not, ways should be sought to help the family toward more adequate command over resources for obtaining the goods, services, and conditions of life deemed essential. Does the gap result from inefficient use of the resources available? If so, information, motivation, and other forms of education may be needed. Finally, are elements of the environment restricting unduly either the supply of resources available or the level of productivity of these resources, or both? For example, relatively high tax rates or excessive inflation tend to limit purchasing power. Under such circumstances, one seeks out and does what is possible to adjust those forces.

Human Needs

Psychologist Abraham Maslow views the requirements of human personality in terms of reductions in deprivation and increments in growth along five general lines. First and most basic are the physical and biological needs fulfilled through food, shelter, clothing, and other means of life. The minimum requirements in the image of the individual himself having been met, he tends to be concerned for emotional and physical security, a sense of belonging, self-esteem and a sense of the respect of others, and self-actualization, i.e., progress in attaining his own personal potentials. Regardless of the assistance given them, impoverished families will not try to help themselves until they approach their own images of minimum essentials of security, belonging, respect, and self-achievement. As noted by Emily Dickinson and others, lack of "hyacinths" and communion with others may be more impoverishing than lack of bread.

Some Economic Profiles

To be impoverished economically means to be actually or potentially short of a desired level of material well-being. Income has been traditionally considered the best single characteristic of well-being. Attention should also be given to other resources, such as property owned, savings, and the outlook for security and regularity of income as well as for its level.

In the depth of the depression, one third of the population was "ill-fed, ill-clothed, and ill-housed." In 1962, the median income of our forty-seven million families was $5956, appreciably higher in purchasing power than in the mid-thirties. Yet, in January, the President's Council of Economic Advisers stated that 9.3 million, or one fifth of our families, had incomes under three thousand dollars and 15 per cent, or about one out of every eight families, incomes below two thousand.

When the 1960 Census was taken, median family incomes were $6040 in Houston, $6687 in Boston, $7092 in San Francisco, and $7342 in Chicago. The percentage of families with incomes under three thousand dollars was 10.6 in Chicago, 11 in Boston, 11.9 in San Francisco, and 18.8 in Houston. The respective proportions with family incomes under five thousand dollars were 23.7, 28.3, 26.1, and 39.5 per cent.

Incomes must be considered in relation to their power to command goods and services. One example is the Interim City Worker's Family Budget of the U.S. Bureau of Labor Statistics for fifty cities in the autumn of 1959. Costs for a "modest but adequate" budget for goods, rents, and services (not taxes and incidentals) were estimated as $4622 in Houston, $5334 in Boston, $5341 in San Francisco, and $5607 in Chicago. This was for a four person family, living in a rented dwelling, and consisting of a husband employed, a wife and mother not employed outside the home, a boy thirteen, and a girl eight. In light of the proportions of families with incomes under five thousand dollars in these cities, one out of every four probably was vulnerable to impoverishment.

Education and other measures are needed to help such families get greater command of resources and use them more productively. Families with incomes lower than the estimated level of need and with more family members, or special emergency costs, are also impoverished. Some who are retired or only temporarily in the low income brackets may have savings on which they may draw for a while, but this often depletes resources which should be reserved.

Intangible phases of life loom high in each person's image of his tolerable existence. To be human means to be vulnerable to poverty not only of body but also of mind, heart, and spirit.

Each person's philosophy is a complex image of his own requirements. In some phases of life, minimum levels seem adequate. In other phases, growth toward certain goals seems so reasonable and desirable that failure to progress toward them brings feelings of impoverishment.

Poverty in Respect to Time

A person may be *time poor,* because demands far exceed his time potential, even though he does the best he can to use his daily twenty-four hours as productively as possible. Such persons have to work hard on setting priorities, on sorting the wheat from the chaff in relation to the demands upon their time.

For an increasing proportion of people the situation is quite different. The problem is one of striving to fill the hours with satisfying experiences. Such persons have to strive to put more life into their hours. In light of mental health and morale, as well as the development of human potentials, this *poverty of motivation and self-direction in relation to time available* is a most serious problem.

Lack of education is another handicap. Many of our unemployed youth and adults are not able to meet their physical and other human needs because they lack opportunity to be trained for jobs. Many exceptional children and youth, the gifted as well as the handicapped, are not receiving the kind of education suited to their needs and potentials. One solution is to get into our colleges and universities those with special qualities of intellect and leadership. Lack of economic resources and physical space in institutions of higher education should not deprive able young people of opportunity to build on their special abilities and make the contributions to society of which they are capable.

Continuing education is needed by many adults so that they may learn to put more life into living. This is as important as being "retooled" to earn a living. In part, this is helping them to educate themselves for changing roles in our dynamic society. When people don't keep their educational levels tuned to their times as well as to their abilities, both society and the people themselves are the losers.

Our increasing concern for human rights, our evolving sense of interdependence, the ecumenical movement, and other developments require us to assess *poverty in human values.* One of the most serious problems is the gap between what we profess as our values and what we demonstrate in our behavior.

Poverty in the arts is a danger to both creator and spectator. Encouragement should be provided the creator to communicate his ideas through his medium. Opportunities should be provided the spectator to be stimulated and renewed through the artist's message. By taking advantage of such opportunities, our citizens can assuage their creative hunger.

One of the basic differences between man and animal is man's ability to think and reason. Frequently evidence of poor judgment, both individual and group, bears testimony to *impoverishment of reason* in our private and public affairs.

One of our most challenging problems is to get ourselves and others to identify those problems in life which deserve the particular attention of our resources of reason and strive to improve the order and creativity with which we deal with them. Failure to live up to our powers of rationality in the private and public sectors of our lives tends not only to limit the growth of the individual toward his potential for being human, but also to deprive society of the benefits of his thought. Such failure represents a gap between "what is" and "what should be" in the evolution of civilization.

Retrospect

Poverty is a persistent gap between "what is" and "what ought to be" as viewed subjectively by the individual himself, objectively by science, or according to the standards of society.

Poverty is not only the result of resources inadequate to the attainment of essentials; frequently it exists because people do not make reasonably productive use of the resources they do have. Restrictions of the physical, economic, and social environment may also contribute to poverty.

Poverty is not only deprivation, or maintenance of life at levels lower than the acceptable minimum, but also lack of human growth above minimum standards toward realization of human potentials.

Poverty of individuals and families may be humanistic as well as economic. Special problems are poverty of time, lack of education in particular segments of our population, deficiency in human values, poverty in the arts, and poverty of rationality. . . .

For the Child Who Has Nothing

At an international conference held at the National Academy of Sciences in Washington a small group of doctors, scientists, and scholars from twenty countries met to talk about young children — the one-to-five age group —

◇ From an editorial in *The New Republic*, December 26, 1964, pp. 7–9. Reprinted from *The New Republic*, © 1965, Harrison-Blaine of New Jersey, Inc., by permission.

in the so-called developing countries. These preschool youngsters constitute 25 per cent of the two billion population of these nations (compared to less than 10 per cent of the population in this country), and the nutritionists tell us that seven of every ten of them suffer from some form of malnutrition. Papers presented at the conference also said that malnutrition permanently impairs physical growth and that there is now strong evidence that malnutrition and irreparable mental retardation are related. The specialists say that unless it is stemmed, the growing incidence of malnutrition will have a major effect on "what our civilization looks, thinks and acts like — in 1984."

The scientists are speaking, of course, of those who are strong enough to survive. Up to half the children in these countries never make it to their fifth birthdays, a mortality rate some sixty times higher than in more affluent societies. Were the death rate in the pre-school age group in Latin America as it is in our country, for example, almost a third of a million fewer youngsters would die every year. Still more graphic, in a country like Libya a mother must have five children to be reasonably certain that one will ever reach the age of fifteen; and in Vietnam, the cumulative mortality approaches 40 per cent with four years of life. This is a proportion of deaths which is not reached until age sixty in the United States.

As if these figures are not striking enough, the highly regarded Mexican nutritionist Dr. Joaquin Cravioto says, "The true picture of child mortality due to malnutrition is still understated." Reason for such "understatement" may well be the unscientific tabulation of mortality rates. According to Dr. Cecily Williams, the grand British lady who keynoted the conference, the job of registering deaths is often left to policemen and postmasters. "In Malaya," she says, "the police had the responsibility of registering uncertified deaths. In one rural area it was found that deaths under the age of three were blamed on 'convulsions' or 'crying convulsions.' Those between three and thirty were usually ascribed to 'fever', and over thirty to 'senility.'"

It was Dr. Williams, incidentally, who many years ago in Africa first described the symptoms of child malnutrition and tagged to it the name of "kwashiorkor." This word from the Ga dialect in West Africa means "the sickness the older baby gets when the new baby comes." When the older child is replaced by the new baby at the mother's breast, the lack of a suitable diet soon makes the first child irritable and listless. Professor Ritchie Calder of the University of Edinburgh, another participant in this month's conference, says: "The most saddening experience I know is to look into the eyes of kwashiorkor; it is like looking into a dark lantern, in which the glint of childhood is unlit. The muscles waste, the skin cracks and scales, like peeling stucco on a wall. The hair loses its pigment. . . . Liver damage almost always occurs. If the child survives its third year, as an untreated case, it will go through life permanently damaged, with its mental and physical development impaired."

This growth retardation, according to studies conducted in fifteen countries by the National Institutes of Health, is approximately 20 to 30 per cent.

This means that by the time the child reaches the age of twelve, he has the physical development of a normal eight-year-old.

Just as serious in the eyes of the nutritionists as growth retardation is that malnutrition lowers resistance against infection. And once he is infected, the malnourished child is of course more susceptible to severe disease. The death rate due to measles in Guatemala, for example, is 228 times greater than in the United States. In Ecuador, it is 325 times greater.

Not too long ago, the matter of "preschool malnutrition" (a misleading professional label, since most of the children have no schools to be "pre" to) kept only the nutritionists and pediatricians awake at night. In recent years, however, it has been giving insomnia to others also.

The technical know-how exists to overcome the problem. In Mexico, for example, where increased attention is being given to small children, preschool deaths dropped 57 per cent in a decade. Some forward momentum is now sensed by many of the scientists. As suggested by one of the delegates in Washington, "We no longer seem to be trying to walk 'up' the 'down' escalator."

A number of conclusions are emerging, most of a long-range nature. These include nutrition eduation programs ("the way to a young child's stomach is through its mother's mind — and this is frequently blocked by grandma"), control of food wastage ("food loss in India due to rats, insects, poor storage and fungi amounts annually to three times the food deficit there"), and, of course, family planning ("every year, India increases its population an equivalent to the size of Greater New York").

Unfortunately, the current problems can't all wait for long-range solutions. Of the many approaches discussed by the experts, it was apparent that one of the easiest, quickest, and least-expensive steps would be to fortify and further enrich the massive quantities of food already being shipped to the needy abroad through America's Food For Peace Program. As part of this program, up to seventy-five million children are every day given some form of food supplement, much of this through CARE and the religious charitable agencies. However, "the nutritive value of these foods," according to Food For Peace Director Reuter (a former director of CARE himself), "could be considerably enhanced with simple vitamin fortification of the non-fat dry milk, and increased enrichment of the flour. Since the law creating this program was originally passed primarily as a surplus disposal measure," Mr. Reuter said, "no legislative authority exists to use additional funds to give our food the needed boost."

A recent NIH study suggests that in East Pakistan alone, 50,000 infants every year are blind for life because of Vitamin A deficiency. In Indonesia, the disease is said to "assume enormous proportions," with hundreds of thousands of children having markedly impaired vision. Vitamin A deficiency is reportedly "widespread," and "a grave threat to sight and survival."

One of the towering figures in this field, Dr. Nevin Scrimshaw of MIT, points out that to provide skim milk to areas already short in Vitamin A serves only to exaggerate the already existing nutritional imbalance. "The United States by sending skim milk to such areas," he says, "runs the risk of precipitating acute Vitamin A deficiency and even blindness. This would be both inhumane and politically dangerous."

"We in the United States have it within our power to prevent this kind of thing from happening," said Vice President . . . Hubert Humphrey in one of his final floor statements as a member of the Senate. One of the originators and long one of the staunchest supporters of Food For Peace, Senator Humphrey told his colleagues: "We can do this at a very minor cost. . . . We ought to find a way to make this minor adjustment in our Public Law 480 program [Food For Peace] to fortify our donated foods. . . ."

The cost has been estimated, for milk as an example, at two one-hundredths of one cent per child per day. Over a year-long period, this comes to something less than seven cents per child for enough Vitamin A and D in his milk to prevent possible blindness, to check rickets (a Vitamin D deficiency which affects the bone structure of up to 50 per cent of children in certain tropical countries), and increase resistance to infection.

Food For Peace Director Reuter points out that aside from the obvious moral concerns related to such an issue, the U.S. aid program has developed foreign markets for U.S. farmers (Japan is now the U.S. farmers' chief overseas customer), but "how can we expect a mother to buy American milk for her child when she can buy fortified milk from other countries at the same price?"

Vice President Humphrey has suggested that we must weigh the cost of fortifying our Food For Peace donations against the costs which may result from the consequences if we don't. "In East Pakistan alone," he says, "we are speaking of 50,000 potential invalids in *one* year in *one* small part of *one* country, who may well end up requiring some type of major welfare assistance. To the budget of that country — and the budget of this country which through its aid program supports that country — it seems a reasonable investment to spend pennies to prevent this kind of thing."

Such fortification and enrichment of our Food For Peace donations is by no means the answer to the problem of malnutrition among so-called preschool children, but according to Mr. Reuter, "it is a good step in that direction. We can feed them all we want when they're six years old — but by then it may well be too late; the damage has been done. Their tomorrows depend on today."

Characteristics of the Disadvantaged

In the opening selections for Part Two, Millard H. Black and Frank Reissman discuss the many characteristics of disadvantaged children. The disadvantaged have a slow mental style that may give the impression of stupidity, but they often perform intellectual tasks well if given enough time. They are typically physical-oriented, one-track learners but may have considerable creative potential. Much verbal diversity is evident in out-of-school and peer-group activities or in role-playing situations, but the quality of language employed has severe limitations. There is some evidence that disadvantaged groups have a much more positive attitude toward education than is generally believed.

The weaknesses of disadvantaged youngsters revolve around the problem of "know-how." Included here is the academic know-how of the school setting and of the middle class in general. Deficiencies are rooted in ineffective habits of perception (auditory and visual discrimination), reinforced by conditions of crowded living, the absence of basic need fulfillment, and loss of hope and aspiration. Riessman suggests special teacher training, special classes for children, and longer periods of time in school and college without "invidious connotations."

Robert D. Strom and Earl C. Kelley focus on school dropouts, who are concentrated among disadvantaged groups. Annually, seven hundred thousand students drop out of school, many to take their places on the human scrap-heap of frustration and failure. Although the potential dropout can be identified as early as nursery school or kindergarten, little concentrated effort has been devoted to early treatment of the problems which lead to failure and discouragement later on, or to follow-through programs. Strom suggests that schools have resisted the integration of new knowledge and research with school programs, especially in the area of individual differences. He warns, "Until potential dropouts are individually helped to succeed, schools collectively will fail." Kelley suggests that teachers must see themselves in a helping role rather than in a role of doing something *to* people, something determined before the one needing help is even seen. If all teachers do first things first, he says, many of the other goals, such as literacy, can then be realized.

The increasing recognition of the effect of social class on teaching and learning in the schools has resulted in a "damned-if-you-do, damned-if-you-don't" dilemma for teachers. Eleanor and Leo Wolf, who believe that exaggerated claims and expectations have contributed to frustration and failure among the teaching profession, caution against certain pitfalls:

> There is sometimes a tendency to overgeneralize and oversimplify the problems of minorities by focusing mainly on the similarities between groups while neglecting crucial differences. . . .
>
>   . . . .
> There is a tendency to exaggerate the nature and scope of the influence that schools can wield. . . .
>
>   . . . .
> We must guard against a tendency to scapegoat the individual classroom teacher. Teachers are often confronted by contradictory admonitions. . . .

Finally, James E. Heald presents an admirable defense of middle-class values. He emphasizes that the values held by middle-class teachers have been "castigated, convicted, and condemned." But what kind of value system should be substituted? Several logical choices for teachers are noted:

1. They may accept the values of another class.
2. They may reject the values of the middle class without substituting a new value system. (This would seem a psychological impossibility.)
3. They may replace their current value system with a new one, the nature of which is yet undetermined.

The case for the defense of middle-class values is built by refuting the first possibility and by supplying some determinants for the third.

Characteristics of the Culturally Disadvantaged Child

MILLARD H. BLACK

Who is the educationally or culturally disadvantaged child? What are his characteristics? What are some of the factors of his environment which affect his educational achievement? These questions, together with a determination of procedures which will compensate for or ameliorate his disadvantage, are areas of great and grave concern, not only in Chicago, Los Angeles, New York, and other great cities, but in many other areas which are in economic and social transition.

Who Is the Educationally or Culturally Disadvantaged Child?

The answer varies from state to state, from city to city. He lives not only in the central area of our great cities. One southern governor in January 1964 declared that 20 per cent of the citizens of his state can neither read nor write, that 50 per cent of the state's young people fail to complete high school. The disadvantaged child is of no single race or color: poverty, delinquency, failure to achieve the goals established by the main stream of society are shared by peoples of all colors and national origins.

The disadvantaged individual may derive from a culture which is rich in its own tradition, but which no longer prepares its members for successful participation in society. The change in economic patterns apparent over the past half-century was intensified by World War II. People from submarginal farms have been forced into cities, while in the cities jobs for the unskilled are decreasing. Thousands have learned that their older ways of life no longer are effective.

What Are the Characteristics of the Culturally Disadvantaged Child?

He is no stranger to failure and to the fear that continued failure engenders. He knows the fear of being overpowered by teachers who are ignorant of the culture and mores of his society, and who may not expect success of him. He fears lack of recognition and understanding from teachers

✧ From *The Reading Teacher*, March, 1965, pp. 465–470. Reprinted with permission of Millard H. Black and the International Reading Association. Millard H. Black is Elementary Reading Supervisor, Curriculum Branch, Los Angeles City School Districts.

whose backgrounds are totally dissimilar and who either misinterpret or fail to recognize many of his efforts to achieve and to accommodate himself to demands which are basically alien.

Riessman (8) describes these characteristics of the deprived individual: (a) is relatively slow at cognitive tasks, but not stupid; (b) appears to learn most readily through a physical, concrete approach (often is slow, but may be persistent when the content is meaningful and valued); (c) often appears to be anti-intellectual, pragmatic rather than theoretical; (d) is traditional, superstitious, and somewhat religious in a traditional sense; (e) is from a male-centered culture, except for a major section of the Negro subculture; (f) is inflexible and not open to reason about many of his beliefs (morality, diet, family polarity, and educational practice are examples of these beliefs); (g) feels alienated from the larger social structure, with resultant frustration; (h) holds others to blame for his misfortunes; (i) values masculinity and attendant action, viewing intellectual activities as unmasculine; (j) appreciates knowledge for its practical, vocational ends, but rarely values it for its own sake; (k) desires a better standard of living, with personal comforts for himself and his family, but does not wish to adopt a middle-class way of life; (l) is deficient in auditory attention and interpretation skills; (m) reads ineffectively and is deficient in the communication skills generally, has wide areas of ignorance, and often is suggestible, although he may be suspicious of innovations. Other delimiting characteristics reported by Riessman have been included among the factors discussed in later paragraphs.

In assessing some of the strengths of this group of children, Riessman describes them as: (a) being relatively free of the strains which accompany competitiveness and the need to establish oneself as an individual; (b) having the cooperativeness and mutual aid which marks an extended family; (c) being free of self-blame; (d) enjoying other members of the family and not competing with them; (e) having the security deriving from an extended family and a traditional outlook; (f) enjoying games, music, sports, and cars.

The following factors, reflecting the conclusions of many persons who have studied the causes and results of cultural disadvantage, are believed by Dr. Newton S. Metfessel (6) to be operative in the lives of children from disadvantaged homes.[1] The grouping of these factors and the remarks relative to them are the work of this writer.

LANGUAGE FACTORS. One such grouping may be termed language factors:

1. Culturally disadvantaged children understand more language than they use. This comparison between understanding and usage does not imply a wide hearing or understanding vocabulary. Figurel (5) reports that at grade two the vocabulary of such children is approximately one-third that of normal children, while at grade six it is about one-half.

---

[1] Reported with the permission of Dr. Metfessel, Director of the Center for the Study of the Education of Disadvantaged Youth at the University of Southern California.

2. Culturally disadvantaged children frequently use a great many words with fair precision, but not those words representative of the school culture. Figurel states that "less than half of the words in the vocabulary of pre-school children are known by second-grade children in slum areas." He also states that "common name words, such as *sink, chimney, honey, beef,* and *sandwich* are learned by culturally disadvantaged children one or two years later than by other children."

3. Culturally disadvantaged children frequently are crippled in language development because they do not perceive the concept that objects have names, and that the same objects may have different names. The impoverished economic conditions under which these pupils are reared, with a scarcity of objects of all types, and the absence of discussion which characterizes communication in the substandard home prejudice against the development of labels and of the concept of a specific name (or names) for everything.

4. Culturally disadvantaged kindergarten children use fewer words with less variety to express themselves than do kindergarten children of higher socioeconomic classes. The use of language by the child chiefly to express his concrete needs, and by parents and other adults to command the child to perform some function, may contribute to the severe limitation of self-expression.

5. Culturally disadvantaged children use a significantly smaller proportion of mature sentence structures, such as compound, complex, and more elaborate constructions. This is not limited to the non-English-speaking child, but occurs among most children who come from culturally disadvantaged areas.

6. Culturally disadvantaged children learn less from what they hear than do middle-class children. The importance of teaching all children the skills of listening has often been pointed out. This appears to be particularly true for disadvantaged children, who come from a milieu in which the radio, television, and the sounds made by many people living in crowded quarters provide a background of noise from which the individual must retreat.

LEARNING PATTERNS. The next grouping of the factors assembled by Metfessel have to do with learning patterns:

1. Culturally disadvantaged children tend to learn more readily by inductive than by deductive approaches. It appears reasonable to assume that low self-esteem, induced by long economic deprivation, discrimination, or both, may cause pupils to distrust their own judgment or conclusions; they need the support of an authoritarian figure in the classroom. The difficulties in using a discovery technique in teaching disadvantaged pupils are obvious.

2. Culturally disadvantaged children generally are unaccustomed to "insight building" by external use of lectures and discussions at home. In homes where families are preoccupied with supplying the elemental needs,

there may be little opportunity to help children learn the techniques of discussion or to move from observation to conclusions. Deutsch (3) reports that "the lower class home is not verbally oriented," and the result is a diminution of the child's general level of responsiveness.

3. Culturally disadvantaged children are frequently symbolically deprived; for example, imaginary playmates are much less acceptable to the parents of culturally disadvantaged children when compared to their middle-class counterparts. The average middle-class parent appears to accept the imaginations of his children, whether or not he understands their educational and psychological import. On the other hand, parents from less affluent circumstances tend to look upon such imagining, even in very young children, as "lying" and to punish when it is observed.

4. Culturally disadvantaged children need to see concrete application of what is learned to immediate sensory and topical satisfaction. This is of particular importance in a school culture in which primary emphasis is placed on long-term goals, which can be met only by foregoing immediate satisfactions. The importance of a series of well defined instructional tasks and attendant goals, continued verbalization, and frequent evaluation of progress is implied by this factor.

5. Culturally disadvantaged children tend to have poor attention span and consequently experience difficulty in following the orders of a teacher. Several authorities have reported the great amount of time children spend listening in the classroom. Research shows that pupils "tune in and out" on the teacher, supplying from context and from their own experience much that they miss during these brief periods of inattention. The lack of connected discourse and generally inadequate communication processes in the disadvantaged home foster the inability of children to attend. This environmental deficiency is reinforced by differences in the vocabulary and syntax used in the classroom and in the home. The pupil whose cultural background is the same as that of the teacher is in a position to supply through context much that he may have missed during intermittent periods of inattention. The sparseness of furnishings in the homes of the very poor, the general drab visual quality of the environment, tend to deny the pupil needed exercise in organization, perception, and reorganization of the objects in the environment.

READINESS FOR INSTRUCTION. Four additional factors included by Metfessel are related to this concept:

1. The culturally disadvantaged child often is characterized by significant gaps in knowledge and learning. Entering school from a background which has not adequately prepared him for success in a traditional curriculum, the pupil participates in communication procedures and patterns alien to him. These disadvantages are multiplied by frequent changes of residence and school, particularly in the lower grades.

2. Culturally disadvantaged children generally have had little experience of receiving approval for success in a task. Born into a community in which relatively few adults have been successful in school, the disadvantaged child

hardly can be expected to be self-motivated in his work in the classroom. The teacher's commonest motivation — "You read that well, John," or "Mary, that was a good report" — fails with this pupil because he has rarely experienced praise in his home. Lack of responsibility in the home is not to be inferred. Child care and housekeeping tasks are assumed regularly and successfully by many of these children who are not yet in their teens.

3. Culturally disadvantaged children are characterized by narrow experience outside the home. Children's participation in activities which are assumed by almost every teacher may be nonexistent among lowest-income groups. Without background to promote understanding, how much will the pupil gain from studying about these activities?

4. Culturally deprived children have very little concept of relative size. Limited in the communication skills, deprived of many experiences which help to build concepts of things to which he must react in the classroom, comprehension of much about which he studies will be severely limited.

SCHOOL BEHAVIOR. Three factors are directly related to behavior in school:

1. Culturally deprived children generally are unaware of the "ground rules" for success in school. The ignorance of *how* to be successful does not imply unawareness of the values of education. Although their reasons may differ from those given by persons in other social groups, many adults and adolescents among low-income groups express their need for education.

2. Culturally disadvantaged children frequently end the reading habit before it is begun. Metfessel continues, saying that "the cycle of skill mastery which demands that successful experiences generate more motivation to read which in turn generates levels of skill sufficient to prevent discouragement, and so on, may be easily reversed in direction and end the reading habit prior to its beginning." Books, magazines, and newspapers are more easily dispensable than food and clothing; among very low income groups they do not represent necessities.

3. Culturally disadvantaged children are placed at a marked disadvantage in timed test situations. Efforts to apply objective measures to almost every phase of school interest and activity have doubtful value for the children from a very low income home. Accurate determination of their potential and their achievement must be obtained through some technique which does not penalize them with rigidly defined time limitations.

4. Culturally disadvantaged children need assistance in perceiving an adult as a person of whom you ask questions and receive answers. The growing tendency of teachers to act as *directors* of classroom activity and to perceive themselves as resource persons implies an area in which culturally disadvantaged children will need specific help. They must be helped to accommodate themselves to an adult role which is unfamiliar to them.

What Are the Characteristics of a Disadvantaged Area?

We can round out the description of our culturally disadvantaged chil-dren by citing some characteristics of a large area in Los Angeles County, which appear to be similar to the characteristics of other very low income areas. Agencies which are seeking to ameliorate cultural disadvantage state that in this area: (a) the percentage of broken homes is almost three times that of the total county; (b) family income is 25 per cent below the county median; (c) population density is approximately double that of the entire county; (d) housing is substandard, and continues to decline in quality; (e) the school dropout rate is 2.2 times as large as the average of the city; and (f) youth delinquency rates are higher in almost all offense categories than for the county generally.

REFERENCES

1. Ausubel, David P., and Pearl Ausubel. "Ego Development Among Segregated Negro Children," in A. Harry Passow (ed.), *Education in Depressed Areas*. New York: Bureau of Publications, Columbia University, 1963. Pp. 109–141.

2. Conant, James B. *Slums and Suburbs*. New York: McGraw-Hill Book Co., 1961.

3. Deutsch, Martin P. "The Disadvantaged Child and the Learning Process," in A. Harry Passow (ed.), *Education in Depressed Areas*. New York: Bureau of Publications, Columbia University, 1963. Pp. 163–179.

4. Educational Policies Commission, National Education Association. *Education and the Disadvantaged American*. Washington: The Association, 1962.

5. Figurel, J. Allen. "Limitations in the Vocabulary of Disadvantaged Children: A Cause of Poor Reading," in *Improvement of Reading Through Classroom Practice*, Proceedings of the Annual Convention of the International Reading Association, Vol. 9. New York: Scholastic Magazines, Inc., 1964.

6. Metfessel, Newton S. Unpublished research, Center for the Study of the Education of Disadvantaged Youth, University of Southern California, 1964.

7. Passow, A. Harry (ed.), *Education in Depressed Areas*. New York: Bureau of Publications, Columbia University, 1963.

8. Riessman, Frank. *The Culturally Deprived Child*. New York: Harper & Row, Publishers, 1962.

9. ———. "The Culturally Deprived Child: A New View," *Education Digest*, 29: 12–15; November, 1963.

✧ ✧ 6 ✧ ✧

The Overlooked Positives of Disadvantaged Groups

FRANK RIESSMAN

I have been interested in the problems of lower socioeconomic groups for about fifteen years, during most of which time there has been a lack of concern for the educational problems of children from low-income families. In the last five years, however, this attitude has changed markedly. There is now an enormous interest on the part of practitioners and academic people in this problem. I think we are on the point of a major breakthrough in terms of dealing with this question.

After appraising a good deal of the recent work that has been done on the education of disadvantaged children, I feel that there is a considerable agreement regarding many of the recommendations for dealing with the problem, although there are some very different emphases. What is missing, however, is a theoretic rationale to give meaning and direction to the action suggestions. I should like to attempt to provide the beginnings of such a rationale.

I think that a basic theoretic approach here has to be based on the culture of lower socioeconomic groups and more particularly the elements of strength, the positives in this culture. The terms "deprived," "handicapped," "underprivileged," "disadvantaged," unfortunately emphasize environmental limitations and ignore the positive efforts of low-income individuals to cope with their environment. Most approaches concerned with educating the disadvantaged child either overlook the positives entirely, or merely mention in passing that there are positive features in the culture of low socioeconomic groups, that middle-class groups might learn from, but they do not spell out what these strengths are, and they build educational programs almost exclusively around the weaknesses or deficits.

I want to call attention to the positive features in the culture and the psychology of low-income individuals. In particular, I should like to look at the cognitive style, the mental style or way of thinking characteristics of these people. One major dimension of this style is slowness.

✧ From the *Journal of Negro Education*, Summer, 1964, pp. 225–231. Used by permission of the author and the publisher. Frank Riessman is a psychologist on the staff of Mobilization for Youth, Inc., and Professor of Psychology, Bard College.

This is a revision of an opening address before the Conference on the Education of Disadvantaged Children sponsored by the U.S. Office of Education, May 21–23, 1962, in Washington, D.C.

Slow *vs.* Dull

Most disadvantaged children are relatively slow in performing intellectual tasks. This slowness is an important feature of their mental style and it needs to be carefully evaluated. In considering the question of the slowness of the deprived child, we would do well to recognize that in our culture there has probably been far too much emphasis on speed. We reward speed. We think of the fast child as the smart child and the slow child as the dull child. I think this is a basically false idea. I think there are many weaknesses in speed and many strengths in slowness.

The teacher can be motivated to develop techniques for rewarding slow pupils if she has an appreciation of some of the positive attributes of a slow style of learning. The teacher should know that pupils may be slow for other reasons than because they are stupid.

A pupil may be slow because he is extremely careful, meticulous, or cautious. He may be slow because he refuses to generalize easily. He may be slow because he can't understand a concept unless he does something physically, e.g., with his hands, in connection with the idea he is trying to grasp.

The disadvantaged child is typically a physical learner and the physical learner is generally a slower learner. Incidentally, the physical style of learning is another important characteristic of the deprived individual and it, too, has many positive features hitherto overlooked.

A child may be slow because he learns in what I have called a one-track way. That is, he persists in one line of thought and is not flexible or broad. He does not easily adopt other frames of reference, such as the teacher's, and consequently he may appear slow and dull.

Very often this single-minded individual has considerable creative potential, much of which goes unrealized because of lack of reinforcement in the educational system.

Analysis of the many reasons for slowness leads to the conclusion that slowness should not be equated with stupidity. In fact, there is no reason to assume that there are not a great many slow, gifted children.

The school in general does not pay too much attention to the slow gifted child but rather is alert to discover fast gifted children. Excellence comes in many packages and we must begin to search for it among the slow learners as well as among the faster individuals.

My own understanding of some of the merits of the slow style came through teaching at Bard College, where there is an enrollment of about 350 students. There I had the opportunity of getting to know quite well about forty students over a period of four years. I could really see what happened to them during this time. Very often the students I thought were slow and dull in their freshman year achieved a great deal by the time they became seniors. These are not the over-all bright people who are typically selected by colleges, but in some area, in a one-track way, these students did some marvelous creative work. It was too outstanding to be ignored. I discovered in talking with students that most of them had spent five or six years in order to complete college. They had failed courses and made them up in summer school. Some had dropped out of college for a period of time and taken courses in night school. These students are slow learners, often one-track learners, but very persistent about something when they develop an interest in it. They have a fear of being overpowered by teachers in situations where they don't accept the teacher's point of view, but they stick to their own particular way of seeing the problem. They don't have a fast pace, they don't catch on quickly, and they very often fail subjects.

At the present time, when there is a measure of public excitement for reducing the four-year college to three years, I would submit that many potentially excellent students need a five- or six-year span to complete a college education.

The assumption that the slow pupil is not bright functions, I think, as a self-fulfilling prophecy. If the teachers act toward these pupils as if they were dull, the pupils will frequently come to function in this way. Of course, there are pupils who are very well developed at an early age and no teacher can stop them. But in the average development of the young person, even at the college level, there is need for reinforcement. The teacher must pick up what he says, appeal to him, and pitch examples to him. Typically this does not occur with the slow child. I find in examining my own classroom teaching that I easily fall into the habit of rewarding pupils whose faces light up when I talk, who are quick to respond to me and I respond back to them. The things they say in class become absorbed in the repertoire of what I say. I remember what they say and I use it in providing examples, etc. I don't pick up and select the slower pupil and I don't respond to him. He has to make it on his own.

In the teacher training program future teachers should be taught to guard against the almost unconscious and automatic tendency of the teacher to respond to the pupil who responds to him.

Hidden Verbal Ability

A great deal has been said about the language or verbal deficit supposedly characteristic of disadvantaged children. Everybody in the school system, at one time or another, has heard that these children are inarticulate, nonverbal, etc. But is not this too simple a generalization? Aren't these children quite verbal in out-of-school situations? For example, that the educationally deprived child can be quite articulate in conversation with his peers is well illustrated by the whole language developed by urban Negro groups, some of which is absorbed into the main culture via the Beatnik and the musician, if you dig what I mean.

Many questions about the verbal potential of disadvantaged children must be answered by research. Under what conditions are they verbal? What kind of stimuli do they respond to verbally? With whom are they verbal? What do they talk about? What parts of speech do they use? Martin Deutsch of New York Medical College is doing some very significant research trying to specify these factors and I surveyed some of his findings in my book, *The Culturally Deprived Child.* I think Deutsch is getting at some very interesting things. One technique he uses is a clown that lights up when the children say something. "Inarticulate" children can be very verbal and expressive in this situation.

Disadvantaged children are often surprisingly articulate in role-playing situations. One day when I was with a group of these youngsters, sometimes mistaken for a "gang," I asked them, "Why are you sore at the teachers?" Even though I was on good terms with them, I could not get much of a response. Most of them answered in highly abbreviated sentences. However, after I held a role-playing session in which some of the youngsters acted out the part of the teachers while others acted out the parts of the pupils, these "inarticulate" youngsters changed sharply. Within a half-hour they were bubbling over with very verbal and very sensitive answers to the questions I had asked earlier. They were telling me about the expressions on the teachers' faces that they did not like. They reported that they knew the minute they entered the room that the teacher did not like them and that she did not think they were going to do well in school. Their analyses were specific and remarkably verbal.

However, the quality of language employed has its limitations and I think herein lies the deficit. As Basil Bernstein indicates, the difference is between formal language and public language, between a language in a written book and the informal, everyday language. There is no question in my mind that there is a deficit in formal language. Since this deficit is fairly clear, the question might be asked, why make such an issue of the positive verbal ability to these children.

The reason is that it is easy to believe, that too many people have come to believe, that this formal deficit in language means that deprived people are characteristically nonverbal.

On the other hand, if the schools have the idea that these pupils are basically very good verbally, teachers might approach them in a different manner. Teachers might look for additional techniques to bring out the verbal facility. They might abandon the prediction that deprived children will not go very far in the education system and predict instead that they can go very far indeed because they have very good ability at the verbal level. In other words, an awareness of the positive verbal ability — not merely potential — will lead to demanding more of the disadvantaged child and expecting more of him.

Education *vs.* The School

There is a good deal of evidence that deprived children and their parents have a much more positive attitude towards education than is generally believed. One factor that obscures the recognition of this attitude is that while deprived individuals value education, they dislike the school. They are alienated from the school and they resent the teachers. For the sake of clarity, their attitude toward education and toward the school must be considered separately.

In a survey conducted a few years ago, people were asked, "What did you miss most in life that you would like your children to have?" Over 70 per cent of the lower, socioeconomic groups answered, "Education." The answer was supplied by the respondents, not checked on a list. They could have answered "money," "happiness," "health," or a number of things. And I think this is quite significant. Middle-class people answer "education" less frequently because they had an education and do not miss it as much.

A nation-wide poll conducted by Roper after World War II asked, "If you had a son or daughter graduating from high school, would you prefer to have him or her go on to college, do something else, wouldn't care?" The affirmative response to the college choice was given by 68 per cent of the "poor," and 91 per cent for the more prosperous. The difference is significant, but 68 per cent of the poorer people is a large, absolute figure and indicates that a large number of these people are interested in a college education for their children.

Why then do these people who have a positive attitude towards education, hold a negative attitude towards the school? These youngsters and their parents recognize that they are second-class citizens in the school and they are angry about it. From the classroom to the PTA they discover that the school does not like them, does not respond to them, does not appreciate their culture, and does not think they can learn.

Also, these children and their parents want education for different reasons than those presented by the school. They do not easily accept the ideas of expressing yourself, developing yourself, or knowledge for its own sake. They want education much more for vocational ends. But underneath there is a very positive attitude towards education and I think this is predominant in the lower socioeconomic Negro groups. In the Higher Horizons program in New York City the parents have participated eagerly once they have seen that the school system is concerned about their children. One of the tremendously positive features about this program and the Great Cities programs is the concern for disadvantaged children and the interest in them. This the deprived have not experienced before and even if the programs did nothing else, I believe that the parents and the children would be responsive and would become involved in the school, because of the demonstrated concern for them.

Some Weaknesses

A basic weakness of deprived youngsters which the school can deal with is the problem of "know-how." Included here is the academic "know-how" of the school culture as well as the "know-how" of the middle class generally. Knowing how to get a job, how to appear for an interview, how to fill out a form, how to take tests, how to answer questions, and how to listen.

The last is of particular importance. The whole style of learning of the deprived is not set to respond to oral or written stimuli. These children respond much more readily to visual kinesthetic signals. We should remodel the schools to suit the styles and meet the needs of these children.

But no matter how much we change the school to suit their needs, we nevertheless have to change these children in certain ways; namely, reading, formal language, test taking, and general "know-how."

These weaknesses represent deficiencies in skills and techniques. However, there is one basic limitation at the value level, namely the anti-intellectual attitudes of deprived groups. It is the only value of lower socioeconomic groups which I would fight in the school. I want to make it very clear that I am very much opposed to the school spending a lot of time teaching values to these kids. I am much more concerned — and in this I am traditional — that the schools impart skills, techniques, and knowledge rather than training the disadvantaged to become good middle-class children.

However, I think there is one area indigenous to the school which has to be fought out at some point with these youngsters; that is their attitude toward intellectuals, toward knowledge for its own sake, and similar issues.

These children and their parents are pretty much anti-intellectual at all levels. They do not like "eggheads." They think talk is a lot of bull. I would consciously oppose this attitude in the school. I would make the issue explicit. There would be nothing subtle or covert about it. I would at some point state clearly that on this question the school does not agree with them and is prepared to argue about the views they hold.

Other Positive Dimensions

In my book, *The Culturally Deprived Child,* and in various speeches, I have elaborated more fully on these and other positive dimensions of the culture and style of educationally deprived people. A brief list would include the following: cooperativeness and mutual aid that mark the extended family; the avoidance of the strain accompanying competitiveness and individualism; the equalitarianism, in informality and humor; the freedom from self-blame and parental overprotection; the children's enjoyment of each other's company and lessened sibling rivalry, the security found in the extended family and a traditional outlook; the enjoyment of music, games, sports, and cards; the ability to express anger; the freedom from being word-bound; an externally oriented rather than an introspective outlook; a spatial rather than temporal perspective; an expressive orientation in contrast to an instrumental one; content-centered not a form-centered mental style; a problem-centered rather than an abstract-centered approach; and finally, the use of physical and visual style in learning.

Summary and Implications

I have attempted to reinterpret some of the supposedly negative aspects — e.g., slowness — that characterize the cognitive style of disadvantaged individuals. I have given particular attention to the untapped verbal ability of these individuals and have indicated the basic weaknesses of the disadvantaged child which the school must overcome, such as the lack of school know-how, anti-intellectualism, and limited experience with formal language. Others which should be noted here are poor auditory attention, poor time perspective, inefficient test-taking skills, and limited reading ability.

The school must recognize these deficiencies and work assiduously to combat them. They are by no means irreversible, but even more important, because neglected, the positive elements in the culture and style of lower socioeconomic groups should become the guide lines for new school programs and new educational techniques for teaching these children.

There are a number of reasons why it is important to emphasize the positive:

1. It will encourage the school to develop approaches and techniques, including possibly special teaching machines, appropriate for the cognitive style of deprived children.

2. It will enable children of low-income backgrounds to be educated without middle-classifying them.

3. It will stimulate teachers to aim high, to expect more and work for more from these youngsters. Thus, it will constrain against patronization and condescension, and determinate, double-track systems where the deprived child never arrives on the main track.

4. It will function against the current tendency of overemphasizing both vocational, nonacademic education for children of low-income background.

5. It will provide an exciting challenge for teachers if they realize that they need not simply aim to "bring these children up to grade level," but rather can actually develop new kinds of creativity.

6. It will make the school far more pluralistic and democratic because different cultures and styles will exist and interact side by side. Thus, each can learn from the other and the empty phrase that the teacher has much to learn from deprived children will take on real meaning. General cultural interaction between equal cultures can become the hallmark of the school.

7. It will enable the teacher to see that when techniques such as role-playing and visual aids are used with deprived children it is because these techniques are useful for eliciting the special cognitive style and creative potential of these children. All too often these techniques have been employed with the implicit assumption that they are useful with children who have inadequate learning ability.

8. It will lead to real appreciation of slowness, one-track learning and physical learning as potential strengths which require careful nurturing. The teacher will have to receive special training in how to respond to these styles, how to listen carefully to the one-track person, how to reward the slow learner, etc. Special classes for slow learners will not culminate in the removal of these youngsters from the mainstream of the educational process on a permanent second track, and longer periods of time in school and college can be planned for these students without invidious connotations.

Dr. Irving Taylor, who has been concerned with various types of creativity in our American society, has observed that the mental style of the socially and economically disadvantaged learners resembles the mental style of one type of highly creative persons. Our schools should provide for the development of these unique, untapped national sources of creativity.

$$\diamond \diamond \; 7 \; \diamond \diamond$$

The School Dropout and the Family

ROBERT D. STROM

> Two roads diverged in a wood, and I —
> I took the one less traveled by,
> And that has made all the difference.
>
> —ROBERT FROST, "THE ROAD NOT TAKEN"

There was a time when it mattered less what road a person chose in life, for many paths held promise of success. But today the traveled road of education, be it preparation for vocation, training for a skill, or learning to be what one might become, makes all the difference. Knowing this, educators are justly concerned about the annual loss of seven hundred thousand students, "the dropouts," those who have chosen the road less traveled.

Any major reduction of dropout incidence will be contingent upon increased understanding about the homes from which such youngsters come. Although one cannot assess the extent to which misconceptions regarding parental influence have served to delimit progress, few would deny the amount as influential. This has been especially true with reference to homes of dropouts in lower socioeconomic neighborhoods.

Where the so-called "culture of poverty" exists, there are familial tendencies which induce conditions that foster dropout. Here one finds a high proportion of disrupted and broken homes where the father often is absent and in which an emotional distance between parents results in dilution of affection for the young. Where no father is present during the evening, there is usually no organized meal, no organized opportunity for language exchange, no real interaction. A common result is cumulative deficit in the language component of a child's development. Since this deficit is qualitative and not quantitative, it is erroneous to believe these children are characteristically nonverbal.

There is a dearth of family activity outside the home, so many youngsters never have been to the country, to another city, or, in some instances, even out of their neighborhood. Recognizing the inadequacy of life space in

◇ From *School and Society*, April 18, 1964, pp. 191–192. Used by permission of the author and the publisher. Robert D. Strom is Associate Professor of Education, The Ohio State University.

Based on a paper presented at the Annual Home Economics Convention, University of Kentucky, Lexington, November 8, 1963.

which such children function, educators have attempted to compensate for "cultural deprivation" by initiating early school enrichment programs designed to include a dimension of experiences which are comparable to the background usually brought to school by children from middle-class families. Ostensibly, this exposure will allow the child from a poor neighborhood a more adequate chance to compete in school.

If, in fact, competition is a virtue of school programing, it is unfortunate that we eliminate much competitive potential of youngsters from slum areas. We do this failing to recognize certain strengths emerging from their background. When these strengths are declared off-limits, they become nonfunctional and the child is forced to compete at a disadvantage by using strengths characteristic of the middle class. For example, youngsters of poverty often have a richness of language expression which is unacceptable in classrooms. Though high in verbal output, such a child usually has poor command of syntax and verb form and thus is unable to say what he would like to say because class rules demand proper expression.

Moreover, students from slums manifest a remarkable degree of independence, seldom needing continued adult approval for their actions. They are ready for responsibilities in the classroom, but, under the current system, anyone with poor grades is denied such an opportunity. These children have a lengthy interest span for that which is familiar to them. Lamentably, most of the materials in texts do not represent the type of life to which they have been exposed, so their attention span is unfairly considered as shorter than that of middle-class kids. It is hoped that some of the strengths of children from the culture of poverty may become functional in the school if our aims to encourage and enhance self-esteem is to be realized.

Finally, the social image of low-income parents as held by teachers serves to restrict pupil learning. John Niemeyer, president, Bank Street College, New York City, asserts that a major reason for low achievement among children in poor neighborhoods is the low expectation regarding their learning capacity as held by teachers. However, the converse is equally disappointing. Parents, who believe that all teachers are emotionally distant from lower-class pupils, perpetuate a myth.

Some parents in low-income areas may be naïve, but they do have deep hope that through the school their children will achieve a better life than they and their parents have had, even though they may not know how to give the support which is the logical concomitant of this attitude. In terms of fundamental motivation which can serve to aid learning, what more can a school ask?

The magnitude of problems in the culture of poverty ought not to prompt one to assume that the desired parent-student and home-school relationships exist in the middle class. For many parents in this segment of society who live through their children as extensions of themselves, somehow hoping to accomplish through their progeny what was not possible in their own life, the concept of preparation for college becomes a paramount concern from the day a child enters kindergarten to the senior prom. Realizing that promotions, honors, awards, and scholarships are contingent upon marks, many parents choose grades for their child rather than growth as a goal in school. The student, if successfully indoctrinated, relocates his interest from subject to grade. In middle-class neighborhoods, report cards are used by parents as status symbols; a premium is put on marks, and parents often bribe, cajole, or threaten a child to obtain them.

Underlying the pressure imposed on the child is an assumption that most if not all can have high grades if they just work hard enough. In many cases, this results in a student making lower marks than his industry normally would permit him to make because his concern impedes effective concentration. Some whose school work has become grade-oriented are unduly disappointed as they perceive a failing grade as complete failure and, hence, lose even that which is within their reach. The unnecessary anxiety, disappointment, and parental disfavor accompanying report time for some youngsters is a first step toward dropout.

As parent surrogate operating *in loco parentis*, how does the school affect dropout? In some ways the affect has been to stimulate enrichment and remedial programs, but by and large it has been negligible or negative. Before the potential dropout can realize his appropriate educational opportunity, certain views must undergo alteration. Popular acceptance is needed for a concept which allows quality to occur within a framework of quantity. Presently, quality is viewed solely as academic rigor and necessarily is confined to those whose intellectual prowess has been demonstrated. Adherence to this limited view of quality finds expression in schools which perpetuate a restricted formalized curriculum that was appropriate in the 19th century when only the so-called "cultured few" were represented in secondary schools. When one prescribed then that "everybody" should study certain subjects, "everybody" meant anybody who was somebody, but today the term "everybody" is coming to mean "everyone."

Actual curricular change has not kept pace with changes in educational objectives as our schools ostensibly have moved from serving a select clientele to the future body politic. In some cases, educators have shown a remarkable ability to resist new knowledge and research findings. This has been especially true in the area of individual differences, where resistance to innovations of proven value would seem to indicate a belief that it might be easier for youngsters to modify their needs than for the school to change its requirements.

Every year a significant number of basically sound young Americans discover that they are not really wanted and that neither their teachers nor their curricular experiences seem to pay any attention to who they are, what they have and what they have not, and what they can do and what they cannot do. Instead, imposed upon them is a nonsensical experience which goes under the name of education.

Arthur Koestler's "Darkness at Noon" has the chief character, Citizen Rubashov, state the following dilemma of one who has fallen victim to his own political party: "The party denied the free will by the individual and at the same time expected his willing self sacrifice. It denied his capacity to choose between two alternatives and at the same time demanded that he should constantly choose the right one. It denied his power to distinguish good and evil and at the same time spoke pathetically of guilt and treachery." Perhaps analogy is not amiss at this point. Do we not overwork the language or doctrine of individual differences and yet seldom employ this practice in teaching and evaluating children? Do we not insist that children remain in school because it is good for them when, in fact, for those whose history of failure is constant, this is socially sadistic? Do we not tell the student he ought to choose what's right and yet limit his right of choice by giving him no alternative within the curriculum? Is tyranny a word for events on foreign soil or does it include the practices of some public schools? Until potential dropouts are individually helped to succeed, schools collectively will fail.

Seeds of Dropouts

EARL C. KELLEY

There is a good deal of valid research which shows that high school dropouts can be identified very early. Some say that they can be located in the third grade; some contend that they can be detected as early as the kindergarten. Therefore, the dropout is not strictly a secondary school problem but also an elementary school one. Perhaps different and better treatment in the elementary school might be one of the most fruitful ways of reducing the number of youths who leave school before graduation. The loss of so many by the secondary schools is one of our most serious social problems.

Future Dropouts

Briefly, the future dropout is over-age for his grade, at least by the time he gets to the third grade. This means that he has already been told that he is a failure. He already feels rejected and alienated. He is out of school a

✧ Reprinted by permission of the Association for Childhood Education International, 3615 Wisconsin Avenue, N.W., Washington, D.C. "Seeds of Drop-Outs," by Earl C. Kelley. From *Childhood Education*, May, 1963, Vol. 39, No. 9, pp. 420–422. Also used by permission of the author. Earl C. Kelley is Professor of Education, Wayne State University.

good deal. It may be due to excessive illness, lack of suitable school cloth-ing, or the fact that he does not have anyone at home who can or wants to make an effort to get him to school. His irregular attendance is one reason he is no longer with his age group. Of course, it is not possible for anyone to be over-age except in relation to an adult standard, such as the cherished grade-level concept.

The future dropout is behind others in reading, arithmetic, spelling, and any other academic achievement which may be expected in his particular grade. He is probably slow in developing ability to deal with abstract concepts, concerning which so many adults are so frenetic.

He is likely to come from a home that is culturally deprived. This con-spires to help to give him a low I.Q. It is true that people are unique — that they vary in intelligence, in creativity, and in many other ways. We have known for thirty years that starved environments lower I.Q.'s while rich environments raise them. Since the I.Q. — arrived at by testing — does not represent intelligence at all but cultural background, the children from crowded areas are less able to do well on I.Q. tests than other children of equal intelligence. Dullness, then, is only partly due to lack of native ability. In considerable degree it is caused by the quality of the life a child is forced to live.

Perhaps the most significant change that has occurred in America in the last half century is that we have moved from being an agrarian nation to an industrial one. This has caused people by the millions to move into cities to be near their work. It is why so many millions of Americans live in crowded conditions. Many problems arise when people live too closely to-gether.

The central parts of our cities are the most crowded because when these parts were built, extra space was considered a detriment rather than a value. Old housing never did have what we now consider minimal facilities for decent living, and these buildings have been allowed to deteriorate. So it has come about that the American city is a great slum surrounded by a belt of more modern and more spacious structures. Efforts are now being made to rebuild the central parts of our cities, but the task is so great that it will take a whole generation to bring about appreciable improvement.

Not all deprived and alienated children come from crowded areas. Many of them live in good physical conditions in the parts of our cities with more space and in our suburbs. However, it is probably true that the worse the living conditions, the poorer the chance a child has.

What kinds of people live in these places? Why does not everybody just move out and leave them to fall down? Why are they so crowded?

Poverty and Deprivation

The most compelling reason why we have so many people crowded into the deteriorated sections is poverty. It is cheaper to live there even though the rents are often exorbitant considering the conditions. And the greater the number who crowd into one establishment, the more there are to share in expense. Poverty *causes* crowding. A related reason for having to live so poorly is segregation. Some people would move to better sections of the city if they were welcome. We have laws against discrimination in housing, but there are not many people in any ethnic group with the courage of a Meredith. Segregation causes poverty because it denies the segregated the opportunity to escape from it. I do not mean to imply that crowdedness is a racial problem. Poverty knows no racial differences. People of all colors and creeds live in our slums. But there are more Negroes in our substandard housing than there would be if it were not for segregation.

Who are the poor? Generally, they are the uneducated, the unskilled. Usually they are the people who have never known good living. Some of them come from sections of our country where decent education was unknown when they were children and is unknown today. Some of them are our dropouts of the recent past.

Children are born to these people, often under shocking conditions. These children are born in poverty, some of them with a skin pigmentation which marks them as inferior in our culture. The day they are born they start far, far behind. They start out behind, so we need not be surprised to find them "not up to grade level."

School — The Best Hope

These are *our* children — not somebody else's. There is no one else to whom we can point. We cannot deny them, because the social consequences which we must bear are too great, if for no better reason. These children are born into an ever downward spiral of poverty, deterioration, degradation, and alienation from self and society. Somehow this vicious cycle must be broken. For this, the school is our best hope.

There are many in our country who stoutly contend that helping our young out of this downward cycle is not the function of the school. They say that the school is for the purpose of teaching the three R's, to be followed by the rest of what is known as academic learning. They say that poverty and deprivation are not our business but that of the home or "society." This was the *original* purpose of the school. When the conditions under which children are born and grow change, the functions of our institutions have to change. As we are now situated, the school is the institution which has the best chance to affect and improve the lot of our unfortunate young. We cannot teach them academic matters until we have done what we can to ameliorate the conditions which have caused deprivation. We cannot cling to the purposes of the school in an agrarian society when that society no longer exists.

It would be good if we could have a wand and improve the conditions under which these children are born. This we cannot do. But we can start with these damaged ones when we get them and try to mend as much as we can.

Teachers in a Helping Role

Since space is limited, I will make just one suggestion. If teachers would see themselves in a helping role rather than in the role of doing something *to* people, something predetermined before the one needing help is even seen, many of the damaged ones could break out of the "jams" they are in.

What does one do when he wants to help someone who is in trouble? He looks first to see *what* is the trouble. If he saw a person in a car by the side of the road, obviously in trouble, and he stopped to help, he would first try to find out whether the person was sick, had had a flat tire, or had run out of gasoline. One would not say, "The trouble with this fellow is that he's illiterate. I will first teach him to read and write and cipher. When he has learned these, all of his other troubles will vanish."

The damaged one may not have had anything to eat. He may not have a mother or a father; or having them, he may still be bereft. He may be starving to death for love — an essential for every human being, especially for the young. When we come at him with our own purposes, we do not help him. We build in him more feelings of rejection and hostility; we cause more alienation.

So I urge all teachers — and especially teachers of our damaged ones — to assume a helping relationship. Let us do first things first; and many of the other goods, such as literacy, can then follow.

✧ ✧ 9 ✧ ✧

Sociological Perspective on the Education of Culturally Deprived Children

ELEANOR P. WOLF AND LEO WOLF

During the past few years there has been an increasing recognition of the importance of social class as a variable that affects the processes of learning and teaching in the public schools. Not only have a great many educators in administrative, training, and supervisory positions learned the language of sociology, but many classroom teachers as well as students in colleges of education have become more aware of pertinent sociological research and have been alerted to the implications of these findings. After years during

✧ Reprinted from *The School Review,* Winter 1962, pp. 873–887, by permission of The University of Chicago Press. Copyright © 1962, by the University of Chicago. Also used by permission of the authors. Eleanor P. Wolf is Associate Professor of Sociology, Wayne State University, and Leo Wolf is Assistant Principal, Moore Elementary School, Detroit.

which many school people considered the term *social class* part of the vocabulary of a snob rather than a concept useful in understanding behavior, interest in social stratification has assumed almost the proportions of a fad in some school systems. Undergraduates in training speak knowingly (and disapprovingly!) of the middle-class biases of teachers, and in classroom discussions they remind one another that many behavior patterns of lower-class children (sexual precocity, physical aggression, profane language) are likely to disturb teachers and create barriers between them and the children they are trying to teach.

At the same time a number of the school systems in our great metropolitan centers are attempting to launch attacks on the deficiencies in the education of the so-called culturally deprived or culturally disadvantaged children. There has never been greater interest or more discussion of sociocultural variables in personality development and educational growth. In-service training programs, workshops, conferences, and committees are grappling with the special problems of such children, and there is much talk of stimulus-deprivation, urban-assimilation, middle-class values, and negative self-images. Sociologists cannot but be gratified at this recognition of the tremendous importance of sociocultural factors. Increased sensitivity to social factors in learning and a deepened knowledge of the consequences of class position are immensely valuable, and the spread of this information throughout the teaching profession represents a great step forward. Even more encouraging is the determination of many dedicated persons on all levels of the school system to develop programs designed to improve the education of those children who seem to be in greatest need of such assistance.

Because these efforts are important and because they have engaged the energies and stirred the hopes of many of the most valuable members of the teaching profession, it is necessary to maintain proper perspective. Exaggerated claims and expectations only contribute to a sense of frustration and failure when unrealistic goals prove unattainable. Closely related to this danger is the problem of the distortion of knowledge as it is transferred and incorporated from the parent discipline to the applied field. Thus, the educational philosophy associated with John Dewey became at times almost unrecognizable by the time it was articulated at the level of certain practitioners. The observations that follow are made in the hope of avoiding these pitfalls.

1. *There is sometimes a tendency to overgeneralize and oversimplify the problems of minorities by focusing mainly on the similarities between groups while neglecting crucial differences.* A recent call to an excellent "education for opportunity" conference illustrates this orientation very well:

> The newcomer into the Northern, urban industrial social milieu generally encounters subjective and objective problems, and we believe that *these problems are similar for those from predominantly white Southern hill sections, the Negro from Southern rural areas, the new in-migrant to the United States, as well as for local citizens of lower socioeconomic groups* [(3) italics ours].

There are certainly some points of similarity, but there are even more striking crucial differences that are of considerable importance to the schools. Teachers who have recently encountered "new immigrants to the United States" from Europe, for example, have typically found such children to be suffering mainly from language difficulties and the sense of strangeness and dislocation that is the lot of all newcomers. (Many have had more rigorous training in some subjects than most American children.) It would puzzle a teacher to suggest that the educational problems he confronts with such children are similar to those he faces with a group of poverty-stricken Negro children whose whole life and background represent deprivation and subordination. It is true that present-day European newcomers are in many respects an unusual group. But more than twenty years ago John Dollard, to mention but one example, called our attention to the significant differences between immigrants and Negroes in American society. Speaking of European immigrants he said:

> They came here under the spur of ambition and with the intention to take every advantage of American opportunities. . . . They know America as the "land of opportunity" — the land of rapid rise in economic position and social status and their anticipations are organized around this conception. Once here there are no categorical barriers put in their way and they are able to continue their determined fight for social advancement. (6)

Gunnar Myrdal documents this thesis in many sections of *An American Dilemma* (11). The authors of *Who Shall Be Educated?* noted in 1944 that "the theory of the melting pot does not work for the Negro. . . . The school cannot help him as it has the immigrant, *for his problem is different* [our emphasis]. If American education could have functioned for the Negro as it did for our ethnic groups, the Negroes as variant people would have long since disappeared from American life" (16:139). Warner, Havighurst, and Loeb do not suggest that the schools cannot help the Negro child in his struggle for advancement — indeed they indicate how this can be done — but they do point out that they cannot help in the same way, because the problems are vastly different (16).

We have so little European immigration now that this is a relatively minor phase of our problem. The few who do come to our shores are usually urbanized, many are prepared to work at a trade or profession, and they have some resources, either personal or organizational assistance. There seems no point in including this small and strikingly different group in the umbrella concept of "newcomers to the city." Mexicans and Puerto Ricans (if they can escape the designation *Negro*) have problems somewhat more like those of the masses of low-status European immigrants of the past, made more acute by the declining need for unskilled labor and other changes in the American economy. The special case of the southern white in-migrant has been described by William Simon as "standing . . . on the very borders of ethnicity . . . they are characterizable by three factors that tend to facilitate access to desirable status positions. They are white, Anglo-Saxon and Protestant . . ." (15:21). After discussing some of the problems now faced by these people in our big cities, Simon goes on to predict for them a probable course of development different at once from both the Negro and the foreign-born:

> Mobility will tend to be an individual occurrence within a context that provides little necessity for continued group identification or participation. It is almost a matter of definition; with upward mobility one merely ceases to be a hillbilly and becomes a southerner — the two are not the same [(15):22].

The assertion by sociologist Nathan Glazer that "there is no natural history of migration" may seem to some an overstatement (7). But there is no doubt that the combination of visibility — the physical marks of race — and the history of slavery, later transformed into a caste-like system of social relations, is unique in American society. No other minority group in our nation has problems comparable in severity to those of the Negro. Even when economic status is held relatively constant, the inferior social status of the Negro appears to have a depressing effect on educational achievement (5). These uncomfortable truths ought not be obscured by euphemistic references to newcomers and minority groups.

2. *There is a tendency to exaggerate the nature and scope of the influence that schools can wield.* It has often been pointed out that the public schools are peculiarly vulnerable to attack. Certain structural features of the institution make the system accessible; at the some time there are widely shared beliefs within American culture that attribute great power to the educative process. Thus, the anxiety of the public over Communism found some segments of society fearfully scrutinizing the schools for evidence of subversion, while other groups insisted that the school play a more active role in immunizing against the infection. Shock at sputnik was instantly translated into a widespread attack on school failure and efforts to greatly increase school emphasis on the physical sciences. Racial tensions during World War II were largely responsible for the development of widespread programs of intercultural education in the schools, designed to promote intergroup understanding. Periodic concern over the alleged increase in mental illness often results in the focusing of attention on the psychological traits of teachers and provokes demands that they assume certain quasi-therapeutic or diagnostic functions.

It is worth noting, at least, that some scholars believe that we cherish excessive expectations of what schools can accomplish. For example, in a recent discussion of the effectiveness of school programs designed to improve intergroup relations, H. D. Schmidt, of the Institute for Advanced Study, reminded us that these programs are based on the assumption "that it is primarily the schools which transmit the heritage of the past to the young, and that the schoolroom is therefore the place where group antagonism can most effectively be rooted out" (13). He goes on to say:

But these beliefs are based on an exaggerated estimate of the influence of teachers and preachers in Western society generally, and in particular of their influence on the minds of the young. . . . Evidence both of a sociological and psychological character now exists, in fact, which strongly suggests that the school plays only a minor role in the development of basic social attitudes among children, and that the *teacher is almost powerless in this area unless his work is visibly substantiated and backed up by the society in whose midst he operates* [(13) italics ours].

In the present movement the schools are being asked to solve many problems that American society has failed to solve. (This is perhaps epitomized by the "bus-ing" of school children in New York City to achieve racial integration, an effort made necessary by the failure of our cities to substantially alter segregated patterns in housing.) Generally, the schools are being asked to improve the economic and social position of deprived children through education, to break through the vicious circle of low education–low socioeconomic status that now exists. Specifically, the schools are being asked to compensate for the massive deprivations from which these children have suffered and to stimulate and motivate them to learn and achieve. Such a program, it seems to us, can be of tremendous significance if careful distinctions are made between what the schools can and cannot do.

We might consider some of the limitations that must be faced in developing a workable program for the schools.

First, the schools cannot create aspirations on the part of the overwhelming majority of deprived and apathetic children if the surrounding society gives the lie to such hopes. In his study of today's urban poverty Michael Harrington observes:

The decline of aspiration among slum dwellers partly reflects a sophisticated analysis of society: for the colored minorities there *is* less oportunity today than there existed for the white population of the older ethnic slums, and the new slum people know this. *The poverty of their myths reflects the poverty of their reality* [(9) 120–121; italics ours].

Many educators are not aware of the extent to which marked differentials between income of Negroes and white persist at varying levels of education (2). For example, if we compare all families where the family head has completed only eight years of schooling, the median family income is $4487 for whites, $3167 for nonwhites. Nonwhite median family income is thus seen to be approximately 70 per cent of white family income. If we compare only families where the head has completed high school, the gap still remains: median family income for whites is $5742, for nonwhites it is $3929, about 68 per cent of white family income. Current unemployment statistics show a similar disproportion. A recent study prepared for the National Urban League summarizes this problem: "Unemployment rates for nonwhite males since 1951 usually have been twice as high as rates for white males, and frequently two and one half times as high."(12)

Parenthetically, it is ironic that even in some school systems that are much involved in programs to increase aspiration levels of culturally deprived children one can find evidence of discrimination against Negroes. The presence of Negro teachers in all-white schools and their employment, when qualified applicants are available, as administrators and supervisors of white subordinates might be more effective as spurs to lagging ambition than many other methods being discussed.

Second, there is little the schools can do to compensate for the fact that the new slum dwellers are often fatherless families, in contrast to the immigrant families of the past, which, though under stress, were usually intact. Further, in a great many cases, problems of family instability are compounded by the effects of residential mobility. This movement (which often, though not always, involves school changes) is at present being intensified in many areas by displacement because of urban renewal programs. Some of the talk heard at conferences and meetings is a bit glib and overly optimistic. Father images are not supplied by contacts with men teachers; self-conceptions are not re-formed by words of praise, nor is a sense of emotional security restored by a friendly smile. All these are desirable in and of themselves, but the school is not a primary group, and thus far there is little evidence that teachers can, in a school setting, restructure basic personality (1).

Third, how many social-welfare functions can the school assume? There is a tendency to take other aspects of our social structure as given and concentrate our fire on the most vulnerable institution — the public school. Thus we note the many suggestions that the local elementary school in the slum or multiproblem area become the focal point of neighborhood organization, the instrument for adult education, the recreation center for adults as well as children, and the co-ordinating agency for all children's social services. It has been suggested that teachers visit the homes of all pupils regularly and participate in local neighborhood affairs and action programs. Yet research indicates that pupils in such schools already suffer from inadequate time devoted to teaching; the actual number of minutes of instruction is startlingly low in some classrooms (5:23). Teachers are already burdened with a number of seemingly unavoidable tasks such as saving-stamp sales; sale and distribution of milk; collection of lunch money; vision checks; hall, playground, and lunch duties; and general record-keeping. All these tasks drain time and energy.

There is undoubtedly merit in some of the plans for the use of the school as the co-ordinating center of a many-faceted program for children, but these functions cannot be piled on the duties of the present staff. The problem of staffing the difficult school has already begun to assume serious proportions. It must be made clear that such proposals would require considerable reorganization as well as additional staff trained in these fields. However, the use of other facilities ought to be seriously considered. It might well be that aggressive programs in family casework, for example, could be conducted much more effectively by augmented and expanded social-work agencies quite apart from the school system.

3. *We must guard against a tendency to scapegoat the individual class-room teacher. Teachers are often confronted by contradictory admonitions.* For example, those who work with deprived children are frequently criticized for expecting too much of them:

> We know that by and large teachers are middle class in value orientation and tend to treat all children "alike" or to assume they are "normal." . . . The demands of the traditional middle-class-value geared and middle-class socially functioning school are unrealistic and punitive for too many of the disadvantaged children. (10)

In his distinguished monograph, Martin Deutsch, discussing the poor test performance of lower-class Negro children, notes that such children do not expect "future rewards for present activity" and goes on to say:

> This inconsistency between the lack of internalized reward anticipations on the part of the Negro child and *his teacher's expectations that he does have such anticipations* reflect the disharmony between the social environment of the home and the middle-class oriented demands of the school [(5):23; emphasis ours].

However, another observation frequently encountered is that expressed by Eleanor Leacock, in her commentary in the same monograph: "teachers' *low expectations* for these children are reflected by the children's lack of expectations for themselves" [(5):31; emphasis ours].

Obviously, if teachers' expectations are high, they are unrealistic and may be punitive. But if expectations are low, they reinforce the child's low esteem and reflect what is sometimes (not, we hasten to add, in the materials quoted) alleged to be teacher prejudice. This dilemma is reflected in the plaint frequently heard from teachers who work in schools in changing neighborhoods. They often report that if they adhere to the same grading standards they used with previous (more privileged) populations they may be accused of prejudice, or at least harshness, as demonstrated by a large number of failures and poor grades. But if they alter their grading system, they may be accused of relaxing standards to the detriment of their new pupils.

Another example of the damned-if-you-do, damned-if-you-don't dilemma is the contention that the middle-class background of teachers, with their ingrained propriety and respectability, seriously hampers their effectiveness with deprived children. But some (often within the same speech or article) assert that even worse is the teacher from a lower-class background, anxious to establish social distance between himself and his lower-class pupils. Similarly, it is stated that the lower-class child is handicapped in school and under-achieves academically because he lacks middle-class work habits and values that stress order, neatness, and punctuality. Yet the presentations of these values, their display and demonstration by teachers, are often held to be a handicap in the educational process and an occasion for reproaches to be hurled against them. Just how important are these behavioral factors in their effect on the role of the school as an instrument for social mobility?

We are in no position to answer the question we have raised. But it may be an aid to better perspective to recall that although some observers have attributed much importance to the role of the schools in assimilation of European immigrants, their success could hardly be traced to the desirable behavior of the teachers of that era:

> From the desk the teacher looked down, a challenge they dared not meet. . . . What an arsenal was at her command to destroy them! The steel-edged ruler across the knuckles was the least of her weapons. Casually she could twist the knife of ridicule in the soreness of their sensibilities; there was so much in their accent, appearance, and manners that was open to mockery. . . . As she snapped shut the closet upon the symbols of her ladyhood within — the white gloves, the rolled-up umbrella, and the sedate hat — she indicated at once the superiority of her own status. There was visible evidence of her correctness in her speech and in her bearing, in her dress, and in the frequent intimations of the quality of her upbringing. Perhaps a few were touched with sympathy at the condition of their charges. But what these offered was pity, nobler than contempt, but to the children no more acceptable. It was rare indeed to find the dedicated woman whose understanding of her students brought a touch of love into her work. After all, it was not this they had dreamed of in normal school . . . that they would devote the rest of their lives to the surveillance of a pack of unwashed ruffians. Mostly the teachers kept their distance, kept flickering the hope that a transfer might take them to a nicer district with nicer pupils from nicer homes. When that hope died, bitterness was born; and there was thereafter more savagery than love in their instruction. [(8):247–248]

In this vivid passage the historian Oscar Handlin recreates for us the public school in the era of great immigration. Yet apparently it did function fairly effectively as an instrument of acculturation for the immigrant pupil:

> If it did nothing else to the child, the school introduced into his life a rival source of authority. The day the little boy hesitantly made his way into the classroom, the image of the teacher began to compete with that of the father. The one like the other laid down a rigid code of behavior, demanded absolute obedience, and stood ready to punish infractions with swift severity. The day the youngster came back to criticize his home (*They say in school that . . .*) his parents knew they would have to struggle for his loyalty. [(8):244]

What enabled the schools to exert influence, if the teacher's attitude toward the pupils was often as unsympathetic as the quoted passage (17) suggests? The key can be found, we believe, in the fact that the child was surrounded by enough examples of success, enough instances of upward movement, to really believe in these possibilities. Herein lies an all-important difference. As Schmidt has pointed out, "the teacher is almost powerless . . . unless his work is visibly substantiated . . . by the society in whose midst he operates."(13:253) The school that taught the immigrant's children reflected the basic approach of American society toward the European immigrant. This approach encouraged assimilation and amalgamation; it was the theory of the melting pot. The prevailing American attitude toward the Negro, by contrast, as Myrdal and others have pointed out, is still one of antiamalgamation and social segregation. In addition, a decreased demand for unskilled labor has made it much more difficult for disadvantaged groups to get an initial foothold on the economic escalator. These factors, rather than the shortcomings of individual teachers, appear to be of considerably greater importance in explaining our difficulties in the education of lower-class Negro children.

The literature is replete with exhortations to teachers in today's slums to try to overcome the apathy and listlessness of their disadvantaged pupils. Yet there is ample evidence that such children typically come to school (or stay home from school) undernourished, inadequately clothed, without sufficient sleep (partly because of severe overcrowding of their dwellings), and with untreated physical ills, sometimes of an acute nature — such as toothaches. A dramatic illustration of the significance of these conditions was recently seen in the Detroit area when a thousand low-income Negro pupils from the Carver school district were placed under the judisdiction (after considerable controversy too lengthy to be reported here) of a middle-class, all-white suburb, Oak Park. Little notice had been taken of the conditions under which these children were trying to learn until they became the responsibility of the Oak Park system. Then, in the words of J. N. Pepper, superintendent of schools: "It looks as if we'll have to begin at the beginning. In this case the beginning is to get these children healthy enough to learn."(4) The school officials went on to call attention to "nonexistent health records," to the fact that only a few of these children had been inoculated against serious contagious disease, and to evidence of malnutrition (4). These conditions had long existed in the Carver school district, and they are common in slum schools in our great cities. But one rarely hears any demands that the medical or dental profession do something about the health needs of these children. Ordinarily it is teachers who hold meetings and conferences where they wonder rather hopelessly what they can do to teach these children who come to them hardly fit to learn.

One cannot help noting that the practice of focusing attention on the shortcomings of teachers and on educational materials and techniques serves to distract attention from more basic (and less easily attacked) problems. For example, a subject currently much discussed at teachers' conferences on underprivileged children is the extent to which illustrations and story content of textbooks should reflect middle-class life. We noted earlier that we tend to attribute exaggerated powers to the educational system, partly, at least, because it seems more accessible to our intervention rather than because it truly plays the role we ascribe to it. Similarly, in considering the ways in which our educational system itself meets the learning problems of deprived children, there is a tendency to concentrate on the variables that are most readily manipulated. Especially attractive are the programs (like those designed to change teachers' attitudes) that do not require substantial expenditures. Unfortunately, these are not necessarily the programs that will be most effective.

It is far from our purpose to provide any kind of rationale for a do-nothing policy or a defeatist attitude toward the problems of disadvantaged children. Their special needs confront us with all the unsolved problems in American education, problems that have begun to bore us with their wearisome recalcitrance, their stubborn refusal to go away: not enough good teachers, too-large classes, not enough facilities for emotionally disturbed or mentally retarded children, not enough money for trips, equipment, remedial teaching, and other enrichment programs — and all the rest. Children who have been deprived at home and in the community need more of all these aids to learning, but they usually get less (14). Even more disturbing is the way these children accuse us of our continued failure to solve basic problems of American society — inadequate health care, slum housing, prolonged unemployment, segregation, and discrimination.

Despite all this, much can be done, and is being done every day, by gifted and compassionate teachers, working against great odds. The present pioneering efforts of the Higher Horizons programs and the Great Cities project will provide invaluable information for future planning. There has long been a tendency for many gifted and sensitive teachers to avoid the slum school, not because they are lazy or indifferent, but because they feel inadequate and helpless in the face of overwhelming odds. We need to remember the magnitude of problems they face and not add to these burdens by excessive expectations. Rather, as educators who can also act vigorously as citizens, we must redouble our efforts to improve the social and economic conditions under which slum children live and which so profoundly affect their learning.

REFERENCES

1. In this connection see *Husbands and Wives* by Robert Blood and Donald Wolfe (New York: Free Press, 1960), chapter ii, for suggestive evidence that even the intimate relations of family life do not offset the powerful impact of societal status on the role of the husband in marriage. Regardless of the presumably endless variations in family climate and wife's personality, low-status husbands in this study tend to be weak in their decision-making power in the home.

2. This information and the data that follow are taken from Table 13, P–60 Series, Bureau of Census, United States Department of Commerce, 1958.

3. *Conference Call*, Michigan Fair Employment Practices Commission, February 9, 1961.

4. *Detroit News*, December 4, 1960, p. 23A.

5. Deutsch, Martin. *Minority Group and Class Status as Related to Social and Personality Factors in Scholastic Achievement.* Ithaca, N.Y.: Society for Applied Anthropology, Cornell University, 1960.

6. Dollard, John. *Caste and Class in a Southern Town,* pp. 428–29. New Haven, Conn.: Yale University Press, 1937.

7. Glazer, Nathan (in book review of Oscar Handlin's *The Newcomers*). *Commentary,* 29: 266; March, 1960.

8. Handlin, Oscar. *The Uprooted.* Boston: Little, Brown and Company, 1951.

9. Harrington, Michael. "Slums, Old and New," *Commentary,* 30: 119–124; August 1960.

10. Kerber, August. "An Experimental Project To Improve the School Experiences of Culturally Deprived Children and the Inservice Education of Their Teachers." Mimeographed memorandum. Detroit: College of Education, Wayne State University, no date.

11. Myrdal, Gunnar. *An American Dilemma.* New York: Harper & Brothers, Publishers, 1944. See especially chapter iii, sections 1 and 2. See also chapters i and ii of James B. Conant's *Slums and Suburbs* (New York: McGraw-Hill Book Co., 1961), which appeared some months after the Wolfs had completed their manuscript.

12. Orshansky, Mollie, and Thomas Karter. *Economic and Social Status of the Negro in the United States, 1961.* New York: National Urban League, 1961. P. 20.

13. Schmidt, H. D. "Bigotry in Schoolchildren," *Commentary,* 29: 253–257; March 1960.

14. For impressive evidence of inequalities in the educational facilities provided for lower-class children in a large school system see Patricia C. Sexton, *Education and Income* (New York: Viking Press, 1961).

15. Simon, William R. "Southern White Migrants: Ethnicity and Pseudo-Ethnicity," *Human Development,* I: 20–24; Summer, 1960. Student publication, Committee on Human Development, University of Chicago.

16. Warner, W. Lloyd, Robert J. Havighurst, and Martin B. Loeb. *Who Shall Be Educated?* New York: Harper & Brothers, 1944.

17. An abundance of anecdotal material indicates that the educational methods and teacher attitudes of the old-country Jewish *cheder,* for example, would scandalize modern educators. Yet it would be hard to exaggerate the high regard in which learning and scholarship were held by the over-all community, and these factors were apparently far more influential than teacher behavior in developing children's attitudes toward education. See Mark Zborowski and Elizabeth Herzog, *Life Is with People* (New York: International Universities Press, Inc., 1962).

✧ ✧ 10 ✧ ✧

In Defense of Middle-Class Values

JAMES E. HEALD

Increased educational concern for the culturally deprived child has been attended by innuendoes to the effect that something is inherently wrong with middle-class values. From pens of scientists, sociologists, and educa-

✧ From *Phi Delta Kappan,* October, 1964, pp. 81–83. Used by permission of the author and the publisher. James E. Heald is Assistant Professor of Education, The University of Chicago.

ors have come charges that teachers with middle-class values must change hem in order to succeed in educating the lower-class child.

The values held by middle-class teachers have been castigated, convicted, and condemned. However, before condemnation through allegation becomes final, middle-class values deserve a defense.

THE ALLEGATIONS

1. . . . if we want to help lower-class children we will have to reorient our thinking and philosophy. We will have to adopt fundamental reforms, radical and crucial in nature, so that the school as an institution will be more nearly in conformity with the cultural and behavioral patterns of this [lower] class. (4)

2. . . . Allied to this general problem is the need in many cases to retrain teachers who, used to one type of pupil from middle-class families, suddenly find themselves engulfed with slum-area children whose values run directly counter to those of teachers. Unless such teachers readjust their thinking, an impossible situation is at hand. (1)

3. . . . Hasn't our middle-class culture produced a society with more than its share of tensions, anxieties, neuroses, and psychoses? How many souls have been blighted, twisted, and distorted by its impossible demands? (4)

The reader of these and similar allegations must conclude that only by laying aside middle-class values can the slum-area teacher expect to become effective. In fact, all society might be better for the loss of such a restrictive set of values! (4)

OPENING STATEMENT FOR THE DEFENSE

When teachers with middle-class values "reorient," "readjust," or in fact deny their value system in order to become more effective, what will the substitute value system look like? The plaintiffs, in preparing the allegations, fail to define a new value structure for teachers which would assure effectiveness. Several logical possibilities seem to exist: (a) Teachers may accept the values of another class; (b) teachers may reject values of the middle class without substituting a new value system (this would seem a psychological impossibility); and (c) teachers may replace their current value system with a new one, nature yet undetermined.

Therefore, the defense will build its case by refuting the first possibility and by supplying some determinants for the third.

THE CASE FOR THE DEFENSE

Acceptance of a value system from a society other than middle-class has been suggested as an alternative. Tenenbaum (4) suggests the lower class, and he has also suggested that schools "be more nearly in conformity with the cultural and behavioral patterns of this class." Before adopting these proposals, it now seems appropriate to revisit the value structures of the classes as determined by Havighurst and Taba (3) in order to recall the values supporting their cultural and behavioral patterns.

Exhibit I

Members of the middle class value:
1. civic virtue and community responsibility;
2. cleanliness and neatness;
3. education as a potential for solving social problems;
4. education as a preparation period for adulthood;
5. good manners;
6. honesty in all things;
7. initiative;
8. loyalty;
9. marital fidelity;
10. responsibility to church;
11. responsibility to family;
12. self-reliance;
13. sexual morality;
14. thrift.

Members of the lower class value:
1. honesty, when friends and neighbors are involved;
2. responsibility, when friends and neighbors are involved;
3. loyalty, when friends and neighbors are involved.

Members of the lower class:
4. overlook or condone stealing and dishonesty;
5. are less restrained in acts of aggression;
6. are less restrained in sexual activity;
7. view juvenile delinquency as normal behavior;
8. feel little compulsion to stay in school. (3)

These, then, are the value systems under consideration. Teachers holding the first set have been warned to "reorient" or "readjust," and it has been suggested that movement toward the second would indeed be desirable if education for the culturally deprived is to be improved.

What needs to be considered in making a judgment?

1. Serious examination of Exhibit I should leave little doubt about the folly of abandoning middle-class values for those of the lower class. Such a movement would place schools in the position of attempting to stand for the moral and the legal while condoning the immoral and the illegal. Only the unthinking would contend that morality can best spring from a society if its leaders are immoral or that the "means" would justify the "ends." The hypocrisy of such a position would make teaching an even more impossible and uninviting profession than it currently is.

2. Human behavior tends to improve as expectations improve. To condone dishonesty, unrestrained sex activity, and juvenile delinquency as acceptable behavior is to establish conditions conducive to such behavior remaining normative. To expect humans to rise above such behavior is to offer hope for changing behavior which is considered immoral and judged illegal. Unfortunately, the teacher trying to change behavior away from the immoral and the illegal may find herself in the unenviable position of having knowledge which makes her an accessory both before and after the fact. In this position, what does represent moral and legal behavior on the

part of the teacher to whom society has not yet granted the legal protection of privileged communication?

3. One of the most serious indictments made about the values of the middle class concerns the inflexibility and rigidity associated with the structure itself. A member of the middle class *must* be of a particular value pattern to be acceptable, and deviation from the perceived pattern of acceptability is cause for peer rejection. The cause is not just and deserves its criticism.

However, rigidity of structure *per se* is insufficient evidence for rejecting the values attached thereto, despite the entreaties of the moral relativists. It may be recalled that the same arguments were used by the relativists as they begged for release from the rigid Victorian concepts about sex on grounds that the rigidity itself was responsible for the guilt feelings contributing to much mental illness. With the campaign successfully concluded, the relativist is embarrassed by the increased number of neuroses arising from the lack of a stable structure in a changing society. The individual has nothing to which he can attach his personal anchor and from which strength of conviction can be derived.

Rigidity alone cannot be inherently evil unless one accepts as a basic tenet that every good is flexible. To carry moral flexibility (relativity) forward is to remove guilt, and simultaneously to destroy human conscience. No description is available of the society which would arise from the ashes of the pyre for the human conscience, but I believe the description would be frightening beyond comparison.

4. To assess the merits of the value systems under consideration, a comparison might be drawn against an older system so secure that "whatever may have been the original source or sanction, the insights have been thoroughly validated by the long experiences of mankind" (2). Such security resides in the Hebraic-Christian ethic. It is offered as Exhibit II with the hope that it will subsequently serve a benchmark function.

Exhibit II

Precepts embodied in the Hebraic-Christian ethic, as offered by Counts, are:

1. "Every man is precious . . . because he is unique." Therefore, "All institutions and social arrangements . . . are to be judged, accepted or rejected, preserved or modified, as they affect the lives of individual beings."

2. Man is a "moral creature in a moral order." He is to fulfill his nature by "striving to do good and make[ing] the good prevail in the family, the community, the nation, and the world."

3. There shall be a brotherhood of equality and essential unity among the races of mankind.

4. There shall be no privileged castes or orders and no man shall exploit another or his property.

5. For the perfection of human society, man is:
   a. to do justice;
   b. to be generous;

    c. to show mercy;
    d. to be honest;
    e. to be truthful;
    f. to cultivate a humane spirit;
    g. to love his neighbor;
    h. to be accountable for his actions;
    i. to be true to his conscience. (2)

Counts concludes his analysis of the ethic by stating,

> These ethical insights are both simple and profound. Even a skeptical and cynical generation must know that the teachings and practices which flow from them are the essence of any good society. Only as we introduce them more fully into the closer relationships of our American community and into the wider relationships of nations can we hope to build a better country and a better world. *In the measure that we ignore or violate them we open the door to savagery and barbarianism.* (2) [Italics are added.]

The defense rests!

SUMMATION

Professional educators seeking to help the culturally deprived have been deluged with helpful hints for solving the learning problems of impoverished children. Among the solutions has come the suggestion that movement away from a middle-class value structure by teachers would be desirable — in fact, necessary. The defense has denied this contention and has asked that the values of the middle classes be weighed, examined, and scrutinized before final judgment is pronounced.

When examined in the time-honored light of an older ethic, the values revered by the American middle class take on new luster because of the numerous similarities. However, the fact remains that the values do not emerge completely untarnished, and the defense, now denied a perfect case, must enter a new, three-part plea in behalf of the defendant: (a) Middle-class values are acceptable as guides to the conduct of teachers engaged in the education of the culturally deprived; but (b) middle-class values are not all-encompassing, and their weakness lies not in what they include but what they omit; therefore, (c) the new value structure proposed for consideration by the jury encompasses all of the middle-class values and the high expectations attached thereto.

But in addition, new values of even higher order should be gleaned from the older ethic: (a) There shall be value in treating all persons as beings of supreme worth; (b) there shall be value in living as a brother to men of all races, creeds, and social positions; (c) there shall be value in actively working for improvements in all social arrangements affecting the lives of men; and (d) there shall be value in striving to make good prevail in the family, the community, the nation, and the world.

Such a value structure might spawn a profession of teachers who would overlook the grime and pox of poverty, who would see beyond the impoverishment of the unenriched intellect, and who could come to dwell in the hearts of the lowliest children. Teachers with these new values would love children more than they hate dirt, and no child could be relegated to genus *subhomo*. As a member of the family of man, his worth would be inherently supreme and independent from social class, economic condition, or ethnic membership.

Condemn middle-class values? No, be proud of them! "Readjust" or "reorient" them? No, but recognize their lack of inclusiveness and expand them to the point where the entire class, including its teachers, can find value and pleasure in improving the culture, the education, the morality, and the social usefulness of the deprived, the impoverished, the destitute, and the abandoned.

The case is remanded to the profession.

REFERENCES

1. Conant, James B. *Slums and Suburbs.* New York: McGraw-Hill Book Co., Inc., 1961.
2. Counts, George. *Education and American Civilization.* New York: Teachers College, Columbia University, 1952. Pp. 222–227.
3. Havighurst, Robert, and Hilda Taba. *Adolescent Character and Personality.* New York: John Wiley & Sons, Inc., 1949.
4. Tenenbaum, Samuel. "The Teacher, the Middle Class, the Lower Class," *Phi Delta Kappan,* 45: 86; November, 1963.

Intelligence Testing and the I.Q.

In the first selection in Part Three, J. McVicker Hunt cites weighty evidence indicating that our concept of intelligence needs much revision. There is no evidence that nature is more important than nurture. These two forces always operate together to determine the course of intellectual development. This modern view of the role of intelligence is basic to understanding the implications of modern enrichment programs. Furthermore, much of the rationale for working with very young children is built upon the idea that intelligent functioning is related to early experiences.

Darwin's theory was a factor in the persistent idea of ethnic and racial differences in intelligence. It has been, and to a great degree still is, popularly believed that Negro intelligence is inherently inferior to Caucasian intelligence. In his selection, Thomas F. Pettigrew attacks this notion on the basis of scientific findings and the implications of modern theory. His discussion of the use racial segregationists have made of this idea of inferiority is well developed. Until we accept the findings of modern science regarding intelligence as it relates to racial and ethnic groups, we will continue to have a loophole through which we can justify, however falsely and selfishly, the second-class citizenship of a large portion of our population. The problem of the disadvantaged must be attacked at this very basic level.

Harold M. Skeels and Samuel A. Kirk report significant research projects concerned with educational intervention and the intellectual development of mentally retarded children. Together, they provide a powerful case for the educability of intelligence. Skeels' studies of the effects of adoption on children from institutions reveal rapid intellectual growth of children placed in stimulating environments at an early age, in contrast to the continuing retardation of institutionalized children not receiving differential stimulation. Kirk presents a documented report suggesting ". . . that the intellectual development of some retarded children is partly contingent upon child rearing practices and the extent of educational treatment at an early age."

The case for and against intelligence testing is discussed by Arthur Hughson and Julius Yourman. Their presentation grows out of the decision of the New York Board of Education to dispense with intelligence testing. It is an emotion-laden problem, but Hughson and Yourman approach the controversy

81

with solid and logical arguments. It is safe to conclude that the controversy will not end here, for there is much to be said for both points of view.

According to Hughson, there is no justification for dispensing with this educational device when it has served education for many years so very well. Achievement testing, valuable in its own way, does not give a picture of an individual's potential. Teachers need intelligence tests in order to motivate pupils and to set reasonable expectations for them. Furthermore, says Hughson, if intelligence tests discriminate against minority groups — and he believes they do — then the tests must be revised so that this built-in factor is eliminated. This is better than abandoning the testing, Hughson feels. He also suggests that the logical way to proceed is to upgrade home and cultural environments rather than to dispense with intelligence testing.

Yourman argues that efforts to remedy the weaknesses of mass intelligence testing should be directed toward the substitution of achievement measures which will appraise the child's learning potential. These measures must be "culture-fair" and based on a person-to-person contact which takes into account all facets of the child's development. This could and should be done on an experimental basis, Yourman contends. The situation is so desperate and acute that new thinking must be developed and tried out. He further contends that until this is done, we will continue to use most of the old formulae which have led us to this position of crisis.

Undoubtedly something as basic as intelligence and its relation to academic achievement deserves our wholehearted attention. Few will deny that our outmoded concept of intelligence and its role in cognitive development has been a strong factor in developing the cycle of failure which constantly plagues the disadvantaged child.

❖ ❖ 11 ❖ ❖

How Children Develop Intellectually

J. MCVICKER HUNT

The task of maximizing the intellectual potential of our children has acquired new urgency. Two of the top challenges of our day lie behind this urgency. First, the rapidly expanding role of technology, now taking the form of automation, decreases opportunity for persons of limited competence and skills while it increases opportunity for those competent in the use of written language, in mathematics, and in problem solving. Second, the challenge of eliminating racial discrimination requires not only equality of employment opportunity and social recognition for persons of equal competence, but also an equalization of the opportunity to develop that intellectual capacity and skill upon which competence is based.

During most of the past century anyone who entertained the idea of increasing the intellectual capacity of human beings was regarded as an unrealistic "do-gooder." Individuals, classes, and races were considered to be what they were because either God or their inheritance had made them that way; any attempt to raise the intelligence quotient (I.Q.) through experience met with contempt. Man's nature has not changed since World War II, but some of our conceptions of his nature have been changing rapidly. These changes make sensible the hope that, with improved understanding of early experience, we might counteract some of the worst effects of cultural deprivation and raise substantially the average level of intellectual capacity. This paper will attempt to show how and why these conceptions are changing, and will indicate the implications of these changes for experiments designed to provide corrective early experiences to children and to feed back information on ways of counteracting cultural deprivation.

Changing Beliefs

FIXED INTELLIGENCE. The notion of fixed intelligence has roots in Darwin's theory that evolution takes place through the variations in strains and species

❖ From *Children*, May-June, 1964, pp. 83–91. Used by permission of the author and the publisher, the Children's Bureau, U.S. Department of Health, Education and Welfare. J. McVicker Hunt is Professor of Psychology, University of Illinois.

The work on which this article is based has been supported by the Russell Sage Foundation, the Carnegie Foundation, and the Commonwealth Fund; and its writing by a grant (MH K6–18567) from the U.S. Public Health Service.

which enable them to survive to reproduce themselves. Finding in this the implicit assumption that adult characteristics are determined by heredity, Francis Galton, Darwin's younger cousin, reasoned that the improvement of man lies not in education, or euthenics, but in the selection of superior parents for the next generation — in other words, through eugenics. To this end, he founded an anthropometric laboratory to give simple sensory and motor tests (which failed, incidentally, to correlate with the qualities in which he was interested), established a eugenics society, and imparted his beliefs to his student, J. McKeen Cattell, who brought the tests to America.

About the same time G. Stanley Hall, an American who without knowing Darwin became an ardent evolutionist, imparted a similar faith in fixed intelligence to his students, among them such future leaders of the intelligence testing movement as H. H. Goddard, F. Kuhlmann, and Lewis Terman (13). This faith included a belief in the constant intelligence quotient. The I.Q., originally conceived by the German psychologist Wilhelm Stern, assumes that the rate of intellectual development can be specified by dividing the average age value of the tests passed (mental age) by the chronological age of the child.

The considerable debate over the constancy of the I.Q. might have been avoided if the work of the Danish geneticist Johannsen had been as well known in America as that of Gregor Mendel, who discovered the laws of hereditary transmission. Johannsen distinguished the genotype, which can be known only from the ancestry or progeny of an individual, from the phenotype, which can be directly observed and measured. Although the I.Q. was commonly treated as if it were a genotype (innate capacity), it is in fact a phenotype and, like all phenotypes (height, weight, language spoken), is a product of the genotype and the circumstances with which it has interacted (13).

Johannsen's distinction makes possible the understanding of evidence dissonant with the notion of fixed intelligence. For instance, identical twins (with the same genotype) have been found to show differences in I.Q. of as much as 24 points when reared apart, and the degree of difference appears to be related to the degree of dissimilarity of the circumstances in which they were reared. Also, several investigators have reported finding substantial improvement in I.Q. after enrichment of experience, but their critics have attributed this to defects in experimental control.

When results of various longitudinal studies available after World War II showed very low correlation between the preschool I.Q. and I.Q. at age eighteen, the critics responded by questioning the validity of the infant tests, even though Nancy Bayley (2) had actually found high correlations among tests given close together in time. Blaming the tests tended to hide the distinction that should have been made between cross-sectional validity and predictive validity: What a child does in the testing situation correlates substantially with what he will do in other situations, but attempting to predict what an I.Q. will be at age eighteen from tests given at ages from birth to four years, before the schools have provided at least some standardization of circumstances, is like trying to predict how fast a feather will fall in a hurricane.

PREDETERMINED DEVELOPMENT. Three views of embryological and psychological development have held sway in the history of thought: preformationism, predeterminism, and interactionism (13). As men gave up preformationism, the view that the organs and features of adulthood are preformed in the seed, they turned to predeterminism, the view that the organs and features of adulthood are hereditarily determined. G. Stanley Hall in emphasizing the concept of recapitulation — that the development of the individual summarizes the evolution of his species — drew the predeterministic moral that each behavior pattern manifest in a child is a natural stage with which no one should interfere. The lifework of Arnold Gesell exemplifies the resulting concern with the typical or average that has shaped child psychology during the past half century.

The theory of predetermined development got support from Coghill's finding that frogs and salamanders develop behaviorally as they mature anatomically, from head-end tailward and from inside out, and from Carmichael's finding that the swimming patterns of frogs and salamanders develop equally well whether inhibited by chloretone in the water or stimulated by vibration. Such findings appeared to generalize to children: The acquisition of such skills as walking, stair climbing, and buttoning cannot be speeded by training or exercise; Hopi children reared on cradleboards learn to walk at the same age as Hopi children reared with arms and legs free (4).

Again, however, there was dissonant evidence. Although Cruze found that chicks kept in the dark decreased their pecking errors during the first five days after hatching — a result consonant with predeterminism — he also found that chicks kept in the dark for *twenty* days failed to improve their pecking. Moreover, studies of rats and dogs, based on the theorizing of Donald Hebb, suggest that the importance of infantile experience increases up the phylogenetic scale (10).

Evidence that such findings may apply to human beings comes from studies by Goldfarb (8) which indicate that institutional rearing (where the environment is relatively restricted and unresponsive) results in lower intelligence, less ability to sustain a task, and more problems in interpersonal relations than foster-home rearing (where the environment provides more varied experiences and responsiveness). Wayne Dennis (3) has found that in a Teheran orphanage, where changes in ongoing stimulation were minimal, 60 per cent of the two-year-olds could not sit alone and 85 per cent of the four-year-olds could not walk alone. Such a finding dramatizes the great effect preverbal experience can have on even the rate of locomotor development. Presumably the effect on intellectual functions would be even greater.

STATIC BRAIN FUNCTION. In 1900, when C. Lloyd Morgan and E. L. Thorndike were attempting to explain learning in terms of stimulus-response bonds, they used the newly invented telephone as a mechanical model of the brain's operation. Thus they envisioned the brain as a static switchboard through which each stimulus could be connected with a variety of responses, which in turn could become the stimuli for still other responses.

Soon objective stimulus-response methodology produced evidence dissonant with this switchboard model theory, implying some kind of active processes going on between the ears. But it took the programing of electronic computers to clarify the general nature of the requirements for solving logical problems. Newell, Shaw, and Simon (21) describe three major components of these requirements: (a) memories, or information, coded and stored; (b) operations of a logical sort which can act upon the memories; and (c) hierarchically arranged programs of these operations for various purposes. Pribram (25) found a likely place for the brain's equivalents of such components within the intrinsic portions of the cerebrum which have no direct connections with either incoming fibers from the receptors of experience or outgoing fibers to the muscles and glands.

So, the electronic computer supplies a more nearly adequate mechanical model for brain functioning. Thus, experience may be regarded as programing the intrinsic portions of the cerebrum for learning and problem solving, and intellectual capacity at any given time may be conceived as a function of the nature and quality of this programing (13, 14).

As Hebb (10) has pointed out, the portion of the brain directly connected with neither incoming nor outgoing fibers is very small in animals such as frogs and salamanders, whence came most of the evidence supporting the belief in predetermined development. The increasing proportion of the intrinsic portion of the brain in higher animals suggests an anatomic basis for the increasing role of infantile experience in development, as evidenced by the greater effect of rearing on problem solving ability in dogs than in rats (14). Frogs and salamanders have a relatively higher capacity for regeneration than do mammals. This suggests that the chemical factors in the genes may have more complete control in these lower forms than they have further up the phylogenic scale.

MOTIVATION BY NEED, PAIN, AND SEX. Our conception of motivation is also undergoing change. Although it has long been said that man does not live by bread alone, most behavioral scientists and physiologists have based their theorizing on the assumption that he does. Freud popularized the statement that "all behavior is motivated." He meant motivated by painful stimulation, homeostatic need, and sexual appetite or by acquired motives based on these; and this concept has generally been shared by physiologists and academic behavioral theorists.

Undoubtedly, painful stimulation and homeostatic need motivate all organisms, as sex motivates all mammalian organisms, but the assertion that all behavior is so motivated implies that organisms become quiescent in the absence of painful stimulation, homeostatic need, and sexual stimulation. Observation stubbornly indicates that they do not: Young animals and children are most likely to play in the absence of such motivation; young rats, cats, dogs, monkeys, chimpanzees, and humans work for nothing more substantial than the opportunity to perceive, manipulate, or explore novel circumstances. This evidence implies that there must be some additional basis for motivation.

REFLEX *vs.* FEEDBACK. A change in our conception of the functional unit of the nervous system from the reflex arc to the feedback loop helps to suggest the nature of this other motivating mechanism. The conception of the reflex arc has its anatomical foundations in the Bell-Magendie law, based on Bell's discovery of separate ventral and dorsal roots of the spinal nerves and on Magendie's discovery that the dorsal roots have sensory or "input" functions while the ventral roots have motor or "output" functions. But the Bell-Magendie law was an overgeneralization, for motor fibers have been discovered within the presumably sensory dorsal roots, and sensory fibers have been discovered within the presumably motor ventral roots.

The most important argument against the reflex as the functional unit of the nervous system comes from the direct evidence of feedback in both sensory input and motor output. The neural activity that results when cats are exposed to a tone is markedly reduced when they are exposed to the sight of mice or the smell of fish, thus dramatizing feedback in sensory input. Feedback in motor output is dramatized by evidence that sensory input from the muscle spindles modulates the rate of motor firing to the muscles, thereby controlling the strength of contraction (14).

INCONGRUITY AS MOTIVATION. The feedback loop which constitutes a new conceptual unit of neural function supplies the basis for a new mechanism of motivation. Miller, Galanter, and Pribram (19) have called the feedback loop the Test-Operate-Test-Exit (TOTE) unit. Such a TOTE unit is, in principle, not unlike the room thermostat. The temperature at which the thermostat is set supplies a standard against which the temperature of the room is continually being tested. If the room temperature falls below this standard, the test yields an *incongruity* which starts the furnace to "operate," and it continues to operate until the room temperature has reached this standard. When the test yields *congruity,* the furnace stops operating and the system makes its exit. Similarly, a living organism is free to be otherwise motivated once such a system has made its exit.

Several classes of similarly operating standards can be identified for human beings. One might be described as the "comfort standard" in which incongruity is equivalent to pain. Another consists of those homeostatic standards for hunger (a low level of glycogen in the bloodstream) and for thirst (a high level of hydrogen ion concentration within the blood and interstitial fluids). A third class, which stretches the concept of incongruity somewhat, is related to sex.

Other standards derive from the organism's informational interaction with the environment. Thus, a fourth class appears to consist of on-going inputs, and, just as "one never hears the clock until it has stopped," any change in these on-going inputs brings attention and excitement. Repeated encounters with such changes of input lead to expectations, which constitute a fifth class of standards. A sixth class consists of plans quite independent of painful stimulation, homeostatic need, or sex. Ideals constitute a seventh class.

There is evidence that incongruity with such standards will instigate action and produce excitement (14). There is also evidence that an optimum of such incongruity exists. Too little produces boredom as it did among McGill students who would remain lying quietly in a room no more than three days, although they were paid twenty dollars a day to do so (14). Too much produces fearful emotional stress, as when a baby chimpanzee sees his keeper in a Halloween mask (9), a human infant encounters strangers, or primitive men see an eclipse.

While this optimum of incongruity is still not well understood, it seems to involve the matching of incoming information with standards based on information already coded and stored within the cerebrum (14). Probably only the individual himself can choose a source of input which provides him with an optimum of incongruity. His search for this optimum, however, explains that "growth motivation" which Froebel, the founder of the kindergarten movement, postulated and which John Dewey borrowed; and it may be the basic motivation underlying intellectual growth and the search for knowledge. Such motivation may be characterized as "intrinsic" because it inheres in the organism's informational interaction with the environment.

EMOTIONAL *vs.* COGNITIVE EXPERIENCE. Another fundamental change is in the importance attributed to early — and especially very early — preverbal experience. Traditionally, very little significance had been attached to preverbal experience. When consciousness was believed to control conduct, infantile experience, typically not remembered, was regarded as having hardly any effect on adult behavior. Moreover, when development was conceived to be predetermined, infantile experience could have little importance. While Freud (7) believed that preverbal experiences were important, he argued that their importance derived from the instinctive impulses arising from painful stimulation, homeostatic need, and especially pleasure striving, which he saw as sexual in nature.

Freud's work spread the belief that early emotional experiences are important while early cognitive experiences are not. It now appears that the opposite may possibly be more nearly true. Objective studies furnish little evidence that the factors important according to Freud's theory of psychosexual development are significant (12, 22). Even the belief that infants are sensitive organisms readily traumatized by painful stimulation or intense homeostatic need has been questioned as the result of studies involving the shocking of nursling rats.

Rats shocked before weaning are found to be less likely than rats left unmolested in the maternal nest to urinate and defecate in, or to hesitate entering, unfamiliar territory, and more likely to be active there. Moreover, as adults, rats shocked before weaning often require stronger shocks to instigate escape activity than do rats left unmolested; they also show less fixative effect from being shocked at the choice-point in a T-maze (28). Evidence that children from low socioeconomic and educational classes, who have frequently known painful stimulation, are less likely to be fearful than middle class children, who have seldom known painful stimulation, suggests that the findings of these rat studies may apply to human beings (11).

While such observations have contradicted the common conception of the importance of early emotional experience, the experiments stemming from Hebb's theorizing (10) have repeatedly demonstrated the importance of early perceptual and cognitive experience. At earlier phases of development, the variety of circumstances encountered appears to be most important; somewhat later, the responsiveness of the environment to the infant's activities appears to be central; and at a still later phase, the opportunity to understand the causation of mechanical and social relationships seems most significant.

In this connection, a study by Baldwin, Kalhorn, and Breese (1) found that the I.Q.'s of four- to seven-year-old children tend to increase with time if parental discipline consists of responsive and realistic explanations, but tend to fall if parental discipline consists of nonchalant unresponsiveness or of demands for obedience for its own sake, with painful stimulation as the alternative.

MOTOR RESPONSE AND RECEPTOR INPUT. One more important traditional belief about psychological development which may have to be changed concerns the relative importance of motor response and receptor input for the development of the autonomous central processes which mediate intellectual capacity. A century ago, the "apperceptive mass" conceived by Herbart, a German educational psychologist, was regarded as the product of previous perceptual input; and Froebel and Montessori both stressed sensory training. However, after World War I, the focus of laboratory learning-studies on response, coupled with the notion of brain function as a static switchboard, gradually shifted the emphasis from the perceptual input to the response output. It is hard to make the great importance attributed to the response side jibe with the following findings:

1. Hopi infants reared on cradleboards, where the movements of arms and legs are inhibited during waking hours, learn to walk at the same age as Hopi infants reared with arms and legs free (4).

2. Eighty-five per cent of the four-year-olds in a Teheran orphanage, where variations in auditory and visual input were extremely limited, did not walk alone (3).

Such observations and those of Piaget (23, 24) suggest that the repeated correction of expectations deriving from perceptual impressions and from cognitive accommodations gradually create the central processes mediating the logical operations of thought. Wohlwill (29) and Flavell (6) have assembled evidence which relates the inferential processes of thought to experience and have given this evidence some formal theoretical organization.

Counteracting Cultural Deprivation

The intellectual inferiority apparent among so many children of parents of low educational and socioeconomic status, regardless of race, is already evident by the time they begin kindergarten or first grade at age five or six (17). Such children are apt to have various linguistic liabilities: limited vocabularies, poor articulation, and syntactical deficiencies that are revealed in the tendency to rely on unusually short sentences with faulty grammar (16). They also show perceptual deficiencies in the sense that they recognize fewer objects and situations than do most middle-class children. And perhaps more important, they usually have fewer interests than do the middle-class children who are the pace setters in the schools. Moreover, the objects recognized by and the interests of children typical of the lower class differ from those of children of the middle class. These deficiencies give such children the poor start which so commonly handicaps them ever after in scholastic competition.

So long as it was assumed that intelligence is fixed and development is predetermined, the intellectual inferiority of children from families of low educational and socioeconomic status had to be considered an unalterable consequence of their genes. With the changes in our conception of man's intellectual development, outlined in the foregoing pages, there emerges a hope of combating such inferiority by altering, for part of their waking hours, the conditions under which such children develop. The question is "how?"

CLUES FROM INTRINSIC MOTIVATION. A tentative answer, worthy at least of investigative demonstration, is suggested by the existence of a change during the preschool years in the nature of what I have called "intrinsic motivation." An approximation of the character of this change has been supplied by the observations which Piaget made on the development of his three children (15, 23, 24). At least three stages in the development of intrinsic motivation appear. These may be characteristic of an organism's progressive relationship with any new set of circumstances and seem to be stages in infant development only because the child is encountering so many new sets of circumstances during his first two or three years.

In the first stage the infant is essentially responsive. He is motivated, of course, by painful stimulation, homeostatic need, and, in Freud's sense, by sex. Russian investigators have shown that the orienting response is ready-made at birth in all mammals, including human beings (27). Thus, any changes in the on-going perceptual input will attract attention and excite the infant. During this phase each of the ready-made sensorimotor organizations — sucking, looking, listening, vocalizing, grasping, and wiggling — changes, by something like Pavlov's conditioning process, to become coordinated with the others. Thus, something heard becomes something to look at, something to look at becomes something to grasp, and something to grasp becomes something to suck. This phase ends with a "landmark of transition" in which the infant, having repeatedly encountered certain patterns of stimulus change, tries actively to retain or regain them (15).

During the second stage the infant manifests interest in, and efforts to retain, something newly recognized as familiar — a repeatedly encountered pattern of change in perceptual input. The infant's intentional effort is familiar to anyone who has jounced a child on his knee and then stopped his jouncing only to find the child making a comparable motion, as if to invite the jouncing adult to continue. Regaining the newly recognized activity commonly brings forth such signs of delight as the smile and the laugh, and continued loss brings signs of distress. The effort to retain the newly recognized may well account for the long hours of hand watching and babbling commonly observed during the child's third, fourth, and fifth months. This second stage ends when, with these repeated encounters, the child becomes bored with the familiar and turns his interest to whatever is novel in familiar situations (15).

The third stage begins with this interest in the novel within a familiar context, which typically becomes noticeable during the last few months of the first year of life. Piaget (23) describes its beginnings with the appearance of throwing, but it probably can be found earlier. While he throws, the child intentionally shifts his attention from the act of throwing to the trajectory of the object that he has thrown.

Interest in the novel is also revealed in the infant's increasing development of new plans through an active, creative process of groping, characterized by C. Lloyd Morgan as "trial-and-error." It also shows in the child's increasing attempts to imitate new vocal patterns and gestures (15, 24).

Interest in the new is the infant's basis for "growth motivation." It has also been found in animals, particularly in an experiment in which rats in a figure-eight maze regularly changed their preference to the more complex loop.

Thus Piaget's (23) aphorism, "the more a child has seen and heard, the more he wants to see and hear," may be explained. The more different visual and auditory changes the child encounters during the first stage, the more of these will he recognize with interest during the second stage. The more he recognizes during the second stage, the more of these will provide novel features to attract him during the third stage.

EFFECTS OF SOCIAL ENVIRONMENT. Such development prepares the child to go on developing. But continuing development appears to demand a relationship with adults who enable the infant to pursue his locomotor and manipulative intentions and who answer his endless questions of "What's that?" "Is it a 'this' or a 'that'?" and "Why is it a 'this' or a 'that'?" Without these supports during the second, third, and fourth years of life, a child cannot continue to profit, no matter how favorable his circumstances during his first year.

Although we still know far too little about intellectual development to say anything with great confidence, it is unlikely that most infants in families of low socioeconomic status suffer great deprivation during their first year. Since one distinguishing feature of poverty is crowding, it is conceivable that an infant may actually encounter a wider variety of visual and auditory inputs in conditions of poverty than in most middle- or upper-class homes. This should facilitate the intellectual development of the infant during his first year.

During the second year, however, crowded living conditions would probably hamper development. As an infant begins to move under his own power, to manipulate things, and to throw things, he is likely to get in the way of adults who are apt already to be ill-tempered from their own discomforts and frustrations. Such situations are dramatized in Lewis's *The Children of Sanchez,* an anthropological study of life in poverty (18). In such an atmosphere, a child's opportunity to carry out the activities required for his locomotor and manipulative development must almost inevitably be sharply curbed.

Moreover, late in his second or early in his third year, after he has developed a number of pseudo-words and achieved the "learning set" that "things have names," the child in a crowded, poverty-stricken family probably meets another obstacle: His questions too seldom bring suitable answers, and too often bring punishment that inhibits further questioning. Moreover, the conditions that originally provided a rich variety of input for the very young infant now supply a paucity of suitable playthings and models for imitation.

The effects of a lower-class environment on a child's development may become even more serious during his fourth and fifth years. Furthermore, the longer these conditions continue, the more likely the effects are to be lasting. Evidence from animal studies supports this: Tadpoles immobilized with chloretone for eight days are not greatly hampered in the development of their swimming patterns, but immobilization for thirteen days leaves their swimming patterns permanently impaired; chicks kept in darkness for as many as five days show no apparent defects in their pecking responses, but keeping them in darkness for eight or more days results in chicks which never learn to peck at all (13).

POSSIBLE COUNTERACTING MEASURES. Such observations suggest that if nursery schools or day-care centers were arranged for culturally deprived children from age four — or preferably from age three — until time for school at five or six, some of the worst effects of their rearing might be substantially reduced.

Counteracting cultural deprivation at this stage of development might best be accomplished by giving the child the opportunity to encounter a wide variety of objects, pictures, and appropriate behavioral models, and by giving him social approval for appropriate behavior. The setting should encourage him to indulge his inclinations to scrutinize and manipulate the new objects as long as he is interested and should provide him with appropriate answers to his questions. Such varied experiences would foster the development of representative imagery which could then be the referents for spoken words and later for written language.

Children aged three and four should have the opportunity to hear people speak who provide syntactical models of standard grammar. The behavioral models would lead gradually to interest in pictures, written words, and books. The objects provided and appropriate answers to the "why" questions would lead to interest in understanding the workings of things and the consequences of social conduct. Thus, the child might gradually overcome most of the typical handicaps of his lower-class rearing by the time he enters grade school.

There is a danger, however, in attempting to prescribe a remedy for cultural deprivation at this stage of knowledge. Any specific prescription of objects, pictures, behavioral models, and forms of social reinforcement may fail to provide that attractive degree of incongruity with the impressions which the toddler of the lower class has already coded and stored in the course of his experience. Moreover, what seems to be appropriate behavioral models may merely produce conflict. Therefore, it may be wise to re-examine the educational contributions of Maria Montessori (20, 26). These have been largely forgotten in America, perhaps because they were until recently too dissonant with the dominant notions of motivation and the importance attributed to motor responses in development.

Montessori's contributions are especially interesting, despite some of the rigid orthodoxy that has crept into present-day Montessori practice, because she based her teaching methods on children's spontaneous interest in learning, that is, on "intrinsic motivation." Moreover, she stressed the importance of teachers' observing children to discover what things would most interest them and most foster their growth. Further, she stressed the need to train the perceptual processes, or what we would today call the information processes. The coded information stored in culturally deprived children from lower-class backgrounds differs from that stored in children with middle-class backgrounds. This difference makes it dangerous for middle-class teachers to prescribe intuitively on the basis of their own experiences or of their experiences in teaching middle-class youngsters.

Montessori also broke the lockstep in the education of young children. She made no effort to keep them doing the same thing at the same time. Rather, each child was free to examine and work with whatever happened to interest him, for as long as he liked. It is commonly believed that the activity of preschoolers must be changed every ten or fifteen minutes or the children become bored. But Dorothy Canfield Fisher (5), the novelist, who spent the winter of 1910–1911 at Montessori's Casa de Bambini in Rome, observed that three-year-olds there commonly remained engrossed in such mundane activities as buttoning and unbuttoning for two hours or more at a time. In such a setting the child has an opportunity to find those particular circumstances which match his own particular phase of development and which provide the proper degree of incongruity for intrinsic motivation. This may well have the corollary advantage of making learning fun and the school setting interesting and attractive.

Montessori also included children from three to six years old in the same group. In view of the changes that occur in intellectual development, this has the advantage of providing younger children with a variety of novel models for imitation while supplying older children with an opportunity to teach, an activity which provides many of its own rewards.

Conclusions

At this stage of history and knowledge, no one can blueprint a program of preschool enrichment that will with certainty be an effective antidote for the cultural deprivation of children. On the other hand, the revolutionary changes taking place in the traditional beliefs about the development of human capacity and motivation make it sensible to hope that a program of preschool enrichment may ultimately be made effective. The task calls for creative innovations and careful evaluative studies of their effectiveness.

Discoveries of effective innovations will contribute also to the general theory of intellectual development and become significant for the rearing and education of all children. Effective innovations will also help to minimize those racial differences in school achievement which derive from cultural deprivation and so help to remove one stubborn obstacle in the way of racial integration.

Although it is likely that no society has ever made the most of the intellectual potential of its members, the increasing role of technology in our culture demands that we do better than others ever have. To do so we must become more concerned with intellectual development during the preschool years and especially with the effects of cultural deprivation.

REFERENCES

1. Baldwin, A. L., J. Kalhorn, and F. H. Breese. "Patterns of Parent Behavior," *Psychological Monographs,* vol. 58, 1945.

2. Bayley, Nancy. "Mental Growth in Young Children," in *Thirty-Ninth Yearbook of the National Society for the Study of Education,* Part II. Bloomington, Ill.: Public School Publishing Co., 1940.

3. Dennis, W. "Causes of Retardation Among Institutional Children: Iran," *Journal of Genetic Psychology,* vol. 96, 1960.

4. ———, and Marsena G. Dennis. "The Effect of Cradling Practice Upon the Onset of Walking in Hopi Children," *Journal of Genetic Psychology,* vol. 56, 1940.

5. Fisher, Dorothy Canfield. *A Montessori Mother.* New York: Henry Holt & Co., 1912.

6. Flavell, J. H. *The Developmental Psychology of Jean Piaget.* New York: D. Van Nostrand Co., 1963.

7. Freud, S. "Three Contributions to the Theory of Sex," in A. A. Brill (ed.), *The Basic Writings of Sigmund Freud.* New York: Modern Library, 1938.

8. Goldfarb, W. "The Effects of Early Institutional Care on Adolescent Personality," *Journal of Experimental Education,* vol. 12, 1953.

9. Hebb, D. O. "On the Nature of Fear," *Psychological Review,* vol. 53, 1946.

10. ———. *The Organization of Behavior.* New York: John Wiley & Sons, 1949.

11. Holmes, F. B. "An Experimental Study of the Fears of Young Children," in A. T. Jersild and F. B. Holmes, *Children's Fears*, Child Development Monographs, No. 20. New York: Teachers College, Columbia University, 1935.

12. Hunt, J. McV. "Experimental Psychoanalysis," in P. L. Harriman (ed.), *The Encyclopedia of Psychology.* New York: Philosophical Library, 1946.

13. ———. *Intelligence and Experience.* New York: Ronald Press, 1961.

14. ———. "Motivation Inherent in Information Processing and Action," in O. J. Harvey (ed.), *Motivation and Social Interaction: Cognitive Determinants.* New York: Ronald Press, 1963.

15. ———. "Piaget's Observations as a Source of Hypotheses Concerning Motivation," *Merrill-Palmer Quarterly,* vol. 9, 1963.

16. John, Vera P. "The Intellectual Development of Slum Children," *Merrill-Palmer Quarterly,* vol. 10, 1964.

17. Kennedy, W. A., *et al. A Normative Sample of Intelligence and Achievement of Negro Elementary School Children in the Southeastern United States.* Monographs of the Society for Research in Child Development, Serial No. 90, vol. 28, 1963.

18. Lewis, O. *The Children of Sanchez.* New York: Random House, 1961.

19. Miller, G. A., E. Galanter, and K. H. Pribram. *Plans and the Structure of Behavior.* New York: Henry Holt & Co., 1960.

20. Montessori, Maria. *The Montessori Method* (1907). New York: Frederick A. Stokes, 1912.

21. Newell, A., J. C. Shaw, and H. A. Simon, "Elements of a Theory of Human Problem-solving," *Psychological Review,* vol. 65, 1958.

22. Orlanksy, H. "Infant Care and Personality," *Psychological Bulletin,* vol. 46, 1949.

23. Piaget, J. *The Origins of Intelligence in Children* (1936). (Translated by Margaret Cook.) New York: International Universities Press, 1952.

24. ———. *Play, Dreams, and Imitation in Childhood* (1945). (Translation of *La formation du symbole chez l'enfant* by C. Gattegno and F. M. Hodgson.) New York: W. W. Norton & Co., 1951.

25. Pribram, K. H. "A Review of Theory in Physiological Psychology," *Annual Review of Psychology,* vol. 11, 1960.

26. Rambusch, Nancy McC. *Learning How to Learn: an American Approach to Montessori.* Baltimore, Md.: Helicon Press, 1962.

27. Razran, G. "The Observable Unconscious and the Inferable Conscious in Current Soviet Psychophysiology: Interoceptive Conditioning, Semantic Conditioning, and the Orienting Reflex," *Psychological Review,* vol. 68, 1961.

28. Salama, A. A., and J. McV. Hunt. " 'Fixation' in the Rat as a Function of Infantile Shocking, Handling, and Gentling," *Journal of Genetic Psychology,* vol. 100, 1964.

29. Wohlwill, J. F. "Developmental Studies of Perception," *Psychological Bulletin,* vol. 57, 1960.

Negro American Intelligence: A New Look at an Old Controversy

THOMAS F. PETTIGREW

Introduction

Following the Supreme Court's school desegregation decision in 1954, white supremacists mounted a major revival of racist doctrines. These claims, centering on the alleged genetic intellectual inferiority of Negro Americans, have received considerable publicity in the mass media. But American public opinion is far less receptive to such reasoning now than it was a generation ago. Public opinion poll data reveal that, while only two out of five white Americans regarded Negroes their intellectual equals in 1942, almost four out of five did by 1956 — including a substantial majority of white Southerners. Much of this change is due to the thorough repudiation of racist assertions by the vast majority of modern psychologists and other behavioral scientists. Indeed, the latest research in this area lends the strongest evidence yet available for this repudiation. The present paper takes a new look at this old controversy and presents a summary of the relevant research.

The "Scientific Racist" Position

The dominant scientific position on this subject has been termed an "equalitarian dogma" and described as "the scientific hoax of the century" by one psychologist, Professor-Emeritus Henry Garrett. He charges that other psychologists have prematurely closed the issue for ideological, not scientific, reasons.

Garrett is publicly joined by two other psychologists out of the roughly twenty thousand who belong to the American Psychological Association. Frank McGurk, of Villanova University, has conducted research with an unvalidated intelligence test of his own design and concluded that "Negroes as a group do not possess as much (capacity for education) as whites as a

✧ From *The Journal of Negro Education*, Winter, 1964, pp. 6–25. Used by permission of the author and the publisher. Thomas F. Pettigrew is Lecturer in Social Psychology, Harvard University.

Thorough documentation for this article will be found in Thomas F. Pettigrew, *A Profile of the Negro American* (Princeton, N.J.: D. Van Nostrand Co., Inc., 1964).

group." In 1956 this work gained wide attention when the *U. S. News and World Report* featured an article under the imposing title of "A Scientist's Report on Race Differences," in which McGurk surveyed six investigations that he claimed to be "the only existing studies that relate to the problem."

The crowning production of this small band is Audrey Shuey's *The Testing of Negro Intelligence.* Shuey, a psychologist at Randolph-Macon Woman's College in Lynchburg, Virginia, provides a large, though carefully selected, review of over two hundred studies bearing on racial differences in intelligence. She ignores the newer conceptions of intelligence and instead relies heavily upon the earlier, less sophisticated investigations, with over half of her references dated prior to World War II. She also concentrates on research performed in the South, with three-fourths of her studies on students coming from tightly segregated Southern and border communities. The great bulk of this research found most Negroes lower in I.Q. tests than most whites. Shuey unhesitatingly interprets this fact as pointing "to the presence of some native differences between Negroes and whites as determined by intelligence tests."

In addition to this "sheer weight of uncontrolled data" argument, these three psychologists attempt to show that the impoverished environment of the typical Negro cannot account for the observed test differences. One favorite example, prominently cited by all three, is Tanser's 1939 investigation of intelligence among the Negro and white children of Kent County, Ontario, Canada. Tanser found that his white sample obtained a higher average I.Q. than his Negro sample; and the three "scientific racists" maintain that this is convincing evidence for their position, since in Kent County "the social and economic conditions of the whites and Negroes were substantially the same."

The Modern Psychological Position

These arguments have not altered the dominant opinion of modern psychology on this topic. In the first place, the studies repeatedly cited by the "scientific racists" in defense of their position are not, upon closer scrutiny, critical tests of their contentions. Consider the Tanser work in Canada. As in investigations in the United States, the "social and economic conditions" of the two groups were *not* equal. Tanser himself admitted that the socioeconomic status of Negroes in Kent County was then and had always been below that of whites and that the Negro children had not attended school as regularly as the white children. Finally, it cannot be said that Southern Ontario is free of racial prejudice and discrimination. Ever since the close of the American Civil War, the position of the Negro Canadian has steadily declined, with violent outbursts against Negroes occurring in Kent County itself. The racial differences in I.Q. observed by Tanser, then, cannot be interpreted apart from the area's racial situation.

These difficulties point up the severely limiting methodological problems that confront this research realm. Any test of native intelligence must of necessity assume equivalent backgrounds of the individuals and groups under study. But until conditions entirely free from segregation and discrimination are achieved and the floor of Negro poverty is raised to that of whites', the definitive research on racial differences in intelligence cannot be performed. Meanwhile, psychologists must conduct their work in a culture where training and opportunity for the two groups are never completely equal.

Other fundamental problems complicate the scene. The very concept of "race" raises special issues. Since Negro Americans do not even approach the status of a genetically pure "race," they are a singularly inappropriate group upon which to test racist theories of inherent intellectual inferiority of the Negroid subspecies. And Anastasi observes that still further confusion is introduced by the ambiguity of the term "race differences." To find that many descriptive investigations using intelligence tests elicit differences between the "races" does not necessarily mean that these differences *result* from race.

Empirical efforts are also hampered by the operation of selective factors in sampling. That is, Negroes and whites in the same situation — such as those inducted into the armed forces — may have been selected differently on intelligence, thus biasing the comparison of test scores between the two groups. For instance, Hunt found that the Navy during World War II did not employ the same screening and selection standards for the two groups, permitting a far higher proportion of mental defectives among Negro than among white acceptances. Such a finding renders any comparisons in test scores between Negro and white sailors of dubious value. Much has been made of the intelligence test performances of the two "races" in both World War I and II, but such selective factors make these data difficult to interpret.

Despite these limitations, however, modern psychology has managed to achieve significant theoretical and empirical advances in this realm. These advances strongly favor a nongenetic interpretation of the typically lower intelligence test score averages of Negro groups. This work can be conveniently summarized under four general rubrics: (1) new theoretical conceptions; (2) the mediators of intellectual underdevelopment; (3) varying opportunities and group results; (4) the individual versus the group.

New Theoretical Conceptions

Since World War II, psychologists and other scientists have seriously reviewed earlier notions about such basic concepts as "the environment," "heredity," and "intelligence." Instead of the older nature *versus* nurture conception, the emphasis is placed on nature *and* nurture. Rather than asking which set of factors — environmental or hereditary — contributes the most to a particular trait or ability like intelligence, investigators ask how the environment and heredity combine to form the observed characteristic. Genes not only set broad limits on the range of development, but also enter into highly complex interactions with the environment, interactions which have not been emphasized enough in the past.

An ingenious animal experiment by Cooper and Zubek illustrates this genetic-environmental interaction. These investigators employed two genetically distinct strains of rats, carefully bred for thirteen generations as either "bright" or "dull." Separate groups of the two strains grew up after weaning in three contrasting environments: a restricted environment, consisting of only a food box, water pan, and otherwise barren cage; a natural environment, consisting of the usual habitat of a laboratory rat; and an enriched environment, consisting of such objects as ramps, swings, slides, polished balls, tunnels, and teetertotters plus a decorated wall beside their cages. Figure 1 shows the maze-learning performances of the six groups of rats (the fewer the errors, the more "intelligent" the behavior). Note that the two genetically diverse groups did almost equally well in the enriched and restricted environments, sharply differing only in the natural situation. In fact, the environment masks genetic potential to the point where it is impossible to distinguish the enriched dulls from the natural brights or the natural dulls from the restricted brights.

The data of Figure 1 bear important implications. *Genotypes*, the true genetic potential, often do not coincide with *phenotypes*, the actual, expressed trait. Similar genotypes may have different phenotypes (e.g., Figure 1's bright rats in the restricted and enriched environments), and similar phenotypes may have different genotypes (e.g., Figure 1's restricted bright and dull rats). Any phenotype is the composite product of the geno-

■ **FIGURE 1** *Maze Error Scores for Genetically Bright and Dull Rats Reared in Three Contrasting Environments*

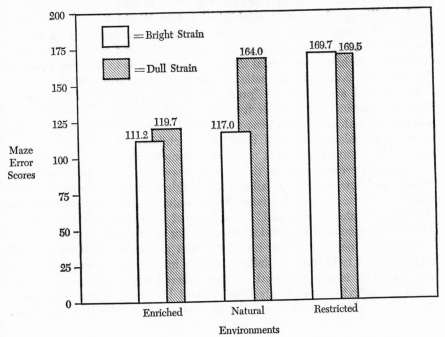

type and the environment in which the genetic potential must be realized. Relevant nature-nurture questions thus become: how environmentally modifiable is the phenotypic intelligence of each genotype? And what is the contribution of heredity to the intelligence score differences among a group of individuals on a specific test *in a specified environment?*

This newer view of the nature-nurture controversy and a mounting accumulation of new developmental evidence has resulted in a revised conception of the nature of intelligence. J. McV. Hunt presents this modern thinking in his volume, *Intelligence and Experience.* Taking his cue from the strategies for information-processing that are currently programed for electronic computers, Hunt prefers to define intelligence as central neural processes which develop in the brain to mediate between the information coming into the individual via the senses and the return signals for motor reaction. Moreover, he maintains that the initial establishment and subsequent capacity of these processes are probably rooted in the child's earliest encounters with the world around him. Intelligence, then, is not merely an inherited capacity, genetically fixed and destined to unfold in a biologically predetermined manner. It is a dynamic, on-going set of processes that within wide hereditary limits is subject to innumerable experiential factors.

Hunt's view upsets two long-unquestioned dogmas about intelligence, dogmas critical to the area of race differences. He terms them the assumptions of "fixed intelligence" and "predetermined development." The first of these has its roots in Darwin's theory of natural selection. It accepts intelligence as a static, innately given quantity, and it causes intelligence tests to be so designed as to render artifactually constant mean I.Q.'s from large populations of children of differing ages. Indeed, the assumption of fixed intelligence became so established before World War II that many psychologists regarded all evidence of substantial shifts in I.Q. as merely the product of poor testing procedures. But, objected Stoddard in 1943, "to regard all changes in mental status as an artifact is to shut one's eyes to the most significant and dramatic phenomenon in human growth."

The second assumption of "predetermined development" refers to the idea that, barring extreme interference from the environment, intelligence will unfold "naturally" with gene-determined anatomical maturation. Classic work on salamanders and Hopi Indian children was cited to demonstrate this maturational effect and that prior experience was unnecessary for normal development. In this era, mothers were told to avoid over-stimulating their children, to allow their children simply to grow "on their own." Hunt considers such advice "highly unfortunate," for it now appears that proper matching of a child's development with challenging encounters with the environment is a critical requisite for maximizing ability.

Notice this new outlook in no way denies an hereditary influence well established by twin studies. Rather, it views intelligence in much the same way longevity is now regarded. A strong hereditary component is recognized in longevity; consistently long or short life spans typify many families. Yet, despite this component, the life expectancies at birth of Americans have almost doubled in the past century. Better medical care, better diets, and a host of other environmental factors converge to enable Americans to make fuller use of their longevity potential. Likewise, the modern view of intelligence holds that we have not begun to expand our phenotypic intelligences even close to our genotypic potentials. From this vantage point, it appears our society has placed too much emphasis on personnel selection and eugenics at the expense of effective training programs and euthenics.

Some of the most imaginative experimentation behind this new thinking is that of the eminent Swiss psychologist, Jean Piaget. His ingenious and detailed studies with children of all ages provide abundant evidence that intelligence is the very antithesis of a fixed, predetermined capacity. And a wide range of other types of investigations amply bears out this conclusion. Even animal intelligence seems to be importantly affected by environmental opportunities. The previously cited rat work of Cooper and Zubek shows how diverse cage environments affect later learning. In addition, pet-reared rats and dogs, with backgrounds of richly variegated experience, later evidence considerably more intelligent behavior than their cage-reared counterparts. And Harlow has demonstrated that monkeys can "learn to learn"; that is, they can develop learning-sets which enable them to solve general classes of problems almost at a glance.

Similar effects of early environmental enrichment on the intelligence of young children have been noted. Kirk has shown that early educational procedures can often produce sharp increments in intellectual functioning among mentally retarded children, sometimes even among those diagnosed as organically impaired. Other studies on normal children, both white and Negro, suggest that preschool training in nursery and kindergarten classes may act to raise I.Q.'s. Among criticisms of this research is the contention that a selection factor could be operating. The natively brighter children may be those who tend to have preschool education. But among deprived children in an orphanage, the beneficial results of early schooling have been noted in a situation where selection factors did not operate. Also relevant is the tendency for orphans to gain in I.Q. after adoption into superior foster homes, the gain being greatest for those adopted earliest.

After reviewing research on cognitive learning in these early years, Fowler concludes that this is the period of human "apprenticeship." The infant is acquiring the most elementary and basic discriminations needed for later learning; like Harlow's monkeys, the infant is "learning to learn." Fowler speculates that conceptual learning-sets, interest areas, and habit patterns may be more favorably established at these early stages than at later stages of the development cycle. Indeed, emphasis on "practical," concrete, gross motor learning in these early years may even act to inhibit later abstract learning.

In any event, research has documented the intellectually damaging consequences of deprived environments. Two English studies found that the children of such isolated groups as canal-boat and gypsy families achieve exceptionally low intelligence test scores, scores considerably below those typically found among Negro American children. Interesting, too, is the fact that as these children grow older their I.Q.'s generally decline, though this is not the case for children of more privileged groups. In a similar fashion, children in orphanages and other institutions tend to have lower I.Q.'s and more retarded motor and linguistic development than children in stimulating home environments.

A related finding concerns the trend toward lower I.Q.'s of children raised in large families. One common explanation of this phenomenon is simply that parents who have large families are natively less intelligent. Yet, as Hunt points out, other findings strongly suggest that it is partly because parents of large families have less time to spend with each child. Thus, twins and doubles born close together reveal a similar tendency toward lower I.Q.'s in otherwise small families. And the negative relationship between family size and intelligence does not appear among wealthy families who can afford servants to provide stimulating attention for each child.

Finally, the extreme effects that can ensue from an impoverished environment are dramatically illustrated in a series of sensory-deprivation experiments. These investigations reveal that normal people respond with marked psychological disturbances when severely restricted in activity and stimulation. They typically experience temporal and spatial distortions and pronounced hallucinations; and they evidence sharply impaired thinking and reasoning both during and after their isolation.

The Mediators of Intellectual Underdevelopment

Within this new perspective on intelligence as a relatively plastic quality, a series of environmental mediators of the individual Negro child's intellectual under-development has been determined. In fact, these mediators exert their effects upon even the Negro fetus. One study found that dietary supplementation by vitamins supplied during the last half of pregnancy had direct beneficial effects on later I.Q. scores of the children. In a sample of mothers from the lowest socioeconomic level, 80 per cent of whom were Negro, the group fortified with iron and vitamin B complex had children whose mean I.Q. at three years of age averaged five full points above the children of the unfortified control group, 103.4 to 98.4. One year later, the mean difference had enlarged to eight points, 101.7 to 93.6. The same researchers failed to find a similar effect among white mothers and their children from a mountain area. Presumably, the largely Negro sample was even poorer and more malnourished than the white mountain sample. Dire poverty, through the mediation of *the mother's meager diet*, can thus begin acting to impair intelligence before the lower-class Negro child is born.

Economic problems also hamper intelligence through the mediation of *premature births*. Premature children of all races reveal not only a heightened incidence of neurologic abnormalities and greater susceptibility to disease, but also a considerably larger percentage of mental defectives. A further organic factor in intelligence is *brain injury* in the newborn. And both of these conditions have higher incidences among Negroes because of their greater frequency in the most economically depressed sectors of the population.

Later complications are introduced by the impoverished environments in which most Negro children grow up. At the youngest, preschool ages, race differences in I.Q. means are minimal. Repeated research shows that in the first two years of life there are no significant racial differences in either psychomotor development or intelligence. Racist theorists deny the importance of these findings on two conflicting grounds. They either claim that infant tests have no predictive-value whatsoever for later I.Q. scores, or cite an older study by McGraw that found Negro infants retarded in comparison with white infants. Neither argument is adequate. Two recent investigations provide convincing evidence that properly administered infant tests *do* predict later scores. And the 1931 McGraw study is no longer regarded as a critical experiment. It was a pioneer effort that compared white infants with Negro infants of markedly smaller stature on an unvalidated adaptation of a European test. Furthermore, later Northern investigations show little or no Negro lag in intellectual development through kindergarten and five years of age when thorough socioeconomic controls are applied.

It is only after a few years of inferior schooling have passed that many Negro children begin to drop noticeably in measured I.Q. Part of this drop is due to the heavier reliance placed by intelligence tests at these ages upon verbal skills, skills that are particularly influenced by a constricted environment. Thus, one Southern study of *"verbal destitution"* discovered that those Negro college students most retarded in a reading clinic came from small, segregated high schools and exhibited language patterns typical of the only adult models they had encountered — poorly educated parents, teachers, and ministers.

Another factor in the declining test averages over the school years is simply *the nature of the schools* themselves. Deutsch gives the example of an assignment to "write a page on 'The Trip I Took'" given to lower-class youngsters in a ghetto school who had never been more than twenty-five city blocks from home. Deutsch maintains: "The school represents a foreign outpost in an encapsulated community which is surrounded by what, for the child, is unknown and foreign."

This tendency of the measured I.Q.'s of Negro children to diminish with increasing age is interpreted by racists not as evidence of the eroding effects of ghetto living but as proof that Negroes mature rapidly and begin to decline earlier than whites. Such an idea, based on the belief that Negroes as a "race" are less evolved, is seriously embarrassed by the often-demonstrated fact that environmentally deprived Caucasian groups reveal precisely the same phenomenon — mountain and other rural children in America and the canal-boat and gypsy children of England. Furthermore, the positive relationship between socioeconomic status and tested I.Q. among

Negroes increases with age, again suggesting that environmental factors become ever more vital as the child matures.

The nature of the *disrupted family life* of many lower-status Negro youths adds to the slum's lack of environmental stimulation. Most of these youngsters are reared in large families, with reduced parental contact. In addition, many of them are in fatherless homes. And Deutsch and Stetler have each demonstrated that Negro children raised in such broken homes score significantly below comparable Negro children from intact homes on intelligence measures.

Other research pinpoints which tasks tested by intelligence tests are most impaired by this restriction of stimulation. Woods and Toal matched two groups of Negro and white adolescents on I.Q. and noted subtest differences. While superior to the whites on some tests, the Negroes were noticeably deficient on tasks such as detection of errors and drawing pictorial completions which required ability to visualize spatially. A series of similar studies reached the same conclusion; one demonstrated that this difficulty with perceptual and spatial relations was considerably more marked in a southern-reared Negro sample than in an I.Q.-matched northern-reared Negro sample. This *breakdown of spatial performance* among otherwise intelligent Negro children, especially in the more restrictive South, offers a suggestive parallel with the comparable spatial breakdown noted in the sensory-deprivation research. In any event, two additional studies provide evidence that this disability is correctable. Both studies gave groups of Negro and white children special training in spatial perception and found that the Negro subjects benefited more from the practice. I.Q. test scores were markedly higher for the Negro subjects five months after the training. Anastasi believes this work supports the idea that the Negroes tested suffered from an unusually barren perceptual experience in early life.

Organic complications and environmental impoverishment are not the only mediators depressing Negro American intelligence. Both the "functioning intelligence" and the measured I.Q. of an individual are inseparably intertwined with his personality. Weisskopf has given case evidence of the great variety of ways *personality problems* can deter normal intellectual development. A child may do poorly in learning situations in a conscious or unconscious desire to punish his parents, to inflict self-punishment, or to avoid self-evaluation. And Roen has demonstrated that such personality problems are more highly related to intelligence test scores among Negroes than among whites. He equated two racial groups of soldiers on a wide range of social variables and found that a series of personality measures were more closely correlated with intelligence for the Negroes than for the whites. In particular, he noted that Negro soldiers who scored low on a self-confidence questionnaire had unusually low intelligence scores.

Racist claims of Caucasian superiority contributes to the Negro's lack of intellectual self-confidence. This insecurity is especially provoked by any direct comparison with white performance. One investigation administered a task to Negro Southern college students with two different sets of instructions. One set told how other students at their college did on the task, while the second told how whites throughout the nation did. Those subjects who anticipated white comparison performed significantly poorer on the task and indicated stronger concern and anxiety about their performance.

The *role of "Negro"* is also a critical factor. Put simply, the Negro is not expected to be bright. To reveal high intelligence is to risk seeming "uppity" to a white racist. And soon a self-fulfilling prophecy begins to operate, for the Negro who assumes a façade of stupidity as a defense mechanism against oppression is very likely to grow into the role. He will not be eager to learn, and he will not strive to do well in the testing situation. After all, an intelligence test is a middle-class white man's instrument; it is a device whites use to prove their capacities and get ahead in the white world. Achieving a high test score does not have the same meaning for a lower-status Negro child, and it may even carry a definite connotation of personal threat. In this sense, scoring low on intelligence measures may for some talented Negro children be a rational response to perceived danger.

In addition to stupidity, the role of "Negro" prescribes both passivity and lack of ambition as central traits. And these traits have been found to be crucial personality correlates of I.Q. changes in white children. The Fels Research Institute found that aggressiveness and high need for achievement differentiate those children whose scores rise between six and ten years of age from those whose scores recede.

Another protective device is slowness. This trait assumes major importance in the speed instruments typically employed to estimate intelligence. In the Negro lower class there is no premium on speed, for work is generally paid by the hour and there are realistically few goals that fast, hard endeavor can attain. Consequently, a number of experimenters have noted that differences in speed of response are primarily responsible for racial differences in I.Q. estimated by timed performance tests.

Playing "Negro" is made especially critical when the examiner is white. Even two-year-old Negroes seem verbally inhibited when *tested by a white*. In fact, this verbal inhibition may be the principal factor underlying the common observation that Negro children generally evidence verbal comprehension quite superior to their verbal communication. One investigation had students of both races tested alternately by Negro and white examiners. For both groups, the mean I.Q. was approximately six points higher when the test was administered by an examiner of their own race. Similarly, adult Negroes in North Carolina were significantly more accurate in rendering the names of the candidates for governor in a recent election to a Negro poll interviewer than to a white interviewer.

Varying Opportunities and Results

If all of these mechanisms are operating to mediate the influence of a lean, hostile, and constricted environment upon the individual Negro's tested intelligence, certain group trends under conditions of varying opportunities can be predicted. These testable hypotheses are: (1) in environments which approach being equally restrictive for children of both races, the intelligence test means of both will be low and will approach equality; (2) in environments which approach being equally stimulating for children of both races, the intelligence test means of both will be high and will approach equality; and (3) when any racial group moves from a restrictive to a comparatively stimulating environment, its measured I.Q. mean will rise.

The first of these hypotheses was tested on an isolated Caribbean Island, offering little stimulation to its youth. It had "no regular steamship service, no railroad, motion picture theatre, or newspaper. There were very few automobiles and very few telephones. The roads were generally poor. There were no government schools above the elementary level and no private schools above the secondary level. . . . People of all colors, then, were restricted to a rather narrow range of occupational opportunity."

Even here, however, complete equality of status between whites and Negroes was not achieved. White skin was "highly respected," whites typically held the better jobs, and, while almost half of the white students attended private schools, nine-tenths of the Negroes attended government schools. Nevertheless, there were no significant color differences on nine of the fourteen intelligence measures. The Negroes did best on tests which were less class-linked, less threatening, and less dependent on uncommon words. Thus, socioeconomic status was a more important factor than race on four of the five instruments which did yield racial discrepancies, and "lack of confidence," as rated independently by teachers, was highly related to three of them. In general, the island youngsters scored rather low on the tests, with race a relatively insignificant consideration. And the selective migration possibility that the brighter whites were leaving the island is not an explanation for these findings, since there was apparently little out- or in-migration. These data, gathered in a locality which approached being equally restrictive for both races, do "not lend support to the conclusion that colored inferiority in intelligence tests has a racial basis."

The second hypothesis has also received support from a number of studies. Three investigations testing young children in Minneapolis, grade school students in a Nevada city, and adolescents in the Boston area revealed that once social class factors are rigorously controlled there are only minor black-white mean I.Q. differences. In these relatively stimulating, educationally desegregated urban communities, both racial groups secured test averages equal to the national norms.

An additional study was conducted in West Germany. A representative sample of fifty-one "Negermischlingskinder" — the mulatto children of Negro American soldiers and German women — was administered a number of intelligence tests and its performance contrasted with a comparable group of twenty-five white German children. There were no significant differences. Two counterbalancing factors complicate the interpretation of this research. The Negro fathers of these children are undoubtedly an intelligent, highly selected group, selected not only in terms of being chosen to serve in the United States Army in Germany but also in terms of acculturating enough to establish an intimate relationship with a German woman. But this factor is balanced by the fact that the children are mostly illegitimate and viewed as such in the German culture almost by virtue of their color. Furthermore, most of their mothers are probably of lower-status backgrounds and have not been able to provide them with the cultural enrichment of the typical German home. And, finally, German culture, even in this post-Hitler era, can hardly be described as totally free of racist thinking. All in all, the satisfactory test performance of these mulatto Germans appears quite remarkable.

Thus, I.Q. means of groups are retarded when there are constrictive environmental conditions and elevated when there are at least average conditions. Three ecological projects provide further evidence for this generalization. One project correlated home rentals with the I.Q. average of the school children in three hundred New York City neighborhoods. Moderately high and positive relationships were found; the more expensive the neighborhood, the higher the test scores. Another noted very close and positive associations between such variables as per capita income and the mean I.Q. level of sixth-grade pupils in thirty American cities. The third project discovered that these ecological correlations tend to be higher for intelligence scores than for scholastic achievement, demonstrating again the extreme sensitivity of the measured I.Q. to the total social environment.

This research is confirmed by additional investigations conducted exclusively on Negroes. Especially since World War II and its attendant expansion of social class differentiation among Negro Americans, socioeconomic variables correlate highly and positively with I.Q. in Negro samples. For example, the I.Q. means of groups of Negro third-graders in Washington, D.C., tended to be highest in areas where radios were most often present in the homes and rents most expensive.

These results suggest the third hypothesis: when any group moves from a restrictive to a comparatively stimulating environment, its measured I.Q. mean will rise. Dramatic evidence for this proposition comes from the unique situation of the Osage Indians. Like many other Indian groups, the Osage were ceded land that they did not choose for the establishment of a reservation. But oil was later discovered on their land, and the Osage became relatively prosperous. Since the Osage did not choose their land, the oil discovery was not an indication of native ingenuity beyond that of Indian groups in general. But now they could afford living standards vastly superior to other Indians and on both performance and language tests were found to meet the national norms and be the equal of comparable whites in the area. This finding is all the more impressive when it is remembered that Indian children generally have measured I.Q.'s considerably below that of Negroes.

Similar improvements are recorded from white mountain children in East Tennessee, public school students in Honolulu, and white enlisted men in World War II. Wheeler gave tests to over three thousand mountain children in 1940, and compared their performance to that of children in the same areas from virtually the same families in 1930. This ten-year span had witnessed broad economic, social, and educational changes in East Tennessee, and the median I.Q.'s reflected these changes in an increment of 11 points, from 82 to 93. Equally remarkable gains are reported for children of many racial groups in Honolulu after a fourteen-year period of steady improvement in the city's schools. And, finally, 768 soldiers, representative of white enlisted men in World War II, took the old Army Alpha verbal test of World War I and provided striking evidence of the nation's rising intelligence between the two wars. Tuddenham shows that the typical white World War II enlisted man did better than 83 per cent of the enlisted men of the first war.

This last study, incidentally, refutes reasoning put forward by McGurk concerning the intelligence test performances of Negroes in the two world wars. He has argued that if environmental factors are responsible for racial differences in intelligence scores then Negro scores should have steadily approached the white scores between the two wars; yet "the various differences in socioeconomic environments of the Negroes, between 1918 and 1950, have not altered the Negro-white test score relationship." Such "logic" assumes that the socioeconomic standards of whites have not changed over these same years. But in fact the prosperity of whites throughout the nation has been improving in many ways faster than that of Negro Americans. If the old Alpha test had been administered to World War II Negroes, they would have most certainly done significantly better than World War I Negroes. "The Negro-white test score relationship" McGurk refers to has only remained constant because Negroes have made giant strides in intellectual growth when environmental improvements allowed it. Meanwhile, as the Tuddenham data demonstrate, the white median intelligence has also been climbing with environmental improvements. Intelligence, like longevity, is not a fixed capacity for either Negroes or whites.

Another curious assumption made by racist theory arises from interpreting regional as well as racial results on the World War I Alpha. A number of social scientists noted that Negro recruits in such states as Ohio and Illinois had higher median scores than white recruits from such states as Arkansas and Mississippi. These extreme comparisons provided an example of where the environmental deprivations of Southern whites clearly exceeded even those of some Northern Negroes. Garrett hesitated to apply his usual explanation for low scores and concludes that whites in these Southern states were innately inferior intellectually. Instead, he emphasized that Negroes scored below whites within each state; he argued that the low white scores in the South were environmentally induced, but that the even lower Negro scores in the South were a combination of environmental factors and genetic inferiority. To make this argument, Garrett had to assume that Negroes and whites in the South were *equally* deprived — even before World War I. This assumption, of course, is absurd. The period 1890 to the First World War was the lowest ebb of Negro fortunes since slavery. Today the remnants of that era ensure that Negro Southerners as a group are the most environmentally impoverished of all Southerners. And while there were often no public schools for Negroes whatsoever in some rural areas of the South before World War I, the belatedly improved facilities of today still lag behind those of the whites.

Once the Negro American escapes these inferior conditions, however, his improved performance parallels that of the Osage Indians and East Tennessee mountain children. Service in the Armed Forces is one of the most important sources of wider experience and opportunities for Negroes, including those who are illiterate. The Army in the Second World War operated Special Training Units and provided a basic fourth-grade education in eight weeks for 254,000 previously illiterate soldiers — roughly half of them Negroes and the great majority Southerners. A slightly higher percentage of the Negroes than whites successfully completed the intensive course, though how this bears on larger questions of Negro intelligence is a matter of debate because the men given this special training were selected. There is no debate, however, that the success of these units proves the educability of many apparently retarded men of both races.

Another mode of improvement for many Negroes is to migrate North. Negro Northerners routinely achieve higher test medians than comparable Negro Southerners; and Negro children born in the North achieve higher medians than those who come to the North from the South. But do the Negro children who migrate improve their group performance as they remain in the North? This was the central question Klineberg set out to answer in 1935 with perhaps the best known research in the field of race differences. Over three thousand ten-to-twelve-year-old Harlem Negroes took an array of individual and group intelligence instruments. These data clearly indicate that the longer the Southern-born children had resided in New York City, the higher their intelligence scores. Those who had been in the North for a number of years approached the levels attained by the native-born Negroes. Smaller studies with less elaborate designs obtained parallel results in Cleveland and Washington, D.C.

More recently, Lee replicated these findings in Philadelphia with the most rigorous research on the topic to date. Employing large samples in a variety of different schools, Lee analyzed the test scores of the *same* children as they progressed through the city's school system. Though never quite catching up with the Philadelphia-born Negro students, the Southern Negro migrants as a group systematically gained in I.Q. with each grade completed in Northern schools. And the earlier they began in the Philadelphia system, the greater their mean increase and final I.Q. The effects of the more stimulating and somewhat less discriminatory North, then, are directly reflected in the measured intelligence of the youngest of Negro migrants.

The major complication in interpreting the Klineberg and Lee work is again introduced by possible selection biases. Those Negro Southerners who migrate North in search of a better life may be selectively brighter and rear brighter children. Such a possibility is emphasized by the "scientific racists," though Shuey concedes this factor could reasonably account for only one-third to one-half of the I.Q. increases observed. But other possibilities also exist. Many of the more intelligent Negroes in the South gain some measure of success and establish roots that are more difficult to break than those of the less intelligent. This phenomenon would operate to make the Klineberg and Lee data all the more impressive. Or, perhaps, intelligence has little or nothing to do with the decision to migrate; personality traits, such as aggressiveness or inability to control hostility over racial frustrations, may be more decisive. Klineberg found the Southern school grades of 562 Negro youths who had since gone North were typical of the entire Negro school populations from which they migrated. More research is needed, but it seems that selective migration cannot begin to account for the dramatic improvement in test performance demonstrated by Negro children who move to the North.

Further evidence that Negro ability goes up when environmental opportunities expand derives from the great diversity of educational enrichment programs current in many major cities. The best known of these is New York City's "Higher Horizons" project. This effort has provided a selected and largely Negro student body with an expensive saturation of skilled specialists — remedial reading teachers, guidance counselors, psychologists, social workers. Its results have been striking; in the first year, the program cut third-graders' retardation in reading from six months to a single month. Backed by major foundation grants, other cities have also begun to experiment. Detroit and Philadelphia tried sending "school-community agents" into ghetto schools in an attempt to win parental support for education. Kansas City's Central High School and Tucson's Pueblo High School initiated imaginative new programs. And Washington, D.C., launched in 1959 a "talent search" project for two hundred deprived seventh graders, 92 per cent of whom were Negro. Similar to Higher Horizons in its concentration of staff and exposure of students to new cultural experiences, "talent search" was soon declared a success. Contrasted with a matched control group, the students of the program evidenced a sharply reduced scholastic failure rate and notable instances of I.Q. increments.

Perhaps the most remarkable demonstration of all is Dr. Samuel Shepard's "Banneker group" work in St. Louis. Shepard, a large, forceful educator, has performed his "miracles" on the most underprivileged school children in the city without the vast expenditures of other efforts. The Banneker group consists of twenty-three elementary schools with over sixteen thousand slum and public housing children, more than 95 per cent of them Negro. A Negro who overcame serious economic disadvantages himself, Shepard adamantly rejected the old dogma that substandard school work is all you can realistically expect from ghetto children. He bluntly challenged the pupils, parents, principals, and teachers of the district to perform up to national standards; he appealed to race pride and resorted to continuous exhortations, rallies, contests, posters, and meetings with teachers and par-

*nts. Students who made good grades were asked to stand in assemblies *or the applause of their classmates. Teachers were asked to visit the homes *f their charges. And parents were asked to provide their offspring with *ncouragement, study space, a library card, and a dictionary, and to give *hem books as gifts. For a concrete incentive, Shepard pointed out the new and better jobs now open to Negroes in St. Louis and the lack of qualified Negroes to fill them.

The results of the Banneker effort speak for themselves. Despite an unending stream of poorly educated migrants feeding the area from the South, all test indicators have risen. In the first four years of the program, the median I.Q. increased from the middle 80's to the 90's; median reading, language, and arithmetic levels all climbed; and the percentage of Banneker graduates accepted for the top ability program in St. Louis's desegregated high schools tripled.

The striking results of these imaginative demonstrations may not be directly due to the exact procedures introduced. Given their vast variety of techniques and their uniform success, the demonstrations probably achieve most of their gains because of the sheer fact of intervention — any kind of thoughtful intervention. Often the rate of initial progress slows once the beginning enthusiasm cools. But this is irrelevant to the larger issue of Negro American intelligence. Dramatic improvements in Negro performance for whatever reason is evidence of the underlying potential for learning heretofore stifled by lack of opportunity and attention. This potential for learning is also evident in the findings of a recent experiment at the University of Texas. Negro children learned series of paired material as rapidly and well as white children, even though they came from lower socioeconomic backgrounds and had significantly poorer I.Q.'s.

Such demonstrations arouse speculation concerning the effects of desegregation of public school systems. Segregationists have long voiced the unsubstantiated opinion that "school mixing" would mean educational chaos, with the Negroes dragging down the higher white standards. But the experience of a great diversity of communities indicates that these fears are unjustified. Administrators of seventeen desegregated school systems appeared before the U.S. Civil Rights Commission in March of 1959 and candidly discussed their problems. Twelve of the educators dealt with the question of academic standards. Ranging from Logan County, Kentucky, and Muskogee, Oklahoma, to Baltimore and Nashville, all twelve reported unequivocally that their academic standards had not been lowered — in fact, many maintained that their standards had improved for both races.

Washington provided the acid test. It embarked upon a sweeping process of educational desegregation in 1954 with Negroes comprising three-fifths of the students, many of them with limited Southern backgrounds. The U.S. News and World Report soon published articles claiming that the District of Columbia's public school system was well on its way to ruin, and these tracts were widely quoted by segregationists. But such dire consequences never materialized. A four-track system of ability grouping and other fresh innovations were adopted. Five years later, in 1959, a factual assessment of the changes was made. Though Negro students, swelled by migrants, now comprised three-fourths of the student body, achievement test scores had risen significantly for each grade level sampled and each subject area tested approached or equaled national norms. Furthermore, both Negro and white students shared in these increments. Such results are not unique to Washington. Louisville reported substantial gains in Negro performance and slight gains in white performance after only one year of desegregation.

Clearly, desegregation *per se* does not accomplish these feats. The Banneker demonstration in St. Louis took place in virtually all-Negro schools; Washington and Louisville witnessed sharply improved test medians among their Negro students, whether in biracial or uniracial schools. The principal factor seems to be the new and healthier self-image Negroes acquire in the process. The act of community desegregation operates to bolster and encourage Negro pupils, parents, and teachers alike. Also important is the sudden interest Negro education finally wins from the whole community. As long as it is a separate system, dominant white interests can and do forget it. But once desegregation forces the community to handle the education of its youth in one package, to consider Negro education as an integral part of the whole process, new attention is attracted. Indeed, the increase in white scores suggests that public education as a whole benefits from the greater public interest.

Washington offers an illustration. Prior to desegregation, survey testing was only done with the white pupils; Negroes were ignored. But immediately after desegregation, testing throughout the system was instituted and the same standards applied at last to both races. Certainly, desegregation is no panacea for the immense problems faced by public school systems with large percentages of environmentally impoverished children. But it does prepare the path for tackling these *real* problems of modern education.

Thus, an array of stimulating circumstances — service in the armed forces, migration to the North, and participation in revitalized school systems — all act to lift substantially the intelligence and achievement levels of Negroes. Often these improvements still do not bring the average Negro performance completely up to white norms, but this is no evidence for genetic racial differences until *all* racial discrimination is abolished.

The Individual *Versus* the Group

The discussion so far has concentrated on group results, yet many of the most important considerations involving Negro American intelligence concern the individual. Not even racists deny the existence of outstanding Negro Americans. Usually, however, the same individuals are cited — Marian Anderson, Ralph Bunche, George Washington Carver — and are considered "exceptions" and special "credits to their race." The truth is that a surprising number of such "exceptional" Negroes have somehow managed to overcome the formidable obstacles of discrimination. Many have naturally entered the struggle for equal rights. But others achieve such stature in nonstereotyped work that they are no longer thought of as Negro. For instance, the originator of the Hinton test for syphilis, the late Professor William A. Hinton, was well known as a bacteriologist and immunologist at Harvard Medical School but not as a Negro.

Superior intelligence comes in all skin colors. While the intelligence test means of the two races are still divergent, the range of performance — from the most retarded idiot to the most brilliant genius — is much the same in the two groups. Some Negro children achieve I.Q.'s into the gifted range (130 plus) and right up to the testable limit of 200. To be sure, the frequency of such bright Negroes is smaller than that of whites, but this, too, can be explained by differential environmental factors. The great majority of these superior Negroes are located in biracial schools in the urban North and West, which suggests that many potentially gifted Negroes go either undiscovered or undeveloped in the segregated schools of the South. Proof that such children do exist in the South comes from programs which intensively seek talented Negro Southerners. Once found, they receive scholarships and attend a variety of desegregated high schools and colleges in the North, and the great majority of them accommodate well to their new and challenging situations.

A further embarrassment to racist theories is created by the fact that the degree of white ancestry does not relate to Negro I.Q. scores. Among intellectually superior Negroes, for example, the proportions of those with varying degrees of white ancestry correspond closely with those of the total Negro American population. Indeed, the brightest Negro child yet reported — with a tested I.Q. of 200 — had no traceable Caucasian heritage whatsoever. "Race per se," concludes Martin Jenkins, "is not a limiting factor in psychometric intelligence."

There exists, then, a considerable overlap in the I.Q. distributions of the two groups. A few Negroes will score higher than almost all Caucasians, and many Negroes will score higher than most Caucasians. Figure 2 shows two typical intelligence test distributions with an overlap of 25 per cent, that is, 25 per cent of the Negroes tested (shaded area) surpass the performance of half of the whites tested. Notice how the ranges of the two distributions are virtually the same, even though the means are somewhat different. This figure illustrates one of the most important facts about "race" and measured intelligence: individual differences in I.Q. *within* any one race greatly exceed differences between races.

■ FIGURE 2   *Typical Test Distributions with "25 per cent Overlap"*

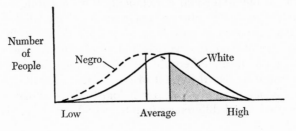

There are two practical consequences of this phenomenon for desegregated education. First, when a school system institutes a track program of ability grouping, there will be Negroes and whites at all levels. Second, some gifted Negroes will actually lead their biracial classes even during the initial stages of desegregation. Thus, Janice Bell, a seventeen-year-old Negro girl, led the first graduating class of track 1-A superior students at Beaumont High in St. Louis; Julius Chambers, a twenty-four-year-old Negro Southerner, became the 1961–1962 editor of the University of North Carolina's *Law Review* in recognition of his leadership of his law school class; and Charles Christian, a thirty-seven-year-old Negro Virginian, academically led his Medical College of Virginia senior class in 1962. "In the study of individuals," summarizes Anastasi, "the only proper unit is the individual."

The Current Conclusion

Intelligence is a plastic product of inherited structure developed by environmental stimulation and opportunity, an alloy of endowment and experience. It can be measured and studied only by inference, through observing behavior defined as "intelligent" in terms of particular cultural content and values. Thus, the severely deprived surroundings of the average Negro child can lower his measured I.Q. in two basic ways. First, it can act to deter his actual intellectual development by presenting him with such a constricted encounter with the world that his innate potential is barely tapped. And, second, it can act to mask his actual functioning intelligence in the test situation by not preparing him culturally and motivationally for such a middle-class task. "Only a very uncritical psychologist would offer sweeping generalizations about the intellectual superiority or inferiority of particular racial or ethnic groups," comments Tuddenham, "despite the not very surprising fact that members of the dominant racial and cultural group in our society ordinarily score higher than others on tests of socially relevant accomplishments invented by and for members of that group."

The principal mechanisms for mediating these environmental effects vary from the poor nutrition of the pregnant mother to meeting the expectations of the social role of "Negro." Some of these mechanisms, like fetal brain injuries, can leave permanent intellectual impairments. Consequently, the permanency and irreversibility of these effects are not, as some claim, certain indicators of genetically low capacity. Fortunately, many of these effects are correctable. Moving North to better schools, taking part in special programs of environmental enrichment, and benefiting from challenging new situations of educational desegregation have all been shown to stimulate Negro children to raise their I.Q. levels dramatically.

From this array of data, the overwhelming opinion of modern psychology concludes that the mean differences often observed between Negro and white children are largely the result of environmental, rather than genetic, factors. This is *not* to assert that psychologists deny altogether the possibility of inherited racial differences in intellectual structure. There may be a *small* residual mean difference — small not only because of the demonstrably sweeping influence of experience but also because the two "races" are by no means genetically "pure" and separate.

Psychology is joined in this conclusion by its sister behavior sciences, sociology and anthropology. Witness the following professional statements:

There are differences in intelligence test scores when one compares a random sample of whites and Negroes. What is equally clear is that no evidence exists that leads to the conclusion that such differences are innate. Quite to the contrary, the evidence points overwhelmingly to the fact that when one compares Negroes and whites of comparable cultural and educational background, differences in intelligence diminish markedly; the more comparable the background, the less the difference. There is no direct evidence that supports the view that there is an innate difference between members of different racial groups. . . . We regret that Professor Garrett feels that his colleagues are foisting an "equalitarian dogma" on the public. There is no question of dogma involved. Evidence speaks for itself and it casts serious doubt on the conclusion that there is any innate inequality in intelligence in different racial groups. . . . (The Society for the Psychological Study of Social Issues, a division of the American Psychological Association, 1961)

. . . The great preponderance of scientific opinion has favored the conclusion that there is little or no ground on which to assume that the racial groups in question are innately different in any important human capacity. . . . The conclusion of scientists is that the differences in test performance by members of so-called racial groups are due not to racial but to environmental factors. This is the operating assumption today of the vast majority of the competent scientists in the field. . . . (The Society for the Study of Social Problems, a section of the American Sociological Association, 1961)

The American Anthropological Association repudiates statements now appearing in the United States that Negroes are biologically and in innate mental ability inferior to whites, and reaffirms the fact that there is no scientifically established evidence to justify the exclusion of any race from the rights guaranteed by the constitution of the United States. The basic principles of equality of opportunity and equality before the law are compatible with all that is known about human biology. All races possess the abilities needed to participate fully in the democratic way of life and in modern technological civilization. (American Anthropological Association, passed by a unanimous, 192 to 0, vote, 1961)

The final definitive research must await a racially integrated America in which opportunities are the same for both races. But, ironically, by that future time the question of racial differences in intelligence will have lost its salience; scholars will wonder why we generated so much heat over such an irrelevant topic. Yet the results of this belated research should prove interesting. Even if small inherent differences are found, their direction cannot be taken for granted. Racists never consider the possibility that the "true" Negro capacity might actually average somewhat above that of the white. Certainly, there are enough environmental barriers operating in the present situation to mask any such Negro superiority. If this possibility should actually be demonstrated, one wonders if white racists would be thoroughly consistent and insist that white children be given separate and inferior education.

The important conclusion for the present, however, is that if there are any inherent distinctions they are inconsequential. Even now, differences in I.Q. within any one race greatly exceed differences between races. Race as such is simply not an accurate way to judge an individual's intelligence. The *real* problems in this area concern ways to overcome the many serious environmental deprivations that handicap Negro youth. To return to the analogy with longevity, the problem is akin to that which faced medicine in the nineteenth century. Automatized America needs to expand the intelligence level of its underprivileged citizens in much the same way it has expanded the life potential of its citizens in the past one hundred years. The success of such programs as "the Banneker group" in St. Louis demonstrates this job can be accomplished when American society decides to put enough of its resources into it. "The U.S. must learn," writes Charles Silberman in *Fortune*, "to look upon the Negro community as if it were an undeveloped country."

✧ ✧ 13 ✧ ✧

Effects of Adoption on Children from Institutions

HAROLD M. SKEELS

The National Institute of Mental Health is presently carrying on three follow-up studies of adults who were reared away from their own parents. The purpose is to determine the adult status of children previously studied by the Iowa Child Welfare Research Station, State University of Iowa, in cooperation with the Children's Division, Iowa Board of Control of State Institutions, which initiated modes of intervention in infancy or early childhood. These include follow-up studies of:

I. A longitudinal study of one hundred adopted children (3). The follow-up of this study is being carried on by the original investigators.

II. A study of the effects of differential stimulation on mentally retarded children (1). The follow-up of this study is also being carried on by the original investigator.

✧ From *Children*, January-February, 1965, pp. 33–34. Reprinted by permission of the author and the publisher, the Children's Bureau, U.S. Department of Health, Education and Welfare. Harold M. Skeels is recently retired from the position of Chief, Special Program Development Section, Community Research and Services Branch, National Institute of Mental Health.

III. A study of the mental development in adoptive homes of children whose biological mothers were mentally retarded (2). The follow-up of this study is being carried on by Lowell W. Schenke, psychologist, Iowa Board of Control of State Institutions, with one of the original investigators (the writer) serving as consultant.

In all three of these studies, the children selected for study were considered to be biologically sound and without demonstrable abnormality as determined through diagnostic evaluation by competent pediatricians. With the inclusion of the present follow-up studies, they cover a life span of thirty years, the present ages of the subjects being within a range of twenty-five to thirty-five years.

Adopted Children

In regard to the follow-up of Study I, all adoptive parents and adopted children have been located after a lapse of sixteen years since the last contacts of the earlier study. Interviews with adoptive parents and their adult adopted children are nearing completion. Analysis of the data will start in the near future.

Preliminary indications are that these adoptive children as adults are achieving at levels consistently higher than would have been predicted from the intellectual, educational, or socioeconomic level of the biological parents, and equal to the expectancy for children living in the homes of natural parents capable of providing environmental impacts similar to those which have been provided by the adoptive parents.

Mentally Retarded Children

In regard to follow-up of Study II, all subjects have been located after a lapse of twenty-one years, all interviews completed, with the data presently being processed.

Preliminary findings of this follow-up study are particularly startling. In the original study, thirteen children in an experimental group, all mentally retarded at the beginning of the study, were at an early age transferred from one institution to another which provided a much higher degree of one-to-one emotional relationship between mother-surrogates and the children. Later, eleven of these children were placed in adoptive homes.

A contrast group of twelve children, initially at a higher level of intelligence than those in the experimental group, remained in a relatively non-stimulating institutional environment over a prolonged period of time. In the initial study, the children in the experimental group showed a decided increase in rate of mental growth, whereas the children in the contrast group showed progressive mental retardation.

In the adult follow-up study, the two groups continued to be remarkably divergent. All thirteen children in the experimental group are self-supporting, and none is a ward of any institution, public or private. Eleven of the thirteen children are married, and nine of these have children.

Of the twelve children in the contrast group, one died in adolescence following continued residence in a State institution for the mentally retarded; four are still wards of institutions — one of these is in a mental hospital, and three are in institutions for the mentally retarded. Among those no longer wards of institutions, only two have married, and one of these is divorced. Two of the four females in the contrast group were sterilized in late adolescence to preclude the possibility of procreation if later placed out to work.

In education, disparity between the two groups is great. In the experimental group, the median grade completed is the twelfth; in the contrast group, the third. Four subjects in the experimental group have had one year or more of college work, one of the boys having received a B.A. degree. Occupationally, the experimental group ranges from professional and semiprofessional positions to semiskilled labor or domestic work. In the contrast group, 50 per cent of the subjects are unemployed, and those that are employed are, with the exception of one person, unskilled laborers.

One girl in the experimental group who initially had an I.Q. of 35 has subsequently graduated from high school and taken one semester of work at a college. She is married and has two boys. These boys have been given intelligence tests and have achieved I.Q. scores of 128 and 107.

If this girl had had the continuing experience characteristic of those in the contrast group, she would have remained all these years on a custodial ward in an institution for the mentally retarded, or have been sterilized in late adolescence or early adulthood and subsequently placed out on a nonskilled labor type of domestic employment.

In fact, "but for the grace of God," any one of the cases in the experimental group might have experienced the impact of deprivation of those in the contrast group, and vice versa.

Cost to the State

We are also studying the cost to the State of each subject in the experimental group and the contrast group of Study II — based on information as to per capita cost for institutional care per month or year for each of the years from 1932 to 1963. Preliminary indications are shocking.

In the experimental group the median total cost is less than $1000, whereas in the contrast group it is ten times that, with a range from $7000 to $24,000. One case in the contrast group can be cited of a person who has been a ward of the State institution for over thirty years. The total cost to the State in this instance has been $24,113.

In the 1930's, the monthly per capita cost at State children's institutions and at mental hospitals ranged around seventeen dollars per month. This has progressively increased over the years until the present figure is considerably more than $200 per month. We can speculatively extrapolate on the cost to the State of the subjects in Study II had our comparisons started in 1963 instead of 1932. Assuming that costs were constant from 1963 to 1993, the case in the example cited would have cost the State $100,000.

Mentally Retarded Parents

As already mentioned, Study III involved children whose biological mothers were considered to be mentally retarded. The children had been separated from their natural mothers in early infancy, either by voluntary release or by court commitment, and had been placed in adoptive homes before they were two years old. The study included a total of eighty-seven cases. I.Q. scores were obtained on each of the mothers, none of whom achieved higher than 75. The range extended down to an I.Q. of 32.

After a time interval of twenty-one years, efforts are under way to locate the adoptive parents and children of this study, and indications are that all or most of them will be found. Several interviews have already been completed.

In the follow-up, in addition to securing information on the adult status of the children, intelligence tests are being administered to the second generation — the grandchildren of the mentally retarded, biological grandmothers.

Preliminary findings in this follow-up study suggest that the first generation (the children of the original study) compares favorably in occupational status as adults with the Iowa population of comparable ages according to 1960 census figures. The second-generation children are scoring average and above on intelligence tests.

Some Implications

Since the preliminary findings of these three follow-up studies are substantiated by reports of many supporting studies published in the past twenty years, it would seem that we have adequate knowledge for designing programs of intervention to counteract the devastating effects of poverty, sociocultural deprivation, maternal deprivation, or a combination of these ills. This means making expenditures for prevention, rather than waiting for the tremendous costs of a curative nature. It does not, of course, preclude further research and exploratory studies to determine the optimum modes of intervention and the most appropriate ages for initiating such procedures.

REFERENCES

1. Skeels, Harold M., and Harold B. Dye. "A Study of the Effects of Differential Stimulation on Mentally Retarded Children" (proceedings and addresses of the American Association on Mental Deficiency), *Journal of Psycho-asthenics,* vol. 44, no. 1, 1938–1939.

2. ———, and Irene Harms. "Children with Inferior Social Histories: Their Mental Development in Adoptive Homes," *Journal of Genetic Psychology,* June, 1948.

3. Skodak, Marie, and Harold M. Skeels. "A Final Follow-up Study of One Hundred Adopted Children," *Journal of Genetic Psychology,* September, 1949.

✧ ✧ 14 ✧ ✧

Effects of Educational Treatment

SAMUEL A. KIRK

During the eighteenth century, Dr. Itard, imbued with the philosophy of the effects of training, strove to treat the Wild Boy of Aveyron through education. He was followed in the nineteenth century by other physicians, namely Seguin, Montessori and DeCroly, all of whom devised educational methods for the intellectual development of the mentally retarded. The efforts of these physicians were stimulated by the idea that training the senses had a direct influence on the central nervous system and, consequently, on the mental development of retarded children.

During the beginning of the twentieth century the ideas of the empiricists were modified by DeCroly, another physician, and even more so by Binet, an experimental psychologist. In this country we usually think of Alfred Binet solely as the father of intelligence testing. Certainly his contribution in this area has been far reaching. But Binet was not satisfied with only the measurement of intelligence. In 1909, he remarked (1), "After the evil, the remedy; after exposing mental defects of all kinds, let us pass on to their treatment." He, like his predecessors, believed in the educability of intelligence, for he stated that the I.Q. was not necessarily constant and that the intellectual functions which could be measured could also be trained. He regretted to find a prejudice against the concept of the educability of intelligence and felt that this prejudice should be dispelled by systematic training of these children. He referred to his method of teaching as "mental orthopedics."

American psychologists reacted very rapidly to the development of the testing movement initiated by Binet. They concentrated on the development of intelligence tests and measures of all kinds. Few psychologists, however, took cognizance of Binet's ideas about the educability of intelligence.

In general, American psychologists and educators were pessimistic concerning the educability of intelligence. This pessimism developed from three influences: first, the studies of Dr. Henry Goddard which purported

✧ Reprinted from *Mental Retardation*, Vol. 34, pp. 289–294, Research Publications, A.R.N.M.D. Copyright ©, 1962, Association for Research in Nervous and Mental Disease. Used by permission of the author and the publisher. Dr. Kirk is Director of the Institute for Research on Exceptional Children, University of Illinois, Urbana.

to show that mental deficiency is inherited along recessive Mendelian lines and consequently cannot be affected by training or environment; secondly, the prevailing definition of mental deficiency advanced by Dr. Edgar Doll, stating that mental deficiency was of constitutional origin, existing at birth or an early age, obtaining at maturity, and incurable; and thirdly, the concept of pseudo-feeblemindedness which indicated that if a mentally deficient child changed his functional level, he had never been mentally deficient, but had been misdiagnosed. These influences made it unpopular for anyone to talk about the educability of intelligence.

In the 1930's, the controversy once more reared its ugly head, and complacency was again challenged. Studies from the University of Iowa Child Welfare Research Station began to suggest that environment and training may have something to do with the functional and measured intellectual level of children, including the mentally retarded. Skeels and Dye (6) reported an interesting experiment in 1939 in which young children were taken out of an orphanage and placed singly in wards of an institution for the mentally deficient. These babies, ranging in age from seven to thirty months, were placed in separate wards where the mentally deficient older girls were allowed to play with them and give them attention, thus stimulating their development. A control group similar to the experimental group remained in the orphanage. On retests of these children, it was found that those who were sent to the institution for the mentally deficient increased approximately 27 points in I.Q. whereas those who remained in the orphange dropped 26 points. This experiment was criticized because of its use of tests of questionable reliability, but enough evidence was present to suggest the advisability of further study.

As the Iowa studies were gradually losing favor, Schmidt (5) reported an experiment so spectacular that it raised many doubts. Two hundred and forty-five children of the educable type, with an initial average I.Q. of 52.1, were reported to have increased their I.Q. scores to 89.3 on the Stanford-Binet in a period of five years. Similar progress was reported on other tests including the Vineland Social Maturity scale. This experiment published in a Psychological Monograph in 1946 created considerable sensation in the United States, Canada and in European countries. Newspaper reports and magazine articles referring to this experiment indicated that "feeblemindedness can be cured."

Because of the questionable nature of the study and its widespread publicity, I was requested to investigate and report on it (4). Although Dr. Schmidt was not permitted to give me any data or any names of the children in her study, some information was available from the files of the schools and the Chicago Child Study Bureau. I found that in a number of classes taught by Dr. Schmidt, the initial average I.Q. scores as recorded in the files of the child study department averaged approximately 70 at the beginning of the experiment (instead of the 52 reported) and on repeat tests three years later the I.Q. scores continued to be 70. This evaluation and review of the study indicated that the data as reported were not authentic and that the report was in great question. This evaluation and other analyses of the study tended to discredit it.

At the University of Illinois, we have conducted two studies on the educability of intelligence. One was a longitudinal study of the educability of intelligence with children at a young age (3). Eighty-one children between the ages of three and six and with I.Q. scores roughly between 45 and 80 were studied. Two training groups, one in the community and one in an institution, were evaluated along with comparable preschool children in communities and institutions who did not receive preschool training.

The purpose of this experiment was to determine whether the rate of development of retarded children can be displaced by stimulation or deprivation at the preschool level. Theoretically, the rate of development should follow one of the grids presented in Figure 1. In this graph are presented theoretical growth curves for the different classifications used in education from average to uneducable. Any change in channel of development is considered a significant change. Thus, if a child changes in rate of development from high educable to borderline, it is considered a

■ FIGURE 1   *Mental Growth Grid*

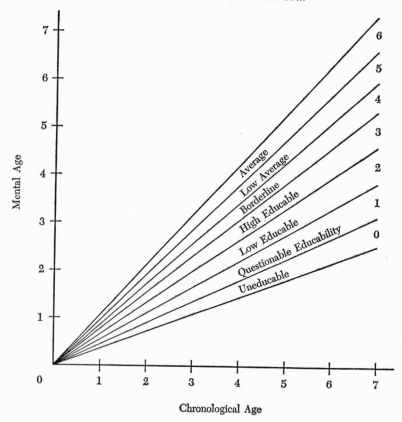

■ TABLE 1   *Development of Children in Foster Homes Plus Preschool, and*
Comparison of Experimental Preschool Group with
Siblings and Twin Controls Living in the Same Home

	Foster Home plus Preschool Education N = 4		Experimental Preschool Children N = 12		Twins and Sibling Controls N = 14	
	No.	Ratio	No.	Ratio	No.	Ratio
Increased in rate of development ...	4	1.0	8	⅔	2	⅐
Held original rate of development ...	0	0.0	3	¼	7	½
Decreased in rate of development ...	0	0.0	1	¹⁄₁₂	5	⁵⁄₁₄

positive change of one level. If the child drops to the low educable channel
or grid, he has made a negative change of one level. The evaluations of the
children at each level were made by a series of psychometric tests and
clinical observations.

Table 1 shows the results of education and home environment on the
changes in developmental rates of young mentally retarded children.

1. Column 1 shows that of four children taken out of inadequate homes
and placed in foster homes and in a specialized preschool at the average age
of 4, all increased their rate of development. Two increased one level, one
increased two levels and one increased three levels. These levels were retained for an average of three years after the preschool experience.

2. Column 2 shows the results of training children who remained in their
own psychosocially deprived homes but received preschool training. Here
two-thirds of them increased their rate of development, one-quarter of them
remained in their channel, and one child decreased in rate of development.
The records show that this child attended the preschool only half the time
because her mother did not have her ready when the taxi came to take her
to school.

3. Column 3 shows the development of fourteen twin and sibling controls
of the twelve children receiving preschool education (Column 2). These
siblings did not attend preschool but attended the regular school after the
age of six. Here we find that only two or one-seventh of the children increased in rate of development, seven or one-half retained their original
rate, and five or nearly one-third dropped in rate of development. These
differences between the experimental children and the twin and sibling
controls are statistically significant.

The conclusions from this data indicate that children from inadequate
homes tend to retain their rate of development or drop in rate of development as they grow older. If society offers compensatory environments such
as a preschool, a reversal of this tendency is accomplished. If the children
are placed in foster homes and in preschools, a more marked change in

developmental rate is produced. These results lend support to the thesis that educational treatment at an early age can accelerate the rate of mental growth of children reared in psychosocially deprived homes.

Another aspect of the experiment compared fifteen preschool children in an institution who had intensive training at the preschool level with twelve children who remained in the wards and did not attend school in the institution until the age of six. The mental and social age growth curves of these two groups showed that neither group followed the theoretical growth curve. The trained group showed displacement of rate of development upwards, whereas the group that remained in the wards during the preschool period showed displacement downwards.

From age four years and four months to age seven years and four months, the fifteen children in the training group increased from an average I.Q. of 61 to 71 on the Stanford-Binet scale, from 57 to 67 on the Kuhlmann-Binet scale, and from 72 to 82 on the Vineland Social Maturity scale. In contrast, the twelve children who did not receive preschool training dropped in Stanford-Binet I.Q. scores from 57 to 50, in Kuhlmann-Binet scores from 54 to 50 and on the Vineland Social Maturity scale, from 73 to 61. These differences were all statistically significant. In addition, six out of the fifteen children in the training group were paroled from the institution, whereas none of the twelve children without training was paroled. These data are further evidence that educational treatment is effective in displacing the rate of development of institutionalized mental defectives.

An interesting result of the experiment related to a comparison of organically involved children with those without a definitive diagnosis of organic etiology. Although 50 per cent of those with organic etiologies displaced their rate of growth, approximately 80 per cent of the familial or cultural group increased their rate of growth. This means that it is more difficult for the group methods of instruction used in this experiment to increase the rate of growth of children with organic diagnosis. It raised the question of whether these children did not require individual tutoring with specific mental exercises in the areas of major deficits.

Professor James Gallagher (2) of our staff has followed this idea with a controlled experiment on the tutoring of brain-damaged mentally defective children. In an institution for mental defectives he selected forty-two children who were diagnosed as having a definite central nervous system involvement. By randomization he selected twenty-one of the children, ages seven to twelve, for the experimental group and twenty-one for the control group. All children attended an institution school for a half-day session. The only differing variable between the groups was one hour of tutoring for the experimental group. Among some of the conclusions reached by Professor Gallagher are: (a) there are some positive effects on the intellectual development of mentally defective brain-injured children from tutoring experience; (b) the effects of tutoring appeared to be greatest with children at the younger ages; and (c) when tutoring ceased, there appeared to be a tendency for the children to drop back to their original rate of development.

Professor Gallagher concluded that the institutional environment may not be sufficiently stimulating to continue the development of the children after tutoring ceased. This is comparable to results of the previous study cited in which children who were paroled from the institution tended to retain their rate of growth, whereas the children who were not paroled from the institution tended to drop to their previous rate of development. Gallagher states that intellectual training of these children must continue for a long time and under a total push program if results are to be achieved on a permanent basis.

Summary

The prejudice against the educability of intelligence has been fostered by the rigid concepts of the inheritability of intelligence and the concepts of incurability and pseudo-feeblemindedness. The results of recent research, my own as well as others, indicate that the intellectual development of some retarded children is partly contingent upon child rearing practices and the extent of educational treatment at an early age. Furthermore, among the higher grades of the retarded, the evidence points to a cultural etiology rather than a genetic one for many of the retarded children in our society. Thus far, it has been found that those with brain damage are more difficult to displace in mental growth by educational treatment than those mental defectives who are not so diagnosed.

REFERENCES

1. Binet, A. *Les Idées modernes des enfants.* Paris: E. Flamnarion, 1909.

2. Gallagher, J. J., *The Tutoring of Brain Injured Mentally Retarded Children.* Springfield, Ill.: Charles C Thomas, Publisher, 1960.

3. Kirk, S. A. *Early Education of the Mentally Retarded.* Urbana, Ill.: University of Illinois Press, 1958.

4. ———. "An Evaluation of the Study by Bernardine G. Schmidt Entitled: 'Changes in Personal, Social and Intellectual Behavior in Children Originally Classified as Feeble-Minded,'" *Psychological Bulletin, 45:* 321–333, 1948.

5. Schmidt, B. G. "Changes in Personal, Social, and Intellectual Behavior in Children Originally Classified as Feebleminded," *Psychological Monograph, 60:* No. 5., 1946.

6. Skeels, H. M., and H. N. Dye. "A Study of the Effects of Differential Stimulation on Mentally Retarded Children," in *Proceedings and Addresses of the American Association on Mental Deficiency,* 44, No. 1.: 114–136, 1939.

✧ ✧ 15 ✧ ✧

The Case For Intelligence Testing

ARTHUR HUGHSON

New York City recently abolished the I.Q. as a measure of intelligence. In place of intelligence tests, the use of achievement testing and teacher judgment for classifying pupils is proposed. This seems very much like substituting *handful* for ounces and pounds and *span* for the more exact measure of inches and feet.

Major arguments and queries in support of my contention that the I.Q. test should not be thus summarily dispatched are these:

1. Achievement tests can help measure educational attainments, but some indicators of academic potential are also needed.

2. Intelligence tests are the most promising and most useful instruments of measurement in this area.

3. Intelligence tests have proved their worth in measuring the potential of average and above-average students. Must the teaching profession be deprived of valid instruments for these groups simply because below-average students do not perform well on them?

4. The decision to drop intelligence tests does not have the wholehearted support of school supervisors and teachers, who were not consulted in advance.

5. Must we toss away instruments that were developed over several generations, in the hope that we can develop more adequate substitutes overnight?

6. The scores made by minority group children on intelligence tests do *not* prove these children to be inferior, but that their environment lacks elements basic to a good education. Instead of destroying the measuring instrument, why not concentrate on improving the environment?

Indicators of Academic Potential Needed

No one claims that intelligence tests are the only criterion found useful, but students of classification of children (and adults), especially those who have worked with bright children, agree that these tests are the best single measure of academic potential available.

✧ From *Phi Delta Kappan*, November, 1964, pages 106–108. Used by permission of the author and the publisher. Arthur Hughson is the recently retired Assistant Superintendent of the New York City Schools.

We have known for a long time that, in the elementary schools, teacher judgments are valid in about 70 per cent of the cases tested — a good average. But what of the other 30 per cent where their judgment is incorrect? Intelligence tests help corroborate and correct teacher judgment.

Again, achievement tests depend for their validity upon the adequacy with which they sample the subject-matter field for which they are intended. The New York authorities plan to use reading as the safest subject field for discovering child potential. It is true, of course, that reading ability shows a high correlation with intelligence, but there is more to intelligence than just reading ability, and these tests cover a broader area than reading. And what of the children who have not learned to read?

Wechsler has pointed out that "Intelligence is the aggregate of global capacity of the individual to act purposefully, to think rationally, and deal effectively with his environment" (4). According to Freeman, "Tests must be appropriate to the environment of those for whom they are intended" (3). One gathers that the underlying motive for scrapping intelligence tests (as well as the I.Q.) is to placate parents with a non-English background whose offspring cannot do well on tests assuming a middle-class, Anglo-Saxon dominated environment. Similar problems arose when the Binet-Simon scale was introduced to America. But the answer then was found in the 1916 Stanford Revision and in the 1937 Revision of the Stanford Binet scale. In fact, the history of the testing movement shows that intelligence tests have been successfully adapted to new purposes when changes were necessary.

Intelligence Tests Are Proven Indicators

It is obvious to students of tests and measurements that intelligence testing must be based on accepted and validated theory and practice. One important consideration is the proper selection of the population sample on which the tests or scales are standardized, and it is true that most tests now in use have failed to include the Spanish-speaking Puerto Rican and the Southern Negro in their sampling. The answer, then, is not to throw out the tests, which remain useful for more than 80 per cent of our pupils, but rather to ask test makers to prepare and, if possible, include in their tests valid materials for testing our children with Spanish backgrounds, as well as those who come from less privileged areas of the continental U.S.

Eliminate Our Best Measuring Instruments?

On April 26, 1963, Calvin E. Gross, New York City superintendent of schools, said:

> We need to exercise more precision as we consider the talents of each student. We need to stop gearing our whole enterprise to the average student. I have no patience with those people to whom ability grouping is still a dirty word or who have begun to say that we are concentrating too much on the gifted child.
>
> I want to apply the concept of precision in education in three ways:

1. I think that for the foreseeable future we can make the most progress by focusing our energies on the children who lie at the two extremes of the ability continuum.

2. We ought to stray less and less from the central business of the schools, which is intellectual development.

3. Now is the time to tackle the problem in the first item, according to the guiding principle in the second item, by applying the technologies and new patterns of organization to the instruction process.

It seems that the objectives listed by the superintendent call for the development of more and better tests rather than the elimination of our most refined instruments.

Supervisor and Teacher Protests

The following editorial appeared in the *C.S.A. Bulletin* (organ of the Council of Supervisory Associations) for April 1964:

The decision to discard group intelligence tests because of their alleged unfairness to underprivileged children and to bilingual children is another example of a hastily adopted unsound policy, reflecting a lack of adequate consultation with supervisors. Psychologists and educators have been working for years to develop nonverbal and culture-free tests without much success. To drop group intelligence tests and to expect the development of adequate substitutes in the form of guides for teacher judgment and new culture-free tests is like selling one's Buick because a *Popular Science* article promises a hydrofoil automobile.

Group intelligence tests are useful and valid predictors of success in school, particularly when used with caution and in combination with other factors. Indeed, official directives to the schools accompanying all city-wide testing programs, in consonance with practices endorsed by test experts, have always cautioned principals against administering the tests to children with language, cultural, social, emotional, or physical handicaps. Principals have always been cautioned to interpret results with care and to be especially alert to instances of discrepancy between various estimates of pupil ability such as formal or informal assessment of achievement.

If tests have been used on children who should not have taken them, then administrators must be reeducated. If test results have been misinterpreted, then teachers and administrators need reeducation. It is strongly recommended that an educational program on the uses and limitations of tests be instituted. But to throw all group intelligence tests out because of alleged unfairness to some children is utterly unsound and will be a negative influence on the effort to adapt educational programs to the differing needs of pupils.

Product of a Half-Century of Experiment

In the middle of the nineteenth century Charcot and Seguin, two French physicians working with cretins in Switzerland, found need for a measure of mental development. They constructed a crude instrument which they used extensively in their studies. They are probably the fathers of mental testing.

In Germany, Wundt attempted to study human behavior objectively. In 1897, Hermann Ebbinghaus tackled the problem of investigating fatigue in learning. He developed his "Completion Test," which was probably the first intelligence test.

In France, continuing interest in identifying mental defectives led Alfred Binet (1904) to use Wundt's laboratory tests. During the next year (1905), with Theodore Simon, he developed an individual intelligence test to measure judgment, reasoning, and comprehension. The 1908 revision introduced "mental age."

American revisions of the Binet Scale started with Henry H. Goddard, who translated the scale into English and adapted it to American children. The first American revision was made in 1910.

Fred Kuhlmann published another Binet Scale in 1912 and revised it in 1922.

In 1916, Lewis Terman finished the Stanford Revision, which became the standard measure of intelligence for more than twenty years. Terman developed MA norms from two years and six months to twenty years.

In 1912, William Stern suggested computing the ratio of mental age to chronological age to get the mental quotient. Terman adopted this suggestion and called it the "Intelligence Quotient" or I.Q.

In 1918, the Otis General Intelligence Test was constructed. This was the first test created for specific use in high schools.

The Delta I and Delta II, published in 1919 by Haggerty, were the first intelligence tests for elementary school pupils.

Actually, group intelligence tests originated during World War I with the Army Alpha and Army Beta tests. These were used to classify our soldiers for the best utilitarian assignments. The Army Alpha and the Army Beta (nonlanguage) tests demonstrated:

1. That mental tests are valuable because they reveal individual differences in mental ability among people of normal intelligence.
2. That mental testing need not be costly or individualized.
3. That these tests can help in the practical job classification of men.

The work of Terman, Hollingsworth, Kuhlmann, Tyler, and others, and the thousands of bright children (as well as slow) who have been steered into proper channels of life work, argue for the retention of intelligence tests and the I.Q.

Summary and Conclusions

It has been suggested earlier in this paper that the real reason for eliminating intelligence tests as well as the I.Q. is to placate parents of children who for a variety of reasons are incapable of achieving favorable results on these tests. In many cases, the claim is made, correctly or incorrectly, that the language problem is too difficult to overcome. Henry Goddard had a similar problem to overcome when he translated the Binet-Simon scale and adapted it for American children. Is it not possible that a similar adaptation can be achieved now? Certainly an attempt might be made. Let us concentrate on getting test adaptation started. It is no doubt true that the milieu in which children find themselves has an important impact on their knowledge and learning ability. As Colvin has said, "Intelligence itself is not inborn, but only the capacity to become intelligent" (2). Modification of the environment does bring effective results. A number of studies indicate that nature and nurture of individual development play an important role in learning and development.

A study by Burks gives these results relating to the contributions of nature and nurture to mental development:

1. Home environment contributes about 17 per cent of the variance in I.Q.; parental intelligence alone accounts for 33 per cent.

2. The total contribution of heredity is probably not far from 75 to 80 per cent.

3. Measurable environment one standard deviation above or below the mean population does not shift the I.Q. more than 6 to 9 points above or below the value it would have under normal environment conditions.

4. The maximal contributions of the best home environment to intelligence is apparently about 20 I.Q. points or less, and almost surely lies between 10 and 30 points. Conversely, the least cultured, least stimulating kind of American home environment may depress the I.Q. as much as 20 or 30 I.Q. points (1).

To sum up, there is no justification for eliminating intelligence testing and the I.Q. On the basis of Miss Burks' findings, it would seem desirable to modify the environment of those who have been doing poorly on intelligence tests.

In our "Higher Horizons" program we learned that desirable results are obtainable by modifying the pupil environment. Let us give our children the benefit of what we have learned from that program.

REFERENCES

1. Burks, B. S. "The Nature and Limit of Improvement Due to Training," in the *28th Yearbook* of the National Society for the Study of Education, Part I. Chicago: The Society (distributed by the University of Chicago Press), 1928.

2. Colvin, S. S. "Principles Underlying the Construction and Use of Intelligence Tests," *61st Yearbook* of the NSSE, Part I. Chicago: The Society (distributed by the University of Chicago Press), 1962.

3. Freeman, F. S. *Theory and Practice of Psychological Testing.* New York: Holt, Rinehart & Winston, Inc., 1960. P. 112.

4. Wechsler, D. *The Measurement of Adult Intelligence.* Baltimore: Williams and Wilkins, 1944. P. 3.

✧ ✧ 16 ✧ ✧

The Case Against Group I.Q. Testing in Schools with Culturally Disadvantaged Pupils

JULIUS YOURMAN

Because the decision of New York City's Board of Education to discontinue group intelligence testing has its roots in several major social forces, it has generated considerable heat from some professional and public groups. The social forces relate to: (1) the difficult task of resolving some *de facto* school segregation of pupils that results from housing and residential area discriminations, preferences, and economic factors; (2) the popular attacks on testing of all kinds, both in schools and in industry (as in *The Brain Watchers* and *They Shall Not Pass*); (3) the social, emotional, and ethical turmoil of the Negro social revolution and civil rights movement generally; and (4) a growing opinion among educators and psychologists that group intelligence tests do not have high predictive validity in measuring *capacity* to learn when pupils tested differ significantly in cultural experiences from those for whom the tests and norms were developed.

History of Intelligence Testing

In an effort to approach this emotion-laden question objectively, a quick review of the historical development of intelligence testing is useful. The basic hypothesis of Binet and Simon, sixty years ago, was that, since experiences could not be discovered for testing problem-solving ability that *no* child had been exposed to previously (within the ability range for children of his age), the next best solution was to provide tasks that *all* children had had *sufficient* opportunity to experience, directly or indirectly, at a given age, since overlearning is not an advantage. The selected tasks would test the child's ability, compared with norms of children representative of his age group. After revisions in 1908 and 1911, the Binet was standardized.

Of course, the tasks finally selected to test French children would not classify U.S. pupils, so the Stanford Revision was constructed in 1916. It had to be brought up to date in 1937 and again in 1960, as children's

✧ From *Phi Delta Kappan*, November, 1964, pp. 108–110. Used by permission of the author and the publisher. Julius Yourman is Lecturer, Brooklyn College, and Consultant for Personnel Research.

representative experiences changed. Stanford Binet I.Q. no longer is determined by the mental age — chronological age ratio. Now the I.Q. is determined from a table of deviations from mean scores of each age group — the Standard Score — because the ratio was found not to be constant, as earlier psychologists had assumed. Psychological and environmental factors *do* affect "intelligence."

Note that intelligence measurement theory rests on comparing each child's score with norms of children in his age group that are *representative.* Recall, also, that all intelligence tests are validated against Stanford Binet scores — the criterion of "general intelligence," which, by design, makes no claim of including all important life and school success factors.

Some opponents of the decision to discontinue group intelligence testing argue that if poor readers, nonreaders, and those with English language handicaps were not included, the group intelligence test would be valid and useful. It is true that reading comprehension and intelligence test scores provide the highest correlations in educational measurements, *other things being equal.* But, when culturally dissimilar children are compared, using norms derived from *the same representative age group,* other things are *not* equal.

The evidence from cumulative research makes it clear that: (1) There are consistent differences in intelligence score distributions of U.S. Negro and white pupils; (2) there is no support for the assumption that there are any inherent racial differences in capacity to learn; (3) cultural and personality differences *do* affect group intelligence scores to the extent that they become low in predictive validity when used for cross-cultural comparisons of capacity to learn; and (4) the labeling of a child with a "permanent" stratification index (I.Q.) is likely to affect his self-concept, his goals, his motivations, and his achievements.

No Racial Differences in Capacity

The question of *inherent* racial differences in capacity to learn is answered in strong negative conclusions in all reports of official scientific opinion, including the UNESCO international committee of sociologists, anthropologists, psychologists, and geneticists, which said in conclusion:

> It is now generally recognized that intelligence tests do not themselves enable us to differentiate safely between what is due to innate capacity and what is the result of environmental influences, training, and education. . . . In short, given similar degrees of cultural opportunity to realize their potentialities, the average achievement of the members of each ethnic group is about the same.

A similar conclusion was reached by the American Association for the Advancement of Science committee on science in the promotion of human welfare (*Science,* 142:558–561; November 1, 1963).

The Journal of Social Issues (April 1964) provides one of the most direct presentations of current evidence of the effects of culture on educational aspirations and achievement of U.S. Negroes. As a supplement, the *Journal* reports the findings of the work group for the psychological study of social issues (Division 9 of the American Psychological Association). The committee concludes flatly that "social deprivation challenges the validity of tests." In part, it explains:

National norms do not permit adequate differentiation at the lower end of aptitude or ability scales.

Predictive Validity: For example, no inequality is necessarily involved if a culturally disadvantaged child is simply reported to have an I.Q. of 84 and a percentile rank of 16 on national norms for a certain intelligence test. However, if this is interpreted as meaning that a child ranks as well or will rank no higher in learning ability than does a middle-class, native-born child of the same I.Q., the interpretation might well be erroneous.

The analysis from the series of researches reported in the *Journal* includes:

Social deprivation, racial discrimination, caste, more frequent absence of a father — family cohesion and pre-school experiences represent two possible environmental modifiers of intelligence test performance that would seem to account for a portion of the differences found between ethnic, class or experimental groups. (p. 34)

Among Negro children in Philadelphia, children living longest in the North had the highest I.Q.'s and those most recently migrating from the South had the lowest I.Q.'s, Lee found. He explained the finding in terms of cultural inequalities (1).

As *The Journal of Social Issues* work group report concludes:

The misuse of tests with minority group children, or in any situation, is a serious breach of professional ethics. Their proper use is a sign of professional and personal maturity.

This, then, is the basis for approving or disapproving the Board of Education's decision to discontinue group intelligence testing. Close to half of the city's public school pupils might be called culturally deprived, with home and community experiences not comparable to those of the *representative* children of their ages against whom their native learning ability has been measured. While psychologists recognize the grossness of group measurements, many teachers use reported group test I.Q. scores as fixed bench marks by which to determine learning expectations and the rate and level of instruction for a child or a class. With the security of a reported below-average I.Q. score, the teacher may be relieved of feelings of responsibility and guilt when a child does not learn, despite the uncertainty of the measure, especially with culturally deprived pupils.

Emphasis on Achievement Testing

Unless there is assurance that teachers can consistently interpret and use tests properly, despite their middle-class norms (which may become ethnocentric), supported by standardized intelligence norms of uncertain predictive validity, there is strong support for the substitution of *achievement* measurements (which do not have the fetish characteristics of exactness and permanence, and which can be improved by mutual pupil-teacher efforts).

The experimental effort to develop personalized, face-to-face, "culture-fair" appraisals of each child's learning potential, in actual or simulated learning situations, is an effort to remedy the weaknesses of mass testing. When a teacher has any doubt about a child's potential, she should have the assistance of a psychologist who can measure the child's intelligence in a controlled, individualized examination of the pupil as a person. The Board of Education promises to extend these services.

The decision to discontinue group intelligence testing and to substitute measurements more directly related to the teacher's interactions with and effects on her pupils seems justified now in New York City, at least as an exploratory measure to meet near-crisis conditions in parts of the school system. The outcomes of this decision will depend, in large measure, on the success of the professional dialogue between proponents and opponents of the decision as they earnestly seek the best next step.

REFERENCES

1. Lee, E. S. "Negro Intelligence and Selective Migration: A Philadelphia Test of the Klineberg Hypothesis," *American Sociological Review*, Vol. 16:227–233, 1951. *See also:* M. Deutsch, "Minority Groups and Class Status as Related to Social and Personality Factors in Scholastic Achievement," *Society for Applied Anthropology Monograph*, No. 2, 1960; G. J. Klopf and I. A. Laster (eds.), *Integrating the Urban School*. New York: Teachers College, Columbia University, 1963; K. Eells, *et al.*, *Intelligence and Cultural Differences*. Chicago: University of Chicago Press, 1951; and E. Haggard, "Social Status and Intelligence: An Experimental Study of Certain Cultural Determinants of Measured Intelligence," *Genetic Psychology Monographs*, 49:141–186, 1954. *And for fun:* H. J. Eysenck, "Testing," *Encounter*, 22: 52–55; June, 1964. (Despite support of the British Psychological Society, the psychological tests to screen applicants to universities are being discontinued, because of social class differences in "educational innovation and motivation in the working-class environment.")

PART FOUR

Education and the Young Child

The word "early" has taken on new meaning in educational circles in the past few years. Research on experimental programing points to early childhood as a time when the child is most susceptible to training and to learning. Increasingly, one hears the term "early intervention" to describe programs holding promise of circumventing the problems centered around the disadvantaged population. Moreover, the consequences of the lack of sensory stimulation during the early years has a cumulative effect in the educational development of the child. If he lacks opportunity to learn, he falls behind, with the deficiency becoming larger and larger each year.

In the first selection in Part Four, Jerome Bruner describes the consequences of such deprivation from both a learning and developmental point of view. Not only does the individual pay a phenomenal price for such deprivation, but society is also the loser. The consequences are of such a nature that it is almost impossible to make up for the loss. This is particularly true when the deprivation is allowed to exist over long periods of time. Bruner contends also that the earlier the intervention, the less dire are the consequences. This selection is of particular significance because much of the rationale for Project Headstart was drawn from Bruner's work.

The contribution of Martin Deutsch to changes in early childhood education, especially as it pertains to the child from the disadvantaged home, is a foregone conclusion. One cannot fully understand the foment in this field without being aware of the thinking and the experimental work being done by Deutsch and his co-workers. In the selection on nursery education reprinted here, he lays the groundwork for the teacher working in the language area particularly well. He also discusses the need of teachers for high expectations and for a thorough understanding of the family milieu in which these children are raised. Deutsch is indebted to William Fowler for some of the approaches used in his experimental groups.

The importance of early childhood in the development of achievement motivation is discussed by Virginia Crandall, who cites provocative and enlightening research in this field but makes it quite clear that further insights must await additional knowledge, which can come only when more research attention is turned in this direction. Certainly, achievement motivation is critical in the learning process.

The challenge of imaginative curricula development is great for educators in the field of early childhood education. These educators cannot accept much of this challenge, however, if school administrators are not aware of the implications of their attempts to bring about innovations into an already misunderstood field. The search of workers in the field of early childhood education for a fresh and workable approach may seem to some critics to be an exercise in trivialities, for they must deal with such mundane matters as trips to the store, trips to the farm, and even (for city children) trips to the city; and they must work with mothers on such commonplace educational problems as sanitation, nutrition, and "buymanship." If the programs are to succeed, however, they must work at this visible and effective level.

Vigorous and imaginative programs are being carried out in many places. We have chosen to highlight these programs by presenting samples from across the country (see the selections by Helen Heffernan, James L. Olson and Richard G. Larson, Bernard Spodek, and Erma Clark, and the article from *Grade Teacher*). In reading the descriptions of these programs, one cannot help but be struck by the fact that though there are many similarities among them, they all have a certain freshness of approach.

Erma Clark's article reports on the setting up of a nursery school program for a group of American Indian children in Utah. The education of Indian children has received little or no attention except by dedicated people who have approached the problem with a rare combination of wisdom and compassion. In many ways, the knowledge gained from working with the Indian has much relevance because he truly represents the classic case of the disadvantaged American.

The tentative conclusions from Connecticut, Florida, and Maryland are much like the conclusions presented to President Johnson by Sargent Shriver at the conclusion of the first Headstart program:

> In Project Headstart, children who had never spoken learned to talk; parents who were frightened of the school authorities came and stayed to help the teachers; volunteers gave hours of time to work with the children, drive them to the classes, and do a myriad number of things that would otherwise not have been done to enable more than 550,000 children of low income families to enter school on an equal basis with their colleagues this fall.[1]

[1] Report to the President on "Project Headstart," August, 1965.

✧ ✧ 17 ✧ ✧

The Cognitive Consequences of Early
Sensory Deprivation

JEROME S. BRUNER

Growth in any field of science is almost always uneven. The past decade, for example, has been a period of turbulent growth in the field of perception; a period in which parallel inquiries in neurophysiology, physics, and psychology have each, in turn, thrown light upon the nature of the perceptual process, light of such an order as to dazzle us all a bit with respect to the fundamental nature of perceiving. I should like briefly to review some of these developments before turning to the problems of sensory deprivation.

Let us consider first the field of physics. The classical metrics of physics up to the end of the nineteenth century were the centimeters, grams, and seconds of classical mechanics. Until very recently in psychology, our description of ambient stimuli and of their effect at a sensory surface has been couched in terms of this system. The effort, moreover, to construct a set of experiential attributes for any modality has been guided by this classical system of physical mensuration, and it is not surprising that Titchener (216)[1] and later Boring (24) ended with the ensemble of intensity, protensity, quality, and attensity (the last a never-ending source of embarrassment!). Today, physics has revolutionized its way of looking at the physical world of potential stimulation. In quantum theory, for example, one specifies the state of a system and the set of transitional probabilities leading to next states. Emphasis upon probability of events and transitional probability has become central. These developments in physics have telegraphed themselves into psychology largely by way of the development of the mathematical theory of communication or information theory — an approach to the analysis of the reduction of uncertainty in physical systems that rests upon Boltzmann's insight that entropy in a system is best de-

[1] The numbers in parentheses throughout refer to citations given in the bibliography of *Sensory Deprivation*, edited by Philip Solomon.

✧ Reprinted by permission of the publishers from Philip Solomon, editor, *Sensory Deprivation*. Cambridge, Mass.: Harvard University Press, Copyright, 1961, by the President and Fellows of Harvard College. Also used by permission of the author. Jerome S. Bruner is Professor of Psychology, Harvard University.

scribed as residual uncertainty. The result of all of this ferment in physics is that attention has been focused on two related and hitherto neglected features of the physical stimulus: first, the set of *possible* stimulating states that might have occurred at any given moment, and, second, the bias in their likelihood of occurrence. The importance of this probabilistic metric for an understanding of the development of environmentally appropriate sets or attitudes will shortly become apparent.

Developments in neurophysiology have also provided a new challenge to the psychologist interested in perception. As in the case of our contact with physics, we as psychologists have been operating until very recently with a 19th or early-20th century conception of the nervous system — an image of a switching and transmission system made up of an afferent or sensory side, a central segment, and an efferent or motor outflow. The work of Granit (75), of Galambos (67), of Magoun and his associates (154), and of Pribram (180) has brought seriously into question whether such a simple input-output model corresponds with the findings of electrophysiology over the past decade and a half. Indeed, we know now that even in so simple a case as the flexion reflex of the spinal mammalian cat, close inspection indicates that a third of the fibres in the efferent nerve trunk going to a muscle have nothing whatever to do with motor activity but with the programming or gating of the sensory stretch receptors in the muscle — setting these receptors to feed back to the spinal cord on the afferent side either a lot or a little sensory information about the state of the muscle. And Granit (75) has shown that centrifugal control fibres operate from the center to the periphery in altering the sensitivity of retinal cells to stimulation. Indeed, Galambos has recently shown that fibres of central origin operate outward to the periphery of the auditory system, serving to "turn off" the sensitivity of hair cells in the organ of Corti when attention is turned elsewhere. Some of these fibres have already been traced back as far as the superior olive and experiments have been done on the effects of severing them, the result of such section being to prevent centrifugal control from operating. Add to this work the continuing experimentation on the boosting operations of the reticular system in facilitating sensory input to the cortex — discharges which, as Lord Adrian puts it (2), clear the cortex of alpha activity in order to give sensory messages a clear field — and still another blow is struck in the interest of freeing psychologists from the rigid model of neural activity that is a heritage from the early Sherrington. What this work indicates, as Robert Oppenheimer put it in his first William James Lecture at Harvard in 1957, is that the price of perceiving anything at all is that not everything is perceived that can potentially be perceived. And so, if you will, the problem for an organism who would hope to minimize the surprise of his environment to a level where he might survive, is to match his programing to the likelihood and significance of events in the environment.

Now consider some of the developments in psychology, for we on our part have not been quiet. I want to single out only two of these. The first is the shift in emphasis in the study of perception from a consideration of classical problems of space-time-quality organization, as is so well represented by the work of the Gestalt psychologists, to what Prentice (179) has called a functional emphasis. I should take a functional emphasis to mean that interest has shifted to the manner in which perceiving relates to and is instrumental in the various ongoing enterprises of an organism, whether these enterprises be simply getting around in a familiar environment or as seemingly complex as looking for food or for a mate or for the Holy Grail. What has been healthy about the new emphasis is that, first, it has confused us out of our smug assumption that perception involved some sort of fixed relationship between an impinging pattern of physical energy on the one side and certain enduring and highly stable properties of the brain on the other, leaving the variability in perception to that favorite American vehicle of variance, the Response. The second and more positive effect of the shift in emphasis is that we have been sent scurrying for independent variables that lie outside the comforting stimulus metric of centimeters, grams, and seconds.

A second development in psychology — new work on the effects of early experience — brings us to the heart of the problem to which we are addressing ourselves: the development of perception. It is a problem with a tortured background, tortured by the pains of yesterday's metaphysical deadlocks. One such deadlock is the so-called nativist-empiricist controversy which has about it some of the scent of a wrongly formulated dichotomy. I say this unkind thing about the so-called controversy simply because it has had no issue, and because it yields on the very margins where it should stay firm. Nobody in his right mind has ever urged that an organism begins with no built-in equipment for perceiving, nor has anybody been so brashly foolish as to claim that experience has no effect whatever on the nature of what we perceive. If the controversy had any real meaning in the study of space perception, where it originated, it certainly has none in the study of perception generally. Or rather, I should say, it has about the same meaning as a quarrel in physics between those who would proclaim that weight was more important than the force-fulcrum distance in Archimedean Type II levers. It is not a controversy but a question of plotting functions.

For bringing this matter into a proper empirical perspective, we must be grateful for the work of Hebb and his students in investigating the effects of early sensory deprivation in animals. I do not propose to review the work, for it is well known. In general, an impoverished environment, one with diminished heterogeneity and a reduced set of opportunities for manipulation and discrimination, produces an adult organism with reduced abilities to discriminate, with stunted strategies for coping with roundabout solutions, with less taste for exploratory behavior, and with a notably reduced tendency to draw inferences that serve to cement the disparate events of its environment such as between the light of a candle flame and the likelihood of its burning when you put your nose into it. To these evidences of reduced capacities, which may indeed be irreversible, although there has not yet been a full-scale attempt to provide adequate therapy toward overcoming these deficits, we should add the fact that there seem to be critical periods operative. Unless certain forms of stimulation-cum-learning take place before a certain point in a puppy's life or a rat's life, there appear to be certain very intractable changes.

We may speculate here a little about the meaning of these challenging findings. Before doing so, however, let us consider first the parallel findings on prolonged sensory deprivation in adult organisms that have the effect of disorganizing cognitive function, upsetting the constancies, even disrupting the perception of continuous contours that extend beyond the immediate focus of attention at the center of the visual field. These matters are mentioned in advance of setting forth some speculations to underline the likelihood that perception and cognitive activity generally depend upon a dynamically stable though ultimately disruptible equilibrium that depends, even in adult life, upon contact with stimulus heterogeneity and a shifting environment. Indeed, even more dramatic evidence is given by Ditchburn and his associates (55) indicating that if a visual pattern is stabilized on the retina such that it is not even displaced by the natural tremor of the eye, it will disappear from view within six or so seconds.

Pulling the threads of the discussion together, we may say that to operate effectively in an environment, an organism must develop a model of the environment, and this for at least two reasons. In the first place, it is a way of conserving information in the form of concepts or universals, the means whereby — to use the ancient Aristotelian language — we separate essences from accidents, or, in modern terms, signal from noise. If you will, the recurrent regularities and the higher probability relationships between and among events are conserved in this model. Given such models — call them trace systems or assemblies or templates or whatever term seems most appropriate to your imagery — it becomes possible, secondly, for an organism to extrapolate and interpolate on the basis of partial information, to perform the kind of inference that may be called, "going beyond the information given." This is a task that is learned gradually at first and then, as the grammatical character of learning develops, to use Lashley's phrase (133), proceeds at an accelerated pace as we convert masses of connected or associated events into more highly ordered systems, as when children in the ingenious experiments of Inhelder and Piaget go from trial-and-error concreteness in bouncing a ball off a wall at a target to the reorganization of the situation as one in which the angle of incidence and the angle of reflection are recognized as equal. This kind of learning is neither S–S nor S–R in the usual senses of those shopworn terms. It consists of a process of organizing "rules" or "transforms" that conserve and represent the redundant structure of the environment.

Without such prior learning, the centrifugal control functions of the nervous system are without a program, without a basis for predicting that certain events are more likely than others or preclude others, and have no basis for selectivity toward stimuli. I would make a small wager at this point. Consider the cast in the experiment of Hernandez-Peon *et al.* (92). Click stimulation produces large spike discharges in the cochlear nucleus. If now the click stimulation is continued but some white mice are introduced into the field under a bell jar, the electrical discharge produced by continuing click stimulation is markedly reduced. Attention is directed elsewhere with attendant gating of the auditory system. The wager is this: if cats are reared in a highly restricted sensory environment, one with a minimum of stimulus variation in either the visual or auditory fields, the selective gating found will be considerably less marked than in normally reared cats. The prediction is based upon several considerations about the nature of perceptual development as perceptual differentiation — a point of view most intimately associated with the Gibsons (69). Continued contact with a rich sensory environment, the view would hold, permits the development of differentiation of spheres of activity, of sensory modalities, of events within modalities. Sensory deprivation prevents such differentiation, prevents the development of selective gating.

This leads to another prediction: part of the process of perceptual development consists of the capacity to utilize cues, to extract information from cue-significate encounters. One of the more interesting forms of information utilization is to be found in the weighing of probable, in contradistinction to certain cues, for the process requires a sorting out and evaluation of negative and positive instances. A given sign leads not *always* but *sometimes* and in excess of chance to a given significate. To master such cues requires either the gradual buildup of excitatory strength as required by such learning theories as Hull's (107) or Spence's (207) or it requires the use of a strategy like that proposed by such analysts of the decision process as Marschak (158) or Savage (194). In the first case, the process would be very slow and informationally very inefficient, particularly if one worked with a two-cue discrimination situation where, say, a white signal led to food 70 per cent of the time and to non-food 30 per cent, and a black cue to food 30 per cent and to non-food 70 per cent. In the second, more informationally efficient strategy, as soon as the animal discriminated the difference in the probability of payoff, he would spot the more probable cue and ride with it. Let us take a group of normal animals and a group with sensory deprivation and set them two-choice discrimination tasks where the two cues lead 100:0/0:100 to their respective consequences, then 80:20/20:80, and finally 70:30/30:70, as in the well-known experiment of Brunswik (32). I would predict that the two groups would differ least on the certain cues, and as one moved in the direction of the equiprobable case, the groups would diverge more and more. The reason for the prediction is based on a quite simple premise. Not only does early deprivation rob the organism of the opportunity of constructing models of the environment, it also prevents the development of efficient strategies for evaluating information — for finding out what leads to what and with what likelihood. Robbed of development in this sphere, it becomes the more difficult to utilize probable rather than certain cues, the former requiring a more efficient strategy than the latter. Then there is the matter of the unsuccessful attempt to order the unorderable environment perceptually.

We may conclude by referring to the problem of transferability in learning. The McGill experiments and those inspired by the work at McGill have given us a striking example of what has been called "nonspecific transfer of training." Savings effected in learning something new by virtue of having learned something before cannot in such instances be credited to the transfer of specific responses or of priorly established associations. Yet it is precisely this type of so-called nonspecific transfer that is perhaps the most typical and the most ubiquitous. It consists of the establishment of models or constructs or concepts that represent the environment in such a way that when one encounters a new task it is possible to handle it as an exemplar of an old concept in connection with which appropriate responses have already been learned. Such transfer has the function, almost, of saving us from having to do much new learning and it is indeed the case that after a certain age in life, we do indeed get saved from much new learning.

But nonspecific or generic transfer also involves the learning of general rules and strategies for coping with highly common features of the environment. And it is here that I think Piaget's vision is the clearest. He remarks upon the fact that cognitive growth consists of learning how to handle the great informational transformations like reversibility, class identity, and the like. In his most recent writing, he speaks of these as strategies for dealing with or, better, for creating usable information. I would propose that exposure to normally rich environments makes the development of such strategies possible by providing intervening opportunity for strategic trial and error. Whether failure to master the elements of such strategies for transforming information before a certain period of growth produces an irreversible loss, I cannot say, nor do I have a clue as to why critical periods are so critical. That there is impairment of strategy under a deprived regimen seems, however, to be fairly evident.

One word of conclusion about the effects of early deprivation. Little is served by fighting over the stale battlegrounds of yesterday's theorizing. There *has* been a greatly increased interest in the manner in which cognitive functioning and perception are shaped by the instrumental role they play in the enterprises of an organism. There have in the past been pleas of protest that this instrumental bedding of perception played no role in shaping its character or laws, that only responses are altered by virtue of instrumental requirements. Such a view comes from the ancient and honorable assumption that all there is to perceiving is the pattern of intensities, durations, and sensory qualities. It is obvious that inference is also a formidable factor in perceiving, else there would not be such a huge difference in recognizing the random word YRULJZOC and the fourth-order word VERNALIT, or frequent and infrequent words would be recognized with equal ease. Inference depends upon the establishment of rules and models, and it also depends upon the development of strategies for arriving at rules and models. I have proposed in this paper that early experience with a normally rich perceptual environment is needed for such learning — that deprivation prevents it.

Let us, finally, explore the implication of work on early deprivation for our understanding of the effects of sensory deprivation on the functioning adult organism. It would seem, first of all, that not only are there critical problems of the development of adequate models of the environment and adequate coping strategies, but that there are also maintenance problems of an order of delicacy that were not even imagined before the pioneering experiments of Hebb and his associates at McGill. The work reported by the contributors to the present volume emphasizes not only the need for variable sensory stimulation as a condition for maintaining a functioning organism, but also the need for continuing social contact and stimulation. We have yet to study the relative effects of each of these sources of maintenance, but it would appear as if they may serve a vicarious function for each other: Where social contact is maintained, as in the efforts at Mt. Sinai in New York to keep up the family contacts of children in respirators, the cognitively debilitating effects of reduced stimulation are notably reduced. It would not be unreasonable to guess that social contact provides a symbolic analogue or vicar for sensory intake.

What is this maintenance problem? I would like to suggest that it perhaps relates to a kind of continuing feedback-evaluation process by which organisms guide their correction strategies in perceiving, cognizing, and manipulating their environments. Let me suggest that the unhampered operation of this evaluation process is critical in the continuing adaptation of the organism, both in the development of adequate cognitive functioning, as I have suggested, and also in moment-to-moment functioning. Consider the massive effects that occur when the evaluation process is interfered with by various means. Distort auditory feedback in speech by the conventional technique of delaying the return of the speech pattern to the speaker's ear by a fraction of a second, and the effect is highly disruptive. Stuttering occurs and the speaker reports a lively discomfort, sometimes bordering on panic. So, too, with the discomfort of a visual Ganzfeld, where virtually all orienting cues are removed and only a white unstructured space remains. Distorting spectacles often have the same effect of disrupting and preoccupying the organism, setting him off on a battle for adequate feedback that makes all else seem trivial. One may suggest that one of the prime sources of anxiety is a state in which one's conception or perception of the environment with which one must deal does not "fit" or predict that environment in a manner that makes action possible. If there is anything to this view of anxiety, then it follows that when one prevents an organism from monitoring the fittingness of his percepts and his cognitive structures, one is cutting him off from one of his principal sources of maintaining adjustment.

The work reported by Goldberger and Holt (Chapter 9) on individual differences in reaction to experimental interference with reality contact and also by Bennett (Chapter 11) on the effect of sensory isolation in high-altitude flying suggests that people respond differently to the initial stages of isolation, some finding it exciting and even intoxicating, others terrifying and disrupting. I do not know what bearing this has on our present problem, save that when one is isolated from external stimulation, one is thrown on internal resources and people differ in the degree to which they live comfortably and confidently with their inner impulses and cognitive models. Over and beyond this important distinction, I would make one other in the form of a guess. It is this: to get any pleasure from being cut off temporarily from adequate evaluation of one's coping, whether by sensory deprivation or by "nonproblem drinking" of five martinis, say, suggests that one is able to rely more on criteria of congruence and consistency in testing one's notions about the world, that one is less fearful of errors of over-daring and overgeneralization. The "strategies of evaluation" of such a person will tend to be more nominalistic and relativistic in the philosophical meaning of those terms. The person who is more easily thrown off by isolation and sensory deprivation and interference will be more the empiricist and realist, oriented outward for testing ideas. Each will show a different developmental pattern with respect to strategies for dealing with reality. We have seen such differences developing in eleven-year-old children whose cognitive patterns are now being studied intensively by the Cognition Project at Harvard, and as I read the findings of Goldberger and Holt I am tempted to make the guess I am reporting here. Perhaps its only virtue, however, is that it is a testable guess that can be rejected easily!

In conclusion, then, I have suggested that early sensory deprivation prevents the formation of adequate models and strategies for dealing with the environment and that later sensory deprivation in normal adults disrupts the vital evaluation process by which one constantly monitors and corrects the models and strategies one has learned to employ in dealing with the environment.

Nursery Education: The Influence of Social Programing on Early Development

MARTIN DEUTSCH

There is a convergence today of knowledge and of social problems which I believe will place increasing importance on early childhood and preschool education.

One converging current comes from social necessity, from the rapid urbanization of our cities and the patterns of substandard living conditions that exist for so many children in the cities. Another current derives from the present status of the psychological and behavioral sciences and the increasing implication in the work being done, especially in the developmental and social psychological areas; that early systematic intervention is the most effective means for alleviating or eliminating later social and learning disabilities.

Currently, 40 to 70 per cent of the total school population in our twenty largest cities consists of children from the most marginal economic and social circumstances. By the time these children reach junior high school, 60 per cent are retarded in reading by one to four years. We know that this academic retardation carries with it a much broader social retardation and that it represents a tremendous loss to America of very needed resources.

It is a simple fact that unskilled jobs are decreasing rapidly and that it will be increasingly necessary for people to enter the job market highly prepared to perform skilled tasks. This is well-nigh impossible for people who were alienated from school at an early age. Thus current social necessities demand attention to the educational process, and especially to the participation in it of the children from the most deprived circumstances.

Let me say a few words about the kinds of backgrounds these children come from. First, one must remember that the slums in our large cities are generally segregated institutions. This means that the mainstream of American life has been denied to these children. They have not had the oppor-

✧ From an address presented at a conference of the National Association for Nursery Education, Philadelphia, October 27, 1962, as published in *The Journal of Nursery Education*, April, 1963, pp. 191–197. Used by permission of the author and the publisher. Martin Deutsch is Professor and Director, Institute for Developmental Studies, Department of Psychiatry, New York Medical College.

tunity to share its values, to internalize the motivational systems that may or may not make the child a successful student. The middle-class child has had school held up to him as a goal with an emblem and as a means, a vehicle, for his own advancement. Writing, books, and reading have played very important roles in his life from the time he could understand simple speech.

This is not at all true for the slum child. Many of the children from lower socioeconomic circumstances come into the school situation and go through a kind of cultural trauma. They have entered a foreign land. There is a teacher speaking in continuous sentences for longer periods of time than they have been spoken to before, often speaking in a different dialect, and expecting and anticipating attention from the children, and assuming that they are functioning in terms of the same parameters as she.

These children have come from a different cultural context, and have had no real preparation to meet the demands of the school. It is not simply that the children lack skills — there is an incongruity between the skills that the children have and the kinds of skills that the school demands. And the school cannot appropriately use and functionally attach the skills of the children to it.

It might be that some changes in curriculum would help in establishing a continuity between the child's previous experience and the demands of the school, but essentially, it is the child who is going to have to make the major adjustment in order to handle the school materials. It is highly important that the child be able to handle these materials, not only because of the kinds of social problems mentioned earlier, but because emotional health is based on achieving the individual dignity associated with competence and success.

If a child begins early to experience largely failure in his contacts with the broader culture, his relationship to it and its various institutions cannot but deteriorate, and simultaneously his sense of self, his emotional growth and health, will suffer. If school becomes more and more a place of failure and stimulates feelings of inadequacy, school will be more and more avoided — mentally if not physically — and will come to have little influence.

The sequence of events described and the individual and social problems to which they relate point up the importance of preparing the child for his first school experience. As was indicated earlier, the middle-class family seems to do this quite adequately for the middle-class child. But for the lower-class child, some social intervention is strongly indicated. This points squarely at preschool programing for these children.

The importance of preschool experience, however, does not derive solely from the fact that it is preschool — i.e., before school — but largely from what is known about the greater resiliency and accessibility of children of preschool age. While there are few specific studies of the effects of early training on later school performance, nearly all cited by Fowler (1) demonstrate substantial gains coming from early training. In a preliminary analysis of some of our own recent data at the Institute, we find higher group intelligence test scores among children who had preschool and kindergarten experience, as compared with those whose initial contact with school was in the first grade. (These data are on children from low socioeconomic status, and will be reported fully in a separate publication.) Data adduced by Scott (5) also point to early childhood as a time of maximum plasticity and accessibility to training and to learning.

This means that the preschool situation can serve as a real stimulant to development and learning, as well as a socio-cultural bridge between the background of the slum child and the demands of the school. This does not imply that the attempt should be to regulate the cultural values of people who come from different social and cultural histories and circumstances, but that the children must be helped to understand the values that motivate the school philosophy and its demands for achievement and accomplishment.

The use of the preschool experience as both a bridge between the two cultures with which the child must deal and as a stimulant to his development, dictates that its program be carefully planned to accomplish these goals. There must be a balance between the social and the cognitive; between the cultural and the emotional. I must say at the outset categorically that planning by educators does not mean regimenting the children. It means organizing a program that will best accomplish the ends in view by supplying the most effective bridge and the most effective early stimulation.

What program content will be most effective can be determined in part by a careful examination of where the cultural discontinuities are most evident in first grade performance, and of the kinds of experiences the middle-class child has which seem best to facilitate his early school learning and adjustment. Much of the kind of enrichment experience I will suggest for children from deprived circumstances is actually common procedure in the experience of middle-class children, and the core of it is daily procedure in the kinds of activity and of training that are put into situations where middle-class children are found. Certain improvements could be introduced into these middle-class situations but the focus here must be on the large body of children who come into our school situations fundamentally not properly prepared for the educational experience.

I would like to put several factors in the building up of a program into the context just discussed. These relate to the motivational, linguistic, memory, and general cognitive areas which seem most crucial in the planning of successful preschool programs.

First, we must recognize that the children from these deprived environments live under very crowded conditions and have few toys or even household objects to play with and to use, to develop the perceptual and spatial understanding taken for granted in school. These children will be coming to a school situation much richer in these objects than any they have experienced before. They cannot be expected to make use of them in the same way, or with the same minimal need for external direction that middle-class children will; they must be helped to play with and use these unfamiliar objects.

This brings us immediately to the problem of the teacher's expectation of children's performance. Usually, these expectations are built on the behavior of middle-class children, and the tendency is to look upon children from the lower socioeconomic groups as being quite slow; they just don't perform in the same way or with the same alacrity and understanding as the child from the more privileged background. Yet one must remember that these children have the same range of potential as any group of children who come from more favorable circumstances. The teacher's expectation that a child will fail or do well is communicated to the child in various ways, even if the teacher is unaware of it. Therefore, for any program for these children to be successful, teachers must be educated to be aware of the particular deficiencies most likely to be encountered in children from underprivileged backgrounds, and to adjust their expectations accordingly.

These children have somewhat different expectations of adult behavior than do middle-class children. Many more slum children come from broken homes, and have had family experiences qualitatively different from those of middle-class children. Frequently the parents, because of economic and social pressures and lack of education themselves, have not been able to reinforce the child in an appropriate way so that he will develop a constructive relationship to his own intellectual and psychomotor behavior, where he will set goals, work toward them, and be disappointed when he fails to receive concrete rewards when he is successful. Native intellectual potential tends to be artificially reduced in the absence of feed-back mechanisms.

When we consider what kinds of experiences and motivational systems can be introduced into a preschool experience, we can first specify a whole process of real feedback. This would mean insuring that the teacher responds to the child, permits him to make demands on her, and indicates by her behavior that she is there not only to offer emotional warmth but also to answer questions and to provide a larger perspective and introduction to the world.

It is important to respond to each child individually, because with these children, there tends to be a major deficiency in the whole area of self-identification. While I believe this to be largely class-based, rather than racially based, most urban Negro children belong to the lower socioeconomic groups, so that often the problem of self-concept and self-awareness is complicated by the realities of social inferiority thrust on Negro children.

Discrimination plays a devastating role in the developing consciousness of the child, and if this role is to be minimized we need, on one level, extensive social engineering. On another level, we need direct work with the child in the school and preschool years which can be extremely effective in at least limiting the kinds of violence done to a child's self-concept by these invidious characteristics of the larger culture.

I would like to turn to the whole question of cognitive development — what the opportunities are for early cognitive development and its stimulation in a preschool program. I mentioned in the beginning that the behavioral sciences are coming increasingly to the realization that there are common opportunities for the early cognitive development of children if it is systematically programed. The child must first develop the expectation that he can complete a task, and that he can explore the environment and ask questions. The program of cognitive stimulation must give opportunity for the child to express curiosity, to explore, and to learn that he can expect feedback and reward from adults.

I should like to quote a short section from a major article in the Psychological Bulletin by Fowler (1), which indicates the importance and the history of cognitive stimulation of young children. While he was not dealing necessarily with children from lower socioeconomic circumstances, the conclusions remain pertinent for all children. The exciting aspect of this article and of others on the subject is the kind of minimal intervention at these early ages that seems to result in maximum changes. Fowler says, near his conclusion,

. . . Much if not most of the energy in child psychology and development in late years has been concentrated on the child's personality, perceptual motor, and socioemotional functioning and development. Originating primarily as a reaction to historically inadequate and stringent methods, fears have generalized to encompass early cognitive learning per se as intrinsically hazardous to development. As legitimate areas of study, the contributions of studies on perceptual-motor and socioemotional problems are obvious. But in the field of child guidance, interest in these areas has come to permeate and dominate work in child development almost to the exclusion of work on cognitive learning. In harking constantly to the dangers of pre-mature cognitive training, the image of the "happy," socially adjusted child has tended to expunge the image of the thoughtful and intellectually educated child. Inevitably, in this atmosphere, research (and education) in cognition has lagged badly, especially since the 1930's, not only for the early years of childhood but for all ages.

Even prior to the more recent era, however, very little careful research was done on early cognitive learning. As historical evidence shows, most studies have comprised the work of those "beyond the pale" of formal psychology. Yet, taken collectively, the findings are so provocative as to make us entertain hopes that many, if not all, children can and indeed should be offered much more cognitive stimulation than they have been generally receiving.

There is, however, a further problem, at once a derivative of and an important contributor to the failure to undertake work on cognitive learning. Few systematic methods have been devised for educating young children, especially in complicated subject matter. We have in mind methods for simplifying and organizing the presentation of cognitive stimuli. Equally important, methods must be sufficiently flexible and play oriented to be adaptable to the primary learning levels and personality organization characteristic of the infant and young child.

Among the kinds of organized stimulation necessary for the cognitive development which we would promote, one of the most important is language stimulation. (By organized stimulation, we mean a systematic introduction of stimuli in a way that is congruent with what is known about the maturational development of the child, and which will offer the child opportunity for the facilitation of what might be passively developed or hypodeveloped cognitive operations.)

Language is probably the most important area for the later development of conceptual systems. If a child is to develop the capabilities for organizing and categorizing concepts, the availability of a wide range of appropriate vocabulary, of appropriate context relationships for words, and the ability to see them within their various interrelationships, becomes essential. Sometimes the most productive training can be done in the third and fourth and fifth years of life in the language area.

Milner recently concluded a study of children who were high in verbal ability and high in reading skill, and of children who were low in both areas. In the kind of observations that one would like to see made also in preschool settings, she points out, in regard to home differences, "There appears to be a radically different atmosphere around the mealtable from a child's point of view for the high scorers than for the low scorers" (4). (This is also a social class difference.)

> More frequently for the high scorers, mealtime at home, particularly the first meal in the day, serves as a focus for the total family interaction. Further, this interaction seems to be positive and permissive in emotional tone for these children, and has a high verbal content. That is, the child is talked to by adults with mature speech patterns and talks back to the adults. The opposite situation apparently exists for the low scorers. There were, in fact, indications in responses of some of their mothers that they actively discourage or prohibit the children's chatter and refuse to engage them in conversation during meals. This prohibition is based on a belief that talking during meals is a bad practice. One low scorer's mother's response to, "Did anyone talk to the child while she was eating a meal" was, "I do not allow her to talk while she is eating, it is a bad habit." To what extent the apparently more limited opportunities for low scorers to interact verbally with personally important adults has contributed to a low degree of verbal skill is unknown.

Other data on this point indicate that an element lacking in the environments of children from slum areas is the failure of adequate and continuous, sustained, connected, and relevant verbal communication. Somehow, in the verbal interaction matrix of the home, the child is not considered a participant; and in not being a participant, he does not give exercise to those incipient processes that must receive the nourishment of experience and active participation. Within the context of the school and the preschool situations this can be reversed; a child can become familiar with language, can increase tremendously his ability to identify and label different aspects of the environment, and can organize these aspects and catalogue them into certain conceptual categories.

Language training will take careful programing if it is to be done most effectively. We have found that children often have a much greater language capability and knowledge of language than is ever evident in a school situation with an adult present. Through experimental techniques, we are able to record language of a child with no adult present, and we — and the child's teacher — are often amazed at the richness of the language that comes out. To stimulate this language so it will be available to the child in a school situation, in a situation where an adult is present, enrichment programing must be carefully planned.

Memory training is another area I want to mention briefly. This is really an adult-child kind of interaction. It is the ability of adults to refer the child to the past and to demonstrate or show him things in the past that have relevance in the present or the future. This interaction depends largely on language training, too. If the child has not had sufficient language, or if language is not a major element within the child-adult interaction, there will be a certain retardation in the development of memory systems. Here, too, specific and detailed programing by educators in the preschool context can play an important role.

Time does not permit me to go into a number of techniques and methods that can be developed, but let me say that if such methods are used (and we hope within a year or so to publish some of the specific methods we are now using), they must be used in terms of the basic principles of the individuation of the child. The child must have individual opportunities to relate to adults, and the stimuli presented to him must be consistent with his own development and history.

If the child is able to remember three or four elements from a problem established for him, and if he is rewarded for it, one doesn't next jump to a six-element problem or give him a one- or two-element problem. Not knowing where a child stands in relationship to a particular and delineated intellectual area can result in a great deal of frustration for the child. One must keep a very accurate accounting of the child's accomplishments and experiences.

The development of perceptual mechanisms is another area for preschool enrichment. This closely relates to the lack of environmental opportunities. The lack of artifacts in the environment and the absence or reduction of language training in the home, can lead to a deficiency in development of auditory and visual modalities. Here, too, early auditory training, and particularly semantic discrimination training, using tape recorders and organized sound systems, should help to compensate the child for his deficiencies. The same is true for the visual area, but again, both these types of training have to be closely meshed with the child's language ability. One must present only words and labels for objects already in the child's vocabulary. It is not possible to teach either visual or auditory discrimination in the absence of an external anchor in the child's language system; he must know the object or word that is being used for the visual or auditory training.

One other factor must be mentioned before concluding this discussion. That is, whatever the means of establishment of the nursery school situation, be it by a board of education, by a neighborhood house, or by any other kind of organizational system, it should be meaningfully related to the community it serves. We have found very often that parents of children from the low socioeconomic environments feel very self-conscious about their own lack of understanding and lack of knowledge and formal education, and sometimes look upon teachers as a competitive threat in their relationship with the child. One parent said recently, "My child comes home and I want to read to him, but the teacher reads so nicely it makes me look stupid."

There is a necessity to see if parallel programs in reading and in library work can relate the child's parents to the essentials of the school situation. This means one has to understand the sociology of the family and the social sensitivities that have developed. Yet it is extremely important to give the parent some insight into what is expected in the school, and even more so to let the parent know it is important for the child's education for him to be a participant in the language interaction in the home and that he receive a certain degree of individuation, attention, and reinforcement. Recently reported research indicates that just the reading to a child by the parent for twenty minutes an evening when the child is two or three years old results in significant changes in the child's language abilities (2).

There is a larger role in interpreting to the community the necessity of preschool experience, so that such education on a systematic basis becomes an indigenous part of the community structure, especially in our metropolitan areas. On this point, and particularly on the special responsibilities of preschool educators to recognize the potential of each child, some recent remarks of Martin (3) are most pertinent. He said,

> . . . there is evidence from a variety of sources that there is in the making a cognitive theory of behavior and development. It would view the child not merely as a passive victim of either his environmental history or of his biological nature, but as one who strives to be the master of both his nature and his history. It will thus emphasize the unique characteristic which makes that mastery a possibility, namely, intelligence. It will be a science of man that includes man. To the development of such a science, research workers and field workers in child development should have a significant contribution to make. For they are by training and commitment, both scientists and humanists. As such, they are in a most favorable position to humanize science and to bring an end to the mechanization of the human being. We face the question of whether man is to be the master or slave of his technology. The answer lies in the extent to which we can succeed in developing and utilizing our most important human resource, the ability to think. That we seem to be rediscovering in our research and theory the mind of the child provides hope that the answer will be in our favor.

Essentially, what is being said here — and I think this makes a good summary for my remarks today — is that the child, as a thinking organism and as a potential contributor to society, must be reached at as early an age as possible, particularly if he is marginal to our major cultural streams.

He must be reached by educators with scientific knowledge, working in consort with behavioral scientists, and recognizing the underlying social necessities that make it imperative for America to solve the problems that will be associated with mass youth unemployment if children are not integrated into the school context.

This integration must be accomplished during the children's first school experiences, and the attempt to do it must be made then, rather than at a later stage, where, unfortunately, it has so often proved a failure.

REFERENCES

1. Fowler, W. "Cognitive Learning in Infancy and Early Childhood," *Psychological Bulletin*, 59:116–152, 1962.

2. Irwin, O. "Infant Speech: Effect of Systematic Reading of Stories," *Journal of Speech Hearing Research*, 3:187–190, 1960.

3. Martin, W. "Rediscovering the Mind of the Child: a Significant Trend in Research in Child Development," *Merrill-Palmer Quarterly*, 6:67–76, 1960.

4. Milner, Esther. "Study of the Relationship Between Reading Readiness in Grade I School Children and Pattern of Parent-Child Interaction," *Child Development*, 22:95–112, 1951.

5. Scott, J. "Critical Periods in Behavioral Development," *Science*, 138:949–955, 1962.

❖ ❖ 19 ❖ ❖

Achievement Behavior in Young Children

VIRGINIA CRANDALL

No one knows exactly why or when children begin to want to do something *well*. Although observers often note that the infant of a year or less struggles to turn himself over, to pull himself up, to walk, to grasp an object, and to acquire speech, most investigators concerned with "achievement motivation" or "achievement behavior" would not classify these early efforts as motivated by a desire to "achieve." What criteria, then, distinguish certain purposeful behaviors as achievement behaviors? Crandall, Katkovsky, and Preston (10) suggest that "achievement behavior is behavior directed toward the attainment of approval or the avoidance of disapproval [from one-

❖ From *Young Children*, November, 1964, pp. 77–90. Used by permission of the author and the publisher. Virginia Crandall is Research Associate in Psychology at the Fels Research Institute for the Study of Human Development.

The preparation of this paper was supported in part by research grant M-2238 from the National Institute of Mental Health, U. S. Public Health Service.

self or from others] for competence of performance in situations where standards of excellence are applicable." Somewhat similarly, in describing achievement *motivation,* McClelland and his colleagues (41) state: "The child must begin to perceive performance in terms of standards of excellence" and to experience pleasant or unpleasant feelings about meeting or failing to meet these standards. Early efforts at locomotion, prehension and speech are not usually categorized as achievement behavior because children of such very young ages do not yet have the cognitive ability to apply "standards of excellence" to their own behavior. Psychologists would generally agree that the child must be able to note a discrepancy between his present level of competence and a higher level of skill and to predict that more proficiency will produce greater pleasure, pride, or approval from others than his present skill will now permit. Thus, it is at the point when the child attempts to *perfect* a skill, to accomplish something *more efficiently* or *quickly,* to produce a *better* product, to do something *well,* that his efforts are defined as achievement behavior.

Achievement motivation would seem to have its origin in learning experiences during early childhood. McClelland, et al. (41) maintain that feelings of pleasure originally attendant upon mild changes in sensory stimulation become associated with early efforts at independent mastery. That is, the child learns to anticipate that certain levels of skill will produce feelings of pleasure if they are perceived as moderately above his present performance level just as he tends to enjoy moderate increments in kind, quality, intensity, and patterning of other forms of stimulation. But these authors state further that "stronger achievement motives probably required for most (though not necessarily all) children some structuring of performance standards, some *demands* by the parents, and the surrounding culture" (41, p. 78; see also (40), pp. 437–452). Crandall, Preston, and Rabson (14) place primary, rather than secondary, emphasis on such demands, rewards, and punishments when considering the genesis of the achievement need. They argue that direct social reinforcement of the child's accomplishment is necessary if the child is to learn to value achievement activities as potential sources of satisfaction and security. Only later, and for some children, does approval from others for good performance become unnecessary and feelings of pride or self-approval constitute sufficient reinforcement to maintain or increase their achievement behaviors.

Individual differences have been found by Crandall, Preston, and Rabson (14) among three-, four- and five-year-olds in the frequency and persistence with which tasks requiring skill and effort are attempted. Sears and Levin (54) also report that four- and five-year-old children varied in their aspirations to tackle succeeded or failed tasks, and Tyler, Rafferty, and Tyler (59) found individual differences among nursery school children in their attempts to get recognition for achievement behavior. Finally, McClelland (39) reports that individual differences in achievement motivation (measured with a test involving the drawing of "doodles") had appeared by the age of five. These studies suggest that the desire to achieve must have been established to some degree by the time these children were tested or observed, but that it is more fully developed in some preschool children than in others. No research, however, has attempted to investigate the approximate age or conditions under which achievement behavior *begins* to emerge.

First-, second-, and third-grade children spend more time and strive more intensely in some kinds of achievement activities than in others (7). Thus, achievement efforts of young grade school children not only vary from child to child, but also vary for any one child from one achievement area to another (*i.e.*, intellectual, physical skills, mechanical and artistic activities). It is possible that similar differentiation occurs even earlier, but no research of this nature has been reported.

Early Environmental Stimulation

Recent investigations by Bruner (4), Deutsch (17), and Hunt (27, 28) have focused on stimulation in the preschool child's physical and social environment as a possible determinant of intellectual achievement.

A group of researchers under the direction of Martin Deutsch (17, 18), for example, Cynthia Deutsch (16) and Vera John (29, 30), have studied Negro and white children on the edge of a large slum area in New York. These investigators found concept formation, auditory and visual discrimination, language acquisition, and I.Q. scores related to such factors as race, social class, nursery school or kindergarten attendance, and father's presence or absence from the home. One of the elements common to all these factors, they reason, is the social and physical stimulus deprivation or enrichment concomitant to the child's status on each of these dimensions.

Forgays (20) presented four-year-old children with discrimination problems in which their only incentive was the opportunity to obtain tactual, visual, or auditory stimulation. Middle-class children learned these problems more rapidly than lower-class subjects, presumably because of their early exposure to more stimulating surroundings.

Most of the researchers associated with these studies have recommended that environmental intervention might increase the achievement of children from deprived backgrounds. The idea is not new. As early as 1907, Montessori (43, 44), in her work with three- to six-year-old children from the slums of Rome, provided her pupils with a wide variety of materials to play with and tasks of graded difficulty to choose from at will. By the time these children were five years of age, many of them were reading and writing. Fowler (22, 23) demonstrated that two-, three-, and four-year-old children can be taught to read by providing a very shallow gradient of stimuli consisting primarily of printed verbal and pictorial material. In his excellent review (22) of earlier attempts to teach children of preschool ages to read, Fowler states ". . . of twenty-five children who learned to read before the age of three . . . 72 per cent had definitely enjoyed a great deal of unusually early intellectual stimulation. . . . There was no evidence of a child reading early where stimulation was absent."

Nursery school attendance is an obvious source of enrichment of the child's environment and, thus, of his intellectual achievement. Results from studies of preschool attendance are too complex, however, to be reviewed here. In general, they seem to indicate that substantial increases in I.Q. cannot be expected from nursery school attendance unless the child has come from an environment which is unusually static and unstimulating (e.g., an orphanage). Even then, results attributed to the environmental stimulation of nursery school may have been artifacts of test unreliability, practice effects of repeated testing, and/or the greater rapport of nursery school children with adult examiners who tested them. Wellman's summary (60) of studies conducted at the Iowa Child Welfare Research Station and the reviews of Hunt (27), Jones (31), and Swift (58) are recommended to the interested reader. Now let us focus directly on the achieving child himself.

Achieving Children

PERSONALITY CHARACTERISTICS. What are the personality attributes of children who display more achievement behavior than their peers? A longitudinal study by Sontag, Baker, and Nelson (56), based on ratings of children's behavior in nursery and elementary school, as well as in the home, showed that both boys and girls whose I.Q.'s increased during the preschool years were independent of adults and competitive with peers. In addition, the girls were less "feminine" in their behavior than girls with decreasing I.Q.'s and did not need immediate rewards for good behavior, but could delay gratification until some more distant time. Later, during the elementary school years, both male and female I.Q. "ascenders" were again found to be competitive in the scholastic situation and independent, initiating more activities on their own and more frequently attempting to overcome obstacles by themselves. Boys with increasing I.Q.'s were also more aggressive and more anxious than boys whose I.Q.'s declined. "Ascending girls displayed more sibling rivalry, had parents who emphasized the importance of school achievement and, at the preschool ages, these girls were able to delay gratification." This ability to delay rewards for more long-term goals has also been shown, by Mischel (42), to be associated with higher achievement motivation scores.

Independence, then, was a consistent characteristic of children who showed increases in I.Q. scores. Such independence was also present in the three- to five-year-old achieving children of another study, one by Crandall, Preston and Rabson (14). That is, the more time these children chose to spend in achievement activities during nursery school, the less they sought emotional support and instrumental help from the staff or from their mothers in the home.

In spite of the fact that independence is related to achievement, a similar sample of children who displayed more achievement efforts in nursery school were found by Crandall, Orleans, Preston, and Rabson (13) to be compliant to the requests and demands of the adult staff. Haggard (25) also reports that compliance to adult pressures and values was found among children at the elementary age level who were high academic achievers. In this longitudinal study of gifted children, Haggard investigated a variety of personality characteristics associated with academic achievement and reports that to some degree these factors change with age. In the third grade,

> High achievers were sensitive and responsive to socialization pressures . . . and were striving to live up to adult expectations. . . . Their conformity in this respect seems to have given them a high degree of security and confidence in their relations with adults, even though they expressed some underlying resentment toward authority figures. In general, however, they showed a high degree of inner harmony, being rather adept at emotional control. . . . In their behavior with others, they were somewhat more tense, competitive, and aggressive; had developed good work habits and were persistent in them; got along better with their parents, teachers, and peers; and showed a higher level of over-all adjustment than did the low academic achievers. . . .
>
> By Grade VII, various changes had taken place in the children who remained high academic achievers. Although they continued to respond to the socialization pressures of adults and to strive toward adult standards of behavior, they had developed strong antagonistic attitudes toward adults. . . . They increasingly rejected adults as persons. At the same time, they showed a marked increase in the level of their anxiety and a corresponding decrease in their intellectual originality and creativity. Although there was no such difference in anxiety and creativity between high and low achievers in Grade III, a marked difference existed between these groups by Grade VII. . . . They also became more aggressive, persistent, hard driving, and competitive, and they showed signs of willingness to be aggressive and destructive in order to defeat and win over other persons. . . .

It would appear, then, that achieving children, in contrast to peers who perform less well, do not need to depend upon adults but are somewhat compliant and conforming to their demands and accept and incorporate adults' high evaluations of the importance of achievement. They are also able to work without being immediately rewarded for their efforts, show initiative, self-reliance, and emotional control. While achieving children of preschool and early elementary age are somewhat aggressive and competitive, their social relationships are generally good. Achievement, however, seems to be exacting its toll. By later elementary school or junior high age, aggression and competition have become accentuated; relationships with siblings, peers, and adults show some disruption; and the children are less creative and more anxious. Research on high school students, beyond the scope of this paper, indicates that these attributes become increasingly pronounced at later ages. Does this mean that the effort to achieve "produces" the less desirable personality attributes? Or does it mean that only if children have acquired such a personality constellation will they then be able to achieve in our highly competitive, post-Sputnik educational system? Cause and effect relationships cannot be determined from these data, but it is obvious that our "education for excellence" is accompanied by certain psychological costs.

ANXIETY AND TEST PERFORMANCE. Much research has been directed toward determining the effects of anxiety on achievement performance. High levels of anxiety seem to impede optimum performance on the complex problem-solving tasks presented in intelligence tests and scholastic-achievement tests. The process is assumed to be one in which the anxious child is overly concerned with the tester's or teacher's evaluation of his performance and is thus less free to attend to the material presented to him in a learning situation and less able to report it in a testing session. It may also be that the less intelligent or less academically proficient child has had more difficulty, fewer rewards, and more failure experiences and, as a result, has *become* more anxious.

[The relationship between anxiety and test performance in elementary school children has been demonstrated in studies by Crandall, Katovsky, and Preston (11); Feldhusen and Klausmeier (19); Keller and Rowley (36); Lunneborg (37); McCandless and Castaneda (38); Reese (47); Sarason, Davidson, Lighthall, Waite, and Ruebush (51); and Stanford, Dember, and Stanford (57). Hafner and Kaplan also did studies on this subject in 1959.] Among *early* elementary school children the findings generally show that more anxious children tend to perform more poorly on achievement and intelligence tests, although the relationships are weak and vary greatly from one investigation to the next. Among fifth- and sixth-grade students, greater anxiety has been found to relate somewhat more frequently to poor test performance, and the relationships are usually stronger for girls than for boys. Where differences in anxiety scores are reported for the two sexes, girls are consistently more anxious, or at least admit to more anxiety, than boys. The lack of strong and consistent inverse relationships between anxiety test scores and achievement test scores except in sixth-grade girls, led Keller and Rowley (36) to maintain that anxiety may only affect academic achievement in relatively high-anxious groups. Since the two longitudinal studies cited previously found that achieving children were more anxious than their nonachieving peers, it may be that moderate amounts of anxiety do not interfere with intellectual performance. There may be, however, some critical level of anxiety (such as that attained by sixth-grade girls) beyond which intellectual efforts are adversely affected.

The characteristics of the learning or testing situation and of the task must also be taken into account. Grimes and Allinsmith (24) found that anxious or compulsive children in highly structured classrooms performed as well on standardized reading and intelligence tests as their less anxious peers but were not as productive in classrooms where less structure was imposed on the learning situation. Sarason *et al.* (51) report that high-anxious children performed better on a "game-like" intelligence test than on a more typical "test-like" instrument. Thus, it might be concluded that when the task or the situation is so structured that it does not engage the anxiety of the usually anxious child, he will be freed to perform more optimally.

ACHIEVEMENT MOTIVATION AND ATTITUDES DIRECTLY RELATED TO ACHIEVEMENT ACTIVITIES. In addition to general personality attributes which have been found to distinguish achieving from nonachieving children, some studies have also shown that achieving children score higher on measures of achievement motivation. Usually an index of achievement motivation is obtained by asking the child to tell stories about pictures or about dolls or to complete a story after a situation has been described to him. Winterbottom (61) found that eight- to ten-year-old boys who obtained the highest achievement motivation scores on a story-telling measure were rated by their teachers as showing more motivation to achieve in general, and in sports and schoolwork in particular. Achievement motivation scores, however, did not differentiate the boys who were rated as actually performing more successfully in those activities from the boys who were rated as less successful in their attempts. In a longitudinal study of six- to ten-year-old children, Kagan, Sontag, Baker and Nelson (33) have shown that higher achievement motivation scores were obtained by children whose I.Q. scores had increased over that age period, while those children with decreasing I.Q. scores had lower scores on the motivational measure. Rosen and D'Andrade (49) have shown that high achievement motivation also characterized nine- to eleven-year-old boys who displayed greater proficiency on achievement tasks consisting of block-stacking, anagrams, and constructing patterns. Finally, Cox (6) reports that fourth- and fifth-grade Australian children with higher achievement motivation scores were superior on school examination performance and were more often in the "superior stream" than in the "inferior stream" (comparable to ability groups in this country).

On the other hand, Crandall, Katkovsky, and Preston (11) did not find achievement motivation scores to be any higher among early elementary children who performed more adequately on reading and arithmetic achievement tests and I.Q. tests. Nor did children with high achievement motivation scores choose to spend more time or strive harder in intellectual achievement activities than did children with lower scores. Murstein and Collier (46) also report that seventh-grade children with higher motivation scores did not perform better on arithmetic problems or a canceling task than did children with lower motivation scores.

These disparities may arise in part from difficulty in the method by which achievement motivation has been assessed. That is, among very young children the stories told to pictures or doll play situations are often so meager as to allow for only the crudest scoring. Or it may be that findings vary by such situational factors as whether or not motivation has been "aroused," and the probability of reward which the situation offers. Little work of this nature has been done, however, with subjects under college age.

It may be that more specific attitudes, beliefs, and expectations concerning achievement activities of different kinds would also contribute to the understanding of achievement behavior. For example, the degree to which children expect that they will be successful in intellectual achievement attempts has generally been found to influence their actual intellectual achievement performance. In studies conducted at the Fels Institute, junior high students who expected to obtain good grades in mathematics and English were, in fact, those students who did perform better in these courses, particularly where high success-expectancy was combined with high I.Q. But, when I.Q. and expectancy were in conflict, the children's expectations of success were even more highly related to their grades than were their intelligence test scores! Children who were confident about being successful also actually performed more competently on standardized achievement tests, and Battle (2) found that if a child expected to do well in mathematics he persisted longer on a difficult mathematics problem.

It should be pointed out, however, that among the junior high students studied by the Fels group and the first- and second-grade pupils studied by Sears (53), the positive relationship of expectancy to performance was somewhat weaker for the poor students than for those who were doing well in school, thus leading to the conclusion that some of the poorer students were giving unrealistically high estimates of their own ability.

SEX DIFFERENCES. Girls seem to have more difficulty than boys in evaluating their ability accurately. Additional findings from the Sears study (53) indicate that fifth- and sixth-grade girls' concepts of their own mental ability are rather inconsistently related to their performance on intelligence and achievement tests, and the author also states that "girls generally show *less good* self-concepts than boys." Brandt (3) also finds that girls are less accurate or realistic than boys in their self-concepts. Crandall, Katkovsky, and Preston (11) even report that among first-, second-, and third-grade girls, the brighter the girl, the less successful she expected to be on intellectual tasks, and the lower her I.Q. score, the more successful she expected she would perform in intellectual activities!

In the same study, the authors also observed the children in free play. They report that the girls who spent most time and were striving hardest in intellectual activities had received higher scores on a measure of their desire to be good at intellectual activities. Thus, the extent of their effort seemed to be determined by their *wish* to do well. Among the boys, however, expectancy of intellectual success was closely and realistically related to I.Q. scores, and boys who thought they could do well were those who were observed to strive hardest in intellectual activities in free play. In addition, these boys held higher standards for their own performance and thought that they, rather than fate, luck, or other people, caused their own intellectual successes and failures. This belief in self-responsibility for, or control over, intellectual successes and failures was also found by Crandall, Katkovsky, and Crandall (9) in elementary children who had higher report card grades and achievement test scores.

An investigation by Crandall and Rabson (15) of both nursery school and early elementary school children revealed that there were no differences between boys and girls in the *amount* of achievement efforts they displayed at either age level, but among the elementary children boys chose more often than girls to return to a previously failed task in an attempt to master it. The girls, however, avoided returning to the previously failed task and were more dependent on both peers and adults for help and approval and more often withdrew from threatening situations in free play.

There is some possibility that girls achieve for different reasons than boys. A number of studies suggest that girls' achievement efforts may more often be directed at obtaining affection or approval from others than from the self-approval attendant upon successful task accomplishment. For example, Sears (52) found that among elementary school boys there were consistent, moderate relationships between achievement motivation and the boys' scholastic achievement test scores. Among the girls of that study, however, *affiliative* motives, rather than their achievement motivation, related most directly to their academic achievement test scores.

Tyler, Rafferty, and Tyler (59) demonstrated that girls who made more attempts in nursery school to obtain recognition for achievement also made more attempts to obtain love and affection. Boys' behavior, however, showed no such relationships. Similarly Crandall, Dewey, Katkovsky, and Preston (8) have shown that elementary school girls who displayed more achievement efforts were those who sought the most approval from the staff of the Day Camp where they were being observed, while achievement efforts and approval-seeking showed no such relationship among the boys.

Thus, young girls may be using achievement striving to obtain love and approval from others. If this is the case, it is not surprising that in our culture which values achievement so highly, girls have become anxious regarding achievement, attempt to obtain approval for their achievement efforts, are prone to avoid the risk of failing, are dependent on adult help, and cannot rate their own competence accurately, often "underselling" it. For girls, the effort to achieve seems to exact fairly strong psychological penalties as the necessary price of affection and approval.

Parental Influences on Children's Achievement Behavior

While there are many aspects of the social environment which contribute to children's achievement behavior, perhaps the most crucial of these for the very young child is found in interaction with his parents. Since it has already been noted that achieving children are also independent, it might be assumed that parents of these children make early and strong demands for independent behavior. Studies on this point, however, show inconsistent results. On the one hand, Winterbottom (61) found high achievement motivation in eight- to ten-year-old boys whose mothers reported on a questionnaire that they had expected early independent behavior and Siss and Wittenborn (55) found that high intelligence and achievement test scores were obtained by third-grade boys whose mothers had expected early or moderately early independence. Yet Chance (5) reports that first-grade children performed more proficiently on academic achievement tests if their mothers expected independent behaviors to occur relatively *late* in childhood. When Rosen and D'Andrade (49) observed parents as their boys (nine-to-eleven) worked on achievement tasks, they discovered that fathers of boys with high achievement motivation allowed their sons more independence, but mothers allowed them less. Still another study, by Crandall, Preston and Rabson (14), did not find independence training, as observed in the home, to be related in either direction to the children's achievement efforts in nursery school.

Part of the disparity in these findings may lie in the differences between mothers' retrospective reports on written questionnaires (see Chance [5]; Siss and Wittenborn [55] and Winterbottom [51]) and the direct observation of mothers' current independence training techniques used in the latter two studies. Part of the difference may be due to the ages of the children studied. In addition, a recent investigation by Rosen (48) has found that boys who received early independence training evidence greater incorporation of their mothers' achievement values — whether these values are strong or weak, positive or negative. Thus, if, by chance, the groups of mothers tested in the foregoing investigations happened to vary from study to study in the achievement orientations they held, the relationships found between independence training and the achievement motivation or behavior of their sons might well be affected. It is interesting to note, however, that mothers' direct reinforcement of achievement attempts (i.e., training specifically aimed at encouraging achievement behavior), was effective in producing higher achievement motivation according to Rosen and D'Andrade (49) and more achievement efforts according to Crandall *et al.* (10).

Mothers' attempts to accelerate their children's cognitive and motor development have also been investigated. Moss and Kagan (45) found that mothers who "pushed" their children's development had sons whose intelligence test scores at three years of age were higher than those of less acceleratory mothers; and Sontag, Baker, and Nelson (56) found that I.Q. ascenders in the elementary years also had more acceleratory mothers.

Investigations by Crandall, Katkovsky, and Preston (12) indicate that parental influences differ greatly depending on the sex of parent and child and the area of achievement behavior under consideration. For example, children's efforts to achieve in the mechanical area were most often associated with attitudes the parents held toward their children of the *same* sex, while parental influences in the physical skills area seemed to come from both the same-sex and the opposite-sex parent. That is, both boys and girls spent more time and worked harder at sports and gross motor activities if their parents of the same sex had participated frequently with them and instigated them toward these pursuits. The physical skills efforts, however, of both boys and girls were also associated with the importance fathers placed on their children's competence in this area, and high-achieving boys had mothers who were rejecting and non-nurturant while girls had fathers who were low in affection.

In the intellectual area the children's efforts were most often associated with attitudes held by parents of the opposite sex and with the context of the child's relationship to that parent. The intellectually striving boys had *mothers* who considered intellectual competence highly important for their sons and whose relationships with them were ones of active involvement. That is, these mothers not only praised their sons' intellectual achievement efforts and were especially nurturant and affectionate, but they were also overtly rejecting and punitive. Conversely, girls who displayed such intellectual efforts in the free-play situation had *fathers* who were generally affectionate and nurturant but criticized, as well as praised, their daughters achievement efforts. The girls' fathers were also more satisfied than dissatisfied with their daughters' efforts and they, as well as the mothers, evaluated the girls' intellectual competence as high. However, like the boys' mothers, these girls' mothers were also overtly rejecting.

The Rosen and D'Andrade (49) study found that both parents of those boys with high achievement motivation scores held high standards for their sons and were more competitive, more interested, and demonstrated more involvement during the sons' performance. The mothers (but not the fathers) were likely to reward their sons with warmth and approval and showed some tendency, also, to punish with hostility and rejection. The authors conclude, "In a way, it is this factor of involvement that most clearly sets the mothers of high *n* Achievement boys apart from the mothers of low *n* Achievement boys."

In sum, the foregoing studies suggest that high levels of active parental involvement, particularly along cross-sex, parent-child lines provide the basis for achievement motivation, performance on intelligence tests, and intellectual achievement behaviors evidenced in free play. It should be noted that in each case, part of that involvement was reflected in negatively valued parental behaviors or attitudes such as rejection, criticality, hostility, or "pushing" the child beyond his ability, and that this was particularly true of *mothers* of achieving children of either sex.

Other investigations of the parental behaviors associated with high academic achievement in children have also found proficiency in the classroom associated with parent-child relationships usually characterized as undesirable. For example, Crandall, Dewey, Katkovsky, and Preston (8) found that mothers of achieving girls were less affectionate and less nurturant, while Barwick and Arbuckle (1) found that mothers of achieving boys were less accepting, and Hoffman, Rosen, and Lippitt (26) found that they were more coercive than were those of other children who performed more poorly. Haggard (25), too, reports that high-achieving children in the early elementary years "saw their parents as being somewhat overprotective, pressuring for achievement, and lacking in emotional warmth (frequently they were correct)."

The attitudes which parents hold about their own personal achievements have been found to affect their attitudes toward their children's achievements and to influence their own behavior with their children in achievement activities. Since neither of these analyses is directly concerned with the *children's* achievement behavior, they will not be discussed here. The interested reader is referred to Katkovsky, Preston, and Crandall (34, 35).

The salience of early maternal behaviors to achievement development was demonstrated in a longitudinal study by Kagan and Moss (32). Intellectual achievement in adult males was strongly related to high maternal protection and low maternal hostility during the first three years of the boy's life, followed by acceleration of the child's achievement efforts during ages three to ten. The achieving adult women, however, had had mothers who were hostile toward them and lacking in protectiveness during the first three years of life while they simultaneously accelerated their daughters' achievement development during that period and again during the ages six to ten. Thus, variations in maternal behavior in the very early years have effects so far-reaching as to produce differences in achievement behavior many years later in adulthood.

Conclusion

This discussion has not attempted to present a comprehensive picture of all the social and cultural, peer, sibling and school factors which have been found to relate to children's achievement behavior. This summary has focused principally on the achieving child himself since it is ultimately the orientations he has developed which determine whether he will attempt to achieve when he is faced with a potential achievement situation. External forces can have impact only indirectly as they influence his motivations and attitudes.

Similarly, in studying the determinants of children's achievement behavior, it seems imperative that we must eventually establish the specific orientations the young child holds which promote, guide, or limit his achievement efforts. Then the link can be established between social and environmental factors and these orientations and we will better understand how and why such external forces are influencing his behavior. While research of this kind has been done with older subjects, almost none has been attempted with preschool children. The difficulty here is primarily one of measurement, and does not reflect indifference to the developmental aspects of achievement attitudes. Attitudes and motivations have previously been assessed almost exclusively through verbal measures, and very young children lack the necessary verbal skills. In addition, our real attack on the origins of achievement orientations, facilitating or impeding effects on their emergence, and their specificity or generality across kinds of activity as they make their initial appearance cannot really be investigated until nonverbal measures are developed.

This report has reflected the almost exclusive emphasis on behaviors of an intellectual nature which characterizes research in achievement. Some few research attempts reveal that many children seek approval for, or feel proud of, their competence in sports, crafts, leadership ability, art, and many other fields of endeavor. We know very little about the determinants of these kinds of achievement efforts. The paucity of research in these domains of behavior is probably a reflection of the overweening emphasis on intellectual achievement which has grown out of present international rivalries; it is indeed unfortunate that such exigencies have turned our attention away from such important aspects of achievement development.

REFERENCES

1. Barwick, Janice, and D. Arbuckle. "The Study of the Relationship Between Parental Acceptance and the Academic Achievement of Adolescents," *Journal of Educational Research*, 56:148–151, 1962.
2. Battle, Esther. "Motivational Determinants of Academic Task Persistence," *Journal of Abnormal Social Psychology*, 2:209–218, 1965.
3. Brandt, R. M. "The Accuracy of Self-Estimate: a Measure of Self-Concept," *Genetic Psychology Monographs*, 58:55–99, 1958.
4. Bruner, J. S. "The Cognitive Consequences of Early Sensory Deprivation," in P. Solomon (ed.), *Sensory Deprivation*. Cambridge, Mass.: Harvard University Press, 1961.
5. Chance, June E. "Independence Training and First Graders' Achievement," *Journal of Consulting Psychology*, 25:149–154, 1961.
6. Cox, F. N. "An Assessment of the Achievement Behavior System in Children," *Child Development*, 33:907–916, 1962.
7. Crandall, V. "Parents as Identification Models and Reinforcers of Children's Achievement Behavior." Progress Report, NIMH Grant M-2238, January, 1961 (mimeographed).
8. ———, Rachel Dewey, W. Katkovsky, and Anne Preston. "Parents' Attitudes and Behaviors and Grade School Children's Academic Achievements," *Journal of Genetic Psychology*, 104:53–66, 1964.
9. ———, W. Katkovsky, and V. J. Crandall. "Children's Beliefs in Their own Control of Reinforcements in Intellectual-Academic Situations," *Child Development*, 36:91–109, 1965.
10. ———, W. Katkovsky, and Anne Preston. "A Conceptual Formulation of Some Research on Children's Achievement Development," *Child Development*, 31:787–797, 1960.
11. ———, W. Katkovsky, and Anne Preston. "Motivational and Ability Determinants of Young Children's Intellectual Achievement Behaviors," *Child Development*, 33:643–661, 1962.
12. ———, W. Katkovsky, and Anne Preston. "Parent Behavior and Children's Achievement Development," paper read at [meeting of] American Psychological Association, Chicago, 1960.
13. ———, Sonya Orleans, Anne Preston, and Alice Rabson. "The Development of Social Compliance in Young Children," *Child Development*, 29:429–443, 1958.
14. ———, Anne Preston, and Alice Rabson. "Maternal Reactions and the Development of Independence and Achievement Behavior in Young Children," *Child Development*, 31:243–251, 1960.
15. ———, and Alice Rabson. "Children's Repetition Choices in an Intellectual Achievement Situation Following Success and Failure," *Journal of Genetic Psychology*, 97:161–168, 1960.
16. Deutsch, Cynthia. "Auditory Discrimination and Learning: Social Factors." Paper presented at Arden House Conference on Preschool Enrichment of Socially Disadvantaged Children, December, 1962.
17. Deutsch, M. "Facilitating Development in the Preschool Child: Social and Psychological Perspectives," *Merrill-Palmer Quarterly*, 10:249–263, 1964.

18. Deutsch, M., and B. Brown. "Social Influences in Negro-White Intelligence Differences," *Journal of Social Issues*, 20:24–35, 1965.
19. Feldhusen, J. F., and H. J. Klausmeier. "Anxiety, Intelligence and Achievement in Children of Low, Average, and High Intelligence," *Child Development*, 33:403–409, 1962.
20. Forgays, D. G. "Subject Characteristics and the Selective Influence of Enriched Experience in Early Life." Symposium paper presented at [meeting of] American Psychological Association, Philadelphia, August, 1963.
21. Fowler, W. "Cognitive Stimulation, I.Q. Changes and Cognitive Learning in Three-Year-Old Identical Twins and Triplets," *American Psychologist*, 16:373 (abstract, 1961).
22. ———. "Teaching a Two-Year-Old To Read: An Experiment in Early Childhood Learning," *Genetic Psychology Monographs*, 66:181–283, 1962.
23. ———. "Structural Dimensions of the Learning Process in Early Reading." Symposium paper presented at [meeting of] American Psychological Association, Philadelphia, August, 1963.
24. Grimes, J., and W. Allinsmith. "Compulsivity, Anxiety and School Achievement," *Merrill-Palmer Quarterly*, 7:247–271, 1961.
25. Haggard, E. A. "Socialization, Personality, and Achievement in Gifted Children," *School Review*, Winter Issue, 1957, pp. 318–414.
26. Hoffman, Lois, S. Rosen, and R. Lippett. "Parental Coerciveness, Child Autonomy, and Child's Role at School." Paper read at [meeting of] American Psychological Association, Washington, August, 1958.
27. Hunt, J. McV. *Intelligence and Experience*. New York: Ronald Press, 1961.
28. ———, "The Epigenesis of Intrinsic Motivation and the Stimulation of Early Cognitive Learning." Paper read at [meeting of] American Psychological Association, Philadelphia, August, 1963.
29. John, Vera P. "The Intellectual Development of Slum Children: Some Preliminary Findings," *American Journal of Orthopsychiatry*, 33:813–822, 1963.
30. ———, and Leo S. Goldstein. "The Social Context of Language Acquisition," *Merrill-Palmer Quarterly*, 10:265–275, 1964.
31. Jones, H. E. "The Environment and Mental Development," in L. Carmichael (ed.), *Manual of Child Psychology*. New York: John Wiley & Sons, 1954, pp. 631–696.
32. Kagan, J., and H. A. Moss. *Birth to Maturity: A Study in Psychological Development*. New York: John Wiley & Sons, 1962.
33. ———, L. W. Sontag, C. T. Baker, and Virginia L. Nelson. "Personality and I.Q. Change," *Journal of Abnormal Social Psychology*, 56:261–266, 1958.
34. Katovsky, W., Anne Preston, and V. J. Crandall. "Parents' Attitudes Toward Their Personal Achievements and Toward the Achievement Behaviors of their Children," *Journal of Genetic Psychology*, 104:67–82, 1964.
35. ———, Anne Preston, and V. J. Crandall. "Parents' Achievement Attitudes and Their Behavior with Their Children in Achievement Situations," *Journal of Genetic Psychology*, 104:105–121, 1964.
36. Keller, E. D., and V. N. Rowley. "Anxiety, Intelligence and Scholastic Achievement in Elementary School Children," *Psychological Report*, 11:19–22, 1962.
37. Lunneborg, P. W. "Relations Among Social Desirability, Achievement, and Anxiety Measures in Children," *Child Development*, 35:169–182, 1964.
38. McCandless, B., and A. Castaneda. "Anxiety in Children, School Achievement, and Intelligence," *Child Development*, 27:379–382, 1956.
39. McClelland, D. C. "The Importance of Early Learning in the Formation of Motives," in J. Atkinson (ed.), *Motives in Fantasy, Action and Society*. Princeton, N.J.: D. Van Nostrand Co., Inc., 1958. Pp. 437–452.

40. McClelland, D. C. "Risk Taking in Children with High and Low Need for Achievement," in J. Atkinson (ed.), *Motives in Fantasy, Action and Society*. Princeton, N.J.: D. Van Nostrand Co., Inc., 1958. Pp. 306–321.
41. McClelland, D. J. Atkinson, R. Clark, and E. Lowell. *The Achievement Motive.* New York: Appleton-Century-Crofts, Inc., 1953.
42. Mischel, W. "Delay of Gratification, Need for Achievement, and Acquiescence in Another Culture," *Journal of Abnormal Social Psychology*, 62:543–552, 1961.
43. Montessori, Maria. *The Montessori Method.* New York: Frederick A. Stokes, 1912.
44. ———, *Education for a New World.* Wheaton, Ill.: Theosophical Press, 1959.
45. Moss, H. A., and J. Kagan. "Maternal Influences on Early I.Q. Scores," *Psychological Report*, 4:655–661, 1958.
46. Murstein, B. I., and H. Collier. "The Role of the TAT in the Measurement of Achievement as a Function of Expectancy," *J. Proj. Tech.*, 26:96–101, 1962.
47. Reese, H. W. "Manifest Anxiety and Achievement Test Performance," *Journal of Educational Psychology*, 52:132–135, 1961.
48. Rosen, B. C. "Family Structure and Value Transmission," *Merrill-Palmer Quarterly*, January, 1964, pp. 59–76.
49. Rosen, B., and R. D'Andrade. "The Psychosocial Origins of Achievement Motivations," *Sociometry*, 22:185–218, 1959.
50. Ruebush, B. K. "Interfering and Facilitating Effects of Test Anxiety," *Journal of Abnormal Social Psychology*, 60:205–212, 1960.
51. Sarason, S., K. Davidson, F. Lighthall, R. Waite, and B. Ruebush. *Test Anxiety in Elementary School Children: A Report of Research.* New York: John Wiley & Sons, 1960.
52. Sears, Pauline S. "Correlates of Need Achievement and Need Affiliation and Classroom Management, Self-Concept and Creativity." Unpublished manuscript, Laboratory of Human Development, Stanford University, 1962.
53. ———, "Self-Concept in the Service of Educational Goals," *California Journal of Instructional Improvement*, Spring, 1964.
54. ———, and H. Levin. "Level of Aspiration in Preschool Children," *Child Development*, 28:317–326, 1957.
55. Siss, R., and J. R. Wittenborn. "Motivational Attitudes of Mothers and Teachers and Their Influence upon the Educational Achievement of Third Grade Boys." Paper read at [meeting of] American Psychological Association, St. Louis, August, 1962.
56. Sontag, L. W., C. T. Baker, and Virginia Nelson. "Mental Growth and Personality Development: a Longitudinal Study," *Child Development Monographs*, 1958, No. 2 (Whole No. 68).
57. Stanford, D., W. Dember, and L. Stanford. "A Children's Form of the Alpert-Haber Achievement Anxiety Scale," *Child Development*, 34:1027–1032, 1963.
58. Swift, Joan W. "Effects of Early Group Experiment: the Nursery School and Day Nursery," in *Child Development Research*, M. L. Hoffman and L. W. Hoffman, eds. New York: Russell Sage Foundation, 1964.
59. Tyler, F. B., Janet Rafferty, and Bonnie Tyler. "Relationships among Motivations of Parents and their Children," *Journal of Genetic Psychology*, 101:69–81, 1962.
60. Wellman, Beth L. "The Effects of Preschool Attendance upon Intellectual Development," in R. G. Barker, J. Kounin, and H. F. Wright (eds.), *Child Behavior and Development*. New York: McGraw-Hill Book Co., Inc., 1943. Pp. 229–243.
61. Winterbottom, Marian. "The Relation of Need for Achievement to Learning Experiences in Independence and Mastery," in J. Atkinson (ed.), *Motives in Fantasy, Action and Society*. Princeton, N.J.: D. Van Nostrand Co., Inc., 1958.

A Challenge to the Profession of Early Childhood Education

HELEN HEFFERNAN

Current interest in the problem of the dropout has focused public attention on the socioeconomically deprived child in our society. In all the studies of disadvantaged children and youth currently going on throughout the country, great emphasis has been put on the early years of life. The earlier we can get these children into school, the greater our hope of compensating for their cultural deprivation. Studies indicate that we cannot compensate at five or six or seven for developmental experiences which children have been deprived of at three and four. At three and four, children are normally making great strides in language development. Denied normal opportunities for such development constitute an almost insurmountable handicap in an education that gives high prestige to verbal achievement.

Statewide recognition of the learning problems of culturally disadvantaged children and youth of school age was given by the passage of the McAteer Bill in a recent legislative session in California. No such recognition has been shown the accumulating evidence that the preschool years in the lives of children from impoverished environments are at the root of their problems. Children from poverty-stricken neighborhoods have difficulties all through their school years because of lack of intellectual stimulation during the early years of their lives.

Studies by Martin Deutsch (1), J. McV. Hunt (4), and by others, show that socioeconomically disadvantaged children are not prepared by their early experiences to handle the curriculum and style of thinking required for success in school. Since birth they have lived as part of a socioeconomic group which differs in codes of behavior, patterns of language, and modes of living from the majority middle-class group in America. Their understanding of the world is shaped by the life of their socioeconomic group. It is becoming clear that the narrowness and poverty of their early experiences put a ceiling on their ultimate potentials for growth.

✧ From *The Journal of Nursery Education*, September, 1964, pp. 237–241. Used by permission of the author and the publisher. Helen Heffernan is Chief of the Bureau of Elementary Education, California State Department of Education.

Providing stimulating experiences in a nursery school appears a promising way to help these young children break through to deeper understandings. The nursery-age years are especially crucial since it is at this point in their development that children usually begin to recognize social situations as such. As this sense of awareness develops, each fresh experience comes with a sharpness that leaves deep and lasting imprints upon adult character.

"Our Invisible Poor"

Professional people who work with upper socioeconomic groups in American society find it difficult to believe we are not what J. K. Galbraith called "The Affluent Society." Mass poverty continues in this country.

Michael Harrington in his book, *The Other America: Poverty in the United States*, "estimates that between forty and fifty million Americans, or about one fourth of the population, are now living in poverty. Not just below the level of comfortable living, but real poverty, in the old-fashioned sense of the word — that they are hard put to it to get the mere necessities, beginning with enough to eat. This is difficult to believe in the United States of 1963 but one has to make the effort and it is now being made." (11)

We are justified in supposing that a fourth of our three- and four-year olds are suffering the effect of poverty which these studies and other comparable studies reveal.

The United States Lags in Provision for Care of Young Children

A news column in the New York Times of October 26, 1963, reports Admiral Rickover, that great expert on the superiority of European education, again deriding American schools to his old friends in the Council on Basic Education. Intellectual honesty should impel this authority on atomic-powered submarines to report on the prevalence of nursery school education abroad. In most cases the preschool program is optional with the parents but an integral part of the total school system. This would be comparable to our kindergartens in California. Attendance in kindergarten is not compulsory. However, in 1962 a comparison between kindergarten and first-grade enrollments reveals 336,421 in attendance in kindergarten and 342,185 in attendance in first grade. Parents do seem to wish to take advantage of every educational opportunity furnished their children.

In France a law dating back to 1881 sets up the Ecole Maternelle as an establishment of first education for boys and girls two to six years old. The Ecole was integrated into the general organization of education as part of primary education at that time and continues so. Attendance is optimal; compulsory education begins at six. The teachers are paid by the State and have the same status as primary teachers (8).

The Ecoles Maternelles or Jardins d'Enfants of Belgium provide for chil dren from three to six years of age. They are under the Ministry of Educa tion and are attached to the nearest primary school staff. Active method: of teaching are used, based on needs of children. In a country of 9,000,000 total population, there are more than 5000 such schools with more thar 10,000 classes. Practically all the children in Belgium attend: 96 per cen spend one year there, 85 per cent two years, and 76 per cent three years (9)

Great Britain provides nursery schools and nursery classes that are legally within the field of the primary education system. They are publicly pro vided and maintained by local authorities. One half of the costs is granted by the Ministry of Education which requires conformity to certain regula tions. Three is the minimum age of entry for nursery classes and at five the child goes to the compulsory infant classes. For nursery schools two is the minimum age.

The British program provides a wide range of materials for children to experiment with, plenty of opportunity for oral expression along with a large supply of pictures and books. There is also much provision for vigor ous outdoor play (5).

Canada too, provides education for preprimary children which is an in tegral part of the school system. There are day nurseries and nursery schools for children from two to six years of age and kindergartens for those five and six years old. The kindergarten age of entry is usually four years by December 31. Research concerning preprimary education is undertaken at four main centers, two in Ontario and two in Quebec. Monographs and bulletins are published frequently and advice is given at any time local schools wish to call upon the centers (6).

The Union of Soviet Socialist Republics, well known for the early training given its children, organizes the system of public education so that pre primary education constitutes the first stage. Usually there is a kindergarten in which pupils are divided into four age groups (children three, four, five, and six years old). The basic task of the kindergarten here is to provide children with complete and harmonious education while at the same time enabling mothers to work. Children entering the eight-year schools must be age seven as decreed in 1959.

The program is prescribed by the Soviet Ministry of Education. Tasks and content of the children's physical, intellectual, moral, and aesthetic education are defined in the program. The teaching of reading is not in cluded in the kindergarten curriculum and does not begin until age seven. The preparation of children for school education is given by means of exer cises in language, in counting aloud up to ten, in music, in drawing and painting, and the like (7).

And so in truth, the United States of America, a nation with about 7 per cent of the world's population but with 55 per cent of the world's wealth lags far behind other countries in provision for the education of young children.

Do these other countries value their children more than we do, or do they value their wealth less? Certainly here is a cultural lag that reflects no credit on the provisions we are making for the care and education of our children.

Records of Abuse of Young Children a National Disgrace

Elizabeth Elmer, Director of the Fifty Families Project, Children's Hospital of Pittsburgh, begins an article in the September-October, 1963, issue of *Children* (2) with the astonishing statement:

> The amount of systematic research on the problem of child abuse and neglect is conspicuously scant. Abundant material is available about individual mistreated children and particular abusive families but data are lacking on comparable groups of children or families selected for study according to carefully defined criteria. This means that few objective guidelines for child protection have been firmly established; for example, little is known about the long-term effects of abuse on the child or about the nature of the factors which determine the outcome of rehabilitative efforts with families.

In seeking the reason for lack of this type of information, Dr. Elmer believes that it is due to

> . . . the taboo in contemporary society regarding abuse and gross neglect. The acute discomfort aroused by the topic leads to extremes of emotion and unquestionably accounts for the disregard of the subject by research workers.

In this study supported by the National Institute of Mental Health an appalling amount of objective evidence on abusive action against very young children is established by pediatricians and bone specialists by means of x-ray pictures of fractures suffered by injured children. Dr. Elmer also appends to this article a bibliography of reports published by reputable doctors in the past five years of infants and young children "brutalized or killed through the negligence or assault of their caretakers."

Quite properly, the Children's Bureau and the Welfare Administration of the U.S. Department of Health, Education, and Welfare which publishes *Children* as an "interdisciplinary journal for the professions serving children" suggests state legislation which should be enacted to protect children from abuse (3) requiring "mandatory reporting by physicians and institutions to police authorities of physical abuse of children based on medical findings." But important as such legislation is, it will not provide for the prevention of such extreme forms of deviant child care, much less curtail the abuse of children which does not show up in bone injuries or hospital records.

Society has a dual responsibility which currently is tragically neglected. First, the responsibility of providing in the curriculum of junior and senior high schools and colleges content on human growth and development and effective child-rearing practices which will provide basic knowledge, habits, and attitudes related to socially acceptable parental behavior. And, second, the responsibility of providing nursery schools where children whose parents are culturally, emotionally, or socioeconomically disadvantaged may be provided an environment in which they may have relatively undisturbed opportunity to achieve the developmental tasks essential to normal maturation.

The current records of the abuse of infants and young children are a national disgrace. Let us not disregard the evidence because it is personally painful to us and because we would prefer to live in a world, even if it be a totally unrealistic world, in which no adult is ever guilty of aggression against a defenseless child. Rather let us have the courage to face these grim and savage facts with determination to support an intelligent course of action for the protection of children by means of legislation and education at all appropriate levels.

This is what democracy means. It means that the resources of the strong are always available in the defense of the weak. We are the strong; especially strong as we have a group commitment through our professional association as persons concerned about the welfare of young children. We are strong because we have a personal commitment because of intelligence and education to know how the growth and development of children can best be served. We have a clear call to personal and professional action which we dare not disregard because ignoring needed action which we know to be right diminishes our stature as worthy persons.

Activities and Studies Under Way

In a recent Public Affairs Pamphlet, Edith G. Neisser describes the program for socioeconomically deprived nursery school age children in New York City in these words:

> The assumption has been that five-year-olds come to kindergarten or six-year-olds to first grade, equipped to profit by a curriculum designed to draw out their abilities. Even kindergarten routines demand more than youngsters who have spent five years under the most debasing and unfortunate conditions can contribute.
>
> Some communities are starting with three- and four-year-olds to prevent the academic grief that results in early leaving. Children whose vocabularies are limited to "Huh," "Shut up," "Go away," and a few choice obscene epithets, who do not even know their own names, who have never listened to a story or looked at a picture book, are being given the chance to catch up with their contemporaries to whom such matters are literally child's play.
>
> The New York City Board of Education in cooperation with the Welfare Department of the City of New York is giving pre-kindergarten children experiences with language that will help them take their places in kindergarten and be ready to read in first grade. One hundred and twenty children, three and four years of age, have been selected for the first year of the undertaking. They will be given two-hour periods four times a week in small groups for intensive "conversation." They will hear stories, listen to records, become familiar with picture books, learn to speak in sentences, and enjoy the kinds of experiences with language that are taken for granted in middle-class homes or, for that matter, in many warm, close-knit slum families.
>
> These children will gain more than the feeling of being at home with books and at ease in talking. They will absorb, it is believed, the attitude "learning

is for me," for there is a connection between listening to the "Three Bears" or its equivalent at three and being able to handle English composition and algebra ten years later. Both indicate an identification with learning (10).

Other noteworthy studies currently under way include:

1. Committee on Human Development, University of Chicago. An environmental study of preschool children to learn how economic and cultural deprivation affects the child's mental growth. Federal grant: $34,500.
2. Ford Foundation studies now being conducted in Baltimore and New York City schools in building three- and four-year-old nursery groups into the public school system.
3. Oakland City Schools Ford Foundation Project in which the Stonehurst Child Care Center is included. The purpose is to provide some comparisons relating to the success in public school of children in a child care center who are given special planned curriculum with regular child care center experience, and with children who have not attended a child care center.
4. New World Foundation, study is being directed by Ruth Updegraff, State University of Iowa, and Shirley Moore, University of Minnesota. An intensive evaluation of nursery school curriculum for typical middle-class children. Study will include a review of nursery education literature and related material in elementary education in psychology, sociology, and other disciplines. Study to be completed in 1964.

Exploratory Committee Studies Needs of Young Children

In view of this evidence and more, an exploratory committee of persons interested in the protection and education of young children has been formed and proposes to study ways and means of extending nursery school education to socioeconomically disadvantaged three- and four-year-olds in California school districts and otherwise to improve conditions for young children in American society.

The proposed project would in no way interfere with existing nursery-type programs, such as parent participation preschools, private nursery schools, and child care centers that are now available to many families. It would serve a group of children, who because of eligibility factors, cost, or social barriers are not included in any of the established services. It would serve a group whose need for the experiences offered in such programs is far greater than that of children from average American families.

The exploratory committee has avoided any effort to prepare actual legislation because it hoped first to clarify purpose and need and then to attract a working group of perhaps a hundred or more people who would give attention to the specific elements in planning, launching, and promoting enabling legislation. This, then, is an invitation to socially minded persons concerned about the young in our society to join with exploratory groups in developing programs designed to meet the needs of young children.

REFERENCES

1. Deutsch, Martin. "The Disadvantaged Child and the Learning Process." Paper prepared for the Ford Foundation Work Conference on Curriculum and Teaching in Depressed Urban Areas, July 10, 1962.
2. Elmer, Elizabeth. "Identification of Abused Children," *Children*, 10:180, September-October, 1963.
3. *Ibid.*, p. 202.
4. Hunt, J. McV. "The Psychological Basis for Using Preschool Enrichment as an Antidote for Cultural Deprivation." Speech at Arden House Conference, Harriman, New York, on Preschool Enrichment of Socially Disadvantaged Children, December 16, 1962.
5. International Bureau of Education, UNESCO. *Organization of Pre-Primary Education*, Report of the International Conference on Public Education, XXIV. Geneva: UNESCO, 1961. Pp. 257–263.
6. *Ibid.*, pp. 105–110.
7. *Ibid.*, pp. 250–253.
8. Leibert, S. Herbiniere. "The French Ecole Maternelle," OMEP, World Organization for Early Childhood Education, No. 10, July 1963.
9. Libotte, M. "From Nursery to Primary School," OMEP. World Organization for Early Childhood Education, No. 10, July 1963.
10. Neisser, Edith G. "School Failures and Dropouts," Public Affairs Pamphlet No. 346. New York: Public Affairs Pamphlets, July 1961. P. 17.
11. Quoted from "Our Invisible Poor," *The New Yorker*, January 19, 1963.

SUGGESTED READINGS

BOOKS AND MONOGRAPHS

American Psychological Association. *Today's Educational Programs for Culturally Deprived Children.* Report of Section II — The Seventh Annual Professional Institute of the Division of School Psychologists. St. Louis: The Association, 1962.

Deutsch, Martin. *Minority Group and Class Status as Related to Social and Personality Factors in Scholastic Achievement.* State University of New York: Research Center in Learning Disabilities (Monograph No. 2, 1960).

Hunt, J. McV. *Intelligence and Experience.* New York: The Ronald Press, 1961.

Passow, Harry. *Education in Depressed Areas.* New York: Columbia University Press, 1963.

Riessman, Frank. *The Culturally Deprived Child.* New York: Harper & Row, 1962.

ARTICLES

Hosley, Eleanor. "Culturally Deprived Children in Day Care Programs," *Children* (U.S. Children's Bureau) September-October, 1963. P. 175.

Levine, D. V. "City Schools Today — Too Late With Too Little," *Phi Delta Kappan*, 44:81–83, 1962.

Norman, Sherwood. "Children Deprived of Belonging," *The Journal of Nursery Education*, September, 1963. P. 285.

✧ ✧ 21 ✧ ✧

An Experimental Curriculum for Culturally Deprived Kindergarten Children

JAMES L. OLSON AND RICHARD G. LARSON

There is a pressing need for urban educators to develop sensible curricula for culturally deprived children. Traditional curricular concepts do not seem to meet this need. Content is inappropriate and reflects the lack of an adequate theoretical curricular structure. If efforts to meet the demands of educating deprived children in depressed area schools are to proceed with logic and efficiency, then controlled attempts to meet these problems must be explicitly described and carefully evaluated.

This article describes the curriculum structure and implementation of a pilot project undertaken in Racine, Wisconsin, which represents one approach to the education of culturally deprived kindergarten children. An experimental group of 20 kindergarten children was identified. This group participated in the curricular activities described in this paper while a like group from a similar school setting was identified for purposes of evaluation.[1]

Theoretical Framework

The writers agreed that both subject selection and curriculum development needed to be based on some logically consistent rationale so that hypotheses could be constructed and tested. Cultural deprivation was defined as having its most notable effects on school children along four dimensions:

1. *Language development:* Underdeveloped expressive and receptive language skills will be evident among deprived kindergarten children, and will

[1] A general description of this project, supported by the Johnson Foundation and Western Foundation of Racine, was reported in the *NEA Journal*, May 1962. The procedures used in identifying deprived children were described in the November 1963 issue of *Exceptional Children*.

✧ From *Educational Leadership*, May, 1965, pp. 553–558, 618. Reprinted with permission of the Association for Supervision and Curriculum Development and James L. Olson and Richard G. Larson. Copyright © May 1965 by the Association for Supervision and Curriculum Development. James L. Olson is Associate Professor of Exceptional Education, University of Wisconsin, and Richard G. Larson is Assistant Curriculum Coordinator, Unified School District No. 1, Racine, Wisconsin.

negatively affect their school achievement. Speech patterns will conflic: with the dominant language norms of middle-class teachers, thus heighten ing the improbability of a successful start in school.

2. *Self concept:* An inadequate self-image may characterize childrer raised in a substandard environment. Self-doubt or insecurity may result in low school achievement and a lessened feeling of personal worth.

3. *Social skills:* The deprived child will have had minimal training in the conventional manners and social amenities accepted by his middle-class teachers. He will be unskilled in relating socially to his peers or to author- ity figures, and will lack ability to function effectively in a school group.

4. *Cultural differences:* Most deprived children will come from lower socioeconomic strata. Many will be members of minority group subcultures. Therefore, their behavior and beliefs may differ from those of the dominant groups in the schools, and will be less readily understood and accepted.

Instruments were selected or designed to assess these four areas. Those children measuring lowest on composite test results were selected and arbitrarily defined as a sample of "culturally deprived" children (5).

The four dimensions also served as the framework for curriculum devel- opment. The investigators and the project teacher identified skills and understandings within each area which were assumed to be vital to school success. Thus, language development yielded receptive and expressive lan- guage skills; these were in turn subdivided, providing reasonably specific curricular objectives which could be translated into teaching plans with relative ease. This analysis is presented in Table 1 [see pages 178–179].

The reader may wonder whether concentrating curricular efforts upon those factors which were assumed to differentiate culturally deprived chil- dren is a naïve attempt to accomplish the impossible — that is, to super- impose middle-class values and patterns of living upon children whose behavioral norms are solidly imbued with the values of a lower-class culture. One may justifiably question whether middle-class standards form a solid enough base upon which to structure a plan for satisfying the social, psycho- logical, and intellectual needs of any man. The writers agree.

The purpose of this curricular structure was to aim instruction at those skills which deprived children lack, but which seem to be universal requi- sites to school success.[2] This may explain the purpose of the column headed "Persisting School Situations."[3] The criterion for entry in this column was the supposed potential for maximizing success in later school experiences.

A further criterion for analyzing the four differentiating areas was a con- sideration of those things which the writers assumed were expected of all students by their middle-class teachers. There was an attempt, therefore,

---

[2] The deep influence of lower-class culture on language development (2), on men- tality (1), on mental health (3, 7), and on school achievement (4, 7) combine to form a grim portrait of deprivation. Bernstein observes that the environmental influences on language may be the most crucial, since school success so greatly depends on that single factor.

[3] This phase is an adaptation of Stratemeyer's (8) curriculum-building concept of "Persisting Life Situations."

to select those persisting school situations which required skills and attitudes which teachers might assume are taught to preschool children in the average middle-class home, but which probably are not taught to culturally deprived children. Thus, the curriculum framework included such entries as the sequential use of words, role adaptation, and belief in one's own success potential.

The preceding description of a curriculum framework for culturally deprived kindergarten children is general; however, at least two qualifications must be observed. First, this framework applied only to one-half of the kindergarten day. Mornings were spent using the recommended curriculum guidelines of the Racine school system. Second, it should be stressed that the theoretical framework was useful only to the extent that it was utilized by the teacher as a guide for the selection of classroom activities. The teacher and the investigators attempted in several ways to maintain a reasonable amount of unity between the theoretical curriculum structure and its practical implementation. All three were involved from the beginning in discussions on curriculum development. All met several times during the school year to review aspects of curriculum and instruction. Finally, the teacher kept a daily log throughout the year in which she recorded activities which seemed appropriate to the academic needs of the experimental subjects.

Activities

A number of classroom activities emerged as particularly promising practices with deprived children. The heavy use of a simple box camera by the teacher paid dividends. After taking candid shots of individuals, of classroom activity, or of the children on their many trips, the photographs were posted on a bulletin board. The photographs immediately stimulated high interest and discussion; many of the children had not seen photos of themselves previously. The teacher frequently changed the snapshots on the board and placed the old pictures in a large class book.

Puppets were used to present dramatizations of well-known stories and to project conversation into imagined characters. Since shyness and inhibited expression typified the speech of some of the children when placed before the class, this medium provided a means of projecting expression and speech without personal exposure.

The class made a monthly "newsletter." Children drew pictures on ditto masters, and the related stories they dictated to the teacher were typed on these sheets. The results were sent home to parents, and single copies were given to other rooms in school. Descriptions of trips, personalities, and special classroom events were favorite subjects. The following example of a newsletter entry reflects the typical expressive style of the children, as well as the nature of the information which seemed important to them:

> I liked the trip to the building. It had lots of windows, and we could see the water. The building was in Milwaukee. The heater felt funny in the bathroom. It was to dry your hands. There were pictures. They were all different. We have some pictures in our house. There is a picture of my

■ TABLE 1   *A Framework for Curriculum Development: Kindergarten*

Developmental Areas Differentiating Culturally Deprived	Persisting School Situations[a]	Classroom Activities

Language Development	Receptive Language
	  Auditory Skills
	    Listening to get meaning from auditory
	    symbols
	      . . . for learning
	      . . . for fun in conversation
	  Visual Skills
	    Interpreting interpersonal meaning from
	    facial and bodily expressions
	    Recognizing relationships between
	    symbolic and concrete concepts and
	    objects
	    Gaining familiarity with traditional
	    cultural symbols
	      Flag
	      Santa Claus
	      Mottoes
	      Slogans, etc.
	Expressive Language
	  Verbal Expressive
	    Development of understandable
	    articulatory habits
	    Using words in sequence
	    Adapting speech to different social
	    situations
	  Motor Expressive
	    Drawing
	    Writing
	    Rhythms
		This column was completed by the classroom teacher as daily lesson plans.

mamma, and my daddy, and me. A lady was putting things in a box. We saw round things in a box. We saw cap waves on Lake Michigan. They were white and went high and low. Some hit the rocks and flashed. There were a lot of cars. Some were parked, some were going. There was a city bus, too. We went on the elevators. We went up and down. We sat down in it, and we were laughing. The building had a lot of windows and steps. They had a kitchen.

In order to give the reader a flavor of other kinds of activities developed by the classroom teacher, the following excerpts have been selected from her daily log.

October 23 — We had quite a good time in the afternoon while Julie frosted her cake. Jeffrey Bogan got hold of the mixer and Julie put the frosting on. The small problem of finding an electrical outlet led to a talk on why we needed one in the first place. How did the use of the electrical mixer make the work easier? Julie didn't know what a birthday spanking was and started to cry when it was mentioned.

TABLE 1 (*Continued*)

Developmental Areas Differentiating Culturally Deprived	Persisting School Situations[a]	Classroom Activities

Social Skills	Relating to peers
	Relating to authority figures
	Developing manners
	Functioning in a group
	  Sharing
	  Taking turns
	  Making choices
	Adapting to required social roles	

Self Concept	Developing:
	  Realization of individual uniquenesses
	  Independence from family
	  Realistic awareness of physique
	  Positive identification with academic success
	  Adjustment to success and failure situations
	  Self-awareness as a group member
	  Feelings of self-worth	

Cultural Differences	Developing an awareness of differences in cultural patterns
	  Eating habits
	  Dress
	  Recreation
	  Home activities
	  Personal relationships
	Expanding geographical limits
	Expanding psychological limits	

[a] This list is by no means complete. The possibilities for expansion are obvious.

December 6 — We went to Milwaukee via the Northshore. All went beautifully, and people were helpful and friendly. Individuals in stores and on the street and in the train were impressed with the manners and attitudes exhibited by the children. The store windows overwhelmed the children. Several said how pretty their mothers would look in some of the dresses we saw.

March 4 — Used the earphones. They picked the songs and stories they wanted to hear. They knew a lot of the songs and I was able to better hear [sic] what they could do along with the phonograph. Omar responded exceptionally well with a loud clear voice.

April 23 — The trip to the Buick dealers. We saw the new cars and watched mechanics at work. The mechanic gave each of them a book and we later looked at the books together.

These samples from the log reflect the teacher's attempts to provide situations which might stimulate growth in the four areas previously described — language development, social skills, self-concept, and cultural differences. The reader will also note references to the most frequent activity — field trips. Trips were assumed to be valuable in eliciting linguistic responses from children; language output could not be expected without provision for input. The planning and evaluation experiences relating to field trips provided key classroom opportunities for the growth of language facility.

Trips also provided chances for social skills to develop in a variety of contexts. Children learned to eat in restaurants and to use transportation facilities. They became adept at altering their behavior to meet the requirements of expected social roles in public places.

Further, trips provided a vehicle for self-concept development. The children were exposed to success in handling social situations, and felt positive responses from others. It was assumed that cultural differences were reduced as the geographic and psychological limits of the children expanded.

One of the most successful field trips took place when a group of university seniors majoring in education accompanied the children on a field trip to Chicago. The only instructions given to the university students were that they should choose a child, stay with him for the day, talk to him, and be good listeners. This experience provided excellent practice in learning to converse with adults. Here was an infrequent opportunity in the lives of most of the children — a chance to receive long and undivided attention from interested persons.

In all, over fifty trips were taken during the eight months the experimental kindergarten was in operation.[4] Total expenses for field trips amounted to $598.00.

Materials

Table 2 [p. 181] presents a listing of the kinds of materials and equipment utilized in this experimental kindergarten program. No attempt has been made to list all of the devices and aids used in the classroom — only those which might be different from the typical kindergarten furnishings have been listed.

Discussion

PARENTAL INVOLVEMENT. The experimenters decided at the beginning of this study that parental involvement would be one variable which could be controlled by simply assuming a typical school policy. That is, if the parents wanted contact with the schools, the schools were ready to provide this contact. If they wanted special help from any services provided by the school, it was provided. In turn, the school initiated routine home contacts which fell within the framework ordinarily assumed by schools in the Racine system. This allowed for a home visit by the teacher, a mid-year parent-teacher conference, and parent contacts for meeting unanticipated problems relating to health, school adjustment, or academic attainment. However, the project teacher and the investigators made a considerable effort to avoid contacts which extended beyond the frequency of those utilized in other local kindergarten classes.

---

[4] The project class began October 15, 1962, and ended in mid-June, 1963. The first few weeks of that school year were used in selecting experimental and contrast subjects.

■ TABLE 2   *Materials and Equipment Used in the Experimental Kindergarten*

Language Development	Self Concept	Social Skills	Cultural Differences

Books
Records
  — Listening games
  — Folk songs
  — Rhymes
Record players
Tape recorders (two)
Listening center
  (Earphones and distributor for small group work)
Montessori sensory education devices
Puppets and puppet stage
Number manipulation devices
	Negro family dolls
	White family dolls
	Puppets
	Full-length mirror
	Camera
	Tape recorder
	Private storage cubicles
		Safety signs
		Family dolls
		Costumes for role-playing
		Lunch tables
		Rhythm instruments
		Dolls representing various occupations
			Records
			Garden and farming tools
			Toys — cars, trucks, trains, tractors
			Sand table
			Cooking utensils
			Farm animals
			Rocking chairs
			Colored cubes
			Model workers

THE CONCEPT OF EXPANDING HORIZONS. As was previously described, field trips were probably the most important curricular vehicle in this pilot program.[5] Before the beginning of the school year, it was decided that, whenever possible, the children would be out of the classroom from one to two days a week. This goal was fairly well achieved; an average of 1.6 trips were taken weekly.

This initial commitment to trips as a catalyst for stimulating academic and psychological development also freed the thinking of project personnel from ordinary channels, and provided a crutch for maintaining a well-paced and stimulating program.

One assumption made by the authors in beginning this study was that the typical kindergarten nap was unnecessary. The school day was lengthened from the half-day kindergarten class to a full five-hour school day. In spite of this increase, the teacher was requested to introduce a nap only if the children seemed to require it. It was decided that naps would be avoided unless the children's behavior gave clear evidence of the need for rest. The experimental classroom teacher reports that throughout most of the school year no nap was required by these beginning kindergarten children despite the fact that they were attending school full days.

THE TEACHER. Miss Eleanor R.[6] was selected as the experimental classroom teacher. Since her background, philosophy, and attitudes undoubtedly had

[5] It is interesting to note that William Raschaert indicates that many of our assumptions about the value of field trips seem to be untested. He found only one paper of significance since 1938 in a recent review of studies on field trips (6).

[6] Miss R. is currently a staff member of the Laboratory School at the University of Chicago.

a great effect upon the curriculum as it was presented to the children, it is necessary to describe her. She had obtained her degree in primary and nursery school education, and was working on a master's degree in mental retardation. Miss R. had nine years' teaching experience.

Her attitudes toward the experimental kindergarten were open and accepting. Her teaching style was informal, with use of a wide range of vocal tones and facial expressions. Often, her face communicated nuances of emotion without the assistance of a spoken word. She laughed and scowled often. She spoke firmly one moment, gently and softly the next.

The preplanning and postevaluation of field trips were marked with Miss R.'s commitment to variety. She activated multisensory stimulation through the use of many projects and techniques within a short time span. Discussion, singing, rhythms, cut-paper projects, taped talks, creative drama, and role-playing were standard. Free play periods were not restricted to a set time allotment.

In summary, this article describes a curriculum specifically designed to meet the assumed educational needs of culturally deprived kindergarten children. A theoretical framework based upon the psychological differences between deprived and typical elementary school children was described. Discussion also considered activities, materials, and the teacher.

REFERENCES

1. Anastasi, Anne. "Heredity, Environment, and the Question 'How?'" *Psychological Review*, 65, No. 4, 1958.
2. Bernstein, Basil. "Social Class and Linguistic Development: A Theory of Social Learning," in A. H. Halsey, J. Floud, and C. A. Anderson (eds.), *Education, Economy and Society*. Glencoe, Ill.: The Free Press, 1961.
3. Harrington, Michael. *The Other America*. New York: The Macmillan Co., 1962.
4. Kirk, Samuel A. *Early Education of the Mentally Retarded*. Urbana: University of Illinois Press, 1958.
5. Larson, Richard, and James L. Olson. "A Method of Identifying Culturally Deprived Kindergarten Children," *Exceptional Children*, November, 1963.
6. Raschaert, William. Personal conversation, Detroit, 1962.
7. Sexton, Patricia. *Education and Income*. New York: The Viking Press, 1961.
8. Stratemeyer, Florence B., *et al. Developing a Curriculum for Modern Living*. New York: Bureau of Publications, Teachers College, Columbia University, 1957.

❖ ❖ 22 ❖ ❖

Poverty, Education, and the Young Child

BERNARD SPODEK

The decade of the sixties might be characterized as the decade of the disadvantaged inasmuch as societal concerns for children and for the poor are converging in public education today. Students of poverty are aware of its cyclical nature as the poor of one generation establish conditions which perpetuate poverty in the next generation. The need to break this cycle has brought the role of education into sharp focus.

Schools are developing programs for the disadvantaged. Programs for dropouts or for youth from the slums who might attend college are becoming familiar phenomena in high schools, as are enrichment and remedial programs in elementary schools in city slums. However, in dealing with the educational problems of the poor, the schools are becoming increasingly aware that they are arriving on the scene of development too late and providing too little to really effect significant change. A "new" approach is being heralded — the development of pre-primary educational programs for children of poverty.

HISTORICAL PERSPECTIVE. The attempt to meet the needs of the preschool disadvantaged children is not, however, a recent concern of early childhood educators. For more than half a century, the nursery school and kindergarten have been viewed by early childhood educators as one answer to the needs of impoverished children. At the turn of the century, Free Kindergarten associations were organized throughout the United States and England. These associations provided kindergartens in slum areas for children whose families could not afford the fees charged by private kindergartens.

The nursery school was originally conceived as an answer to the problems of the young child growing up in an urban slum community. The first nursery school was organized in the heart of a London slum to meet the needs of a disadvantaged population. Over the years, because of the lack of public support in the United States, nursery schools have catered to the middle class. The lack of public funds for nursery education created nur-

❖ From Educational Leadership, May, 1965, pp. 593–602. Reprinted with permission of the Association for Supervision and Curriculum Development and Bernard Spodek. Copyright © 1965 by the Association for Supervision and Curriculum Development. Bernard Spodek is Assistant Professor of Education, University of Wisconsin at Milwaukee.

sery schools which were available only to children whose families could afford to underwrite the total cost of schooling. The day-care center became the "nursery school" of the impoverished. This distorted picture has developed in the United States because of the exclusion of nursery schools and, in some communities and states, kindergartens from public education. Kindergartens are not supported by state aids in some twenty-six states. This has created a situation where at times the school systems in communities with the highest percentage of families in poverty have no kindergartens, while affluent communities in the same states have them.

JUSTIFICATION FOR PRESCHOOL PROGRAMS FOR DISADVANTAGED CHILDREN. If one is not prone to accept the evidence of historical concern, then it is well to look at several theoretical arguments that may be used to justify pre-primary education as a basis for raising the intellectual performance and academic achievement of disadvantaged children. Most of these positions relate to newer conceptions of intellectual development which attack the concept of fixed intelligence and suggest that experiences are the major determinant of a person's intelligence.

Piaget (12) has done extensive studies of intellectual development over the past several decades. His theory suggests that the child progresses through a series of stages in intellectual development. At each stage the child interacts with his environment, through the processes of assimilation and accommodation, bringing new ideas into his developing intellectual schema and changing these schema as they no longer fit the information gathered. While Piaget sees these stages as invariant, the rate at which children move through these stages can differ. Development, states Piaget, is influenced by four main factors: maturation, experience, social transmission, and equilibrium or self-regulation. Piaget reports such variations in a study of Iranian children, in which rural children were reported to be far behind urban children in their intellectual development due to a differentiated environment. In an American replication of one of Piaget's tests, Almy (1) found that, in a comparison of private school and day-care children (who would represent lower-class families), day-care children's thinking was less mature and qualitatively different from that of the private school children.

Hunt (8) has synthesized the theories of Piaget with other studies in learning and intellectual development. Hunt uses the model of the computer for his theory and compares thinking to data processing. Hunt suggests that the early years of development play a significant role in providing the generalized conceptual skills needed for later learning. He further suggests the need to provide environmental enrichment activities that are matched to the child's developmental level at each stage. Hunt's suggestion of the possibility of increasing intelligence for children through environmental manipulation appears to be a direct outgrowth of the evidence he presents. His assertion that Montessori education would be most appropriate for young children, especially those from impoverished background, does not necessarily follow from his data.

Bloom's recent study of human development (4), based upon longitudinal and other studies, presents the proposition that environmental variations can have their greatest effect during the period of rapid change for that characteristic. For many developmental characteristics, including height, intelligence, and intellectuality, as well as aggressiveness in males and dependency in females, fully half of the human organism's total development occurs before the child reaches school age. Even general school achievement is half developed by grade three. This would suggest that in order for environmental manipulation to have its greatest impact in the area of intelligence, it ought to occur during the preschool years. Since school achievement generally begins developing in grade one, educators can only speculate about the potential impact of preschool programs on this characteristic.

The research cited here suggests that a child's intelligence will vary as a function of his environment and that early environmental manipulation can have maximum impact in accelerating intellectual development. It further suggests that children who are impoverished economically are also impoverished in environmental stimulation. In order to develop preschool educational programs for poor children, one needs to know the significant ways in which the environment of poor children is different from that of the rest of society's children, and the particular kinds of intellectual stimulation that these children lack.

Deutsch (5) suggests that the urban slum offers the child a minimum of visual stimuli, with few pictures. The furniture, toys, and utensils of the small child are sparse, repetitious, and lacking in form and color. Few manipulative objects are available to these children, while the urban environment has removed the child from stimulating encounters with natural phenomena which were available to poor children in previous eras. The slum child also comes from a home that is not verbally oriented, causing difficulties in the child's auditory discrimination, just as the lack of visual stimuli creates difficulties in form discrimination and visual and spatial organization. Added to these are deficiencies in memory training, a lack of expectation of reward for performance, and an inability to use adults as a source of information, correction, and reality testing.

Bernstein (3) has studied differences in language development between the lower and middle classes and has defined these as differences in kind. He suggests that entirely different language systems exist within each of these classes. Bernstein has described the language of the lower class as a "public" language (later termed *restricted*), as contrasted with the "formal" language (later termed *elaborated*) of the middle class. The "public" language is characterized by short, grammatically simple sentences. It is limited and condensed, containing symbols of a low order or generality. It is a language of implicit meaning. The "formal" language is more accurate and grammatically correct. It is precise and can express a wide range of thought. The limitation of the "public" language will limit the kind of ideas that can be expressed and communicated, as well as the kind of thought that can be symbolized and ordered within it. The differences in language systems between these two segments of society can also cause a lack of understanding as individuals attempt to communicate between the two.

Hess's (7) studies of the mother-child interaction as a supporter of cognitive style and learning open another dimension to the problem of class-related environmental differences that might affect learning and intellectual development. To date, three aspects of successful teaching in these interaction situations have been identified. First, the mother must provide her young student with the tags or symbols for the important features of the lesson she hopes to teach. Secondly, there must be opportunities for her to receive feedback from the child. Finally, the mother must motivate the child to engage in the learning process. Hess's research tends to place intellectual development within the context of human interaction and suggests that, in a study of environmental differences, the significant human beings in a child's life and their various attributes must be considered as an important variable.

These variables of environmental stimulation, human interaction, and language activities provide the educator with guidelines upon which to propose effective programs for impoverished preschool children. In the past few years, several research or demonstration preschool programs have been developed. A review of these should provide additional insight into the effectiveness of the approach of using preschool education to maximize educational opportunity for the poor.

PRESCHOOL PROGRAMS FOR DISADVANTAGED CHILDREN. The traditions of the nursery school and kindergarten, and the years of experience that these traditions represent, plus the implication of the research reviewed here, provide a valuable resource for developing new programs for disadvantaged children. The rooting of the newer programs to be discussed in these traditions and this research can provide evidence of their appropriateness. Older conceptions of education, including the concept of "nurturance" as education stated by McMillan in her early works on the nursery school (10) need to be tested along with the newer conceptions presently being developed. Some important research on the effects of preschool programs has been done in the past, but this research has often been spotty and poorly designed. Fortunately, recent reviews of research in the area of nursery education, such as those by Sears and Dowley (13) and Swift (15), are readily available.

The research presented here as justification for preschool programs for disadvantaged children would suggest that there might be a different set of practices necessary for the optimum education of the children of the poor. While the projects devised to identify or demonstrate such programs are still in the "progress report" stage, providing at best inconclusive statements of results, a review of these programs should prove fruitful.

Deutsch's project (6) in cooperation with the New York City Public Schools is probably the best known of the preschool programs. This project contains a variety of more basic research studies along with its educational components. Deutsch utilizes a basic nursery school curriculum closely related to those found in high quality preschool programs. In addition to this, a variety of special enrichment techniques are provided. These techniques center around the areas of cognitive functioning, memory training, language development, and motivation. Although Deutsch has described specific elements of his program, a full description of his entire curriculum is not yet available, though it has been promised.

Olson and Larson (11), in their program for disadvantaged kindergarten children, focused on providing an abundance of field trips and supportive language experience for their children. This program was developed on the assumption that the children's limited experience had limited the development of a reservoir of concepts. By increasing the breadth of experience, it was assumed that there would be an increase in the children's accumulation of concepts necessary for successful school achievement.

The Baltimore Early Admissions Project (2) provides school experiences for disadvantaged four-year-olds. Descriptions of the curriculum established reveal a program based upon sound principles of early childhood education appropriate to all children. The focus on individual differences, firsthand experiences, and a sensory-rich learning environment, with particular attention to language development and the development of self-concept, suggest that the Baltimore adaptation is based as much upon individual differences as upon cultural differences.

Klaus and Gray's report (9) on their Early Training Project similarly suggests the use of major elements of the traditional approach to preschool education in their curriculum with some specific differences. The ratio of adults to children in this program is high, as it is in the Baltimore program. Other differences reported pertain primarily to the allocation of time for activities and the specific uses made of some of the materials. Strodtbeck's (14) "Reading Readiness Nursery" suggests by its title a specific program of prereading experiences. His program report indicates, however, that a "conventional nursery" experience was provided. Strodtbeck's suggestion that a particular teaching style, characterized as the "Yiddisha Mama" technique, might be particularly potent for poor children is a provocative one. The question of the effects of various teaching styles on young, culturally disadvantaged children could bear further investigation.

As already stated, these projects are now in progress. Results to date on the effect of these programs have been more indicative than conclusive. The common areas of the curriculum stressed are the development of cognitive skills, language facility, self concept, and motivational patterns, as well as an increase in environmental stimulation. Each of the programs described is firmly rooted in the conventions of the nursery school and kindergarten.

In conclusion, preschool programs for disavantaged children will become more numerous in the next few years. Federal money available through grants from the U.S. Children's Bureau and the Office of Economic Opportunity will provide a powerful stimulus to their development. It will be exceedingly important that the developers of these programs base new curricula on knowledge of the effects of long established traditional approaches to early childhood education as well as on newer practices that are shown to be effective by contemporary research. Presently developing research could be more valuable to the field if there were a concerted effort to factor out the effects of traditional nursery school practices from those of the more innovative practices.

REFERENCES

1. Almy, Millie. "Young Children's Thinking About Natural Phenomena: Interim Report." New York: Horace Mann-Lincoln Institute of School Experimentation (mimeographed).
2. Baltimore Public Schools. *An Early School Admissions Project: Progress Report, 1963–64.* Baltimore, Md.: 1964.
3. Bernstein, Basil. "A Public Language: Some Sociological Implications of a Linguistic Form," *British Journal of Sociology,* Vol. 10, No. 4; December, 1959.
4. Bloom, Benjamin S. *Stability and Change in Human Characteristics.* New York: John Wiley & Sons, 1964.
5. Deutsch, Martin. "The Disadvantaged Child and the Learning Process," in A. H. Passow (ed.), *Education in Depressed Areas.* New York: Bureau of Publications, Teachers College, Columbia University, 1963.
6. ———. "Nursery Education: The Influence of Social Programming on Early Development," *Journal of Nursery Education,* Vol. 19, No. 3; April, 1963.
7. Hess, Robert. "Maternal Teaching Style, Social Class, and Educability." Paper read at the Midwestern Association for Nursery Education Conference, May 2, 1964 (mimeographed).
8. Hunt, J. McVicker. "The Psychological Basis for Using Preschool Enrichment as an Antidote for Cultural Deprivation." *Merrill-Palmer Quarterly,* Vol. 10, No. 3; July, 1964.
9. Klaus, Rupert A., and Susan W. Gray. "Early Training Project: Interim Report." Nashville: George Peabody College for Teachers, November 1962 (mimeographed).
10. McMillan, Margaret. *The Nursery School.* New York: J. M. Dent & Son, 1921.
11. Olson, James L., and Richard Larson. "A Pilot Study Evaluating One Method of Teaching Culturally Deprived Kindergarten Children." Racine, Wisc., August, 1962 (mimeographed).
12. Piaget, Jean. "Development and Learning," in R. E. Ripple and V. A. Rockcastle (eds.), *Piaget Rediscovered.* Ithaca, N.Y.: Cornell University, 1964.
13. Sears, Pauline S., and Edith M. Dowley. "Research on Teaching in the Nursery School," in N. L. Gage (ed.), *Handbook of Research on Teaching.* Chicago: Rand McNally & Co., 1963.
14. Strodtbeck, Fred L. "Progress Report: The Reading Readiness Nursery: Short-Term Social Intervention." Chicago: University of Chicago, August 1963 (mimeographed).
15. Swift, Joan W. "Effects of Early Group Experience: The Nursery School and Day Nursery," in Martin Hoffman and Lois W. Hoffman (eds.), *Review of Child Development Research.* New York: Russell Sage Foundation, 1964.

A Nursery School on the
Ute Indian Reservation

ERMA CLARK

One of the most exciting and stimulating programs of which the writer has had an opportunity to be a part has been the setting up of the Ute Indian Tribe Nursery School in Fort Duchesne, Utah. One reason it has been of special significance is that the Nursery School has been pioneered and entirely financed by the Ute Indian Tribe. This is out of the ordinary because almost all other educational enterprises on other Indian reservations have been government initiated and operated.

We have been together but eighteen months. I wish every educator working with deprived and disadvantaged children could see the daily observable practical learning that is taking place. The increase in amount of verbalization and vocabulary is astounding. Also remarkable is added skill in large and small muscles. One of the greatest noticeable learnings is the increase in attention span. It isn't unusual to find many of the children spending twenty minutes to a half hour at the easel board, whereas when they first came it was unusual if they stayed a minute. Perhaps the biggest behavior change is in the attitudes of the children. We have put much emphasis upon providing an enriched environment in every direction to motivate and help the children to feel good about themselves. Large photos of each child placed beside their lockers have done much to further our objective. Frequently during the day children will be found by their lockers saying each other's names and fingering his or her own picture, thus giving each child a much-needed sense of identity. With a bit of encouragement, the children make a habit of putting their things away in their individual lockers. In the "creative" room the children put each puzzle and game back on the shelf before taking another. The children are learning to accept responsibility for their own actions. It's amazing how children this young have

✧ Reprinted by permission of the Association for Childhood Education International, 3615 Wisconsin Avenue, N.W., Washington, D. C. "A Nursery School on the Ute Indian Reservation," by Erma Clark. From *Childhood Education*, April, 1965, pp. 408–410. Also used by permission of the author. Erma Clark is Director, Ute Tribe Nursery School, Uintah-Ouray Indian Reservation, Fort Duchesne, Utah.

a sense of order and, if given an opportunity, with a little encouragement they like to keep things orderly.

We believe in providing an atmosphere where children can fall in love with life and with learning. We believe in teaching the Three L's — living, loving, and learning. This is a preparation for teaching the Three R's and, when they are ready for it, growth becomes a reality.

Equipment and Materials

Last fall the Ute Tribe leased an old, unused junior high school for the Ute Nursery School, which was housed in the gym and four rooms. In the gym there were a little red car; a pushable boat on rollers; sets of large and small suitcase blocks, tricycles, wagons and a fireman's gym — for big muscle development and dramatic play. In addition, there was a large airplane tire which was the children's delight.

One room was used for a housekeeping room in which everything was child-sized; another was used for creative activities — easel painting, puzzles, pegboards, clay, and games. Here we kept our lizards, hamster, parakeet, turtle, and chicks. Our animals and zoo have been our greatest asset. No matter how reticent a child, he responds to living things in such a way that he verbalizes freely and becomes more sociable as he happily loses his self-consciousness.

Another room was used as a rhythm and story room where were gathered all kinds of rhythm instruments, drums, castanets, bells, maracas, resonator bells, and tambourines, some of which we had made. The scarves, which we used for our rhythm and dance time, were solicited from parents and friends. The writer found that the use of these scarves as accompaniments to the rhythm instruments, played in a permissive atmosphere — with certain limits — where a sense of trust for each child prevailed, did much to help a child find himself.

Program — Attraction to Family

Because our program was novel for the Indians, mothers, grandmothers, sisters, and aunts came with the children. We finally had to have the Indian Home Agent come and set up sewing and cooking classes to keep the extended family occupied while the children were in session. It was our hope upon first coming to the Reservation that we could set up a parent cooperative nursery where mothers would participate one morning a week. We soon found they were not ready to get involved with this project as they had many problems and numerous other children. The first day seventeen mothers came with seventeen children and continued coming for the next two days.

As we went along the program became stronger; but not until after Christmas, when the novelty wore off for the mothers and they began staying home, did the program really develop. Despite a stormy political split within the tribal council and among the three bands of Indians, our program gained strength. Our chief supporter and advocate, director of the program

— the one who really initiated it — accepted a teaching position at a nearby university. This was a loss because he was a man of vision and educational background, fifty years in advance of the tribe in his thinking. At this time all educational and recreational activities of the Tribe were dropped except the Nursery School. But the parents, seeing that the program was really helping the children, voted to keep the preschool program.

Destruction and Restoration

We were just getting back on our feet again after a threatened setback, and we had gone out to visit each parent and child at Christmas. Then, for a reason that has not to this day been determined, on New Year's Day in seventeen degrees below-zero weather, a fire broke out in the Nursery School; within an hour everything was burned to the ground with total loss. The writer, who was away for the Christmas holidays when the news was broadcast, could not believe it. Luckily no children were in the building. The building and all the wonderful equipment were gone, however.

Soon phone calls began coming in from all over the town and state. It seemed that many people were concerned and wanted to know what help could be given to get the Nursery School back into operation again. The Mormon Church lent us a chapel, only recently remodeled. The Ute Business Committee voted funds to replace the lost material and equipment. The Tribe building supervisor with his staff built lockers, cupboards, a sand-and-water table, and other needed equipment and put down linoleum. The maintenance crew hauled from storage near the burned building some things that had escaped the fire. The teachers scrubbed, cleaned, polished, and painted. And in just three weeks we were back in operation again, with more comfortable facilities than before.

Present and Future Status

The Economic Opportunity Program is indeed adding new dimensions to preschool programs. The Navahos have requested funds for twenty-four classrooms. The Jicarilla Apaches, the San Carlos, the Papagos, two Sioux tribes, and the Utes have sent proposals and recommendations for nursery schools. Many more are in the process of writing up their proposals.

Contrary to what is generally believed, the Indian population is growing phenomenally. It is predicted that by 1975 there will be 750,000, or three-quarters of a million. Ten thousand teachers with no special training are teaching the Indians, who need to be taught by persons understanding the Indian value system.

In conclusion, I should like to quote a few lines by Robert Roessel, who is on the President's task force and one of the most knowledgeable persons in the United States on Indian Affairs.

Today, in our age of science and technology, we have become aware, if only slightly, of the interrelatedness of mankind. We have come to realize that what happens in the Congo or in the Fiji Islands intimately affects our life and our future. The oceans are as lakes and the mountains are as hills. The "one-world" concept is time and again commanding our thought and frequently our support.

Yet, despite this global familiarity we have utterly failed to understand our first American, the Indian. The American Indians provide the subject matter for the majority of TV plots, but these only compound the lack of understanding. . . .

Perhaps lessons learned from Indian Education may be an aid in helping our nation to understand and respect differences wherever we find them.

✧ ✧ 24 ✧ ✧

Preschool Programs for the Deprived Child in New Haven, Connecticut, Dade County, Florida, and Baltimore, Maryland

1. New Haven, Connecticut

In New Haven, Conn., pre-K education is deep into its third year. Most of the bugs have been ironed out, and some of the results are already proved. Over-all, the success is summed up this way by Adelaide Phillips, director of the program:

"Children from the pre-K program now enter kindergarten at a level they would normally not reach until January without preliminary schooling."

You get an idea of how important this is to the school system when you realize that many — perhaps most — of the three-year-olds who come into the pre-K program *do not even talk.* Thus, the basic purpose of the program is to bring children of limited advantage up toward the level of the typical school child so they do not find themselves in a situation where they cannot compete.

The New Haven program is part of the regular school system, uses teachers lured by the education department, and operates on methods worked out by Mrs. Phillips and the school curriculum department under Jeanette Galambos, curriculum assistant. It is concentrated entirely in areas of the city where economic and cultural limitations result in a large pro-

✧ From "What the Preschool Programs Learned About the Deprived Child in New Haven, Connecticut, Dade County, Florida, and Baltimore, Maryland," *Grade Teacher,* September, 1965. Used by permission of the publisher.

portion of children who are far from ready for kindergarten when they reach it.

Says Mrs. Phillips: "Of our parents, 27 per cent are twenty-six years old or younger and have eight to ten children. The children may live in two rooms, with four or five adults. Almost before they are a year old, they are on their own because mother is involved with the next baby."

She visited thirty-five homes in a spot check and found one toy: a battered red truck. Children played with the doorknob or climbed up and down on a chair.

"Imagine the way the world opens up for them when they come to school and first lay hands on something as elementary and as wonderful as a crayon!" says Mrs. Phillips.

"For our beginners, a field trip is a walk down the street with a teacher who points out to them that everything that flies is not a pigeon and tells them that the things on trees are called leaves and they are a color and the color is green."

In the schoolroom, the system is halfway between the tightly structured and the freely permissive. Children must know what is expected of them, what they can do, what they cannot do, how far they can go. The emphasis is on play. It must be play with a purpose, but it does not have to be play that produces some specific answer. Any of several answers will do.

As with most primary education, the primary tools are objects — the children's names, colors, purposes, how to handle them. At the beginning, the New Haven system treats the children as if they were just two and a half years old, instead of three or more. Things are kept simple and few, because the youngsters are easily confused. In a few weeks their capacity expands tremendously. Because there are budget problems, classroom equipment never becomes elaborate, but it always seems like a dream world to its small inhabitants.

Naturally, there are discipline problems, frequently those arising from law-of-the-jungle behavior. Patiently, over and over, the teachers talk to misbehaving children, pointing out that there are standards of conduct that must apply to all. Gradually, it takes.

In the opinion of Adelaide Phillips — and to the eye of any observer — the work done with pre-K mothers is at least as important as that done with the children. The program will not accept a child whose mother will not spend two and a quarter hours one day each week at the school. (This is sometimes — but rarely — waived.) During this time, mothers work with parent counselors. One thing stressed is behavior and discipline; the school hopes to instill in parents a respect for the same sort of control the school uses.

The parents observe their children and often feel that they are just playing. Then the counselor points out what the children are learning — why they are playing — how the play helps them. Again, they urge parents to take these ideas home with them.

A major parent-counselor activity is work with books. The counselors go over the children's books (which often are also the proper level for the parent), helping the mothers see how they can further the growth of their children by encouraging book time at home.

The work with parents has been so effective that about two hundred mothers and fathers roused themselves to go to the state capital to present their views at a hearing that involved an appropriation of money for state aid to schools.

There are sixteen centers operating in New Haven, serving about 480 children and their parents. Some of the funds come from the Ford Foundation and the New Haven Board of Education. Additional aid comes from the Office of Economic Opportunity. Centers are located in housing developments, church basements, community house gymnasiums — wherever space can be found. All must be within walking distance of the children who will attend; there are no transportation facilities. In some cases, rent is free, although there may be custodial costs. In other cases, a small rental is paid.

Each center has a staff composed of a regular teacher employed by the New Haven school system, a teacher's aide, a baby-sitting attendant — for parents who come to their weekly sessions and must bring their offspring — and usually a volunteer worker. In addition, there are part-time parent counselors, psychologists, nurses, and a physical education teacher who move from center to center on schedule.

In charge of it all is Adelaide Phillips, a graduate of Wheelock College, Boston, a two-time primary teacher with time out for a family between stints, a former principal of an elementary school in Glastonbury, Connecticut, and a grandmother.

During the past two years, the New Haven staff has made some basic discoveries in working with children of limited advantage:

1. Children do not do as well under total permissiveness in pre-K as they do when they know there are controls — and respect them.

2. Elaborate equipment and a wide range of materials do not stimulate creative activity as much as do a few fairly common and familiar items that do not puzzle the child.

3. A slow start is vital. A few weeks or months must be allowed for the child of limited advantage to get used to the idea.

4. The program is a loss unless it is based on some sort of verbalization or expression, even though it may be a poorly pasted picture of a dog.

5. Encouragement of thought — any thought — is important.

For now, Mrs. Phillips says she gauges the success of the program more on the relative uniformity of a "graduating class" than on its as yet short history in later grades. Some of her teachers' pupils enter the pre-K room average-bright. Others arrive terrified, speechless, or unresponsive. When, at the end of the year, these children are willing and eager to stand up in front of the class and sing a song, Adelaide Phillips believes she has accomplished something.

2. Dade County, Florida

Kindergarten is not a basic part of the public school system of Dade County (Miami area), Florida. Yet last year, for the first time, more than one thousand five-year-olds answered the clang of school bells. They were pioneers in what is known as the John F. Kennedy Preschool Program.

The youngsters had one thing in common: underexposure to the better things in life. The JFK program is designed to put them on more equal terms with children from the brighter side of the "Culture Curtain" before they get to first grade.

The program, financed and operated within the framework of the school system, resulted from a proposal made by the superintendent of schools calling for a $90,000 allocation to pay for staff and instructional materials.

However, almost anyone who has something to give to, or something to gain from, the program has become involved. Junior college students, specially trained, are paid class leaders; professional teachers are paid consultants; the staff of a TV show cooperates; volunteers give classroom assistance; parents are taught to help their children.

Counted as a blessing by the preschool class leaders are the "Time for School" telecasts by Miami's Channel 2. Three fifteen-minute "tele-lessons," designed especially for five-year-olds, are presented each day. One is planned for the "culturally different." Another presents arts and sciences for children of normal background. The third offers stories, games, songs, and reading-readiness experiences. All preschoolers must watch this last program.

Studio personnel prepare a *Time for School Guide* and monthly supplements for use by the preschool leaders and parents. In addition to program information, the guide offers supplementary activities.

Initial plans for the JFK program did not spell out rules for parent participation. However, it soon became apparent that everyone would benefit from interest in the homes.

In culturally deprived areas, parents tend to be reluctant to visit schools, yet parents of the JFK preschoolers soon began to do such things as accompany classes on field trips, furnish and serve refreshments, attend PTA meetings.

As a result of such voluntary cooperation, a "Preschool Parent Pilot Program" was developed. Only parents of pupils who had shown especially good progress were invited to participate. They met frequently with school personnel to discuss their children.

One of the devices used was a "Work Study Sheet." The work sheets offered conversation ideas ("talk to your child about color, such as *red* socks . . ."); they listed the names of inexpensive books available in supermarkets; and they offered ideas for home games.

End result: a better home and school relationship for the parents, as well as their children.

3. Baltimore, Maryland[1]

A child asks excitedly, "Did you see our chicks? First they were in the eggs."

Then other children chime in:

"But they pecked and pecked and they got out. It took a long time."

"They were ugly."

"Yes. Wet and ugly. But then they got dry."

"And fluffy and beautiful."

"They're soft. And they were tired. They got tired 'cause it was hard to peck so long."

Ideas come quickly, spilling from the lips of bright-eyed four-year-olds. They press foward eagerly to share an exciting experience with a visitor to their classroom.

This is new behavior for these children who, a few months earlier, had been inclined to depend heavily on gestures for communication, who could not identify chicks in picture books, and who did not use words such as "ugly," "beautiful," "fluffy," or "soft" to describe objects. These are some of the 328 youngsters who have participated in the Early School Admissions Project, an experimental program initiated in Baltimore schools in 1962 by Dr. George B. Brain, superintendent of public instruction.

The Early School Admissions Project is an attempt to discover to what extent early admissions to school can assist children from depressed areas to overcome limitations on learning imposed by factors in their environments. It is a research project designed to discover ways to:

1. Accelerate the achievement of children limited by environmental factors beyond their control.

2. Increase parental understanding of the values of education.

3. Facilitate communication between the school and community agencies as they work together to help children.

There are currently four Early Admissions Classes, one in each of four elementary schools located in areas of the city populated by low-income families, many of whom are dependent upon public assistance. A class contains approximately thirty children and is staffed by two teachers, a teacher's aide, and volunteer personnel. Children who participate are selected on the basis of age, environmental privation, and freedom from gross mental or physical impairments.

WHAT THEY DO. In an Early Admissions Center, children participate in a wide variety of firsthand experiences. These experiences are occurring throughout the entire time the children are in school. Some are initiated by children, some are initiated by the teacher, and some arise from situations in the environment.

[1] This section was written by Catherine Brunner, Project Coordinator, Early School Admissions Project, Baltimore Public Schools.

For example, Vernon came to school wearing new shoes. He burst into he room and ran to his teacher, bubbling with excitement. Time was pro-ided for Vernon to show his shoes to the children and to talk about them. Children wearing shoes that were the same color or style as Vernon's shoes dentified them. The children described the new shoes as "shiny," not "messed up," and not "beat up." Several children spontaneously placed :heir shoes next to Vernon's to see who had the longest shoe.

On another occasion, the teacher brought a rabbit to school. By means of observation, the children identified distinguishing features of the animal. Several frames of a filmstrip and demonstrations by the teacher helped them learn to handle the animal properly. Pictures and information read from a book by the teacher enabled them to decide what kinds of food rabbits need. Some children helped a teacher prepare a cage for the rabbit. Others helped to obtain food for the rabbit at nearby stores.

An unanticipated event frequently gives rise to a learning situation. One day, while the children were outside playing, heavy winds began to blow. Children saw toys toppling over. They chased hats that blew off, and they observed the effects of the wind on paper, on clothes on wash lines, and on trash cans.

Within the context of each experience, children are encouraged to ques-tion, seek solutions to problems, test ideas, and discover relationships. They are helped to name objects, feelings, or actions accurately and to learn words that will describe them. They are guided to form accurate concepts and extend their knowledge of their environment.

NEW DIMENSIONS. Music, art, and literature add new dimensions of experi-ence. Opportunities for self-expression and for the acquisition of knowledge and skills are provided as children become acquainted with books, music, and the use of a variety of art media. These areas of the curriculum make possible a wide range of vicarious experiences involving people, places, situations, and feelings.

There are opportunities each day for the pleasure of selecting books to enjoy alone, as well as time to share books with others. Frequently, tape recordings are produced in which a child tells his own version of a favorite story or the teacher reads or tells a story.

Through the use of paint, crayons, chalk, and other art materials, children develop an awareness of color, form, and design. Tactile experience is ex-tended as materials of different textures are handled and their possible uses are explored.

No attempt is made to teach children to draw or to use patterns to pro-duce an end result. Each child is encouraged to use materials in ways that are meaningful for him. When he wishes to talk with others about his work, he is encouraged to speak freely.

Songs, rhythmic response to music, and the use of rhythm instruments to interpret movement and feelings provide additional means for self-expres-sion. No effort is made to establish stereotyped movement in rhythmic response; the child is encouraged to respond as he sees fit in terms of the music. Children learn to discriminate differences in pitch, tempo, and intensity.

MATHEMATICAL RELATIONSHIPS. The meanings of mathematical relationships begin to emerge as children solve problems each day. How many cups of cocoa do we still need? How many children can work with the clay at one time? How many are at the clay table now? How many more may come? Who will take the second turn to slide? Into which space will the big blocks fit best?

Children are encouraged to learn and to use an accurate vocabulary in order to express ideas related to quantitative relationships, time, space, position, or size.

A portion of each day is reserved for self-selected activities. During this period, children move from one activity to another as they wish, selecting their own pursuits and spending as much or as little time with an activity as their interests and needs require. Children select from a wide variety of activities. They work with puzzles, beads, and other manipulative materials. They use blocks and large play equipment, look at books, listen to recording stories, and work in the housekeeping area. They talk to one another or to adults, listen to an adult read or tell a story, and examine interesting objects. They observe and care for class pets and participate in water play.

THEY DEVELOP AWARENESS. Permeating the entire Early Admissions Program is the effort to enable each child to develop a positive self-concept. This is fostered by an atmosphere in which each child feels welcome, is free to explore, can question and disagree, and has time to pursue his own interests as well as participate in group activities. He can make mistakes and learn to correct them; he can express his feelings within reasonable limits and grow in his ability to cope with them; and he can receive recognition for his successes and assistance with his failures.

Self-identity is basic to self-concept. Therefore, children need to hear their names when they are greeted each morning or when they are addressed. They need to become aware of their physical appearance by means of classroom mirrors and pictures or films of activities in which they are involved. Self-identity is strengthened when children have special places to keep their possessions and when the work they do is labeled with their names.

THE PARENTS' ROLE. The building of a self-concept is also an important aspect of work with parents. Parents influence greatly the development of their children. Therefore, parent education assumes great importance in the functioning of the Early School Admissions Project.

Parents of children who live in depressed areas are not always "school-oriented." They may have been unhappy in their own school experiences. They may sense limitations that have resulted from meager educational experiences, and, as a result, find the school environment uncomfortable.

However, they do want their children to experience a better way of life. Education is identified by the parents as a means to the realization of this better life.

One project center is located in a new school building. A meeting was devoted to acquainting parents with the new building so that they might be made aware of the facilities and how both children and adults may use them.

Several meetings have provided opportunities for parents to join their children for lunch. During these luncheons, parents saw how teachers encouraged good eating habits.

The staff of one center learned that many children were not eating adequate breakfasts or had none at all. Time was devoted to helping parents become aware of the importance of breakfast. Suggestions were made as to appropriate foods and foods that could be prepared with a minimum of time and effort.

Group meetings also have been devoted to helping parents gain knowledge on child growth and development. They learned ways in which they could help their children to learn such things as names and addresses, correct names for common objects, correct names for colors, and to speak distinctly.

The Early School Admissions Project represents a program of preventive education. Can it prevent or alleviate impediments to learning that seem to stem from environmental privation? Studies will determine this, but already experience has shown that children who have participated in the program:

1. Attend kindergarten.
2. Make a better start in kindergarten. They have fewer adjustment problems, greater verbal ability, increased independence, and increased ability to participate in group activities.
3. Seem to score better on readiness tests.
4. Seem to make a better start in reading.

One year of the Early Admissions Program can insure a better start in school. Continued achievement on the part of children depends upon each teacher and the quality of the work she develops with the children and the parents.

Early admission to school is just the beginning. The opportunity for a better beginning will be extended to 360 additional children during the 1965–1966 school year as new centers are opened.

Baltimore has taken significant first steps. It is attempting to reinforce this beginning with inservice training for teachers at levels beyond the prekindergarten stage. What will be the end product? Greater equalization of educational opportunity for children from impoverished environments. This is the hope and the goal of the Early School Admissions Project.

✧ PART FIVE

Education and the Older Child

Several pieces of federal legislation relating directly to the disadvantaged have been passed recently. The Economic Opportunity Act of 1964 and the Elementary and Secondary Education Act of 1965 may well prove to be among the most significant educational achievements of this generation. The selection from the *ALA Bulletin* and the one by Robert E. McKay offer the practitioner overviews of these and other acts, with directives for possible action. The April, 1965, issue of *American Education* stated that Title I alone of the Elementary and Secondary Education Act of 1965 would provide for state school expenditures ranging from 1.3 per cent of the total state expenditure in Nevada to 19.3 per cent in Mississippi.

The problem of providing compensatory education for the urban disadvantaged is discussed by Bernard A. Kaplan, Frederick Shaw, and David P. Ausubel. According to Shaw, "The number one problem faced by urban teachers today is how to offer culturally deprived youth an education that meets their needs." Such topics as teaching strategy, consultant help, parent involvement, community involvement, identification of needs, motivation, and guidance are discussed. The Great Cities School Improvement Program and the Higher Horizons Program are described, along with the problems encountered in their implementation. Shaw believes that one possibility for altering the course of intellectual retardation in the disadvantaged pupil is to focus on the cognitive rather than on the motivational aspects of learning; that is, to ignore the student's unmotivated state for a time and concentrate on effective teaching. Then perhaps he will learn, despite his lack of motivation, and the satisfaction of learning may help to develop the motivation to learn more.

A problem that has gained less educational focus than the plight of the urban disadvantaged but one that is of critical concern to the entire nation is the problem of educating the rural disadvantaged. In an article from the *NEA Journal*, Robert M. Isenberg points out that:

> To focus only upon the problems that rural migrants create after they have moved to the city is much the same as treating a disease without concern for its cause. For, whereas many rural disadvantaged will continue to stream into our cities, millions more will remain in the country and seek subsistence there.

201

Joe L. Frost and O. Ray King cite results from a continuing study of rural welfare recipient children that appear to be representative of general findings among very low income rural groups. An additional observation is that the delinquency rate is considerably lower among rural groups than among urban groups. Factors associated with crowded living appear to be largely responsible for the higher incidence of delinquency. Progress in school can be significantly increased by the provision of an enriched environment for the disadvantaged rural student, but environmental restriction in infancy and early childhood imposes indelible effects upon the growing child. The enriched school program can only alter, not erase; by age six, the harm has been done.

Frost, Cyrus Karraker, and George E. Haney direct attention to the education of the migrant child. They discuss the scope of the problem, family living patterns, corrective programs, and practical recommendations. Much that can be done depends upon legislative action and initiation of corrective educational programs. Fortunately, legislative action has been taken and corrective programs have been initiated at an unprecedented rate. The preliminary results of patterns of action that have been established promise the freeing of vast quantities of previously wasted human potential.

Another of the "pockets of poverty" in this country is vividly described by Peter Schrag. The schools of Appalachia still maintain "pot-bellied stoves" and "outdoor privies" as standard pieces of equipment. Teachers hold school in one- and two-room schools where several grades are grouped together and older pupils often teach the younger ones. For teachers in these schools, political alignment may decide job permanence. Although attitudes of suspiciousness toward change will affect the redirection of education in these remote areas, federal support promises hope for better tomorrows.

In the last selection in Part Five, Doxey A. Wilkerson suggests needed emphases in research on the education of disadvantaged children and youth, adding that the disadvantaged child himself may well be a target for change, but perhaps we would do better to modify the school to fit the child rather than to modify the child to fit the school.

✧ ✧ 25 ✧ ✧

Federal Legislation and Programs for Underprivileged Young People

There are several pieces of federal legislation and several different governmental programs that relate directly to the disadvantaged and seriously underprivileged young people about which every professional librarian should be knowledgeable. Chiefly they are embodied in the following pieces of legislation: the 1962 Welfare Amendments, the 1963 Vocational Education Act (certain sections only), the Manpower Development and Training Program, and the provisions of the . . . Johnson Poverty Bill (Economic Opportunity Act of 1964).

In addition to the above there are several other federal programs which deal directly with or at least touch tangentially on the disadvantaged or the "culturally different" child. Some of these are the Kennedy Mental Health Act and the Juvenile Delinquency Act, as well as numerous projects of the National Institute of Mental Health. However, space will not allow these programs to be dealt with in this article.

1962 Welfare Amendments (P.L.87–543)

This act amending the public welfare provisions of the Social Security Act is administered by the Bureau of Family Services of the Welfare Administration. These amendments constitute the first extensive overhauling of our public assistance program from early New Deal days to the present time. They emphasized and gave federal support to the concept of public assistance as a program designed to save, recast, and reeducate welfare families so as to make as many of them as possible self-supporting. The amendments are aimed especially at doing something for families receiving welfare aid under the program of aid to families with dependent children (AFDC). Special emphasis is placed on proper education of children in families receiving public assistance so that the children do not in their turn fall into the pattern of public dependency. Some of the noteworthy provisions of these amendments are:

AID TO FAMILIES WITH DEPENDENT CHILDREN — UNEMPLOYED PERSONS (AFDC–UP). The amendments extended a temporary program which had been en-

✧ From the ALA Bulletin, September, 1964, pp. 705–711. Used by permission of the publisher, the American Library Association.

acted the previous year. Under this program the federal government will share in assistance payments to families with children under eighteen where the family is in need because of the father's unemployment. The expansion of the older AFDC program to encompass these families of the unemployed is optional with the states and requires state enabling legislation; so far eighteen states have qualified under the AFDC–UP provisions. As the program becomes better known, and as more fathers seem to be somewhat permanently unemployed, it is expected that additional states will avail themselves of this new welfare program.

COMMUNITY WORK AND TRAINING PROGRAMS (CWT). This is an innovative and enterprising method for giving constructive work and training experience to heads of households and other adults in public assistance families. Work and training of employable, adult welfare recipients is chiefly in public service type of employment. CWT has proven to be immensely popular among those involved in the program (and with welfare officials) in the places where it has been tried, particularly in the state of Kentucky which has extended this program to most of its severely impoverished counties. Some adults have been trained through this program for rather significant private employment opportunities. But whether employable after a CWT training program or not, the morale and attitude factor alone should be sufficient to recommend this type of public assistance formula over the older type of straight "relief" formula.

SPECIAL DEMONSTRATION PROJECTS. The 1962 amendments permit special demonstration programs; among those in progress are various youth programs designed to keep young teen-agers from public assistance families enrolled and achieving in junior and senior high schools. In one of these special demonstration programs, young boys and girls from AFDC families and from welfare families are given subsidized public service type employment, mostly within the school itself, which adds immeasurably to their ability to keep themselves on a social and economic par with their more economically fortunate schoolmates. This subsidized employment continues only as long as they continue in high school or in a high school equivalent vocational training program. This program helps to develop good work habits and attitudes toward future private employment.

These special demonstration programs, unlike the other 1962 welfare amendment programs can be 100 per cent federally financed for a period of time not to exceed three years. Federal financing for other welfare programs is on a federal–state matching basis.

While these special "welfare" youth programs are quite new, those in progress in several states seem to indicate that young people in public assistance families have as much academic talent as their nonwelfare peers — if they are properly motivated to stay in school and strive.

DAY-CARE CENTERS. During World War II mothers were encouraged to venture out of the home and to accept employment connected with the war effort. To assist mothers to do this, day-care centers were opened in almost every urban area in the country. After the war, however, federal financing for these centers was eliminated for economy reasons. Still another reason was that they were thought to be unnecessary because mothers were supposed to be able to stay home in the model postwar world. As a result of the withdrawal of federal financing, public day-care centers ceased to exist in nearly all states except a few which continued to extend help on their own.

Day-care centers are again very necessary, however, because the truth is that ever increasing numbers of married women with children do (and for various reasons, must) work outside of the home. Under the 1962 amendments federal funds are earmarked for state use in developing day-care services for public assistance mothers.

With their children placed in day-care centers, many mothers who wish to avail themselves of the opportunity are free to participate in basic education and training programs which can also be established for AFDC mothers under the new programs encompassed in the 1962 amendments.

1963 Vocational Education Act (P.L.88–210)

Congress acted swiftly after the assassination of President Kennedy to enact several long pending educational provisions, which he had advocated, as a sort of educational memorial to this young education-minded president. This act was one of the educational measures so enacted last December.

Congress made it plain in this act that any disadvantaged person could be given vocational education under this act whether still in school, out of school, or merely in need of retraining. Congress realized that there are many young people out of school and out of work who need additional training in order to make themselves employable. This program can even be utilized by local educational authorities to set up training programs for those who are now employed but who seek additional training so as to upgrade their skills.

Four provisions of this 1963 Vocational Education Act are directly applicable to disadvantaged young people:

WORK–STUDY PROVISIONS. The law provides several million dollars for a nationwide work-study program for needy young people between the ages of fifteen and twenty-one who are enrolled full time in vocational programs. This part-time employment must be public service type employment and can include both school libraries and public libraries. This aid is limited to a maximum of $350 per academic year or $500 per year if the young person is a resident student.

RESIDENTIAL VOCATIONAL SCHOOLS. The same section of the act which provides for the work-study program also provides for the building of five experimental residential vocational schools. These schools would be built and completely equipped with federal funds, as well as maintained with federal funds up to a maximum of $2000 per pupil per year. They would be operated by state and local school authorities.

In filling these schools, boys from unwholesome urban slum environments who need better environmental conditions as a prerequisite for study are to be given priority consideration. The schools are to be considered model vocational education schools in every way, and can be expected to pioneer new teaching methods and programs. Congress requested that one school be built in the Washington, D.C., area; the locations of the other four residential schools have not yet been announced.

AREA VOCATIONAL SCHOOLS. A large percentage of the funds payable to the states under this vocational program are earmarked for the first few years for the construction and equipping of area vocational schools. These schools represent a rapidly developing concept in American public education. It constitutes recognition by Congress that in many parts of the country small, inefficient, poorly supported educational units, such as we relied upon in the past, cannot do the vocational and technical educational job required for today's world. Hence an area vocational school concept is being explored.

Where the school districts are now large and geographically comprehensive, such as cities, only minor administrative changes will be brought about by the construction of new area type schools, but in some states the combined cooperation of several school districts or even multiple-county cooperation will be required.

COMMISSIONER'S ROLE. The Commissioner of Education will receive 10 per cent of all vocational education funds appropriated under this act ($118,-500,000 authorized in fiscal 1965, $225,000,000 authorized after fiscal 1966) for purposes of research into the field of vocational and technical education. This will include the ability to fund demonstration programs. It is anticipated that the commissioner may well give initial consideration of this vocational research and demonstration money to finding new ways to involve "hard core" youth who are known to be concentrated at the lower end of the I.Q. scale.

The Manpower Development and Training Act of 1962 (MDTA) and the 1963 Amendments to this Act

This is the principal adult manpower development and youth training program of the federal government for out-of-school youth who are already in the labor force. Passed by Congress as part of the 1961 antirecession program, MDTA has been difficult to operate to its maximum potential because it calls for such a high level of intrabureau federal cooperation between the Labor Department and the Department of Health, Education, and Welfare. It also requires considerable state and local cooperation since all certification and training are on the local level by state agencies and local educational bodies.

SOLANO COLLEGE
100 Whitney Avenue
Vallejo, California 94590

The 1963 Congress authorized extensive improvements in this program, mostly so that it could be utilized to train larger numbers of unemployed out-of-school youth. The 1963 amendments permit local utilization of this program to be largely directed at disadvantaged youth. They also permit additional basic literacy training of any adult up to a maximum of twenty-two weeks (hence previously untouchable functional illiterates can now be included in MDTA training programs).

After fiscal 1965, the states that wish to continue taking advantage of this important program for unemployed men, women, and young people will have to match a portion of the federal funds, but up to that time the federal government underwrites 100 per cent of the cost of the training. Up to the present time most of MDTA training has been in established educational institutions; this institutional-based training has been quite expensive, often because the size of the class or the project was so small. Forty-nine states have used MDTA training to a greater or lesser degree, depending on the ability of local educational officials to initiate training projects.

LABOR DEPARTMENT YOUTH OPPORTUNITY CENTERS. The Labor Department, using MDTA funds, has just embarked on a multimillion dollar program to open special youth opportunity centers in the slums of 105 urban areas across the country. The 105 Standard Metropolitan Statistical Areas (SMSA) have been so selected that every state will have at least one center. Fifty-five centers will be located in fifty-five large metropolitan areas of 500,000 or more population. Thirty additional centers will be in SMSA's of 200,000 to 500,000 population.

These centers are to be staffed with men and women uniquely qualified to deal with the dropout and other marginally educated youths who need "special handling" in order to place them in jobs or (mostly) in suitable job training programs. The centers are to be located in city slum and urban "gray" areas. The idea here is to recruit actively and be available to seriously disadvantaged youths who are not presently availing themselves of present state employment offices. These centers will be a special youth project part of the local state employment office.

Certainly this national experiment by the Labor Department to deal realistically with hard core unemployed youth before they become seriously alienated is to be both applauded and anxiously watched.

The Antipoverty Program
(Economic Opportunity Act of 1964)

R. Sargent Shriver has been designated by President Johnson as the White House anti-poverty man who will be appointed to head this important new economic program once Congress approves his nomination. President Johnson approved the Act in a signing ceremony at the White House August 20, and a supplemental budget will be requested to implement the program.

The final version, passed by the House on August 8, is essentially that approved by the Senate on July 23 with the addition of several amendments, including extension of the veto power of state governors to cover private as well as public agency programs under Titles I and II, and a loyalty oath requirement. The disclaimer would apply only to three categories: enrollees in the Job Corps; an individual, like a consultant, who receives some direct benefit from appropriated funds; and, possibly, members of the new volunteer corps named VISTA.

There are four parts of the Economic Opportunity Act which should have special significance for school librarians, whether rural or urban, who seek to keep informed on important economic opportunities for both young people and unemployed or underemployed adults in their community. These special parts or provisions are:

> Under Title I ($412,500,000)
> Part A — Job Corps
> Part B — Work Training Program
> Part C — Work-Study Program
> Under Title II ($340,000,000)
> Part A — Urban and Rural Community Action Programs
> Part B — Adult Basic Education Programs
> Under Title V ($150,000,000)
> Work Experience Programs (for Adults)
> Under Title VI ($10,000,000)
> The Volunteer Program (Volunteers in Service to America — VISTA)

JOB CORPS. The administration expects that thirty to forty thousand young people between the ages of sixteen and twenty-one will be enrolled in this camp program by the end of the first year of operation. For those who volunteer and are selected, the Job Corps will offer a rewarding opportunity for education, vocational training, useful work, physical training, and recreation. The enrollees will live in either conservation or training centers in both rural and urban areas. The conservation centers of approximately 100 to 200 youths each will offer a healthy, out-of-door type of life where the discipline of work and new skills will be learned while our nation's parks, forests, and other natural resources are being improved. In some centers it is expected that educational and vocational training will be provided through local public educational agencies or private vocational or institutional agencies. Similarly, some centers will be planned and managed by other institutions which have appropriate resources to contribute to youth education and guidance programs for disadvantaged youth.

While library people at the national level naturally will be interested in making certain that an adequate budget for books and librarian assistance is included in the national planning entailed by this vast peacetime camp program, librarians at the local level, where these camps or centers are to be located, should also be concerned about library facilities for these camps.

The camp program is expected to attract dropouts who will require considerable reeducating and basic employment readiness type of training. The federal government is committed to try to establish a certain number of these Job Corps camps for girls who likewise require residential type preemployment readiness training.

THE WORK TRAINING PROGRAM. The work training program under Title I is designed to give unemployed young men and women aged sixteen through twenty-one (including both those in school and those out of school) a chance to escape poverty by providing them with an opportunity to work and to receive training experience not now available to them in private employment or under any existing federal program.

The work training programs, which will be started in hundreds of local areas in the country under this program during the next two years, are designed to occupy young people who might not have been significantly involved in vocational education programs or might not yet qualify for an MDTA training program — in other words, they are designed to catch young people who have fallen between the cracks of existing training programs.

The work offered young people in this program is designed to increase their chances for eventual private employability by enabling them to acquire new skills and work habits on a job. It will also give them a feeling of belonging to their community through significant public service type of work projects, performing important public services which are necessary but which might otherwise never be performed or provided. Under present plans many of these training projects and centers will be actually run by public and private nonprofit agencies. These agencies will act as official sponsors and will contract with the federal government for operational funds, etc.

The projects will be distributed equitably among the states, taking into account the needs of youth. The distribution of work training places within states will depend both on the severity of the state's poverty problem and local interest. Work places can be in libraries, hospitals, playgrounds, and local government offices and departments such as recreation, health, sanitation, public works, schools, county parks and forests, settlement houses, and other places where public services can be performed without displacing other workers from existing jobs.

Those enrolled in the Job Corps described above will receive compensation of $50 per month over and above all food, clothing, and complete living expenses such as health services and travel expenses, etc. Those who participate in the local work training programs are to be paid rates which are "appropriate and reasonable in the light of relevant factors." (This will probably mean something like 75 cents per hour.) The entire cost of recruiting, transporting, housing, training, and paying the enrollees of the Job Corps will be borne by the federal government, but the cost of the local youth work training program will be shared. The federal share cannot exceed 90 per cent for the first two years of the program; thereafter the federal contribution cannot exceed 50 per cent. The local contribution may be either in cash or in kind, including rent or educational services, etc.

It is anticipated that the Labor Department will utilize the services of the 105 special Youth Opportunity Centers located in urban slums and gray areas to help recruit for these work training program positions. The administration expects to be able to accommodate 200,000 young people in this program during the first year at these local training centers.

As for library inclusion on a systematic basis, it will be up to the local library authorities to seek local participation in their community's planning program for a work training center or project.

WORK-STUDY PROGRAM. This will be largely a reconstitution of the prewar National Youth Administration program which aided countless thousands of young people to complete their college education. (It will be limited to college level education.) One hundred forty-five thousand young college students will be assisted by this work-study program during the first year of operation. Colleges and universities will be urged to permit only young people who are in actual financial need to be employed with federal subsidy under this program. The program is directed toward those young students who require this kind of financial assistance in order to enroll in a college or to continue in a college program once enrolled. The earnings of an undergraduate will be $500 per year and of a graduate student, $1000 per year. The number of graduate students envisioned the first year is 15,000 (included in the 145,000 figure). Ninety per cent of the cost of this program would be underwritten for the first two years by the federal government and 75 per cent, in succeeding years, providing the work performed is for the college itself; if the work is performed outside of the college the subsidy cannot exceed 50 per cent.

With this kind of student-assistant help in the offing, life should soon be somewhat brighter indeed for many college librarians.

COMMUNITY ACTION PROGRAMS (CAP) AND ADULT BASIC EDUCATION PROGRAMS. Outside of the vast Job Corps program and the enterprising work training center program, the CAP program is by far the most imaginative both in its concept and in its importance. It could turn out to be the most important new utilization of library services and abilities in decades. With $315 million to spend for urban and rural programs (90 per cent federally financed for the first two years) along with twenty-five million dollars earmarked for adult basic education, many communities where there are sizeable impoverished groups that desire an action program will be able to qualify. In cases of extreme regional poverty, the director of the Office of Economic Opportunity can forgive the local 10 per cent share (again, either in cash, in services, or in kind). While it is intended that these local community action programs are to be many faceted and comprehensive (i.e., schools, public welfare, libraries, social agencies, etc., utilizing a many-sided approach), money can be given for initial action programs or projects while planning for greater local agency and organizational involvement.

It is assumed that every comprehensive CAP program in either an urban or a rural area will include the schools in some form or another. Certainly it is the desire of those planning the operation of the poverty program on the national scene that schools be included in all community action programs designed to combat poverty.

The language of the bill as it stands at the time of the publication of this article provides that CAP can conduct programs in the fields of employment, job training and counseling, health, vocational rehabilitation, housing, home management, welfare, and certain kinds of educational programs, namely "special remedial programs" and "noncurricular educational assistance for the benefit of low income individuals and families." It is believed that this language will permit all kinds of "noncurricular" educational programs of both a remedial and enrichment nature. While general aid to a school system is specifically prohibited, programs with special emphasis on reading and library usage, preschool programs (including nursery programs), and after-school programs (with the library again involved) will be possible in communities where there are substantial numbers of poor people. Preservice teacher training and in-service teacher training might also be permitted in order to serve the pressing needs for qualified teachers in schools in low-income areas.

Certainly the inclusion of schools in CAP programs on a par with health, welfare, and employment groups should serve to encourage forward-looking educators to plan for wider community involvement and cooperation in helping schools to solve existing educational shortcomings of a long standing nature. The possibilities for new types of special educational programs for assistance to disadvantaged youth which can be funded under the poverty bill is truly exciting, and school librarians should have an increasingly large role to play in these new programs.

FAMILY UNITY THROUGH JOBS. The welfare administration will administer this part of the poverty bill and will have $150 million to implement adequately the 1962 welfare amendment program of Community Work and Training (CWT) in many more states than have previously availed themselves of this type of welfare program.

It is estimated that approximately twenty thousand men who would be responsible in turn for about 114,000 dependents could be accommodated during the first year of an expanded CWT program. In addition to the male-centered CWT program, about thirty thousand AFDC mothers who are seeking employment and who could benefit from basic education and work training will be accommodated under Title V. It is estimated that at the present time 100,000 AFDC mothers are employable if they had proper re-education and training (i.e., their family responsibilities permit outside employment and their personal health and age offer no employment bar).

VOLUNTEERS IN SERVICE TO AMERICA (VISTA). The VISTA program is a re-naming of President Kennedy's previously proposed Domestic Peace Corps. Five thousand volunteers working at local, state, and federal levels are envisioned, costing a total of $5 million. Half of the volunteers would be subject to state approval and will be paid by the state or local community following their period of training. The state and local communities are expected to draw on some of these VISTA individuals to help staff the teaching and administrative positions to undertake the local work and training program and some of the CAP programs. All volunteers, whether state or federal, will receive fifty dollars per month plus living allowances and maintenance.

The programs briefly sketched above constitute the chief federal programs concerning the culturally disadvantaged now in existence or in the process of being planned. While several have direct significance for school librarians, all of these programs should be understood (if only in part), if the school library is to fulfill its proper school informational and educational role. The public schools are about to undertake a vastly expanded role of providing leadership, of doing something about cultural deprivation and generation after generation of dependence and idleness. School librarians must be prepared to play their proper role in this exciting leadership movement.

✧ ✧ 26 ✧ ✧

The President's Program: "A New Commitment To Quality and Equality in Education"

ROBERT E. MC KAY

When all the arguments over formula have been forgotten and current concerns over constitutionality resolved, enactment of the Elementary and Secondary Education Act of 1965 will, without question, go into the books as the most significant educational achievement of any Congress in this century, indeed if not in the entire history of the nation.

The action marks the assumption by the federal government of its appropriate and long-overdue role in assuring adequate educational opportunity for all American children.

It reflects recognition at the highest levels of what citizens across the country have insisted for years, that educational needs in an increasingly complex society are national in scope and cannot be met from state and local financial resources alone.

The decision of the Eighty-Ninth Congress, by overwhelming majorities in both houses, to approve President Johnson's education program tran-

✧ From *Phi Delta Kappan*, May, 1965, pp. 427–429. Used by permission of the author and the publisher. Robert E. McKay is Chairman of the National Education Association's Legislative Commission and Assistant Executive Secretary, California Teachers Association.

THE PRESIDENT'S PROGRAM 213

scends in importance the more than $1.3 billion the bill will pump into elementary and secondary financial arteries the first year of its operation or the considerably larger amounts it will provide in each of its subsequent years.

It constitutes, as the President said after the House had approved the measure by a vote of 263 to 153 the night of March 26, "the greatest breakthrough in the advance of education since the Constitution was written."

Allowing for what critics might consider as political or even partisan exuberance, none can contend that the legislation is routine. Most dispassionate and perceptive observers will agree that the President's program is unique if not revolutionary in some of its approaches.

The concept that educational inadequacies be attacked on a measured basis of the financial status of the family from which the child comes had not heretofore been wrapped into an aid-to-education law. The relationship of poverty and ignorance, long acknowledged, is being applied for the first time in Title I of the bill.

Likewise, the provision of textbooks and instructional material to *all* children and the establishment of supplementary educational centers and services for the *entire* community are clearly not of the customary pattern.

There is, however, in the judgment of some of the best legal minds in the country, no breach of constitutional guarantees of separation of church and state in the program, nor is there any violation of the principle of state and local control of education. The United States Attorney General is one who has reached this conclusion.

Premature and inaccurate statements on what President Johnson planned to recommend last January led to confusion and in some cases condemnation of the plan before it was ever proposed. A few trigger-happy publications editorially damned the program for things which at no time were ever contemplated.

What the Elementary and Secondary Education Act of 1965 is and how it came about should be understood clearly before conclusions are reached.

The legislation, signed into law by the President at a moving ceremony at the old country school in Texas where he had his first lessons, provides a grand total of $1.3 billion in aid to the elementary and secondary schools of the country, starting next July 1.

A major part of the money provided by the act will be distributed to the states on the basis of the number of children from low-income families. The formula whereby $1.06 billion will be made available under Title I takes into account two factors. They are the number of children aged five through seventeen who come from families with incomes of $2000 or less a year and the number from families receiving assistance from the aid-to-dependent-children program. For each such pupil the allotment to the state will be 50 per cent of the average per-pupil expenditure in the state. School districts will receive funds from the state educational agency under plans developed by local school boards for special programs designed to meet the needs of children from low-income families.

Apportionments of $100 million each are provided under Titles II, III, and IV for library resources and textbooks, supplemental educational centers and services, and expanded national and regional educational research activities.

An important though relatively low-expenditure portion of the program is the provision of $25 million in grants to strengthen state departments of education.

NEA Developed Pattern for Johnson

The President's program was patterned after a plan developed by the National Education Association. It is based primarily on an expansion of the concept of "impact" involved in Public Law 874, which up to now has been limited to the effect on schools of the presence of federal military and defense establishments.

The NEA Legislative Commission conceived this approach two years ago, brought about the introduction of a "trial balloon" bill (S 2528, by Senator Wayne Morse) last year, and refined it into a major proposal for this session. The Administration plan, recommended by the President in his educational message in January, adopted this approach and, with proposed expansion of higher education facilities contained in separate legislation, was for exactly the amount, $1.5 billion, suggested by the NEA last December.

The National Education Association, representing nearly a million members of the profession, has been in the forefront of the battle for passage of the legislation.

Capitol Hill observers credit the NEA, through its massive nationwide campaign in support of the measure, with having produced the votes which made passage of the bill an overwhelming bipartisan victory instead of a nip-and-tuck partisan achievement.

Strong support of the program was voted by the NEA Legislative Commission after careful analysis of the proposal. Acutely conscious of its long-time role in protection of state and local autonomy and of separation of church and state, the NEA laid the provisions of the President's program down alongside established NEA policy. The commission decided that the President's proposal did not violate NEA policy, which insists that legislation providing general or specific aids be consistent with the constitutional provision respecting an establishment of religion and with the tradition of separation of church and state.

Scattered discussion of whether the President's program violates the First Amendment appears to be based on a lack of understanding of the Constitution or the effect of the legislation.

The bill makes no provision whatsoever for grants to private or parochial schools. The program established by HR 2362, authored by Rep. Carl D. Perkins (D-Ky.), is totally in the hands of public school officials. Title to all property is vested in the public agency and any use by nonpublic school pupils is solely on a loan basis.

Some die-hard critics who disagree with the Supreme Court approval of the now widely recognized and utilized "child benefit" principle of providing services to children rather than funds to institutions are still insisting, thirty-five years later, that the court in effect didn't know what it was doing when it handed down its decisions.

Second guessing the Supreme Court seems to have become the favorite indoor sport of a few whose professional talents lie in fields other than that of law. Some pedagogues, junior and senior grade alike, profess to have legal knowledge superior to that of the United States Supreme Court. They sound as though they think they know better than the chief tribunal of the nation what was intended by the Founding Fathers when they wrote into the Constitution the guarantees of separation of church and state.

Perhaps they should be considered when next there occurs a vacancy on the court.

Not a Dime to Parochial Schools

With respect to parochial institutions, here are the facts:

Not one dime of the $1.3 billion provided by President Johnson's program will be paid to private or parochial schools.

Public school authorities will retain legal possession and control of all property provided by the program.

No nonpublic school as such will be aided by the provision of services — preschool, after school, or summer school — which are available *to the children* who may be enrolled in those institutions.

Research funds may not be used for parochial or sectarian purposes. None may be utilized for the benefit of any institution for training in sectarian instruction or for the preparation of students to become ministers of religion or to enter upon some other religious vocation or to prepare them to teach theological subjects.

Library books and textbooks made available by Title II to *all* pupils in a community must be those used by or approved for use by the public schools. Use must be on a loan basis, the same as in the use of materials from public libraries.

Who will maintain that the long-established right of any child to borrow and use a book from a public library is a violation of the First Amendment or an aid to a private or parochial school?

With respect to books, the President's program merely extends this practice to materials owned and controlled by the public schools. If this be a violation, then every public library in the land is in contempt of the Constitution. Obviously, they are not. And neither will the public schools be in providing textbooks to *all* children in the community.

Despite the critics, despite some parts of the bill which undoubtedly will need perfecting, despite the legal questions raised by nonlegal minds, the Elementary and Secondary Education Act of 1965 will stand as one of the all-time great educational achievements of Congress.

27

Issues in Educating the
Culturally Disadvantaged

BERNARD A. KAPLAN

Culturally disadvantaged youth — and by this we usually mean poverty-stricken youth — are the subject of growing interest among the nation's educators. For the most part, the problem of educating this group is an ancient one, but it is becoming more and more visible as rural slums are transplanted to the great city, where they grow and fester. (The problem still exists in rural areas, of course, in all its depressing forms [5]. Because urbanization and migration to the cities continue unabated, concern will mount.

Recognition of the problem and initiation of steps to solve it are manifest in many districts across the country. The April 1963 issue (V. 52, no. 4) of the *NEA Journal* devotes fifteen pages to seven articles on programs and approaches. The progenitor of these programs began as the Guidance Demonstration Project in New York City in 1956. Eminently successful, it was later expanded and renamed Higher Horizons.

The Higher Horizons program served as a model for myriad other programs, including the Ford Foundation Great Cities Grey Areas programs, Houston's Talent Preservation project, Phoenix's Careers for Youth, and Seattle's Disadvantaged Student program. The first state-wide program based on the Higher Horizons formula was started as Project ABLE by New York state in 1961. It provides $200,000 annually in state funds on a fifty-fifty matching basis to sixteen different city, village, and suburban communities. Four other states are now planning or considering similar programs: Maine, Rhode Island, Pennsylvania, and California. The California legislature recently approved a proposal for an Environment Enrichment program in which $324,000 in state funds will go to school districts.

While many communities are becoming aroused to the needs and are showing interest, a number of issues connected with establishing Higher Horizons-type programs need discussion.

ISSUE I. WHO ARE THE DISADVANTAGED AND HOW ARE THEY IDENTIFIED? Are all pupils who live in slum neighborhoods disadvantaged? Do all pupils from

✧ From *Phi Delta Kappan*, November, 1963, pp. 70–76. Used by permission of the author and the publisher. Bernard A. Kaplan is Coordinator, Project ABLE, Bureau of Guidance, New York State Education Department, Albany.

minority groups and urban areas qualify for such programs? Should we call them "culturally deprived," "impoverished," "disadvantaged," or something else? Can entire "culturally deprived" schools be selected for such programs, or do we work with only selected cases within these schools?

Frank Riessman, in his recent book titled *The Culturally Deprived Child* (7), uses these terms interchangeably: culturally deprived, educationally deprived, underprivileged, disadvantaged, lower-class, lower socioeconomic. He points out that by 1970 one out of two public school pupils in these cities will be "culturally deprived." Indeed, this is already the case in Washington, D.C., Baltimore, Wilmington, and Philadelphia.

Whether we choose to call these pupils disadvantaged, culturally deprived, or economically impoverished, they usually exhibit two characteristics: they are from the lower socioeconomic groups in the community and they are notably deficient in cultural and academic strengths. The latter characteristic is usually, but not always, a consequence of the first factor. The parents of these children have simply been unable to provide the quality of background, outlook, initial grounding, and readiness for formal learning that middle- and upper-class parents provide as a matter of course. And all too often our schools have been almost exclusively geared to the mores of the latter group.

Identifying or designating certain pupils or schools as culturally disadvantaged remains a local problem. Sometimes 90 per cent or more of the student body may unquestionably fit this designation, and consequently the entire school may require a special program. In other cases, perhaps 50 per cent of the student body can be regarded as culturally disadvantaged, while in most schools the ratio is more likely one disadvantaged pupil to three up to ten not underprivileged. These latter schools face the problem of how to provide a program for only a portion of the school's enrollment (usually scattered throughout all grade levels), how to select and exclude specific individuals (borderline cases are the toughest), and finally, how this group should be designated. One Project ABLE elementary school in a New York state village has students dispersed throughout the school, with anywhere from one to six in a class of twenty-five to thirty. Another Project ABLE program in a small city not far away has identified its sixth-grade disadvantaged youngsters and brought them together in a pilot program in one classroom under one highly competent male teacher.

As to what terms to use, the impact of labeling individuals or schools as culturally deprived, no matter how accurate this term may in fact be, is best illustrated by what happened to an elementary principal in New York state. As a project director of a "culturally deprived" school, he had so termed it to teachers and board members. At a meeting of representatives from all Project ABLE schools in the state, he found that the neighborhood school he had attended as a boy was a Project ABLE school. When he heard this, his first reaction was, "That's ridiculous! My old school? That neighborhood's not culturally deprived!" The character of the neighborhood may have changed since his day, but the important point is that an intelligent, dedicated individual directing his efforts and ingenuity to improving the educational level of his culturally disadvantaged students failed to recognize the denigrating effect of the phrase until it was applied to *him*.

Most programs for culturally deprived pupils are now being given euphonious (or euphemistic) titles, frequently chosen by the pupils themselves. These titles can be indicative of the purpose and spirit of the programs without overtones of denigration: Higher Horizons, Project ABLE, Operation Bootstrap, Springboard, New Frontiers, Wings, Project Mercury, Project HELP, Talent Demonstration.

ISSUE II. ARE PROGRAMS FOR THE DISADVANTAGED "FAIR" TO OTHER SCHOOL CHILDREN? In districts where special programs have been developed, the provision of extra teachers and counselors, special services, supplies and materials, cultural enrichment trips, and the like are eyed enviously by pupils, teachers, administrators, and parents from non-project schools. This is especially so when the special program is designed for only a segment of the school's enrollment. Some administrators have felt that this is an insuperable handicap and hesitate to develop special programs for this reason. It is also argued that these programs are unfair to non-project children because they cost more on a per-pupil basis.

Such objections are not new to education. They have been raised with regard to special education for the physically handicapped, mentally retarded, gifted and academically talented, and emotionally disturbed. Few people now feel that special educational problems do not merit special programs and additional costs. It is true that a compensatory educational experience for the disadvantaged group almost always entails additional expenditures. However, it can be argued that *equal* educational opportunity for these youngsters does not necessarily mean the same *kind* of education; in most cases, it means equal *plus* more of the same in greater depth, quality, and appropriateness.

If some school board members are reluctant to allocate additional funds to certain subgroups, let them calm their doubts in the knowledge that almost without fail, these programs bring sparkling dividends which benefit the rest of the school program and the wider community. For example, practices, approaches, and experiences developed by teachers in these programs are often transferable, with little or no additional cost, to other classes and schools in the district. The impact on the school's morale is evident in this excerpt from a Project ABLE director's report:

> When the project began, a few teachers in the project schools were skeptical of its value. At the end of the first year of operation everyone associated with the project — students, parents, school and community personnel alike — is enthusiastic and hopeful it will be expanded. The most frequently expressed comments are "This is wonderful; let's have more of it!" or "At last we are able to do what we've always known should be done."
>
> At first it was a little difficult to interest teachers in giving the extra time required. Now we have lists of teachers, many from faculties other than those of the project schools, who are anxious to participate.

Finally, school board members and community leaders are beginning to see clearly, especially with regard to school dropouts, that a greater investment *now* constitutes a saving to the community in the long run, when this investment is balanced with resultant lower costs for welfare, unemployment benefits, institutional and rehabilitative services, and greater earnings and citizen productivity.

ISSUE III. ARE PROGRAMS FOR THE DISADVANTAGED JUST ANOTHER METHOD OF MAINTAINING DE FACTO SEGREGATION? Some educators and observers have wondered whether these programs might not be an attempt to maintain *de facto* school segregation. This is because students in most of the programs are overwhelmingly from minority groups, especially in Northern cities where housing and neighborhood residential patterns have operated to produce *de facto* school segregation in supposedly integrated schools. Segregated schools serving segregated neighborhoods will be excused and even condoned, these people infer, if the programs and services offered by these schools are outstanding and attractive.

These programs, once instituted, in fact tend to produce the reverse effect. Project pupils are given the chance to participate in activities with pupils from all over the school district, often for the first time. Since the purpose of programs for the disadvantaged is to lift the sights and aspirations of these youngsters, the resultant effect, when these attempts are successful, is for greater numbers to select and qualify for academic and honors courses at the high school level. At this point they associate with white students from middle-class and privileged backgrounds much more frequently and intimately than they otherwise would.

In addition, in view of what has happened to the "separate but equal" doctrine, it is unlikely that the Negro community will tolerate the extension of this practice in a new form, even on a "separate but better" basis.

Programs for the disadvantaged serve to accelerate pupil adjustment, growth in achievement and ability, and readiness, so that these pupils can assume full-fledged membership status in the schools. They develop the ability to benefit from and aspire to whatever opportunities the community's educational system and the future may offer. This is why such organizations as the National Scholarship Service and Fund for Negro Students (NSSFNS) and the National Urban League endorse them enthusiastically.

ISSUE IV. SHOULD PROGRAMS FOR THE DISADVANTAGED CONCENTRATE ON ONE SPECIFIC GRADE LEVEL, E.G., THE ELEMENTARY GRADES? Some educators argue that programs for the disadvantaged can be most effectively and economically operated if they concentrate at one level, for example, Grades 1–3, rather than at a higher level. It is not at all unusual to hear recommendations that "this approach is unquestionably a good one at this level but a far superior job could be done if it had been in effect for these same children one, two, or three years earlier."

Successful or promising programs have been inaugurated at *all* levels (8). Prekindergarten programs for disadvantaged children have been conducted in New York City, Baltimore, and by the state of Pennsylvania's Environment Enrichment program. Kindergarten programs for this group are underway in Racine (Wisconsin), Dayton (Ohio), White Plains (New York), and in Texas for Mexican-American children. Other programs for the disadvantaged cover the full range of grades one through twelve. Project ABLE schools in New York state have programs underway at all levels, although most of them concentrate on grades four through eight. The Higher Horizons program is now operating in grades three through ten.

Indeed, a few colleges have started experimentation with programs and admissions policies and procedures for disadvantaged youth. Bronx Community College in New York City has experimented with special precollege evening courses in literature, composition, mathematics, and basic study skills. Intensified guidance and counseling has been provided for these youngsters. Southern University (Baton Rouge), Dillard University (New Orleans), and Whitworth College (Spokane, Washington) are experimenting with precollege orientation for these students. Harvard, Brown, and Rhode Island College have relaxed admissions requirements for, and are carefully following up, selected cases.

Since programs are serving the disadvantaged at all levels from prekindergarten through college, the important question is not the best grade level on which to focus these activities but rather the most appropriate place to *begin*.

The level at which a school system chooses to introduce its program will depend, of course, on a number of factors, among them staff readiness and leadership, facilities, community resources, and parental support.

ISSUE V. DO PROGRAMS FOR THE DISADVANTAGED REQUIRE FOUNDATION FUNDS OR OUTSIDE FINANCIAL SUPPORT? Admittedly, foundation grants and outside funds are a great asset in getting a program underway, not only because of the extra monies provided but for the aura of approval and support the staff and the community attach to a foundation program. The Ford Foundation's Great Cities Grey Areas program has provided sizeable amounts of money to metropolitan school districts. The College Entrance Examinations Board and the National Service and Scholarship Fund for Negro Students donated funds to get the original Guidance Demonstration project underway in New York City. The Johnson and Western Foundations have made grants to the Racine, Wisconsin, school system for its experimental program. State funds in New York state and Pennsylvania have permitted their respective state education departments to develop projects.

Nevertheless, in a number of cases school systems have begun their programs with little extra expenditures or with the additional funds provided entirely by the local community. In Norfolk, Virginia, a recent replication of the Higher Horizons program was attempted at that city's Jacox Junior High School without outside support. According to a study by Brazziel and

Gordon, programs to help disadvantaged children make better use of public education can be carried out in any school at a modest cost (2).

Some school systems have already developed special activities for the culturally disadvantaged without outside assistance. The National Urban League's Talent Search Bank approach, utilizing community volunteers and resources, has done this for some time.

Sometimes a small or token appropriation is sufficient to launch a successful demonstration. In New York state during the last few years, the State Education Department has sponsored Talent Search programs in thirty city, village, and suburban school districts. For the most part these are small-scale demonstration projects. NDEA Title V-A funds provided intensified guidance services for underachieving students at the junior high school level.

In the future, it appears, school systems desiring programs for their culturally disadvantaged students will have to rely primarily on local funds and resources. As with other educational innovations, from programed learning to language laboratories, once educational merit has been established, the introduction of the new program becomes the joint responsibility of the school district and the state.

ISSUE VI. IS ADDITIONAL MONEY ALL THAT'S NEEDED TO LAUNCH A SUCCESSFUL PROGRAM? Obviously an effective comprehensive program for disadvantaged children requires additional funds. While there may be disagreement about the amount, there is a general consensus that compensatory educational experiences and provisions demand additional expenditures. However, a school district must provide more than money if it is to develop a successful program.

For one thing, even if specialists are added, much will need to be done in the way of orientation and in-service training for the entire staff. Special curricular materials will have to be developed. Program activities, particularly those pertaining to cultural enrichment, work-study experiences, and group guidance will require planning and coordination. If, in addition, team teaching, ungraded primary programs, and other such innovations are to be simultaneously introduced, even greater care must be exercised in making plans. This planning takes time.

Hunter College, Yeshiva University, Newark State Teachers College, and Queens College have each been developing specialized educational programs for their students who will be teaching disadvantaged pupils. The Detroit Public Schools and Bank Street College (New York City), working independently, are developing special materials for teaching reading to culturally disadvantaged pupils at the primary level. One school in Chicago developed its own elementary school readers "replete with slums instead of suburbs as motifs and mixed ethnic groups as characters" (2).

Especially important is the need to work with the entire staff of the schools involved. Many teachers, often unconsciously, may be psychologically rejecting these students; all teachers in such a program should have the opportunity to participate in in-service training to examine their attitudes, expectations, and practices with regard to these youngsters.

ISSUE VII. IS THERE A STANDARD TYPE OF SCHOOL PROGRAM FOR THE DISADVANTAGED THAT A COMMUNITY CAN ADOPT? Some administrators assume that programs for the disadvantaged can be introduced in much the same way that a new educational practice such as television is added. However, the depth, breadth, and exact form that characterize successful programs vary considerably community to community. Some aspects are highlighted in some schools but assume secondary roles in others. Perhaps the best illustration of the variety that can occur is shown by the forty-two programs described in the . . . February 1963 publication, School Programs for the Disadvantaged, prepared by the NEA's Educational Research Service. While these programs share basic similarities, each is unique and must be viewed as reflecting local needs and local leadership. Each school must design and develop its own. Even the Higher Horizons program provides for variation among schools. No two programs in Project ABLE are just alike, though all were planned and initiated during 1961 under State Education Department auspices.

One community can learn from another engaged in a similar program. Visits by teachers and administrators to programs-in-action help to transplant program techniques and rationales from one community to another. In addition, a growing body of research and progress reports is available to interested districts.

ISSUE VIII. ARE PROGRAMS FOR THE DISADVANTAGED UNDULY INFLUENCED BY THE "HAWTHORNE EFFECT"? These programs, it is claimed, are effective not because of the specific techniques and activities employed but because the children involved feel that they have been selected for special consideration. Given a sugar pill which he thinks is an aspirin, the child reports that his headache has disappeared (the "Hawthorne effect"). It is asserted that it's not *what* is done but merely that something "special" is done and that students know they have been selected for this something special; the end result will still produce substantial improvement in behavior, although the changes may be only temporary.

The research now underway with experimental and control groups will eventually illuminate the validity of these charges. However, it does appear from the evidence already reported that substantial gains in the performances of pupils (test scores, class marks and standings, attendance, educational and vocational goals) and of schools (holding power, discipline, scholarship awards, teacher retention) are achieved merely by the introduction of these programs. Such gains as improved reading skills and increased holding power are not ephemeral in their effect on student achievement and accomplishments. Though student performance *may* no longer continue to improve with a cessation of program activities (thereby supporting the thesis that the "new" motivation is not fully integrated), it is likely that this criticism applies equally well to other facets of the school program, e.g., extracurricular activities or guidance services.

The goal of most Higher Horizons-type programs is to convey to each disadvantaged pupil the feeling that he is the focus of the school's concern and attention. This may be a distinct revelation for many of these pupils. Unless correspondent traits are manifested by the staff and effectively communicated to the pupil and his parents, these programs fall short of their objectives. Some observers feel it is this aspect of the program more than any other that produces the desired changes. Others feel that improved techniques and methods and new opportunities are the key components. Still a third group contends that it is a combination of these two approaches. Of course the two approaches are not mutually exclusive. The Hawthorne criticism, however, applies mainly to the first and third views, i.e., heightened motivation, no matter how it is produced, will bring about (similar) change in student performance. If this is true, a logical question is, What alternative (more effective, less costly, or more efficient) "sugar pill" activities might realistically be substituted?

Some experts suggest that these programs can accomplish their objectives by eliminating all but one or two features, these varying with the needs or resources of the community. Recent research evidence regarding motivation and underachievement suggests that these two phenomena are highly complex; therefore, it appears unlikely that oversimplified or "shortcut" solutions will produce similar changes in student behavior. In fact, even in full-scale Higher Horizons programs, where activities are multiple and varied, a minority of students make no gains.

The importance of motivation, attitudes, and the student's self-image in these programs must not be minimized. The frequency with which these programs report noticeable positive change, first in student demeanor (dress, attendance, interest, speech), and subsequently in academic accomplishments (grades, levels of achievement, skills) emphasizes the importance of including consideration of student attitudes in programs for the disadvantaged.

ISSUE IX. DO PROGRAMS FOR THE DISADVANTAGED OVERLOOK OR MINIMIZE THE ATTRIBUTES OF THE CULTURE OF THESE CHILDREN AND THEIR FAMILIES? The term "culturally deprived" is now viewed with some disfavor by certain sociologists and educators; more accurate terms, they submit, are "culturally different" or "economically deprived." They maintain that children from impoverished families are *not* culturally deprived in the sense that they are culture*less*. Rather, their cultures and heritages *differ* from those cultivated by the middle-class schools they attend. Programs for the disadvantaged, they say, disregard the special strengths of this group, e.g., their folk humor, physical or manipulative propensities, pragmatism, etc., and condescendingly regard these children as having little if anything positive to offer or to build on in the classroom.

Some critics scold the schools for their rejection of the "culture of poverty" and insist that many of these youths who, in turn, reject the schools by dropping out are wiser and more realistic than their peers who choose to remain (4).

The claim that school personnel in general and programs for disadvantaged specifically minimize potential non-middle-class contributions and meritorious qualities is probably a fair appraisal. However, there is evidence now that many programs are attempting to foster in their staff a better understanding of the community's disadvantaged and to adapt and develop materials and methods accordingly. For instance, primary readers and materials more realistically attuned to the actual experiences and backgrounds of these children are being developed. (The Board of Education of New York City has recently served notice on textbook publishers that it would no longer purchase social studies texts which do not adequately treat minority groups and deal realistically with intergroup tensions and efforts to relieve them. Other large city systems are considering similar stands.) The New York State Education Department has developed curriculum materials pertaining to the Negro in American history and American society today (6). The Washington, D.C., public schools are developing similar materials.

Special courses for teachers in training and teachers in service help school personnel gain a better understanding of varying cultural and ethnic groups and their problems. Some programs for the disadvantaged make provision for home visits by teachers and counselors or arrange for periodic, informal discussions with small groups of parents (numbering four to six) in the school. These attempts at improved parental communication and participation also give school personnel more accurate perspective and insight regarding the backgrounds, values, and orientations of disadvantaged families.

Do programs for the disadvantaged, by their mere existence, indicate that the cultures and values of these groups are meaningless and unworthy of consideration in the schools? Are these programs set up primarily to stamp out cultural differences and to fill the void with values, goals, and habits deemed more acceptable to "society" by school board members or administrators? If this were the case, it would do great violence to the American democratic tradition. It seems more likely that the real aim of these programs is not the blurring and subjugating of differences so much as providing underprivileged pupils with the tools of an education adequate to guarantee them the competence to make their own choices and decisions regarding how they wish to live, to work, to play. Otherwise, their choices are restricted by immediate circumstance and limited environments. As the Educational Policies Commission has pointed out (3), "If the problem of the disadvantaged is to be solved, the society as a whole must give evidence of its undifferentiated respect for all persons."

The commission further asserts:

> The problem of the disadvantaged arises because their cultures are not compatible with modern life. One of the greatest challenges facing the United States today is that of giving all Americans a basis for living constructively and independently in the modern age. *The requirement is not for conformity but for compatibility.* To make all people uniform would be as impractical as it

would be inconsistent with American ideals. *To give all people a fair chance to meet the challenge of life* is both practicable and American. [Italics added]

Jacob Landers, coordinator of New York City's Higher Horizons program, in answer to the question, What makes a successful Higher Horizons school? (1) said:

> No amount of increased appropriation, and no change in procedures or organization, can be effective without a fundamental faith in the ability of the children. It is not enough to know intellectually that Negro and Puerto Rican children can learn as well as other children. It must be felt in the marrow of the bones and in the pit of the stomach.
>
> This belief in the children and pride in their accomplishments must run like a golden thread through the fabric of the school's daily existence. With this feeling, the school poor in services can yet be rich in achievement; without it, the richest services yield but the poorest results.
>
> Our great enemy is the phrase "as well as can be expected." It implies that the school merely reflects the community, but cannot affect it. It implies an acceptance of the *status quo*, rather than a struggle to change it.
>
> The true Higher Horizons program spreads faith in children and hope for their future.

The variety of programs which have been developed illustrates that this faith in children and hope for their future can be expressed and fostered in different ways. There will naturally be questions about the most practicable, economical, and beneficial kind of program to develop in a given community. These questions are embraced by the issues discussed here. Only by confronting these squarely and unequivocally will school districts be able to develop successfully their own programs for disadvantaged pupils.

REFERENCES

1. Board of Education of the City of New York. *Higher Horizons Bulletin*, December, 1962.
2. Brazziel, W. F., and Margaret Gordon. "Replications of Some Aspects of the Higher Horizons Program in a Southern Junior High School," *Bulletin of the NASSP*, Vol. 47, No. 281; March, 1963.
3. Educational Policies Commission, National Education Association. *Education and the Disadvantaged American*. Washington: The Association, 1962.
4. Friedenburg, Edgar. "An Ideology of School Withdrawal," in Daniel Schreiber (ed.), *School Dropouts*. Washington: National Education Association, 1963.
5. Isenberg, Robert M. "The Rural Disadvantaged," *NEA Journal*, Vol. 52, No. 4; April, 1963.
6. New York State Education Department. *Intergroup Relations, Resource Handbook for Elementary School Teachers: The Negro in American History*. Albany, N.Y.: Division of Intercultural Relations in Education, State Education Department, 1963.
7. Riessman, Frank. *The Culturally Deprived Child*. New York: Harper & Brothers, 1962.
8. Schreiber, Daniel. "The Dropout and Delinquent: Promising Practices Gleaned from a Year of Study," *Phi Delta Kappan*, Vol. 44, No. 5; February, 1963.

28

Educating Culturally Deprived
Youth in Urban Centers

FREDERICK SHAW

The number one problem faced by urban teachers today is how to offer culturally deprived youth an education that meets their needs. In 1950, about one child out of ten attending public schools in the nation's fourteen largest cities was culturally disadvantaged. In 1960, the proportion had risen to one of three. Some authorities believe that by 1970 it may be one out of two. These figures underscore the urgency of the problem.

The purpose of this article is to trace the origins of the problem, show how some of the nation's larger school systems are trying to handle it, and explore the issues involved.

In terms of sheer numbers, American population movements in the middle years of this century dwarf the tribal invasions of the early Middle Ages and the westward surge in American history. During the years 1940 through 1960, for example, more than twenty-six million people were added to the populations of the suburbs of our large cities. The entire country did not contain that many people in 1850.

By 1960, about 62 per cent of all Americans were concentrated in 212 "standard metropolitan areas." Such a region is defined by the Bureau of the Census as "one or more contiguous counties containing at least one central city of over fifty thousand population as the core of an economically and socially integrated cluster of people." In more colorful language, these areas have been called a "galaxy of urban solar systems." The combined population of these metropolitan areas now exceeds 108 million inhabitants, and almost one-third of the nation now lives in suburban areas.

Suburb and central city, however, have not grown at the same pace. Between 1950 and 1960, the outskirts of our great cities grew by more than seventeen million, an increase of 47.2 per cent. At the same time, the central cores gained scarcely four million, only 8.2 per cent. Millions have deserted the central areas for the suburbs, seeking attractive homes and surroundings, more play space for children, and lower taxes. Those who

✧ From *Phi Delta Kappan*, November, 1963, pp. 92–97. Used by permission of the author and the publisher. Frederick Shaw is Research Associate for the New York City Board of Education.

left were usually in the above-average income brackets, for they could afford to buy a house and pay commuting costs. The poorer families, of course, were unable to build or purchase homes or rent "garden apartments."

As a result, some of our more affluent suburbs have tended to become homogeneous in economic status and occupation, and sometimes in ethnic background as well. Dan W. Dodson, professor of educational sociology at New York University, has pointed out the consequences of this selectivity. Suburbanites, he declared, lead an "antiseptic" way of life: "nice families, segregated into nice homes, away from the pollution of both industry and the heterogeneous masses of the inner city."

Economic homogeneity can operate most advantageously for a community's educational system, if its affluent citizens are school-minded and willing to tax themselves. Some of the best American school systems today are found in wealthy suburban areas. School districts near New York, Chicago, and Philadelphia have built up top-ranking systems. They have pioneered in teaching methods, school administration, and school architecture. Schools like these are sometimes called "lighthouse schools," because they serve as beacons to guide less favored communities in educational progress.

Who replaces suburban-bound citizens in the core cities? Throughout American history, the chief source of unskilled urban labor has been Europeans. Today, trans-Atlantic immigration has been reduced to a trickle, and the principal newcomers are natives of the Western hemisphere. Thousands of Puerto Ricans and Negroes from our Southern states have settled in such Northeastern cities as Newark and New York. Southern Negroes and Appalachian whites have migrated to Baltimore, Detroit, Cincinnati, Chicago, and other cities in the Middle West. Mexican-American and reservation Indians have flocked to western cities, such as Oakland, California, and Phoenix, Arizona. Between 1950 and 1960, New York City lost about 1,300,000 middle-class whites, a population greater than that of Cleveland, Ohio. They were replaced by 800,000 Negroes and Puerto Ricans, an underprivileged group larger in size than Washington, D.C. New York's experience in the Fifties was not typical in numbers, but it *was* characteristic of population shifts other major cities have experienced.

James B. Conant believes that the "very nature of the community determines what goes on in the school." The neighborhoods in which these immigrants settle are often characterized by bad housing, high population density, and a lack of privacy. Incomes tend to be low and uncertain, and many residents may be on public relief rolls. Most have limited vocational and economic competence and low social and economic expectancy. Not infrequently, the community lacks trained leadership. Crime rates are high and conditions ripe for juvenile delinquency. Cultural resources are minimal. Family patterns are disoriented.

Neighborhoods of this kind have a marked impact on their schools, for the children who live in such areas are poorly prepared and poorly motivated for formal education. Mel Ravitz, professor of sociology at Wayne

State University, has explained why the conventional courses taught in urban schools often seem to have little relevance for them:

> Many of these children of the depressed areas come from home situations that are deplorable, where the primary need is for the services of a nurse, a dentist, a dietician, where there is abject poverty, where there is much physical overcrowding in poor housing, where many kinds of psychological problems beset members of the family. Often, too, the families are split, with the mother assuming responsibility for both parents. Even if the family is not split, the controls that once applied in the rural setting have been broken in an urban setting that is hostile, uncaring, anonymous, and which has forced the restructuring of the family. The parental images the children now see are images of despair, of frustration, and of enforced idleness. It is absurd, too, for a middle-class teacher to set these children down each day to try to focus their attention on ancient history or on the multiplication table or on nouns or verbs, when simple good common sense demands a concern with situations and circumstances under which these children live, conditions which they cannot ignore sufficiently to concentrate on what to them are really otherworldly matters. (1)

Research studies have consistently shown lower average I.Q.'s among children in such depressed areas than those from more favored homes. Often scores on such tests decline as the children grow older. Here are the median scores in certain disadvantaged districts in New York City: grade 1 — 95; grade 3 — 92; grade 6 — 87; grade 8 — 82.

Children from low socioeconomic areas also tend to fall farther and farther behind their peers in achievement. In one large district in New York, the average child was found to be retarded one year in reading in the third grade, almost two years in the sixth, and two and one-half in the eighth.

These children often have great difficulties in personal adjustment. Delinquency is more concentrated, and destructive aggression more widespread in problem areas; psychoses and completely disabling breakdowns are disproportionately high. One reason is that they receive relatively little of the ego satisfaction, the rewards, and the feeling of belonging that society has to offer. Almost from the very beginning, however, many fail to master the conventional academic curriculum. This lowers their already shaky self-esteem. School dropouts are also highest among children from neighborhoods of this kind, and relatively few get to college.

Basically, these children have the same drives for achievement, recognition, and acceptance as their peers; but deficiencies in early experiences and in motivation, and frequently family and social difficulties as well, weight the odds against academic success. Often their parents work at jobs requiring little education, and the children get the impression that school is not particularly important in preparing them for life. These influences seem to weigh most heavily on the boys. In low socioeconomic areas, they consistently score lower on intelligence tests and achievement tests than the girls.

Difficulties like these are further aggravated by the high turnover of newcomers in the schools. Children frequently shift from neighborhood to neighborhood and from school to school, disrupting their own schooling as well as the education of their less-traveled classmates. In Manhattan, where the pupil population of the elementary schools is higher than 76 per cent Negro and Puerto Rican, the mean mobility rate in a recent year was 51 per cent. In three schools that were almost completely Negro, the turnover was 100 per cent that year.

Some authorities believe that the whole environment in these slum areas must be improved and that the schools must play a vital role in this endeavor. What they need is more special services, greater efforts to help pupils solve their personal problems, and a boost in their parents' cultural aspirations. This is precisely what the Great Cities Grey Areas School Improvement program and the Higher Horizons program have set out to do. Each will be discussed in turn.

The "great cities" include the fourteen largest public school systems in the country. Ten are now experimenting with the Grey Areas program, assisted by the Ford Foundation. Program aims are to help disadvantaged children in many ways: to raise their school achievement levels, to identify and help able youngsters, to raise the level of their aspirations, to equip them for modern urban life by developing their competencies, to increase parental responsibility, and to mobilize community support in their behalf.

It is worthwhile to focus briefly on the pilot project which began in the public schools of Detroit in 1959. Basic elements in the Detroit project are: (1) The classroom teacher's work is reinforced by assistance from specialized professional workers and smaller class size. (2) The school tries to show parents that education can open new doors to opportunity for their children, particularly if they are convinced this is possible and willingly cooperate. (3) The community is involved in upgrading the education of its children. (4) Additional funds are provided. Each of these elements will be discussed in turn.

1. *Reinforcing the teacher's work:* The classroom teacher is the kingpin of the educational process. Without effective teaching, no educational endeavor, whether conventional or pioneering, can succeed. That is why the following efforts were made to assist the teacher:

a. Competent consultants in the areas of education, social work, sociology, and psychology gave in-service courses, and local workshops on local school curricular problems were organized.

b. Each school involved in the project added three full-time specialized persons to its staff: a school-community agent, a visiting teacher, and a coaching teacher. The school-community agent acted as a liaison officer between community and school. He interpreted the school to the community and vice versa. Some community agents worked with block clubs, community councils, or parents' groups. Others took charge of after-school and evening programs for youth and adults. The visiting teacher was really a social worker. Trained in case work, she handled children and parents of children who had serious school-adjustment problems. The visiting teacher is no stranger to the Detroit schools, but normally serves several schools. In the Great Cities project, however, she was assigned full-time to a single school, thereby enabling teachers to make referrals of children with physical or emotional difficulties more readily. Finally, children with pronounced reading disabilities were referred to a coaching teacher, specially trained in language arts. She worked with small groups of five to fifteen children, helping them overcome reading deficiencies. She also helped train other teachers in this area.

2. *Involving parents:* It would be a mistake to consider parents in low socioeconomic areas hostile to academic training. Many whose origins are rural, however, are indifferent or see relatively little need for it. Those eager to have their children well educated often lack formal schooling themselves and are unable to help.

The Detroit project attempted to involve parents in school activities in order to raise their educational and social aspirations for their children and give parents a better understanding of the educational process. First, free classes in such practical subjects as speech, shorthand, typing, sewing, and millinery were offered. Then refresher classes in reading and arithmetic were organized. This enabled the parents to help their children in school work. Other activities, such as clubs or courses in how to budget, prepare food, repair furniture, and become generally efficient in household tasks and family relations bolstered the parents' self-esteem and raised family aspirations.

3. *Community involvement:* In addition to organizing activities for parents, the schools included in the pilot project set up comprehensive programs of after-school and evening activities to serve the needs of the community. Some emphasized afternoon enrichment programs for youth; others, evening adult programs. In a sense they became real community schools. In addition, public and private agencies offered the help of their personnel and resources. The Neighborhood Service Organization of Detroit, for example, conducted day camps for fifty-five emotionally disturbed children from project schools during the summer of 1961. The YMCA and YWCA generously offered the use of their physical facilities and carried on a variety of programs. The city's public libraries took children to distant libraries in "library caravans" by bus.

4. *Special appropriations:* The activities described above required more funds than are provided in conventional schools. Generally speaking, the extra cost of the demonstration project did not exceed 10 per cent of the normal costs of schooling in the Detroit schools.

One of the best known school programs for disadvantaged youth is New York's Higher Horizons project. Like the Detroit project, it began operating in 1959. It originated three years earlier, however, in the Demonstration Guidance project, organized in Harlem's Junior High School No. 43 and George Washington High School, the school to which its graduates are fed. J.H.S. 43's pupil population was 48 per cent Negro, 38 per cent of Puerto

Rican background, 2 per cent of other Spanish-speaking origin, 1 per cent Oriental, and 11 per cent white. In George Washington High School, 28 per cent of the total student body was Negro and 10 per cent Puerto Rican. The general purpose of the Demonstration Guidance project was to "identify and stimulate able students from a culturally deprived area to reach higher educational and vocational goals." More specifically, it was a pilot program "aimed at raising levels of aspirations and achievement by compensating for limitations stemming from cultural deprivation and motivating pupils to achieve their full potential."

In 1956, Junior High School 43 had fourteen hundred students in the seventh, eighth, and ninth grades. Half these pupils, the most promising, were selected for the project. Their mean I.Q. score was 95. On the average, they were one and one-half years retarded in reading. Some dropped out of school; others entered vocational high schools; still others left the city. The 375 who remained and entered George Washington High School comprised the project students. The students were admitted in 1957, 1958, and 1959, the years they were graduated from J.H.S. 43.

The program of New York's Demonstration Guidance project will be considered under the same four headings as the Detroit project.

1. *Reinforcing the teacher's work:* Students who were deficient in reading entered special remedial classes of five and six. All teachers, regardless of subject, spent the first ten minutes of class time in reading exercises. In George Washington High School the students were placed in small classes of not more than fifteen. They took English twice a day because they had difficulty with the written and spoken language.

Counseling services were considerably expanded. In place of the usual counselor-pupil ratio of one to 1400 in the city's junior high schools, the proportion was one to two hundred in Junior High School 43, and one to 125 in George Washington High School. In most high schools it is one to 550. This meant almost four and one-half times the usual number of counselors.

At George Washington High School an intensive program of individual counseling was carried on. Each student was interviewed at least twice a year. Some had more than twenty counselor contacts. Counselors uncovered many personal problems, such as the difficulties of the girl whose stepfather kept throwing her books out of the window, or the boy whose mother would not allow him to accept a college scholarship. These clinical services helped children cope with environmental difficulties interfering with school achievement.

A dynamic program of group guidance was also instituted. Its chief purpose was to raise the students' levels of aspiration by impressing on them the fact that they could finish high school, enter college, and get decent jobs. Specific prevocational and vocational training were provided. Counselors also helped children find special services, both inside and outside school, such as remedial mathematics, special clubs, after-school centers, college coaching, and the like. Finally, counselors worked closely with teachers, giving them pertinent and detailed information about the scholastic and personal needs of their charges.

2. *Involving parents:* Parents who were recent arrivals from the rural South or Puerto Rico often lacked an understanding of the dynamics of urban living or of the specific needs of their children. Many were uninterested in or unaware of the educational and cultural opportunities available to their children. Counselors tried to persuade parents like these to be reasonable in the assignment of home chores, to provide privacy for study, and to encourage good school work. Strenuous efforts were made to give parents faith in their offspring. School personnel spent considerable time in parent interviews, parent meetings, parent workshops, and even trips for parents.

3. *Community involvement:* A New York state employment counselor was assigned to the high school to help pupils plan occupational careers and to aid in placement. In addition, counselors from the National Scholarship Service and the Fund for Negro Students visited the senior classes, making positive suggestions for college and giving some scholarship winners special grants.

For the most part, however, the children were brought to the community rather than the other way around. Trips to museums, libraries, industrial plants, concerts, the ballet, the theater, and colleges were a regular part of the program. One group of pupils spent a weekend at Amherst; another visited the University of Massachusetts, getting firsthand experience with campus life. Each class made a trip to Washington, D.C., where one group conferred with the Commissioner of Education himself.

As a result, some students became devotees of the Philharmonic or *aficionados* of the ballet and the theater. It was no longer considered "square" to attend a symphony concert or "sissy" to carry a paperback book.

4. *Special appropriations:* The program could not be regarded as inexpensive. The per-pupil cost in Junior High School No. 43 was increased by $100 per annum, in George Washington High School by $250. This was more than 40 per cent higher than the academic high school expenditure of $600 per capita.

The Demonstration Guidance project has generated great enthusiasm among educators. Frank Riessman, author of *The Culturally Deprived Child,* wrote: "There is no question that the program did a splendid job in demonstrating . . . that educationally deprived children can learn."

In 1959, 114 pupils in the project entered George Washington High. Of these, eighty-five, or 74 per cent, remained in school and were graduated in June 1962, a proportion almost 50 per cent higher than preproject students from Junior High School 43. Before the project began, the highest rank of any student from Junior High School 43 in his Washington High graduating class was forty-one. But in the class of June 1962, project students obtained ranks two, four, and nine. Students in the 1960 project class were one, four, and six. Out of the eighty-five project students graduating in 1962, fifty-one went on to some form of higher education, almost three times the preproject number. Fourteen obtained scholarships and attended such institutions as Dartmouth, Radcliffe, New York University, the University of Maine, and Western College for Women.

The success of this pilot project led to its expansion in a less intense form. The Higher Horizons program, as it is now called, served 25,000 pupils in fifty-two elementary schools and thirteen junior high schools during the 1961–1962 school year. Unlike the Demonstration Guidance project, it included all grades from three through nine. It also served *all* pupils in project schools, whatever their academic potential. Costs were reduced to $35 per pupil, partly because of experiences gained in the pilot project. Instead of one counselor to 200 pupils, for example, the ratio became one to 385. The results of this extended program are now being appraised by the school system's Bureau of Educational Research. In 1962 it was extended to eleven high schools, largely schools fed by Higher Horizons junior high schools.

John H. Fischer, formerly superintendent of schools in Baltimore and now president of Teachers College, Columbia, has suggested that culturally deprived children be given "compensatory educational opportunities" to help them overcome their initial cultural deficiencies. In essence, this is what both the Great Cities School Improvement program and the Higher Horizons program are trying to provide.

The Demonstration Guidance program did not come in a bargain basement package. "Some boards of education and some superintendents seem to think that all you need for a Higher Horizons program is hope, faith, and a little retooling," Jacob Landers, coordinator of New York's program, once declared. "The fact of the matter is that compensatory inequality of education is an expensive theory." Indeed, it costs more to raise a disadvantaged child from a slum area to a given standard of educational achievement than the typical child living in a more favored suburb. Unfortunately, the central cities in which the majority of disadvantaged pupils are found are usually financially hard pressed. Their more affluent suburbs, however, often have greater tax resources to support their school systems.

In recent years, New York's public schools have endeavored to fulfill the needs of disadvantaged children in many other ways. A few are outlined briefly below.

1. *"Special Service" schools:* All school systems have favored schools and problem schools. In New York, the latter are called "special service" schools because they get extra help. The criteria for classifying these schools are based on their pupils' I.Q.'s (a guide to their potential), their reading age (an index of achievement), the number of pupils receiving free lunch (an indicator of socioeconomic status), pupil mobility (a clue to administrative and instructional complications), the number of non-English-speaking pupils (a signal of special reading difficulties), and the per cent of teachers

on permanent tenure (inverted, a warning of personnel difficulties). In 1962, 201 out of the city's 584 elementary schools, or 34 per cent, were classified as "special service" schools. (In 1956, only forty-three out of 592 elementary schools, or 7 per cent, were in this category.) Those schools get priorities in the appointment of regular teachers and the assignment of guidance counselors. Class size is appreciably smaller than in the more favored schools and they are served by an expanded program of remedial reading to upgrade their pupils' reading skills. Some schools have special "teacher-training" consultants to help newly appointed teachers. All schools in the Higher Horizons program are in the "special service" category, but not all "special service" schools are in the Higher Horizons program.

2. *The Early Identification and Prevention program.* This program is based on the familiar adage, "An ounce of prevention is worth a pound of cure." If children who show evidence of maladjustment can be helped in the early grades, their problems can be overcome more readily or minimized later in life. Under this program, teams of guidance counselors, social workers, and psychologists try to find children in the first three grades with potential physical, learning, emotional, or behavioral problems and refer them to remedial classes, clinical services, family agency services, health services, and the like. Talented or gifted children are also identified, but they are distinctly in a minority. Any child can be maladjusted, but the incidence is highest in problem areas. Indeed, a number of "E.I.P." schools, as those serviced by the program are called, are also Higher Horizons schools.

3. *Junior Guidance classes:* This is a two-year pilot program being conducted in a small number of elementary schools, in which emotionally and socially disturbed children are handled by special teachers, with the help of counselors and clinical psychologists. In many instances pupil behavior patterns reflect disturbed homes. Research has indicated that emotional instability cuts across class lines, but is more widespread in low socioeconomic areas than in privileged homes.

4. *Programs for non-English-speaking children:* New York, traditionally the nation's melting pot, has assimilated millions of foreigners. Today, the principal foreign tongue is Spanish, spoken chiefly by Puerto Ricans. From 1953 to 1957, a "Puerto Rican Study" developed test techniques, teaching methods, and instructional materials for teaching English to Puerto Ricans. The school program for these children is based on this study. Recent arrivals may be placed in so-called "C" classes, where they remain up to a year. Non-English coordinators and substitute auxiliary teachers are assigned to schools with many non-English-speaking pupils to work with teachers, interview new arrivals, follow up pupils when they are placed in regular classes, and improve cooperation between school and community.

5. *Career guidance and potential dropouts:* Other programs handle potential dropouts. The children most likely to leave school are those who are unsuccessful in their studies. Many are intellectual, emotional, or social misfits. The Career Guidance program attempts to salvage junior high

pupils of this kind. The work is carried on largely by extra guidance counselors and corrective reading teachers whose services supplement the work
of the regular class teacher. This project, which is carried on in "special
service" schools, has shown that pupils who are apt to drop out of school
because of limited academic success may be dissuaded by specially designed programs of prevocational education and effective guidance.

When James B. Conant visited slum schools in big cities, he found
teachers and administrators struggling against "appalling odds." These
schools are too difficult and the rewards too small for many teachers. As
a result, the need for teachers in such schools tends to outrun the supply.
Measures have been taken to help the teachers in these schools. Alertness
courses, some partly on open-circuit TV, have trained teachers in such
areas as the techniques of teaching reading. Specially trained coordinators
recently conducted a training program for teachers of non-English-speaking
children. Finally, teacher assistants have taken over some of the teachers'
burdens. Volunteers provided by the Public Education Association have
assisted classroom teachers for several years. A key part of this experiment
has been helping pupils improve their reading and giving special assistance
to the non-English-speaking child.

Some teacher preparatory institutions have attempted to inculcate future
teachers with the idealism of the Peace Corps. Hunter College, a munici-
pally supported institution in New York, has been developing a promising
program of training teachers to staff multiproblem schools. Student volunteers are assigned to a particular school in a depressed neighborhood, usually in Harlem. They familiarize themselves not only with the schools but
with the community as well. They visit Negro homes, read Negro newspapers, confer with community leaders, talk with local ministers, and in-
spect local housing projects, hospitals, and police stations. They observe
teachers for two weeks before they gradually "break in" to a regular classroom assignment. More thorough than most pupil-teacher courses, this program includes mutual exchanges of experiences among student-teachers,
periodic conferences with key personnel in the school, and intensive guidance by the Hunter College teacher preparatory staff. Comprehensive
preparation of this kind helps ready them for later service in schools in depressed areas. It enables them to face their tasks with realism and understanding instead of shock and frustration.

The "Bridge Project," conducted at Queens College, another college-level
municipal institution, is a demonstration project established to discover how
teachers can be prepared to help slum children learn. (Bridge stands for
"Building Resources of Instruction for Disadvantaged Groups in Education.") Its approach is many-sided. Three recent graduates of the
teacher-training program, for example, will teach the same classes in a Negro
neighborhood continuously for the entire three years of junior high school.
Secondly, an experiment in supervision centers about a "coordinating
teacher," who will suggest possible improvements in teacher preparation

and supervision in schools of this kind. Finally, new teaching techniques, and a modified organization of subject matter are being tried out.

We have only a beachhead of knowledge on how to teach disadvantaged children. The college experiments and demonstration projects described above are hopeful signs. Intelligent efforts are being made to prepare teachers to handle assignments of this kind with confidence and skill.

In the past, one of the principal tasks of the American public schools has been to assimilate and Americanize the European immigrant and to help him take his place in an industrial society. Today it is to educate millions of newcomers in the slums of our big cities. The preservation of our democratic way of life, the demands of our economy, and the mental health of our people all require that we learn how to educate their children effectively. Thomas Jefferson hoped this nation would remain agricultural, because he distrusted city mobs. If millions of newcomers in our big cities are alienated because they are inadequately prepared to cope with the dynamics of urban living, Jefferson's prophecy may be partly realized.

Again, this country has been shifting to occupations that require more skill. With automation already on the horizon, the demand for unskilled labor is inevitably declining and the need for trained workers is rising. This suggests that we must look to the culturally deprived to fill shortages of skilled manpower. Otherwise, declares Conant in an oft-quoted remark, we are "allowing social dynamite to accumulate in our large cities." More than half the youth in some slum neighborhoods, he discovered, were unemployed.

Finally, we must offer these children the best opportunities to develop a wholesome respect for themselves and society. Failure to do so will inevitably produce heavy costs, in the form of police protection, courts, jails, and mental institutions. It will surely be less expensive, in the long run, to organize schools which can meet the needs of disadvantaged youth.

REFERENCE

1. Ravitz, Mel. "The Role of the School in the Urban Setting: Depressed Areas." Paper delivered at Work Conference on Curriculum and Teaching in Depressed Urban Areas, Teachers College, Columbia University, July 2–13, 1962.

29

A Teaching Strategy for Culturally Deprived Pupils: Cognitive and Motivational Considerations

DAVID P. AUSUBEL

The possibility of arresting and reversing the course of intellectual retardation in the culturally deprived pupil depends largely on providing him with an optimal learning environment as early as possible in the course of his educational career. If the limiting effects of prolonged cultural deprivation on the development of verbal intelligence and on the acquisition of verbal knowledge are to be at least partially overcome, better-than-average strategies of teaching are obviously necessary in terms of both general effectiveness and specific appropriateness for his particular learning situation. Yet precisely the opposite state of affairs typically prevails: the learning environment of the culturally deprived child is both generally inferior and specifically inappropriate. His cumulative intellectual deficit, therefore, almost invariably reflects, in part, the cumulative impact of a continuing and consistently deficient learning environment, as well as his emotional and motivational reaction to this environment. Thus, much of the lower-class child's alienation from the school is not so much a reflection of discriminatory or rejecting attitudes on the part of teachers and other school personnel — although the importance of this factor should not be underestimated; it is in greater measure a reflection of the cumulative effects of a curriculum that is too demanding of him, and of the resulting load of frustration, confusion, demoralization, resentment, and impaired self-confidence that he must bear.

Cognitive Considerations

An effective and appropriate teaching strategy for the culturally deprived child must therefore emphasize these three considerations: (a) the selection of initial learning material geared to the learner's existing state of readiness; (b) mastery and consolidation of all on-going learning tasks before new tasks are introduced, so as to provide the necessary foundation for successful sequential learning and to prevent unreadiness for future

✧ Reprinted from *The School Review*, Winter, 1963, pp. 454–463, by permission of The University of Chicago Press. Copyright © 1963 by the University of Chicago. Also used by permission of the author. David P. Ausubel is a staff member of the Bureau of Educational Research, University of Illinois.

learning tasks; and (c) the use of structured learning materials optimally organized to facilitate efficient sequential learning. Attention to these three factors can go a long way toward insuring effective learning for the first time, and toward restoring the child's educational morale and confidence in his ability to learn. Later possible consequences are partial restoration of both intrinsic and extrinsic motivation for academic achievement, diminution of anti-intellectualism, and decreased alienation from the school to the point where his studies make sense and he sees some purpose in learning. In my opinion, of all the available teaching strategies, programed instruction, minus the teaching-machine format, has the greatest potentialities for meeting the aforementioned three criteria of an effective and appropriate approach to the teaching of culturally deprived pupils.

READINESS. A curriculum that takes the readiness of the culturally deprived child into account always takes as its starting point his existing knowledge and sophistication in the various subject matter areas and intellectual skills, no matter how far down the scale this happens to be. This policy demands rigid elimination of all subject matter that he cannot economically assimilate on the basis of his current level of cognitive sophistication. It presupposes emphasis on his acquisition of the basic intellectual skills before any attempt is made to teach him algebra, geometry, literature, and foreign languages. However, in many urban high schools and junior high schools today, pupils who cannot read at a third-grade level and who cannot speak or write grammatically or perform simple arithmetical computations are subjected to irregular French verbs, Shakespearean drama, and geometrical theorems. Nothing more educationally futile or better calculated to destroy educational morale could be imagined!

In the terms of readiness for a given level of school work, a child is no less ready because of a history of cultural deprivation, chronic academic failure, and exposure to an unsuitable curriculum than because of deficient intellectual endowment. Hence, realistic recognition of this fact is not undemocratic, reactionary, or evidence of social class bias, of intellectual snobbery, of a "soft," patronizing approach, or a belief in the inherent uneducability of lower-class children. Neither is it indicative of a desire to surrender to the culturally deprived child's current intellectual level, to perpetuate the status quo, or to institute a double, class-oriented standard of education. It is merely a necessary first step in preparing him to cope with more advanced subject matter, and hence in eventually reducing existing social class differentials in academic achievement. To set the same *initial* standards and expectations for the academically retarded culturally deprived child as for the nonretarded middle- or lower-class child is automatically to insure the former's failure and to widen prevailing discrepancies between social class groups.

CONSOLIDATION. By insisting on consolidation or mastery of on-going lessons before new material is introduced, we make sure of continued readiness and success in sequentially organized learning. Abundant experimental research has confirmed the proposition that prior learnings are not transferable to new learning tasks unless they are first overlearned (4). Overlearning, in turn, requires an adequate number of adequately spaced repetitions and reviews, sufficient intratask repetitiveness prior to intra- and intertask diversification (6), and opportunity for differential practice of the more difficult components of a task. Frequent testing and provision of feedback, especially with test items demanding fine discrimination among alternatives varying in degrees of correctness, also enhance consolidation by confirming, clarifying, and correcting previous learnings. Lastly, in view of the fact that the culturally deprived child tends to learn more slowly than his nondeprived peers, self-pacing helps to facilitate consolidation.

STRUCTURED, SEQUENTIAL MATERIALS. The principal advantage of programed instruction, apart from the fact that it furthers consolidation, is its careful sequential arrangement and gradation of difficulty which insures that each attained increment in learning serves as an appropriate foundation and anchoring post for the learning and retention of subsequent items in the ordered sequence (2). Adequate programing of materials also presupposes maximum attention to such matters as lucidity, organization, and the explanatory and integrative power of substantive content. It is helpful, for example, if sequential materials are so organized that they become progressively more differentiated in terms of generality and inclusiveness, and if similarities and differences between the current learning task and previous learnings are explicitly delineated (1). Both of these aims can be accomplished by using an advance organizer or brief introductory passage before each new unit of material, which both makes available relevant explanatory principles at a high level of abstraction and increases discriminability. Programed instruction can also be especially adapted to meet the greater needs of culturally deprived pupils for concrete-empirical props in learning relational propositions.

Although programed instruction in general is particularly well suited to the needs of the culturally deprived child, I cannot recommend the small-frame format characteristic of teaching-machine programs and most programed textbooks. In terms of both the logical requirements of meaningful learning and the actual size of the task that can be conveniently accommodated by the learner, the frame length typically used by teaching machines is artificially and unnecessarily abbreviated. It tends to fragment the ideas presented in the program so that their interrelationships are obscured and their logical structure is destroyed (7). Hence it is relatively easy for less able students to master each granulated step of a given program without understanding the logical relationships and development of the concepts presented (3). In my opinion, therefore, the traditional textbook format or oral didactic exposition that follows the programing principles outlined above, supplemented by frequent self-scoring and feedback-giving tests, is far superior to the teaching-machine approach for the actual presentation of subject matter content (7).

Motivational Considerations

Thus far I have considered various environmental factors that induce retardation in the culturally deprived child's intellectual growth, as well as different cognitive techniques of counteracting and reversing such retardation. These factors and techniques, however, do not operate in a motivational vacuum. Although it is possible separately to consider cognitive and motivational aspects of learning for purposes of theoretical analysis, they are nonetheless inseparably intertwined in any real-life learning situation. For example, school failure and loss of confidence resulting from an inappropriate curriculum further depress the culturally deprived pupil's motivation to learn and thereby increase his existing learning and intellectual deficit. Similarly, although a number of practice and task variables are potentially important for effective learning in a programed instruction context, appropriate manipulation of these variables can, in the final analysis, only insure successful long-term learning of subject matter provided that the individual is adequately motivated.

Doing without being interested in what one is doing results in relatively little permanent learning, since it is reasonable to suppose that only those materials can be meaningfully incorporated on a long-term basis into an individual's structure of knowledge that are relevant to areas of concern in his psychological field. Learners who have little need to know and understand quite naturally expend little learning effort; manifest an insufficiently meaningful learning-set; fail to develop precise meanings, to reconcile new ideas with existing concepts, and to formulate new propositions in their own words; and do not devote enough time and energy to practice and review. Material is therefore never sufficiently consolidated to form an adequate foundation for sequential learning.

The problem of reversibility exists in regard to the motivational as well as in regard to the cognitive status of the culturally deprived pupil, inasmuch as his environment typically stunts not only his intellectual development, but also the development of appropriate motivations for academic achievement. Motivations for learning, like cognitive abilities, are only potential rather than inherent or endogenous capacities in human beings; their actual development is invariably dependent upon adequate environmental stimulation. Cognitive drive or intrinsic motivation to learn, for example, is probably derived in a very general sense from curiosity tendencies and from related predispositions to explore, manipulate, and cope with the environment; but these tendencies and predispositions are only actualized as a result of successful exercise and the anticipation of future satisfying consequences from further exercise and as a result of internalization of the values of those significant persons in the family and subcultural community with whom the child identifies.

INTRINSIC MOTIVATION. The development of cognitive drive or of intrinsic motivation for learning, that is, the acquisition of knowledge as an end in tself or for its own sake, is, in my opinion, the most promising motivational strategy which we can adopt in relation to the culturally deprived child. It is true, of course, in view of the anti-intellectualism and pragmatic attitude toward education that is characteristic of lower-class ideology (8), that a superficially better case can be made for the alternative strategy of appealing to the incentives to job acquisition, retention, and advancement that now apply so saliently to continuing education because of the rapid rate of technological change. Actually, however, intrinsic motivation for learning is more potent, relevant, durable, and easier to arouse than its extrinsic counterpart. Meaningful school learning, in contrast to most kinds of laboratory learning, requires relatively little effort or extrinsic incentive, and, when successful, furnishes its own reward. In most instances of school learning, cognitive drive is also the only immediately relevant motivation, since the greater part of school learning cannot be rationalized as necessary for meeting the demands of daily living. Furthermore, it does not lose its relevance or potency in later adult life when utilitarian and career advancement considerations are no longer applicable. Lastly, as we know from the high dropout rate among culturally deprived high-school youth, appeals to extrinsic motivation are not very effective. Among other reasons, the latter situation reflects a limited time perspective focused primarily on the present; a character structure that is oriented more to immediate than delayed gratification of needs; the lack of strong internalized needs for and anxiety about high academic and vocational achievement, as part of the prevailing family, peer group, and community ideology (5); and the seeming unreality and impossibility of attaining the rewards of prolonged striving and self-denial in view of current living conditions and family circumstances, previous lack of school success, and the discriminatory attitudes of middle-class society (5).

If we wish to develop the cognitive drive so that it remains viable during the school years and in adult life, it is necessary to move still further away from the educational doctrine of gearing the curriculum to the spontaneously expressed interests, current concerns, and life-adjustment problems of pupils. Although it is undoubtedly unrealistic and even undesirable in our culture to eschew entirely the utilitarian, ego-enhancement, and anxiety-reduction motivations for learning, we must place increasingly greater emphasis upon the value of knowing and understanding as goals in their own right, quite apart from any practical benefits they may confer. Instead of denigrating subject-matter knowledge, we must discover more efficient methods of fostering the long-term acquisition or meaningful and usable bodies of knowledge, and of developing appropriate intrinsic motivations for such learning.

It must be conceded at the outset that culturally deprived children typically manifest little intrinsic motivation to learn. They come from family and cultural environments in which the veneration of learning for its own sake is not a conspicuous value, and in which there is little or no tradition of scholarship. Moreover, they have not been notably successful in their previous learning efforts in school. Nevertheless we need not necessarily despair of motivating them to learn for intrinsic reasons. Psychologists have been emphasizing the motivation-learning and the interest-activity sequences of cause and effect for so long that they tend to overlook their reciprocal aspects. Since motivation is not an indispensable condition for short-term and limited-quantity learning, it is not necessary to postpone learning activities until appropriate interests and motivations have been developed. Frequently the best way of motivating an unmotivated pupil is to ignore his motivational state for the time being and concentrate on teaching him as effectively as possible. Much to his surprise and to his teacher's, he will learn despite his lack of motivation; and from the satisfaction of learning he will characteristically develop the motivation to learn more.

Paradoxically, therefore, we may discover that the most effective method of developing intrinsic motivation to learn is to focus on the cognitive rather than on the motivational aspects of learning, and to rely on the motivation that is developed retroactively from successful educational achievement. This is particularly true when a teacher is able to generate contagious excitement and enthusiasm about the subject he teaches, and when he is the kind of person with whom culturally deprived children can identify. Recruiting more men teachers and dramatizing the lives and exploits of cultural, intellectual, and scientific heroes can also enhance the process of identification. At the same time, of course, we can attempt to combat the anti-intellectualism and lack of cultural tradition in the home through programs of adult education and cultural enrichment.

EXTRINSIC MOTIVATION. The emphasis I have placed on intrinsic motivation for learning should not be interpreted to mean that I deny the importance of developing extrinsic motivations. The need for ego enhancement, status, and prestige through achievement, the internalization of long-term vocational aspirations, and the development of such implementing traits as responsibility, initiative, self-denial, frustration tolerance, impulse control, and the ability to postpone immediate hedonistic gratification are, after all, traditional hallmarks of personality maturation in our culture; and educational aspirations and achievement are both necessary prerequisites for, and way-station prototypes of, their vocational counterparts. Hence, in addition to encouraging intrinsic motivation for learning, it is also necessary to foster ego-enhancement and career-advancement motivations for academic achievement.

As previously pointed out, however, the current situation with respect to developing adequate motivations for higher academic and vocational achievement among culturally deprived children is not very encouraging. But just as in the case of cognitive drive, much extrinsic motivation for academic success can be generated retroactively from the experience of current success in schoolwork. Intensive counseling can also compensate greatly for the absence of appropriate home, community, and peer-group support and expectations for the development of long-term vocational ambitions. In a sense counselors must be prepared to act *in loco parentis* in this situation. By identifying with a mature, stable, striving, and successful male adult figure, culturally deprived boys can be encouraged to internalize long-term and realistic aspirations, as well as to develop the mature personality traits necessary for their implementation. Hence, as a result of achieving current ego enhancement in the school setting, obtaining positive encouragement and practical guidance in the counseling relationship, and experiencing less rejection and discrimination at the hands of school personnel, higher vocational aspirations appear to lie more realistically within their grasp. Further encouragement to strive for more ambitious academic and vocational goals can be provided by making available abundant scholarship aid to universities, to community colleges, and to technical institutes; by eliminating the color, ethnic, and class bar in housing, education, and employment; by acquainting culturally deprived youth with examples of successful professional persons originating from their own racial, ethnic, and class backgrounds; and by involving parents sympathetically in the newly fostered ambitions of their children. The success of the Higher Horizons project indicates that an energetic program organized along the lines outlined above can do much to reverse the effects of cultural deprivation on the development of extrinsic motivations for academic and vocational achievement.

REFERENCES

1. Ausubel, D. P. "The Use of Advance Organizers in the Learning and Retention of Meaningful Verbal Learning," *Journal of Educational Psychology*, 51:267–272, 1960; D. P. Ausubel and D. Fitzgerald, "The Role of Discriminability in Meaningful Verbal Learning and Retention," *Journal of Educational Psychology*, 52:266–274; 1961, and their "Organizer, General Background, and Antecedent Learning Variables in Sequential Verbal Learning," *ibid.*

2. Ausubel, D. P., and D. Fitzgerald. "Organizer, General Background, and Antecedent Learning and Retention," *Journal of Educational Psychology*, 52:266–274, 1961; and *chology*, 53:243–249, 1962.

3. Beane, D. G. "A Comparison of Linear and Branching Techniques of Programed Instruction in Plane Geometry," "Technical Report," No. 1. Urbana: Training Research Laboratory, University of Illinois, July 1962.

4. See Bruce, R. W. "Conditions of Transfer of Training," *Journal of Experimental Psychology*, 16:343–361, 1933; C. P. Duncan, "Transfer in Motor Learning as a Function of Degree of First-task Learning and Inter-task Similarity," *Journal of Experimental Psychology*, 45:1–11, 1953, and his "Transfer after Training with Single versus Multiple Tasks," *Journal of Experimental Psychology*, 55:63–72, 1958; L. Morrisett and C. I. Hovland, "A Comparison of Three Varieties of Training in Human Problem Solving," *Journal of Experimental Psychology*, 55:52–55, 1958; and J. M. Sassenrath, "Learning without Awareness and Transfer of Learning Sets," *Journal of Educational Psychology*, 50:202–212, 1959.

5. Davis, A. "Child Training and Social Class," in R. G. Barker, J. S. Kounin, and H. F. Wright (eds.), *Child Behavior and Development*. New York: McGraw-Hill Book Co., Inc., 1963. Pp. 607–620.

6. See Duncan, *op. cit.;* Morrisett and Hovland, *op. cit.;* and Sassenrath, *op. cit.*
7. Pressey, S. L. "Basic Unresolved Teaching-Machine Problems," *Theory into Practice,* I:30–37, 1962.
8. Riessman, F. *The Culturally Deprived Child.* New York: Harper and Brothers, 1962.

The Rural Disadvantaged

ROBERT M. ISENBERG

To focus only upon the problems that rural migrants create after they have moved to the city is much the same as treating a disease without concern for its cause. For, whereas many rural disadvantaged will continue to stream into our cities, millions more will remain in the country and seek subsistence there.

As yet, rural school systems, except in a few scattered instances, have not taken direct steps to develop programs for their disadvantaged comparable to the experimental efforts under way in many cities. Nor is articulation between rural and city schools sufficient to assist substantially with mobility adjustments. Such a simple thing as the transfer of pupil records, for example, would help, but even this has not been worked out with any consistency.

The challenge to both city and country is to develop in the disadvantaged the ability to adjust to a society and a future for which they are, at present, largely unprepared. Among the characteristics of the rural disadvantaged — both children and adults — are a low level of aspiration, a tendency to set only short-term goals, values which differ somewhat from acceptable norms, and a general unfamiliarity with cultural activities which lead to enriched living.

School district reorganization and consolidation have done much to help rural schools attack the problems confronting them. Because relatively large numbers of students can be taught in consolidated schools, rural areas are able to afford more well-qualified teachers, more guidance counselors, and

◇ From the *NEA Journal,* April, 1963, p. 27. Used by permission of the author and the publisher. Robert M. Isenberg is Director, Division of Rural Service, National Education Association, and Executive Secretary of the NEA Department of Rural Education.

more school psychologists than ever before. Furthermore, an increasing number of summer school programs, bookmobiles, outdoor education programs, recreation programs, and other efforts give promise of reaching more of the rural disadvantaged who previously had no access to such opportunities.

Some help from outside the school is also coming. Significant federal and state programs designed to increase employment opportunities in rural areas and to develop employable skills on the part of the unemployed are now under way.

Nonetheless, much of what should be done in rural areas for the culturally disadvantaged must be undertaken by schools. In many rural communities, the school is the only social institution with resources and personnel to give real and substantial help to young people, whether they migrate to the city or remain at home. The chief hope for eliminating poverty and social disadvantage thus rests with education.

❖ ❖ **31** ❖ ❖

Educating Disadvantaged Children

JOE L. FROST AND O. RAY KING

Arkansas shares with the nation a burden of educating many thousands of disadvantaged Americans. The disadvantaged live in every geographical area of the country — big city and rural — and they represent every ethnic group. They live in slums, in rural mountain areas, on reservations, or in trucks, cars, shacks, and tents as they follow the crops. They have been called culturally deprived, restricted, and disadvantaged. But basically they are the poor — the unskilled, the welfare recipient, the illiterate, and frequently, the unwanted.

The disadvantaged in Arkansas form three rather distinctive educative groups: the economically restricted (often welfare recipient) child in regular schools, the Negro in segregated schools, and the migrant child in regular and special summer schools. Many come from homes receiving

❖ From *The Journal of Arkansas Education*, November, 1964, pp. 6, 28. Used by permission of the authors and the publisher. Joe L. Frost is Assistant Professor of Education, University of Texas, and O. Ray King is Professor and Head, Department of Elementary Education, Sam Houston State Teachers College.

welfare grants, either food or money. During 1961–1962, over ninety thousand Arkansas people were dependent upon public welfare monetary grants, while 265,732 received surplus commodities. It appears pertinent that these members of society become more productive when we consider that over fifty-one million dollars was spent by the Arkansas State Department of Public Welfare alone during the year July 1, 1961, to June 30, 1962. Most important, however, is the impact of economic restriction upon the education of children, for poverty breeds poverty.

Disadvantaged youth present a unique set of problems for educators. They are usually retarded in school achievement, poorly adjusted to school living, have unique value systems, and are more likely than other children to become delinquent or drop out of school. Offering an education that meets their needs may well be the number one problem facing teachers today.

Results of studies conducted in three rural Arkansas elementary schools during a two-year period ending in August, 1964, offer insights into improving the education of disadvantaged children. For clarification we call these schools A, B, and C with enrollment as follows:

School A: A special summer school for children of migrant workers; most were residents of Arkansas and attended Arkansas schools during the regular school terms. One hundred and twenty children were subjects for this study.

School B: A rural elementary school located in a community of six thousand. Three hundred fifty-six children were enrolled; sixty-two were welfare recipients and subjects for this study. An enriched curriculum was in operation with emphasis upon total development of children and provision for individual differences. Special provisions were made for disadvantaged children — showers, food facilities, clothing, medical care, and special health instruction.

School C: A rural Negro elementary school. Forty-six children were subjects (every child enrolled for which data could be obtained).

Data were collected from standardized tests, interviews, observations, sociometric techniques, informal tests, and rating scales. A 650 computer was used to facilitate computation. The results of the investigation revealed a number of common problem areas existing among the three groups. Approaches to alleviating these should prove to be similar. On the basis of the data and direct observation, conclusions and recommendations were made.

Academic Achievement

With few exceptions, low-income children were retarded in school achievement — reading, arithmetic, and language. The degree of retardation was more severe with each passing year (the welfare children in school B showed slight gains for each successive grade level). Fewer than 5 per cent of all disadvantaged children studied achieved above the national norms. They achieved highest in arithmetic and lowest in reading. The achievement of girls was significantly superior to that of boys.

The welfare children in school B enrolled in multigrade (two grades in one room) classrooms earned higher academic achievement and personality scores on the California series than children in one-grade classrooms. They scored lower on mental maturity tests.

Placement in special classrooms reflects the cultural influence upon learning in general and I.Q. and academic achievement in particular. Fourteen of the fifteen children enrolled in School B's special classroom were from disadvantaged homes. In some respects the effects of cultural deprivation and mental retardation upon learning are similar. A critical re-examination of the concept of mental retardation may be in order.

Personality Development

Disadvantaged children achieved below average on the California Test of Personality. Here again, the children enrolled in School B scored significantly higher than the other groups with near average scores.

Disadvantaged children were less acceptable for friendships by their peers, and teachers tended to score them less preferable to teach (School B). Lack of preference is no surprise to teachers accustomed to the problems associated with teaching disadvantaged children in the regular classroom.

Home Factors

For School B only (sixty-two welfare children, Grades 1–6), data were collected for a number of variables associated with the home life of disadvantaged children.

Factors reflecting participation in total family social activities (church attendance and taking vacations with parents) correlate significantly (1 per cent level) with the academic achievement of welfare children.

The typical welfare recipient child is absent from school eight days per semester; he has attended two schools, and rides a school bus. The chances are one in four that he has visited a dentist during his lifetime. He has seven siblings (this mean was the same for over sixty migrant families interviewed) and lives in a five-room house; church is attended twice a month. The chances are one in three that the home has running water but nine in ten that it is serviced by electricity.

Parents exhibit little concern for their children's school progress, evidenced by the fact that only 11 per cent ever attended a P.T.A. meeting, and only 16 per cent have visited their child's classroom. On the other hand the chances are one in two that parents have taken the child on a family vacation or have attended a regularly scheduled parent-teacher conference.

Recommendations

1. Research studies to date emphasize that deprivation of certain contacts — language, affectional, physical, and material — in infancy and early childhood appear to impose severe restrictions upon the growing child. Further, disadvantaged children are retarded in ability to profit from common school experiences upon entry to first grade and become increasingly

retarded through time. Therefore, special efforts should be made to provide rich preschool experience through nursery schools and kindergartens.

2. College curriculums should provide special training for prospective teachers of disadvantaged children.

3. Class size should be reduced proportionately to increased numbers of disadvantaged children in attendance.

4. Multigrade and ungraded classes should be used to provide for close contacts among children of similar interests and talent, and to reduce peer-group pressures upon slow learners.

5. Attention should be directed toward obtaining parent involvement in school functions.

6. School transportation should be used for frequent trips to give children multiple opportunities for concept development and for gaining increased language facility.

7. In-service programs should be conducted for helping teachers develop techniques for teaching the disadvantaged child. Emphasis should be given to understanding attitudes, values, and aspirations of low socioeconomic groups.

8. The basic needs of food, clothing, rest, and affection must be met before efficient school learning can take place. The effective school curriculum will contain provisions for these necessary ingredients.

Finally, we believe that curriculum, philosophy, and practice must diverge from narrow emphases toward supplying a rich educational environment that is consistent with the necessities as well as the peculiarities of disadvantaged children.

✧ ✧ 32 ✧ ✧

School and the Migrant Child

JOE L. FROST

Each year 150,000 children move with their parents across the croplands of this country, harvesting as they go. They are burdened by poverty and disease, deprived of education and legislation which could alleviate their

✧ Reprinted by permission of the Association for Childhood Education International, 3615 Wisconsin Avenue, N.W., Washington, D.C. "School and the Migrant Child," by Joe L. Frost. From *Childhood Education*, November, 1964, Vol. 41, pp. 129–132. Joe L. Frost is Assistant Professor of Education, University of Texas.

condition. These are the migrants — rejected by communities and unwelcomed in schools. Temporary residence makes them ineligible for public assistance[1] and other legal benefits. Many are illiterate; most are educationally retarded.

Child labor and school attendance laws are inadequate and often ignored as children (at times as young as four years of age) work in the fields beside their parents. Deprived of cultural experiences which contribute much to success in schools, these children are frequently destined for failure in school and become misfits in adult living. They subsequently bear other generations of migrants. Thus the vicious cycle proliferates.

Most educators agree that the task of the school is to build upon a child's prior learnings while developing fully functioning individuals. There is further agreement that methods employed toward this end be consistent with the innate potential of the child and a democratic view of living. Appropriate procedures for educating the migrant child are elusive, for each child brings a unique set of problems to school. He may have a value system dissimilar to that of the teacher, a low level of aspiration, limited language facility, little knowledge of or concern for sanitation, and even less familiarity with generally accepted cultural patterns. These problems appear to be common, with some modifications, to all economically restricted groups in this country. Schools and communities must somehow develop compensatory approaches.

Summer School for Migrant Children

One rural Arkansas community, with the cooperation of churches and other agencies, has attempted to provide for the educational needs of migrant farm laborers' children during summer months. These children offered a unique opportunity for study by educators and sociologists — all were Caucasian; most were residents of Arkansas; all attended regular schools either full time or sporadically during the regular term. The school activities described below took place during the summer sessions, 1962 and 1963.

This school for migrant children was conceived and organized by local United Church Women and supported by the State and National Council of Churches. The Department of Elementary Education at the University of Arkansas provided assistance with the instructional program.

A camp for migrant workers with 160 cabins was maintained by the community. Only the barest of necessities was available. Living conditions were substandard yet better than those of families living in cars, trucks, tents, and shacks during the harvest season.

After a grueling day in the fields picking beans, strawberries, or grapes, the children (ages four to sixteen) came to school. Their work day began as early as 4:30 a.m. and ended in early afternoon upon arrival at school,

---

[1] *Editors' Note:* It is hoped that The Economic Opportunity Act of 1964 will soon alleviate the problems of the migrant child. This article was written before the recent passage of the bill.

where a hot lunch was provided, followed by a period of rest and sleep. Then the children were divided into age groups for instruction. Experiences were shared; group and individual activities were planned. There was time for creative expression utilizing various media — leather crafts, woodworking, and mechanics for the older boys; art, dramatics, music, and literature activities for everyone. Reading, writing, arithmetic, science, and social studies taught in a creative manner were integral parts of the total program. The degree of structure was dependent upon the maturity level of participating children.

Real Experiences

Units of work were developed around real-life experiences of the children. An especially profitable unit was initiated during the first week of school as children shared travel experiences. Questioning and exploring ideas led to writing experience stories and working with maps and books. Thus momentum developed. Little imagination was required to move from this stage into studies of science close to the living of these youngsters — health, animals, and crops. In each area, numbers were important. To the migrant child, arithmetic made sense. In the words of Freddie, "You have to know how to count or you might get beat out of your money."

Home Life of Migrant

A check of sixty families showed that the average number of children per migrant family was five, making a total family group of seven. These family groups often lived in one-room cabins. Not only was there crowded living, but food was often limited; clothing was passed from child to child or worn day after day by the same child until discarded; sanitation was difficult because of lack of running water, electricity, and screen doors; children's activities varied from "just loafing" or scuffling with siblings to fishing and playing improvised games. Books and other educational materials were luxuries. Parents, worn out from a day in the fields and primarily concerned with providing sustenance for large families, had little time or energy to spare for their children. Money was not readily available for cultural pursuits. It is to be expected that a child coming from this environment has a view of life considerably different from that of the typical middle-class child, especially in respect to self-concept; sex roles; responsibilities to family, school and community; peer-group roles; goal setting and educational aspirations.

These children were friendly, affectionate and intensely loyal to their families. Hostility, when present, was violent but quickly forgotten. Boys were particularly proud of their physical ability. Four- and five-year-olds spoke with pride of picking twenty pounds of beans in one morning. Fourteen-year-olds often did the work of grown men. Delinquency was rare. The teachers participating in this program constructively utilized this knowledge in classroom living.

Basic Human Needs

A crucial factor in the life and education of the migrant child is the provision of basic human needs — rest, food, clothing, shelter, and affection. These must be satisfied before many school experiences can have real meaning. The resources of the tired, hungry, cold, or unwanted child cannot be channeled toward educative pursuits. No child, deprived or otherwise, will achieve according to his potential if he is continually rejected by children and teachers. The migrant child is often rejected because his appearance, behavior, and attitudes are somewhat foreign to teachers' and classmates' concepts of what children should be like. Teachers almost unanimously assert their belief in the value of uniqueness and individuality, but their actions or classroom practices often do not support their beliefs. To repeat, sincerely valuing and accepting these children pays a tremendous educative bonus.

Language

The language skill of migrant children is severely limited. Results of the Peabody Vocabulary Test administered to thirty-two randomly selected individuals, ranging from six to sixteen years, revealed raw scores strikingly similar across chronological age lines. The child of six or seven had essentially the same vocabulary as the youngster of fifteen or sixteen. Limited cultural experiences in the home, poor adjustment to and progress in school were major causative factors.

The average degree of retardation for all migrant children attending the summer school was about three years, ranging from less than one year for six- and seven-year-olds to about five years for sixteen-year-olds. Many migrant children drop out of school permanently. A portion of these become failures in adult living. Large-scale retardation of migrant children in school would superficially appear to be due to subnormal intelligence if scores on I.Q. tests were considered valid estimates. Conventional group I.Q. tests cannot profitably be utilized. Poor language facility on the part of the youngsters precludes validity. The Davis-Eells Games, a "culture fair" test of problem-solving ability, was administered to thirty children, ages eight to fourteen. The range of I.Q. scores was 54 to 100 with a mean of 78.[2] (Other nonverbal tests have produced similar results.) Scores indicated that most of the children in this group were subnormal in intelligence. However, this was not necessarily true. Educators working with the children were convinced that, despite test results, most were bright, capable and willing to learn. This conviction was supported over and over again in actual classroom practice.

[2] Low I.Q. scores appear to be due to restriction of cultural experiences which contribute to success on I.Q. tests. Raw scores on the Davis-Eells Test increased disproportionately with increased chronological ages of the children. Therefore, older children tended to earn lower I.Q. scores due to chronological age differential affecting the conversion of raw scores to I.Q. scores.

Jimmy, with a measured I.Q. of 69, perceived and described possibilities for improving techniques in leather and metal craft before the instructor had completed the initial explanation.

Sue, I.Q. 75, quickly and accurately computed daily and weekly earnings from picking beans without resorting to the use of pencil and paper.

Billy, I.Q. 78, demonstrated proficiency in explaining road map symbols.

It is generally agreed that a culture-free I.Q. test has yet to be developed.

We have learned a great deal over a period of time about the living and learning of these children who harvest the crops. We need to know much more about factors that affect their progress in and adjustment to the typical middle-class-oriented schools which they will attend during the winter months. The knowledge gained thus far gives us some guidelines for action.

Good Teachers, Time, Space, Materials

The successful teacher of migrant children will practice good human relations. He will develop sensitivity to and awareness of problems inherent in substandard living. There will be no public evaluations of children by segregation of individuals and groups because of ability, behavior, or offensive odors; there will be no chastisement of children with learning deficiencies through brutalizing, ignoring, or giving low marks; there will be no telling through ingenious, teacher-created techniques that they are failures. As if they didn't know it!

More attention will be given to the variables — time, space, and materials:

- more time allocated by teachers to learning about and providing for unique needs, interests and abilities
- more time for building upon and extending limited backgrounds of experiences
- more time for providing basic needs of food, shelter, clothing, rest and affection
- more time for genuine understanding and acceptance
- more time for developing acceptable habits, attitudes, and social maturity
- more time for administrative planning and action in developing better programs for migrant and other deprived children
- more space (and fewer children) for individual and group activity
- more variety in materials to provide for diverse interests and abilities.

Creating an optimum learning environment for the migrant child is indeed difficult and demands much of teachers and social agencies. Extraordinary effort is required. The ordinary is scarcely good enough for the typical child and is practically useless for the migrant.

While the school needs to adapt programs along with social agencies, the total problem of the migrant worker needs to be attacked by local, state, and national agencies simultaneously. Concern for the migrant and other deprived groups is rapidly increasing. Much that can be done depends upon legislative action and initiation of corrective educational programs. Meanwhile, society continues to share the shame of "cheap" migrant labor and to pay the price in wasted human potential.

33

Can We Afford Misery?

CYRUS KARRAKER

One thousand day-care centers were needed for fifty thousand migrant children in 1963, but the government provided no more than fifty. This number, small as it is, fails to show how great is the neglect of these children since the states of New York, Ohio, and Pennsylvania operated thirty-one of the fifty, while in the three states with the largest migrant populations — Texas, California, and Michigan — only one center was operated. The one was the signal achievement of California. In addition to the fifty centers provided by the government were the centers provided by religious groups. These were often decidedly beneficial though reaching only a very small percentage of the children in need.

The states in 1963 with well-established programs of day care for migrant children, supported from public funds were: New Jersey (state funds), four; New York (state funds), fourteen; Ohio (federal), six; Pennsylvania (federal and state), eleven; and Wisconsin (federal), four. Other states which include in their child welfare services plans for migrant day care through federal assistance are: California, Florida, Indiana, Maryland, Michigan, Minnesota, North Carolina, and Oklahoma. Colorado's one day-care center receives state support. Day care for migrant children in these states is in a somewhat pilot stage.

Our Hidden Children

The difference a day-care center makes in the life of a migrant child can scarcely be grasped without visiting a migrant camp where the children live. Be prepared to have your heart broken when you see the injuries inflicted on their personalities. In this forbidding place the child has no privacy, no playthings, scarcely any care, and perhaps worst of all, no one to appreciate or admire him for anything he may do. You may read articles and view films on migrant life — all they tell you will soon be forgotten — but once you see the little children at a camp they will never let go of your conscience.

✧ From *The Journal of Nursery Education*, January, 1964, pp. 89–95. Used by permission of the author and the publisher. Cyrus Karraker is Professor of History, Bucknell University.

Finding the children is a problem, for the camps are located on isolated farms far from the public view. Factory children of a half century past were not hard to find. These children with sad, tired faces, and many with twisted limbs, were readily observed as they entered or left the factories by people walking along the adjoining streets. Today's migrant children are out of sight and out of the public's mind. Their rescue requires a great amount of your determination.

Whose Responsibility?

Who is responsible for the welfare of these children? The growers, primarily, because they import migrant families into the county to harvest their crops. Yet the invariable reply of these men to every appeal for their aid is: "I've no time for the kids; my crops have to be harvested." At the same time, a large degree of responsibility also rests on the neighboring community. For example, a playground is the obvious need at every camp where children live.

These children, like all children, love to have fun; their health and happiness depend on it. The setting up of a playground with sandbox, combination slide and swings would cost a civic or church group no more than twenty-five dollars, yet can you imagine the great amount of happiness from this small investment? Curiously enough, many people who are quick to help the underprivileged in foreign lands can overlook them in their own backyard. This happens to the migrant child. A playground at a migrant camp is such a rarity to behold that on seeing one you wonder when St. Christopher had passed that way, and whether anyone raised an objection to his playground, such as "It is a waste of good money to help these children; they'll just destroy everything you give them."

The prevailing condition of migrant children over the nation was described by a migrant woman who was brought in to testify at hearings conducted on farm wages by the Industrial Welfare Commission of California in 1961. She was asked how old she considered her children must be before taking them to the fields? She replied,

> 'Course, we never did believe that the girls should be in the fields, but there has to come a time for everybody. So then we had a little boy, he was about, oh, he was about a year old. We didn't take him to the fields, but we had him in the camp which is worse enough, in that kind of heat and the mosquitoes. It is not the same as when you are in your own home. And then that next year he was about two years old and that is when we took him into the fields.

When asked how old they were when they started to work, she replied, "I never did put my children to work very little. The littlest one was seven. She did whatever she could. You know, no rush" (4).

The life of children at these camps and in the fields bears a striking resemblance to life in factory slums and to child labor of a half-century ago, which caused such a storm of protest in that day. The difference is that today's "factory children" are on wheels and their salvation depends on the establishment of day-care centers and summer schools, with health services, wherever they can be found.

The Center's Contribution

For these bereft children the day-care center is a haven of joy. Anna Mary Reed, Director of the Migrant Child Care Center for Potter County, Pennsylvania, gives us this happy picture:

The center provided care five days a week, Monday through Friday, from 8:00 a.m. to 5:00 p.m. Breakfast, dinner, and an afternoon snack were served. Regular and well-planned meals erased hunger pangs. Each day consisted of play, meals, rest, and again play.

Professional workers were provided by the Departments of Health and Public Welfare. The public health nurse called at the center every day for one and a half months. The social worker enrolled the children, kept records, and helped the parents understand the value of the center. . . .

The warm, sunny outdoors beckoned each child. Here a variety of equipment was provided to stimulate play experiences. Here there was room for a release of boundless energy and enthusiasm. The red and white tricycles proved a main attraction. From the swings came high-pitched voices, "Teacher, come push me; push me high!" The wagons were fine carriers for hauling people and carrying sand from the sandbox. Those with domestic interests could be found in the weather-beaten treehouse cooking a pork and bean dinner. The sandbox provided much interest, particularly for making mudpies and cakes.

Quiet moments were had before and after meal times. The children rapidly learned simple songs and tunes. Fingerplays and poems were enjoyed. A familiar piece was chanted in unison, each one keeping perfect rhythm. They liked to hear and repeat the expressive lines of the "Three Bears." Learning and singing songs were a definite joy to these children. And what is more expressive and indicative of a happy heart than a song? (1).

This report is not of a model day-care center, one found superior to all others. The same benefits to children in care, education, health, and social adaptation are being repeated in centers wherever they are operated. Then, why is it that day care is not being provided in all areas of need, wherever there are migrant children? Why are there so few over America? Is it lack of money? If so, how do Pennsylvania, Ohio, Wisconsin, and the few other states manage to obtain the necessary funds to set up centers for their migrant children?

Funds Are Not Lacking

The answer to the question of scarcity is that funds are not lacking, but deep concern for these children's welfare is sadly lacking. Federal funds have long been available to all the states for day care centers for migrant children, but only a small number used them in 1963. Two states, New York and New Jersey, rely on state appropriations. In New York, the oldest in migrant day care, the state provides 90 per cent of the funds required and the growers contribute 10 per cent. In 1963 fourteen centers were operated under this arrangement. The same year New Jersey operated four centers entirely from state funds, these in combination with the summer school program.

Pennsylvania, which operated eleven day-care centers in 1963, has experienced three stages of financing. The first center, a pilot type, was set up in 1954 and was financed in part by the state and the remainder by private means. In the succeeding years federal funds were used exclusively until 1958. Since that year state funds have been added to the federal. Ohio, on the other hand, has financed its day-care centers exclusively from the federal resource, as does Wisconsin. Colorado's day-care center at Platteville was operated by the local citizens' committee on migrants with assistance from the State Department of Education.

What is the source of the federal funds? Their availability is wholly unknown to a host of high-minded citizens who are anxious to set up day-care centers for these children as the greatest service they can render the migrants, but who see no way of financing them. The federal government provides the needed financial assistance through the Child Welfare Services Fund from which the U.S. Children's Bureau makes allotments annually to the states (7). Migrant children, as well as resident children, are entitled to its benefits, though this fact has never been over-publicized. If Pennsylvania, Ohio, and Wisconsin can use these funds extensively for day-care centers, so, of course, can the other states. Perhaps the answer lies with the state agency, which bears the responsibility for these children but is apathetic about it. An example of what a group of citizens can accomplish by forcing the issue of migrant day care may be found in the welfare annals of Pennsylvania.

The Pennsylvania Story

In Pennsylvania the program of day-care centers for migrant children was initiated soon after the organization of the Pennsylvania Citizens' Committee on Migrant Labor in 1952. This committee was organized for the main purpose of providing day-care centers for migrant children. An investigation of camps showed this to be the most urgent need of the children. But that old bedeviling question arose: "Money, money, money, where do we get the money?"

The Citizens Committee demanded a center immediately to meet the emergency and, as a result of its agitation, money was found and a pilot program of small dimensions set up. This program was made possible only by the Committee using its own funds to supplement the insufficient funds provided by the state. The Committee located a school building for the center and arranged with members of an American Friends Service Committee work camp to provide the staff, whose orientation for their work with migrant children was arranged at Cornell University in connection with the New York Day Care Program.

The pilot program served in 1954, but when the season closed the prospects for a permanent day-care program for Pennsylvania looked pretty bleak. Then it was that a member of the Committee, who had gone to Washington looking for a ray of hope in some department, returned with the joyful news of the availability of federal day-care funds through the

U.S. Children's Bureau for setting up day-care centers for migrant children. This money would assure the continuance of the program. The request for its use from the state's allotment was promptly made of State Child Welfare; its director responded to the challenge and since 1955 Pennsylvania has operated a program of day care for migrant children with federal assistance.

The responsibility for operating the centers is contracted by the Department of Public Welfare to the Child Development Department of the College of Home Economics of the Pennsylvania State University. The day-care center held at Ulysses in Potter County in 1955 was the first to use federal funds. It had an enrollment of fifty children. The eleven day-care centers operated in many parts of the state in 1963 served nearly three hundred. Meanwhile, the program has been vastly expanded and improved in day care, personnel, and equipment, in health and social services. Not only are a large number of children aged three to seven benefited, but also their families at adjacent camps.

The supervisor of the Day Care Program of Pennsylvania is Mrs. Marion Sheridan of the Office of Children and Youth, while its coordinator is Mrs. Naomi Naylor, instructor in the College of Home Economics of Pennsylvania State University.

The action taken by Pennsylvania in behalf of its migrant children appears all the more significant when it is realized that not only was it the first state to make use of federal funds for day care for migrant children, but it did so at a time when ten other states, which provided no form of aid to these children, heartlessly returned the unused remainder of their allotments, totaling almost $300,000 to the Children's Bureau at the end of the fiscal year.

This sum, if it had been used, would have operated a chain of day-care centers with incalculable benefit to thousands of children. In 1958 the Children's Bureau adopted the rule of reallotting the funds that are returned to those states which apply for them, and this policy has resulted in an expansion of services to the resident children, although it is not evident that many migrant children have been benefited.

This is the Pennsylvania Story. It tells how the Pennsylvania Citizens' Committee on Migrant Labor and the state's Bureau of Child Welfare cooperated in the use of federal funds to establish a day-care program for migrant children. The program operates under approved standards and possesses the prerequisite character of stability and permanence. Why have not the other states done likewise? If it is not discrimination against the migrant children because of their class, then what is the reason?

The answers one hears most frequently at the Capitol are these: "The state's allotment has already been used up for resident children"; "The need of day-care centers for migrant children in this state has not been officially established"; and "No citizens' group has ever requested the use of these funds for migrant children." Are these the real reasons, or nothing more than the standard excuses for official inaction?

Government officials, as a class, have an unenviable reputation of frigidity toward embracing new programs. Some, it seems, are fearful of the demagogic politician, the type who screams and beats his breast at the very mention of the expenditure of pennies for welfare or education. Some appear to delay action until they can discern a tidal wave of popular sentiment for the children. They are well aware of the fact that migrant families are nonresident, unorganized, alone, and completely helpless at the Capitol. Their helplessness, indeed, in most states, is equal to that of the [serfs in medieval England or France].

Besides the narrow-minded professional types, one is privileged to meet others who are conscientiously trying to set up day-care programs for migrant children. They insist, and rightly, that these be based on a broad involvement of citizen interest to insure success of the project. Members of the citizens' committee, in answer, will protest that they cannot get the thing off the ground without more forceful state leadership. The facts of the situation in several states would seem to place a large share of responsibility for setting up a day-care center on the state welfare agency. This is where leadership is to be expected.

When a citizens' committee, one undeniably representative of the community, makes a request for a center, the State Welfare Department should send one of its staff to lend assistance, if possible, someone with experience in composing community differences and promoting indigenous civic leadership. As the situation now stands, in several states, members of the citizens' committees and welfare officials are discussing the problem avidly from all angles, but, like stationary running, there is no forward motion and no day-care center.

California

One citizen who has kept her eyes steadily on the children is Mrs. Emma Gunterman of Gridley, California, a crusader to whom all parties give most credit for the official day-care center and summer school that were operated in California last summer. The center was the first in the state to be operated for these children with the use of federal funds. The program was conducted under the State Departments of Education and Social Welfare and County Welfare of Butte county at the Gridley Farm Labor Camp. It had an enrollment of about twenty children. The beginnings are small but all persons involved, at Sacramento and in the county, are enthusiastically planning improvements. The summer school for the children was operated by the Department of Education of neighboring Chico State College as a workshop for its students. Its program was original and of decidedly high quality. The enthusiasm of the students was delightful to see (3).

This is an encouraging beginning in California for a predicted chain of day-care centers next year. California, which surpasses all other states in its health services to migrants, should be expected to move forward rapidly with day-care and education programs now that the ice has been broken at Gridley and the ordeal of the pilot stage is past. Such was the experience of Pennsylvania and Wisconsin.

Wisconsin

As a guest of The Governor's Committee on Migratory Labor on tour I was privileged to observe Wisconsin's day-care program, which began in 1962 and developed rapidly during 1963. There was only one center at Spring Lake in 1962; in 1963 there were four, three in Waushara County and one in Door County, caring for about 140 children ranging in ages from three to seven. The program has progressed under the leadership of Jenny Lind, Supervisor of Field Services and Community Services of the Division for Children and Youth, with the support of the Governor's Committee, whose chairman is Dr. Elizabeth Brandeis Raushenbush (6).

The program includes particularly interesting features that are worthy of emulation elsewhere. Some of these are:

The enrollment of resident children with the migrant children.

Motion pictures of the children shown to them, to their great merriment.

The Family-Visitor, who at camps performs the functions of the social worker.

The employment in the Division of Children and Youth of a staff member with special training in organizing community groups.

If anything is needed in Wisconsin, it appears to be an added summer school program for the older brothers and sisters of the little ones who are so happily cared for at day-care centers.

New Jersey

The combination of day-care and summer school programs appears to be the wave of the future. In New Jersey the day-care program recently has been combined with the summer schools, operating at Cranbury, Woodstown, Cedarville, and Deerfield Township, already well established; while in New York the day-care centers came first, and the summer school program combined with day-care at Sherrill, Westmoreland, Clinton, and North Norwich (5). The total number of children enrolled at New York's fourteen centers in 1963 came close to seven hundred.

The manifest advantages of combining two programs under one roof are economic. The same bus provides transportation, the same cook serves both groups, and a recreational director (when there is one) supervises the play of both age groups. Such a day-care center obviates the need for older brothers and sisters to act as baby sitters; they are freed to come to school, and while learning, they will escape the injurious effects of day-long toil in the fields.

Ohio

Ohio is another state to make rapid progress both in day-care and summer school programs. Strong leadership has been provided in this state since 1957, when the programs were inaugurated by the Departments of

Child Welfare and Education (2). At the same time local citizen participation in the programs and the encouragement of the Ohio Consumers' League have proved most helpful.

One of the most interesting of Ohio's day-care centers is at Hartville, near Cleveland. This center was good when first visited in 1961; now with further improvement it is brilliant! On arrival we saw to our joy, standing in front of the center, a shiny new mobile dental clinic. In the chair was a young adult migrant worker with a dentist peering in his mouth and a nurse standing by. The patient appeared to be enjoying his "ordeal," though, no doubt wondering about all the commotion. A half-mile away was Day Care Center No. 2 for more children and a section of the building set apart for family clinics. These, together with other health services, are provided under the Migrant Health Law, enacted by the 1962 session of Congress, from which Ohio obtained $65,000 for health projects in fourteen counties. Our pleasure over the progress made in migrant child care during the past two years was heightened by a visit to an attractive day camp operated in the same area for somewhat older children by the Migrant Ministry.

Each state's day-care program may be said to possess features which merit consideration for adoption by other states. If only each state knew what the other states were doing. As it is, state education and welfare departments, when giving serious consideration to the initiation of a program of day care or a summer school, are inclined to set up research committees on the subject and then hold numerous conferences, as if its migrant child-care problems were totally new and wholly different from those of Wisconsin, Ohio, Pennsylvania, or New York, or those of education were wholly foreign to Colorado, Ohio, New Jersey, or Oregon. This form of parochialism is delaying progress in migrant child welfare. Those states which already possess successful programs in migrant child welfare should be promptly consulted as the first step.

As one special contribution, all states should consider the adoption of a social worker such as the one who features Pennsylvania's day-care program. She is an employee of Public Welfare, with a college degree, whose duties are manifold. A member of the staff of the day-care center, she assists in the enrolling of children from the nearby camps. She also transports children to clinics, doctors, and hospitals, and gives consultation to their families when needed. Social workers also reach out to help children in the more isolated camps who are too far away to be enrolled at a center. In effect, they provide a very helpful liaison between the day-care centers and the camps, and make the center what the place should be, a center of service to all migrant families of the area.

Snail-Like Pace

So much has been written on the blessings of a day-care center to the children who are forced to live in migrant labor camps, but as yet with such minimum results. The question persists: How long will the American public be satisfied with this snail-like pace of providing care for these children of misery, when after a decade the states and communities have provided care and education for not more than 10 per cent of their number? At this rate the migrant people will never have civil rights, not even an Emancipation Proclamation.

National leadership is required, from both the federal government and a national committee of citizens. The latter should be selected from those who possess a burning desire to end the neglect of these children.

Congress would accomplish a great deal for the children if it would pass a bill authorizing day-care centers. The sum provided in the bills introduced the past two sessions by Senator Harrison Williams was only $750,000, but even this small amount would accomplish a great deal of good by serving as a catalyst to those states which show a mounting interest in setting up day-care centers. The recently enacted Migrant Health Bill has already served this useful purpose in several states.

A second bill of great importance to migrant children would authorize the setting up of a Domestic Peace Corps, or National Service Corps. The Domestic Peace Corps would be soundly based, like the Peace Corps, on familiar practices of religious groups over a decade in assisting the underprivileged, yet it has been subjected to highly emotional attacks, seemingly devoid of any humane consideration. The volunteers of a Domestic Peace Corps would be the answer to the prayers of thousands of migrant families for sanitary housing, recreation, health services, day care, and education.

Finally, if Congress fails to pass legislation for the welfare of migrant children, the President of the United States should intervene to help these children. Surely the President of our great nation has the power to protect his helpless children from a commerce that makes profits more important than their lives. These children must not be thought of as Negroes, Indians, or Spanish-Americans, and thus cast out of our society. They are our own American children whom we must save before it is too late.

REFERENCES

1. Department of Public Welfare. "Migrant Child Care Centers and Services." Harrisburg, Pa.: Office of Children and Youth, 1960.

2. A Report by the Governor's Committee. "Migratory Labor in Ohio Agriculture," Columbus, Ohio: Division of Labor Statistics, 1962.

3. Gunterman, Emma E. "Children Count." Available at Route 1, Box 746, Gridley, Calif.

4. Karraker, Cyrus H. "Agricultural Seasonal Laborers of Colorado and California." Lewisburg, Pa.: Pennsylvania Citizens Committee on Migrant Labor, 1962.

5. Report of New York State Interdepartmental Committee on Farm and Food Processing Labor. Albany, N.Y.: The Committee, 1962.

6. Raushenbush, Elizabeth Brandeis. "The Migrant Labor Problem in Wisconsin." Madison, Wisc.: Governor's Commission on Human Rights, 1962.

7. U.S. Department of Health, Education and Welfare, Social Security Administration, Children's Bureau. "Children in Migrant Families." Washington: Government Printing Office, December, 1960.

34

Problems and Trends in Migrant Education

GEORGE E. HANEY

The most educationally deprived group of children in the Nation — these are the children of our domestic agricultural migratory workers (3). Most migrant children enter school late, their attendance is poor, their progress is slow, and they drop out early. The result? Most of them are far below the average grade level for their age, their achievement is usually under the fourth grade, and the illiteracy rate among them is high.

The sorry plight of these children has become a critical national problem since illiteracy or lack of an elementary education can condemn them to a life of ignorance, poverty, and dependence on society.

For more than a decade the public has been aware of the plight of these children. In 1951, the President's Commission on Migratory Labor said:

> This Commission wishes to reiterate its conviction that the education of the children of migratory farmworkers (and their parents also) is one of the most urgent and most esssential of many steps which the Nation can and should take to improve the lot of migrants who have for so long been deprived of what the rest of us take for granted.

Even though local and State educational agencies have made considerable progress in improving educational programs for these children in the decade since the Commission spoke, recent studies and reports indicate that tens of thousands of migrant children still do not have an opportunity for education equal to that of other American children.

Just how many thousands of migrant children there are is hard to determine because they are on the move so much of the time. In 1954, the U.S. Department of Agriculture estimated that the number under eighteen years old ranged between 175,000 and 225,000. In 1962 in hearings before the Senate subcommittee, the number was put at 150,000.

It is not hard to believe that the vast majority of these migrant children are being denied their birthright. There is ample evidence that they are among the most educationally deprived in the country: surveys and studies by federal and State agencies and local school systems report facts too much alike to be questioned. For example:

✧ From *School Life*, July, 1963, pp. 5–9. Used by permission of the author and the publisher. George E. Haney is a Specialist in Education for Migrant Children, U.S. Office of Education, Department of Health, Education and Welfare.

A 1960 survey by the U.S. Department of Agriculture found that migratory farmworkers twenty years old and older had completed a median of 6.9 years of school, compared with ten years for all Americans in the same age group (5).

A survey paper prepared for the 1960 White House Conference on Children and Youth says that these children are far below grade level and that their average achievement in school generally is under fourth grade — the minimum standard for literacy.

The Department of Labor says that, among 2301 migrant children found employed on farms in violation of the child-labor provisions of the Fair Labor Standards Act, 72 per cent were enrolled in grades below the normal level for their ages.

A 1959 study by the Colorado State Department of Education found that 16 per cent of all parents surveyed had no formal education, and less than 25 per cent had completed only the grades in the first to fourth level.

A 1961 report from New Jersey says "Though complete data are not available, school reports from several states show that possibly as few as one in fifty enters high school and fewer than this graduate. Consequently vocational training courses and school guidance services usually offered in the high school are virtually out of reach of these youngsters" (1).

The states of Ohio, Oregon, Pennsylvania, and Texas and others have made similar studies of the educational achievement of migrant children, and all indicate a high rate of retardation among them. The studies also indicate that they become progressively more retarded, that they fall further behind until they drop out of school in the elementary grades, and that few enroll in high school.

Studies and State surveys have found that migratory pupils are not educationally retarded because they lack intelligence or ability, but because they lack the opportunity to attend school regularly and to receive a continuous program of education.

The schooling of the migrant child is frequently interrupted by movements of his parents from one community to another. Studies indicate that most migrant families do not spend more than five months, or at the most seven months, in any one place. Each time the family moves during the regular school year, the child loses time from school.

Each year these 150,000 children accompany their parents from community to community and from state to state. And each year they confront local and state school authorities with serious educational problems. The high rate of retardation and the low educational attainment of migrant children compound the schools' problems of providing for them. In turn, the inability of some schools to meet these problems contributes to the further retardation of the children.

Problems

Providing for the education of migrant children during the regular school year creates many difficult and complex problems which have many social and economic ramifications. The seasonal impact of migratory children on school systems along the routes creates problems of finance, school transfer records, grade placement of pupils, and provision of teachers and school facilities. There is, in addition, the problem of getting migratory children to enroll and attend school regularly.

SEASONAL IMPACT. In some communities it is not uncommon for the number of school-age children to increase by more than 100 per cent during the harvest season. Lack of financial support to provide additional classrooms, teachers, transportation, equipment, textbooks, and supplies often makes them an unacceptable burden. Since the numbers of workers vary greatly from year to year, school officials find it difficult to plan provision for the migratory children who will reside in their community during the harvest season. This presents a most serious problem to officials with restricted budgets. If officials have no assurance of the number, they may decide that expenditures for additional facilities are not economically advisable.

SCHOOL TRANSFER RECORDS. It is not uncommon for migrant children to be told on arriving home from school at the end of the day that they must immediately get ready to move on to the next community. Since school officials have had no advance information about the children leaving or where they are going, they do not send transfer records along. If the children enter school in the next stop on the road, their new teachers may write to former teachers for transfer record cards. Many children, however, do not re-enter schools in other communities while they are on the trek. By the time they arrive at their home base in November, some have forgotten the names or addresses of the schools they attended.

Educators say that many migrant children still do not bring transfer records, and that those they present do not contain sufficient information for grade placement. In 1955 the U.S. Office of Education developed a transfer record form for children to carry from school to school. Several districts have used this form, but because of the difficulties of migrant life and state variations in regulations, it has had limited use. Some communities in California and Colorado have agreements with other communities in and out of their own states to send records by mail when children move.

Although more migrants than formerly are presenting transfer records, a survey of seven State programs found that interstate agreements were needed on the type of information to be supplied and the methods of sending records from school to school (2). It has also been suggested that a clearinghouse be established for the school records of migratory children in the east coast stream (6).

GRADE PLACEMENT OF PUPILS. One of the serious obstacles to officials in planning a suitable program for a migrant child is their not knowing the level of his academic achievement and the grade in which he should be placed to enable him to progress and benefit the most from his educational experience. When a migrant does not bring a record from the previous schools he has attended, an evaluation can be made on the basis of such factors as his chronological age, achievement, reading ability, physical maturity, and social adjustment. Much time is lost in this procedure by both the pupil and the teacher. If migrant children carried their school records with them, schools could plan suitable programs for them and place them without loss of time and effort.

PROVIDING TEACHERS FOR MIGRANT CHILDREN. One of the critical problems in the education of migrant children is to provide teachers who understand their cultural background and their socioeconomic and educational needs. It is difficult for teachers with overcrowded classrooms to adapt the established curriculum to children who enter school late or to initiate a different program of studies for them. This presents a difficult task to the experienced teacher and an almost impossible problem to the unprepared or inexperienced teacher.

When school districts have an unusually large influx of children, providing teachers as well as classrooms for them may seriously handicap the school program. The children may enter a community in late September or early October, from two to eight weeks after the opening of school. Unless the district has already made plans for them, it may have difficulty in finding qualified teachers to augment the regular staff.

THE SCHOOL ATTENDANCE PROBLEM. It is estimated that a large number of school-age children do not attend school from the time they leave their home-base state early in April until they return in November or December. The Office survey of seven state programs (1961) found that approximately 50 per cent of the migrant children who resided in Ohio and Oregon and 25 to 30 per cent of those who resided in Colorado during the regular school sessions never enrolled in school.

A study in Michigan reports that 17 per cent of 917 children did not attend school during the year 1956–57. Reports from home-base schools in Florida and Texas reveal that most migrant children arrive at school two and three months late and leave as much as six and eight weeks before school closes in the spring, and that most of them do not enter school from the time they leave their home base until they return.

The Office survey also revealed a number of reasons why migrant children do not attend school regularly or never enroll during the regular school year. Among the most important are the following: The parents' lack of education or their attitude toward the importance of education for their children; their need for the children's earnings or for older children to care for their younger brothers and sisters while the mother works in the field; and the language barrier in areas where Spanish-speaking migrants are working. Other reasons reported by the survey, though less important, kept children out of school: The communities' attitude of rejection or indifference toward migrants; attendance laws of some communities, which bar transients; failure of local officials to enforce attendance and child labor laws; lack of school facilities to provide for a large influx of migrants; lack of proper food or clothing for children of school age; lack of school transfer records; lack of financial assistance to provide school supplies and facilities for the migrants.

Some communities along the migrants' routes declare "crop vacations" and close schools during the peak of the harvest season so that children can help gather crops. Local children have an opportunity to make up lost time, but migratory pupils do not. They move on to the next community where schools may also be closed for crop vacations.

NEED FOR EDUCATIONAL CONTINUITY. The variations between school districts and states in textbooks, curriculums, and programs of study make it difficult to provide migrant children with a continuous and sequential educational program. Different teachers, textbooks, methods of study, and achievement standards confuse and shake the self-confidence of children who may enroll in as many as four or five schools each year. This situation encourages dropouts.

In order to provide more continuity and articulation in the educational program of children on the move, some educators have proposed that short-term units in basic skills be developed for use in both regular and summer sessions. With an outline of such units, the children would have a better opportunity to progress from one unit to another in each school where they enroll. The units would provide a guide to a more continuous program of study and would help avoid duplications and omissions in their educational programs.

Short units could be developed through experimentation and cooperation among school districts and states along specific migratory routes. Such cooperation would, however, call for interstate agreements, which are hard to obtain. In addition funds would be required for curriculum research and experimentation.

FINANCING SCHOOL PROGRAMS. It is difficult for some school systems to solve financial problems created by children who cross district and state lines. It is especially difficult for rural schools: "The seasonal impact of these children produces an acute fiscal problem for rural educational systems which, in comparison to urban school systems, already face the most serious handicap in our educational system" (4).

The many problems teachers and administrators face in trying to provide for migrant children has made state action and support necessary in some states. In 1962 nine states were providing financial assistance to school districts for the operation of summer schools. Other states were providing financial assistance to local school districts on the basis of average daily attendance of migratory children at the regular school session. For example, Pennsylvania reimburses the school districts one dollar per day per child attending regular sessions, up to forty days.

Summer Programs

Since most migrant children attend school six or seven months during the school year and must adjust to several new schools each year, they are seldom able to earn promotion from grade to grade. Local communities and states have made several notable efforts to provide a more continuous program of education for these children.

Several Northern states are supporting summer session programs to provide migrant children with an opportunity to make up time lost from school. These schools were first organized by voluntary and religious groups in the early 1940's, most of them as experimental pilot projects. But as the schools gave evidence of meeting the migrants' urgent need for education, the states began to assume the responsibility for their operation as early as 1947.

During the summer of 1961, seven states (California, Colorado, New Jersey, New York, Ohio, Oregon, and Pennsylvania) were providing financial assistance to school districts for the operation of summer schools for migrant children. In 1962 the State of Washington operated a pilot summer school for them, and Wisconsin operated summer sessions for all children to which they were eligible.

In spite of the fact that classes were held during the summer months when children were not forced to attend and when their wages were needed, the enrollments increased and many children returned the following year. Case studies in several of these states reveal that many children have been able to make up one or more grades of schooling. A 1962 report on the summer program in Oregon says that children who attended regularly for three weeks or more made scholastic gains of from two to four months, that two boys advanced a full grade in reading, and that all made some progress.

It has been estimated that 205 summer schools would be needed for the twenty states using the largest number of migrant workers with children (hearings on S. 1124).

Trends in Migrant Education

Progressive leadership is being exercised at the local, state, and federal levels to improve the educational programs for migratory children. Increased public awareness of the need for improvement has stimulated research and study by various educational agencies. The problems of teachers and administrators in trying to provide opportunities for these children have made organization and coordination of educational services necessary at the local and state levels in some states.

LOCAL LEADERSHIP. In order to provide for the seasonal impact of large groups of migratory pupils, some districts have organized small classes at the beginning of the school year so that the children can be absorbed without overloading classes. In some districts temporary facilities, such as gymnasiums, auditoriums, and music rooms, are converted into classrooms. Other schools change to double sessions in order to accommodate the migrants. Some districts have employed additional attendance officers to enforce the school attendance and child labor laws. Several districts have made agreements with other districts to transmit information on school transfer records.

STATE LEADERSHIP. In addition to providing financial assistance to districts for migrants' education, several state departments of education have designated staff members to provide leadership on the problem. Three state departments (Colorado, New Jersey, and Oregon) have full-time coordi‐ nators of migrants' education. Other states have staff members (mostly elementary supervisors) with divided responsibility for planning and co‐ ordinating programs to provide better opportunities for the children.

In at least twenty-eight states, Governor's committees on migratory labor are concerned with housing, wages, transportation, schools, child labor health, and other measures. Many of these committees have made con‐ siderable progress in these vital areas and in promoting correctional state legislation. Legislation for the education of migrant children has been en‐ acted in nine or more states (California, Colorado, New Jersey, New York Ohio, Oregon, Pennsylvania, Texas, and Wisconsin).

FEDERAL LEADERSHIP. Because of the awakened interest in agricultural mi‐ grants and their families, national voluntary organizations have requested correctional legislation by the federal government. Five migratory labor bills (introduced by Senator Harrison Williams of New Jersey) dealing with child labor, education, health, crew leader regulation, and the creation of a national advisory council to aid migrants were passed by the Senate in the first session of the Eighty-seventh Congress. The education bill would have provided financial assistance to the state and local committees for the education of migrant children during the regular and summer school ses‐ sions, for state and interstate planning and coordination, and for pilot proj‐ ects on the education of adult migrant workers.

The health bill was the only one of the five bills approved by the Con‐ gress. It provides federal grants for the next three years to finance clinics and health services for migrants. The clinics are scheduled at times and places accessible to the migrants.

Six migratory labor bills have been introduced in the Eighty-eighth Con‐ gress. One of the bills would provide for improved educational opportu‐ nities for migrant agricultural employees and their children.

REFERENCES

1. Gatlin, Curtis. *The Education of Migrant Children in New Jersey.* Trenton, N.J.: Department of Labor and Industry, 1960. P. 2.

2. Haney, George E. *Selected State Programs in Migrant Education,* U.S. Department of Health, Education, and Welfare, Office of Education. Washington: Government Printing Office, 1963.

3. Hearings Before the Senate Subcommittee on Migratory Labor, April, 1961. Wash‐ ington: Government Printing Office, 1961, p. 16.

4. *Ibid.,* p. 9.

5. Survey of U.S. Department of Agriculture, *Monthly Labor Review,* vol. 85, 1960, p. iii.

6. U.S. Department of Health, Education, and Welfare and U.S. Department of Labor. *Report of East Coast Migratory Labor Conference.* [In press at the time this article was written.]

✧ ✧ **35** ✧ ✧

The Schools of Appalachia

PETER SCHRAG

Goldie Bell is an experienced American elementary school teacher who has never been asked about phonics, the new math, or the college potential of her pupils. The Scuddy School, where she works, can be reached only by crossing a muddy creek from an unpaved road which winds its way into one of the many blind valleys of eastern Kentucky. Down the road from the school live the coal miners — many of them now unemployed — who would be eligible for the Scuddy School PTA, if the school had one.

Mrs. Bell teaches five grades — fourth, fifth, sixth, seventh, and eighth — in her half of the wooden building that comprises the school. In the adjacent room a younger woman teaches grades one, two, and three. The walls are painted gray and brown, bare bulbs provide light, and a pot-bellied, coal-burning stove affords an uneven heat in the winter. There is a constant murmur in the room; most of Mrs. Bell's thirty-eight children must work on their own, the older ones helping the younger, the faster giving aid to the slow. One child has no shoes, many have no socks, and several look prematurely old. They are the children of some of the poorest people in America. A few are reading a story:

> Jane and Spot were going up the street as fast as they could. So were Jack and Jim. [Jane is blond and wears a blue dress; two boys follow on roller skates.]
> "Get out of the way," called the boys. But just then Jane stopped. The boys stopped, too.
> "Look boys," said Jane. "See what I have in my pocket."
> "Pennies!" said Jack.
> "What are you going to buy with them? Is it a toy for Spot?" [Later in the story they go for a spin in the family's green and white cabin cruiser.]

As they read, Mrs. Bell is asking another group about a different story. "Who is it that's driving the big tractor?" she asks.
"Jack," says one of the pupils.
"What's the girl doing?"

✧ From the *Saturday Review*, May 15, 1965, pp. 70–71, 87, and Peter Schrag, *Voices of the Classroom* (Boston: Beacon Press, 1965). Reprinted by permission of the Beacon Press, copyright © 1965 by Peter Schrag. Also used by permission of the *Saturday Review* and the author. Peter Schrag is Assistant Secretary of Amherst College.

"Washing dishes."

"What would she like to do?"

"Be out with the boy."

"They had one of those dishwashers," Mrs. Bell says. "Not many of us are lucky enough to have one of those."

The Scuddy School is one of twenty-odd one- or two-room schools in Perry County, and one of several thousand in Appalachia; many have been closed in recent years, but hundreds will remain because transportation over the "hollows" is difficult and because — strangely enough — local pride and suspicion of the world outside demand that they be kept open. Many are built of wooden slats, though some have been replaced since World War II with cinder block structures — usually because "the old school burned down." The pot-bellied stove and the outdoor privy are the only standard pieces of equipment. A miscellany of old desks, benches, tables, and chairs comprise the furniture; decorations come from old magazines and calendars.

The one-room schools of eastern Kentucky are staffed by a mixture of people — some, like Mrs. Bell, are dedicated veterans, others are women who have not met certification requirements, and still others are persons who once taught in the better consolidated schools but who were "sent up a hollow" for an academic or, more commonly, a political offense. Teachers are rarely fired, but if they identify themselves with the wrong faction in a local election, they will be sentenced to an inferior school, sometimes as much as fifty miles from home.

The presence of the one-room schools, and the fate of some of the teachers, are symptoms of the problems that plague education in Appalachia. In eastern Kentucky, which has never had a tradition of public education beyond the three R's, schools mean jobs as bus drivers, teachers, and lunchroom employees; they mean contracts for local businessmen, and they represent power for county politicians. In Breathitt County, for example, Mrs. Marie Turner has been superintendent of schools since 1931; her husband held the office for six years before, and several in-laws controlled it before that. The Turners own the building in which the Board of Education is located, and they take rent from the Board. According to the *Lexington Leader,* which ran a series of articles on school politics in Kentucky — with little apparent effect — the Turners have profited from the schools' purchase of coal, gasoline, and school buses, and from the deposit of school funds in local banks. Elsewhere in Kentucky school boards purchase real estate from the sons and daughters of board members, and hire each other's children and wives as teachers. In Perry County, where Goldie Bell teaches, and where the Board followed common practice by naming a new school for the superintendent, Dennis G. Wooton ("We don't wait till they die," someone said), Mr. Wooton's son-in-law, Curtiss Spicer, is principal of the Wooton School, and his daughter, Mrs. Spicer, is one of its teachers.

This kind of nepotism is almost inevitable in an area as ingrown as eastern Kentucky: of the nineteen pages in the Hazard telephone book, the Perry County seat, two are filled with listings for people named Combs, four persons named Combs teach at the Dilce Combs High School, and recently a high school science teacher named Combs was exiled to a one-room school for supporting a school board candidate named Combs against an incumbent named Combs. Virtually all the teachers in the Perry County Schools grew up in the county, or within a few miles of its borders, and many are teaching in the classrooms where they sat as students not many years before. Even if an outsider wanted a job in eastern Kentucky — and few do since the average salary is just over three thousand dollars — he would have difficulty obtaining one. "Outsiders just wouldn't be happy here," said one of the county superintendents.

The consequence of the inbreeding is that few new ideas have reached the schools of the area. Even the consolidated high schools operate largely with antiquated equipment, irrelevant textbooks, and obsolete material. Although many teachers sincerely strive to teach children in the best possible way, the years of previous miseducation make the task difficult. Sharon Barnett, a young, attractive English teacher at M. C. Napier High School near Hazard (Napier was superintendent when the school was built) spends the first semester in her senior course diagramming sentences; in the second semester she hopes to have her students read Macbeth. She knows that such an undertaking is difficult, but she desperately wants to bring something of the culture of the outside world to her community. She has come back to teach in Perry County because "my life is here," because "I love these people." And she knows what she's up against. "We could do so much more for these kids if their background were not so poor," she said. "They've had poor teaching in the country schools; some of the teachers are disliked so much that the kids are determined not to learn in order to hurt the teacher."

Yet despite all efforts — and there are other teachers like Sharon Barnett — the schools remain irrelevant for most of the students. Of those who started first grade in Perry County in 1948, about 12 per cent graduated in 1960. Many boys drop out, as a teacher said, "to get a job, a car and show off," and the girls quit to get married. A substantial number leave school and do nothing other than stand on the street corners of the towns. In Perry County, where the unemployment rate is about 17 per cent, the children fall into two groups: those who are ambitious and want to go north, especially into Ohio and Indiana, and those who see no value in any education, and have given up. When a grade school teacher recently asked her pupils what they wanted to do when they grew up, several answered, "to get on the welfare."

The content of the school curriculum provides little incentive for academic effort. Students are rarely challenged to work on their own, laboratory equipment is scarce and rarely used, and the courses in social studies are largely devoted to the clichés of American history and American life. The required civics book in Perry County proclaims, characteristically:

> Our economic system is founded on these basic principles: free private enterprise, competition, the profit motive, and private property. Businessmen and others must compete against one another in order to earn profits. These

profits become their private property. This system is known as *capitalism*. By means of our capitalistic system we have built the most productive economy, bringing Americans the highest standard of living that the world has ever known.

Since the county does not furnish free books in the high schools, students who use the civics text are not only required to read it but to pay for it. When relevant issues come up they fall outside the formal curriculum. In a discussion of civic responsibility and community planning, a high school teacher told his class: "In case something goes wrong in city government, the citizens should protest, they should write letters, and keep the officials on their toes."

"My uncle says he'll lose his job if the Democrats don't get in," a student exclaimed. Another student interrupted to say "In Hazard they don't care . . . if they cared they'd fix it up."

"It's not that bad," a third student said. "You just don't appreciate what we have."

"That's because there's nothing to appreciate. . . ."

"All the money goes to the hifalutin' big shots. You know the clothes they sent in after the flood, it didn't go to the people that needed it. They got a little bit so they could take pictures for the newspapers."

Discussions like this are rarely encouraged or channeled. Some teachers are nervous because others have been exiled to one-room schools, and because the community tolerates few heresies. The textbooks are safe and therefore irrelevant — the best teachers will admit privately that "we're not giving the kids what they should have."

Many teachers and principals are now making serious efforts to keep children in school. Sharon Barnett challenges her students to visualize themselves in ten years. "I ask them about what kind of job and home they think they'll have, and I tell them that the drunks on the street once had dreams like theirs. They've been protected by their parents and by the mountains. They don't know what the world is like. The mountains are terribly high." These efforts sometimes mean that a principal must find shoes for a boy who has none, or a loan for this year's books, repayable at twenty-five cents a week, or a special trip to a cabin in a ravine to convince a family that staying in school is important.

Many of the mountaineers value education even though most never went beyond the eighth grade themselves. They want lives for their children that are better than they have had, but they do not know, and cannot know, what a good education is, or the kind of effort it requires. Although eastern Kentucky, with substantial amounts of state aid, has made great progress in education in the past five years, eliminating one-room schools, raising teacher salaries, and increasing the proportion of teachers who are certified with a degree from a college, the education its schools provide is still far behind most of the nation. Perry County has some new elementary schools that are bright and well-equipped, and the Hazard Vocational School, which children from the county high schools can attend, provides training in a number of useful trades. But even the most recent advances have failed to bring education in Appalachia to an effective level. In an age of technical sophistication, most high schools in eastern Kentucky have little laboratory equipment, and sometimes no laboratories at all. A biology student in one school said that his experimental work in biology consisted of "looking through a microscope once." There are few school libraries and few schools with gymnasiums, language laboratories, films, tapes, or records. For many, the most elaborate equipment is the coke machine, and in an area as carbonated as Kentucky, there are many of those. Meanwhile, school authorities confront incredible problems of transportation. Schools open in mid-August because snow in the winter often makes the roads impassable, forcing the schools to close sometimes for several weeks. Perry County, with about 7800 public school children, spends $144,000 a year busing them.

Despite these difficulties, the respectable citizens of the county towns — some of which have separate school systems — remain smug and provincial; many of them deny that there is any poverty in Appalachia, and they resent outside help. Hazard, which is surely one of the ugliest small towns in America, is ringed with signs, sponsored by a local bank, proclaiming "We Like Hazard" and "We Like Perry County." While thousands of tons of coal flow almost untaxed from mechanized mines, and the region's top-soil flows down the muddy rivers, and the ambitious kids move to the north, no one takes much local interest in the problems of education in the county. School officials shrug with a kind of hopelessness about their overcrowded, inadequate buildings, saying they are "bonded to the hilt," but rarely mentioning the incredibly low county tax structure; the town burghers say the schools are fine, that "they're doing a good job," and the women's church groups resent the idea that some of the clothing they gave for the poor was actually returned to the same counties in which it was donated.

Local pride rests in high school football and basketball teams, but few take any active interest in the minds of the kids. In those schools where Parent-Teacher Associations are active, the parents help raise funds for library books and team athletic equipment, without much protest about the fact that the Board of Education provides neither books nor a program in physical education. With the exception of the Hazard *Herald*, which has criticized some of the more flagrant manifestations of school politics, there is not one organization in all Perry County that is critical of the schools. Ever since the coal companies began to exploit eastern Kentucky and its people, outsiders have been suspect, and no one wants their advice now. Thus even those with the best intentions must work carefully and cooperate with the local politicians. To do otherwise is to be ineffective.

Although large amounts of state and federal money are going into public education and welfare programs in Eastern Kentucky — 90 per cent of the Perry County School budget comes from the state — attempts to achieve educational reform at the state level have been frustrated. Harry Caudill, the Whitesburg attorney who is the author of *Night Comes to the Cumberlands*, was a member of a special legislative committee that proposed, among other things, a strong educational Hatch Act to prohibit teachers from engaging in school politics, and the election of school board members on a countywide basis, rather than from intracounty districts. "A great howl went up," Mr. Caudill said. "We were called agents of the Pope and a whole lot of other things." Since other political issues diverted the attention of those who might have supported them, the committee's proposals were never enacted.

Despite its poverty, Appalachia remains perhaps the most typically American region; its people have not entirely shaken their frontier attitudes about the conservation of resources, about the value of education, and about relations with the outside world. Rivers are polluted with trash and garbage, refuse dumps foul scenic valleys, and the hulks of abandoned cars line many highways. While most of the nation has become more European, more cosmopolitan, Appalachia has changed but little, remaining behind its protective mountains. Thus there remains a suspicion of change, and of anything but the most conservative education.

Nevertheless a few voices have been raised recently to challenge the old isolation, the brightest of them being Harry Caudill's. And even conservatives like Mrs. W. P. Nolan, the editor of the *Herald*, are expressing a new consciousness. Like some of her fellow citizens, she is worried about Communist infiltration and outside interference in Kentucky. But she also concedes that something is drastically wrong with the schools. "Someone should talk about short-changing the kids," she said. "If we'd had good education in this state fifty years ago, we wouldn't be so embarrassed now before the nation and the world. A lot of this welfare money goes down the drain. We really need help on just three things: flood control, highway construction, and education. If we got that, we could take care of ourselves." Indications are that federal support will be forthcoming for the first two items. If it is, then perhaps there is also a chance for the schools.

36

Prevailing and Needed Emphases in Research on the Education of Disadvantaged Children and Youth

DOXEY A. WILKERSON

The essays which comprise this Yearbook[1] are replete with citations and analyses of a wide range of studies relating to the education of disadvantaged children and youth. To attempt at this point a detailed summary and critique of research developments in this field would be somewhat redundant, and no such attempt is here made. Rather, attention is directed to some prevailing and needed emphases in relevant research. The concern is not for the specific findings and technical adequacy of the studies, but for the problem areas with which they deal.

Specifically, a conceptual framework is suggested as a basis for interpreting and appraising emphases in research on the education of disadvantaged youth; prevailing emphases are described and evaluated; and what appear to be needed emphases are defined and illustrated.

TARGETS OF CHANGE

Special educational planning for socially disadvantaged children and youth is concerned with effecting changes; prevailing practices are assumed to be inadequate. This is likewise true of research which undertakes to guide such planning. Probably the most fundamental question to be answered as a point of departure for both is: What are the targets of change? The concern here is for systematic studies, and the answer an investigator gives to this question necessarily influences the formulation of his problem and the kinds of data he seeks.

The targets of change which are of major relevance in this field may be classified in three categories: the child, the school, and the society. Func-

---

1 *Editor's Note:* The Yearbook referred to here and on page 278 is the regular Summer, 1964, issue of the *Journal of Negro Education* cited below. The 200-item bibliography referred to on page 278 and on other pages throughout this selection is entitled "The Education of Socially Disadvantaged Children and Youth," by Doxey A. Wilkerson, and appears on pages 358–366 of this same issue of the *Journal.*

✧ From *The Journal of Negro Education*, Summer, 1964, pp. 346–357. Used by permission of the author and the publisher. Doxey A. Wilkerson is Associate Professor of Education, Ferkauf Graduate School of Education, Yeshiva University.

tionally, they are inseparably interrelated; but they represent alternative *foci* of attack. The distribution of investigative emphasis among them is suggestive of investigators' perceptions of what needs to be changed for the more effective education of disadvantaged children and youth.

The Child

The disadvantaged child, of course, is a prime target of change. Directly or indirectly, all research in this field is concerned with modifying the characteristics and developmental patterns of young people who do not succeed at school tasks and whose general behavior is often at odds with the normative demands of the larger society. Overwhelmingly they are lower-class youth who live in urban slums. Very large proportions of them are also minority-group youth, mainly Negroes, Puerto Ricans, and Mexican-Americans. Their disadvantages are socially induced, functions of the life experience generally associated with lower-class status in the society; and where there is a confluence of the negative correlates of both lower-class status and minority-group status, such handicaps tend to be most acute.

Positive changes in the cognitive learning ability, emotional-personality development and general behavior of these young people are very much in order. There is general recognition that the disadvantaged child is a proper target of change.

The School

Less widely recognized, or admitted, is the need to change the school. Indeed, school administrators and teachers tend to bristle at any suggestion that they are not already doing the best possible job, "under the circumstances." Aside from overcrowding and inferior equipment, which are common in depressed areas, they are reluctant to concede that there are inadequacies in the nature and quality of the school experiences provided for disadvantaged young people.

Yet, as Havighurst, Riessmann, and many others have pointed out, the prevailing pattern of school life in our country was cast in a middle-class mold, and is largely alien to the experiences of lower-class youth. This is true of the school's administrative organization, its curriculum, its instructional methods and materials, and the education of its professional personnel. To assume that, somehow, lower-class children must be made to slough off most of the characteristics developed in *their* encounters with the environment and to "fit into" school structures and processes developed in response to presumed middle-class needs is unconscionable.

It is now established that the principle of equality of educational opportunity calls for adapting school programs and procedures to individual differences. There is every reason to hold that it also calls for adapting the school to class differences. Otherwise, especially in the context of urban slum environments, "equality of educational opportunity" will remain largely devoid of meaning.

Note should be made of the fact that research which is directed toward positive changes in disadvantaged children generally implies some modification of the school, at least in teaching methods. The dominant thrust of such studies, however, is to change what is "wrong" with the child, not the school. There are substantial grounds for insisting that the school, too, is a proper target of change. It needs to become more responsive than it now is to the conditions and needs of lower-class life.

The Society

The area of needed changes to which least attention is given in educational circles is the society itself. This is understandable. Nevertheless, it is important to emphasize that substantial changes are necessary in social structure and processes as a basis for truly effective education for disadvantaged children and youth.

This is true, first of all, as regards the social circumstances into which such children are born and in which their primary socialization takes place. Poverty, slum homes and neighborhoods, family disorganization, adult illiteracy, considerable crime and delinquency — these are some of the common features of the social situation in which disadvantaged children are nurtured. The school should do all it can to "compensate" for the negative influences involved, but the fundamental need is to eliminate such conditions from American social life.

There is also the basic need to expand the opportunity-structure for lower-class youth entering the labor market. It is coming to be recognized that the negative attitudes of many disadvantaged youth toward school and the widespread delinquency among them are very largely — probably mainly — a function of an economy in which, increasingly, they have no place.

The impoverished circumstances under which most socially disadvantaged young people live and the increasingly limited employment opportunities to which they can look forward tend largely to negate current efforts to improve their education. In these and other important respects, the society itself is a proper target of change.

Thus, sound, effective education for disadvantaged children and youth entails the making of important changes in the young people themselves, in their schools, and in the larger society. It follows that all three "targets" should be of concern to educational researchers in this field. The question of moment here is the extent to which relevant systematic studies are addressed to needed changes in each of these areas.

EMPHASES IN RESEARCH

The general literature on education for socially disadvantaged youth gives substantial attention to all of the areas of change here defined, but this is not the case with research in the field. It is concentrated overwhelmingly in only one area — indicated changes in young people.

This general pattern of concentration is evident from inspection of the accompanying bibliography.[2] Further illustrative are the results of a rough classification here made of the 126 items in Silverman's "Selected Annotated Bibliography of Research Relevant to Education and Cultural Deprivation," the most careful selection of important studies now available. Subjective judgments based on titles and annotations suggest that about six of these studies do not relate directly to any of the three "target" areas here used. Of the remaining 120 studies, about 82 per cent are addressed to needed changes in disadvantaged children and youth, about 8 per cent to needed changes in the school, and about 10 per cent to needed changes in the society.[3]

Insofar as the nature of the research problems attacked may be taken as an index of investigators' perceptions of where changes are needed, it appears that very few researchers in the field are concerned about inadequacies in the school and in the society. Rather, their preoccupation is with modifying the disadvantaged child.

It is instructive to note, even in summary fashion, the nature of prevailing emphases *within* the several target-areas of change, and also what appear to be important types of problems that are largely neglected. Generalizations are based upon the review of a wide range of systematic studies relating more or less directly to education for disadvantaged children and youth.

The Child

Studies addressed to needed changes in disadvantaged children may be grouped into two broad, interrelated categories. One relates to special cognitive-learning problems of such youth, and the other to their special problems of emotional-personality development.

COGNITIVE-LEARNING STUDIES. Most numerous among studies in the cognitive-learning group are those concerned with assessing the intellectual ability of disadvantaged children, especially Negroes. There has been a notable increase in the number of such studies during recent years. Most of them, although highly relevant to the learning problems of disadvantaged youth, seem to have been inspired by the "new" ideological offensive through which race-difference advocates seek to forestall meaningful school integra-

---

[2] Incidentally, that bibliography of about 200 items [see footnote 1, p. 275] is selective; many other works might have been included. Part A includes a somewhat arbitrarily selected group of important studies which are fairly representative of research emphases in the field. Part B includes a wide range of other studies, reports and discussions, many of which might well be included in Part A. Thus, although Part A is the more selective, no sharp distinction is to be drawn between the two sections of the bibliography.

The bibliography is restricted mainly to areas suggested by the titles of chapters in this Yearbook. Thus, it does not include the vast and related literature on intergroup relations education or that on school segregation and integration.

[3] Other classifiers would undoubtedly differ in their assignments of these bibliography items [see footnote 1, page 275] to the several categories, but such variations could not be of such dimensions as to negate the general tendency here noted.

tion. Illustrative are the "new look" studies of Klineberg, Pettigrew, Tumin and others.[4] Marshalling the evidence on Negro-white comparisons, they discredit thoroughly, once again, the fraudulent pseudo-theory that Negro youth are inherently limited in their capacity to learn.

It should be pointed out, however, that even these studies are largely predicated upon a conception of "intelligence" that is becoming obsolete. As the basic theoretical studies of Hunt and Piaget have shown, ability to learn ("intelligence") can no longer be conceived as an entity — or even a "potential" — that is genetically given; rather, it must be understood as a mental function which develops *in the process* of interaction between the organism and its environment. To alter the nature and variety of an individual's encounters with his environment is to modify the course and extent of his intellectual development; hence, mere assessment of outcomes yields but limited understanding. Although this insight is generally acclaimed by researchers in the field, its implications for methodology focused upon the *process* of intellectual development are not yet reflected in the literature.

In addition to these Negro-white "intelligence" studies, there are other studies which are addressed more directly to school problems of cognitive learning. They deal mainly with such variables as social class, bi-lingualism, and primary socialization. Most of these studies, together with those previously discussed, are concerned with the technical problems involved in measuring intellectual ability among disadvantaged children.

Another large group of studies in the cognitive-learning area includes investigations of the general scholastic performance of disadvantaged pupils, together with associated influences. Attention is given mainly to such variables as age, grade, social class, test "intelligence," motivation, family status, mobility, teachers' perceptions and attitudes, and certain organic factors. Into this category might also be grouped the substantial number of studies of the incidence and correlates of school dropouts.

Relatively few studies are addressed to the specific cognitive-learning deficits, or handicaps, of disadvantaged children. Those that are relate mainly to language development, especially reading. There is a substantial number of such studies, apparently reflecting the vital importance of language in intellectual development and the prevalence of speech and reading problems among disadvantaged youth. They deal with social-class differences, auditory and visual discrimination, auditory-visual shifting, early language behavior, readiness, "enrichment," bi-lingualism and other variables, together with technical problems of testing and prognosis. There are also a few studies which are concerned with specific learning problems in other areas, especially arithmetic, and several which are concerned with the reversibility of cognitive-learning disabilities among disadvantaged youth.

One of the greatest needs in this cognitive-learning area is for more studies of the specific characteristics and processes of learning among disad-

[4] Unless otherwise noted, citations are to authors and titles listed in the accompanying bibliography [see footnote 1, page 275].

vantaged children. As Gordon points out in his discussion of behavioral theory and learning:

> If we view the learner as a product of the interaction between organism and environment, psycho-educational design in directed learning for socially and culturally disadvantaged children must be dictated by the topography of the learner (an analysis of the specific and detailed character of the learner) and the topology of the learner's experience (an analysis of the specific and detailed history of the learner's experience).

There are many unanswered questions in this area to which research efforts might profitably be addressed. Attention is here called to only a few illustrations.

The general literature is full of assertions about the nature of disadvantaged children's specific learning disabilities, but in most cases systematic documentation is lacking.

It is occasionally suggested that disadvantaged children are also characterized by certain distinctive learning assets, such as complex symbolization in in-group language, selective motivation and creativity, and accuracy of perception and generalization around some social, psychological and physical phenomena. Here, too, however — even more than in the case of their handicaps — systematic documentation is still to be made.

Riessman and others have suggested that styles and modes of perception among disadvantaged children differ significantly from those of middle-class children. Generally, however, their studies are descriptive, and do not inquire into the causal influences which are operative. Moreover, there is need for considerably more research which further defines and documents this and related characteristics of the intellectual functioning of disadvantaged children.

The negative acceleration of the learning curve among disadvantaged pupils as they move through the elementary-school grades, with a tendency toward plateau beginning about fourth grade, has often been charted. Here is an important phenomenon the understanding of which probably requires careful study of interactions between the child and the home, school, and community. Its causal influences are yet to be established.

There is also the related question: Why do some disadvantaged children perform much more satisfactorily in school than others from apparently comparable socioeconomic circumstances?

Hunt, following Piaget, suggests that intellectual capacity is based upon central processes which are hierarchically arranged and sequentially developed, and hence that it is important to "match" the learner's encounters with the environment with this developmental configuration. What does this principle of "match" imply for the development of cognitive-learning ability among disadvantaged children, especially for nontraditional approaches to motivation and the arrangement of curricular content?

A few studies have demonstrated the importance of multisensory input in learning, but further exploration along this line is needed. For example, what are the relative effects upon learning of sequential as opposed to simultaneous stimulation of several senses?

Are there some areas of cognitive-learning in which the handicaps of social disadvantage can be overcome more readily than in others?

Probably the most crucial need for research in this whole area is for studies addressed to the question of *how* the cognitive functions develop among disadvantaged children; this is the key to remedial, or "compensatory," effort. Many studies have identified a number of psychosocial variables of learning, but there are few insights into how they operate to influence learning. What is the process, for example, by which elements of the socioeconomic milieu of disadvantaged children affect their growth in cognitive learning?

Incidentally, we really know very little about the *process* of intellectual growth in children generally. Further research with disadvantaged children along this line — and along other lines as well — may be expected to help illuminate the whole field.

EMOTIONAL-PERSONALITY STUDIES. There are fewer studies of emotional-personality development among disadvantaged youth than there are in the cognitive-learning area. One substantial group of such studies relates to self-concept and ego-development, especially (but not exclusively) among Negro youngsters. For the most part, these studies deal with the development of color-consciousness and racial attitudes; the relationship between self-concept and such variables as social class, affectual relations in the family, and absence of a father in the home; and the relationship between self-concept and academic motivation and achievement.

Another substantial group of studies relates to the aspirations of disadvantaged children. They are concerned mainly with the assessment of aspiration levels, as regards education, occupations, and social mobility; the relationship between aspirations and rejection, in home and in school; and the relationship between aspirations and academic motivation and achievement.

Still another group of studies relates to the social attitudes and values of disadvantaged youth — their moral ideology, attitudes toward generally accepted behavioral norms, subcultural values, and attitudes toward school. There is also a miscellany of studies concerned with meaningful incentives, tendencies toward aggression, time-orientation, friendships and informal group relationship, and a number of specific personality characteristics.

As in the case of cognitive-learning characteristics of disadvantaged children, there is need for much more detailed topographical documentation of their emotional-personality characteristics than is now available.

Similarly also, there is need for much more study of the process of development of negative (and also positive) attitudes, values, self-concepts and aspirations among disadvantaged children, not merely their assessment.

In this connection, it appears that the Negro Nationalist movement, despite objectionable tenets of its political ideology, is more successful than most of our schools in developing among disadvantaged Negro youth a sense of personal dignity, pride of race, and behavioral changes in the direction of acceptable norms. Analysis of the influences and processes involved might yield insights of value for school practice.

To cite another example, it is commonly observed that minority-group youngsters who are alert, cooperative, eager and able to learn in the first grade often become apathetic, overtly hostile, and academic failures after about three years in school. What is the process of this development? Does their low-level academic motivation develop mainly in response to home and community experiences, or to school experiences?

As in the case of cognitive-learning studies, almost all of the research on the emotional-personality development of disadvantaged children consists of assessment studies, restricted largely to measuring end-products as reflected by test and scale performance. There are extremely few process studies, involving analysis of behavioral changes as they take place. Such studies, of course, would need to give major attention to children's perceptions, evaluations, and feelings as related to their experiences as they develop, an approach which is almost entirely lacking in the field.[5]

The School

There is a large and growing literature on changes that are needed or are being made in school programs and personnel to the end of improving the education of disadvantaged children and youth, but the bulk of it is descriptive and speculative; it includes very little research.

Such systematic studies as there are in this target area consist mainly of the following: several evaluations of early childhood enrichment programs and dropout-prevention programs; a few analyses of the treatment of minority peoples in textbooks; several studies of the effectiveness of specified teaching procedures and counseling programs; several studies of teachers' attitudes and perceptions; at least one study of the classroom activities of teachers who are "effective" with lower-class pupils; evaluations of one significant demonstration project; and at least three studies of segregation-integration as a variable of scholastic achievement.

The relative dearth of research on school functioning in relation to disadvantaged children is consistent, of course, with the general lack of systematic studies of the school. Universal assessment of pupils is not paralleled by evaluation of school programs and procedures. The fact is that very little the school does has been validated by research.

There is evident need, however, for considerable research on the school as it functions in relation to disadvantaged children — along some lines which have already begun, and along many others which appear largely to be ignored.

One area in which studies of the school are much needed is that of the current demonstration projects for the education of socially disadvantaged

[5] One notable exception to this generalization is Coles' psychiatric study of school desegregation in the South. In certain respects, another is the comprehensive study now under way in Newark, N.J., of "Social and Cultural Factors Related to School Achievement," sponsored by the Urban Studies Center of Rutgers–The State University. Among other things, it seeks "to gain from the children a view of what it is that makes up their world, and how they define the various things in that world."

children and youth. Such projects have been launched during recent years in several score cities, but only in the case of one of them — New York City's "Demonstration Guidance Project" — has there been any substantial report of systematic evaluation. Moreover, even the New York report fails to identify the particular approaches, among the many used, to which the very salutary development of the children involved can be attributed. Most of these demonstration projects are still quite young, and it may be that they will report research findings in the period ahead.

A second area of needed studies about the school is that of teacher education, characteristics, and behaviors. In almost every depressed neighborhood, for example, there are one or more teachers who are reputed to be notably effective with disadvantaged pupils. What are their distinguishing characteristics and behaviors?

Most all school systems conduct fairly substantial programs of inservice education for teachers. Do the courses and other activities involved help to improve teachers' performance with disadvantaged children?

A number of colleges and universities are developing preservice programs of teacher education which are designed specifically to prepare professional personnel for depressed-area schools. Do beginning teachers from such schools perform more successfully than other beginning teachers?

There is need for much more study than has thus far been made of the quality and effects of interaction between teachers and their disadvantaged pupils, especially as regards teachers' perceptions of lower-class pupils' intellectual ability and teachers' attitudes toward such pupils.

There is an extensive research literature in psychotherapy on the dynamics of group interaction in learning, and considerable also in social psychology; but there appears to be very little in the area of academic learning. School-related studies of the use of group dynamics as a teaching method might suggest approaches of much significance in the education of disadvantaged youth.

Somewhat incidentally, a number of school-related programs around the country are using non-professional youth in tutoring younger disadvantaged children.[6] Evaluation studies, if the results are positive, might point a way toward expanded educational services as well as increased employment opportunities for disadvantaged youth, with minimal demands on school budgets.

A third area of needed studies about the school is that of curriculum content and organization. For example, does the sequential arrangement of curricular content that prevails in the elementary school, especially after third grade, have any relationship to the observed tendency of disadvantaged children's learning curves to flatten out during the middle grades?

A few systems have introduced, or are developing, textbooks and other instructional materials which include minority-group people among their illustrations, and also which include heretofore omitted content about the history, life, and culture of minority peoples. Does the use of such ma-

---

[6] An example is the Homework Helper Program of Mobilization for Youth, Inc., New York City.

terials improve the cognitive learning of disadvantaged minority-group pupils, or their emotional-personality development? What effect does its use have on white pupils?

Additional studies are needed of the effects of early childhood enrichment programs upon the subsequent cognitive and emotional development of disadvantaged children, and also of the effects of the ungraded sequence in the elementary school.

The current process of school desegregation suggests a fourth area of important questions about the school which research could help to answer; and in the case of some of them, optimum conditions for investigation may obtain only during the next two or three years.

For example, is there a qualitative change in intellectual performance as a function of ethnic integration in the classroom? How does such integration affect the learning of disadvantaged minority-group children, and of other children? Aside from the theoretical significance of this problem, its current political importance becomes apparent wherever school segregation is attacked, which now means almost everywhere. Yet, except for Katz's recent and able review of what is mainly tangentially related evidence, St. John's somewhat relevant dissertation in 1962, and the Hansen and Stallings studies of four and five years ago, there seems to have been no substantial research around this issue.

Related to this question is that of the effect upon learning of homogeneous *vs.* heterogeneous grouping in the classroom, where heterogeneity involves not only a wide range of individual differences but also social-class and ethnic differences. The grouping variable, *per se*, has been the subject of numerous studies, but not with the added variables of class and ethnic differences.

The extension of school desegregation also invites process studies of its meaning for white and minority-group pupils and their teachers, and of the mechanisms through which genuine integration develops. Only the Coles study, mentioned previously, appears to be addressed to this problem.

Finally, there is the area of school-home relationships. Parental support of school efforts is generally recognized as of special importance in the education of disadvantaged children and youth, and substantial numbers of demonstration projects and regular school programs include activities designed to enlist such support.[7] It appears, however, that none of these programs has been evaluated systematically. Studies in this area are much needed.

In this connection, the approaches to school-community relations which were developed by the "community school" movement of several decades ago probably warrant re-examination in the context of today's educational planning for disadvantaged youth. They may offer fruitful suggestions for school practice and related research.

---

[7] Probably the most widely heralded program along this line is that of the Banneker Project in St. Louis.

It cannot be emphasized too strongly that important changes are required in the school if substantial improvement is to be made in the education of disadvantaged children and youth. As Parsons notes, the secondary socialization function of the school is to train individuals "to be motivationally and technically adequate to the performance of adult roles;" and its selection function is that "of 'manpower' allocation," especially in the world of occupations (2). The manner in which the school performs these functions decisively influences the life chances of the young people it serves. Thus, insofar as the school is geared to the values and apparent needs of middle-class life, and is unresponsive to those of lower-class life, it operates to guarantee continuing generations of disadvantaged children and youth. Probably the area of research most needed, and most neglected, in this whole field is that concerned with modifications of the school to the end of more effective functioning with lower-class youth than now prevails.

The Society

How to develop a society in which there are no millions of "disadvantaged children and youth" is not, of course, a researchable question; the big answers in this area will have to be found through other methods. There are subsidiary questions, however, to which systematic studies might well be addressed.

Most of the few studies previously mentioned as classifiable in this area could just as well be assigned to the other two target areas. They relate mainly to the socioeconomic status of disadvantaged children's homes, internal family organization and relationships, community influences on character building, and environmental variables in school attendance and achievement. All have at least implicit implications for social reconstruction, and others even more pointed in this regard can be cited or suggested.

Illustrative are studies of how poor performance in school is related to such socioeconomic phenomena as malnutrition. Pasamanick and Knobloch, for example, have shown the close relationship between prenatal inadequacies (especially in maternal nutrition) and paranatal disturbances (especially premature birth), on the one hand, and school retardation among lower-class Negro children, on the other. The hypotheses they advance on the basis of such findings, if verified through further research, argue powerfully for special governmental programs to assure at least that lower-class children are not handicapped by socioeconomic influences even before or at the time of their birth. More analyses of such relationships are needed.

Also needed are studies of what current technological trends imply for the education and careers of disadvantaged young people. It is generally recognized that the on-rush of automation has rendered much of vocational education nonfunctional and obsolete. Both industry and the armed forces now train workers with little education for a wide range of jobs, some fairly technical, in short periods of time. Moreover, demands for marketable skills in the 1970's will probably differ considerably from current demands. Studies which undertake to forecast future job requirements and to define their educational implications cannot help to provide the vastly expanded work opportunities that are urgently needed, but they might help to facilitate the transition of disadvantaged young people from school to such jobs as there are.

There is also need, finally, to bury beyond resurrection the still prevalent notion that the lower classes are largely "uneducable." Modern theoretical knowledge about the development of intellectual ability makes it clear that our society can have a highly educated general population whenever that goal is backed by the political forces necessary for its attainment. More and more studies demonstrating this fact may facilitate the emergence of such forces.

There is also the question of the meaning for education of an international political climate which tends to restrict the democratic process and which carries the continuing threat of annihilation. The negative impact of the Cold War on the values and outlook and even the intellectual development of young people — and also their teachers — is probably more marked than is generally realized. Progress studies to chart and interpret this development might help not only to illuminate the tasks of educators, but also to strengthen the fight for peace.

As in the case of studies of needed changes in the school, one cannot emphasize too strongly the need for studies of indicated changes in the society. It is unrealistic to hope significantly to alter many of the negative characteristics of disadvantaged young people without substantial enlargement of the opportunity-structure with which our society confronts them.

For example, it is commonly observed that disadvantaged youth lack "academic motivation," and tend to drop out of school early. But in doing so, they may be responding to quite realistic appraisals of what continued schooling means for their adult careers. As Goodman notes: "Negro college graduates average in a lifetime the same salary as white high school graduates. After seven or eight years, the salary increase of Negro and Puerto Rican high school graduates over those who have dropped out is perhaps $5 a week. Is this worth the painful effort of years of schooling that is *intrinsically worthless and spirit-breaking?*" (1)

Similarly it is commonly observed that disadvantaged children tend to be "present-oriented," and are but little motivated by deferred rewards. However, considering the erosion during this period of even the limited employment opportunities once available to such youth, the skepticism of these young people about educational values to be realized sometime in the future is warranted. As Pearl once remarked: "The problem is not that these youngsters have no 'future-orientation;' they have *no future*. We are almost in the position of counseling them to 'Stay in school so you can be an unemployed high school graduate.'" (3)

Special educational planning for disadvantaged youth and research designed to help guide such planning need increasingly to consider the social implications of the goals they seek.

SOLANO COLLEGE
100 Whitney Avenue
Vallejo, California 94590

CONCLUSIONS

It is not very difficult to sit at a desk and suggest studies for other people to make, and it may not be very meaningful either. Researchers will continue to tackle those problems which correspond to their interests, skills, and available methodology. Nevertheless, there may be some value in recording one observer's judgments about prevailing and needed research on the education of disadvantaged children and youth, even though he does not purport to have examined all of the significant studies in the field.

First, current preoccupation with the assessment of children should give way to much increased evaluation of the school. Although studies in both areas are functionally interrelated, the prevailing tendency is to assess the child outside the context in which learning proceeds.

There is need for substantially greater investigative attention than now obtains to the school, as such, — its curriculum content, and organization; the democratic quality of its interpersonal relations; and the values and perceptions and competencies of its professional personnel. Indeed, this observer's experiences in the field lead increasingly to the conviction that the *main* focus of efforts toward change should be the school, not the disadvantaged child.

Second, there is also need, of course, for many more studies of the characteristics and developmental patterns of disadvantaged young people. Desirably, studies in this area should place greater emphasis than they now do on the *specific* deficits and assets of such youth, in cognitive learning, and in emotional-personality development. Desirably also, they should place much greater emphasis on the *process* of development, rather than maintain the prevailing emphasis on the assessment of outcomes.

Third, educational investigators would do well to give increased attention to the needs of a society which creates and maintains vast numbers of socially disadvantaged children and youth. Quite apart from their responsibilities and activities as citizens, researchers, *qua* researchers, can contribute significantly to the improvement of that society.

REFERENCES

1. Goodman, Paul. "Don't Jail the Young," *American Child*, 46: 3–7; May, 1964.

2. Parsons, Talcott. "The School as a Social System: Some of Its Functions in American Society," Chapter 31 in A. H. Halsey, Jean Floud, and C. Arnold Anderson, (eds.), *Education, Economy and Society*. New York: The Free Press of Glencoe, 1961.

3. Pearl, Arthur. Address to the Workshop on Guidance for Socially Disadvantaged Children, Forty-First Annual Meeting of the American Orthopsychiatric Association, Chicago, Ill., March 18–21, 1964.

Teaching Communicative and Problem Solving Skills

All areas of reading instruction are currently in a state of ferment, but one area of imperative need — improving the reading achievement of disadvantaged children — *will*, in the opinion of Helene M. Lloyd, be given priority. In the first selection in Part Six, Lloyd discusses eight avenues of attack:

- New types of tests will be developed.
- All-out efforts will be made to encourage earlier language development and to build the necessary language concepts.
- The development of urban-oriented materials will be accelerated.
- The preservice and inservice education of teachers will be improved.
- There will be an increase in the quality and the quantity of the special personnel provided for upgrading reading in schools in areas in which there are large numbers of disadvantaged citizens.
- The reading program will be stabilized by the use of adequate records describing children's progress in developing reading skills.
- There will be a special focus on more and improved research studies in beginning reading.
- Ways will be found to stretch the school day and school year to provide the required reading instruction time for disadvantaged children.

One of these points, the development of urban-oriented materials, is given attention by Gertrude Whipple in her discussion of the development and use of readers for the disadvantaged in Detroit. Action by determined people over a brief period of time is currently accelerating progress in producing literacy among the disadvantaged.

The importance of school library programs is stressed by Charles G. Spiegler, Alexander Frazier, and Harriett B. Brown and Elinor D. Sinnette. Through good literature fitted to their cultural and intellectual levels, children learn that reading can be fun, that unexplored vistas await them. Books are an excellent way to introduce the concept of a multi-cultural society. They provide heroes with whom children can identify, goals toward which to aim, and rational methods for attaining these goals. Searching questions are asked of librarians:

Does the library room have the air and atmosphere of a special place? Does it have the best books of all times for the children of today? Have the best of the new materials dealing with the Negro, Puerto Rican, and other minority groups been added to the collections? Have outdated and inaccurate materials been discarded?

The writers would add other questions: Does the school have a central library with enough books to satisfy the needs and appetites of the children it serves? Are books circulated freely? Are children restricted in their choice of books and in the number they may borrow? What attitude does the librarian and teacher take toward the child who accidentally soils, tears, or loses a book? Answers to questions like these may provide significant insights into the success or failure of library programs.

Herbert Fremont, Natalie Mintz and Herbert Fremont, and B. L. Israel focus on the teaching of mathematics to disadvantaged groups and offer practical suggestions to teachers for improving mathematics programs. Fremont says that an almost indestructible wall of indifference toward mathematics has been built by the disadvantaged as a result of personal troubles, lack of motivation, and past failures. The mortar binding these blocks of indifference together is the attitude of teachers that ". . . the disadvantaged are a lower form of life." Israel describes the efforts of the Minnesota Mathematics and Science Teaching Project to develop curricular materials.

Recommendations for an elementary-school science program based on the positive elements of the characteristics, environments, and expectations of disadvantaged children are made by Samuel Malkin. Such a program must be based on real problems and should not depend on skills such as reading but should reinforce basic academic skills and afford children opportunities to use appropriate materials and equipment.

Lorenzo Lisonbee reports on the Biological Sciences Curriculum Study (BSCS) efforts to prepare programs for the limited learner. With regard to the question, "What is the best subject matter for disadvantaged children?" two schools of thought are explored. One school favors a program oriented to health and human physiology, since many youngsters will not complete high school. The second school advocates teaching a relatively few basic scientific concepts. According to Lisonbee, Jerome Bruner's conclusion that any concept can be taught at any level has had considerable influence in recent curricular developments. The editors of this volume would add a brief postscript to this opinion, however, in the form of a question. Can any concept be taught at any level *if pupil commitment is absent?*

37

What's Ahead in Reading for the Disadvantaged?

HELENE M. LLOYD

Today all aspects of reading instruction are in a state of ferment, and we who are caught up in this ferment find it difficult to separate trends from fads or to know exactly what is ahead in reading. Being part of the school system of a great city, however, I do see one major area of obvious need concerning which action *will* be taken because it *must* be taken. This imperative need is to improve the level of reading achievement of socially disadvantaged children. What can be done?[1]

There are, I believe, at least eight avenues of attack in meeting the reading needs of the socially disadvantaged child. We cannot rank the eight in order of priority; we cannot guarantee that each will function independently or will function in every circumstance. But in our all-out assault on the problem in New York City, the greatest promise of progress seems to be offered by these eight avenues.

Avenue 1

New types of tests will be developed to give a more valid picture of the disadvantaged child's capacity to learn to read. We must rapidly replace our present group intelligence and reading readiness tests with measuring rods that do not militate against the disadvantaged and that, at the same time, give a true picture about the abilities and needs of all the other children in our schools.

A start in this direction has been made by New York City schools. We are developing in cooperation with the Educational Testing Service a new type of test for use with our first grade children next year in lieu of the group intelligence test. If the new test proves successful in grade one, similar tests will then be developed for upper grade levels. The New York City reading readiness test is also undergoing revision to take into account the affirmative assets of the socially disadvantaged.

[1] This paper reports (with minor changes) remarks delivered by the author at a meeting of the American Association of School Administrators.

✧ From *The Reading Teacher*, March, 1965, pp. 471–476. Reprinted with permission of Helene M. Lloyd and the International Reading Association. Helene M. Lloyd is Assistant Superintendent, Board of Education of the City of New York.

Other examples of similar efforts to break free of the testing vise that binds us and militates against one group of children could, I am sure, be reported by others. Now that resolute action has been initiated, it is inevitable that we shall see in the years ahead a tremendous effort by school systems, publishers, and researchers for the development of new means and materials of appraisal.

Avenue 2

All-out efforts will be made in the years ahead to *encourage earlier language development* and to build necessary concepts. We know that language patterns are firmly implanted by the time a child is six years old. Therefore, the socially disadvantaged child must have our help with language and concept development in the preschool years.

This means that school systems in urban areas will have increasing numbers of nursery schools, summer playschools for preschool children, workshops for their parents. James B. Conant said that the more disadvantaged the neighborhood, the more important it is to have kindergarten and pre-kindergarten schools.

A pilot study using selected four-year-old children, now underway in six New York City elementary schools, is highlighting some of the values of a special preschool program for disadvantaged children. This study is being made in cooperation with the Institute for Developmental Studies, Department of Psychiatry, New York Medical College. The basic curriculum includes a regular nursery program with special emphasis in certain areas of cognitive development. Auditory and visual discrimination, concept formation, and language development are being stressed. The effect of this preschool program on later school achievement is being studied with mounting interest.

A special facet of the preschool enrichment program is the attempt to stimulate interest among the parents and to enlist their cooperation. Efforts are being made successfully to help the parents to understand the school experiences of their children, to develop a positive orientation to school, and to increase the reading skills and storytelling abilities of the parents themselves.

Teaching procedures in kindergarten are also being evaluated and analyzed in a companion program undertaken by the New York City Board of Education and the Institute for Developmental Studies. Additional studies of similar types are under way in other parts of our country. The results of studies to date emphasize that the kindergarten day should be lengthened, to five hours from the present two, two-and-a-half, or three hours. In addition, kindergarten should no longer be considered optional in urban areas but must be considered mandatory because of its contribution to language-concept development. Mandating kindergarten attendance will overcome the ironic circumstance that those children most in need of kindergarten experiences are frequently not even registered in our urban cities.

Avenue 3

The development of *urban-oriented materials* will be accelerated. This reading material must not be today's material with a few new stories, a few new words, or a few new photographs added. This material must be largely new, growing out of the interests, vocabulary, and experiences of *every* type of city child, including the socially disadvantaged. The material will include more than a series of basal readers; it will include a full and powerful gamut of skill kits, tapes, recordings, filmstrips, packaged materials, programed materials. New materials will be prepared in all areas of the curriculum — social studies, health education, science, and others. Special emphasis will be placed on audio-visual materials and on materials the child can use independently, thus freeing the teacher for teaching other children to read. The need for new materials is great; all of us know we shall have to run in the years ahead to catch up with today's and tomorrow's needs in this area.

Avenue 4

The preservice and inservice *education of teachers* in the area of reading will be improved. Today's drive for improvement in the quality of reading instruction, the need for which was underscored by the results reported in Mary Austin's book, *The First "R,"* will continue with increased momentum in the years ahead.

We know the classroom teacher is the key factor in any reading improvement program. In teaching reading to the socially disadvantaged, this teacher must not only be a skilled reading technician but also must have a sound background in mental hygiene and child guidance and an understanding of and respect for varying cultural and ethnic groups.

In urban centers, televised courses in the teaching of reading, with emphasis on mental hygiene and human relations, will be expanded and become a standard part of both inservice and preservice training; for example, eight thousand New York City teachers enrolled in such a course on the teaching of reading at the primary level; six thousand, in a course at the intermediate grade level. These television courses, however, cannot be the main answer. Teachers and teacher trainees must get guided experience in teaching reading under the direction of highly qualified reading specialists.

At the preservice level, I believe this need will be met in the future by the expansion of the type of program Dr. Donald Durrell is using at Boston University, i.e., taking busloads of students to public schools on a regular schedule for work with children on a one-to-one basis in reading, or by an expansion of a program which we have initiated in New York City and which I shall describe later, the Campus School Program.

On the in-service level, the teacher will obtain highly qualified guidance in three ways:

First, and foremost, from his supervisor who, because of certification requirements or because of professional interest and need, will increase his skill as a reading technician. This increased skill in the teaching of reading will be necessary because of the ever-increasing leadership role of the supervisor in developing a quality reading program. The increased ability in reading will also be necessary because the supervisor will be and must be held directly accountable to the Board of Education and to parents for each child's progress in reading *regardless* of the number of reading specialists in the school.

Second, the teacher will receive help from a special teacher of reading assigned to his school to assist in the improvement of reading instruction. We have 539 such specialists in our New York City elementary schools and look forward to their working for some type of certification in order to ensure adequate backgrounds in reading.

Third, the teacher will receive help from college specialists working in and with the public schools.

The planned involvement of college personnel will result, I forecast, in the initiation of language arts resource centers located within clusters of schools in disadvantaged areas. It is to such a center that a teacher will come alone, or with colleagues, or with a few children. He may come for professional consultation, for demonstrations of new procedures, for assistance with special reading problems.

Two years ago in New York City, we facilitated preservice and inservice growth through college involvement by the initiation of the Campus School Program, in which nineteen colleges now work closely with thirty-one of our elementary schools. We look forward to having this program expanded at all levels as a basic phase of our long-range program for the education of teachers of reading.

Avenue 5

There will be an *increase in* the quality and the quantity of the *special personnel* provided for upgrading reading in schools in disadvantaged areas. Just a few of these special personnel will be considered.

SPEECH SPECIALISTS. We shall see within the next few years a new utilization of speech specialists in all schools in disadvantaged areas. We know that there is a close relation between speech problems and reading problems. The relation is such that one cannot readily solve the reading problem without first solving the speech problem.

In New York City, we are participating in a most promising study: instead of reserving the services of speech therapists to the elimination of stuttering and other deep-rooted problems of individual children, we are also using these specialists in a pilot project to upgrade the general speech levels of whole classes. The professional reaction to this project has been so affirmative that additional positions have been requested so the project may be expanded — another breakthrough toward reading progress.

TEACHERS OF LIBRARY. We foresee the day when the library will serve as the coordinating hub of every elementary school's reading program. The teacher of library will not only perform all the usual librarian services but will also maintain a rotating flow of books from the library to each classroom.

New York City, with other cities, is conducting a long-range drive to have school libraries with at least ten books for every child and a teacher of library assigned to each school. We now have 237 such positions in our 590 elementary schools and have requested 287 additional positions for next year.

READING CLINICS. To meet the needs of the retarded reader who is emotionally disturbed, we will need more reading clinics in disadvantaged areas. From these areas particularly come children with grave, deep-seated problems that can be resolved only by the clinic team. Included on this team are the following: a reading counselor, speech therapist, social worker, psychologist, and when needed, the psychiatrist. These team members work with the individual child and/or his parents. We have eleven such reading clinics in New York City and are so gratified by their success that we are striving to increase this number to twenty-five.

Avenue 6

The reading program will be stabilized, particularly in disadvantaged areas, by the use of *adequate reading records*. A basic characteristic of children in socially disadvantaged areas is the excessive mobility of their families. Some children move seven, eight, ten times in one school year.

The shifting of children from neighborhood to neighborhood and from school to school, disrupting their own schooling as well as that of their less mobile classmates, has a disastrous effect on reading progress. In Manhattan, for example, the mean yearly mobility rate is 51 per cent. In several disadvantaged schools, the turnover is over 100 per cent a year.

To combat the ill effects of this mobility and to ensure systematic progress, New York City is using, on an experimental basis, a Reading Record Card, which is sent with the child's other records to his next teacher or his next school. This card provides a ladder of the reading skills and the child's progress up that ladder, as well as a record of the materials he has used. It provides orientation for his next teacher and eliminates his using reading materials he has already read satisfactorily in his former class or school.

Avenue 7

We will focus on more and improved *reseach studies in beginning reading* for all children, with special emphasis on the disadvantaged. I refer to the studies in first-grade reading being encouraged by the United States Office of Education. Several studies have been approved, and researchers and reading specialists are working with some of New York City's first-grade children, especially those disadvantaged children who are having difficulty understanding the meanings of words and who lack adequate skill in listening and speaking.

I urge that before any one of us makes drastic changes in our first-grade reading program because of pressures from those who believe in more phonics, we wait until the fall of 1965, when the results from this nation-wide focus on first-grade reading can be carefully analyzed in light of implications for our own school systems. After taking a hard look at these research results, then I urge that we take action if needed.

Avenue 8

We will find means to *stretch the school day and school year* to provide the required reading instruction time for socially disadvantaged children.

New York City has already taken giant steps in this direction by establishing After-School Study Centers in 163 elementary schools, 52 junior high schools, 40 high schools (13 academic, 27 vocational). These centers reinforce the reading programs in all schools with a percentage of 75 or more of Negro and/or Puerto Rican children. The centers are open from Tuesday through Friday from 3 to 5 p.m., and on Saturday from 9:30 to 11:30 a.m. Teaching is done by members of the day school staff who are familiar with the children's needs. Emphasis at the elementary level is placed on remediation in reading and mathematics, on homework help, and library activities. Requests are arriving daily for the establishment of these centers in other schools in New York City where the need is great. Correspondence received indicates that the pattern will probably spread in the near future to other cities faced with similar problems.

In the years directly ahead, other changes will be effected to improve reading. Boards of education in urban centers will, of necessity, also initiate plans for a twelve-month attack on reading improvement in school areas where the need is great. Yes, we are realists. We know that the cost will be great, too. The alternative, however, is to continue today's practice of having to use the fall months to retrieve the learning lost as a result of a two- or three-month vacation period and, thereby, reduce instruction time by approximately one third. Stretching the school year will be another way of helping the disadvantaged child make progress in reading.

What's ahead in reading? I have enumerated eight avenues so promising that they seem certain to develop into tomorrow's throughways. The important thing in this discussion, however, is not any one of these avenues, or even all of them together, but rather the assurance they offer that the situation can be corrected by people who are determined to correct it. What lies ahead in reading? *Action by people who are determined.*

✦ ✦ 38 ✦ ✦

A Cure for Allergy to Reading

CHARLES G. SPIEGLER

Culturally, he is bounded on the north by comic books, on the south by the pool parlor, on the east by the racing form, on the west by neighborhood small talk. Living in an intellectual ghetto, he sits in my classroom — annoyed to the point of hostility. I have asked him to read a book — any book — for a first report of the term.

"He" is Barry Saltz, a sixteen-year-old future butcher of America (one of many such in my classroom); a present reluctant reader (one of many such in my classroom). It doesn't dismay him that in his sixteen years he has not read a book cover to cover. I search my mind for a book that might appeal.

"How about *Questions Boys Ask?*" I recommend.

"Naaah."

I try sports, hobbies, deep-sea fishing — everything from prehistoric man to the stars millions of light years away. But I get a look that warns me, "Mister, you're wasting your time."

I am losing heart when, one day, a small area of hope appears. It is no bigger than the cluster of warts on Barry's index finger.

Those warts really worry the butcher-to-be, because, "They're gonna drive away my customers." I asked him one day, "Why don't you get rid of them?" I learned that he believed he got them from touching frogs' and that if he was lucky that they would vanish one day, as if by magic.

I recommended a book, *Superstitions? Here's Why!*, urging him to read the section on warts. I agreed to accept this as a report. Barry read the book through in one four-hour sitting. He memorized the paragraph on warts. Moreover, he became aware of other books in the library on health and strength. Before the semester was over, he could tell all about *The Wonders Inside You* by Cosgrove, *Magic Bullets* by Sutherland, and *Boy's*

✧ From *Improving English Skills of Culturally Different Youth*, U.S. Office of Education (Washington: Government Printing Office, 1964), pp. 91–99, as reported in *Education Digest*, April, 1964, pp. 35–38. Used by permission of the author and the publishers. Charles G. Spiegler is chairman of the English department of a New York City high school and a member of the English Department of The City College (Baruch Center), New York.

Book of Body Building by Pashko. He still refers to De Kruif's *Hunger Fighters* as "*Hunger Pains*," but who cares? Barry Saltz is on his way!

Does it matter? Does it really matter that the Saltz nose now goes between the covers of a book? Yes, indeed! For, of all youth's divine rights during the precious period we call "the school years," I place the enjoyment of books very high. Just as we learn to write by writing, we learn to read by reading. And I'm glad I got Barry Saltz to read because I'm convinced that the meat on which our Caesars feed is anti-intellectualism, "know-nothingism."

In the growing struggles between freedom and authoritarianism, it is better for all of us that the Barry Saltzes be thinking, questioning, probing citizens — not vacuums. Though there are many paths to this end, I respect reading as one.

I have had the opportunity to study hundreds and hundreds of Barry Saltzes in their raw, untutored state. Coming from homes where the bedtime story is unknown, where the television set takes the place of the reading lamp, they sat in my classroom with all the symptoms of cultural blight.

Family ties, as the ordinary middle-class youngster enjoys them, were unknown to many of my boys. Fully 20 per cent lived at home with but one parent, the second having vanished, run off, or died. I had boys who had never been served a warm breakfast by a mother since they could remember, boys who never had a heart-to-heart talk with a father. If mother or father were called to school on some matter of discipline, we were often invited to "Hit him! Whack him! I mean treat him like he was your own!"

Spawned in such homes, the Barry Saltzes never go much beyond talking of "Who's gonna win the fight next week?" or watching crime shows on TV, going to movies on dates, ogling the girlie magazines. Offer one a ticket to a Broadway play or a concert at Carnegie Hall, within easy distance, and the response would be, "That's for eggheads," or "You come home too late."

Small wonder that when we talk to them of *Silas Marner* they hear us not. Their ears are tuned to the change-of-period bell. Desperate, we bring out the great, beloved classics which are on the world's permanent bestseller lists. With pomp and ceremony, we introduce children to these classics. They are unmoved. In quiet resignation, we label them "retarded readers"; and that great cultural divide between the middle-class teacher (reared on Shakespeare, Browning, and Eliot) and the sons and daughters of "blue-collar" America (so often raised on comics, movies, and TV) becomes deeper and wider.

The Remedy

We have to heal that breach, and we can. But it can be healed only with understanding — the understanding that the Barry Saltzes are allergic to print; that much of what his teachers choose for him to read is not only not a cure for this allergy but is an extension of it; that only the book which packs a wallop for him may hope to effect a cure. The remedy? Begin with a book that hits him where he lives.

I learned this ten years ago when, as a new departmental chairman, I walked into the middle of a cold war between most of the nine hundred students and most of the English teachers. The main issue was books, required books for classroom study.

You walked into classes where teachers were devoting a full term to *Silas Marner*, and you saw children with heads on desks and eyes shut. You walked into the library and rarely saw a youngster except with a prescribed booklist based on the predilections of his teacher. The children were not reading, and the teachers had thrown in the sponge with the excuse, "They can't!"

I believe they could. Let them begin with what they like, I begged. Appeal to their interests — and they will read.

We inaugurated a three-day book fair, displaying two thousand books dressed in jolly jackets and written on hundreds of lively subjects I was sure youngsters liked. There was a shaking of faculty heads. "I'll bet you won't sell a hundred books. All these kids want is comics and girlie books. They won't buy anything decent!"

But they did. For three days, while English classes were cancelled, they browsed, read at random, bought or not as fancy struck them. And when the fair was over, we knew that these were the three days that had shaken our smug little world. Those students who would read only comics and girlie books spent hard-to-come-by change to take home 1123 books.

Granted, Bill Stern's *My Favorite Sports Stories* and *The Real Story of Lucille Ball* were best sellers, but not far behind were the *Burl Ives Song Book*, *The Red Pony*, and books of science fiction. And higher than anyone dared predict were *The Cruel Sea* and *Mutiny on the Bounty*.

Though no teachers were panting down the students' necks to "read this!" they did guide student choice in a few instances. One broad-shouldered lad was about to buy *The Scarlet Letter*, thinking it was a football story.

We relegated *Silas Marner* to the basement. Booker T. Washington in his struggles for an education became a far more genuine superman than the comic-book man with wings. *Kon-Tiki*, on the perilous Pacific, replaced Eliot's nineteenth-century England. By the end of the year, the majority of our nine hundred students were reading at least a book a month. Many were doing far better. Library circulation was up from six hundred to fifteen hundred.

Neither "climax" nor "denouement" cluttered up book reports. They reported in terms they know: "I like," "I love," "I hate," "I get mad," "It's great," "heartwarming," "exciting."

Success was not absolute and universal. We still had lads like Lenny Kalter who equated the carrying of books with the role of the sissy. It wasn't until Miss Isenberg (a public librarian assigned to visit our classes regularly to bestir the reluctant dragons) introduced Kalter to Felsen's *Hot Rod* that Lenny could identify with a character in a book — in this case, Bud Crayne, *Hot Rod's* hero and lover of speed. Lenny devoured *Hot Rod*, then *Street Rod*, *Mexican Road Race*, *Thunder Road*, and *The Red*

Car were finished within two weeks. He was searching the stacks all ove the city for "anything by Mr. Felsen." When he heard we were plannin to invite an author to visit our assembly to keynote our next book fai Lenny volunteered to write the first formal letter of his life — a letter o invitation to Mr. Felsen.

As for television, far from proving a menace to reading, as is often al leged, it can be a boon. To the culturally deprived children, television i a new window to look out on a new world. Through it they view the fullest richest array of new interests man has ever known. Teach a little "dial manship" and TV can become an Aladdin's lamp far more wondrous tha the original. Our librarian recognized that and arranged a bulletin boar entitled "If You Watch: Why Not Read?"

If we really want to introduce the culturally deprived youngster to book he can read on subjects he wants to read about, we are living in a bounti ful age. In truth, this is the Golden Age of Writing for Youth, with man magnificent series by excellent writers available to them.

The job of preparing the proper materials for the customer we are talk ing about is far from complete. The task is formidable, with both the text book and the trade book. As a first piece of advice to anyone approachin the task, I would urge: "Listen to the children you are serving." Here ar their answers:

> The subject has to be worth it to us. We like books about animals, aviation careers, hobbies, sports, the sea, westerns. We love lots of adventure, plenty o excitement, slews of interesting facts about science and things.
>
> Don't treat us like babies. We may not be such hot readers, but that doesn' mean if you give us an easy book about ducks on a farm we'll cackle over i gleefully. We had that stuff in the third grade.
>
> . . . .
>
> Give us lots of good pictures, good drawings, and big print.
>
> . . . .
>
> You have to know how to write. Maybe the fellow who likes to read a lot will stand for some boring parts, but not us. If you want us to read, don' beat around the bush but come to the point. Give us a story that pushes on to the next page and the next page — and we'll stay with it.

Only in the faith that there are no "second class" citizens in our schools, a faith conceived, nurtured, and cherished in pride for nearly two centuries, can we hope to rise to the urgent tasks ahead. I am supremely confident that we shall.

Multicultural Primers for Today's Children

GERTRUDE WHIPPLE

For 277 years — from 1685 until 1962 — no Negro characters appeared in first-grade basic readers used in American schools. Over the years, as developments in printing permitted, the mechanical features of readers approached high standards of excellence. Along with these mechanical improvements, the Caucasian culture depicted was steadily refined until, in most instances, it became upper middle class.

In 1962, the Detroit City Schools Reading Program introduced three preprimers illustrated with multiracial characters, prepared with the culturally deprived child in mind. The books had several unique characteristics.

From the very beginning, story characters in the books represent races other than Caucasian, on the premise that children can identify more readily with the characters representing the peoples they see in multicultural neighborhoods. The first three preprimers introduce a Negro family and a boy representing a white family. People of various nationalities and races are represented in other books now being prepared.

The program promotes the development of correct speech patterns in different ways. It is recognized generally that the difficulty many children in multicultural neighborhoods encounter in learning to read is primarily a language problem. Many children lack ability to speak in grammatical sentences, to use descriptive adjectives, and to develop their ideas beyond a noun or rudimentary phrase. The authors of the preprimers strove to use the natural, familiar speech patterns of the culturally disadvantaged children, gradually and in accord with good usage. Words commonly misused were repeatedly employed in correct, simple sentence patterns.

Words for the basic vocabulary were chosen with great care — selected from a reservoir of words which are widely but incorrectly used. Active verbs were employed frequently, for the child can act them out in the process of learning their meanings. The authors gave preference to words helpful in developing a strong, sound phonetic program.

Each story is designed to satisfy the child by developing suspense, which is resolved on the last page in a surprise or humorous ending. The authors

✧ From *Appraisal of the Detroit City Schools Reading Program* (Detroit, Mich.: The Public Schools, 1963), pp. 1–2, 30–32, as reported in *Education Digest*, February, 1964, pp. 26–29. Used by permission of the author and the publisher. Gertrude Whipple is Assistant Director, Language Education Department, Detroit Public Schools.

decided that stories for culturally disadvantaged children must have high interest value. Unlike the privileged child, the culturally disadvantaged children come from meager homes with few, if any, newspapers, magazines, or books. Having had no pleasurable experiences in reading, they lack the desire to learn. The illustrations in the books were designed to stimulate their interest.

The books are shorter and more numerous than the corresponding books of other series. The purpose of this innovation was that of giving the child the pleasure of accomplishment at the earliest possible moment, since he comes from a home in which long-term goals are seldom sought.

The *Teacher's Manual* for the series places emphasis on social objectives as well as skill objectives, since it is urgent that all children develop proper attitudes toward others.

The value of these innovations was tested in an appraisal, through classroom experiment, of the new Detroit City Schools Series as compared with another widely used series, considered one of the best of its kind on the market. The second series is referred to in the following paragraphs as the Standard Series.

Appraisal

The five innovations of the City Schools Series are appraised below in the light of experimental findings and the reactions of teachers:

RACIALLY MIXED SETTING. How does the appearance of Negro and white characters affect children? Reports from teachers show that the children make no mention that the characters appearing in the readers are racially mixed. In all classes — Caucasian, mixed, Negro — the children indicated a marked preference for the new series. When asked individually to indicate the child character they preferred as schoolmate and playmate, the children gave highest rank to the Negro characters of the new series. All evidence indicated that the choices were not made on the basis of race. Instead, the children were intrigued by the realistic stories featuring exciting adventures such as they might have.

Evidence indicates that first-grade children are generally not conscious of race; this race consciousness develops later in the elementary school years. With the use of the series, Detroit's children read books in which characters of different races mingle freely on equal terms. The preprimers are now in use in every Detroit school. Teachers are enthusiastic about using the books. This investigator has encountered no complaints from parents.

VERBAL COMPETENCE. With all the pupils, the City Schools Series was significantly more effective than the Standard Series in promoting word recognition. For both series, the same teachers taught the same number of words in the same amount of time. Complete mastery of the vocabulary was shown by 68 per cent of the children on the City Schools test as against 50 per cent on the Standard test. In oral reading, although differences were slight, the differences consistently favored the City Schools Series.

The new series was much more successful in promoting verbal ability among boys — an encouraging result since remedial-reading classes include many more boys than girls. Sixty-nine per cent of the boys recognized every word in the City Schools vocabulary; as against 49 per cent in the Standard vocabulary. In oral reading, 36 per cent of the boys had perfect scores on the City Schools test to 23 per cent on the Standard test.

The Negro group revealed the most striking increase in verbal ability through use of the City Schools Series. The number of perfect scores on the City Schools word-recognition test was more than twice that on the Standard test. Furthermore, the average number of errors which the Negro pupils made in reading a fifty-word test was two less for the City Schools than for the Standard Series. This indicates that reteaching is required less through use of the City Schools Series.

DESIRE TO READ. The appraisal of the Detroit City Schools Series exhibited two unmistakable findings: In interest appeal, the City Series far exceeds the Standard Series; and the City Series was especially popular with boys and with culturally disadvantaged pupils.

Statistical data revealed high-interest value in all of the participating schools, including schools in high and low socioeconomic areas, in all Negro, all Caucasian, and mixed areas.

The reactions of the pupils during the experiment added impressive evidence. They showed no overt reactions with the Standard Series. But with the City Series, as they read they chuckled and laughed with pleasure. The teachers confirmed the observations. One teacher of a class for bright children said, "The books are so constructed that the children seemed to grasp the humor, surprise, mystery or whatever at the first glance. Spontaneous laughter would burst forth just on seeing the picture for the first time — no belaboring the point."

Another teacher reported that during the experiment with the City Series the children flocked to the library tables searching for further reading.

A most significant finding was the exceptional popularity the City Series found with boys. The Series was popular with girls, but the extreme popularity with boys was markedly evident. The City Series also found a far higher popularity with Negro pupils than the Standard Series — exceeding the increased favor the City Series found with Caucasian pupils. The significance lies in the promise of increasing the proportion of children who want to learn to read successfully.

SHORTER BOOKS. What is the effect on reading of providing beginning readers that are shorter than usual? Altogether, the City Series has five preprimers against the usual three of other series. Each of the five preprimers is shorter than the average.

Comments of the teachers on this aspect best show how this relates to the higher interest value and productive learning: "The children felt a sense of accomplishment in having read three books in so short a time." "Because of the small number of stories in the books, the children enjoyed success early in the semester."

SOCIAL RELATIONSHIPS. Reading can change the outlook of a child and deepen his understandings of his relationships to others. This does not mean that stories in a reader should be used as a basis for moralizing, but rather that the stories should furnish worthwhile content for thinking and living as well as for teaching reading.

No objective answer can be given as to how successful the books in the City Schools Series are in the development of greater sensitivity to social problems and relationships. A few responses from teachers might serve to indicate their judgments: "These books help to develop many desirable social attitudes. The children were aided in developing feeling for and understanding of others." "Sharing and cooperation among friends is emphasized throughout. . . . Children must learn these (values) if they are to interact successfully in a school situation and throughout life."

The data collected during the experiment, and the comments from parents, teachers, and pupils show clearly that this series, oriented to city life, is used successfully by culturally varied children. It meets the needs of urban children in general, and is recommended for integrated use because it is truly representative of city life.

✧ ✧ 40 ✧ ✧

Broadening the Experience
of the Culturally Disadvantaged

ALEXANDER FRAZIER

This is a third-grade classroom in a downtown school. The children are reporting on a science experience that had to do with the conditions favorable to the nurture of living things. The tallest and darkest boy in the room is standing before us with a waterless flask over the rim of which droops the wilted top of a rather elderly carrot. "I brought this in last week," Ted reports as he holds it up for us to see, "and it's getting worse."

In another situation, this time a four-room school far back in the mountains, a reading group clusters around the teacher. These are first graders

✧ From the *ALA Bulletin*, June, 1964, pp. 523–526. Used by permission of the author and the publisher, the American Library Association. Alexander Frazier is Professor of Education, The Ohio State University.

who have been reading a story about hide-and-seek. "What other meaning do we have for 'hide'?" asks the teacher, recalling the advice of the manual. The children are puzzled "Let me give you a few hints," she proffers. Finally she points to their shoes; she has leather in mind.

"Now where does this kind of hide come from?" she persists. "Giraffes," one child hazards. Another, "Hippopotamuses." A third, "Crocodiles." The teacher beams; they are getting closer. Then one last contribution is offered. Becky waves her hand wildly. "Yes?" the teacher asks. "Leprechauns!"

These are mountain children, but many of their unpainted shacks have a new adjunct: a multifingered tower attuned to the world beyond the hollows.

Another vignette. In this urban second grade, half the children are members of hill families who spend their weekends with kinfolk across the river. Mrs. Dane has found that she can stimulate the flow of talk on Monday mornings by starting off with news about herself. Since they met last, she reports, she has been working in her rose garden, spading up the soil and spreading fertilizer to feed the roots. "Why, Mrs. Dane," one bright-eyed little fellow exclaims, "I didn't know you knew about fertilizer!"

These are some of the children we have become concerned with these days as we ask ourselves whether we can do more to help disadvantaged children succeed in school.

Compensation and Remediation

One of the ways we are trying to help them is by enriching their experience through what is coming to be called compensatory education. The program we have is all right, we seem to say, but these children are not ready for it. They need so many experiences they haven't had.

They need all kinds of encounters with the unfamiliar. If they're city children, they need to be taken to the country to see where milk comes from and how fields are plowed. If they live in the country, they should be taken to the city to ride up and down on an escalator or visit the zoo and feed peanuts to the monkeys. At school, the environment may be deliberately enriched for these children. Books of all kinds; pictures, films, and filmstrips; persons who can serve as resources and perhaps as models; a great range of concrete materials for manipulation — variety and abundance in all of these are to be valued.

Eventually, through such compensation, children who have come to school with too little will have gained enough to get started. Then they will move through our program with greater expectation of success. Or so it is hoped.

However, if they don't succeed once they do get started, we can always work on their deficiencies by a program of remediation or adjustment. After all, compensation can be carried just so far. Finally we have to start teaching, wherever our children come from. And if instruction doesn't "take," we will do whatever we must to make up for lack of learning. We know a good many things to try:

• We may group the poor learners within a class or work with them in-dividually.

• We may farm them out to the teacher of the next younger group for a period a day.

• We may send them out to meet three times a week with the reading specialist.

• Or, if we have a good many such children, we may decide to reorga-nize our primary program around reading levels and give the children more time to move through the established sequence.

In most of these ways of remedying or adjusting the slow-moving child to our regular program, we need all the help we can get in finding stimu-lating materials for reading and learning. We want books of many kinds, nonprint materials of many kinds. The more varied and abundant our re-sources for teaching, the more likely we are to bring deficient children up to snuff. Or so we hope.

Trying To Do Much More

But surely, as we think of what library services may do for the culturally disadvantaged, we must feel that there is something more to be done than getting them ready for things as they are or cleaning up after their failure to learn (or ours to teach). Experience with richness of resources for learn-ing ought not to be regarded as preparatory for our regular program or as being provided peripherally for those who don't respond within it to our satisfaction. Compensation may strike us as too little, remediation as too late.

Rich resources, we would agree, ought to be in the middle of the pro-gram; perhaps that may mean some changes in things as they are or as sometimes they may be. Ted's carrot, as he can observe from a carefully planned experience, is certainly "getting worse." But he is ready now to move from direct observation and from his present level of language to resources that may help find more of the reasons why and more discrim-inating ways of reporting on these reasons.

The children who know at least a little about giraffes and hippos and crocodiles and even leprechauns happen to be living in a classroom that has by actual count 162 trade books collecting dust on a bottom shelf under a couple of rows of supplementary readers and unused health and science textbooks. All these are perceived somehow as being there to be read if there is still time after the necessary classroom work has been done.

Mrs. Dane's boy from the hills has a new respect for his teacher because he has found that she knows something that really matters. And her con-cern for his growth has a broader base as she moves to bring him together with resources, either in her classroom or accessible to it, that will help him learn how to build on what he already knows.

A Rich Situation for Learning

We know what a situation in which richness of resources is central to learning looks like and how library services can relate to it. But let us look at one example simply as a reminder of the need to demand more of ourselves than compensation and remediation.

It is ten o'clock and all the children in this second-grade room except three are reading in books they chose. The three are on the floor lettering a report on a large sheet that is headed "Our Weather Experiment." It is April and this class has been making instruments to keep track of the rainfall.

The teacher is reading with one boy who is having some trouble with word endings; they are using one of the supplementary literary readers from a well-known series. At the teacher's elbow another boy appears with his book held out and a finger on one word. "What does 'fragment' mean?" he asks. "A piece of something," the teacher tells him.

Around the table where the teacher happens to be working, children are reading these books: *Freddy the Magician, The Marshmallow Ghosts, The Real Book about the Texas Rangers, Spring Things,* and *Smokey.* Elsewhere the visitor finds children at work on *A Book to Begin on Time; Ghosts, Ghosts, Ghosts; It Happened One Day; What Is Weather; Rodeo; Stories to Remember; Christopher Columbus; Betsy and the Circus;* and *Annie Oakley: The Shooting Star.* In a window seat two girls are sitting together; one is reading *Eddie and His Big Deals* ("It's my second Eddie book," she volunteers); the other, *Peter Pan.* Why are they sitting here? "Oh, we just like to read together."

At the end of a table, where he has plenty of room to spread the book out flat, a seven-year-old Civil War buff is carefully studying the pictures in *Divided We Fought: A Pictorial History of the War, 1861–1865,* borrowed from the high school collection just for him.

The visitor accompanies one small reader upstairs to the elementary collection to get a book about people of other lands. The general topic of group study has been how things began, and she is interested in learning more about where the people of this country came from in the early days. The librarian tries to help her find just the right book. His help is especially valued in getting hold of titles on the higher shelves. At each book in turn she glances quickly. "No . . . no . . . no . . ." She is taking a look inside each to assess its readability in terms of what she knows she can do. "That's it," she says firmly when she is offered *Where in the World Do You Live.*

Later the teacher says of this class, "They're reading all kinds of books, of course, for all kinds of purposes. One boy has just started on the Hardy Boys series. But we've all been reading this week for our group study in particular. We've used many films and filmstrips, too. Next week we are going to the museum to find more answers to our questions. We have a lot of interest in pioneers and the Old West. We'll try to pull things together soon and perhaps develop a simple time line, relating it to some of our arithmetic concepts."

And as the visitor prepares to leave, the teacher offers a last word: "The main thing is to develop purposes for finding out. That's two-thirds of the battle."

Guidelines

What we have been saying is that library services need to be kept in the middle of the picture from the beginning for all students, privileged as well as disadvantaged.

We might contend, too, that the concerns learners bring with them should be honored if we are to help them discover the range of resources besides direct personal experience through which their needs may be satisfied. Sometimes we think we already know what these interests and needs are. But do we? There is so much that might be learned about, well, fertilizers or maybe kinds of hunting dogs other than those down home or possibly about boys of another time who were born into families that lived in a log cabin set high on a ridge far off at the end of a dirt road that got lost winding up into the hills.

We may agree that sometimes such interests are difficult to bring into the open at school or elsewhere. We tend, perhaps, to try to fit the seekers of new experience to our program, whether in the school or in the community library. Is there effort in both places to help all kinds of seekers find ways to express and to satisfy the many more or less personal and relatively unique concerns that they may bring with them?

We may recognize that much stimulation may be needed to arouse new concerns and interests. In schools, these purposes can be derived — and are in the best teaching situations — from planning for the search in many fields of knowledge. The purposes so derived will then call for the use of all the resources we can possibly muster. Exciting new interests in the nonschool setting involves other problems but is no less essential if we are to serve the special needs of the disadvantaged or the different. Certainly merely placing a placard above a shelf of books that everyone ought to know will not be enough.

Whatever the difficulties are in trying to become more effective in bringing library services to such children and youth, we must certainly resist confining our efforts to compensation and remediation. Let us do what we can there, surely, but let us add a third approach to this new campaign. Let us be, as we always have been, concerned chiefly with the use of our full resources for the achievement of satisfaction.

The School Library Program for Children in a Depressed Area

HARRIETT B. BROWN AND ELINOR D. SINNETTE

The Negro or Puerto Rican child or the child of other minority groups living in depressed areas, who enters the New York City schools in 1970, will find that much ground work has been done making it possible for him to achieve his full potential. In September, 1956, the Board of Education took an important step toward vitalizing the elementary library program by appointing twenty-five librarians, one to each of the city's district superintendents' offices. These district librarians helped to set up libraries, build new collections, and weed old ones; aided teachers in planning library periods; worked with parents and community agencies; and promoted district library activities.

The importance of books is always stressed in the program. The task is to help each child realize that the mastery of books is essential to success in the school world. The program attempts to find material suitable for the child who is already retarded in reading and materials to stimulate those whose aptitudes and abilities know no bounds. Teachers are shown how library materials can best be used, and parents are guided to help children become familiar with the world of books.

In addition to programs of storytelling, story reading, book talks, and visits to public library branches for children, there are programs for parents. Through the school newspaper, talks at workshops, parent-teacher meetings, and book fairs, the librarian can encourage parents in building home libraries and understanding the importance of books in the lives of their children. Puerto Rican parents were made aware of the free facilities of the public library through a meeting planned with the district guidance counselor and the district librarian.

Librarians use music, films, and a variety of devices to introduce books and reading to the children. The film, *The Red Carpet*, led to some excellent discussion about people who deserved the "red carpet" treatment. This

❖ From the *ALA Bulletin*, July-August, 1964, pp. 643–647. Used by permission of the authors and the publisher, the American Library Association. Harriett B. Brown is Supervisor, Bureau of Libraries, Board of Education of the City of New York. Elinor D. Sinnette, District Librarian, Board of Education of the City of New York, is at present on leave to the University of Ibadan, Nigeria, where she is conducting a study of new African children's literature.

in turn stimulated creative writing. The reading of *My Mother Is the Most Beautiful Woman in the World* showed the children that children of all nationalities see beauty in their mothers. The discussion that followed culminated in a Mother's Day program on a local radio station, where the children discussed physical and spiritual beauty. The district mathematics coordinator, a gifted folk singer and guitarist, will use her special talent this fall, at the request of the district librarian, to introduce attractive library books with mathematics concepts. Reading biographies of Frederick Douglass and Prudence Crandall has helped the children realize the courage and fortitude that people have shown in working toward American ideals. Through all of these media, children are realizing the power of books for inspiration and information.

Library activities take on new and essential meanings in a neighborhood where association with books is frequently lacking. A child's first introduction to books is often through the school library. This introduction, if it is to produce a reader who enjoys reading, must be pleasurable and meaningful. The book collections try to represent the best of all cultures and groups. The library program aims to provide children with the best kind of library service. But program workers are aware that too many youngsters know little about different peoples. Their day-to-day existence is in a section set apart — an all Negro and Puerto Rican section. Their society is all Negro and all Puerto Rican. Heretofore, only a limited number succeed in breaking through the invisible barriers and achieve recognition based on merit. Books are an excellent means of introducing the child to the concept of a multicultural society.

Racial and Cultural Pride

As the library program was developing in the schools, a tremendous movement developing outside of the schools had a direct influence on the children, their curriculum needs, and the school library program. The impact of this movement was seen in the 1963 march on Washington.

At district conferences, the guidance consultant and the school community coordinator reaffirmed the belief that the children were very aware of the problems of civil rights movements. Faced with daily stresses and the panorama of their peoples' struggle shown vividly on television and in newspapers, it is quite easy for a youngster in this area to become disillusioned.

The district library list of resource people has proven very helpful. A battalion chief of the fire department (the second Negro in the community to reach the rank) returned to his alma mater to speak. A well-known runner, now captain of the Yale track team, spoke of track and scholarship in one of the school libraries.

Sculptors, poets, painters, and chalk talk artists are among those called upon to help. Many live in or near the Harlem area and some are products of the Harlem schools. They have been eager to cooperate in the goals of the program. It is hoped that their messages will help some young people set and attain their goals and develop worthwhile life-time attitudes. All children need heroes with whom to relate. Children need to know their people's contribution to the growth of their country. This has been a long-neglected area for the Negro and Puerto Rican child. Therefore, a good deal of library work centers around seeking out and providing many books and materials in these fields.

For instance, the library contribution to the Science Fair was an exhibit of biographical materials, mounted pictures, and books about noted scientists. (The Science Fair is developed by the schools of Districts 10 and 11 and exhibited in a hall at Teachers College, Columbia University, attracting college students as well as parents and school people.) The contributions of Negro and Puerto Rican scientists were emphasized. The Puerto Rican agencies helped with source material about their scientists. The exhibit showed the children that their cultures have played a role in the development of this country and that these cultures need not be a barrier to achievement in any selected field.

This year, National Library Week was observed by extending activities into the community. School librarians and auxiliary teachers in the district who speak Spanish, in cooperation with the Harlem Branch of the New York Public Library, sponsored an exhibit called "Roads to Richer Understanding; Contributions of the Negro and Puerto Rican to Our American Heritage." The second floor of the library was arranged with paintings, works of art, books, posters, photographs of original documents, artifacts. Authors, artists, sculptors, community people, and bookshops all joined in this celebration. The opening reception emphasized the essential role of both school and public libraries in education for cultural understanding, and indicated aids in the selection of books for home and school libraries.

A great deal of emphasis has had to be placed on remedial work in this area. An after-school tutorial program, newly introduced into many of the city schools in the fall of 1963, opens the library for informal use four days during the week and Saturday mornings. In many district schools, the library has become the center of the program. It is used for homework, for teaching remedial reading, and as a circulating library for the children. In one school on a hot Friday afternoon, large numbers of children were returning books and checking them out for weekend reading. Others worked on homework assignments, using the reference collection. During one lull, the librarian took three first graders over to a quiet corner and read *My Dog Is Lost.*

Librarians have participated in a program of intervisitation between schools whose students are from different cultures. In one school, art was the basis for research and discussion. Each school had received a set of prints, and, through the school library program, the classes learned about the artists represented. Two other schools used units on New York and Canada from the social studies curriculum for their intervisitation meetings. This program indicates that children of different ethnic groups and economic levels, when motivated by mutual interest, can meet and exchange ideas and develop appreciation of each other.

From time to time, the Bureau of Libraries issues excellent bibliographies for all schools which have been invaluable guides in book ordering. A long bibliography, "Focus on One America, Using Books for Better Human Relations," was published in the spring of 1960 and supplemented in the fall of 1962, with a second supplement this fall. Another, on books of interest to the non-English-speaking child who is just being introduced to English language books, has had extensive use. In 1963, the bureau issued basic lists of books on and about the Negro and Puerto Rican people for teachers and for elementary, junior, and senior high schools.

Higher Horizons Program

A city school program which has given particular emphasis to what the school and the community want for every child has been the Higher Horizons Program. Like the new elementary school library program in the city, it began in 1956. At that time, a pilot project was started in a junior high school in Districts 10 and 11 to find methods of developing talents and resources of minority group children. The success of the pilot project led to its expansion into the Higher Horizons Program, which has now attained national prominence and has been extended to school grades above and below the original age group.

The original aims of the Higher Horizons Program were to develop the potential of all children and to prevent waste of human talent. The project's concept that improvement in a pupil can best be effected by direct influence upon the child, the teacher, and the parent was variously implemented within the school districts.

In Districts 10 and 11, the approach was through an emphasis on curriculum: proficiency in reading, writing, oral expression, mathematics, and science. The district superintendent believed that the best way to give our children a feeling of accomplishment and security was to make them academically proficient.

The Higher Horizons Program, when developed, included grades 3 through 12. Of the original thirty-one elementary schools in the project, eight were in Districts 10 and 11. By 1962 there were programs in fifty-two elementary schools and eleven of these were in these districts. Lack of academic achievement, especially in reading, had become a matter of grave concern to school officials and the community. The superintendent knew that academic proficiency would help these children to feel secure in the school world and aid in their adjustment to the world at large. Therefore, proficiency in the "basic" was stressed. However, time was also allotted for cultural activities with trips to the ballet, the theater, and museums.

The Bureau of Libraries gave the Higher Horizons schools extra allotments to help build up their book collections and the Elementary Division of the Board of Education assigned Teacher of Library positions to every elementary school in the Higher Horizons Program in September 1962, when the first 110 such positions were granted. These assignments made quite a difference in library activities within each school and within the district.

Each person selected for this position is an enthusiastic librarian (at heart, if not as yet with a degree). Under the guidance of the district librarian, they have concentrated on making their rooms attractive and the programs inviting and stimulating. They have shown that a capable librarian can coordinate the research and informal reading activity of the entire school. They supervise the professional collections and make the use of books and materials meaningful to teachers and children. The theme, "Let's ask the librarian," echoes throughout the district.

Teacher Orientation

Because teachers' attitudes in the education of children with different backgrounds from their own is so important, librarians are concentrating on providing the school with professional collections of books about Negro and Puerto Rican life and culture. These collections include not just sociological treatises full of statistics, but books that reflect the attitudes and aspirations of the children in the East and Central Harlem area. A teacher will get more in the way of feeling and understanding from reading *The Poetry of the Negro* by Hughes and Bontemps, *On Being Negro in America* by Saunders Redding, *The Fire Next Time* by James Baldwin, and *Puerto Rico in Pictures and Poetry* by Cynthia Maus, than from struggling through some of the more technical presentations and analysis of the American problem as it relates to the Negro and Puerto Rican in New York.

The cooperation of the faculty is essential in the development of the school library program. When Higher Horizons started, every teacher in the district who taught in the Higher Horizons Program at the elementary level participated in an after-school in-service course conducted by district specialists in reading, mathematics, science, and library and with the district curriculum and guidance coordinators. Each session was devoted to a different phase of the curriculum. The district staff were then able, through classroom visits, to guide the teachers in the implementation of the program.

What was developed and practiced in the Higher Horizons schools which had more staff and larger budgets because of the special project, has gradually been applied to other schools throughout the district and all programs, therefore, including the library, have been enriched.

The in-service course is a good method of interchanging ideas among teachers and faculty. This year, the district librarian and the school community coordinator directed a course open to all teachers entitled The Negro: His Role in the Culture and Life of the United States. Much dynamic thinking was engendered from this course. An outstanding psychologist, Dr. Kenneth Clark, a dynamic civil rights leader, Constance Baker Motley, and the well-known author, James Baldwin, were among the guest lecturers.

The second half of the course was devoted to writing a handbook for teachers entitled *We Too Sing America* (from Langston Hughes' poem). This will serve as a guide to the presentation of subject matter related to the Negro. A similar handbook on resources in the field of Puerto Rican culture is being planned. With the use of these aids, teachers may not only add to their knowledge, but also direct children in the use of the potential and varied resources of the school library.

In January, 1964, the district superintendent and the district librarian arranged a meeting with principals, the district staff, and school librarians, in the Schomburg Collection. This reference branch of the New York Public Library, located in the heart of the Harlem community, contains the greatest depository of books and materials on the Negro and African in the world. Arthur Schomburg, a Puerto Rican, had been told at an early age that black people had no history. He refused to believe this and began to gather documentary proof to the contrary. The nucleus of his collection has grown into the famous library named in his honor.

At the meeting, each principal and each librarian received two bibliographies, "Books about Negro Life for Children," by Mrs. Augusta Baker, now coordinator of work with children at the New York Public Library and "The Negro: A List of Significant Books," by Mrs. Dorothy Homer. Mrs. Baker formerly served as children's librarian and Mrs. Homer as branch librarian in the circulating branch adjacent to the Schomburg Collection. A kit was also distributed which contained a list of selected books recommended for purchase for the school professional libraries of the districts, some suggestions of resources for picture and poster materials, and names of people in the community who are available to address assemblies and classes. The guest speaker at the meeting was Ernest Crichlow, Negro artist and illustrator.

At another principals' conference in the districts, a junior high school librarian read a paper on "Developing a Lifetime Habit of Reading," telling about the library program in her school and how the guidance counselor and other teachers cooperate with her in making books meaningful to the children. This paper was later published in *The School Library Bulletin*, a publication of the Bureau of Libraries.

Librarians must take a searching look at their libraries and tools. Does the library room have the air and atmosphere of a special place? Does it have the best books of all times for the children of today? Have the best of the new materials dealing with the Negro, Puerto Rican, and other minority groups been added to the collections? Have outdated and inaccurate materials been discarded?

Librarians must employ new ways of making the faculty and school administration more aware of library resources and their place in the school curriculum. The use of the library during school hours and beyond should be encouraged. In this time of strife, all children must be guided to use the materials that will help them to understand themselves, their community, and their country better. Plans for children to share and exchange ideas and ideals with neighboring communities must be made. They must be provided with inspiration and encouragement, models on which to fix their sights, and rational methods by which to attain them. And finally, parents and the community must be encouraged to aid librarians in promoting and carrying out the very best in library services.

BIBLIOGRAPHY

Materials of Interest to Adults

BIBLIOGRAPHIES

Baker, Augusta. "Books about Negro Life for Children." New York: The Public Library, 1963.

Bureau of Libraries, Board of Education of the City of New York. "Suggested List of Books Useful in the Program of Instruction for the Non-English Reader." New York: The Bureau, 1963.

————. "Focus on One America," *School Library Bulletin,* February, March, 1960.

Homer, Dorothy. "The Negro: A List of Significant Books." New York: The Public Library, 1960.

BOOKS

Baldwin, James. *The Fire Next Time.* New York: Dial Press, 1963.

Hughes, Langston, and Arna Bontemps (eds.). *Poetry of the Negro, 1746–1949.* Garden City, N.Y.: Doubleday & Company, Inc., 1949.

Maus, Cynthia. *Puerto Rico in Pictures and Poetry.* Caldwell, Idaho: The Caxton Printers, Ltd., 1941.

Redding, J. Saunders. *On Being Negro in America.* Indianapolis: The Bobbs-Merrill Company, Inc., n.d.

Materials of Interest to Children

BOOKS

Bontemps, Arna. *Frederick Douglass: Slave — Fighter — Freeman.* New York: Alfred A. Knopf, Inc., 1959.

Keats, Ezra, and Pat Cherr. *My Dog is Lost.* New York: The Crowell-Collier Publishing Co., 1960.

Reyher, Becky. *My Mother Is the Most Beautiful Woman in the World.* New York: Lothrop, Lee & Shepard Co., n.d.

Yates, Elizabeth. *Prudence Crandall: Woman of Courage.* New York: E. P. Dutton & Co., Inc., 1955.

FILMS

The Red Carpet. Weston, Conn.: Weston Woods Studio.

❖ ❖ 42 ❖ ❖

Some Thoughts on Teaching Mathematics
to Disadvantaged Groups

HERBERT FREMONT

It is difficult to teach mathematics effectively to any child. The need of most children for concrete learning experiences, coupled with the inherent abstract nature of mathematics, makes for difficult teaching in the best of situations. Add to this the many personal troubles that the student from a low socioeconomic neighborhood brings to school with him, and you begin to get a sense of the immensity of the challenge facing the teacher of mathematics with disadvantaged children.

The children of Junior High School 40 in the South Jamaica section of Queens in New York City are a typical disadvantaged group. Many times I have been asked the question, "What are the abilities of these children generally in mathematics?" Perhaps the most accurate answer at this time is, "We do not know!" In actuality, we have had little opportunity to uncover the real mathematical abilities of these children. The number of blocks that prevent our accurate estimation of ability can almost be likened to the Berlin Wall. Perhaps we should call these blocks the Indifference Wall. Of what kind of brick is this wall constructed? It consists of a variety of materials. Lack of motivation to learn what is taught in school is a sturdy building block for this wall. How many of our middle-class children come to school with a strong desire to learn as a result of having lived in homes rich in books, music, and interested adults? Part of the strong motivation to learn may very well be the result of a desire to get high grades, but the desire is there. It is in definite evidence as one visits classrooms in the more affluent sections of our city. It has always amazed me that students will sit still for some of the most inept teaching. What in heaven's name makes them take it? Could it be that students know only too well that the good grade is paramount? One thing is certain: children of disadvantaged groups do not share the intensity of this desire for a high grade. The homes

❖ From *The Arithmetic Teacher*, May, 1964, pp. 319–322. Used by permission of the author and the publisher. Herbert Fremont is Professor of Education, Queens College.

This article was prompted by Dr. Fremont's work as a mathematics consultant to the research project, Building Resources of Instruction for Disadvantaged Groups in Education (BRIDGE), Queens College.

from which too many of them come have not fostered the strong desire to learn that is present in so many of the more advantaged children. Thus, lack of desire is one of the building blocks of the wall of indifference.

Another part of this wall is made up of the numerous past failures of these disadvantaged children. By the time most of these children reach junior high school they are quite convinced that school holds little of value for them, and even fewer satisfactions. They are stupid. They know it because their teachers know it and have worked hard to impress them with this fact. They simply cannot do the work that is required of them. Not only are these children well aware of their plight, but they have actually resigned themselves to it. There is little desire left in them to try to overcome their numerous past failures in mathematics because slowly, but surely, they have been brainwashed with the idea that they cannot be taught and will not learn. What better foundation upon which to build a wall of indifference than lack of motivation and lack of success? And of what is the mortar made that binds these blocks into a wall of strength?

To begin with, there is the often-found hostility and prejudice of teachers. Mix in the attitudes that the only joys in teaching come from working with the bright child and that the desire to learn is not the teacher's responsibility, and the mortar takes shape. These are the attitudes of the same teachers whose fear and lack of understanding of children result in the harsh, repressive measures of strict control. With a minimum of contact and experience with any but the well-scrubbed, well-fed children of middle-income homes, the teachers feel that the disadvantaged are a lower form of life. Their negative attitudes are the stuff of which the mortar is made that binds the blocks into an almost indestructible wall of indifference.

Destroying the Wall of Indifference

But the wall must come down. There are many ways to undertake its destruction. The teacher, of course, is the key to any move that may be considered. This person must know her mathematics, must have an understanding of how children behave and learn, and must know how to present lessons effectively. These things are provided for in current teacher-training programs. They are not enough. The teacher of the disadvantaged must also be actively interested in children. She must genuinely care for them, and constantly be anxious to learn more and more about the children and how to work well with them.

When it is communicated to the students that the teacher cares, that the teacher feels each student is important, that she feels each student can and will learn, the wall of indifference begins to weaken. Through it all, the teacher must be human in her dealings with her students. There may be times when she will raise her voice and shout at a student; she may get angry; she may even lose her self-control in a brief moment of great frustration. In spite of this, each student knows that these reactions do not mean that she is less concerned about him. Anger, shouting, and frustration are all human emotions, and the teacher is a human being, not a saint. She laughs, cries, and gets angry just like everyone else. Above all, she is herself in the classroom, completely honest with her children. They are treated as fellow human beings of infinite worth and importance. Without this, there is no beginning in the teaching of disadvantaged groups.

This is the place where teacher-training has thus far been ineffective. We must undertake the careful development of attitudes and values designed to give the prospective teacher the feeling that the students are primary. Our present structure of courses does not seem to be effective enough in this area.

Basic approaches to teaching mathematics to the disadvantaged take on meaning in the framework described. Sit-down teaching, with the teacher hiding safely behind her desk, can be expected to achieve little in this situation. The psychological distance between teacher and pupil has to be reduced and the involvement of the teacher with each of his students increased. Many teachers are quick to point out that group work with these students is foolhardy. This is the attitude of the frightened ones. When you are working *with* these children, and not *against* them, any approach that enables you to work with individuals is helpful and necessary.

At J.H.S. 40, the mathematics classes were often broken down into smaller subgroups. Sometimes it meant that several students worked together on a math game. Sometimes it enabled the teacher to provide different levels of instruction. Sometimes it offered the opportunity to start different students working on different topics. Whenever grouping was used, a particular purpose dictated the method, but it was always a natural part of the classroom activities. Can these children work in groups? They did, with numerous advantages. Besides the advantages mentioned above, each student began to play a more active role in his or her learning of mathematics. Small-group work necessitates greater student responsibility. The technique of selecting a leader for each group enhanced this value for the students. Within a carefully structured framework the students were working somewhat "on their own." For the first time many students experienced some degree of success in mathematics. A simple maxim was at work: A student who does his work well feels somewhat better about himself and perhaps he can be a bit more charitable with others.

Concrete Representations for Mathematical Abstractions

Mathematical abstractions must be presented in as concrete a representation as possible. At J.H.S. 40, the variety of materials employed was as wide as could possibly be obtained. Automated programs, commercial aids, mathematical games and puzzles, manipulative devices, homemade flash cards, any item with the remotest possibility of helping someone was used. You can never know in advance which device might be the one item to help a particular student. It is a kind of "buckshot" approach where the greater the variety of materials available, the higher the probability of reaching each child. A careful check was kept by both teacher and student of all the work done by each student through the use of a personal folder. The folder contained all test papers, written work, ditto work, and any other item of interest completed by the child. The child's progress was readily apparent to him. From time to time each student received a workbook of his own, and was encouraged to write in it. This book became one of the child's most cherished possessions, a book that was his and no one else's. The pride of owning a book, any book, was a new and exciting experience for many. Perhaps better care for the property of others will result. Commercially prepared ditto master stencils were employed, and helped the teacher gain in her ability to deal with differences. No item was discarded. We kept on hand every bit of material that we could get into our hands. The work was not limited to the classroom. Several trips were arranged, and the students visited the stock exchange and other pertinent areas of interest. Each time they conducted themselves in model fashion. Guest speakers were invited into the mathematics classroom: an insurance agent and an expert on stocks and bonds. The level of student interest and the maturity of their questions and discussions were remarkably high. Bit by bit, these children began to make progress, began to take hold, began to learn and become interested. What their abilities are is still an unknown, but there seems to be a good potential in most of these students.

Somewhere along the line, piece by piece, a wall of indifference has been built between disadvantaged children and the school and the society. The child begins to learn how to live behind this wall, and perhaps he finds it somewhat comfortable. His teachers have played no small role in this process. His teachers are the means for the destruction of the wall. The implications for teacher-training are clear. The training process must construct within each future teacher the understanding that all children deserve a chance. Tomorrow's teachers must accept the fact that every child coming to school has a tremendous desire to learn, that every child would like nothing better than to be able to get the correct answer to the problem given him. If a better understanding of one's self is a prerequisite to the acceptance of others, then this objective must be provided for in the training program. A training experience such as this could result in greater opportunities to build approaches to learning that will break the traditional mold of the teacher-dominated class. The teacher who is afraid cannot create an atmosphere of freedom for those he fears. An outcome of the training program must therefore be a strong respect for all people . . . not just tolerance. Our children do not want merely to be put up with; they want respect and appreciation. At J.H.S. 40 we have seen what such a teacher can accomplish. Not only did she begin to raise her students, but she herself began to grow as she continually learned.

School as a Place Where Important Things Happen

In the future we should attempt to develop curriculum and methods that are designed to give students the feeling that school is a place where important things are going on. In mathematics, we have a big advantage: ease of communication. Despite low reading ability, a student can come to grips with a column of figures. If his answer is correct, he is encouraged. He'll try another. Of course, there is a caution to note. Too much abstract number work without meaning has already been thrown at him. There is a need to develop over-all projects that have mathematical experience as an integral, not an incidental, part of the entire process. The stock market provides one such opportunity. Scale drawings of meaningful objects and places provide another. We must develop and search out more such experiences that place the mathematics to be learned in a meaningful setting. In short, we must establish some purpose for the students to learn mathematics. Perhaps many teachers are not quite sure of the purpose themselves. Does teacher training answer this question? It should. But most important of all, at the junior high level provision must be made for quick success experiences for all children. These must consist of work that is difficult enough to pose a challenge, and yet not too difficult for the student to do. Such experiences can mark the beginning of the destruction of the Indifference Wall. "Nothing breeds success like success."

What a potential source of energy and growth for our nation is stored in these disadvantaged children! The sooner we can get on with the business of destroying for all time the wall of indifference, the sooner society will begin to reflect the benefits this group can contribute.

❖ ❖ 43 ❖ ❖

Some Practical Ideas for Teaching Mathematics to Disadvantaged Children

NATALIE MINTZ AND HERBERT FREMONT

Suggestions to teachers about helping disadvantaged students to learn mathematics are in very short supply. Although the number of articles about these children is on the increase, specific and practical ideas are still sorely needed if teachers are going to open the horizons for these students of currently limited outlook. We have the feeling that much more is at

❖ From *The Arithmetic Teacher*, April, 1965, pp. 258–260. Used by permission of the authors and the publisher. Natalie Mintz is a junior-high-school science and mathematics teacher in the New York City Public Schools, and Herbert Fremont is Professor of Education, Queens College.

stake than the mathematics experience of the disadvantaged. How many average students from middle-class homes have many of the same problems as their less fortunate peers? Is it possible that they too may be troubled children whose needs are not being met by the present school program? Certainly, teachers generally become involved in the personal problems of their students when these problems interfere with the planned instruction. Is it conceivable that many of our less outgoing students can achieve an acceptable level of work in mathematics and yet be troubled by some of the very concerns and frustrations that are so obvious among disadvantaged children? Can it be a matter of similar problems but different intensities? Of course, we cannot supply a definite answer. The feeling does persist, however, that, as we study the difficulties of the children we classify as "disadvantaged," we will begin to gain insights into the troubles of all students and develop the ability to help all children learn about mathematics.

In an attempt to build lessons based upon the notion that school is a place where important things are happening, we decided to use experience-type units in a seventh-grade class in a difficult school. The mathematics learnings involved in this unit, while of an incidental nature to the students, were very carefully planned for by the teacher. The use of a variety of teaching aids is generally a prerequisite in work with children who have a history of difficulty with mathematics experiences.

A useful teaching aid for the teacher who is attempting to give purpose to his instruction in mathematics is the catalogue generally published by large department stores around holiday time.[1]

Teaching children who have great difficulty abstracting mathematical concepts can be a frustrating experience for both teacher and student. Doing per cent problems can be an odious task for students who do not understand the mathematical concepts involved, and who see little purpose in doing such problems in the first place. For the perplexed teacher in such a situation we have a helpful suggestion. Make use of the department store catalogues when they become available, and plan a unit based upon holiday shopping and gift buying.

Such a unit is best planned to begin about Thanksgiving and continue until Christmas. The mathematical concepts to be taught are multiplication and division of decimal fractions; the meaning of per cent; equivalent per cents; converting per cents to fractions, and the reverse; all kinds of problems involving per cents, and general problem-solving techniques.

As an introduction to the unit, each child received a catalogue. The contents of the catalogue, together with the holiday season, generated spontaneous student interest. The children were permitted to look freely through the catalogue and to examine the contents. They were encouraged to talk about the array of gifts they saw. In this discussion of the various items, careful attention was given to the spelling of each name in an at-

[1] In the case described, the Gertz Department Store catalogue was used at the suggestion of Gertrude Downing, Coordinator, BRIDGE [Building Resources of Instruction for Disadvantaged Groups in Education].

tempt to enlarge student vocabulary. We did not limit ourselves to purely mathematical goals.

The class then considered the problem of using the catalogue to buy gifts for friends and relations. On the last page of the catalogue was an order blank listing each of the items in the catalogue. The children understood that the gifts could be bought by completing this form. The form brought forth many questions:

"Do we charge it, or send a check?"
"What does it mean to charge it?"
"What does C.O.D. mean?"
"What is a money order? How do you make one out?"
"Why must we pay tax? How do you figure out how much?"

As the children considered these questions, they began to complete the order form which called for much information, such as item, quantity, description, size, color, price, tax, total cost. The activity generated much student interest. In addition, the students had a real need to learn how to carry out the mathematical computations involved so that they could purchase the items. Thus, before the process was taught, a situation was created that helped each student want to know how to do the necessary work. In addition to the development of the desire to learn, the unit provided meaningful experiences of many kinds: developing vocabulary, writing clearly, completing forms, understanding the importance of taxes, understanding methods of purchasing, learning item names, writing item descriptions, filling out order blanks, computing item taxes, and deciding about payment.

The area of taxation was especially fruitful in the development of concepts. Determining how to compute the tax, deciding how much money must be set aside for taxes, determining what becomes of tax money, differentiating between local and federal taxes (some items had two kinds of taxes on them) all served as a rich fund of valuable mathematical and nonmathematical experiences. This topic suggests other possibilities. Extended studies of income tax, property tax, or amusement tax are but a few of the possible areas for further study.

Thus, our children now had some definite purpose for their work. Per cents to them were concepts to be learned so they could figure costs properly. The catalogue is real. Many students actually bought gifts in the moderate price range, and others had fun doing some additional dreaming. Many of the students began to pick up the topics discussed and ask questions about taxes on cigarettes, leather goods, and toys. The girls were extremely interested in cosmetics. Others who had marketing responsibilities at home recalled the tax on paper goods. A few asked about the restaurant tax. There was a genuine interest in these topics because they had meaning for the students *now*, in their present, everyday world. This is a far cry from the "learn-it-because-you'll-need-it-as-an-adult" approach.

A narrative always tends to give the impression that progress through the unit described was smooth and uninterrupted. Of course, this is seldom the case. For some children the problems were not easy. One of the principal areas of difficulty was the multiplication of decimal fractions. But such problems arising in a meaningful context help the student. It is interesting how the decimal points found their way to the correct position when we were dealing with money.

Learning the basic algorisms is a lot easier when there is a definite need to learn them. In isolation they are meaningless and become rote drill experiences. These children have been drilled, drilled, and redrilled, only to learn how impossible mathematics can be to master, and how useless it is to try to learn. Disadvantaged children especially have been "cooked and fried" in skill work from their first day in school. If they haven't learned fundamental skills by the time they reach junior high school, we must try to invent new experiences to help them learn. It is not simply a matter of providing more drill. One helpful technique is to make the mastery of mathematical skills a stepping-stone to something of immediate interest and use to the student.

Evaluation procedures for this unit involved the completion of numerous forms. To the children this activity was not considered a test. Rather, they saw it as a natural activity growing out of previous work. They thought it was fun.

The entire unit was climaxed by the actual purchase of an item from the catalogue for the fish tank that was in the classroom. As the children completed this task, we began to get a sense of the enjoyment the children experienced as they became aware of their newfound skills. Yes, they seemed to have learned a good deal more than simply "finding the per cent of a number."

✧ ✧ 44 ✧ ✧

An Approach to Teaching Children Handicapped
by Limited Experience

B. L. ISRAEL

While recent findings reveal that even very young children can grasp difficult concepts at a much earlier age than was formerly thought possible, the
reports also indicate that the concepts must be introduced on a level of
understanding compatible with the experiential background of the pupil.
This can often be done through stories or games or by providing material
which is of real interest to the particular age group or maturity level of the
pupil.

Young children do not readily accept material or information unless it is
fanciful or imaginative or related to their immediate living or playing needs.
It makes little difference that adults may be sure that it will prove useful
in years ahead. The material must be significant and meaningful (or challenging) to them. It must be introduced and explained in terms which they
can grasp and comprehend quickly and easily.

This is particularly so for children from economically or culturally disadvantaged areas and backgrounds. While the functional approach and the
social utility of specific mathematical learnings have been relegated to the
background by mathematicians in the teaching of mathematics, the pupils,
nevertheless, consider this factor in the learning of mathematics whether
they do so consciously or unconsciously.

It has been stated on more than one occasion that the various experimental programs working toward a revision and modification of existing elementary school mathematics and science curricula seem to be geared to the
needs of the intellectual elite among the young. These are the college-
bound pupils who, as a result of these changes, will have a greater under-

✧ From *Minnemath Center Reports* (Minneapolis: University of Minnesota Institute of
Technology, Minnesota School Mathematics and Science Center, Autumn, 1964),
pp. 4–6. Used by permission of the author and the publisher. B. L. Israel, while
on leave from his position as assistant principal of Public School 289 in Brooklyn,
N. Y., has worked in the Minnesota School Mathematics and Science Center (Minnemath) to develop supplementary units of instruction for culturally disadvantaged
pupils. These supplementary units are coordinated with regular materials of the
Minnesota Mathematics and Science Teaching Project, the Minnemath Center's major
undertaking, which uses the name Minnemast.

standing of basic mathematics and scientific principles to help them cope more successfully with the advanced courses being offered sooner and earlier in the high schools and colleges. This may or may not be so.

It would appear, however, that the needs, both immediate and projected, of a large segment of the school population located in low socioeconomic areas, rural as well as urban, may be somewhat different from the needs of other pupils who will never be included in the high school "dropout" statistics. The latter, as a result of social pressure, greater motivation, or comparative cultural and/or economic advantage, will complete high school and probably go on to college.

It was, however, with the particular needs of pupils from disadvantaged urban environments in mind that Professor Paul C. Rosenbloom, Minnemath director, suggested I prepare a series of supplementary units which could be coordinated with the materials currently in use in the Minnemast program.

Many of the pupils for whom these materials were prepared have comparatively low levels of verbal facility and limited experiences outside of their immediate environments. Hence, the story sequences and the pictorial representations, to have meaning or reality for them, would have to be closely related to the commonplace and limited experiences of children growing up in crowded urban situations.

I found that the Twin Cities, with a population less than one-tenth that of New York City, nevertheless have certain school and pupil conditions which are similar to those in the East. There are probably analogous situations in every city in the United States with a population of 100,000 or more.

In and around the Hall School area of North Minneapolis, I met many youngsters of various ethnic backrounds, of low verbal facility, low reading ability, and achievement test scores considerably below the norms for the Twin Cities area. Although the congestion, overcrowding, and concomitant frictions and tensions generally found in comparable districts of New York City, Detroit, or Chicago were far less severe in the Hall School neighborhood, the very limited scope of experiences of the pupils was evident in the discussions and conversations of a summer class there. The pupils had little knowledge of local community resources such as the nearby Mississippi River area, parks, lakes, zoos, animal farms, or other similar facilities.

This limited scope of experiences and interaction with their environment is a significant and common characteristic of children in disadvantaged areas, regardless of the nature of the community. In seeking to improve the educational procedure for them, adjustments to the characteristics of the learners would thus seem to deserve top priority in curriculum experimentation. Opportunities for broadening their horizons must not be presented at a level of sophistication which prevents the children from experiencing success in formulating answers, comments, or other responses.

The degree of family mobility seemed somewhat less in Minneapolis than in New York City, although there is a group of itinerant workers (generally of Mexican extraction) who represent an exception. The other minority groups located in that part of Minneapolis are Negroes and American Indians. The Hall School has a regular pupil population of approximately 400, half of whom are white. The other half includes children from the various minority groups in almost equal numbers.

Nearby, modern housing project areas and the garden apartment developments are similar to the low-income and middle-income housing developments in the East. Conspicuously absent from the Minneapolis landscape, however, are the crowded tenement dwellings found around Public School 289 and in slum areas of the larger cities.

Against that neighborhood background, the first of the supplementary units was developed around a shopping trip to a supermarket. The material dealt with weight and measurement. The initial story sequence concerned itself with two boys from the same schoolroom, white and Negro, who met on the way to the supermarket. Similarities between them, rather than differences, were emphasized in the unit. These included similar items to be purchased, similar clothing, and similar speech patterns.

In various situations each boy in the story was able to impart new information to the other. Words such as quart, pint, ounce, dozen, liquid, and dairy are all in the story line as natural elements of a shopping trip. The pictorial representations in this unit proved to be most effective in themselves. When shown to a group of youngsters to whom the story had not been read, it was possible for them to construct a story that turned out to be not very different from the original.

There were other psychological and sociological implications built into the story line. When Bobby and Paul decided to obtain additional information at the library to satisfy their curiosity about the origins of certain weights and measures, the school librarian whom they questioned was pictured as a Negro.

The psychologists on our summer writing project confirmed the expectation that the positive image of professional competence and achievement, as well as the tacit understanding that a white child would be going to a Negro for help and guidance, would be picked up quickly by even very young pupils. This view seems to have been borne out when the materials were tried out at the Hall School during the summer program.

The summer project was under the direction of the school's principal, Mr. Willard Ludford, and Minnemast participation covered a three-week period. The groups involved consisted of pre-first, pre-second, pre-third, and pre-fourth-grade pupils. Many of them had never seen the Mississippi River, we discovered, although it flows through Minneapolis less than ten blocks from Hall School. Several had never been more than just a few blocks away from their homes. One of the aims of the summer project was to provide additional experiences, both verbal and cultural, to enlarge the backgrounds that these children would bring with them to school in the regular fall term.

The group with which I worked consisted of fifteen pre-second-graders. From the comments of observers at our session, it appeared that there was high interest in the material presented, and response to opportunities for enlargement of their limited vocabularies. The children seemed particularly pleased when handling and working with egg cartons, milk containers, coffee cans, scales, and related materials which had been made available to them for the lessons. They had opportunities to weigh items and to compare sizes and quantities.

They rejected one of the illustrations which accompanied the story because there were "no people in it." They discussed the characters in the story and suggested titles for the "book they were helping to write for other children."

In the follow-up lesson a few days later it was found that retention of understanding of the new vocabulary words was limited. This indicated a need for additional reinforcement exercises and activities employing the new phrases and words encountered in the story.

It should be understood that Minnemast does not subscribe to the idea of a separate or distinct curriculum for children from disadvantaged environments. However, we must provide for the introduction of those concepts in the program on a level of understanding which is compatible with the limited verbal capacity of many young school children in low socioeconomic urban areas.

The use of these supplementary units is optional. They can be used in conjunction with the regular units currently in the Minnemast series. The time of their introduction can be decided by the teacher based upon the needs of a grade or a particular group within a grade.

The supplementary units planned to meet this particular need are now undergoing revision for trial use at experimental centers.

45

The Culturally Deprived Child and Science

SAMUEL MALKIN

Educators have always had the problem of adapting the curriculum to the needs of children with special problems. Today teachers throughout the country, particularly in urban areas, are being confronted in ever-increasing numbers by the special problem of the culturally deprived or disadvantaged child. In New York City, it is estimated that 225,000 out of 573,000 elementary school children and 75,000 out of 186,000 junior high school pupils are in that category. Coupled with the disadvantaged or culturally deprived child is the non-English speaking child. About 11.5 per cent of the entire elementary school population of New York City speak English haltingly or not at all (1).

What are some characteristics of these children? In working with them, one quickly becomes aware of their general lack of achievement in the basic academic skills of reading, writing, and arithmetic; their general-low self-image; and their lack of interest. Then one becomes aware of their limited experiences. What we tend to take for granted in youngsters — that they are familiar with gardens, pets, automobiles, trains, bicycles, elevators, and the country — is not necessarily true for these children. Indeed, many have never strayed from their own neighborhood or block, even though they may live in a city with many places to go and things to do.

What are some of the conditions that cause cultural deprivation? Although poverty may not in itself be a cause, most culturally deprived children come from poor areas. Many come from broken homes or from families with deteriorated social standards; many come from areas where there is conflict between their own existing subculture and the standard American middle-class culture. Then, too, these areas may contain a constantly changing population with families moving in, staying awhile, and moving away again. The youngsters may have no roots, no feelings of loyalty, or no sense of responsibility to the community.

Teachers need orientation to work with these children since the children's expectations contrast sharply with the teaching and therapeutic processes which the teacher is normally trained to use. For example, these children desire authority and direction rather than training in self-direction; they desire action rather than introspection; they desire structure and organiza-

❖ From *Science and Children*, April, 1964, pp. 5–7. Used by permission of the author and the publisher. Samuel Malkin is Supervisor of Audio-Visual Instruction, Board of Education of the City of New York.

tion rather than a permissive situation; they desire simple, more concrete, scientifically demonstrable explanations rather than symbolic, circuitous interpretations; and they desire informal, sympathetic, nonpatronizing relationships rather than intensive ones (3).

These desires and expectations of the disadvantaged child are positive elements upon which a functional and developmental curriculum can be built. Frank Riessman, in his book *The Culturally Deprived Child* (2), strongly advocates such an approach. His observations identify other elements which have a direct bearing on the development of a curriculum for these children. These are: ability in abstract thinking, but at a slower rate than middle-class children; skill in nonverbal communication; greater achievement when tasks are motor-oriented; and greater motivation to tasks which have tangible and immediate goals.

An elementary science program for such children must be based on the positive elements of the characteristics, environment, and expectations of these children.

What Are the Features of Such a Program?

AN ELEMENTARY SCIENCE PROGRAM MUST BE BASED ON THE PUPILS' ENVIRONMENT. Children are concerned with the world about them; the sound of bells, thunder and lightning, automobiles, airplanes, trees, birds, and their own bodies. Disadvantaged children are no exception; however, their own world may not be the same as their teacher's world. To the teacher, larva, pupa, and butterfly are part of nature; to the pupils these may be meaningless because they may never have seen these things. Skyscrapers, concrete, and alley cats are more meaningful to these children than the Grand Canyon, sedimentary rocks, and protozoa. The culturally deprived child's environment is quite restricted, and we must seek from his environment those elements familiar to him and build our program upon them.

It is also important to enlarge the pupil's environment. This suggests that he be given direct experiences through audio-visual materials. A trip to the farm or zoo where the urban slum child can see and fondle farm animals, a lesson on magnetism where he and his fellow pupils can handle many different magnets, or a film which shows him what makes night and day are all experiences which enlarge the pupil's concepts about his environment.

AN ELEMENTARY SCIENCE PROGRAM MUST BE BASED ON REAL PROBLEMS. Children ask questions about their environment and want answers to their questions. Some of these questions are: How does the school bell ring? What makes the light go on? Why do we want to explore outer space? How can we keep food from spoiling? How does the weatherman forecast weather? How does a telephone work? How can my skates roll more easily? What makes a car stop? Whereas many children frequently obtain the correct answers to their questions from parents or from books, the culturally deprived youngsters generally do not. Their parents are not able to help them and they are not able or motivated to help themselves. They must rely on the school for the correct answer, or else be satisfied with misinformation or no answer. The implications are clear. The teacher must gear her program to help these children find answers to questions about their environment. Indeed, the teacher may need to help the children verbalize questions which their environment has led them to submerge. Questions, such as those listed above, could and should serve as the aims of lessons in elementary science. By basing the aims of her lessons on real problems, the teacher can capitalize on pupils' interest and compensate for the learning they should, but do not, receive at home.

ELEMENTARY SCIENCE SHOULD NOT DEPEND ON READING OR OTHER ACADEMIC SKILLS. A major weakness of the disadvantaged child is lack of achievement in reading and other academic skills. This lack of achievement in reading probably accounts, in large measure, for lack of success in other curriculum areas which depend on reading. If an elementary science program is to be successful, then the pupils must feel that they can succeed in science. I conceive of elementary science as a truly "democratic" subject — democratic to the extent that every child can participate in, and get a feeling of, achievement and success from it. Therefore, it is important that activities be so chosen that they do not discourage children. One way to do this is to use children's language skills, other than reading, in the elementary science program. Such skills as listening, speaking, reporting, observing, and note-taking (at the pupil's level) should be encouraged.

Teachers should plan lessons which draw on pupils' experiences, and the conclusions to each lesson should be elicited from the class in the pupils' own language. Audio-visual materials should be used extensively to provide basic information and material for research. Children can use film-strips with individual viewers just as they would use books. The formation of soil and the operation of the water cycle can be demonstrated more effectively by films than by books.

Although the basic science program should not depend on textbooks, children should have contact with many science books at their own reading level. Thus, instead of thirty books of a basic series of texts on one grade level in a class, it might be possible to have thirty books of many series at different levels. Trade books on many topics at varying reading levels should be available. In this way, children could select those books which they are able to read, and which do not frustrate them.

ELEMENTARY SCIENCE SHOULD REINFORCE BASIC ACADEMIC SKILLS. Although this may seem contrary to what was previously stated, it is not. Elementary science can and should encourage and motivate growth in reading. As these children get a feeling of success from their science activities, they may be motivated to greater achievement. Thus, they can be encouraged to use some of the trade and textbooks that are to be found in the room. Elementary science can provide even more basic reading experiences. Labeling of specimens, models, and charts provide reading experiences, as do captions on filmstrips. In my own experience, at the end of each lesson I ask the children to tell me what they have learned from that lesson. Their own statements are written on large sheets of paper and the pupils copy these in their notebooks. Many weeks later the pupils are able to read their statements, although they may not be able to read at that level in their basal readers. They are able to read their experience charts because they are motivated to learn to read those statements which arise from their own experience. Elementary science is used to motivate these pupils.

A more formal experiment correlating science and reading is being conducted by Richard Kinney, at Public School No. 188 in Manhattan. In this experiment, reading lessons, based on the children's science experiences, are being prepared on three reading levels. The results so far have been encouraging and point to further study in this area.

ELEMENTARY SCIENCE SHOULD AFFORD CHILDREN OPPORTUNITIES TO HANDLE MATERIALS AND EQUIPMENT. A fundamental concept in teaching elementary science is that all children should have an opportunity to handle materials and equipment. This is especially true for the culturally deprived child since he seems to have greater achievement when tasks are motor-oriented. Teachers, therefore, should provide every opportunity for children to participate in demonstrations and experiments. If possible, there should be enough material so that every child can use the same materials at his seat that his teacher is using at her desk. Kits of materials can be organized which contain, for example, thirty dry cells, thirty switches, thirty bells, and pieces of wire, or thirty sets of different magnets. The materials that are used should be familiar to children. Esoteric and elaborate equipment should be avoided since it may be confusing to children and assume importance rather than the science concepts being demonstrated. Children should be given recognition for their projects by having their exhibits displayed to other pupils as well as to their parents and to the community at periodic science fairs.

Through proper adaptation of the elementary science curriculum to the needs of this large portion of our children, we may bring about an enrichment of their lives which, in turn, will benefit our entire community. We have, so far, failed to tap America's greatest resources, the creative skills and abilities of all its children. Among these disadvantaged children, there is a large reservoir of future high-level, professional, and skilled personnel and we must learn how to help them realize their potential.

Throughout the country, experimentation with curriculum development for the culturally deprived children, such as the "Higher Horizons Program" and "Mobilization for Youth" in New York City are providing insights into the techniques of teaching such children. Through implementation of our new insights both society and the child will benefit.

REFERENCES

1. Board of Education of the City of New York. *Higher Horizons Progress Report.* New York: The Board, January, 1963.

2. Riessman, Frank. *The Culturally Deprived Child.* New York: Harper & Row, Publishers, 1962.

3. ———. "Some Suggestions Concerning Psychotherapy with Blue-Collar Patients." New York: Mobilization for Youth and Department of Psychiatry, Columbia University, 1963. P. 4. (Unpublished mimeographed paper.)

46

Teaching Science to the Disadvantaged Pupil

LORENZO LISONBEE

The Biological Sciences Curriculum Study is investigating the feasibility o
tailoring a program in biology to fit the needs and abilities of the one-hal
million slower learners in the biology classes of the nation's high schools
The study finds that it is impossible to separate the socioeconomic factor
from the task it is attempting. An estimated 30 to 50 per cent of these pu
pils seem to be culturally deprived, disadvantaged Americans. What the
BSCS ought to do and can do for these youngsters, whose reading level:
range upward from the second grade and whose desires to be taught spar
from the highly desiring to the stubbornly resistive, remains a question
That they have worth as becoming productive citizens sharing the respon
sibilities of a democratic society is not doubted. That they need and car
learn the minimal science basic to being informed citizens is the consensu:
of the many who have contributed ideas and suggestions to the BSCS Special Student Project, the first of the major national movements involved
with science curriculum revision to become involved with the limited
learner and, consequently, with the socioeconomic background of its students.

To be disadvantaged is a relative matter. If the most disadvantaged student in our American high school were transplanted to many other groups
elsewhere in the world, he would be recognized as a very advantaged person, literate and intelligent. He would be able to read and write, add and
subtract, and relate a great deal about the so-called civilized world. But in
America he is a limited learner, a disaffected youth, a disadvantaged American; he is culturally deprived.

The relativeness in the situation, of course, is due to the present social,
economic, and educational status of the large majority of people in America.
The median school years completed by adults twenty-five years old and
older in seven states is now beyond the twelfth grade; in three-fourths of
the states it is beyond the tenth (6). The large middle class for the past
two and one-half decades has placed a premium on education and on be-

✧ From a presentation at the Southwestern and Rocky Mountain Regional Meeting of
the American Association for the Advancement of Science, April 29, 1963, University
of New Mexico, Albuquerque, as published in *The Science Teacher*, October, 1963,
pp. 18–21. Used by permission of the author and the publisher. Lorenzo Lisonbee is
a consultant to the Biological Sciences Curriculum Study, University of Colorado.

coming skilled. Our technological society has rapidly become more and more technological, consuming in fantastic numbers skilled professional and semiprofessional men and women. There is hardly a place any more for the unskilled: the machines have taken over the pick and shovel, even the human hand in such skillful "unskilled" labor as cotton harvesting. A distinguishing mark of the disadvantaged is that he does not have the advantage of being skilled in doing something that fits somewhere into the technological pattern of our society.

Who Are the Disadvantaged?

A half-dozen books have been written during the past three years on the subject of the disadvantaged American and the culturally deprived. Recent issues of periodicals have been dedicated to this cause (2). The writers, most of whom are specialists in the field of educational sociology, educational psychology, and psychiatry, seem to agree that our disadvantaged citizens are victims of their environment and have a very limited perspective and understanding of the society of which they are a part. They have limited aspirations, not commensurate with their latent abilities. By being deprived, they are further deprived in school with what usually amounts to a second-rate education even in a first-rate school system. They are not understood by their middle-class teachers. They want to learn, but resist the methods of the ordinary educational system to get them to learn. They are not interested in special favors, but do want, like all human beings, to be respected (2, 7, 8, 9). They lag in school achievement and do not read at or near their grade level (5, 7, 8). It is estimated that nearly one-half of the slow learners — the low 20 to 30 per cent on the academic scale — in our secondary schools come from the ranks of the culturally deprived, a group which harbors far more potential in ability and aptitude than does the advantaged slow learner group.

The disadvantaged pupils' appearance in our large city schools is increasing at a tremendous rate. The Educational Policies Commission predicts that by 1970, if present trends are not reversed, one-half of our large cities will be inhabited by the disadvantaged Americans (5, p. 10). This would mean that at least one-half of the enrollment in the schools would consist of students from disadvantaged homes. This trend has alarmed a number of spokesmen to the point that the culturally deprived are now in the spotlight. Our large cities have received grants and have budgeted local monies to investigate the problem of the disadvantaged. There are the Great Cities Project, New York's Higher Horizons, Cleveland's Hough Community Project, Philadelphia's School Improvement Project, to name a few (3, pp. 17–20).

It is interesting to note that the ranks of the culturally deprived nation-wide have not increased; they only seem to be increasing because, heretofore, they have been isolated in remote rural areas, unnoticed. Now that they are migrating to the cities for a better life, they have become conspicuous.

Even though the school dropout rate for this group is high, large numbers of disadvantaged pupils survive their educational experience into and through high school. Compulsory attendance laws encourage many to remain through the ninth and tenth grade. Many pupils stick with it and graduate, because they have learned from experience that it is much easier to get a job with a high school diploma than without one. The general tendency to remain in school is reflected in the fact that the enrollments in some of our large city high schools are composed almost entirely of disadvantaged Americans.

Science Offerings

Of course, these youngsters take science, and they are enrolled in large numbers in the science classes. If you visited the schools in our large cities, you would find most of them in the "general" classes: general science in the ninth grade and general biology in the tenth. You would find that the science program in which these "generals" find themselves is, in the main, entirely lacking in laboratory work and teacher demonstration. High school buildings in the large cities are usually old and were designed back in the days when one biology laboratory for a high school of two to three thousand students was considered sufficient. Today, in more schools than not, one and only one laboratory remains and is used continuously and exclusively for the honors and college prep classes.

The situation is generally deplored and regretted. One science supervisor in a large city school system remarked that the generals are given a lecture-reading type course, and the higher achievers get an activity program; whereas, perhaps, it should be the other way around. The less able, the less articulate, the less verbal, need the activity in the lab to help them learn. The more able, with a greater power to abstract, are much more at home with textual materials and class discussion than are the less able; but of course, they, too, need the experiences in scientific inquiry provided by the laboratory.

Serious effort is being made in most large city school systems to provide laboratory facilities for all classes in the science program. But the outlook is discouraging. The tax rate in some of our large cities has reached the statute limitation while property within the school district has devaluated. To add three or four laboratories to each of, say, fifty high schools requires finances which seem under the present circumstances not to be available.

Teacher and Pupil

Associated with the effort and the need to provide laboratory facilities for the less able and the disadvantaged, there seems to be a serious sociological problem involving the pupil and the teacher, a problem which, as yet, has not been recognized or clarified in the literature. In visiting schools during the 1963–64 academic year, a correlation seems to have been observed between the quality of the science program and the socioeconomic background of the school community, other factors being equal. In large city school systems, for example, where the minimum teacher preparation and available monies were the same throughout all the high schools in the system, it was observed that the more deprived the school community, the lesser the quality of the science program.

To illustrate this relationship of economic deprivation and quality of the science program, may I describe my observations in one large city school system. In this district, laboratory facilities are available to all science classes. All the school plants are kept in tip-top shape. To teach in this system, a candidate must pass a qualifying examination and have an accumulation of semester hours of credits in his major field beyond the minimum to meet state certification requirements. Teachers throughout the system are on the same salary schedule. School A is located in an area that is comprised of the so-called culturally deprived, disadvantaged Americans. School officials reported that 10 to 30 per cent of the students enrolled are absent each day. About one-half of the students who enter in September are not the same one-half who finish in June. Average reading level in the school is seventh-grade and the average I.Q. as measured by verbal tests is 85. In visiting the biology classes, we found the rooms (lab-classroom combinations) to be barren. The class activity consisted mainly of students' taking turns reading from the text, with the teacher interspersing the procedure with comment. As we moved to schools B, C, D, and E, we progressively moved to schools having higher and higher socioeconomic backgrounds. We observed that the quality of the science program improved from school to school. In school D, a biology teacher and his students were working on a research project supported by the National Institutes of Health. The biology lab-classrooms were alive with "biology." In school E, located in a well-to-do upper middle-class and lower upper-class community, science was being taught as so many these days say it should be taught. The study of biology was being approached through biology as a science. The students were discovering for themselves important concepts through an investigative approach afforded by the laboratory. The biology lab-classroom was a research lab, with student projects located wherever space permitted.

The most significant part of this narrative now follows: In school E, teacher Mr. Doe was asked how he would react to the proposal that he be transferred to school A, over in the deprived part of town, to set up a science program such as he had in school E, with the understanding that at the end of two years he would then return to his present school. The teacher thought a few seconds and replied, "If the administration insisted that I do this, I would resign." "Why?" "When I teach I must as a teacher and as a human being be stimulated by my students through feedback from them. I put a lot into my teaching; here these youngsters are bright and highly motivated. They find science exciting and are responsive. I have taught students like those in School A. I am fully sympathetic with them. But I cannot get the response from them that I must have to find satisfaction in teaching. These youngsters are unresponsive, to me at least, and unmotivated. Most of them don't care whether school keeps or not."

The correlation between the socioeconomic background and the quality of the science program seems to exist quite generally over the country. I have often pondered the causes, especially in those cities which provide well-trained teachers and equal financial resources to all. I believe the situation is a fertile field for research. I am inclined to believe that perhaps Mr. Doe provided the answer. It might well be that when a good teacher, full of good intentions, goes the second mile in providing a first-rate science program for these youngsters, he may eventually give up in despair because these youngsters may seem to be unresponsive, unappreciative, unproductive, thus providing no reinforcement for the teacher.

Science for the Disadvantaged

But, the disadvantaged pupil needs to have a first-rate program in science and other basic subjects, and he needs, perhaps more than anyone else, first-rate teachers, and first-rate teaching, for several reasons.

1. He represents a significant segment of our society — a segment that is important and could be more important as a contributor of worthwhile service to society; he is important as a potential voter and important for the fact he is a human being who shares with others the responsibilities of a democratic society.

2. As a human resource this group in our classrooms across the nation is a gold mine of hidden talent. For example, the Cook County Department of Public Aid recently completed a study of 646 dependent youngsters age sixteen through twenty who had dropped out of school. The reading levels ranged from Grade 2.6 to Grade 10, with 40 per cent measuring below Grade 6. Yet on the Beta nonverbal intelligence test, over one-half of these youngsters had I.Q.'s ranging from 90 to 123 (3, p. 30; 7, Chap. 6).

That these youngsters have a great potential in our technological society apparently is not doubted by those who have studied the problems of the disadvantaged. These youngsters deserve good teaching, and they need good teachers, teachers who will tolerate them and respect them, even though they may come from a different class, a different cult than they. Needed are teachers who understand that these youngsters have different values and different aspirations than they, and that these pupils come from a group that often has different family structuring than their own.

A teacher also needs a strong subject-matter background, especially on the secondary level, and herein lies one of the great weaknesses in our attempts to provide a suitable and meaningful education for these pupils. These pupils are often placed into a program wherein the newest, the youngest, the most inexperienced teacher is assigned to teach them. An experienced teacher, an understanding teacher is needed (5, pp. 19, 20). Too often, teachers who have less than a minor in the subject are assigned to teach these classes. If these youngsters are going to be given a valuable and meaningful program in science, they need a teacher who understands science, a teacher who has a good subject-matter background in science and who understands how to teach science to the disadvantaged.

There are a few teachers who do find teaching these pupils rewarding. If somewhere in the professional training of teachers, prospective teachers become aware of this group and the associated educational and sociological problems, more and more teachers would choose to teach these pupils; and many others would do a better job of teaching them. Every methods course should include an hour or two wherein the teacher in training is given opportunity to explore this problem.

In teaching science to the disadvantaged, it is important to help them acquire an understanding of the importance of science in today's world, how it has contributed to our standard of living and to the culture of modern society. These youngsters also need to know how the scientist goes about his work. They also need to gain appreciations for science. To learn these various aspects of science, the disadvantaged as well as other students need to do some actual "sciencing."

In regard to the question of what is the best subject matter for the group, there are two schools of thought: One school is represented by influential voices saying that these youngsters, many of whom will not be going beyond the tenth grade, could best benefit from a program oriented to health and human physiology. They need to know how to take care of their bodies, to know the rudiments of nutrition and sanitary living, and to know how their body works, it is argued. The other school of thought would say that these youngsters have had enough of this type of instruction by the time they reach the tenth grade. They should now be given the opportunity to become familiar with the important basic concepts in science and to be introduced to the processes of science. They are ready and require something new. It is now time to familiarize them with the basic scientific principles regarding the world and universe surrounding them and of which they are a part. That these youngsters can grasp these concepts is a proposition supported by a number of current spokesmen. Jerome Bruner's notion that any concept can be taught at any level now seems to be commonly accepted (1, pp. 33, 43, 46, 47). Hubert Evans of Columbia University offers additional hope that our disadvantaged pupils can become sufficiently literate in science when he says,

> Scientific literacy does not require a survey and understanding of the whole of science and technology. A relatively small number of fundamental scientific concepts and conceptual schemes can be identified and, when understood, can form a firm foundation for understanding the nature of the sciences and scientific work and for interpreting the newer developments as they come along (3, p. 33).

George W. Beadle, Nobel laureate and president of the University of Chicago, recently wrote,

> As scientific knowledge grows, it tends to become simpler in one important respect: As the facts increase, the principles often become fewer, clearer, and easier to understand (3, p. 34).

The advocates of the second school of thought would say that these relatively few basic scientific concepts would and should be the ones given emphasis in a program for these pupils, and in the study of these concepts these pupils can learn best through a discovery approach as offered through laboratory investigations.

Program Expectations

The Biological Sciences Curriculum Study is attempting to prepare a program for the limited learner (low 30 per cent in our academic classes) which consists of a large number of disadvantaged pupils. It is currently working on the premise that these youngsters need and deserve a program which explores important, basic concepts in modern biology. The consensus of biology teachers generally, especially those who have taught the BSCS biology, supports the BSCS premise. The BSCS holds to the conviction that these youngsters will find more interesting adventures in their school experience in science through traveling new roads related to updated concepts in biology than retraveling the byways of health, disease, and nutrition.

During the summer of 1963, three experimental units were prepared, based on this premise. These units explore important ideas in genetics, ecology, and cellular biology. They will be tried by about one thousand students during the 1963–64 school year. The construction of a complete year's program is scheduled for the summer of 1964. It is hoped that through the materials prepared and the program developed and the quality of teaching provided, these youngsters will find the course fascinating and challenging and will want to come back to class day after day. If this can be accomplished, perhaps this program will contribute to the effort to keep these youngsters in school and to provide a program which they appreciate.

In developing the program, the BSCS is cognizant of the associated sociological problems — those that relate to the pupil and his cultural background and to the pupil and his teacher.

REFERENCES

1. Bruner, Jerome S. *The Process of Education.* Cambridge, Mass.: Harvard University Press, 1961.
2. Conant, James B. *Slums and Suburbs.* New York: McGraw-Hill Book Co., Inc., 1961.
3. *NEA Journal,* April, 1963.
4. *Educational Leadership,* 20:3; February, 1963.
5. National Education Association, Educational Policies Commission. *Education and the Disadvantaged American.* Washington: The Association, 1962.
6. ———, Research Division. *Research Bulletin,* 40:14; December, 1962.
7. Riessman, Frank. *The Culturally Deprived Child.* New York: Harper & Row, Publishers, 1962.
8. Sexton, Patricia. *Education and Income.* New York: The Viking Press, 1961.
9. Taba, Hilda. *Curriculum Development: Theory and Practice.* New York: Harcourt, Brace & World, Inc., 1962. Chaps. 5, 8, and 10.

Training Teachers of the Disadvantaged

In our attempts to carry out the tremendous task of educating all children, say Frank Riessman and Arlene Hannah in the first selection in Part Seven, we have tended to try to standardize two things that cannot be standardized: children and teaching methods. Contending that the art of teaching must be preserved, that we need teachers who have "style," who are not only dedicated and idealistic but also practical, Riessman and Hannah offer practical and ingenious suggestions for making teaching exciting and meaningful.

The ideas presented by Miriam L. Goldberg have great relevance for all teachers, although she particularly addresses herself to teachers of the disadvantaged. She believes that a pupil's learning is, to a very high degree, a function of the kind of teaching to which he is exposed, and that teaching influences not only the child's mastery of subject matter but also his interpersonal relationships.

Goldberg further points out that there are varieties of good teacher style. Some are suited to many different types of students while others are more effective with one type. An awareness of this principle is crucial to the effective administration of any school, but most particularly to the schools attended by large numbers of disadvantaged children.

Children from disadvantaged populations desperately need the services of a good teacher. Their educational deficit is usually so great that only the best offers hope of *any* progress in an educational setting.

Vernon F. Haubrich suggests that the problems surrounding the preparation of teachers for disadvantaged areas lies ". . . in the cultural misunderstandings that exist between many teachers and many children and parents from disadvantaged areas." He describes the dual task of colleges and universities in meeting this challenge: to develop appropriate programs and to employ broader resources of the academic community.

The past four years has seen the development of an increasing controversy regarding the "culturally disadvantaged" child and how to help him. This controversy has been too long in coming before us, but the debate now seems to have reached some degree of maturity. Frank Riessman's book, *The Culturally Deprived Child,* published in 1962, probably should be credited with giving much impetus to the discussions which have permeated government, school systems, teacher education institutions, and the public at large. The selection by Patrick J. Groff is based on a teacher study of the views of Riessman. These are teachers who work at the "firing line," who should have extensive knowledge of the practices and procedures which produce results, and who should have firsthand knowledge of the characteristics of children from pockets of poverty.

Groff's study indicates substantial agreement with most of the opinions of Riessman. Where agreement does not exist, further investigation is badly needed. If we are to find better ways to teach this large group of children, we must know more about them. The areas of disagreement are important enough to challenge some teaching techniques and some ideas concerning subject matter that have been suggested by many authors and educational authorities. Further research must be encouraged at all levels.

Training teachers of the disadvantaged must be given high priority by educational institutions. We are far from being "out of the woods" in knowing how to do the best job. A continuing dialogue should be carried on so that we are able to define the areas for further research and inservice training. Teaching is difficult but very satisfying for those who are suited to it, and the teacher of the disadvantaged deserves all possible support in meeting this extraordinary challenge. The teacher cannot conquer all alone. Society must participate in this social and educational revolution if progress is to be made. And progress must be made, for we are dealing with human lives and potentialities.

47

Teachers of the Poor

FRANK RIESSMAN AND ARLENE HANNAH

Poverty is coming of age; of that there is no doubt. President Lyndon Johnson emphasized this development in his recent statement of commitment to an all-out attack on poverty.

Another President, John F. Kennedy, bespoke his own commitment in many ways. They tell a story about Mr. Kennedy. After a particularly grueling morning in his office, he would open the doors, step out, and clap his hands. Then the children from the White House schoolroom would come streaming in to him from all directions, playing leapfrog, hiding under the presidential desk, and tumbling through the French doors into the sunlit rose garden. After a time, he and the children would return to their duties, refreshed from this interchange. He had a *style* about him, this man, and he knew how to summon the children.

What does all this have to do with poverty? Simply this: that a crucial domestic issue today is the education of all, not some, children. And we have thus far failed in summoning them. Overwhelming statistical evidence — for instance, the dropout and illiteracy rates — bears this out. Our failure, of course, has shown up most markedly in the education of the poor.

The Forgotten Children

What is there in our monolithic school system that has kept us from reaching these youngsters? A piece of the answer is that the system, in the face of its gargantuan task, has attempted to standardize what could not be standardized, to set up "norms" that were middle-class ones, and to reward what was most expedient — conformity to the middle-class measuring stick. But the system is no longer working; the children are no longer learning. The measuring stick is broken, and unless we find another more realistic one, we shall have lost the minds and hearts of countless children.

Another piece of the answer is that the teacher comes to the school ill equipped to teach low-income youngsters. Such a youngster's world is an alien, fearful, and confusing one to the teacher, just as the classroom is to

❖ From *The PTA Magazine*, November, 1964, pp. 12–14. Used by permission of the authors and the publisher. Frank Riessman is a psychologist on the staff of Mobilization for Youth, Inc., and Professor of Psychology at Bard College. Arlene Hannah is a staff member of Mobilization for Youth.

the child. Much of what was taught in college applies only in a limited way to a child who is hungry, is burdened with responsibilities at home, and speaks another language (whether that language is Spanish, Chinese, or the language of the streets).

How do we get these two together? How do we get them to appreciate, respect, and really "dig" each other as human beings? Many innovations have been offered and are already in process in regard to the child — crash remedial courses, preschool programs, increased guidance services, and others. One cannot miss their underlying implication that the problem is with the individual child and his family, whether that problem is labeled psychological impoverishment, subcultural deprivation, or whatever, and that the school is trying to patch up, in some way, what has gone wrong.

The validity and vital necessity of these programs should not be minimized. But this is not a one-way street. Certainly the child is deprived. Yet isn't the middle-class teacher just as deprived, as isolated, and as disconnected from a large portion of our society as the child?

The beginning solution, it seems to us, must stem from our teacher training institutions. We must work out a whole new system of pedagogy geared to the teaching of children from low-income families. Larger doses of sociological and anthropological material must be dispensed to teacher trainees in order to develop an appreciation of other ways of living, other realities. Concurrently, there should be community field trips, home visits, and student teaching in a variety of situations. Teachers should find out what it is like to eat rice and beans every day on a welfare budget, how it feels to wait five hours in a city clinic before being seen, why a family would choose to have a television set before a second pair of shoes all around.

Teachers must be fortified with knowledge of many kinds about low-income culture — particularly its strengths, such as its attitudes toward education, its inventiveness, its cooperativeness. But this learning must not be limited to the reading of relevant material from the behavioral and social sciences. In our breathing, changing society, the use of contemporary art forms is an invaluable device of which we should make full use. Reading Warren Miller's novel *The Cool World* or engaging in a seminar-discussion about the works of James Baldwin might evoke a more honest realization of the way other people view the world than a dozen courses in traditional pedagogy. Contemporary movies, workshops in Negro history, the learning of Spanish, or an understanding of the language of the streets would all contribute sharply to the teacher's "sensitivity training" toward low-income groups.

Infinite Variety

There is yet another fertile area that must be plowed in teacher education, and that is *style*. We said earlier that the late President Kennedy had a style, a distinctive mode of expression that allowed him to summon the children. This art, springing as it does from the unique and intuitive roots of each human being, can be developed by future teachers while they are

in college, and it can also be developed in the in-service programs. In visits
to schools in more than thirty-five cities, in witnessing a myriad of classroom
situations, we have always found at least one teacher in a school who, it
was agreed by everyone (children, parents, colleagues, and administrators),
was a "good" teacher. But the personality of each of these teachers, the
manner of approach, the point of view were vastly different.

One such type of teacher we call "the boomer." She shouts in a loud,
strong voice, "You're going to learn. I'm here to teach you, and there will
be no nonsense in this classroom." She lays down the ground rules early,
and the kids know immediately that with her there is a point beyond which
they cannot go. They may not like her, but they learn. Now some psychologists and educators might call this person hostile; yet she has learned to
use her aggressive quality effectively in the classroom.

Another kind of teacher might be called "the maverick." Everybody loves
this teacher but the boss. He gets upset because the maverick is always
raising "difficult" questions and presenting ideas that disturb. Now this
teacher is convinced that ideas are meant to disturb, to stir up, and consequently develops a close link with young and eager students. He is as surprised and curious as they are at each turn of mind, each new discovery,
and it is this fresh quality that comes through to them.

Then there is "the coach," an informal, earthy person who uses his hands,
his senses, in a very specific way. He sometimes is an athlete himself, but
more basically he is physically expressive — and that is how he conducts
his dialogue with the world. Many low-income youngsters like this. Coming from homes in which the accent is often on activity and motion, they
are able to connect with the quality of physical expressiveness quickly and
in a very natural way — a way more natural for everyone, really, than sitting still at a desk for two or three unbroken hours.

In sharp contrast is "the quiet one," who is able to reach much the same
goal through sincerity, calmness, and definitiveness. This teacher's essential
dignity pervades the classroom and commands both respect and attention
from the pupils.

We also have "the entertainer" — colorful, melodramatic, and, most important, not afraid to have fun with the children. Frequently he makes
mistakes through his sheer flair for the comic. When this happens, he is free
enough to laugh with the children at his own blunders. His inventiveness
may cause furrows in his supervisor's brow when he has children make
western hats instead of writing an essay about cowboys. But they may
learn more about cowboys and may be more interested in reading about
them than if a traditional method had been followed. This teacher actively
involves the children. Their opinions count, and they know it.

A very striking example of another teaching style is what we might call
"the secular type." This fellow is usually very relaxed and informal with
the students. He may have lunch with them or use their bathroom. (You
would be amazed at how many children do not really believe that teachers
eat and sleep and go to the bathroom, just as people do!) He is often very

comfortable in talking turkey with the kids, not in a mechanical or contrived way but through a deep involvement in language, its development and power.

One such teacher in Syracuse recently became quite interested in "hip" language. He is Gerald Weinstein, curriculum coordinator of the Madison Area Project. Rather than using a nineteenth-century poem from a standard school anthology, he used one full of current "hip" jargon by Negro author Langston Hughes as a point of departure for discussion. The students, in sharp contrast to their previously apathetic attitude, now were alive, animated, and involved, since this was on their "turf." For some of them it may have been the first time in their school experience that they could exhibit knowledge and have some sense of success and accomplishment.

The *Syracuse Herald-Journal* for November 11, 1963, reported on this program, noting that "the enthusiasm of that class session led the students into more of Hughes's poetry. Later they moved into other kinds of literature in more conventional language.

> But the students were not the only ones to learn from the exciting class. Weinstein learned, too. He learned the advantage of being familiar with the language of the children you are teaching and establishing a rapport with.
> For if a teacher doesn't start "where the child is," as Weinstein says, "he only reinforces the failure and frustration that has become normal pattern for disadvantaged students."

Thus we begin to see the myriad possibilities of teacher types and styles. Development of a style of teaching may be essential to making contact with these youngsters. This can be done through numerous devices. One of them is role-playing, where other teachers could be the class and the situations could be varied.

For example, the intensity of the discipline problem could be decreased or increased, the number and types of students could be manipulated, and so on. With the change of situations, the discovery gradually comes that each future teacher begins to do things that somehow "fit" him naturally. At the same time he partly takes over and is modified by things he has read, learned, or experienced. As roles are switched, one's repertoire is broadened, and shifts in attitude take place. Through this organic approach, the fledgling teacher learns to mold and strengthen his own techniques and thus to develop a style.

The Heart of It All

The common denominator in all this, of course, is a deep and utter commitment to the involvement of these youngsters. The crucial ingredient is basic human respect. To quote Miriam L. Goldberg in a recent paper on "Adapting Teacher Style to Pupil Differences," delivered at a conference on disadvantaged children at Teachers College, Columbia University:

> Perhaps the answer to this question requires the addition of still another characteristic to our hypothetical model, one that is most difficult to teach:

idealism, dedication to a cause, the desire to help the have-nots, to render service. That this openness to commitment exists in many young people is confirmed by the large numbers applying for the Peace Corps, preparing for missionary work, choosing to work in settlements, in hospitals, in special schools for disturbed or retarded or otherwise handicapped children. These young people feel that they are answering a call, and they rise to its demands. We have also witnessed such behavior, perhaps too often, in times of revolution and war, when young men and women have willingly gone into hardship and danger for what they believe in.

We suggest that we are now in the middle of a revolution and that "dedication" and "idealism" are used in this quotation neither in a sentimental sense nor in a paternalistic, missionary sense. Rather they are used in the full realization that if we are to continue to exist as a society, it is our mandate to light a small candle of hope in the minds of all children.

School today is too often a bookish place — rigid, formalistic, prissy. It is "negative feminine." And unless we take immediate steps to make it "positive human," we will have lost, irrevocably and forever, the tremendous bounty of childhood — and ourselves in the process.

❖ ❖ **48** ❖ ❖

Adapting Teacher Style to Pupil Differences: Teachers for Disadvantaged Children

MIRIAM L. GOLDBERG

It has become a cliché to state that the major effects on pupil learning result from what goes on in the classroom. We recognize that what the teacher and the pupils do during the five or six hours a day when they are in direct contact with each other is the "compass of learning." And yet, until recently, little of our research has addressed itself to the teaching process. We have studied the achievement of pupils under various methods of instruction, we have described and theorized about the personality characteristics of teachers, we have explored various theoretical formulations about the na-

❖ From a revision of a lecture presented at the Merrill-Palmer Institute, March, 1963, as published in the *Merrill-Palmer Quarterly*, April, 1964, pp. 161–178. Used by permission of the author and publisher. Miriam L. Goldberg is Associate Professor of Education, Teachers College, Columbia University.

ture of learning, and the effects of varying the administrative deployment of pupils and more recently of teachers have been investigated. We have examined the effects of class size, the functions of the administrator, the guidance counselor, and other adjunct personnel of the school. But we still could not describe with any degree of accuracy what teaching is all about, what the teacher actually says and does in the process of teaching, and what effect this has on pupil learning.

Although little may be known about the teaching process in general, even less information is available on the "fit" between particular styles of teaching and the learning of particular pupil populations. This question looms especially large as one considers the problems of teaching children from depressed or disadvantaged areas; pupils who, thus far, have not been effectively "reached" by the teaching procedures to which they have generally been exposed. That various teaching procedures now in use are more or less effective with pupils from more affluent or academically motivating environments is undoubtedly true. But these same procedures, typically learned in teacher education programs, have rarely proved effective with disadvantaged youngsters.

Three assumptions underlie this paper: The first maintains that a pupil's learning is, in large measure, a function of the kind of teaching to which he is exposed. Thus, the extent to which a pupil masters a given set of academic tasks reflects not only his aptitudes and attitudes, but also the appropriateness of the particular approach by which he is taught.

The second assumption, implied by the title, rejects the notion of the universally "good" teacher, equally able to adapt his style to varying pupil populations, and substitutes a conception of a variety of "good" teachers, differentially suited (by temperament and training) to teaching differing groups of students.

The third assumption proposes that children from culturally disadvantaged backgrounds, though highly variable, nevertheless represent a describable pupil population in need of teachers who are uniquely "good" for them.

The first portion of this paper presents some of the evidence in support of the first two assumptions, citing studies which point up the variety of teaching styles and their effects on pupil achievement in general and on the achievement of specific categories of pupils in particular. The remainder of the paper proposes a hypothetical model of the successful teacher of disadvantaged pupils and suggests how such a model may be approached.

STUDIES OF TEACHER PERFORMANCE

The last decade has witnessed a number of efforts to study the processes of teaching. The first consideration of most of the studies has been to describe and classify what the teacher and the pupils say and do during a class session. Some of the investigations have gone beyond the descriptive material into a study of the relationships between the teacher's style of performance and the learning patterns of children.

Categorizing Teacher Style

A variety of more and less structured classroom observations have yielded various classifications of teacher style. For example, Flanders (2) classified teachers as those who more often exert "direct influence," through lecturing, giving directions or criticizing student's work, and those who more often exert "indirect influence" through clarifying feelings, providing praise and encouragement, developing and making use of student ideas and asking questions.

Medley (6) divided the teacher's performance into three broad categories: (a) his means of controlling the class, (b) his approach to the content, and (c) the interpersonal climate he creates. In the "control" category fell such behaviors as eliciting large amounts of pupil response, maintaining a high degree of order or permitting a high degree of pupil initiative. "Approach to content" included such procedures as emphasizing individualization or using interesting, original devices and materials. The "class climate" category included the teacher's consideration for pupils' problems and feelings, the degree of support given to pupil statements and responses, and the frequency with which reproof and criticism were used.

More clearly defined perhaps, are the three dimensions of teacher style suggested by Ryans (8). The first is a personal dimension ranging from "friendly-warm-understanding to aloof-restricted." The second is a task dimension, ranging from "responsible-organized-business-like to unplanned-slipshod." The third describes the dynamic quality of the teacher's performance from "stimulating-informative to dull-routine." These categories are similar to those suggested by Warrener (11), who drew his observations from social behavior in non-teaching leadership situations. His categories were: (a) "objective" work orientation, (b) "social relations" orientation, and (c) "subjective" personal, expressive orientation.

The dimensions suggested by Ryans are sufficiently independent of each other so that a teacher may be at a different point along that scale on each one. For example, one teacher may be characterized as warm, businesslike, and stimulating; another as warm, business-like, but dull; or one might even be seen as aloof, business-like, and stimulating. Each dimension represents a continuum, and for most teachers there will be a characteristic point along its baseline.

Categorizing Verbal Behavior

The studies mentioned above have concentrated on the teacher's stance, his characteristic mode of behavior, the flavor of his performance, and his attitudes toward his task. Little attention was paid to the handling of content, the skill of questioning, the organization of material, and the like. For aspects of the teacher's work which relate to the processes of handling content, one must turn to the work of B. Othanel Smith and his associates (9). Here, the concern has been with the "logical operations" of teaching; with discovering ". . . how concepts, norms, laws, etc., are introduced, analyzed and manipulated in the course of instruction" (9, p. 2). Using large samples of electrically taped classroom sessions, the verbal behavior of both teachers and pupils was categorized into thirteen "major acts" — such as defining, stating, reporting, opining, explaining, comparing and contrasting, classifying, etc. Such analyses made possible the description of a teacher's characteristic performance through quantifying the frequency with which his verbal behavior falls into one or another of the various categories. Eventually, it should become possible to discover to what extent the differential frequencies are a function of a pervasive style of teaching, a response to the inherent logic of a particular subject or phase of it or a reflection of the particular group of pupils being taught.

Relating Teacher Style to Pupil Achievement

But the analyses of teaching styles and logical operations, significant though they may be in supplying needed systematic information on the teaching process, have only just begun to shed light on two crucial questions: (a) What difference do these ways of teaching make? Do pupils, in general, come out with different kinds or amounts of learning when taught by teachers using one or another approach to teaching? (b) Does a particular teacher's style have more or less the same effect on all pupils under his tutelage? If not, are there ways of determining the characteristics of pupils who would fare better under one teaching style than under another?

Working with junior-high-school classes in mathematics and social studies, Flanders (2) related teaching style to pupil achievement and degree of dependence. He reported that when learning goals were unclear, as in a new task, lecturing and giving directions increased the dependence of students on the teacher and tended to lower achievement. In general, he found that patterns of "indirect influence" resulted in greater content mastery and in more positive attitudes toward school than did the "direct influence" procedures. However, in classes designated as superior — where pupils' achievement was greatest and attitudes toward the teacher were most favorable — there was an element of flexibility in the teacher's influence patterns not found in below-average classrooms. In superior classes, teacher behavior was less predictable, "shifting from domination and close supervision" on some occasions, to "indirect participation" at other times. These studies also suggest that for pupils who tend to be dependent upon teacher direction and unable to pursue work on their own, a high level of "direct influence" — lecturing, criticizing, giving directions — tends to be associated with lower achievement than is apparent when more independent pupils are exposed to similar "direct" teaching procedures.

In their study of "The Language of Teaching," Bellack and Davitz (1) analyzed tape-scripts of high school social studies classes studying a unit in economics. They identified four basic Pedagogical Moves: structuring, soliciting, responding, and reacting which "describe the verbal maneuvers of students and teachers . . . and set the framework for the analysis of meaning communicated in the classroom." Although the first phase of this research is largely descriptive, as are most of the other analyses of the verbal behavior of teaching, the data analysis will be used not only to cate-gorize and describe but also to relate the linguistic variables to student learning and attitude change. In subsequent phases, Bellack plans to address himself more intensively to studying the functions of the various Pedagog-ical Moves — the recurring patterns or "cycles" of moves characteristic of a given teacher, and the relation between patterns of teacher verbal be-havior and student performance.

Of special interest to the major concern of this paper is the work of Heil and his associates (4). They hypothesized that "in a particular class, the teacher's behavior will evoke a certain amount of achievement with children of a given set of feelings and level of intelligence." On the basis of assess-ment instruments, fifth and sixth grade pupils in a New York City school were divided into four personality categories: (a) *Conformers* — character-ized by incorporation of adult standards, high social orientation, control over impulses and emphasis on mature behavior; (b) *Opposers* — showing disturbed authority relationships, oppositional trends, pessimistic tone, in-tolerance of ambiguity and disappointment and frustration as central dy-namics; (c) *Waverers* — described as anxious, ambivalent, fearful, floun-dering and indecisive, and (d) *Strivers* — showing marked drive for recog-nition, especially in school achievement, and exhibitionistic needs. The teachers were divided into three personality types — the *Turbulent,* the *Self-Controlling,* and the *Fearful.*

Pupil achievement was contrasted for each pupil category under each teacher type. In general, when achievement was controlled for I.Q., the "strivers" achieved most, followed by the "conformers," then the "opposers" and showing least gains, the "waverers." Neither the "strivers" nor the "conformers" were significantly affected by teacher personality; but for the "opposers" and the "waverers," teaching style made a significant difference. For the last two groups, the "self-controlling" teachers, who maintained an orderly, workmanlike class, focused on structure and planning — but, at the same time, showed a sensitivity to children's feelings and emphasized interpersonal relations in the classroom — were most effective. The "turbu-lent" teachers — characterized by greater concern for ideas than for people, freedom of expression of strong feelings and attitudes, little patience with routine tasks, "sloppiness," and inconsistency — were more successful than either of the other types in teaching math and science. In the other sub-jects their success was limited to "strivers" and "conformers." The "turbu-lent" teachers were least successful with the "opposers" who evidenced the highest intolerance of ambiguity. The "fearful" teachers — anxious, de-pendent on the approval of supervisors and of the children, unable to bring structure and order to the teaching task, and highly variable in their behavior — were uniformly ineffective with all kinds of children except "strivers," who fared well regardless of the teacher.

Teachable Groups

A quite different approach to the study of the relationship between teacher style and pupil learning is found in Thelen's (10) recent work on the formation of "teachable" groups. Since the 1930's repeated efforts at assessing the effects of "homogeneous" versus "heterogeneous" grouping or, in more modern parlance, broad and narrow ability-range groups, have produced meager results. The findings, though apparently inconclusive, are consistent in reporting that in the absence of deliberate curricular modifications, grouping, on the basis of ability, has no significant effects on pupil achievement. But all of the grouping efforts were predicated on the assumption that if the class group is "homogeneous" with respect to intelligence or reading level or achievement in a particular subject, then, *ipso facto*, such a group becomes more "teachable." A teacher in such a group would accomplish more with the pupils than would be the case where the range of ability was wide. What was left out of the equation of "teachability" was the teacher's style of working and his perception of the kinds of pupils with whom he tends to be most successful. From Thelen's work (10) it would appear that I.Q. or achievement status are by no means the most significant determinants of the teacher's perception of "teachability." Thelen states that, in general ". . . teachers recognize four kinds of students: the good, the bad, the indifferent, and the sick. But the problem is that each teacher places different students in these categories, so that whatever is being judged is not primarily some characteristic of the student" (p. 226). He urges that ". . . the teachable students for one teacher may be quite different than for another, that the fit between teacher and teachable students primarily results in better meeting the teacher's most dominant needs . . . he is able with the teachable class to do more fully what he tries to do with his other classes . . . that successful grouping must take the teacher himself into account" (p. 220). Despite finding few differences in achievement between "teachable" and random groups, Thelen states: "We remain convinced that any grouping which does not in some way attempt to 'fit' students and teachers together can have only accidental success" (p. 221).

A significant implication of the studies of teacher characteristics, teaching process, and teachable groups is the recognition that variations in pupil attainment in the classroom are related to variations in teacher performance, and that a particular teacher affects different pupils differently. We are forced to question the stereotype of the "good teacher" and the "poor teacher," although there may be some few who would prove excellent for all pupils and many more who would be inadequate no matter what the assignment. Most teachers, however, vary in their effectiveness depending upon the characteristics of the pupils they confront, the opportunity to fulfill their expectations for themselves and for their class, the content of what they teach, and the extent to which the school provides them with what they perceive to be necessary facilitations.

TEACHERS FOR DISADVANTAGED CHILDREN

In discussing the problem of "teachable groups" Thelen (10) points out that despite great individual differences in teachers' perception of who is teachable, there are some pupils — from 10 to 25 per cent of the average school — whom *no* teacher includes among the teachable. His description of this group is reminiscent of what we know about the school behavior of children from disadvantaged areas, from city slums, and rural backwoods. Similarly, Heil's "opposers" and to some extent his "waverers" remind one of typical behaviors of disadvantaged children. In the great cities these children represent an increasing proportion of the total pupil population, far more than the 10 to 25 per cent suggested by Thelen. And it is expected that by 1970 one out of every two pupils in large city schools will be "culturally disadvantaged."

The approach to the problem of staffing schools in depressed areas requires several sequential efforts. The first step is to gain broad public acceptance of the assumption that disadvantaged pupils, though widely variable in their abilities and personal characteristics, nonetheless represent a describable group. That is, they represent a group which, although it overlaps other groups in many ways, has unique characteristics, stemming from common backgrounds, values, and experiences. The second step is to characterize the teacher who is successful with culturally disadvantaged pupils — successful because the pupils in his classes achieve better than similar pupils in other teachers' classes and have more accepting attitudes toward school, toward the teacher, and toward learning. The third step involves re-examinations of teacher selection and education for staffing disadvantaged area schools.

Since there are no systematic data on what such teachers do, it may be worth while to create a hypothetical model of the "successful teacher of disadvantaged children." Our model can be constructed of implications from available research on teacher behavior, insights from impressionistic observations, and inferences from investigations of the characteristics of disadvantaged pupils and their social world. It may well be that several models of successful teachers will be needed to account for the great variety of pupils within the disadvantaged population. What is suggested here is a general outline which may have to be refined and subdivided to achieve optimum "fit" between pupils and teacher.

Hypothetical Model of the Successful Teacher of Disadvantaged Pupils

The teacher who is successful with any group of pupils is the one who respects the children in his classes and they, in turn, respect him. As teachers in slum schools look at their pupils, they see many children who are discouraged and defeated, even in the early grades, children who express their alienation from the school and the society it represents by aggressive acting-out behavior or by a kind of tuned-out lethargy and listlessness. There are frequent transgressions against the ethical, moral, and legal codes of society. Pupils seem to be making little effort to learn, show no desire to better themselves, to break out of the limits imposed upon them by their ignorance. The teacher may feel sorry for them, realizing the limiting circumstances of their lives. Or, he may be angered by their laziness, their lack of effort, believing that they could if they would, but they won't. Or, he may write them off as hopeless, too dumb to learn, taking up time and resources that could be better utilized by pupils with more ability and greater motivation.

But the successful teacher of disadvantaged children does respect his pupils — and not because he sees them through the rose-colored lenses of the romantic — finding "beauty" and "strength" where others see poverty and cultural emptiness. On the contrary, he sees them quite realistically as different from his children and his neighbors' children, yet like all children coping in their own way with the trials and frustrations of growing up. And he sees them, unlike middle-class children, struggling to survive in the ruthless world of their peers, confused by the conflicting demands of the two cultures in which they live — the one of the home and the street and the neighborhood, the other of the school and the society that maintains it.

Like the anthropologist, the successful teacher views the alien culture of his pupils not as a judge, but as a student. He understands the backgrounds from which the children come, the values placed on various achievements, the kind of work and life to which they aspire. He recognizes and understands the reasons for their unwillingness to strive toward future goals, where such efforts provide little reward in the present.

He knows that many of the children bear the scars of intellectual understimulation in their early years. Familiar with the home life of the children, he knows how rarely they are helped to name the things they see and feel and bear, to recognize similarities and differences, to categorize and classify perceptions, to learn the word for the object, and the phrases through which to express an idea or a feeling.

The successful teacher is aware of the various family structures from which the children come: the matriarchal family in which no father is present; the home where there are two parents, but both working; where one or both parents are able-bodied but out of work, recipients of relief; where the father is disabled and stays home while the mother works; where an extended family — grandparents, aunts, uncles, and other relatives — live together. This teacher has seen the physical conditions in which the children live: their lack of privacy, the poor facilities, the absence of basic amenities. He knows the kinds of jobs the parents have, their aspirations for themselves and for their children, and what role they attribute to the school in shaping their child's future.

The teacher is aware of the ethnic group membership of his pupils and how such membership shapes the child's image of himself and of his world. He knows something about the history, traditions, and social structures of the various ethnic groups, their unique culture patterns, their status in American society, the blocks and frustrations which they confront, and their perceptions of what life has in store for them.

He knows that the language of his pupils is closely tied to the life they lead. While it may represent a complete lack or a distortion of acceptable English, he recognizes its functional qualities for the pupils. Though this language is not "the coin of the realm," it often represents the only known and acceptable medium of exchange in the child's home or neighborhood.

In addition to his knowledge about the child in his environment, the successful teacher has a sophisticated understanding of how a child's abilities are assessed and therefore a realistic perception of what these measurements describe and predict. He knows that native potential intelligence is, at least thus far, unmeasurable; that what tests measure is learned behavior, and that the learning results not only from the child's native ability but also from his total experience. Yet he realizes that many intellectual abilities, like some of those which enter into creative functioning are not measured by existing intelligence tests.

He is also aware that the tests provide a fairly accurate description of the child's present ability to handle academic material and, unless there is a significant expansion and reorganization of his experience, the tests will predict with fair reliability how the child will function academically in the future. The successful teacher accepts the test scores as a fair and valid measure of the child's present academic ability, while rejecting them as a measure of native intelligence.

These and many other anthropological and psychological data affect the style of the successful teacher of disadvantaged pupils. But while the anthropologist's task is to describe and compare behavior of various cultures, and the psychologist's to understand individual behavior, the teacher's job is to modify it. Therefore, he must use his knowledge about his pupils and the world in which they live to guide him as he attempts to open more and more doors for them, and to help them acquire the skills and knowledge with which to enter the new and open spaces which lie beyond. The successful teacher sees his task as preparing his pupils to make competent choices among potentially available alternatives. He is aware that with every passing year the rapidly automating economy affords fewer and fewer opportunities to the minimally educated, and more and more to the academically and technically trained, and he communicates this understanding to his pupils.

The successful teacher meets the disadvantaged child on equal terms, as person to person, individual to individual. But while he accepts, he doesn't condone. He sets clearly defined limits for his pupils and will brook few transgressions. He is aware that, unlike middle-class children, they rarely respond to exhortations intended to control behavior through invoking feelings of guilt and shame. He, therefore, sets the rules, fixes the boundaries, and establishes the routines with a minimum of discussion. Here he is impersonal, undeviating, strict, but never punitive. Within these boundaries the successful teacher is businesslike and orderly, knowing that he is there to do a job. But he is also warm and outgoing, adapting his behavior to the individual pupils in his class. He shows his respect and liking for his pupils and makes known his belief in their latent abilities.

He realizes the danger of the "self-fulfilling prophecy" of expecting, and consequently finding a low level of achievement. He, therefore, lets each pupil know that he expects more than the pupil thinks he can produce —

but his standards are not so high as to become too remote to strive toward, and the attempt fraught with frustration. He rewards each tiny upward step, alert to every opportunity for honest praise, and, as much as possible, withholds harsh criticism and censure when progress is slow or entirely lacking. Above all, he is honest. He doesn't sentimentalize, doesn't pretend that a pupil's work is good when it isn't, doesn't condone unacceptable behavior.

The successful teacher is also something of a showman, coming to his task with an extensive repertory of carefully constructed scripts and props into which he breathes a sense of drama and high interest to capture the imagination of his pupils and hold their attention.

His repertory is not only extensive, providing a great variety of materials and teaching procedures tailored to the learning patterns of his pupils, it is also carefully catalogued to allow him to find what he needs quickly and efficiently.

As do other successful teachers, our model teacher has extensive knowledge of the content of the subject he teaches. In fact, he knows it so well, that he has no need to rely on study guides. Like the knowledgeable native, he guides his pupils through his country without a Baedeker, relying rather on his own familiarity with its terrain to take them to the important sights by paths and highways not often known to the less sophisticated.

Like all composite portraits, this hypothetical model presents an idealized version of reality. The hypothetical teacher is described as a mature, well-integrated person who respects his difficult, unmotivated and apparently unteachable pupils. He communicates his respect by setting high but reachable expectations, by his impartial and consistent firmness and honesty, and by his warm personal regard for each individual. He combines the detached but completely accepting stance of the anthropologist observing cultural differences, with the active involvement and manipulative approach of the determined reformer, the educator, in the sense of one who *leads* his pupils *out* into the wider world. Though not a specialist in any one of the behavioral or social sciences, he gleans from each of them knowledge which helps him understand the behavior of his pupils, the meaning of their scores on tests of intelligence and aptitude, the realities of their present and future world, the demands which various social and vocational alternatives will make upon them. In addition, the model requires the teacher to have a wide repertoire of materials and procedures, the ability to devise new ways, to deviate from accepted procedures and courses of study — but always to be aware of the knowledges and skills the pupils must eventually acquire. If the hypothetical "successful teacher" were to be characterized in a single phrase it would be *ordered flexibility*.

Examining the Hypothetical Model

The sketch presented here needs to be examined on two counts. First, it represents a hypothetical model, derived from inference and deduced from theoretical concepts. Before it is accepted, it must be verified through systematic observation, classification, and comparison of successful and unsuccessful teachers in "slums and suburbs."

But if the model in whole or in part does fit reality, if the characteristics described in the portrait do in fact approximate the characteristics which distinguish the successful teacher of disadvantaged pupils, then we must ask: How are we to get such teachers? Although the ideal presumably represented by this characterization can act only as a remote goal, how can it be approached?

It is simply nonsense to suppose that, even if the entire pool of existing teachers were screened, one would find enough people who resemble the hypothetical model to staff even a small proportion of the depressed-area schools. We must, therefore, look to teacher education to produce new teachers more nearly in the image of the model and to reshape the styles of those already in service. We return to the question of teachability, but this time with reference to the teacher as a student.

Approaching the Model Through Education

To what extent are the attributes of the model teachable? At least three of the aspects are of a cognitive nature and, for the reasonably bright and motivated student, can probably be approached through instruction: (a) mastery of subject matter; (b) the acquisition of an understanding of the major concepts from the behavioral and social sciences and their relevance to teaching disadvantaged children; and (c) the development of a repertoire of teaching strategies which hold promise for working with disadvantaged pupils. But to accomplish these three purposes alone would require a considerable reorganization and revision of undergraduate and graduate programs of teacher education, both pre-service and in-service.

DEVELOPING NEW COURSES. The development of appropriate courses would require the intensive collaboration of social and behavioral scientists, faculties of education, and successful classroom teachers. Out of such collaboration can grow not only curricula which would lead to a better understanding of the child in his environment, but also new strategies, new methods, new materials based on the empirical evidence provided by the social scientist and the practical wisdom of the teachers and educators. This has been successfully done in the development of some of the new curricula for the secondary and elementary schools.

LABORATORY EXPERIENCES. Given increased understanding and a repertory of appropriate teaching methods, the teacher can approach his task with greater openness, with less prejudice, and above all, with less fear. But every young teacher needs a bridge by which to cross the chasm which separates "knowing about" from actually doing something. For the teacher confronted by a class of poorly motivated, often discouraged and difficult pupils, continuous assistance and reinforcement in the teaching situation are essential. In *Teachers for the Schools in Our Big Cities*, Harry Rivlin, Dean of Teacher Education of the City University of New York, outlined a variety of desired modifications in existing modes of teacher preparation for large city schools (7). He placed major stress on the importance of laboratory experiences, starting with observation, leading to limited participation, then to student teaching, and finally, to independent responsibility for instruction. At every stage, the future teacher, and then the newly appointed teacher to the difficult school, must work under close supervision, receiving both psychological and practical support from the college staff and from the master teachers in the schools.

Hunter College (3), in an effort to improve the preparation of teachers for depressed area schools, selected a group of students who expressed a willingness to remain as regularly appointed teachers in the same "most difficult" junior high schools in which they had accepted appointments as student teachers. As part of their training, they were seen more often than was customary by a member of the college faculty and worked closely with carefully selected cooperating teachers. They spent the last ten weeks of their student teaching in full command of the class, under constant supervision. A number of these young men and women, in due course, took and passed the required examinations and were appointed as regularly licensed teachers to the same school in which they had taught as students. But the supervision and assistance continued, reinforcing their earlier learning and providing the needed support and encouragement.

SELECTION OF CANDIDATES. But so far, the discussion has not taken account of those less tangible, but perhaps most significant, characteristics of our model: openness to and acceptance of differences in people, firmness and consistency, warmth and respect, and, above all, flexibility. Can courses, laboratory experiences, or field work assignments be devised which will develop these characteristics? The descriptive material on teacher characteristics and teaching style referred to earlier sheds little light on the antecedents of the observed behavior. Do some teachers use more and others less "direct influence," for example, because they are, by nature, more or less directive as people? Were they ever so, from childhood on? Or, does their classroom behavior reflect their teacher training and education? Are some teachers relatively "unplanned" in their approach to teaching because they believe that too much planning restricts the participation of the pupils, and given evidence to the contrary, would become more organized and business-like? Or is their unplanned, "slipshod" approach to the classroom just one case of an unplanned and inconsistent approach to most life situations, a behavioral pattern unamenable to easy change through training?

There are no simple answers to this crucial question. Perhaps the training of teachers for the several areas of special education may be a case in point. In each area of exceptionality, teachers are exposed to technical knowledge of the medical, social, and psychological aspects of the disability with which they will work. Further, the teachers are instructed in ways of changing the general curriculum and adjusting both content and method to their special groups (5). Such training has prepared large numbers of teachers who are successful in working with pupils normally viewed as difficult or unteachable.

But teachers who enter special education do so voluntarily. In fact, they select the special area in preference to teaching normal children. Their own natural styles may thus be suited to the work they select and the training falls on fertile ground. It is probably beyond common sense to expect any training to make of the potential secondary school teacher with a passion for communicating the ideas of the physical sciences, a fine teacher of retarded adolescents. To attempt to retrain the elementary school teacher who thrives on the rapid progress, the quick wit, the deep probing, and ingenious responses of his gifted pupils into a successful teacher of the dull and lethargic would be equally foolhardy.

Consider also: (a) The man or woman threatened by ambiguity, unable to adapt readily to unexpected circumstances, who functions adequately only in a meticulously ordered world; or (b) the basically weak, dominated person who seeks in the classroom, perhaps unconsciously, the opportunity to prove his power by bending others to his will; or, further (c) the bigot who clothes his prejudices in psychological theories of ethnic or class inferiority and is convinced, before he enters a classroom, that for all but a few disadvantaged children, schooling beyond the very minimum is a waste of the taxpayers' money. Such prospective teachers may or may not be adequate for other teaching assignments — the compulsive character may well make a fine college professor somewhere — but they are probably not the kind of people who can be trained to fit the hypothetical model.

But then there are those prospective or practicing teachers who, although not completely free of prejudice, are yet not so bigoted as to resist attitudinal change in the face of new experiences. And some who may not be overly flexible in their approach are yet not immobilized by rigidity. Although somewhat at variance with the hypothetical model, the personalities, attitudes and values of some teachers would not be antithetical to those required by the model. For them we must assume, at least until proven wrong, that teacher education can produce greater consonance, better "fit" between what the pupils need in order to learn and what the teacher does in the act of teaching.

DEVELOPING EMOTIONAL CLOSENESS. Since a considerable portion of teaching style derives from attitudes and values, teachers of disadvantaged children would need, in addition to cognitive learnings, experiences through which to come emotionally close to the feelings, the anxieties, the aspirations of slum children and through which to examine their own feeling and reactions. Such efforts might include role-playing in situations where the teacher alternately takes the part of the child as he copes with various school and out-of-school problems, and of the teacher responding to lifelike classroom situations.

Teachers' feelings and values might also be involved and reshaped through the study of literary works. The novel and the short story which, at their best, provide a penetrating and illuminating exposition of life's fundamental conflicts, often have the power to transport the reader into the lives of people unlike himself but who, nonetheless, share with him many aspects of the human predicament. Books which deal with changing attitudes across generations, with the transition of immigrant groups from their original ghettos to the broader American Society, with adaptations to bicultural life, with the effects of early disability or severe deprivation on the behavior of the adult, with the universal problems of the adolescent as well as with those unique to a given time or place — these and many other literary themes might be used effectively. For the literary art is often able to create acceptance where direct contact may engender rejection or contempt. The "safe remove" of literature enables the individual to view the problems of others with greater openness, especially if his reading is geared toward exploring his own feelings as they became enmeshed with the feelings and strivings of others.

Such special efforts, though desirable for all teachers, are especially needed for teachers of the disadvantaged, since they most often come from backgrounds which provide little familiarity or personal involvement with the life which their pupils live.

In short, it is proposed that if the hypothetical model stands up under rigorous examination as embodying the characteristics, the "style" of the successful teacher of disadvantaged children, then the idealized model can be approached (though rarely reached) through deliberate pre-selection, and by an expanded and reconstructed approach to preservice and inservice teacher education. Given the relatively bright student or young teacher, not completely blocked by deeply rooted attitudes and personality structures antithetical to the desired characteristics, education may help shape him in the image of the model.

Attracting Teachers to Difficult Schools

But even assuming that there are ways to prepare successful teachers for depressed-area schools, why should bright young people want to enter such a vocation? The realities are against such a choice. Teachers today are in a seller's market. There are many more vacancies than candidates, especially at the elementary level and in the sciences and mathematics, and teachers can choose the district in which they want to work. Suburban schools, for example, afford amenities which urban schools so often lack. But above all, because of their size and organization, the suburban schools more often give the teacher a sense that he is a professional, that he is respected in his job and can successfully carry out what he has set out to do. He can teach children and, in most instances, they learn.

What inducement does the slum school offer? The children are difficult; in the perceptions of many teachers now in these schools they are "unteachable." The supervision is inadequate and often hostile. Principals and their assistants are constantly harassed by continuous teacher turnover, uncovered classes, disciplinary problems in the school, involvement with the police and the courts, lack of appropriate or even adequate books and materials. They have little time and less energy to give their teaching staffs the needed help and support. Teachers, frustrated by their inability to induce learning in their pupils, often having no place to turn for help, resort to discipline-maintaining rather than teaching activities. In this process, the teacher loses all sense of professional commitment. Many feel as did a very young woman when asked how long she had taught before leaving the field. She said, "I haven't taught a day in my life, but I served a three-year sentence in junior high school X."

What awaits them in depressed area schools is well known to prospective teachers. In fact, in 1962 better than a third of the new teachers appointed to Manhattan schools declined the appointment. Although they had prepared to teach, they apparently preferred almost any other kind of employment, or none at all, to teaching in a slum school.

No matter how excellent the preparation of teachers of disadvantaged children may become, no matter how much assistance is given both to preservice students and to beginning teachers, teaching in slum schools will remain a difficult, often frustrating and very taxing job — far more so than teaching in the unruffled surrounding of tree-lined suburbia. What, then, will induce young people to become candidates for a hard life, deliberately to choose the slum over the suburb?

Perhaps the answer to this question requires the addition of still another characteristic to our hypothetical model, one that is most difficult to teach — idealism, dedication to a cause, the desire to help the have-nots, to render service. That openness to commitment exists in many young people is confirmed by the large numbers who apply for the Peace Corps, prepare for missionary work, or choose to work in settlements, in hospital schools, and in special schools for disturbed or retarded or otherwise handicapped children. These young people feel that they are answering a call, and they rise to its demands. We have also witnessed such behavior (perhaps too often) in times of revolution and war, when young men and women have willingly gone into hardship and danger for what they believed in. How can this spirit be harnessed for teaching in difficult schools, in the "underdeveloped" areas of our own great cities? Is there, to paraphrase William James, an "educational equivalent of war?"

Perhaps each city needs to designate, as some have already begun to do, one or two schools in each depressed area which become service centers, open to view, for which teachers are carefully selected and in which they feel privileged to teach. Such schools could help to counteract the negative image now in the minds of prospective teachers. Those who are idealistic, who would like to perform a service, will see that there is hope; that the task, though difficult, can be done.

HELPING THE TEACHER IN SERVICE. But even when colleges and universities have evolved the needed curricula and made them part of the total education of prospective teachers, when bright young people are motivated to enroll, even if the graduate programs incorporate the new developments into their courses for experienced teachers, the problem of staffing schools in depressed urban areas will be only slightly alleviated. Assistance must be given to the hundreds of thousands of teachers now serving in depressed-area schools. Obviously, no program of study can reach all teachers now in our schools through direct contact. But they could be reached and helped and encouraged by changing supervisory patterns, by re-educating existing supervisors where they may be amenable to such re-education, or by selecting from each school one teacher who comes closest to the model and exposing him to a special program. Such teachers could return to their schools as supervisors, master teachers, or team leaders. From them could be formed the corps of cooperating teachers responsible for training students.

PROBLEMS OF SCHOOL ORGANIZATION. The problem of staffing disadvantaged-area schools must be attacked simultaneously on many fronts. We must confront the fact that teachers for difficult schools need special training. We must reshape the program of teacher preparation, attract capable young people to such programs, and help them as they move through their apprenticeship into full professional status. And we must also provide a corps of trained master teachers and supervisors who will bring skills and hope to the hundreds of thousands of teachers now in service.

But there is still another front upon which the attack must be launched — making changes in the amenities and management of the schools. Some of these are easy changes to make, because they do not require devising new courses or reshaping attitudes and values. All that they require is some additional money — simple things like providing a safe parking place, a comfortable lunch, and rest room; of giving the teacher, especially at the elementary level, some relief during the day. Each school must make provisions for removing the one or two most difficult children from regular classrooms so that classes may become more teachable, lessening the teacher's sense of frustration and enhancing his sense of fulfilling his professional responsibility.

Somewhat less simple are the needed changes in supervision. Additional supervisory personnel, both in the school and from affiliated teacher education institutions, need to be provided. The presence in each school of staff members — eventually trained in the new approaches — whose sole responsibility would be to help teachers unburdened by administrative or disciplinary matters might prove especially helpful. Perhaps if the supervisory load is spread, principals will be less harassed, less afraid of trouble, less apt to reward the teacher who maintains a quiet classroom, and more respectful of the teachers as people and as professionals.

The solution of any problem requires first, a clear recognition and description of the problem; secondly, a concerted research and experimental effort; and thirdly, the implementation of what is already known or what is learned through systematic study. To approach a solution to the problem of staffing schools in disadvantaged areas and providing competent teachers to work with disadvantaged children requires the following steps: (a) open recognition that slum schools and disadvantaged children need uniquely prepared teachers; (b) systematic study of the personal qualities, knowledge, and skills needed for successful teaching in these situations; (c) development and experimental testing of reconstructed teacher education programs, both on campus and in the field; (d) screening of candidates to eliminate those students or young teachers now in service whose values and personality characteristics are in conflict with the desired teaching style; (e) raising the status of the disadvantaged-area teacher to that of a high calling, by invoking all available reward systems; and (f) initiating systematic changes to make the schools more livable for the teacher, the teaching experience less frustrating, and the supervision more professional. Such efforts can go a long way toward raising the morale and the effectiveness of those presently teaching, and toward bringing into the teaching force many able young people who will not only come but will stay.

It is, of course, a romantic notion to suppose that even the best qualified teachers will, through their efforts alone, solve all the social problems which shape the lives of disadvantaged children. The work of other agencies in the community needs to be integrated with the work of the school. The more effective the school becomes, the more help both the child and the family will need to understand and accept his changed behavior and increased academic success and aspirations. But if the presently disadvantaged child is not to be fettered by his ignorance, not to be relegated to the ranks of the unemployable in a society which provides increasing opportunities to the academically competent and has less and less room for the functional illiterate, then the school has a central role to play. And central to the school, to the development and achievement of the child, is the teacher.

REFERENCES

1. Bellack, A. A. "The Language of Teaching: Relationships of the Linguistic Behavior of Students and Teachers in High School Classrooms to Student Learning." Project Proposal, Teachers College, Columbia University, 1963. (Mimeographed.)

2. Flanders, N. A. "Teacher and Classroom Influences on Individual Learning," in A. H. Passow (ed.), *Nurturing Individual Potential*. Washington: Association for Supervision and Curriculum Development, National Education Association, 1964. Pp. 57–65.

3. Haubrick, V. F. "Teachers for Big-City Schools," in A. H. Passow (ed.), *Education in Depressed Areas*. New York: Bureau of Publications, Teachers College, Columbia University, 1963. Pp. 243–261.

4. Heil, L. M., M. Powell, and I. Feifer. "Characteristics of Teacher Behavior Related to the Achievement of Children in Several Elementary Grades." New York: Author, May, 1960. (Mimeographed.)

5. Mackie, R. P., and H. M. Williams. "Teachers of Exceptional Children," *Review of Educational Research*, 29:395–407; 1959.

6. Medley, D. M. "The Development of Classroom Behavior Dimension for Teachers and Pupils." Paper presented at a meeting of the American Association for the Advancement of Science, 1962. (Mimeographed.)

7. Rivlin, H. N. "Teachers for the Schools in Our Big Cities." New York: Division of Teacher Education, City University of New York, 1962.

8. Ryans, D. G. "Characteristics of Teachers: An Informative Systems Approach to Theory of Instruction with Special Reference to the Teacher." Paper presented at an American Educational Research Association symposium entitled "Theories of Teaching," February, 1963.

9. Smith, B. O., M. Meux, *et al. A Study of the Logic of Teaching*, III. Urbana, Ill.: Bureau of Educational Research, 1963.

10. Thelen, H. A. "Teachability Grouping." Department of Education, University of Chicago, August, 1961. (Mimeographed.)

11. Warrener, C. K. "A Classification of Social Achievement." Paper presented at a meeting of the American Sociological Association, August, 1962. (Mimeographed.)

✧ ✧ 49 ✧ ✧

The Culturally Disadvantaged and Teacher Education

VERNON F. HAUBRICH

The issues and problems surrounding the preparation of teachers for disadvantaged areas are intimately linked to the realities of the social setting of the schools and colleges and the ambitions and motives of prospective teachers. The heart of the matter lies in the cultural misunderstandings that exist between many teachers and many children and parents from disadvantaged areas. Teachers and children are, in many cases, "talking by" one another (5). Far too many children seem not to want to learn those things that the school thinks important.

Before looking at the nature of a teacher education program which could make sense to teachers and lead to effective teaching, we should note that the problem we are concerned with is not unique to our time. Oscar Handlin (2) has noted the history of immigrants to our society, and Edward Krug (3) has indicated the response of educators to the historic demand of newcomers for education in the new society. The problems facing teachers

✧ From *The Reading Teacher*, March, 1965, pp. 499–505. Reprinted with permission of Vernon F. Haubrich and the International Reading Association. Vernon F. Haubrich is Chairman, Department of Education, Western Washington State College.

in the slums and disadvantaged areas were no less important in 1840, 1890, or in 1920 than they are today. The crucial differences between the former immigrant and the present-day in-migrant occur in the qualitative nature of the school response, the nature of the educational problems of the new in-migrant, and the rapidity of the technological change in the society as a whole. Let us take a moment to examine the differences between the former situation and the present one.

First, it is important to note that, by and large, the newcomers to the big cities are American citizens who are demonstrating the amazing mobility of the people in our society (2). The long depression in Appalachia, the closing of opportunities in the rural sections of our country, the growth of the new West, and the migration from Puerto Rico have caused gigantic shifts in population. In the main, the newcomers are moving to the urban centers to seek the good life that is part of the promise in our society. It is also important to note that many of the newcomers are darker in color, and that the big cities have lost, as the in-migration has occurred, corresponding numbers of whites to the suburban areas. The children of the in-migrants tend to have special problems which require special attention on the part of teachers and administrators. For example, Martin Deutsch (1) has noted again and again the special language and cognitive problems of the slum child.

Second, today's colleges have a dual handicap in preparing teachers for service in disadvantaged areas. On the one hand, they tend to prepare teachers for children and for schools which are only rarely found in disadvantaged regions. The educational psychology of the middle-class child, the methods which one uses in the "good" school setting, and the normal constraints one applies in a typical school setting just will not work in the disadvantaged areas of big cities. On the other hand, the prospective teachers who are themselves on the rise in our society are not always eager for the challenges of teaching in disadvantaged areas. The young prospective teacher has an image of what the task of teaching is going to be, and his home, peer group, and college tend to confirm a vague and general rejection of the disadvantaged.

What this all boils down to is that many prospective teachers have a picture of disadvantaged areas as places in which little distinction can be won and little recognition is given. Considering the emphasis in the past few years on "giftedness" and the pressure on the college student, the confusion about and the rejection of the disadvantaged are understandable. Teaching the disadvantaged does not fit into the perceptual pattern the prospective teacher has learned to see and value.

Third, the sociological, anthropological, and political issues which arise in disadvantaged areas are not always as fully understood by teachers as one might hope. The impact of color in our culture, the social and economic status of the Negro and his long fight to attain even marginal recognition, is a story that many young teachers do not understand. The slums of segregated housing, the financial plight of migrant workers, the technological displacement by the revolution in automation, and the range of psychological cuts caused by poverty are usually not part of the apperceptive mass of the typical prospective teacher. Consequently, it would be fair to say that many new *and* experienced teachers are operating under false assumptions and with inadequate and inaccurate information.

In summation, the prospective teacher has not fully understood the social revolution which is under way in America; the schools have not fully participated in this revolution; and, finally, many children will not receive the kind of education to which they are entitled unless and until there are some drastic changes in the patterns of teacher education in colleges and universities.

In the face of this situation, what can colleges and universities do to prepare teachers effectively for schools that serve disadvantaged areas? Are there any guidelines which educators may use in setting up programs for prospective teachers who may teach in disadvantaged areas?

Guidelines for Effective Teacher Training

1. It is critically important for those in teacher education to understand the changes that have been occurring, and they must make provision in the curriculum of the college for the effective use of materials, field trips, and discussions to the end that students will become aware of the conditions and realities surrounding the disadvantaged.

Colleges must begin to look at the wide variability in students, schools, and systems of learning. Colleges and departments of education must begin to use cultural anthropologists, sociologists, historians, and political scientists to aid prospective teachers in understanding the nature of deprivation, the history of the race, and the politics of the slum. Teacher educators must, in short, utilize the full resources of the college to lead the prospective teacher to focus on and understand the nature of the problem he will face. To treat the catastrophic problems in disadvantaged areas in a business-as-usual fashion is to invite disaster.

2. It is time that the colleges and the public schools worked out programs through which able and knowledgeable teachers from the public schools can work with colleges and share their insights and experiences with students *and* faculty. This kind of continuing contact with the practitioners in the field would nourish teacher education programs and give to theory some practical criteria by which to test implications and programs. We should invite, on a regular basis, teachers, administrators, and related personnel to the college to help bridge theory and practice and to aid one another. I am convinced that additional use of public school personnel (for example, joint appointments) would not only aid the teachers in public schools but would be a boon for college students and faculty alike.

3. Colleges in nonurban areas have an equal responsibility in meeting these new challenges. It is absolutely essential that the typical state college or university, which is often located at some distance from severely disadvantaged areas, begin to set up direct and continuing contacts with such

districts and school systems. As an example, Western Washington State College in Bellingham, Washington, is now placing increasing numbers of volunteer student teachers in sections of Seattle (approximately ninety miles distant) which can be called disadvantaged.[1] It is important to the success of such programs that induction seminars precede the actual student teaching. These induction seminars, using personnel from the college, the school, and the community, can effectively pave the way for the inexperienced student teacher. The common problems of the school and community constitute the usual agenda for these induction seminars, and it is crucial that in each school the unique problems of that school and its community be examined and understood.

4. Colleges and school systems must realize that many young teachers feel abandoned in those schools that serve disadvantaged areas. Schools that serve the disadvantaged regions of a city are often considered places to run from rather than places to be sought for the unique challenges they offer. But teachers will not run if they do not feel that the system and the college have abandoned them and that they must, therefore, fend for themselves. After four years in the schools of East Harlem, I am convinced that the apparent difficulty of teaching is only one factor in the teacher shortage that plagues disadvantaged areas. When teachers are convinced that no one cares for their work, when they are convinced that the job is a "dead end" and that little or no recognition will come to their work or to the school, then they want out.

Consequently, it is essential that colleges and schools in disadvantaged areas involve the teachers in conferences, research projects, curriculum workshops, and that they provide a continuing flow of student teachers to aid in the development of sound educational schemes for children who need help. One of the ways this can be assured is by the development of a number of "teaching centers" by colleges and selected public school systems. In these "teaching centers" one would find college personnel, supervisors who would be on joint appointment with the school and the college, and public school personnel who would be conducting seminars for the college in the public school. Colleges and universities must commit themselves to schools in disadvantaged areas and school systems must become centers for inquiry.

5. A hidden assumption that is often made by colleges and universities is that the problems of the elementary teacher and the secondary teacher are essentially different. I say hidden because in many institutions several of the foundation courses for all teachers are the same (psychological foundations, philosophical foundations, etc.). However, it has been my experience that the unique problems of children and teachers in disadvantaged areas are aggravated by the lack of specific skills on the part of some teach-

---

[1] Dr. Harry Harrison now holds a joint appointment with the Seattle Public Schools and Western Washington State College. The college and the Seattle Public Schools share his time and also share the cost. Similar arrangements have been made in Edmonds and Bellingham, Washington.

ers. One of these basic skills is a fundamental knowledge of and an ability to begin a reading program within each classroom *no mattter what the subject field.* In a project in several junior high schools in East Harlem, *not one* of the student teachers had had a course in or an experience with the teaching of reading. (This was in the TRUE Project at Hunter College. Needless to say, a great deal of work in reading was undertaken.)

6. It is crucial for colleges and public schools to realize that children who come from disadvantaged areas have severe educational, social, and emotional problems and that the children often act out these problems at home, in the neighborhood, and at school. This situation means that the beginning or experienced teacher must be equipped with certain skills which are absolutely essential for success in schools serving disadvantaged or depressed areas. The teacher must acquire:

The ability to understand and utilize developmental and remedial reading procedures

The ability to organize and routinize specific classroom procedures

The ability to reconstruct syllabi, textbooks, and reading materials in terms of the background of students

The ability to work effectively with small groups within the classroom and to know when to use such procedures

The ability to adjust new entrants to the classroom situation quickly

The ability to construct and use concrete materials for classroom work

The ability to handle aggression and violence

The ability to use individual and group procedures in gaining classroom discipline

The ability to know when a child should be referred and to whom

A knowledge of the language patterns in an area and the ability to correct such patterns

A knowledge of neighborhood and family to see what effect this has on classroom work and procedures

The ability to translate the "academic" knowledge of children from depressed areas into specific procedures for classroom use

7. Given a program that includes the above kinds of experiences, the student teaching program in a disadvantaged area must include *a maximum amount of actual teaching* on the part of the prospective teacher (6). The student teacher should be, after a careful induction period, given the opportunity to try his wings with organization and procedures which are cooperatively developed.

Weekly conferences in the school with the cooperating teacher, the supervisor, and specialized personnel such as reading specialists are absolutely essential. It is through these conferences that the individual problems of the prospective teacher can be hammered out and the working agenda, based on these problems, be set up for the next week. The concept of the teacher who learns to diagnose learning difficulties and provide for the conditions of effective teaching and learning is the objective that high quality programs should attempt to develop. Colleges and school districts can provide a direct entree to teaching by seeing to it that the student teacher's first permanent teaching position is in the school where he did his student teaching. In many cases schools serving disadvantaged districts have severe teacher shortages. This program of preparation and first appointment, if the student teacher so desires, is a means of holding those whom a school has helped prepare, thus ending some of the drastic teacher shortages in disadvantaged areas.

When one thinks of the necessary guidelines or criteria for establishing effective programs of teacher education for disadvantaged and depressed areas, a number of questions come to mind. The following questions point up much of the foregoing discussion.

1. Are the faculty of the college which is preparing teachers involved in the disadvantaged schools? If the faculty is active in these schools — consulting, supervising student teachers, conducting research — students will be reassured that the need is genuine, not pedantic. If the faculty wants the program to go, they must become involved.

2. Does the curriculum of the preparing institution reflect the necessary modifications in the areas of cultural anthropology, sociology, psychology, and factors of political and historical relevancies? As an example, one cannot teach Puerto Rican or Negro youths without knowing a great deal of their history, their politics, and the things they value.

3. Do public school teachers in the schools serving disadvantaged areas participate in the program both in the school and at the college? An honest two-way street is necessary.

4. Are relevant specialists from the school district and the college utilized to afford the prospective teacher the necessary skills and procedures in teaching the disadvantaged? Here is where the team approach has meaning for prospective teachers.

5. Do prospective elementary and secondary teachers have an understanding of the skills involved in teaching reading, and do they fully understand that in many schools serving disadvantaged areas all teachers are, in some measure, reading teachers? Has the college provided the necessary background and the school the opportunity to test these skills?

6. Are procedures established for the careful induction of the prospective teacher during his first few days in the school?

7. Does the college have a continuing program within these schools so that the young teacher does not feel abandoned during his first years of teaching?

8. Is there an effective understanding by the prospective teacher of the family, neighborhood, and peer group in the particular area where he is about to teach? Are field trips made to community agencies to reinforce his understanding?

9. Are the student teachers volunteers? Is there a provision made that, wherever possible, the student teacher may remain as a regular teacher in the school where the student teaching was completed? If one starts with volunteers, more than half the battle is won.

10. Do the school and the college provide the necessary recognition to teachers for service in disadvantaged areas?

When any program such as this is being considered, one should keep in mind that not all beginning teachers wish to serve in disadvantaged areas. A program at Hunter College attracted between 5 and 10 per cent of the eligible students in student teaching. Additionally, it should be noted that some preliminary research at Hunter indicates that the volunteers for the program were less authoritarian, more open, and less dogmatic than were the non-volunteers (4). All this seems to indicate that the problems associated with finding, preparing, and retaining teachers for schools in disadvantaged areas may be tied together. Continuing research is required as to the teaching skills necessary to enable youngsters from these areas to succeed in school.

Colleges with an eye to the future should consider, as part of their entire program in teacher education, the adoption of selected schools in disadvantaged areas in which research in teacher education can be carried out. It is essential that all the relevant information (concepts and skills) be developed in preservice programs so that *all* teachers, no matter what their objectives or where they will teach, will have the opportunity to understand the basic nature of the problem. Colleges and universities have a dual responsibility in meeting the challenge of the disadvantaged: first, to develop programs for prospective teachers which are accurate, relevant, and helpful; second, to employ all the resources of the academic community to insure equality of educational opportunity for all children.

REFERENCES

1. Deutsch, Martin. *Minority Group and Class Status as Related to Social and Personality Factors in Scholastic Achievement.* Society for Applied Anthropology, Monograph No. 2, 1960. Ithaca, N.Y.: Cornell University, State School of Industrial and Labor Relations.

2. Handlin, Oscar. *The Newcomers.* Garden City, N.Y.: Doubleday, 1959. (It is in this book that Handlin points out the differences between the former immigrants and newer "in-migrants.")

3. Krug, Edward. *The Shaping of the American High School.* New York: Harper & Row, 1964. (See, in particular, chapter 8, "The Children of the Plain People.")

4. Langberg, George, and Philip Freedman. "An Evaluation of Self-Selection in the Recruitment of Student Teachers for Problem Schools." Unpublished paper, Hunter College, 1963.

5. Mannheim, Karl. *Ideology and Utopia.* New York: Harcourt, Brace & Co., 1936.

6. Passow, Harry A. (ed.). *Education in Depressed Areas,* Sect. IV. New York: Bureau of Publications, Teachers College, Columbia University, 1963.

Culturally Deprived Children: Opinions of Teachers on the Views of Riessman

PATRICK J. GROFF

The Culturally Deprived Child by Frank Reissman (New York: Harpers, 1962) has received favorable notice since its publication. Goodwin Watson in his foreword to the book predicted it "likely to be the pioneer in a series of investigations that will reveal to America that we have neglected a major source of man-power and creative talent." Dr. Watson made clear in his introduction that additional research on the culturally deprived is necessary and that an urgent need seemed to be that of developing creative teachers for the culturally deprived child. The book by Riessman is concerned primarily with this objective: To assist in the development of a teacher's understanding of and respect for the CD child; i.e., to encourage the belief that the CD child can make normal achievement under proper school circumstances.

Two related questions emerge from this treatment that are not answered to any extent in the book: (a) How close are present-day teachers of CD children to the levels of understanding and acceptance demonstrated by the ideal teacher of the CD child Riessman describes? (b) With how many of the changes in school curriculum and organization proposed in the book do they agree? This study investigated these points. It attempted to determine the opinions of teachers of CD children.

PROCEDURE

Seventy-eight statements were abstracted from the book, *The Culturally Deprived Child*. These statements were then arranged into four general categories. They were: (a) the background and personality of the CD child, (b) the teacher of the CD child, (c) classroom procedures and pupil management techniques for the CD child, and (d) the curriculum, school organization and school administration in the CD school.

This list of seventy-eight statements was then submitted to each of 373 teachers who taught in sixteen elementary schools in the culturally disadvantaged and socially deprived area of a metropolitan city. The majority of

✧ From *Exceptional Children*, October, 1964, pp. 61–65. Used by permission of the author and the publisher. Patrick J. Groff is Professor of Education, San Diego State College.

the children enrolled in each of these schools lived in Negro or Mexican-American ghettos of that city. This was observed to be so by the writer in visits to the neighborhoods of each school, and/or by reports of teachers or supervisors of student teachers in these schools. Each teacher of CD children was requested, first, to read each statement, and then, on the basis of his experience with CD children, to indicate for each statement that:

5 — He agreed entirely with it.
4 — The statement was more true than false.
3 — It was as true as it was false, or vice versa.
2 — It was more false than true.
1 — He disagreed entirely with it.
0 — He had not enough knowledge of the matter to respond.

To help ensure frankness and objectivity, the teachers were asked to make anonymous responses.

Of the 373 teachers, 294 (or 78.8 per cent) responded. Since the administration of the school district in which these teachers taught declined to participate in the study, it was necessary to mail these statements directly to the teachers' homes for their completion and return rather than distribute them through school channels. This may have been the better procedure in any case. It does suggest the sensitive or controversial nature of such a study.

RESULTS

The per cent of the teachers who responded to each statement with each of numbers 5–0 was calculated. No further weightings for these numbers were made. For purposes of analysis it was decided to pool the per cent of teachers who responded 1 or 2 for each statement and to regard this as the per cent who disagreed with the statement. Accordingly, the per cent of teachers who responded 4 or 5 for each statement was pooled. This was regarded as the per cent who agreed with the statement. The ratio of the per cent of responses 4 and 5 to the per cent of responses 1 and 2, was then calculated for each statement. For example, to the statement, "The CD child typically comes from a poverty stricken home," 69.2 per cent of the teachers responded either 4 or 5, while 29.4 per cent responded either 1 or 2. Consequently, the ratio of teachers who agreed to those who disagreed with this statement was found to be 2.4 to 1.

For fifty-nine of the seventy-eight statements, positive ratios were found. These ratios ranged from 45.3 to 1 agreement with the statement: "Despite his overt hostility and defiance, the CD child seeks respect from his teachers," to a 1.1 to 1 agreement with the statement: "Permissiveness, accent on the self, and introspection are contradictory to the culture of the CD child." The average of the positive ratios for the fifty-nine statements was 5.6 to 1. Therefore, nineteen of the seventy-eight statements turned out to have negative ratios, that is, more teachers disagreed than agreed with them. The average of the negative ratios for these nineteen statements was 2.5 to 1. Eight of the above fifty-nine statements were found to have positive ratios of less than 1.5 to 1. It is with these latter two groups of statements that this report will deal in detail. In summary, these are the statements with which more teachers disagreed than agreed, or ones with which less than 1.5 times as many teachers agreed than disagreed.

AGREEMENT WITH RIESSMAN

For the details of the fifty-nine statements with which the teachers in this study agreed a good deal more than they disagreed, the reader is directed to Riessman's book. Very briefly, these were statements regarding the CD child: his poverty; the lack of corrective action taken in his home; his great respect for physical prowess and physical science; his inability with I.Q. tests; the slow manner in which he works on academic problems; his lack of response to academic challenge; his insecurity and fear of failure with academic problems; his quickness in judging facial expressions and verbalizing in his own idiom; the superiority of his physical or motoric over his word-style problem-solving techniques; the superiority of his thinking in spatial rather than temporal terms; the superiority of his nonverbal over his verbal expression; the superiority of his efforts in spontaneous versus structured situations; his general verbal inadequacies including his short auditory attention span; his search for respect rather than love from his teacher; his lack of interest in knowledge for its own sake; and his ambivalent feelings toward education in spite of his generally negative view of it as a mode of self-realization.

Statements in the book these teachers agreed with regarding teachers of CD children were: teachers underestimate the CD child's intelligence and intellectual curiosity and therefore have too low expectations of him; they should not equate his intelligence with his speed, verbal facility, or test-taking skills; that although there is no need for teachers to give up their middle-class character, teachers should have respect and acceptance for the child's culture and not try to "middle class" him; and that they discriminate, frequently unintentionally, against the child, have too many negative images of him, and therefore should study their rejecting attitudes as much as the child's home environment.

Statements in the book regarding classroom procedures teachers in the study agreed with were: natural leaders of the class should be sought out and won over; strong demands, and firm, unyielding rules are needed from a definite and authoritative teacher, who sets up a highly structured classroom with strict routine and order; meticulous teacher planning is critical; usual ways of teaching grammar and usage are inappropriate; and role playing should be a basic teaching technique.

Statements in the book regarding curriculum and school administration or organization agreed with were: academic standards should not be lowered; reading textbooks are "out of tune" with the child's daily life; more time for instruction in reading is needed; there should be teacher education courses on the CD child; flexible, nongraded classes should be used; smaller classes are imperative; and special consultants on the CD child are needed.

DISAGREEMENT WITH RIESSMAN

The nineteen statements with which the teachers disagreed more than they agreed are listed below. Also included here are the additional eight statements for which there was no strong agreement, that is, with which less than 1.5 times as many teachers agreed as disagreed. For each statement is given its negative or positive ratio as calculated in the manner explained above. Minus ratios indicate disagreements.

The Culturally Deprived Child

1. The CD child at home is generally not expected to assume household responsibilities (−4.4).
2. The CD child peer group rejects the child who pleases the teacher with his conformity, dependence, neatness, and nonaggression (−1.2).
3. Permissiveness, accent on the self, and introspection are contradictory to the culture of the CD child (1.1).
4. The CD child lacks a sense of competition in school (−2.3).
5. Talk, reading, and intellectualism are regarded by the CD child as feminine activities (−1.8).
6. The CD child is anti-intellectual and therefore sees little value in books and discussions (−1.4).
7. The teacher of the CD child should expect initial hostility and nonacceptance from him (−1.6).
8. The CD child has a proclivity for persisting along one line of interest or activity (1.4).
9. The CD child has a colorful, free associative feeling for metaphor in language (−1.5).
10. CD children will make an organized, cooperative effort to break the new teacher or to see how much he can stand (1.2).

The Teacher

11. The white teacher should not treat the Negro CD child with informality. He sees this as disrespect (−3.2).
12. Teachers tend to talk down to the CD child — to speak his language (−1.3).
13. The best teacher of the CD child is one who identifies with the underdog (−2.0).
14. Teachers who are physical, as opposed to word-ridden, are best for the CD child (1.3).
15. There should be more teachers of CD children from the same racial or cultural minorities as the children (1.45).

Procedures

16. Physical punishment fails to deter the aggressive behavior of the CD child (1.2).
17. Teachers of the CD child should give suggestions and demonstrations of their superior physical strength (−8.2).
18. Teaching machines and programed learning should be especially effective with the CD child (−1.1).
19. The CD child does not like to work in short spurts with frequent breaks (−5.1).

20. For CD children the present system of personal marks and like comparisons should be replaced by group competition (−3.6).

21. The teacher cannot take a gentle approach with the CD child (−5.4).

Curriculum, School Organization, or Administration

22. The CD child likes best the three R's, and likes least the social studies, literature, and the arts (−1.2).

23. Group projects and planning with CD children result in much commotion and many discipline problems (1.3).

24. Teachers of CD children should stay with the same class for three years (−1.9).

25. The school should provide an extended school day for the CD children conducted by others than the regular teachers (−1.0).

26. Teachers of CD children should receive higher pay than teachers of middle-class children (1.2).

27. Segregation of CD children on ability or achievement levels should not be undertaken (−1.7).

LACK OF KNOWLEDGE

It should also be remembered that the teachers in this study were given the option of not responding to any statement about which they felt they did not know enough to give a reasonable opinion of its validity. The average per cent of teachers not responding to the seventy-eight statements was 7.97. For seven of the statements, however, it was found that around 20 per cent of the teachers felt so limited in their knowledge of the matter that they could not respond; for one statement 37.4 per cent could not respond. These statements and the per cent of teachers who could not respond to them were:

Permissiveness, accent on the self, and introspection are contradictory to the culture of the CD child (22.4).

The I.Q. of the CD child can be raised if he is shown how to answer I.Q. tests (24.5).

The CD child has a great respect for physical science (19.7).

Teaching machines and programed learning should be especially effective with the CD child (24.5).

For CD children the present system of personal marks and like comparisons should be replaced by group competition (37.4).

The best teacher of the CD child is one who identifies with the underdog (20.4).

Teachers of CD children should stay with the same class for three years (23.1).

The school should provide an extended school day for the CD children conducted by others than the regular teachers (20.4).

DISCUSSION

This "grass roots," teacher validation of the central ideas of an important new book on the culturally deprived child created fresh insights into this matter while at the same time it raised new questions

1. More teachers agreed than disagreed (on fifty-nine of the seventy-eight statements) with Riessman's judgments of the CD child, his school, and his teachers. Moreover, agreement when given was on the average twice as strong as disagreement when it was given (average agreement-disagreement ratios as calculated above were +5.6 versus −2.5). This implies that in many respects these teachers, in their own thinking at least, were well disposed toward an acceptance of Riessman's model teacher, curriculum, and school for the CD child.

2. Nevertheless, at several important points, the teachers in this study either disagreed or agreed only mildly with the authority of the book. It was not possible to collect and analyze the reasons for these disagreements. However, certain inferences as to their origins can be made. For one thing, the disagreement with certain statements (numbers 13, 18, 20, 24, and 25 above) might be partially explained as due to teachers' lack of knowledge of the details of these new ideas; thus the consequent reluctance toward acceptance which this engenders. To these five statements 20 per cent or more of the teachers said they did not have sufficient knowledge to respond. It was noted that over one-third of the teachers did not know enough about statement 20 to respond to it.

In other instances the teachers seemed to contradict themselves, or to have unreliable opinions. The negative ratio as seen for statement 21, for example, was 5.4 to 1. Elsewhere in the list of statements, however, a positive ratio of 29.8 to 1 was found for the statement, "The teacher of the CD child must be definite and authoritative. Strong external demands, firmness, and rules are needed." This statement also conflicts with the negative ratio found for statements 7 and 10. Both contradiction and support can be found elsewhere for the negative ratio of statement 6. For example, there were found positive ratios of over 2 to 1 that the CD child lacked respect for knowledge and education. In another statement, however, a positive ratio of 6.5 to 1 was found that the CD child's attitudes toward education were more positive than is generally believed. On another issue elsewhere in the list teachers gave a positive ratio 17.3 to 1 for the statement, "The CD child has a great respect for physical prowess." This opinion seems in contradiction with the negative ratio seen for statement 17. These examples are shown as exceptions to the general reliability of teacher responses that were given to two similar statements.

3. With some statements it does not seem possible with the evidence on hand to infer the reasons for the essential disagreements between the authority of the book and the teachers. This is especially so with statements 1, 2, 4, 5, 8, 9, 11, 12, 19, 22, and 27. It is with these disagreements that particular interest should be taken as they suggest basically different judgments by the two sources of opinion in this study: teachers of CD children and Riessman. These are disagreements that cannot be easily explained either as instances of simple lack of knowledge or of the unreliability of the teachers' opinions. Investigation of the reasons for these disagreements could form the topic of a further study on the matter. On the one hand,

the teacher opinions expressed here may be erroneous. Whether right or wrong, the important consideration is that they are held. If Riessman's model of the teacher, the CD child, and his school is a valid one, a program designed to change such opinions is undoubtedly called for. If, on the other hand, the teachers' opinions have greater substance, the conclusions of the book need revision. The nature of the issue posed here is critical, and therefore demands clarification.

✦ PART EIGHT

Individual, Family, and Community

The relationship of the individual to the family and the community seems obvious. In many situations, however, society has forced the withdrawal of certain of its members because they have been denied the essential ingredient of hope. They have been compelled to build for themselves psychological walls for protection from what they view as a hostile environment.

It is not safe to assume that all families embrace middle-class values. Robert D. Strom's selection, "Family Influence on School Failure," shatters the illusion that school failure results only because of the child. The student's family and way of living are essential factors in producing the "need" to drop out of a situation which would alienate him from his family *if he were to succeed.* Moreover, the pressure for immediate economic rewards makes it necessary for him to withdraw from school so that he can earn a few dollars now, rather than to remain in school in order to qualify for a job which will earn him perhaps ten times as much later.

Damaris Pease and Louise G. Daugherty develop the framework for seeing the family in its societal setting. They discuss the interrelationships of the family and society, helping the reader to see the many forces which impinge on child and family development. One learns from their presentations that the fight to prevent disadvantaging must begin by creating desirable conditions within the family so that the forces which form attitudes and aspirations within the child will be positive forces. They point out, however, that families cannot "go it alone." They need the backdrop of a facilitating society.

Society has ignored the basic needs of the individual. As Jules Henry observes in the selection, "White People's Time, Colored People's Time," "Among the children of the very poor, survival must take precedence over every other consideration." Where the fight for survival involves the full energies of the child, how can he find the time and the strength to develop the values espoused by his society, such as pride in work, reward for effort, consideration of other people, and courage in meeting life's problems?

A concerted attack should be developed at all levels of community and government. Frank G. Dickey reports on a mode of attack which, though costly and dependent upon the sincere cooperation of the community, the

377

school, and social agencies of all types, seems to hold promise of success. The Southern Association of Colleges and Schools and the College Entrance Examination Board have pooled their resources to aid the Negro citizen in developing a keener sense of his own responsibility for lightening his burden. This is one of several burgeoning programs which are imaginative and stimulating and which may serve to provide clues to the solution of other community problems.

The fascinating work being done at the University of Chicago by Robert D. Hess gives the reader insights into parent-child interaction in various social classes. The minimal communication patterns of the disadvantaged class puts no premium on effective communication and concept development. The style adopted by the "disadvantaged" mother is constrictive in its manner. There is little tendency to allow the child to reflect, to consider, and to choose. He must deal with the immediate present rather than with the future. This pattern has far-reaching implications for his development and his ability to participate in the deliberations of society.

Human needs are a logical basis around which to develop community structures. Glenn R. Hawkes suggests ways in which communities should look at their individual and family building programs for the disadvantaged. Until human needs serve as the guiding force for societal mechanisms, these severe problems will remain. And, in our complex society, they will undoubtedly grow more complex.

✦ ✦ 51 ✦ ✦

Family Influence on School Failure

ROBERT D. STROM

Studies assessing the impact of social class on adolescents have consistently shown that the highest incidence of school failure occurs among children from low-income families.

Hollingshead's extensive investigation of a midwestern city in 1941 showed that by far the largest proportion of dropouts, eight out of nine, were reared in the poorest of socioeconomic circumstances. These findings were duplicated in the 1950's by McCreary, Kitch, and Young. Notable among recent studies are those of Bowman and Matthews, who conclude that perhaps 88 per cent of today's dropouts are members of lower-class homes.

Where the so-called culture of poverty exists, there are familial tendencies inducing conditions that foster dropping out of school. Here one finds a high proportion of disrupted and broken homes where the father is often absent and in which an emotional distance results in dilution of affection for the young. Where no father is present during the evening, there is usually no organized meal, no organized opportunity for language exchange, no real interaction. A common result is cumulative deficit in the language component of a child's development. Since this deficit is qualitative and not quantitative, it is erroneous to believe these children are characteristically nonverbal.

In the absence of positive paternal guidance, one might hope the female parent could provide compensatory influence. Unfortunately, the facts indicate otherwise. Evidence most often points to an inadequacy in the cognitive features of early mother-child exchange that tends to foster later alienation from the educative processes and other basic institutions.

Recent research conducted by R. D. Hess and others at the University of Chicago has considered the problem of maternal competence in preparing children for school. The aim was to determine what facilitating experiences are present in middle-class families that typically do not occur in the lower socioeconomic homes. Through questions directed to mothers and their

✦ From *The Tragic Migration* (Washington: Department of Home Economics, National Education Association, 1964), pp. 5–10, as reported in *Education Digest*, February, 1965, pp. 8–10. Used by permission of the author and the publishers. Robert D. Strom is Associate Professor of Education, The Ohio State University.

379

four-year-old children, representing the several income levels, investigators were able to glean some interesting data with regard to differences in maternal attitudes toward school, perception of educational purpose, and role in preparing children for learning.

One technique was to ask each mother what she would say to her child on his first day of school. This is a typical response from mothers in the lower-income group: "I tell him to do what the teacher says, not get into trouble, not to fight, to come home right after school, and not to get lost." This is a view of school as raising issues of dealing with authority and peers rather than presenting educational content. If learning is mentioned, it is incidental or secondary.

The response is in contrast to the middle-class parent, who was likely to say: "The teacher is like mommy, you learn from her; if you have trouble, go to her; you are going to learn to read and write." This approach views school activity in terms of the child's learning experience.

The female parents were also asked to explain a picture of a teacher and mother in conference. Those from the low-income group most often said that the mother had been called in by the school regarding some disciplinary problem; the middle-class mother more frequently saw the conference as a parent coming to consult with the teacher about a learning problem.

The major difference between these responses is in the view of the school as an institution with which the child must cope, as contrasted with a view of the school as a place of learning. The lower-class child approaches school unoriented toward learning but attuned to a need of getting along with the institution.

To ascertain variations in style of maternal instruction, each parent was asked to teach her child how to assemble a jigsaw puzzle. Most often the middle-class mother would indicate, "This is a jigsaw puzzle which makes a picture. We remove the pieces and then put them together again to make the picture. See where all the pieces are, and look at the colors so you will know where they go." Thus, the task was defined; the child was told how to proceed.

Mothers of the low-income group often dumped the puzzle without directions, saying, "You do it." The only guidance offered was in the frequent phrase, "Turn it around, turn it around . . ." Thirty-five times one mother said this until, in defeat and frustration, her child replied, "You do it."

The mother of the frustrated child was trying sincerely to help her child. She did not know how to teach and was unable to convey the concepts needed to solve his problem. The ability to communicate concepts, to share information, and to program a simple task is seldom present in the low-income family. Imagine the child in repeated interaction with his mother. The reaction of defeat, "You do it," is likely to recur and be magnified. The more favored middle-class child did not know more about the puzzle to begin with but, through experience, realized that with some guidance there was a way to reach a solution. On this kind of motivational base, positive attitudes toward new learning may emerge.

Middle-Class Influences

There should be no assumption that a paragon of home-pupil relations exists in neighborhoods of the middle class. Many parents in this segment of society have in recent years adopted an unfortunate shift in emphasis from child development to scholastic achievement. Youngsters who have been prized for themselves and for what they are find early that more adult value is attached to the dimension of academic behavior than any other. Thus, from the day a child enters kindergarten, grades become a mandate, the report card becomes a status symbol.

Underlying the pressure imposed on youngsters is the assumption that most if not all can have high marks if they just work hard enough. This can result in a student making lower marks than his intelligence and industry normally permit him to make, simply because his concern impedes effective concentration. Some who become grade-oriented are unduly disappointed as they perceive failure to get a certain grade as complete failure and hence lose even that which is within their reach. The unnecessary anxiety, disappointment, and parental disfavor at report time for these students is a first step toward dropping out.

Despite these outcomes, the argument persists that competitive marking in elementary and secondary school is a necessary preparation for the type of life children can expect to encounter in our society. But the real competitive situations of life are chosen when one perceives a possibility of success. The so-called competition of the school is hardly chosen by children but is forced on them by compulsory school laws, anxious parents, and ill-trained teachers.

In a sense, school "competition" becomes a daily punishment for those of lesser ability. Repeated frustration in competitive situations produces a tensional state which makes large demands on a child's emotional balance and may alter his proper relationship with companions, teachers, and parents. Competition is not the way to bring each person to his full potentiality.

The goal of helping youth become adequate to the demands of an uncertain, but not uninviting, future, will not be realized so long as preparation for adulthood is subject to the cultivation of precocity, conditional affection, and adherence to a limited concept of achievement. The goal of education must be broadened from scholastic to personal achievement.

✧ ✧ 52 ✧ ✧

Family Forces Influence Child Behavior

DAMARIS PEASE

Families in our society have the primary responsibility for the socialization of children. It is within the family that the child first begins to understand his relationship to others and to become aware of the world around him. The family helps to prepare the child to assume the responsibilities of adulthood in a democratic society.

To participate successfully in the functions of our society it is necessary for the members to become informed; to be able to shape the values, attitudes, policies, ideals, and aspirations of the society; and to give direction and help to the leaders they have selected. A democratic society is dedicated to the proposition that all men are created equal and have an equal opportunity. Such a proposition represents the ideal — the goal toward which the society strives. In attempting to work realistically toward this goal, equality has been defined in terms of the potential of any given individual and education has been selected as the means by which each individual can reach his potential.

In any society there are subcultures. These subcultures may differ from the society in general in terms of racial, ethnic, religious, and socioeconomic factors. Within our society one way of looking at the subcultures is in terms of social class. The idea of social class in which some groups have the advantage while other groups are denied opportunity is distasteful to most of us. But to refuse to recognize that within our society there are different social classes, even though the differences often are not clearly defined, is to ignore an objective analysis of the family forces influencing the growth and development of children. If, as a society, we are truly striving to establish equality among ourselves, we must recognize the inequalities which exist and are inherent in class structure. Recognition of these differences in social class and an objective evaluation of child-rearing practices emphasize the effects of environmental factors on the growth and development of children and hopefully lead to more effective educational opportunities for them.

There is an inherent danger in categorically defining families as belonging to lower, middle, or upper socioeconomic groups. Social class is not

✧ Damaris Pease is Professor of Child Development, Iowa State University.

determined by a single factor such as amount of income or level of formal education. Consideration must be given to such factors as social participation, type and location of home, stability of marriage, source of income, methods of child-rearing, and degree and direction of motivation. Social class, while manifesting various life-style characteristics, is flexible rather than rigid. It is estimated by combining a number of characteristics which do not contain rigid barriers. Social mobility or movement among classes is a basic feature of social class.

Concern for the effects of the environment on the growth and development of the child is not new. Studies in the area of animal research, maternal deprivation, and institutionalization during early childhood indicate that if the environment is not conducive to growth, development can be arrested. Nor is the awareness of the importance of education and academic success as a means to better living new. What is new is the general awareness that many children are not actually in a position to benefit from the education our society provides. Many children enter school with a cultural handicap which makes it difficult if not impossible for them to take advantage of the opportunity to learn.

It has been estimated that 15 to 25 per cent of the children in this country come from homes with the least formal education, the lowest incomes, and the least stability in occupations (1). In these homes the family structure is unstable. Over half of the families are fatherless and when the father is present he spends little time at home. Family members are numerous and living space limited — privacy is a luxury. Employment is haphazard, since most parents are unskilled in a trade.

Another 25 to 40 per cent of the nation's children (depending upon the location, size, and age of the community) come from families economically solvent but possessing few resources to see the family through an economic emergency. Broken homes are not as prevalent, although about one third of these children come from families in which the parents have been separated by divorce, death, or desertion. These families are hard workers — taking their "blue-collar" jobs seriously. Most of the mothers work. Participation in civic affairs is limited or lacking. Marriage comes early and schooling, while recognized as a means to social mobility, often is not completed.

The remainder of the nation's children come from homes of white collar and professional workers — that group sometimes identified as the great American middle class. Most of the parents are high school graduates and many have college degrees. Marriage occurs somewhat later for these families and broken homes are less frequent. These families are socially upward mobile, striving for financial independence and often attaining it. The family members are energetic and ambitious. They are active in all kinds of social and civic affairs and the parents see to it that the children have opportunities to take music and dancing lessons, join the Scouts, participate in the church choir and other group and community activities which will help prepare them for responsible adult leadership. Decisions are reached through common agreement of both parents rather than authoritative direction of either the father or mother. These families are supportive of their children and work to provide them with opportunities to achieve both academically and socially.

It is for this group that most of our educational programs are designed. Our educational system is future-oriented and rewards hard work; serious attitudes toward learning; cooperation, consideration, and respect for others; acceptance of responsibility; leadership; and the successful attainment of the basic skills of communication necessary to achieve these goals.

The child from the middle-class family experiences few contradictions between his family life-style and the goals of the school. Most teachers come from the middle class and hold the same values and attitudes as his family. Achievement in school is recognized as an important factor in successful preparation for adulthood by both the family and the teacher. The middle-class child is more or less "in tune" with the school.

The educationally disadvantaged children — those whose families are in the lower socioeconomic class in reference to the middle class — share no such continuity of values between home and school. In fact, educationally disadvantaged children are handicapped children. Their handicap is most evident when they are required to function within the framework of middle-class standards, values, and attitudes — particularly those which pertain to cleanliness, obedience, respect for authority, the virtue of hard work, and the subsequent, if somewhat delayed, status-promoting rewards.

How familiar, for example, is the old story theme of the boy from the slums of the great metropolitan city who rises to a position of authority on the local police force and must eventually "turn in" his life-long, boyhood playmate. What scorn and rejection he faces from his old neighborhood! Obviously he is just as "disadvantaged" among his neighbors as his criminal buddy is among the socially acceptable middle class.

Changing middle-class standards will not solve the dilemma. But recognition of the forces affecting the socialization of the child will lead to greater understanding of the cultural environment from which the child emerges and to more effective means of providing him with the skills and knowledge for which he has the potential. The issue has been clearly pointed out by Goldberg:

> The issue is not whether to imbue these children with middle-class values or to strengthen the positive aspects of their own unique cultural forms. The issue is, rather, to provide these children with the skills and knowledges which will enable them to select their future direction rather than be hemmed in by the increasingly limited sphere of operations left to those who lack these skills. (2, p. 89)

The educationally handicapped child is no more responsible for his handicap than the child blind from birth or crippled by polio. His difficulty lies in the fact that his handicap does not show physically and that society subscribes to the philosophy that anyone can succeed if he but tries.

The educationally handicapped child is confronted with a double handicap — the one he acquired within his family and the one society imposes upon him by manifesting negative attitudes and intolerances toward poverty, racial and religious differences, and different family and cultural living patterns. In addition to these handicaps the child is faced with the school society oriented toward the education of the middle-class child.

Like any other child the child from a lower-class family views society within the limits of his immediate family and neighborhood. But often behavior which is sanctioned at home is seen as inappropriate by the middle-class school society. For example, the second-grader who reads in school that for breakfast Dick and Jane and Sally had orange juice, milk, hot cereal, and toast (made of whole wheat bread for good measure) and knows that he had a coke and a doughnut this morning is hardly in a position to feel good about himself, his family, or the society which implies he is out of step.

A family attempting to keep a roof over its head and enough food on the table to sustain life has little time or incentive to encourage and foster inquisitiveness, experimentation, and evaluation. The child comes to school ill prepared in basic concepts and skills necessary for school achievement. Early difficulty in the mastery of basic intellectual skills results in feelings of defeat and failure. The older the child grows the more difficult it is to acquire these basic skills and the gap between himself and his middle-class-oriented peers widens.

More often than not the parents did not finish high school and they fail to see the relationship between years of schooling and later rewards of increased earning power and independence. The fact that there are limited job opportunities for those without a high school education or that our changing economy emphasizes automation and demands academically trained people is not recognized by his parents. The child from the lower socioeconomic family fails to receive support and reinforcement from home to bolster his failing self concept or to compensate for his lack of basic skills in the school setting.

Thus a negative self-image is reinforced in a thousand and one experiences in his school life. Little wonder he rebels against these ever-increasing and mounting failures in his school experiences. In his search for status he turns away from the school, and incidentally from the society which it represents, finding satisfaction, status, and protection from his debilitating negative self-image in the street and gang where he can use the survival skills learned at home (2).

Within recent years there has been a growing body of knowledge about educationally disadvantaged children. These children have been described as lacking motivation to succeed, appearing to have short attention spans, and possessing few if any of the basic skills necessary for academic achievement. They are unable to delay immediate gratification and have acquired negative self-images. To better understand the origin of these characteristics it is necessary to look at the home and school environments in relation to the developmental aspects of growth.

Short attention span in a child may be caused by faulty physical and intellectual development, it may be a result of the age of the child, or it may occur because the child has had little experience in learning to concentrate or attend to a problem. The educationally handicapped child comes from a household of many people living in small, crowded rooms. Noise is everywhere around him — people talk but seldom to him. He may well have learned *how not to listen*. He "tunes out" the teacher and his classmates. Contrast this with the middle-class child who is taught to "stop, look, and listen." The problem for the handicapped child becomes even more significant when it is recognized that he comes from a non-verbal household — that is, the adults tend to speak to him in short sentences or short, directive phrases: "Get out." "Stop that." "Shut up." He has not experienced explanations for these commands nor received conditional reasons for what he is told to do. Contrast this to the middle-class mother who says to her child, "In a few minutes you'll have to pick up your sewing from the table so we can set it for supper." To be sure, the middle-class child is told what she must do but she is told why she must do it and is allowed to assume some responsibility relative to when she will do it.

The educationally handicapped child has a limited perception of the world about him. He has learned the law of survival of the fittest — and fitness for him means getting what you want for yourself by whatever means possible. In a study of social class and parental values, Kohn (3) found that both middle- and lower-class mothers valued honesty for their children. However, the middle-class mothers expected honesty to come from internal standards while the lower-class mothers imposed honesty on their children. The middle-class child was expected to act appropriately, not because his parents told him to, but because he wanted to. This puts the responsibility directly on the child, compelling him to make his own evaluations and decisions. It places high value on inner control and requires him to be considerate of others.

The educationally handicapped child is poorly motivated at school. He has had little experience at home in receiving either approval for success in a task or disapproval for failure. If he is lacking or deficient in the basic academic skills he has little internal drive to continue in school. His middle-class peer is encouraged to bring home school work, often provided with a special place to study at home, and given support and encouragement by his parents to perform well at his school tasks.

Not all educationally handicapped children manifest all these characteristics or each characteristic to the same degree. There are some children who experience an academically enriching environment from birth but who nevertheless are "educational cripples." There are other children who appear to have had no real opportunity to learn who become successful adults and contributing members of society. To be culturally handicapped does not always signify an economically and academically poor environment.

If children are to be helped to help themselves it is important to recognize the strengths as well as the weaknesses of their environment. Children from the lower socioeconomic classes are learning from their parents to cope with a negative environment. In our society the traditional family pattern is patriarchal but frequently in the area of unskilled labor women are able to secure the more stable jobs. This has helped to bring about a female-based, extended family structure. Mother, grandmother, aunts, and other members of the extended family work together to share responsibilities related to the home, child-rearing, and earning a living (5). This represents an attempt, and often a successful one, to maintain family organization and stability.

There tends to be greater sibling interaction in these families, since parents have less leisure time to devote to the children. Often brothers and sisters display strong loyalties toward one another and make personal sacrifices to help each other.

Children tend to be peer-oriented and there are many positive features to be found in the peer culture. Rules and regulations of the peer culture must be obeyed if a child is to be accepted by his gang. Frequently these rules support rather than negate society's values. Honesty and loyalty to the group, cooperation with and consideration for each other, and fair play are all necessary characteristics of peer acceptance.

Often children from the lower socioeconomic families are required to develop their own inner resources at an early age. Children learn from each other, develop independence, and assume considerable responsibility. For example, one boy of ten was getting up every morning at five o'clock to sell newspapers. After school he returned to his street corner to sell the evening papers. He was willing and proud to contribute his earnings to his mother who had three younger children to support.

Just as there is no single criteria for classifying a family as belonging to the middle, lower, or upper strata of our society so there is no single solution to the problem of social class differences in child-rearing practices.

Before a child can learn effectively he must be ready to learn. He must be free to accept new ideas, to be receptive to differences in people's behavior, and to realize the potential within him. Not only must he be ready maturationally to acquire new skills and knowledge but he must have the desire or motivation to learn. One source of motivation is the degree to which basic physiological and psychological needs are met within a child.

Maslow (4) has suggested that the motivating force behind human behavior is a hierarchal system of needs. He postulates that every child in order to be a satisfied and creative individual must find fulfillment for these needs: (a) safety (which is based on the physical as well as the psychological environment), (b) love and affection, (c) esteem or feeling of self-worth, and (d) self-realization or self-actualization.

To experience fulfillment of the safety needs the child must live in a stable, predictable, and orderly world. Too many inconsistencies in his world lead to anxiety and fear. School for many children is a new and strange experience. If the child is not helped to bridge the gap between the unfamiliar and the familiar he will be unwilling to accept or try the new.

While children from both the lower- and middle-class families may have their safety needs threatened, the child from the educationally disadvantaged home experiences greater inconsistencies between home and school. Some of these inconsistencies, and incidentally some of the child's anxiety, can be reduced by recognizing the strengths of the home environment in the classroom.

Love and affectional needs relate to the ability to give and receive love from others. Parents who fulfill this need do so by accepting the child — whatever he may be — regardless of what he does. Families from the lower socioeconomic class love their children just as those from the middle class. But there is less time to devote to children and less of a basis for understanding the goals toward which the children are working in school. In other words, there tends to be less communication between adult and child.

In school these children, perhaps more than others, need to feel the teacher respects their ideas and desires regardless of the techniques they use to convey them. Because they have been required to develop their own resources early, they may find new and different ways of doing traditional school tasks. Both parents and teachers can be alert and receptive to different, but perhaps equally adequate, ways of performing home and school tasks.

Esteem need, according to Maslow, is the feeling the child has about himself as a worthy, adequate, and capable person. This is based on real capacity, achievement, and respect from others. As a child develops skills and acquires knowledge he becomes more capable. When his achievements are reflected in acceptance by and respect from others he comes to accept and respect himself. Teachers can recognize the skills, particularly the physical and visual ones, that children possess and provide opportunities to combine these skills with new ones. As parents recognize and reinforce the importance of learning academic skills children will feel more competent and positive about their own abilities and "learning" will become easier.

The need for self-actualization relates to the child's desire for self-fulfillment — the desire to work toward his potential. To satisfy this need all other needs must be met, at least to some degree. Satisfaction of this need is represented by becoming what one is capable of becoming. Teachers, recognizing the strength of children's backgrounds, and working within this framework, can expect more rather than less from these children. Teachers will be challenged to develop new techniques to bring out the creativity of the children.

The concept of basic needs as the motivating force in the life of a child cannot be and is not the complete answer to the problems arising from social class differences. But with greater understanding of the underlying causes of behavior those who live and work with children can help them to more nearly realize the potential which is within them — "What a person can be he must be." (4, p. 256)

REFERENCES

1. Bernard, Harold W. *Human Development in Western Culture.* Boston: Allyn and Bacon, Inc., 1962.

2. Goldberg, Miriam L. "Factors Affecting Educational Attainment in Depressed Areas," in A. Harry Passow (ed.), *Education in Depressed Areas.* New York: Teachers College, Columbia University, 1963. Pp. 68–99.

3. Kohn, Melvin L. "Social Class and Parental Values," in Paul H. Mussen, John J. Conger, and Jerome Kagan (eds.), *Readings in Child Development and Personality.* New York: Harper & Row, Publishers, 1965. Pp. 345–366.

4. Maslow, A. H. "A Theory of Human Motivation," in Don E. Hamachek (ed.), *The Self in Growth, Teaching and Learning.* Englewood Cliffs, N.J.: Prentice-Hall, Inc., 1965. Pp. 246–268.

5. Riessman, Frank. "Low-Income Culture: The Strengths of the Poor," *Journal of Marriage and the Family,* 26:417–421, 1964.

Working with Disadvantaged Parents

LOUISE G. DAUGHERTY

Impoverished backgrounds, restricted opportunities, and a sense of despair and resignation characterize the parents of the deprived children in our cities. Parental indifference to the value of education is transmitted to the children, whose school careers are naturally characterized by poor attendance, low achievement, and early leaving. Thus, the cycle of hopelessness and despair is repeated from generation to generation.

In considering how to break this cycle, the Research Council of the Great Cities Program for School Improvement proposed that only if these culturally deprived children received specific and concentrated attention would they be adequately prepared to become contributing citizens. The Chicago Project also proposed that the schools could not treat the problems of the children effectively without also treating the problems of the parents.

To test the validity of these proposals the Chicago Board of Education, with a grant from the Ford Foundation and supplementary funds of its own,

✧ From the *NEA Journal,* December, 1963, pp. 18–20. Used by permission of the author and the publisher. Louise G. Daugherty is Superintendent, Chicago Public Schools, District 11.

has launched a Special Project to see what can be done for certain children in District Eleven, one of twenty-one administrative subdistricts.

When the Project began in 1960, its major goal was the motivation of students who had had unsuccessful elementary school experiences. The primary emphasis was on boys and girls fourteen or more years of age who were still in elementary school.

In an effort to increase these youngsters' self-respect and their opportunities for advancement, Project staff and school staff planned cooperative programs designed to increase school attendance, raise levels of achievement, reinforce school experiences, and increase vocational competence. The Project also included programs designed to upgrade the quality of family life and to encourage community participation.

In July 1961 the Project effort was extended downward to embrace pupils between eleven and thirteen years of age, who were overage in grade placement and upward to provide practical programs for dropouts in District Eleven.

Also expanding horizontally, the Project has sought to utilize the services of business groups and community agencies and to involve parent groups at all levels of the program.

The work with parents has proved to be of primary importance. The Project effort has been directed at the most unsuccessful families in a district which is extremely low on the socioeconomic-educational scale. Project interest has centered on parents who need help in understanding their children, in seeing the value of school, in developing homemaking skills, in learning to cope with urban life, in achieving vocational competence, and in accepting the responsibility of parenthood. Since such parents do not usually come to community agencies for assistance other than financial, the Project staff has literally gone into the homes to provide service to all who would accept it.

Such service has been provided in a number of ways by using staff members with special skills.

A *school social worker*, for example, became involved with families in order to help children with problems of adjustment in school. Home visits resulted in family counseling and increased competency on the part of both mothers and fathers.

In one instance, a mother in a housing project started a library in her living room for her teen-age children and their friends. Inexpensive guidance booklets furnished by the Project proved surprisingly popular. Since the youngsters had no public library in their area, the mother learned how to provide this needed service in the home. At the same time, she learned how to discuss with the younger generation the problems outlined in the guidance booklets.

The social worker also formed a Father's Club. Any male figure, in or out of the home, who was willing to represent one of the youngsters in the Project was eligible to attend.

Fathers, uncles, and friends seemed glad to have an all-male group where they could discuss adolescent behavior. After the first meeting, they asked to bring youngsters they were representing, for they felt the discussions would benefit the young people and that it would also help to hear the youngsters' side of any problems. Finally they invited their wives to attend. This group became the host for the first meeting of Special Project parents the following school semester.

A *home economist,* who combined rural approaches with urban know-how, organized sewing groups that met semiweekly in apartments where mothers could bring their preschool children to play while the mothers learned how to sew. While remodeling hand-me-downs and making draperies and furniture covers, the mothers discussed urban ways of family life.

One group organized by the home economist met in the model apartment of a public housing project where mothers learned more about cooking skills. Still another met in Dunbar Vocational High School's cafeteria kitchen where they were taught how to convert government surplus cornmeal and powdered milk into cookies and a chocolate drink.

Mothers involved in the preparation discovered the value and versatility of surplus commodities and learned how to work in a large commercial kitchen. Furthermore, hungry elementary students using the building between four and six o'clock for special cultural, vocational, and remedial classes had the opportunity to feast on an abundance of wholesome snacks.

Using the community and the city as a laboratory, the home economist took groups of mothers to supermarkets in order to teach meal planning, budgeting, and intelligent purchasing; to department store yard goods departments in order to teach about textiles and what makes them good (or poor) bargains; to utility companies' home economics demonstrations in order to learn about resources for homemakers of which they had been unaware.

Although the initial effort of the home economist was made with the parents of the overage pupils (fourteen through seventeen) in Special Project classes, other groups were recruited from among parents whose children had been enrolled in urban 4-H Clubs organized by the Project. Such parents had for their primary interest not sewing, cooking, and home improvement, but aiding their own children in 4-H.

A *youth activities counselor* used an indirect method to develop security and leadership in his groups. Increasing parental involvement was approached through the interests and activities of children in the 4-H groups rather than by working directly with the parent. The parents were willing to participate in the 4-H activities if they were not held totally responsible for a group or an activity; they functioned best as assistants to the regular teacher. Although they lacked talents or skills, they enjoyed and took pride in those of their offspring.

A *parent educational counselor* worked with parents in school-oriented programs. She made home visits when necessary, but did not attempt to set up home-based groups. Instead, she worked with principals and teachers to encourage and then lend a hand with parent activities related to school progress. In addition, she deliberately scheduled meetings at such community agencies as YWCA's and recreation centers in order to expose parents to facilities which were available to them but were not being used by them.

Tours of local business establishments made parents aware of existing employment opportunities and helped them to learn what academic and vocational skills their children would need to enter the world of work. Tours to the City Hall and the Police Headquarters Building helped them understand city government.

Spring tours of two district high schools acquainted parents with the programs and physical plants of the schools where their children would be enrolled the following semester. A mother-daughter workshop to prepare girl elementary school graduates for high school was an outstanding success.

Parent groups organized by the counselor discussed mental health services and care; ways to help children in reading, science, and other school subjects; the importance of adequate diet and sleep for physical well-being.

One of the counselor's most satisfying efforts has been the Large Family Project, the aim of which is to enrich the lives of large families (six or more children) who have no father in the home. Aware that such families have few if any opportunities for taking even short trips as a family group, the counselor arranged for twenty-five of these families to go on tours to interesting places throughout the city in a bus furnished by the Project.

She visited the mothers and invited them to take their families on the tours, starting with a trip to the Brookfield Zoo. When they accepted (and all did), she and the home economist then discussed with them packing of suitable lunch, wearing appropriate dress, and the assignment of responsibilities to each member of the family.

After the second trip, this one to a museum, a mother of nine confided how much the trips meant to her because she and her children had never been out together before as a family group! All families, in fact, enjoyed the expeditions and were deeply grateful.

Another educational counselor helped involve parents of two different types of children in the Special Project. He organized a group of parents of juveniles known to the police and a counseling group for academically talented children. Graduate students in guidance at Chicago Teachers College South counseled whole families and met individually with the parents of able students.

All of these activities for parents were designed to reinforce the educational programs of the schools of District Eleven. Hopefully, such programs will increase parental competency enough to result in improved home life and in increased capability of the children.

Despite the efforts made by the special staff of the Project, however, the school has also had to make its own overtures to the parents in terms of the educational tasks to be performed.

Friendly interviewing of the child and the parent at the time of enrollment has enabled school personnel to explain the goals of attendance and scholarship and the objectives of the special program. It also has helped the school staff to find out whether the parents had obvious interests or needs that could be helped by Project or community resources. One expression of interest in knowledge about the city government, for example, encouraged the Board of Education to sponsor an Americanization class in a local church building.

At one school in the district orientation meetings for parents, an open house and a Parent-Interview Day for graduates stimulated parental thinking in terms of their children's abilities and possible futures. Personal conferences concerned with attendance and scholastic progress further strengthened the school-parent relationship.

One teacher in the same school began a series of after-school visits to homes of his pupils. Parents were so appreciative that he was encouraged to become an after-school staff member of the Project, using the same techniques but visiting all the parents of Special Project students.

Before each visit, the teacher usually phoned or sent a letter home by the child. Sometimes, but rarely, he would arrive unannounced.

These visits established greater rapport between home, school, and community; built closer ties in teacher-pupil-parent relationships; and enabled teachers to obtain firsthand information on the home condition of their pupils. They also helped build a positive image of the school as an agency which reaches out to the disadvantaged family.

Other schools in the district adopted this "reaching out" philosophy and initiated parent education programs of their own. One school implemented a reading program for parents by showing them how children were learning reading grade by grade. This group, under the leadership of the principal, developed a Saturday activity in which parents assumed responsibility for three or four other children as well as their own. These groups convened at the various homes, and on Saturdays the parents took children to theaters and libraries. No teachers were involved on Saturday.

A second school developed a series of meetings based on the interests expressed by parents in vocational opportunities, welfare policies, child health practices, and homework assignments.

What techniques are best in reaching out to the disadvantaged parent? The same techniques used to win the support of the economically advantaged parent also will work with the disadvantaged parent:

- A genuine interest in the child and the parent who loves him.
- An opportunity to bring to the teacher or the administrator any problem hindering the child's progress.

- Patience in listening to a problem and concrete suggestions as to what steps parents (and school) may take to work out a solution.
- Printed communications that are simple enough to be understandable but mature enough to reflect respect for the parents' intelligence.
- Encouragement and appreciation for all parental efforts — even the unsuccessful ones.
- An expressed dedication to excellence in education.

Children in well-to-do suburban areas need quality education, but the children in disadvantaged urban areas need it even more. The schools of District Eleven have been working with this philosophy, helped by Foundation funds and experimental programs made possible by the Chicago public schools. In this effort, parents become of increasing importance to their children — and to themselves and their community — because the school cares enough to reach out to them.

✧ ✧ 54 ✧ ✧

White People's Time, Colored People's Time

JULES HENRY

Among the children of the very poor survival must take precedence over every other consideration. But current motivational theory tends to downgrade immediate and physical motives. It turns its eagle vision instead, like a rising young executive, on "goal-striving," "status-seeking," and "planning." By such elite and middle-class standards the poor must be said to have little or no motivation.

Under a grant from the National Institute of Mental Health we have been studying a large St. Louis housing development inhabited almost exclusively by very poor Negroes. We middle-class observers have noted the pronounced tendency of the tenants toward "random-like" and unrealistic behavior. Their attitudes toward space, time, objects, and persons lack our patterns of organization, lack our predictability — even sometimes seem to lack sense — to us. How do they seem to the project dwellers themselves?

✧ From *Trans-Action*, March–April, 1965, pp. 31–34. Used by permission of the author and the publisher. Jules Henry is Professor of Anthropology, Washington University.

After more than a year of field work with about fifty families we have the strong impression that they are well aware of the differences.

For instance, they make a strong distinction between C.P. (colored people's) time and W.P. (white people's) time. According to C.P. time a scheduled event may occur at any moment over a wide spread of hours — or perhaps not at all. They believe, however, that in the highly organized world of the whites it occurs when scheduled.

The housing project is so isolated from the social and economic life of the city and the white community that the occupational classes of the Census Bureau scarcely apply to it. The tenants work as domestics, or in the nooks and cracks of our economy; employment is uncertain, pay is poor, resources are scarce. Yet unemployed men talk of jobs they do not have, and the women in this "City of Women" speak of husbands dead, fled, or who never existed.

Illusion is thus a way of life. Young and old spend money they do not have for expensive clothes and cars. People with no power and status brag of influence and position and concentrate on getting the better of each other. The illusion of middle-class success settles invisibly over them. Thus a white school teacher working with Negro children remarks that they are not interested in solid accomplishment but only in showing off. Obviously such short-cutting must interfere with learning and with facing school and life realistically.

Casting out the poor and the Negro from white society has resulted in a social life so saturated by illusion that the fancy soon becomes the only possible achievement.

Disorganization and a life of dreams fit into the social dynamic of the school room to create educational underachievement.

The children of disorganization cannot create classroom organization; and the teacher can only work with those who have somehow managed to acquire enough of the necessary motivation. Often we have seen a harassed teacher working with a very few children in a class and trying to ignore the disorder and uproar the others are creating. Here are some notes made in one such sixth grade classroom, with both Negro and white children:

> The teacher was leaning over Paul's desk helping him with arithmetic. Irv and Mike were watching. Alice was talking to Jane and Joan to Edith. Nearby Alan, Ed, and Tom were pushing and shoving. Tom got out of his seat, made a wad of notebook paper and tossed it into the air several times. Tom and Ed suddenly slammed their desks shut, got up, and walked out noisily, Lila and Alice followed. Alan grinned at the observer, waved his hand, and said, "Hi." The teacher took no notice. . . .

This process of *partial withdrawal* — whereby the teacher simply withdrew to those few students she could handle — may occur anywhere an individual tries to cope with a disturbed environment; I have also seen it in mental hospitals. It reflects not so much the relationship between authority and client but the total social situation.

In school pupils have the choice of building status either with their teacher or their friends; to many, reputation among friends may be much more important. The pressure of peer groups is very strong, and self-destructive status choice can occur in any such conflict between the demands of authority figures and the demands of the group. What usually tips the balance toward teacher and self-preservation is a measure of hope in the future. Disorganization can tip the balance the other way.

This is especially true if the disorganization has unique attractions for the children. In integrated classrooms, the approval of white students may become so attractive to Negro children that they gladly risk official displeasure, punishment, or failure. In coeducational classes, attracting the attention and getting the approval of the opposite sex can become much more important than "teacher's dirty looks." All such "split" situations introduce disturbing and competing elements. Students can make status choices that ruin their whole future lives.

Very, very poor children, both by feeling and understanding, lack the structure on which conventional education can build. Their background does not have the elements of order necessary to achieve. Their homes are crowded, full of disturbance, physically and personally disorganized; they do not operate on schedules that pay much attention to school concepts of time. They lack both belief in achievement and fear of no achievement.

When thirty to fifty such children are a class supposed to be run by one teacher, disorganization must result. From it the teacher in sheer self-defense may select only those elements suited to her task — she will teach those considered teachable and let the others go. But even the children most willing and able to learn are under tremendous pressure from their classmates to give up and join them. By pleasing the teacher they can buy success in a vague and distant future only at the probable expense of making their present life lonely, unhappy, and even dangerous.

The poor motivation of the low-achiever is not therefore a demon somehow arising from and locked up inside himself but one effect of a whole sea of pressure and pain which has surrounded him since birth; and in which he himself seldom knows why he gasps.

The Missing Ingredient

But why all this disorder, illusion, and destruction? Does it come about because, as some moralists believe, the poor lack an essential fiber, so that they tack and waver in the wind against which *we* advance?

This view is actually not far wrong. The poor do lack a fundamental vitamin that we others absorb with the smell of food, with the promise of gifts at Christmas, with plans for graduation. *They lack the essential strength of hope.*

Hope is not a simple nutrient. It goes straight to the heart of organization and makes it work.

Among lower animals organization occurs largely through inborn genetic factors. With man, things are not so direct, and the word "culture" has been chosen to designate the complex learnings that determine his behavior.

But "culture" varies between societies and even between groups within societies. For the middle and upper classes in our society, achievement and security are major determinants. They organize behavior — or our behavior is organized around them. They act as carrots; the fear of their opposites — failure and insecurity — acts as a goad. When people do not see success and failure as we do, their behavior will appear to us random and purposeless; and we disapprove of it. But those who cannot *hope* for achievement or security can have no concept of the organization of behavior through time toward goals.

The culture of the middle-class itself has been superficially charted. How, for instance, does the middle-class handle *hope, time,* and the *self?* Achievement depends on hope — and hope rests on time. Some *time* in the future we hope to achieve something. Even to say "Billy has stopped wetting the bed" means that desired change has occurred through time: Billy used to wet the bed but does so no longer.

But the parent with no hope can have only partial understanding of his child's having stopped bed-wetting. He can have no fruitful conception of the conscious movement through time toward desired goals. Relative to large social goals, his actions are undirected.

Flight from Death

Though the poor have little hope for life, they do not wish to die. According to comparative suicide rates they have less taste for final voluntary quietus than any other class. Therefore, they concentrate on those factors that keep them alive — now — that make direct, obvious, and strong contributions to present life. The culture of the very poor is a *flight from death.*

In this setting, the very disregard of common methods of looking at things and objects — such as how to arrange a house — can become institutionalized, a way of life. Such disregard in objects we call disorder; in behavior we call it randomness.

Martin Heidegger in *Being and Time* relates the perception of self to existence through time. When people think of themselves they seem to say, he argues, "*That* is the way I was, *this* is how I am now, and in the *future,* I hope to be something else." These perceptions of self have past, present, and future; and it is from them, he believes, that we conceive time. They presuppose change during time — movement from what used to be toward what will be. Self must therefore exist at least partly as a function of time; it must include organization through time.

But what happens to a person who has no expectations or hopes for himself or his children? His behavior, having neither background nor direction, is disorganized. What is left of him is the irreducible ash — the *survival self* — the flight from death.

The survival self has no real sublimation or higher displacement — nothing but physical life — in a very limited but very intense form. The survival self must concentrate on those experiences which give it continual and vivid reassurance that it is alive — heightened perhaps and smoothed by drugs or alcohol. It must, literally, keep *feeling* its life. Sociologists of middle-class background contemptuously refer to this state as "hedonism" — living for pleasure. It is not — it is flight from death.

The famous second law of thermodynamics states, in paraphrase, that disorder within an isolated system can only increase. Life is not pure physics; but there is a useful parallel. Consider a middle-class neighborhood or suburb. It is not an isolated system. Its members go out into the community, and the community comes in at the door and the mind. The resources of the community are known to and used by it, and it is subject to steady cultural and economic stimulation — which it in turn affects. The interaction brings adjustment and regulation; the disorder or randomness — "entropy" in the language of physics — is low.

The slum or lower-class housing project does not have access to these sources of support and stimulation. A paradox — or vicious circle — exists: because of their disorganization and lack of hope the very poor cannot or do not get to the major sources of economic and cultural stimulation; and their disorganization and hopelessness came in the first place from lack of access to these resources. Cut off from hope, stimulation, and change, the poor neighborhood is an isolated human thermodynamic system, and its disorganization can only increase.

Many middle-class selves are also in flight from death; but they are trained to look at life through the lens of achievement, sustained by hope and expectation, and they can fly along this path — perhaps even to greater achievement. This sustenance is not available to the great majority from the slum and housing project.

Our conclusion then must be that hope is a boundary: it separates the free from the slave, the determined from the drifting — and the very poorest from almost all those above it. A corollary conclusion — even more surprising — follows: *time, space, and objects really exist for us only when we have hope.*

Short of reforming his world, how can we stimulate the slum child to greater school achievement? Certainly it will not be enough to merely improve teaching methods and curricula. We must improve the school as a social system.

Some proposals are in order:

BUILDING UP PERCEPTIONS. Children whose central milieu involves so much disorganization and disorder cannot master mathematics, or any other discipline involving order and direction. I would urge that these children be given preschool training in which the basic perceptions that other children acquire without apparent effort be deliberately taught. For instance, a child must learn fundamental shapes and categories — insideness and outsideness, roundness, straightness, flexibility, rigidity, transparency, opacity, motion in a straight line, motion in a circle, rocking motion, and many other basic perceptions. A child should have this perceptual competence before he starts school.

CALMING DOWN. Poor children often come to school unfed, after wretched nights torn by screaming, fighting, bed-wetting; often they cannot sleep because of cold and rats. They come to class hungry, sleepy, and emotionally upset. To start routine schoolwork effectively at once is impossible. I propose that teachers be specially trained — as they are in the Youth Development Project of the greater Kansas City Mental Health Foundation — to deal with such children, and that they *breakfast with them* in school. The school should, of course, furnish the food, perhaps out of government surplus. School breakfast would accomplish two things: it would feed hungry children, otherwise unable to concentrate adequately on their work; and it would bring teacher and pupil together in an informal and friendly atmosphere, associated with satisfaction, before the strain of classroom constriction and peer-group pressures dictate that teacher become an enemy. It is essential, therefore, that the teacher be present. A program like this suggested by me in Kansas City brought about immediate and sharp improvement in attendance, behavior, and in schoolwork. The more the teachers know about the emotional management of these children, the better.

EXPANSION OF PARTICIPATION. The frequently proclaimed immediate goal of instruction — more personalized attention — is especially important with low-achievers. This can be done by reducing class size, or by increasing the number of teachers. The extra teachers, if not as highly qualified as the regulars, should nevertheless be trained and familiar with the lessons. They can be substitutes, teachers in training, or even members of the domestic counterpart of the Peace Corps whenever that is established. They should be able to help with routine tasks, with keeping order — and with seeing to it that each child has more time, attention, care, and opportunity to learn.

Very poor children need hope in order to achieve. So do those who work with them.

55

A Frontal Attack on Cultural Deprivation

FRANK G. DICKEY

The Southern Association of Colleges and Schools and the College Entrance Examination Board are joining forces in a five-year program designed to prepare the Negro citizen for the fuller responsibilities which are his and which will increase in the coming years. A preliminary grant of $895,000 from the Ford Foundation and $405,000 from the Danforth Foundation are already available for this project.

The College Entrance Examination Board will focus its efforts on readying the culturally isolated yet talented individual for admission to college. The term "Project Opportunity" aptly describes this segment of the project. Identification of students will be made at the seventh- or eighth-grade levels, and special programs will be developed for working with parents, students, and teachers to strengthen educational programs and make students more capable of handling college work.

The Southern Association segment of the program is somewhat more complex and varied in its approach.

At intervals during its sixty-eight-year history, the association has conducted experimentation and research and has engaged in action programs designed to improve the quality of education; but never before has it embarked upon so momentous and far-reaching a program as this one.

Two urgencies require that better educational opportunities be made available to Negro Americans. First, the rights they are successfully claiming are now threatened anew by a coalition of reactionaries, still amorphous, but crystallizing rapidly. The best defense against these forces antagonistic to full citizenship for Negroes will be a strong educational system steadily feeding into the nation more and more qualified Negro leaders. Second, the good name of the United States in the world community will continue to be weakened until a solution to the problem of the Negro minority in education is found.

These are the assumptions upon which this proposal is founded:

1. Integration will only be achieved from strength, not from weakness. Integration must be a two-way street; that is to say, the best trained Ne-

✧ From *Phi Delta Kappan*, May, 1964, pp. 398–400. Used by permission of the author and the publisher. Frank G. Dickey is Executive Director, Southern Association of Colleges and Schools, Atlanta.

groes will move easily into white institutions, and whites will move readily into the best equipped and most promising Negro institutions.

2. Institutions now predominantly or entirely for Negroes represent a capital investment that the nation neither can nor should abandon. Instead we should strengthen them to pave the way for the final complete integration.

3. Many of the schools and colleges now predominantly for Negroes will remain so for the foreseeable future because of economic, political, and social pressures that cannot be eliminated except through careful education and the reorientation of thought and feeling. This is not to say that legal barriers to desegregation should be tolerated, or that any individual should be denied an opportunity for which his individual abilities suit him.

4. It is widely believed in both the white and Negro communities that educational institutions primarily for Negroes are inherently inferior, and that this acceptance is of sufficient strength in the public mind to require a demonstration of its error. Only when both groups know that excellence is possible in institutions predominantly for Negroes, and that it has been achieved by some already, will the possibility of a two-way integration really exist.

5. A partial and piecemeal approach to this problem is no longer adequate to the needs of the Negroes or to the necessities of the United States in this day. The characteristic pressures of our time seem to require a broad-scale and coordinated attack on this problem.

6. The greatest barrier to complete and harmonious integration in education is the cultural deprivation under which the Negro has labored in our country.

7. Any successful approach to this difficulty must engage large numbers of persons from the majority and minority groups in a cooperative relationship. This new relationship must be achieved on a basis of mutual respect and self-respect derived from an awareness of competence in achievement.

8. The total cost of this improvement of educational opportunities for Negroes will be of such magnitude that it can be assumed only by the people themselves through their state and local governments, or through the federal government, if the people so decide.

9. The electorate can be persuaded to accept this burden only if they are convinced that the returns will be compensatory.

The specific aims of the project are:

1. To improve the educational opportunities afforded in the institutions selected.

2. By this improvement to explode the myth of inherent inferiority that has been attached to institutions primarily for Negroes, and thereby to open the path to the two-way integration that represents the only real and permanent solution to the majority-minority problem.

3. To persuade school boards and city and county governments that their best interests will be served by adopting for all their schools the techniques

employed in the schools and colleges selected for this project, and therefore to accept the financial burden of implementing similar programs on a large scale.

4. To explore possibilities and refine techniques to overcome the cultural deprivation that is robbing millions of Americans of the lives that should be theirs, and that prevents the United States from reaching its potential as a nation and as a community.

Two elementary schools, two high schools, and a cluster of colleges, all in the same city or close by, will be selected as a "center." Five to seven centers are to be established, work in the centers being coordinated through the project's central administration. Other schools in each area will be chosen as controls so that evaluation may be made.

One criterion for the selection of a city will be the local school board's willingness to cooperate. The climate of the community must give assurance that the experiment may be completed and its results considered objectively. Cooperative school boards will be urged to budget some support for the work as evidence of their intent to follow up the experiment in other schools if initial efforts prove successful.

Program leadership is to come from three sources: the local school system, the colleges in the center, and the project administration. School superintendents and administrators are expected to provide local cooperation and support. The colleges in each center will bear the burden of leadership in the varied efforts in each center and in the evaluation of results.

The money requested for this project is to be expended in schools and colleges primarily for Negroes. Cooperation of schools that are primarily for white students is expected, and the colleges in each center primarily for whites will be active in the work, but their participation will be advisory and voluntary.

In addition to efforts made through the chosen schools, each center will set up a community development program organized around participating schools. These programs will enlist parents and other members of the school community in a common attack on the cultural deficiencies that cripple many Negro adults. Lack of understanding will hamper the progress of their children unless the parents understand what is being tried and give their assent and assistance.

The majority group in each city will be asked to join in the work through the community development programs. Civic leaders, churches, and community organizations will be recruited for the task of overcoming the psychological and sociological barriers to the establishment of a healthy interrelationship between all elements of the population.

The colleges will have a dual role. First, they are to demonstrate excellence. To this end, they must engage in a complete restudy of their purposes, curriculums, methods, and facilities. Some strengthening of the faculties will be mandatory and further graduate work will be necessary for some faculty members. There must be a total effort to become a home for the love of learning, a place in which students and teachers together are excited by their common task of scholarship and self-education. Second, the colleges must become centers about which the chosen satellite schools undertake the move to excellence.

Through the leadership, advice, and consultative resources of the colleges, the schools will enter into self-analysis, the recruitment of needed personnel, and into the better employment of their resources and those available in the community. In-service training programs for faculties of elementary and secondary schools will be established by colleges. Some of these programs will be held on college campuses; others will take place in the schools themselves. During the summers, colleges will provide institutes and special programs to help solve problems that have been identified during the school year. Refresher programs may be established for school faculty members lacking recent collegiate training in their specialties. Other courses will be arranged to broaden the education of staff members who feel the need for further study and self-development.

The colleges will also become centers for the identification and preparation of unusually able students who will be invited to take advanced special instruction in reading and mathematics.

A major responsibility of the college will be to assist the public schools in student-parent guidance programs and to be active in endeavors to overcome the effects of cultural deprivation. A good part of the colleges' responsibility will be in the area of interpreting the goals and activities of the total program to the communities in which the schools operate.

The elementary and secondary schools, like the colleges, will have a dual role. First, they will be urged and helped to become centers of scholastic excellence. To reach this prime goal, additional personnel will be sought to make student-teacher ratios reasonable; equipment will be purchased to make the most effective teaching possible; and the libraries will be strengthened to reinforce the work of the classroom. Moreover, teachers will be encouraged to participate in in-service training courses, summer study programs, and faculty seminars concerning problems of their school. Leadership in these efforts will come from the colleges whenever appropriate.

Special attention will be given to identifying able children as early as possible and to encouraging them and their parents to set high goals and to persevere in the academic effort. At the same time, remedial programs in reading and arithmetic will be set up to overcome deficiencies that will already have appeared in some students.

Second, each school will be asked to take leadership in the community development program centered around its work. A student-parent counseling service will seek to enlist parents in the effort to better educate their children and in their own improvement. The school will become a cultural center for the geographic area of the city that surrounds it and will take the initiative in stimulating community self-analysis and betterment.

Part of the project will be an incentive and reward program for the schools, colleges, and communities. It is not intended to compete with the many competitive awards now open to Negro students. One of the hopes of the project is to increase the number of Negro students eligible for and interested in already existing programs.

This program, however, is aimed at stimulating better academic performance and at demonstrating to the average Negro family that superior work will be matched with the funds these students will need to pursue their goals successfully.

There will be no effort to require able students to stay in colleges and universities near the center. Watching their progress will be easier if they do, but it is felt that students will do better if allowed to take their awards at the colleges of their choice. Guidance will be offered, of course, but rigid restriction will be avoided.

All of the efforts thus far described could be helpful to the people concerned and to the communities involved. The basic assumption of this proposal is that their effects will be more widespread and their worth far greater if coordinated with an attack on the cultural deprivation that is the greatest problem in any Negro community. The community program becomes, then, the capstone of the total effort.

First of all, this program will involve the parents of the children in the selected public schools. They will be asked and encouraged to assist in raising the educational aspiration of their sons and daughters and to participate actively in the educational process. Not incidental is the hope that the parents themselves will experience a renewal of mind and spirit and that many of them will abandon the apathy and hopelessness characteristic of men and women who have been culturally deprived.

In the second place, through this community development effort, an endeavor will be made to bridge the gap between the environment of the minority and that of the majority. By raising the sights of the minority and by drawing into that effort the resources of the majority, it is expected that distinctions between the groups will weaken and that a new and stronger single community will replace the older divided one.

The community development program will require that schools become centers of cultural life for children, parents, staff members, friends, and relatives. Artists and lecturers would furnish by their appearances a framework for periodic meetings of the community. Some of these should be Negroes who have achieved great success in music, education, law, business, medicine, or the arts. Other meetings would bring together special interest groups to view pertinent television productions, to hear telelectures by appropriate experts, to form workshops in home decoration and improvement, or to learn from invited speakers from the local majority groups about the daily conduct of political, economic, and religious affairs in their city.

Beyond this direct action to overcome cultural deprivation, there should be a matching effort to involve the Negro citizens in civic club, P.T.A., and church programs. College students of both races could be drawn into a system of tutorials for younger students. Special needs will be found in each community to which the people will be sensitive and for which they will want to muster their particular resources.

Out of the community education programs should grow an increased number of potential graduate and professional students, a greater awareness of responsibility and opportunity on the part of both majority and minority, and a new sense of unity and pride in the entire citizenry.

One difficulty hampering most Negro children in the South is their almost complete separation from the literature, art, and music that the majority of the community take for granted. White children take their textbooks home and frequently supplement them with private libraries or with public collections. Negro children in many schools are not allowed to take books home, have no private collections, and do not really have a chance to explore the public libraries. Art galleries, books of prints, record albums of fine performers, and representative ensembles are almost unknown in the homes of the average Southern Negro.

The project includes, therefore, a request for funds to purchase, or to have printed, books, records, and prints suitable for the different grade levels for distribution at a nominal cost. It is believed that such a direct attack on the problem of cultural deprivation will prove its usefulness in a relatively short time. A stipulation with the gift or reduced price might be a report of reading or listening from the student, or from the student and his family.

One of the purposes of the total program is to persuade communities other than those chosen for the project to adopt the methods used and to undertake the upgrading of their own educational systems. Public information reports will be issued to inform citizens of selected cities and towns about the progress made and to tell the story through the region and nation. Reports about the successes of the chosen stipend and scholarship winners, publication of achievements in the testing program, analyses of the communities most successful in lowering juvenile delinquency rates, announcement of enlarged pools of skilled and professional workers, improvement of public health — all these could be invaluable in persuading communities across the region to improve the educational opportunities for their Negro youth and to accept a completely integrated society.

56

Educability and Rehabilitation: The Future of the Welfare Class

ROBERT D. HESS

The question of whether rehabilitation of welfare families is dream or reality is too complex to be answered directly; this paper approaches it by a roundabout although hopefully not a circuitous route.

To begin with a summary, it is this paper's thesis that the behavior which leads to social, educational, and economic poverty is socialized in early childhood, that is, it is learned; and that a long-range program of intervention cannot be effective unless it concerns itself with the socialization or re-socialization of the children of welfare families. This paper also argues that our present policy of dealing with poverty is designed not to eliminate, but to institutionalize it, and that we are in the process of creating a permanent "welfare class"[1] as a lower level of society in the United States.

This paper will attempt to elaborate on these two themes, to show the relationship between them, and to describe a project now under way at the University of Chicago which inquires into a small segment of this enormously complicated problem.

In order to make an argument for this thesis, it is necessary to state several propositions and assumptions, some of which are familiar and some of which may not be readily accepted:

First, that social structure shapes the interpersonal relationships that develop between the family and the community and its institutions.

Second, that the nature of the interaction between the family and the social system affects the structure of the family and the interpersonal and affective exchange within it.

Third, that the verbal communication that emerges within the family as

---

[1] The author first heard this term from Dr. Bettye Caldwell, State University of New York, who is doing some of the most significant work now under way in the analysis of early learning of culturally deprived children.

✧ From a presentation before the Groves Conference on Marriage and the Family, Knoxville, Tennessee, April, 1964, as published in the *Journal of Marriage and the Family*, November, 1964, pp. 422–429. Used by permission of the author and the publisher. Robert D. Hess is Professor of Education, University of Chicago.

central part of interaction affects the cognitive development of the young child.

Fourth, that in welfare families, early deprivation, then, is not only economic and emotional, but is most damaging in the restrictions it places upon the mind and educability of the child.

Fifth, [that] if ameliorative action is not taken in the early years, the child's capability to change his position in the social structure is effectively foreclosed.

This brief and simplified model of the maintenance of a social structure through socialization of the young focuses upon the contribution of cognitive and linguistic rather than economic or emotional processes. If it is a valid model, it follows that our present practices will not eliminate the welfare class but will tend to institutionalize it within a publicly financed bureaucratic structure.

In order to illustrate the point, a fantasy may be used for comparison: in a fiendish plot, a nation has decided to promote mental ill health among a segment of its population with a program designed so that its intent is not obvious. A high-level conference of social scientists, psychiatrists, social workers, educators, and other relevant professionals is called to shape the direction of this program. Some of the recommendations for such a project might include the following principles for the promotion of mental ill health:

1. All families involved should be economically dependent on the state and should be maintained at a level which the society considers to be one of marginal subsistence.

2. The family should be disrupted — the fathers must not be permitted in the home under threat of additional economic deprivation.

3. Attempts at self-help and economic improvement will result in punitive action on the part of the state — that is, income earned by any member of the family, even by the children, will be deducted from the monthly allotment.

4. The natural and normal desires of the mother for social and sexual gratification with the father or other males will be frustrated; and such desires, if expressed, will be punished.

5. All families will be subjected to suspicion and implicit accusation. The state will engage the services of an investigative agency which will enter the homes of these families unannounced at odd and unusual hours, against the will of the family, to conduct inspections of the home in an effort to find evidence that may be used to further reduce the economic deprivation of the family unit.

6. The members of these families will be deprived of self-direction and autonomy — they will be acted upon rather than acting.

7. These families will be given a specific legal definition and identity, using such terms as "welfare cases," "on the relief," or such alphabetical designations as "ADC." A public image of these families will be created

through the mass media which portrays them as dishonest, lazy, immoral, and illiterate; occasional public and publicized investigations will reinforce this image.[2]

It is obvious by now that this is not an entirely hypothetical project, but that it bears some resemblance to the regulations and practices under which our welfare programs are now operating. The intent of these programs, of course, is not to damage these families but to assist them. Perhaps it is time to inquire whether the national intent is being served by our present policies. Welfare programs are growing at a rapid rate. Between 1950 and 1962, federal funds to states for Aid to Dependent Children increased from 256 million dollars to 854 million dollars, an increase of more than 300 per cent. (2) Mr. Percy, in his campaign for the governorship of the State of Illinois, described public welfare as the state's fastest growing industry. President Johnson's attack on poverty is likely to increase the proportion of our national resources that is to be devoted to welfare families. These trends are cited not in opposition, but in concern lest the programs developed and developing emerge as structures to deal with the consequences and products of poverty — dropouts, draft rejects, adult illiterates, delinquency, crime — rather than with its basic causes.

The contemporary national concern over poverty makes this an appropriate time to examine the effects of our welfare programs. Such an examination should attempt to determine whether the immediate goals of these programs may have long-term consequences which perpetuate poverty by creating a vast administrative structure to deal with it on a permanent basis. Our present welfare programs should be planned not only for the effects they will have in 1964, but for the impact they will show by 1984. The evidence available suggests that the possibilities for rehabilitation of adults are exceedingly limited. If this is so, we must turn to the task of eliminating poverty and cultural deprivation. Certainly everything reasonably possible should be done to deal with the effects of economic and educational disadvantage at the adolescent and adult levels, but the long-range investment must be coordinated to maximize the positive effects upon the children in these families. This suggests something more than a preventive program, although it includes preventive measures; it is an argument for a positive program directed at the early years, before the warping and crippling atmosphere of deprivation can permanently impair the physical, cognitive, and emotional faculties of the child and assign him an identity as a member of an inferior segment of our society.

Assuming that this general argument has merit and that we may best think of rehabilitation in terms of the young child rather than the parents, how can we assess the influence of poverty and deprivation on the developing resources of the child?

---

[2] The author is indebted for the discussion of the potentially negative impact of ADC programs upon the mental health of the client to David J. Kallen, Bethesda, Maryland, in his unpublished paper, "Some Comments on the Reports of the Joint Commission on Mental Illness and Mental Health and Some Research Suggestions Relevant to Community Mental Health."

The experimental project described in this paper began in this context.[3] The problem of semiliteracy in adults in the United States, although usually ignored, is not new. One of the difficulties that manpower retraining programs encounter is a frequent failure of applicants to pass qualifying exams for the programs. In some areas, of twenty persons who apply, only about three pass the tests which qualify them to enter courses of training that are now available. The method of dealing with adult illiteracy has been a long-range one — through education of children in the public schools so that illiteracy would gradually and eventually disappear from the society. However, the attempts to raise the general level of education of populations in economically depressed areas of this country are, at the present time, inadequate. There is reason to believe that many, if not most, high school students in economically disadvantaged areas are semiliterate when they drop out or graduate from high school. In addition, reports from principals and teachers indicate that in these areas, this educational retardation is present when the child arrives at school; in some schools, one-half to two-thirds of the first-grade pupils are not ready for first-grade work when they enter the school in the fall. Our present system of education seems unable to overcome this handicap, so that by the eighth grade, pupils in large areas of the great cities may be retarded, on the average, by two and one-half academic years.

These trends seem to support the notion that the early years are critical; the goal of the project, therefore, was to study the impact of the home upon the cognitive and motivational behavior of the young child. Orientation for this research goes back to the well-documented association between social class and both academic performance and intelligence, which consistently shows test scores to be relatively low in working-class groups, especially in that socioeconomic level now termed "culturally deprived." This relative deficit in scholastic competence and educability is the essential problem that is facing the schools in metropolitan areas of the United States.[4]

The question the study presents is this: in what way does social class experience affect mental development and scholarship? What happens in the cultural environment that produces behavior which by Grade 7, 8, or 9 results in educational retardation of two or three years?

In this context, the hypothesis of the research is this: In cultural deprivation, the pattern of communication that develops between mother and child has an effect upon the child's cognitive equipment and communication skills which handicaps him when he begins his school program. This is not so much a theory of deficit as a theory of distortion — that is, these

[3] This project is supported by the Research Division of the Children's Bureau, Social Security Administration, U.S. Department of Health, Education, and Welfare; Ford Foundation Fund for the Advancement of Learning; and grants-in-aid from the Social Science Research Committee of the Division of the Social Sciences, University of Chicago.

[4] For its theoretical orientation, this project is indebted to the work of Basil Bernstein, Allison Davis, and Robert J. Havighurst. It also draws somewhat less directly from the ideas of Bruner, Erik Erikson, J. McV. Hunt, Luria, Schachtel, and Vygotsky.

children learn cognitive patterns of responsive behavior and ways of interpreting stimuli from the external world which are not adaptive or functional for academic learning and which prevent the child from taking advantage of cognitive experiences available in a classroom.

This theoretical position follows from the excellent work of Basil Bernstein of the University of London. In Bernstein's view, language structures and conditions what the child learns and how he learns, setting limits within which future learning may take place.[5] He identifies two forms of communication codes or styles of verbal behavior: *restrictive* and *elaborate*.[6] Restrictive codes are stereotyped, limited, and condensed, lacking in specificity and the exactness needed for precise conceptualization and differentiation. Sentences are short, simple, often unfinished; there is little use of subordinate clauses for elaborating the content of the sentence; it is a language of implicit meaning, easily understood and commonly shared. It is the language form often used in impersonal situations when the intent is to promote solidarity or reduce tension. Restrictive codes are nonspecific clichés, statements, or observations about events, made in general terms that will be readily understood. The basic quality of this mode is to limit the range and detail of concept and information involved. That is, it is predictable.

Elaborate codes, however, are those in which communication is individualized and the message is specific to a particular situation, topic, and person. It is more particular, more differentiated, and more precise. It permits expression of a wider and more complex range of thought, tending toward discrimination among cognitive and affective content.

These distinctions may be clarified by two examples of mother-child communication using these two types of codes. Assume that the emotional climate of two homes is approximately the same — the significant difference between them is in style of communication employed. A child is playing noisily in the kitchen with an assortment of pots and pans when the telephone rings. In one home, the mother says, "Be quiet," or "Shut up," or any one of several short, peremptory commands, and she answers the phone while the child sits still on the floor. In the other home, the mother says, "Would you keep quiet while I answer the phone?" The question the study poses is this: What inner response is elicited in the child, what is the effect upon his developing cognitive network of concepts and meaning in each of these two situations? In one instance, the child is asked for a simple mental response. He is asked to attend to an uncomplicated message and to make a conditioned response (to comply); he is not called upon to reflect or to make mental discriminations. In the other example, the child is required to follow two or three ideas. He is asked to relate his

[5] For a full statement of his position see "Social Class and Linguistic Development: A Theory of Social Learning," in *Education, Economy, and Society*, ed. by A. H. Halsey, Jean Floud, and C. Arnold Anderson, Glencoe, Ill.: Free Press, 1961.

[6] Bernstein has used different terms for these two communication modes. In his chapter in Halsey *et. al.*, he calls them "public" (restrictive) and "formal" (elaborative). The terms used in this summary come from more recent papers.

behavior to a time dimension; he must think of his behavior in relation to its effect upon another person. He must perform a more complicated task to follow the communication of his mother in that his relationship to her is mediated in part through concepts and shared ideas; his mind is stimulated or exercised (in an elementary fashion) by a more elaborate and complex verbal communication initiated by the mother. As objects of these two divergent communication styles, repeated in various ways, in similar situations and circumstances during the preschool years, these two imaginary children would be expected to develop significantly different verbal facility and cognitive equipment by the time they enter the public school system.

The orientation of the project is to view the child as an organism which receives a great deal of information of many kinds, much more than he can accommodate. What the child responds to, how he interprets stimuli, and how he reacts to them, are learned in interaction with the environment. He is taught what to attend to, how to interpret messages, and how to respond. These patterns of cognitive activity are socialized in early experience in the home and become the basis upon which further cognitive development proceeds.

The effects of such early experience are not only upon the communication modes and cognitive structure; they also establish potential patterns of relationship with the external world. It is one of the dynamic features of Bernstein's work that he views language as social behavior. As such, language is used by participants of a social network to elaborate and express social and other interpersonal relationships and used in turn to shape and determine these relationships. The integral association between language and social structure is critical for an understanding of the effects of poverty upon children; within the individual family, this association emerges in terms of the principles which govern the decision-making activities, which themselves help regulate the nature and amount of social exchange.

The interlacing of social interaction and language is illustrated by the distinction Bernstein makes between two types of families — those oriented toward control by status appeal or ascribed role norms and those oriented toward *persons*. (1) In status-oriented families, behavior tends to be regulated in terms of role characteristics — children are told to behave in harmony with status and role expectations. There is little opportunity for the unique characteristics of the child to influence the decision-making process or the interaction between parent and child. In these families, the internal or personal status of the children is not influential as a basis for decision. Norms of behavior are stressed with such imperatives as, "You must do this because I say so," or "Boys don't act like that," or other statements which rely on the status of the participants or a behavior norm for justification.

In the person-oriented family, the unique characteristics of the child modify status demands and are taken into account in interaction. The decisions of this type of family are individualized and less frequently related to status or role ascriptions. Behavior is justified in terms of feelings, pref erence, personal and unique reactions, and subjective states. This philoso phy not only permits, but demands, an elaborated linguistic code and a wide range of linguistic and behavioral alternatives in interpersonal inter action. Status-oriented families may be regulated by less individuated com mands, messages, and responses. Indeed, by its nature, the status-oriented family will rely more heavily on a restricted code. The verbal exchange is inherent in the structure, regulates it, and is regulated by it.

This principle of linkage between verbal behavior and structure can readily be extended into two directions of theory and inquiry. It applies to relations between the family and the institutions of the community. In such interaction, the status of the welfare family is reflected in personal and verbal exchanges which solidify the status positions by reducing the discretion available to the low-prestige, inferior-status participant. The range of alternatives to action is limited by the nature of his position in the system. That is, the status of the welfare client is one in which uniqueness and individuality are lost in the necessity to apply, with equal fairness to all, the regulations of the legislative or institutional program. This is the price we, or rather the clients, pay for bureaucratic efficiency and fiscal responsibility. It is inherent in the structure of a welfare program. It is intensified by racial discrimination; the combination of racial prejudice low-class status, and welfare identity is a multiple burden of such propor tions that the resources many of these families reveal in their refusal to capitulate to despair and depression is amazing. We underestimate the physical and psychic energy absorbed by this inner struggle and tend to interpret as lethargy or passivity what is actually the fatigue of depres sion.

The other route that analysis of language and social structure may take is toward an examination of the consequences of linguistic codes and their accompanying patterns of social interaction upon the developing cognitive faculties of the child. Although these effects will be commented upon later, the argument is briefly that person-oriented families tend to justify be havior and emphasize its consequences; status-oriented families ask for rote learning and acceptance of status quo — that is, they use a more rigid learn ing and teaching model, in which order rather than rationale is stressed.

These results are being analyzed for the effect of maternal interaction and teaching styles upon the child. The project is the first of a series of studies of the socialization of educability in the urban matrix.

The concept of educability, as used in this study, is defined as a readiness to learn (in a formal school setting) resulting from a confluence of achieve ment motivation, attitudes toward the school, and an array of cognitive abilities mediated largely through language and other forms of communi cation. The matrix or schemata of responses that develop are socialized and internalized through usual processes of learning in interaction with others. In the early years, this interaction is, of course, primarily with the mother or mother substitute.

In a sense, the project extends the study of mother-child relationships into more specifically cognitive areas of behavior. Studies of mother-child interaction repeatedly have shown the relevance of two primary factors of love-hostility and of control-autonomy. But because such studies typically have not included inquiry into cognitive aspects of interactive behavior, the relevance of the cognitive dimension in maternal behavior has not been carefully explored. Within this rationale, the project has these specific goals:[7]

1. To identify and measure cognitive aspects of mother-child interaction;
2. To identify and examine maternal teaching styles and the effect of these styles upon the cognitive behavior of the child;
3. To study the relation of affective and other nonintellectual aspects of mother-child interaction to the child's motivational and cognitive behavior;
4. To study the physical resources of the homes and their contribution to the development of educability.

A research group of 160 mothers and their four-year-old children was selected to provide variation along four dimensions: socioeconomic background, type of housing, economic dependency status, and intactness of family. All subjects are Negroes, nonworking mothers, free from any obvious mental or physical disabilities. The criteria for selection of subgroups and the composition of each group are:

Group A (N = 40). Professional, executive, and managerial occupational levels; all families living in private housing.
Group B (N = 40). Skilled blue collar occupational levels; one-half from public housing, one-half living in private housing; all families economically self-sufficient; nuclear family structure intact.
Group C (N = 40). Unskilled or semiskilled occupational levels; one-half living in public housing, one-half in private housing; economically self-sufficient; nuclear family structure intact.
Group D (N = 40). Unskilled or semiskilled occupational levels (last employment); one-half from public housing, one-half from private housing; economically dependent on public assistance (ADC); family structure disrupted by absence of father.

These mothers are interviewed twice in their homes and then are brought to the University for testing and for an interaction session between mother and child in which the mother is taught three simple tasks and then asked to teach these tasks to the child. This session is recorded and observed. The three tasks are: (a) sorting several plastic toys and kitchen implements

---

[7] Although this study is restricted (for practical reasons) to the study of maternal influence and style, the significance of the father in interaction with the child in cognitive behavior must not be forgotten. The patterns of father-child exchange undoubtedly differ from those of the mother, but the process of socializing cognitive behavior is likely to be organized about similar dimensions of behavior.

by color and by function (these are to ride in; these are to eat with; etc.) (b) a more complex sorting task, using blocks of varied shape and mark ing; and (c) drawing designs using an etch-a-sketch toy. An etch-a-sketch in a small, flat box with a screen on which lines can be drawn by a device within the box. The marker is controlled by two knobs — one for horizontal movement, one for vertical. The mother is assigned one knob, the child the other. Together they attempt to copy the design models shown them. The mother decides when their product is a satisfactory copy of the original She also estimates in advance how well she and the child will perform. The products are scored by measuring deviations from the original designs.

The project is still in the data-gathering phase, but some trends are al ready apparent. A small part of the research results may be summarized illustrated from the protocols, and grouped under the following headings (a) the mother's image of herself, her relationship to the school, and the techniques she uses to induct the child into the school system; (b) the mother's communication and interaction styles which she uses in teaching the child simple tasks. In all of these, the focus is not so much upon the mother as upon the consequences her behavior will have for the educa bility of the child. Because of the limits of space, middle-class and welfare families will be discussed without making the distinctions or the qualifica tions that ought to be made. One of the prominent features of the data is the tremendous amount of variability that occurs in each of the social class levels; while social class variation will be discussed as if it represented group differences, these differences are actually individual ones which hap pen to be associated with socioeconomic status.

The image that the working-class mother has of the public school is of an institution that is distant, unresponsive, competent, and authoritarian These views, which are easily revealed in conversation, are supported by a more standard type of instrument designed to measure the mother's atti tudes toward the school. On this instrument, responses are complete from almost one-half of the research group. These responses can be paraphrased as follows: In contrast to middle-class mothers, those from the working class hold the following attitudes: (a) they believe that they can do very little to improve the schools; (b) they believe that most children have to be made to learn; (c) they believe that if they disagree with the principal, there is very little they can do. Incidentally, they also believe that edu cation has both economic and subjective consequences: they feel that peo ple who have a great deal of education enjoy life more than those who do not.

In attempting to apply Bernstein's concept of status-oriented and person-oriented families to the data, the investigators analyzed maternal responses to the question: "Imagine your child is old enough to go to public school for the first time. How would you prepare him? What would you tell him?"

One mother, who is person-oriented and uses elaborated verbal codes, replied as follows:

"First of all, I would remind Portia that she was going to school to learn, that her teacher would take my place, and that she would be expected to follow instructions. Also, that her time was to be spent mostly in the classroom with other children and that any questions or any problems that she might have she could consult with her teacher for assistance."

"Anything else?"

"No, anything else would probably be confusing for her at her particular age."

In terms of promoting educability, what has this mother done in this response? First, she has been specific and informative; she has presented the school situation as comparable to one already familiar to the child; second, she has offered reassurance and support to help the child deal with anxiety; third, she has presented the school situation as one which involves a personal relationship between the child and the teacher; and fourth, she has presented the classroom situation as one in which the child is to learn. This orientation toward school fosters confidence and initiative on the part of the child and helps him gear into the school routine by seeing it as an extension of the home situation.

A second mother responds as follows to this question:

"Well, John, it's time to go to school now. You must know how to behave. The first day at school you should be a good boy and should do just what the teacher tells you to do."

In contrast to the first mother, what has this mother done? First, she has defined the role of the child as passive and compliant. Second, the central issues involved in school are in the area of dealing with authority and the institution, rather than with learning. Third, the relationship and roles portrayed are sketched in terms of status and role expectations rather than in personal terms. Fourth, the entire message is general, restricted, and vague, lacking in information about how to deal with the problems of school except by passive compliance.

A third mother offers essentially the same response:

"I would tell her to go to school and be nice. I'd tell her to obey her teacher and to be very good while she's at school."

These responses illustrate the tendency for status-oriented families and relationships to restrict the linguistic codes used in communication and to further reinforce the social network. The child who comes to school with a status orientation is prepared, at best, to engage in rote learning and passive acceptance of school authority in the learning situation. His initiative and participation in the learning possibilities of the school are meager, and the teacher who attempts to engage him in an exchange of ideas or tries to encourage him to inquire and to ask questions will soon be frustrated and disappointed. Not that all such children accept the authority of the school in this unquestioning fashion; the point is that the restrictive interaction in the home and in the accompanying verbal exchanges give them no alternative except to resist and rebel. The range of choice open to them is limited by the nature of the cognitive and interactional environment in which they have had experience.

Again quotes from the mothers illustrate these dynamic differences in cognitive and interactional style in the mother's attempts to socialize her children into behavior appropriate for a school context. In this item, the mothers were asked what they would do if their child talked in class and disturbed the class by mild forms of misbehavior.

One mother says:

"I would try to find out why she must — why she feels she must do these things?"

"Anything else?"

"No, I would wait for her answer before making a decision."

This is perhaps the model of a person-oriented family. In event of conflict between the institution and the child, the mother supports the child in her assumption that whatever the child has done, there must be a good reason for it. Her attention is on the child, not on the infraction or on her own relationship to the school. A second mother says:

"I would just give him a good spanking."

This is, perhaps, a model of a status-oriented family, with little regard for the subjective experiences that are involved. In event of conflict between the child and the institution, the mother supports the institution and, indeed, reinforces it. Of critical importance to the interest in cognitive development, an additional feature of this response is that the mother offers no rationale, no context of meaning which will prepare the child for future encounters with the teacher or other authority figures. The learning is power-oriented, and its contribution to the child's grasp of the world, to the development of his ability to deal with the world by understanding it, is minimal. This may be the most critical aspect of the maternal behavior — the extent to which her actions and words help the child make sense of the world in which he lives and, by making sense of it, becomes more able to deal with and to adapt to it.

The second major point on which this paper reports comes from the observations and recordings of interaction between the mother and child in a more carefully structured teaching situation. The wide range of difference in linguistic and interactional styles of these mothers may be illustrated by excerpts from recordings. The task of the mother is to teach the child how to group or sort a small number of toys. Parenthetically, since the principle of grouping or classifying is basic to many learning situations and mental operations, this task is not simply an elaborate game.

The first mother, who happens to be middle-class, outlines the task for the child, giving sufficient help and explanation to permit the child to proceed alone. She says:

"All right, Susan, this board is the place where we put the little toys; first of all you're supposed to learn how to place them according to color. Can you do that? The things that are all the same color you put in one section; in the second section you put another group of colors; and in the third section you put the last group of colors. Can you do that? Or would you like to see me do it first?"

Child: "I want to do it."

This mother has given explicit information about the task and what is expected of the child; she has offered support and help of various kinds; and she has made it clear that she impelled the child to perform. A second mother's style is not quite so easily grasped by the child. She says, in introducing the same task:

"Now, I'll take them all off the board; now you put them all back on the board. What are these?"

Child: "A truck."

"All right, just put them right here; put the other one right here; all right, put the other one there."

This mother relies more on physical signs and nonverbal communication in her commands; she does not define the task for the child; the child is not provided with ideas or information that she can grasp in attempting to solve the problem; neither is she told what to expect or what the task is, even in general terms.

A third mother is even less explicit. She introduces the task as follows:

"I've got some chairs and cars, does you want to play the game?"

Child does not respond. She continues:

"O.K. What's this?"

Child: "A wagon?"

Mother: "Hm?"

Child: "A wagon?"

Mother: "This no wagon, what's this?"

The conversation continues with this sort of exchange for several pages. Here again, the child is not provided with the essential information he needs to solve or to understand the problem. There is clearly some impelling on the part of the mother for the child to perform, but the child has not been told what he is to do.

The consequences of this sort of exchange affect both the cognitive ability of the child (in that he is not taught how to deal with problems) and also his motivation for achievement and sense of self-confidence because the experience is essentially frustrating.

To date, the research results identify at least three aspects of successful teaching in these interaction situations.[8] First, the mother must provide

[8] The procedure used in this project is to record all physical and verbal behavior of the mother and child while the mother is teaching the child three experimental tasks. These recordings are rated on 22 variables designed to measure: (1) when and how important concepts are introduced; (2) whether opportunities for feedback are provided; (3) how the mother uses feedback to alter her teaching; (4) the use of rewards or punishment to motivate the child; (5) how many bits (discriminations) of information are in each message; (6) the number of words used; and (7) a rating of the level of difficulty of words employed.

her young student with the tags or symbols for the important features of the lesson she hopes to teach. Second, there must be opportunities for her to receive regular feedback from the child. In other words, she must be able to monitor the communication exchange to find out if her child has decoded the message correctly. Finally, she must motivate the child to engage in the learning process. By either rewards or punishment, she must gain and hold the cooperation of the child.

What are the consequences of these styles for the development of motivation toward learning, cognitive flexibility and complexity, and other resources that lead to educability? It is a little premature to make generalizations since careful relating of the behavior of individual children to the teaching styles of their mothers remains to be done. However, some of the differences between middle- and working-class children are in line with the general hypothesis. For example, even at similar I.Q. levels, the child from a working-class home tends to be less curious and to show less initiative than is essential to participation in a learning situation and, indeed, in a society. This behavior appears in both experimental measures of curiosity and in the interaction situations, where it shows as reluctance on the part of the child to ask for clarification or to assert his own questions and opinions in the situation. In short, teaching styles of the mothers in the working class seem to be socializing a passive attitude toward learning on the part of the child in which his own imagination, curiosity, and assertiveness are discouraged, and he is taught to assume the stance of waiting to be told, to receive, and to be acted upon.

In its implications for rehabilitation, it is the contention of this paper that the socialization of communication and interaction modes by the mother reflects not only educational and cultural deprivation, but the family's place in the social structure as well, and that efforts at rehabilitation cannot afford to ignore this basic feature of early learning. If, indeed, these learned modes of verbal and social interaction reinforce the social system and induct the child into patterns of poverty through restricting the range of verbal, social, ideational, and economic opportunities, a rehabilitation program will of necessity be a futile salvage operation unless it deals with the most basic of family processes — the socialization of the young.

REFERENCES

1. "Family Role Systems, Communication, and Socialization," unpublished papers prepared for the Cross-National Conference on Research on Children and Adolescents, University of Chicago, February 20–28, 1964.
2. *Social Security Bulletin,* U.S. Department of Health, Education and Welfare, quoted in *Statistical Abstracts,* 1962–63.

57

Human Needs and the Community

GLENN R. HAWKES

One of the major purposes of organizing a society is to develop mechanisms by which human appetites can be fulfilled. People form into groups in order that their common good can be fulfilled. If an individual's good is not met he seeks out different groups through which he can and will achieve the satisfaction of his appetites. It cannot be stressed too strongly that people become apathetic toward and anxious about ultimate goals they would like to achieve through societal organizations if they continually sense a lack of reliability in the means offered to accomplish these goals. Obviously any society that is to remain alive must satisfy basic needs, provide security, and allow for the realization of value satisfaction and new emerging satisfactions. Such an organization must become the depository of values, must provide symbols for people's aspirations, and must contain customs, institutions, economic arrangements, and political forms which enable an individual to give concrete reference to his values in his day-to-day behavior.

If the gap between what society actually provides in terms of the effective wherewithal for living and what it purports to provide becomes too great the individual becomes frustrated and skeptical and will sooner or later seek a new society in which he does not perceive this great gap. The effective society is one which enables the individual within it to develop personal loyalties because his needs are being met. Aspirations can then follow which are congenial to social values held by the society. In a pluralistic society such as this one, full account must be taken of the wide range of individual differences that exist.

Just as any living thing has to go through one stage before it can develop to the next, so it appears that some of these appetites of human beings must be accommodated before others can blossom and mature. To put it in concrete terms; if a child comes to kindergarten with an empty stomach he is not about to learn the things we want him to learn! If a society cannot organize in a way that allows the satisfaction of basic physiological needs then that society is in trouble. That is to say, it can-

❖ Glenn R. Hawkes is Dean of Family and Consumer Sciences, University of California, Davis.

not hope to become a building and growing society. It will be torn by strife and despair until changes are made.

We need a philosophical framework on which to build programs which free the individual to become a productive member of society — a member who builds and learns because he is *free* to do so. Abraham Maslow gives us such a framework (3). He states that our basic needs are physiological. If these needs are not met we are not ready to move to the next order of needs. The needs are ordered as follows:

1. Physiological needs, such as hunger, thirst, activity, rest.
2. Safety needs, security, and release from anxiety aroused by threats of various kinds.
3. Love needs, including love, affection, acceptance, and a feeling of belonging.
4. Esteem needs, including both self-esteem from mastery and confidence in one's worth, adequacy, and capacities, and esteem from social approval.
5. Need for self-actualization through creative self-expression in personal and social achievements; need to feel free to act, to satisfy one's curiosity, and to understand one's world.

Only as more basic motives (needs) are satisfied, at least to some theoretical minimum, do motives higher in the hierarchy become potent behavior determinants. But when motives lower in the hierarchy are satisfied, then automatically, because of the inherent nature, motives higher in the hierarchy motivate activity and effort. Motivational needs higher in the hierarchy keep man continuously striving as lower needs are satisfied. His striving, however, is toward self-actualization — toward creativity and toward peak experiences which give full meaning to life. The opportunity to strive toward self-actualization is an opportunity demanded by the enlightened person from a functional society.

If a love-drive is curtailed by fear, the fearful person will not let himself go. If his hunger drive has not been satiated, it will overcome the fear of punishment. Only when the lower, primary needs are satisfied, can the higher needs (motives) come into play. To understand this hierarchy of needs in the human personality is to understand why we cannot expect too much of people living in slums and disadvantaged areas, where daily life is a continual struggle to appease hunger and to ward off fears.

When hunger and fear are reduced, love needs can make themselves manifest. When love needs are permitted gratification, the needs of esteem and self-actualization can develop. But it is nearly impossible to have the higher motives until the lower ones have been gratified.

It is foolish and Utopian to expect disadvantaged people living in degradation to pull themselves up by their psychic bootstraps. True, a few extraordinary individuals seem to have the "stuff" to do this, but the vast bulk are crushed under the weight of their condition.

Wanting the esteem of society, and possessing self-esteem, are later and higher motives in the development of personality. To ask the disadvantaged to care about art, books, science, civic responsibility and financial integrity is like asking a hungry and frightened baby to "act like a grown-up."
As Maslow states:

> From Freud we learned that the past exists now in the person. Now we must learn, from growth theory and self-actualization theory, that the future also now exists in the person in the form of ideals, hopes, duties, tasks, plans, goals, unrealized potentials, mission fate, destiny, etc. One for whom no future exists is reduced to the concrete, to hopelessness, to emptiness. For him, time must be endlessly "filled." Striving, the usual organizer of most activity, when lost, leaves the person unorganized and unintegrated. (3, pp. 199–200)

Hadley Cantril suggests seven requirements the individual places on society (1). He makes it clear that if these requirements are not met then the individual cannot mature to his full capabilities. While all of us have a responsibility to help shape and form our culture it is abundantly clear that leaders exert more influence than others; therefore it follows their responsibilities are greater.

His first requirement is that an individual must have the opportunity to develop a sense of personal identity and integrity. He states that each person craves a sense of his own self-constancy. This constancy he obtains from the transactions he has with other individuals. If these transactions are satisfying he builds up loyalties. These loyalties develop from sharing significances with other people. Loyalties of this sort play a real role in meeting our needs for esteem.

A sense of worthwhileness is listed as the second requirement the individual places on society. This is referred to as an individual's desire for a feeling of self-respect rooted in a faith in his own values and experienced when he confirms the reality of these values in his own day-to-day behavior.

Our senses of self-constancy and of worthwhileness are preserved only if we have the third requirement — a sense of community. It is necessary that the individual recognize the source of his personal identity and strength: from his family, his neighbors, his associates or fellow workers, and his group ties or his nation. Cantril suggests this sense of community is becoming increasingly difficult to experience in the great urban areas of the world, so many of which are burgeoning in planless fashion or are, if planned, often designed with standards of efficiency or technology in mind rather than the need for community participation. Clearly, it is necessary to place a prime value on the needs of human beings in neighborhood and/or civic planning. The symbol of our time should not be the bulldozer but rather the human being with his changing and developing needs — from childhood on through old age.

The fourth requirement is the opportunity to enlarge one's sense of self in both space and time. The opportunity must exist for the individual to develop social, regional, and national loyalties that enable him to extend himself backward into the past and forward into the future. Each one accomplishes this through the opportunity to use and then create symbols, images, and myths which provide focal points for identification and self-expansion. A very real problem of the American Negro is the lack of symbols, images, and myths which are not self degrading. The opportunity is rather for him to diminish his stature if he looks back. Only when he is allowed to participate on equal footing as an American can he use the symbols, images, and myths which allow the middle-class Caucasian American the opportunity for enlargement of self.

A sense of personal development, a sense of direction, a feeling of process and progress, describes the fifth requirement which the individual places on society. This requirement refers to the feeling that one's life is a continuous creation in which one can take an active part. There is a feeling that one has some control over direction of his fate, not necessarily in all ways, but at least often enough to give one a sense of personal development. In our modern and complex society this sense is not always easy to come by. Our society is complex and there are forces which frighten and dismay even the most confident among us. Nonetheless it is vital to the continued development of the individual that he obtain satisfactions in this area often enough to have the feeling of, at least, shared responsibility for his own destiny.

We crave some certainties, some beliefs, some faith if we are not to be overwhelmed by uncertainties and anxieties. This sense of commitment is the sixth requirement the individual places on his society. Such a sense of commitment helps us define what is right and wrong, good and bad, and what direction our actions should take. In an uncertain world one can often be panicked into vigorous effort to find controls which give us these certainties at the expense of allowing for individual differences and beliefs. The maturing person seeks from society some certainties and some room for continued debate and change and knowledge and circumstances change. A society to be fulfilling must provide opportunity for both.

The seventh requirement listed by Cantril is a need for societal mechanisms which will ensure the satisfaction of the human appetites. In effect we are being told that a society must organize itself in such a way that the physiological needs, security needs, love needs, and esteem needs can be met. Our economic system must be such that there is opportunity for the growth and development of each one of us. This requirement, although listed last by Cantril, is basic in an orderly society. Without the mechanisms to meet these basic needs the individual can not be free to become a self actualized agent of his own fate. He becomes, rather, caught up in a cycle of desperation which discourages, inhibits, and finally relegates him to a secondary place in his own existence. The individual becomes ensnared in a drive to fill his time with nonessentials because a responsibility for his own direction is denied him.

In examining the role of society and the role of the individual in attempts to prevent and circumvent disadvantaging conditions, it is necessary to see

the backdrop of the interrelationships between an individual and his society. It is also necessary to examine the forces in the society which may
be used constructively to prevent damaging conditions. The family of the
individual, this primary of all primary groups, is undoubtedly where the
forces have their greatest initial potency. Any society building program
in this culture must have as its primary goal the strengthening of the family
as an institution geared to cope with day-to-day problems. This, because
for all the class differences in family structure and function, the family
bears the first responsibility for the developing child.

The world of the infant is bounded by those who have first responsibility
for his care. His sense of trust, autonomy, and initiative depends upon
his family meeting his needs. His physical health depends upon his family's
ability to buy the necessary foods and their knowledge of how to get this
food to him. Their ability to find medical help, to pay for it, and to know
when to seek it will affect the child's development, perhaps his very survival. If the arrival of another "mouth to feed" carries the threat of trouble
for the other family members it is easy to see why love needs may not be
met.

Duhl and Chayes (2) use an interesting analogy to describe the relationship among the individual, his family, and society.

In a bedspring where each coil is connected to its neighbor, the central
coil might be considered the individual and the coils immediately surrounding it would then represent the nuclear family. From these radiate
the extended family and beyond them the community, the state, and the
nation. Thus, when pressure is put on the individual — on the central coil
— his ability to bear it depends upon both his own strength and the support of the surrounding coils — his family and the coils which surround
and support the family. The pressure might be illness, a psychological
crisis, work, or economic problems. The individual is rarely strong enough
to take the pressure alone and the family — the surrounding coils — must
take some of the strain if the whole network is not to sag. Where there is
a weakening of extended family ties, the support of those coils is reduced
and the stress is shunted outward to the next surrounding ring of coils —
the community and particularly those agencies in the community designed
to help out in such situations.

The need for agency help can be reduced if the strength of the central
coil and the immediately surrounding coils is increased; if the individual
and his family are strengthened and able to bear life's pressures with an
ever-decreasing amount of outside help (2, p. 584).

If strengthening of the child's family can occur early there is much
greater chance of building the kinds of competencies needed for growth
and development. There is ample evidence that the life-style developed
in the first few years largely determines the kind of life-style which will
perpetuate during the person's life. The life-style developed in the middle
class essentially fulfills the current value system espoused by our culture.
That is to say, the child's view of himself is positive and building. He is

led to believe that society will provide the opportunities for him to move toward his full potential. Not so with the child from the disadvantaged segment of our society. He learns early that he will be passed by. He learns early that the endless maze of societies, institutions and agencies seems to circumvent helping him. He has drilled into him the culture of the disadvantaged.

Basically the culture of the disadvantaged is one of hopelessness and despair. A wall is built by the individual and his family to protect him from what he believes to be an unresponsive society. He learns that schools do not speak his language. His interest in achievement is dulled because his older siblings and his parents have found that schools do not equip him for the fight he faces to get his basic needs met. He learns the uselessness of drive and education. He learns jobs are not forthcoming and attempts to get help are frustrated by the cross-purposes of society's helping agencies and institutions. This pattern of despair is reinforced with experience and passed in a kind of social heredity fashion from generation to generation. This life condition constantly widens the gap between the middle-class culture and the culture of the disadvantaged.

Homes of this sort are pervaded by a kind of chronic romance with difficulty. Resources, meager as they are, are not used wisely. People who have not learned to cope with the demands and enticements of our complex economic structure buy worthless and shoddy materials. They are seduced into overextensions of credit and by inefficiency in their planning for the future. They are easy to exploit. And exploiters seem to be all around. It is small wonder that the disadvantaged become disenchanted with the ways of society which our middle-class premises about life have developed.

The mid-1960 approach to diminishing the disadvantaged segment of our society needs to be dualistic in nature. We must refashion our social agencies and institutions on a human and family building nature. Furthermore we need to intervene early in attempt to prevent the pyramiding of social attitudes and learnings which tend to perpetuate the culture of the disadvantaged. The great illiterate minority (children) have the right to ask what their communities can do for them. And children have a right to ask this question because it is at the community level, after the family, where needs are first met or not met. It is at this level where we create programs which will give a child the opportunity to grow and develop to his maximum. It is within the community framework where we institutionalize teaching a child how to learn, that learning is exciting, that it is fun, and that life is worth living.

Social mechanisms must put first things first. We cannot make headway in changing social conditions if we do not set up procedures whereby physiological needs can be met. The old axiom that an army travels on its stomach is as true for a society. Some way needs to be found to reduce the glaring inconsistency of overproduction of foodstuffs and hunger. Both exist in this affluent society. A community attempting to reduce the effects of the disadvantaging conditions would be well advised to make certain food is available for all of its people and that the source of this foodstuff is as secure as modern conditions can make it. Following the theory of Maslow, a community should then turn its attention to the problems of security. The freedom from fear is essential if the individual is to move gradually toward the point of self-actualization. Protective agencies within the community will need to be coordinated in such a fashion that they are nonthreatening to this population who because of previous experience tend to see such protective agencies as a threat to their security rather than as protective of it. The policeman, for example, is often perceived as an impediment to freedom. He curtails rather than facilitates the societal interactions of the disadvantaged group. The many "Don't" signs which we erect to facilitate adequate social intercourse are often perceived as a direct affront to this group because of the restrictive nature of their environment.

The lack of esteem-building experiences can often be construed as a hurdle in the opportunity to properly fulfill the esteem needs. Personal questioning, which middle-class citizens would greatly resent, are common everyday experience. In some public housing developments, for instance, if there is a question about the moral character of the prospective tenant he is not allowed to live there. To insure the proper moral climate questions such as the following are commonplace: "Are your children legitimate?" "Can you prove you are married to your husband (wife)?" "Can you prove all of these children are fathered by the same man?"

Moreover the lack of job opportunities for males often has the net effect of making him feel less than a man. In many cases the wife must become the breadwinner. His ability to protect and care for his family as a husband and father is reduced to a shadow of the commonly held stereotypes of what a mature man should and can be. Small wonder then if he undervalues his own worth when a community has said in effect, "you are not valued." The model a man so buffeted by life can project for his children is greatly curtailed. Their budding concepts of manliness must, of necessity, be distorted from the norms commonly projected by the middle class. A dilution of the potentialities of the male role becomes a part of the child's understanding of husband and father.

To expect an individual to develop to the point of self-actualization is highly unrealistic when opportunities for growth and development are not provided within the community setting. A sense of personal identity, of worthwhileness, and self-constancy, cannot and will not come when the individual is denied the opportunity to participate in the transactions of his own society.

Our society fraught with problems may not be as much in need of redemption as a recognition of the new social problems we are uncovering. We need the vision to see problems and the maturity to face up to them. We are likely to think it is not worth doing the little each of us can do. But all that is done, the greatest that is done, will be made up of the acts of individual people and dedicated groups. We should re-examine our efforts and re-plan the organizations of our communities around human needs and particularly the needs of the great illiterate minority — children. Our chances of success seem to be correlated with our willingness to start early so as to break the cycle of frustration, the cycle of despair, and the cycle of failure.

REFERENCES

1. Cantril, Hadley. "The Individual's Demand on Society," in Seymour M. Farber and Roger H. L. Wilson (eds.), *Conflict and Creativity*. New York: McGraw-Hill Book Co., Inc., 1963.

2. Duhl, Leonard J., and Antonia H. Chayes. "Individual, Family and Community," *Journal of Home Economics*, 56:579–585; October, 1964.

3. Maslow, Abraham. *Toward a Psychology of Being*. New York: D. Van Nostrand Company, Inc., 1962.

✧ BIBLIOGRAPHY

A. BOOKS AND MONOGRAPHS

Allen, James E., Jr. *An Assessment of the All-Day Neighborhood School Program for Culturally Deprived Children.* Albany, N.Y.: State Department of Education, December 8, 1961.

American Psychological Association. *Today's Educational Programs for Culturally Deprived Children,* Report of Section II, The Seventh Annual Professional Institute of the Division of School Psychologists. St. Louis: The Association, 1962.

Association for Childhood Education International. *When Children Move from School to School,* Membership Service Bulletin. Washington: The Association, 1960.

Bagdikian, Ben H. *In the Midst of Plenty: A New Report on the Poor in America.* New York: Signet Books, 1964.

Baker, Augusta. *Books About Negro Life for Children.* New York: The New York Public Library, 1963.

Bayley, Nancy. "Mental Growth in Young Children," in the *Thirty-Ninth Yearbook of the National Society for the Study of Education, Part II.* Bloomington, Ill.: Public School Publishing Company, 1940.

Berea College. *Rural School Improvement Project.* Lexington, Ky.: Transylvania Printing Company, 1958.

Bernstein, Basil. "Social Class and Linguistic Development: A Theory of Social Learning," in A. H. Halsey, J. Floud, and C. A. Anderson (eds.), *Economy, Education and Society.* New York: The Free Press of Glencoe, 1961.

Bloom, Benjamin S. *Stability and Change in Human Characteristics.* New York: John Wiley & Sons, Inc., 1964.

Board of Education of the City of New York, Bureau of Educational Research. *The Demonstration Guidance Project: Annual Progress Report, 1957–1958, 1958–1959, 1959–1960, 1960–1961.* New York: The Board of Education, n.d.

Brooks, Melvin S. *The Social Problems of Migrant Farm Laborers.* Carbondale, Ill.: Southern Illinois University, Department of Sociology, 1960.

Brown, William L., and Ben H. Phelper. *Red, White, and Black.* New York: 20th Century Publishers, Inc., 1964.

Bruner, Jerome S. *The Process of Education.* Cambridge, Mass.: Harvard University Press, 1961.

Burchill, George (ed.). *Work-Study Programs for Alienated Youth: A Casebook.* Chicago: Science Research Associates, Inc., 1962.

Caplovitz, David. *The Poor Pay More.* New York: Free Press of Glencoe, 1963.

Caudill, Harry M. *Night Comes to the Cumberlands, a Biography of a Depressed Area.* Boston: Little, Brown & Company, 1962.

Children in Migrant Families. U.S. Department of Health, Education and Welfare, Social Security Administration, Children's Bureau. Washington: Government Printing Office, December, 1960.

Close, Herman L., and Ruth S. Irvin. "The Cooperative Junior High School: A Program for Disadvantaged Youth," in the *Guidance Bulletin of Florida State University,* Vol. 10, June, 1963.

Conant, James B. *Slums and Suburbs.* New York: McGraw-Hill Book Co., Inc., 1961.

Davis, Allison. "Child Training and Social Class," in R. G. Barker, J. S. Kounin, and H. F. Wright (eds.), *Child Behavior and Development.* New York: McGraw-Hill Book Co., Inc., 1963.

————. *Social Class Influences Upon Learning.* Cambridge, Mass.: Harvard University Press, 1948.

————. "The Future Education of Children from Low Socio-Economic Groups," in T. M. Stinnett (ed.), *New Dimensions for Educational Progress.* Bloomington, Ind.: Phi Delta Kappa, 1963.

Denenberg, V. H. "The Effects of Early Experience," in E. S. E. Hafez (ed.), *The Behavior of Domestic Animals.* London: Balliere, Tindall, and Koch, 1962.

Deutsch, Martin. "Some Psycho-Social Aspects of Learning in the Disadvantaged," in *Mental Health and Educational Achievement.* Englewood Cliffs, N.J.: Prentice-Hall, Inc., 1964.

Dollard, John. *Caste and Class in a Southern Town.* New Haven, Conn.: Yale University Press, 1937.

Education and Poverty. A portfolio of the major addresses delivered at the second annual conference of the National Committee for Support of the Public Schools. Washington: National Committee for Support of the Public Schools, 1964.

Eells, Kenneth W., et al. *Intelligence and Cultural Differences.* Chicago: University of Chicago Press, 1951.

Fiske, D. W., and S. R. Maddi. *Functions of Varied Experience.* Homewood, Ill.: Dorsey Press, 1961.

Flavell, John H. *The Developmental Psychology of Jean Piaget.* Princeton, N.J.: D. Van Nostrand Co., Inc., 1963.

Fraser, D. M. "Experimental Approaches to Preparing Teachers for Work with Culturally Handicapped Children," in the *New York Society for Experimental Study of Education Yearbook.* New York: The Society, 1961.

Frazier, Alexander. *A Program for Poorly Languaged Children.* Columbus, Ohio: The Ohio State University, College of Education Center for School Experimentation, October, 1963.

Fresno County Project. "The Educational Program for Migrant Children," in *Teaching Children Who Move With the Crops.* Fresno, Calif.: Walter G. Martin, Fresno County Superintendent of Schools, September, 1955.

Frost, Joe L. "School Environment and Disadvantaged Children," *Collected Papers of the Inter-Institutional Seminar in Child Development.* Dearborn, Mich.: The Edison Institute, June, 1965.

Giles, H. Harry. *The Integrated Classroom.* New York: Basic Books, Inc., 1959.

Ginzberg, Eli, and Douglas W. Bray. *The Uneducated.* New York: Columbia University Press, 1953.

Gordon, Edmund W. "Social Status Differences: Counseling and Guidance for Disadvantaged Groups," in Daniel Schreiber (ed.), *Guidance and the School Dropout.* Washington: National Education Association, 1964.

Graham, Jory. *Handbook for Project Head Start.* New York: Anti-Defamation League of B'nai B'rith, 1965.

Handlin, Oscar. *The Uprooted.* Boston: Little, Brown & Company, 1951.

Haney, George. *Selected State Programs in Migrant Education,* U.S. Department of Health, Education and Welfare, Office of Education. Washington: Government Printing Office, 1963.

Harrington, Michael. *The Other America: Poverty in the United States.* New York: The MacMillan Co., 1962.

Havighurst, Robert, and Hilda Taba. *Adolescent Character and Personality.* New York: John Wiley & Sons, Inc., 1949.

Hawkes, Glenn R. *Helping Children Understand Themselves.* NEA Elementary Instructional Service. Washington: National Education Association, 1965.

Hebb, Donald O. *The Organization of Behavior.* New York: John Wiley & Sons, Inc., 1949.

Hechinger, Fred M. (ed.). *Pre-School Education Today.* Garden City, N.Y.: Doubleday & Company, Inc., 1966.

Holbrook, David. *English for the Rejected.* New York: Cambridge University Press, 1965.

Homer, Dorothy. *The Negro: A List of Significant Books.* New York: The New York Public Library, 1960.

Hunt, J. McV. *Intelligence and Experience.* New York: The Ronald Press Company, 1961.

Janowitz, Gayle. *Helping Hands: Volunteer Work in Education.* Chicago: University of Chicago Press, 1965.

Jewett, Arno, Joseph Mersand, and Doris Gunderson. *Improving English Skills of Culturally Different Youth in Large Cities,* U.S. Department of Health, Education and Welfare, Office of Education. Washington: Government Printing Office, 1964.

Kerber, August, and Barbara Bommarito. *The Schools and the Urban Crisis.* New York: Holt, Rinehart & Winston, Inc., 1965.

Keyserling, Leon H. *Progress or Poverty.* Washington: Conference on Economic Progress, December, 1964.

Klopf, G. J. and I. A. Laster (eds.). *Integrating the Urban School.* New York: Columbia University Teachers College, Bureau of Publications, 1963.

Landers, Jacob. *Higher Horizons Progress Report.* New York: Board of Education of the City of New York, January, 1963.

Lewis, Oscar. *The Children of Sanchez.* New York: Random House, Inc., 1961.

Migrant Child Care Centers and Services, Department of Public Welfare, Office of Children and Youth. Harrisburg, Pa.: The Department, 1960.

Migratory Labor in Ohio Agriculture, A Report of the Governor's Committee, Division of Labor Statistics. Columbus, Ohio: The Division, 1962.

Miller, Herman P. *Rich Man, Poor Man.* New York: Signet Books, 1965.

Miller, Leonard M. *References on Dropouts,* U.S. Department of Health, Education and Welfare, Office of Education. Washington: Government Printing Office, October, 1962.

Morgan, James N., *et al. Income and Welfare in the United States.* New York: McGraw-Hill Book Co., Inc., 1962.

Myrdal, Gunnar. *An American Dilemma.* New York: Harper & Brothers, 1944.

National Education Association, Educational Policies Commission. *Education and the Disadvantaged American.* Washington: The Association, 1962.

———, Research Division and American Association of School Administrators. *School Programs for the Disadvantaged.* Washington: The Association, 1962.

Orshansky, Mollie, and Thomas Karter. *Economic and Social Status of the Negro in the United States, 1961.* New York: The National Urban League, 1961.

Passow, Harry. *Education in Depressed Areas.* New York: Columbia University Press, 1963.

Patterson, Franklin (ed.). *Secondary Education for Disadvantaged Urban Youth: A Colloquy.* Medford, Mass.: Tufts University, Lincoln-Filene Center for Citizenship and Public Affairs, 1964.

Pettigrew, Thomas F. *A Profile of the Negro American.* Princeton, N.J.: D. Van Nostrand Co., Inc., 1964.

Piaget, Jean. *Play, Dreams, and Imitation in Childhood.* New York: W. W. Norton & Company, Inc., 1951.

———. *The Origins of Intelligence in Children.* New York: International University Press, 1962.

———. *The Psychology of Intelligence.* Paterson, N.J.: Littlefield, Adams & Company, 1960.

Rambusch, Nancy McC. *Learning How to Learn: An American Approach to Montessori.* Baltimore: Helicon Press, 1962.

Raushenbush, Elizabeth B. *The Migrant Labor Problem in Wisconsin.* Madison, Wisc.: Governor's Commission on Human Rights, 1962.

Ravitz, Mel. *The Role of the School in the Urban Setting: Depressed Areas,* paper delivered at Work Conference on Curriculum and Teaching in Depressed Urban Areas, Columbia University Teachers College, July 2–13, 1962.

Ribble, Margaret. "Infantile Experience in Relation to Personality Development," in J. McV. Hunt (ed.), *Personality and Behavior Disorders.* New York: The Ronald Press Company, 1944.

Riessman, Frank. *Alternative Strategies for the Education of the Disadvantaged.* New Brunswick, N.J.: Rutgers University Press, October, 1963.

———. *The Culturally Deprived Child.* New York: Harper & Brothers, 1962.

Rittwagen, Marjorie. *Sins of Their Fathers*. Boston: Houghton Mifflin Company, 1958.

Rivlin, Harry N. *Teachers for the Schools in Our Big Cities*. New York: University of the City of New York, Division of Teacher Education, 1962.

Saltzman, Henry. "The Great Cities Program," in Thomas Shirrard (ed.), *Community Organization*. New York: Columbia University Press, 1961.

Schreiber, Daniel (ed.). *Guidance and the School Dropout*. Washington: National Education Association, 1964.

————. *The Higher Horizons Program: First Annual Progress Report, 1959–1960*. New York: Board of Education of the City of New York, n.d.

Sexton, Patricia. *Education and Income*. New York: The Viking Press, 1961.

Silverman, Susan B. *Selected Annotated Bibliography of Research Relevant to Education and Cultural Deprivation*, Bibliography for Conference on Research Problems of Education and Cultural Deprivation. Chicago: University of Chicago, 1964.

Spodek, Bernard (ed.). *Preparing Teachers of Disadvantaged Young Children*. Summary of a conference of NDEA Institutes for Teachers of Disadvantaged Youth. New York: National Association for the Education of Young Children, 1966.

Stoddard, G. D., and Beth L. Wellman. "Environment and the I.Q.," in the *Thirty-Ninth Yearbook of the National Society for the Study of Education*, Bloomington, Ill.: Public School Publishing Company, 1940.

Strom, Robert D. *Teaching in the Slum School*. Columbus, Ohio: Charles E. Merrill Books, Inc., 1965.

Sutton, Elizabeth. *Knowing and Teaching the Migrant Child*. Washington: National Education Association, Department of Rural Education, 1962.

Taba, Hilda. *Curriculum Development: Theory and Practice*. New York: Harcourt, Brace & World, Inc., 1962.

Thomas, Donald. *Determining an Effective Educational Program for Children of Migratory Workers in Wisconsin: Phase I*. Madison, Wisc.: University of Wisconsin, School of Education, 1961.

Torrance, E. Paul, and Robert D. Strom (eds.). *Mental Health and Achievement: Increasing Potential and Reducing School Dropout*. New York: John Wiley & Sons, Inc., 1965.

U.S. Department of Health, Education and Welfare, Office of Education. *Programs for the Educationally Disadvantaged: A Report of a Conference on Teaching Children and Youth Who Are Educationally Disadvantaged*, Bulletin No. 17, 1963. Washington: Government Printing Office, 1963.

————. *The Education of Migrant Children: Questions and Answers*. Washington: Government Printing Office, 1963.

Utah State Department of Public Instruction. *Utah State Dropout Study, 1962–63*. Salt Lake City, Utah: The Department, October, 1963.

Warner, Lloyd W., Robert J. Havighurst, and Martin B. Loeb. *Who Shall Be Educated?* New York: Harper & Brothers, 1944.

Washington State Department of Public Instruction. *Dropouts: Washington's Wasted Resource.* Olympia, Wash.: The Department, March, 1963.

Whipple, Gertrude. "Culturally and Socially Deprived Reader," in *Underachiever in Reading,* Proceedings of the Annual Conference on Reading, Vol. 24, Supplementary Educational Monographs, No. 92. Chicago: University of Chicago Press, 1962.

Wiener, Norbert. *Cybernetics.* New York: John Wiley & Sons, Inc., 1948.

Woodworth, R. S. *Heredity and Environment: A Critical Study of Recently Published Material on Twins and Foster Children,* Social Science Research Council Bulletin, No. 47. New York: Social Science Research Council, 1941.

Yeshiva University Graduate School of Education. *Guidance for Socially and Culturally Disadvantaged Children and Youth.* New York: The University, 1963.

Yeshiva University. *Northern School Desegregation: Progress and Problems.* New York: The University, 1962.

Young, Leontine. *Wednesday's Children.* New York: McGraw-Hill Book Co., Inc., 1964.

Youth in the Ghetto. New York: Harlem Youth Opportunities Unlimited, Inc., 1964.

B. PERIODICALS

Arnez, Nancy L. "The Effect of Teacher Attitudes Upon the Culturally Different," *School and Society,* 94: 149–152; March 19, 1966.

Asbell, Bernard. "Not Like Other Children," *Redbook,* 121:64–65; October, 1963.

Ausubel, David P. "A Teaching Strategy for Culturally Deprived Pupils: Cognitive and Motivational Considerations," *School Review,* 71:454–463; Winter, 1963.

Baldwin, James. "A Talk to Teachers," *Saturday Review,* 46:42–44; December 21, 1963.

Barber, Bernard. "Social Class Differences in Educational Life-Chances," *Teachers College Record,* 63:102–129; November, 1961.

Baynham, Dorsey. "Great Cities Project," *NEA Journal,* 52:17–20; April, 1963.

Beavers, Irene. "Contributions Home Economics Can Make to Low-Income Families," *Journal of Home Economics,* 57:107–111; February, 1965.

Bellenger, Mary Ellen. "Guidance for the Disaffected," *Educational Leadership,* 20:294–297; February, 1963.

Bender, Louis W., and William G. Sharpe. "Junior High School Course for Disadvantaged Students," *National Association of Secondary School Principals Bulletin,* 47:128–131; March, 1963.

Berlin, Irving N. "Special Learning Problems of Deprived Children," *NEA Journal,* 55: 23–24; March, 1966.

Bernstein, Basil. "Language and Social Class," *British Journal of Sociology,* 11:271–276; 1960.

———. "Social Class, Linguistic Codes, and Grammatical Elements," *Language and Speech,* 5:221–240; October-December, 1962.

Bloom, Sophie. "Improving the Education of Culturally Deprived Children: Applying Learning Theory to Classroom Instruction," *Chicago Schools Journal,* 45:126–131; December, 1963.

Blumenson, G. T. "How To Wipe out Educational and Cultural Blight," *CTA Journal,* 59:16–18; March, 1963.

Boutwell, W. D. "What's Happening in Education: Information on What Various Cities are Doing for Children of the Poor and Less Educated," *PTA Magazine,* 58:25–26; December, 1963.

Brazziel, William F., and M. Gordon. "Replications of Some Aspects of the Higher Horizons Program in a Southern Junior High School," *National Association of Secondary School Principals Bulletin,* 47:135–143; March, 1963.

Brewer, John. "Stirrings in the Big Cities: Pittsburgh," *NEA Journal,* 51:14–17; September, 1962.

Brown, Harriett B., and Elinor D. Sinnette. "The School Library Program for Children in a Depressed Area," *American Library Association Bulletin,* 58: 643–647; July-August, 1964.

Bruner, Jerome S. "The Course of Cognitive Growth," *American Psychologist,* 19:1–15; 1964.

Burchinal, Lee, Bruce Gardner, and Glenn R. Hawkes. "Children's Personality Adjustment and the Socio-Economic Status of their Families," *Journal of Genetic Psychology,* 92:149–159; 1958.

Clift, V. A. "Factors Relating to the Education of Culturally Deprived Negro Youth," *Educational Theory,* 14:76–82; April, 1964.

Cohn, Werner. "On the Language of Lower Class Children," *School Review,* 67:435–440; Winter, 1959.

Crandall, Virginia. "Achievement Behavior in Young Children," *Young Children,* 20:77–90; November, 1964.

Crosby, Muriel. "Portrait of Blight," *Educational Leadership,* 20:300–304; February, 1963.

Cunningham, William. "Stirrings in the Big Cities: Boston," *NEA Journal,* 51:48–50; October, 1962.

Cutts, Warren. "Reading Unreadiness in the Underprivileged," *NEA Journal,* 52:23–24; April, 1963.

———. "Special Language Problems of the Culturally Deprived," *Clearing House,* 37:80–83; October, 1962.

Daniel, William G. "Editorial Comment: Educational Planning for Socially Disadvantaged Children and Youth," *Journal of Negro Education,* 33:203–209; Summer, 1964.

Darling, Richard L. "School Library Services for the Culturally Deprived Child," *School Life,* 46:18–20; October, 1963.

Daugherty, Louise G. "Working with Disadvantaged Parents." *NEA Journal,* 52:18–20; December, 1963.

Della-Dora, Delmo. "Culturally Disadvantaged: Educational Implications of Certain Social-cultural Phenomena," *Exceptional Children,* 28:467–472; May, 1962.

———. "Culturally Disadvantaged: Further Observations." *Exceptional Children,* 29:226–236; January, 1963.

Deutsch, Martin. "Facilitating Development in the Preschool Child: Social and Psychological Perspectives," *Merrill-Palmer Quarterly,* 10:249–263; July, 1964.

———, and Bert Brown. "Social Influences in Negro-White Differences," *Journal of Social Issues,* 20:24–35; April, 1964.

Dickey, Frank G. "Frontal Attack on Cultural Deprivation," *Phi Delta Kappan,* 45:398–400; May, 1964.

"Disadvantaged: A Symposium, The," *NEA Journal,* 52:16–30, April, 1963.

Downing, Gertrude L. "Supervision Experiment with the Disadvantaged," *Educational Leadership,* 21:433–435, 445; April, 1964.

Druding, Aleda. "Stirrings in the Big Cities: Philadelphia," *NEA Journal,* 51:48–51; February, 1962.

Duhl, Leonard J., and Antonia Handler Chayes. "Individual, Family, and Community," *Journal of Home Economics,* October, 1964.

Duvall, Evelyn M., and Daniel Schreiber. "Low-Down on Dropouts," *PTA Magazine,* 58:4–6, 36–37; November, 1963.

"Education and the Disadvantaged American," *NEA Journal,* 51:4; April, 1962.

Educational Leadership, 22 (7); May, 1965.

"Educational Planning for Socially Disadvantaged Children and Youth," *Journal of Negro Education,* 33:203–366; Summer, 1964.

Elam, Stanley (ed.). "Educating the Culturally Deprived in the Great Cities," *Phi Delta Kappan,* 45:70–100; November, 1963.

Elmer, Elizabeth. "Identification of Abused Children," *Children,* 10:180; September-October, 1963.

English, Walter. "Minority Group Attitudes of Negroes and Implications for Guidance," *Journal of Negro Education,* 26:99–107; 1957.

Epstein, Lenore. "Unmet Needs in a Land of Abundance," *Social Security Bulletin,* July, 1963.

Evans, Harley, and George Womer. "Stirrings in the Big Cities: Cleveland," *NEA Journal,* 51:50–53; November, 1962.

"Federal Legislation and Programs for Underprivileged Young People," *American Library Association Bulletin,* 58: 705–708; September, 1964.

Feldman, Shirley. "A Pre-School Enrichment Program for Disadvantaged Children," *New Era,* 45:79–82; 1964.

Foster, Florence P. "Premature Independence in Preschools for the Disadvantaged," *Young Children,* 21: 142–150; January, 1966.

———. "The Song Within: Music and the Disadvantaged Child," *Young Children,* 20: 373–376; September, 1965.

Frazier, Alexander. "Broadening the Experiences of the Culturally Disadvantaged," *American Library Association Bulletin,* 58:523–526; June, 1964.

———. "Teaching the Culturally Deprived," *National Elementary Principal,* 42:16–19; February, 1963.

Fremont, Herbert. "Some Thoughts on Teaching Mathematics to Disadvantaged Groups," *Arithmetic Teacher,* 11:319–322; May, 1964.

Frost, Joe L. "School and the Migrant Child," *Childhood Education,* 41:129–132; November, 1964.

Frost, Joe L., and O. Ray King. "Educating Disadvantaged Children," *Arkansas Education Association Journal*, 37:6, 28; September, 1964.

Fusco, G. C. "Preparing the City Child for His School," *School Life*, 46:5–8; May, 1964.

Goff, Regina A. "Curriculum as a Source of Psychological Strength for the Negro Child," *Educational Administration and Supervision*, 38:293–301; May, 1952.

Goldberg, Miriam L. "Adapting Teacher Style to Pupil Differences: Teachers for Disadvantaged Children," *Merrill-Palmer Quarterly*, 10:161–178; April, 1964.

Goodman, Paul. "Don't Jail the Young," *American Child*, 46:3–7; May, 1964.

Gordon, Edmund W. "A Question of Culture," *American Child*, March, 1963.

Grambs, Jean D. "The Culturally Deprived Child," *Education Digest*, 30:1–4; January, 1965.

Green, Myrtle, and H. B. Gardner. "Stirrings in the Big Cities: Kansas City," *NEA Journal*, 51:34–36; December, 1962.

Groff, Patrick J. "Dissatisfactions in Teaching the Culturally Deprived Child," *Phi Delta Kappan*, 45:70–76; November, 1963.

Haney, George E. "Problems and Trends in Migrant Education," *School Life*, 45:5–9; July, 1963.

Harrison, E. C. "Working at Improving the Motivational and Achievement Levels of the Deprived," *Journal of Negro Education*, 32:301–307; Summer, 1963.

Haubrich, Vernon. "The Culturally Different: New Context for Teacher Education," *Journal of Teacher Education*, 14:163–167; June, 1963.

Havighurst, Robert J. "Conditions Favorable and Detrimental to the Development of Talent," *School Review*, 65:20–26; March, 1957.

————. "Knowledge of Class Status Can Make a Difference," *Progressive Education*, 27:100–105; February, 1950.

————. "Who Are the Socially Disadvantaged?" *Journal of Negro Education*, 33:210–217; Summer, 1964.

Hawkes, Glenn R. "Building Self-Image in Preschoolers," *Instructor*, 75: 27–54; January, 1966.

————. "The Not-Yet-Literate Minority," *Journal of Nursery Education*, 19:98–99; January, 1964.

Hayes, Harry. "Some Ways to Teach Culturally Deprived Children," *Chicago Schools Journal*, 45:221–228; February, 1964.

Heald, James E. "In Defense of Middle-Class Values," *Phi Delta Kappan*, 46:18–83; October, 1964.

Hersey, John. "Education: An Antidote to Poverty," *Young Children*, 21: 66–72; November, 1965.

Hess, Robert D. "Educability and Rehabilitation: The Future of the Welfare Class," *Journal of Marriage and the Family*, 26:422–429; November, 1964.

Hines, R. H. "Social Expectations and Cultural Deprivation," *Journal of Negro Education*, 33:136–142; Spring, 1964.

Hosley, E. "Culturally Deprived Children in Day-Care Programs," *Children*, 10:175–179; September, 1963.

Hott, Irving. "School Administrator and the 'Educationally Disadvantaged' Child," *Bulletin of the National Association of Secondary School Principals,* 48:85–98; March, 1964.

Hughes, Byron O. "Implications of Heredity for Education," University of Michigan School of Education *Bulletin,* 18:41–44; 1946.

Hughson, Arthur. "The Case For Intelligence Testing," *Phi Delta Kappan,* 46:106–108; November, 1964.

Humphreys, Lloyd G. "The Organization of Human Abilities," *American Psychologist,* 17:475–483; 1962.

Hunt, J. McV. "How Children Develop Intellectually," *Children,* 11:83–91; May, 1964.

————. "Piaget's Observations as a Source of Hypotheses Concerning Motivation," *Merrill-Palmer Quarterly,* 9:263–275; 1963.

————. "The Psychological Basis for Using Preschool Enrichment as an Antidote for Cultural Deprivation," (Report of Arden House Conference on Preschool Enrichment of Socially Disadvantaged Children, December 16, 1962, Harriman, New York), *Merrill-Palmer Quarterly,* 110:209–248; July, 1964.

Hunter, Madeline C. "Stirrings in the Big Cities: Los Angeles," *NEA Journal,* 51:18–20; April, 1962.

Isenberg, Robert M. "The Rural Disadvantaged," *NEA Journal,* 52:27; April, 1963.

Israel, B. L. "An Approach to Teaching Children Handicapped by Limited Experience," *Minnemath Center Reports,* 2:4–6; Autumn, 1964.

Jaffa, Neubert N. "The Disadvantaged Child: The Potential Dropout," *The Instructor,* 74:23; December, 1964.

John, Vera P. "The Intellectual Development of Slum Children: Some Preliminary Findings," *American Journal of Orthopsychiatry,* 33:813–822; 1963.

Kaplan, Bernard A. "Issues in Educating the Culturally Disadvantaged," *Phi Delta Kappan,* 45:70–76; November, 1963.

————. "Can We Afford Misery?" *Journal of Nursery Education,* 19:89–95; January, 1964.

Kelley, Earl C. "Seeds of Drop-Outs," *Childhood Education,* 39:420–422; May, 1963.

Kerckhoff, Richard K. "Race and Social Class as Opportunities for Early Childhood Education," *Young Children,* 20: 357–362; September, 1965.

Kirman, J. M. "Teacher Survival in Difficult Schools," *High Points,* 46:69–70; April, 1964.

Klineberg, Otto. "Life is Fun in a Smiling, Fair-Skinned World," *Saturday Review,* 46:75–77; February 16, 1963.

Kornberg, Leonard. "Slum Children and New Teachers," *Journal of Negro Education,* 32:74–80; Winter, 1963.

————. "The Culturally Deprived Child in School," *NEA Journal,* 50:23–24; April, 1961.

Kvaraceus, William C. "Helping the Socially Handicapped Pupil in the Large City Schools," *Exceptional Children,* 28:399–404; April, 1962.

Landes, Ruth. "Cultural Factors in Counseling," *Journal of General Education,* 15:55–67; April, 1963.

Larson, Richard, and James L. Olson. "Method of Identifying Culturally Deprived Kindergarten Children," *Exceptional Children,* 30:130–134; November, 1963.

Lawson, David. "Culture and Education: Definitions and Relations," *Educational Forum,* 28:449–456; May, 1964.

Layton, Warren K. "Special Services for the Dropout and the Potential Dropout," *National Association of Secondary School Principals Bulletin.* 37:72–76; March, 1953.

Lee, Ralph. "Stirrings in the Big Cities: Detroit," *NEA Journal,* 51:34–37; March, 1962.

Levine, Daniel V. "City Schools Today — Too Late With Too Little," *Phi Delta Kappan,* 44:18–83; 1962.

Lewis, Frederick H. "Teachers in a Depressed Area: Most Important Quality for the Teachers of Disadvantaged Children Is Compassion." *Clearing House,* 30:497–498; April, 1956.

Lisonbee, Lorenzo. "Teaching Science to the Disadvantaged Pupil," *Science Teacher,* 30:18–21; October, 1963.

Liston, Margaret I. "Profiles of Poverty," *Journal of the American Association of University Women,* 58:12–14; October, 1964.

Lowrie, Jean (ed.). "Providing School Library Services for the Culturally Deprived," *American Library Association Bulletin,* 58:523–526, 643–647, 705–711; June-September, 1964.

Maleska, Eugene. "Stirrings in the Big Cities: New York," *NEA Journal,* 51:20–22; May, 1962.

Malkin, Samuel. "The Culturally Deprived Child and Science," *Science and Children,* 1:5–7; April, 1964.

Mayer, Martin. "The Good Slum Schools," *Harpers,* 222:46–52; June, 1961.

Mays, J. B. "Social Disadvantage and Education," *Educational Research,* 5:2–9; November, 1962.

McAteer, J. E. "Equality of Opportunity Must be Real," *CTA Journal,* 60:14–15; March, 1964.

Metz, F. Elizabeth. "Poverty, Early Language Deprivation, and Learning Ability," *Elementary English,* 43: 129–133; February, 1966.

Mukerji, Rose, and Helen F. Robison, "Teaching Strategies for Disadvantaged Kindergarten Children," *Young Children,* 21: 195–199; March, 1966.

National Council of Family Relations Journal, November, 1964.

Newton, Eunice S. "Culturally Disadvantaged Child in Our Verbal Schools," *Journal of Negro Education.* 31:184–187; Spring, 1962.

————, and Earle H. West. "The Progress of the Negro in Elementary and Secondary Education," *Journal of Negro Education,* 32:466–484; Fall, 1963.

Norman, Sherwood. "Children Deprived of Belonging," *Journal of Nursery Education,* 18:285; September, 1963.

O'Hara, James M. "Disadvantaged Newcomers to the City," *NEA Journal*, 52:25–27; April, 1963.

Olsen, James. "Children of the Ghetto," *High Points*, 46:25–33; March, 1964.

Ornstein, A. C. "Teacher Training for Difficult Schools," *Journal of Secondary Education*, 39:172–173; April, 1964.

Orshansky, Mollie. "Children of the Poor," *Social Security Bulletin*, July, 1963.

————. "Counting the Poor: Another Look at the Poverty Profile," *Social Security Bulletin*, January, 1965.

Ozmon, Howard A. "A Realistic Approach to the Writing of Children's Textbooks for Deprived Areas," *Elementary English*, 30:534–535; December, 1960.

Paschal, Billy J. "A Concerned Teacher Makes the Difference," *The Arithmetic Teacher*, 13: 203–205; March, 1966.

Passy, Robert A. "Socio-Economic Status and Mathematics Achievement," *Arithmetic Teacher*, 11:459–470; November, 1964.

Patin, H. A. "Class and Caste in Urban Education," *Chicago Schools Journal*, 45:305–310; April, 1964.

Peters, R. M. "Teacher Looks at Culturally Deprived Children," *Chicago Schools Journal*, 45:22–25; October, 1963.

Pettigrew, Thomas F. "Negro American Intelligence: A New Look at an Old Controversy," *Journal of Negro Education*, 33:6–25; Winter, 1964.

Phillips, Waldo B. "Counseling Negro Pupils: An Educational Dilemma," *Journal of Negro Education*, 29:504–507; Winter, 1960.

————. "Role of the Counselor in the Guidance of Negro Students: Reply to D. L. Trueblood," *Harvard Educational Review*, 31:324–326; Summer, 1961.

"Preschool Plan is Ripe Dream Without Funds: School Administrators' Opinion Poll," *Nation's Schools*, 74:48; August, 1964.

"Preschool Programs Strive to Start Deprived Children on Par With Others," *Nation's Schools*, 73:84; June, 1964.

Rabinow, Barney. "Training Program for Teachers of the Emotionally Disturbed and the Socially Maladjusted," *Exceptional Children*, 26:287–293; February, 1960.

Redl, H. B. "What Else Should You Know About Children You Teach?" *Instructor*, 73:108; September, 1963.

Rehage, K. J. "Culturally Deprived Child," *Elementary School Journal*, 63:186; January, 1963.

Riessman, Frank. "The Culturally Deprived Child: A New View," *School Life*, 45:5–7; 1963.

————. "The Overlooked Positives of Disadvantaged Groups," *Journal of Negro Education*, 33:225–231; Summer, 1964.

————. "Styles of Learning," *NEA Journal*, 55: 15–17; March, 1966.

————, and Arlene Hannah. "Teachers of the Poor," *PTA Magazine*. 59:12–14; November, 1964.

Rosen, B. C. "Family Structure and Value Transmission," *Merrill-Palmer Quarterly*, 10:59–76; January, 1964.

Rousseve, Ronald J. "Teachers of Culturally Disadvantaged American Youth," *Journal of Negro Education,* 32:114–121; Spring, 1963.

Schmidt, H. D. "Bigotry in School Children," *Commentary,* 29:253–257; March, 1960.

Sears, Pauline, and H. Levin. "Level of Aspiration in Preschool Children," *Child Development,* 28:317–326; 1957.

Shaw, Frederick. "Educating Culturally Deprived Youth in Urban Centers," *Phi Delta Kappan,* 45:91–97; November, 1963.

Siebert, Edna M. "Stirrings in the Big Cities: Chicago," *NEA Journal,* 51:8–12; January, 1962.

Silberman, C. E. "Give Slum Children A Chance: A Radical Proposal," *Harper's,* 228:37–42; April, 1964.

Silverstein, A. B., and others. "Cultural Factors in the Intellectual Functioning of the Mentally Retarded," *American Journal of Mental Deficiency,* 67:396–401; November, 1962.

Simon, William R. "Southern White Migrants: Ethnicity and Pseudo-Ethnicity," *Human Development,* 1:20–24; Summer, 1960.

Sloane, Frank O., and Pat Tornillo. "Stirrings in the Big Cities: Miami," *NEA Journal,* 52:14–16; January, 1963.

Smiley, M. B. "Who Would Teach Here," *PTA Magazine,* 58:16–19; September, 1963.

Spiegler, Charles G. "A Cure For Allergy to Reading," *Education Digest,* 29:35–38; April, 1964.

Spodek, Bernard. "Poverty, Education, and the Young Child," *Young Children,* 21: 2–8; October, 1965.

Steiner, G. J. "Educating the Culturally Disadvantaged," *Chicago Schools Journal,* 44:31–32; October, 1962.

Stull, E. G. "Reading Materials for the Disadvantaged: from Yaki to Tlingit to Kotzebue," *Reading Teacher,* 17:522–527; April, 1964.

Tannenbaum, Abraham. "Family Living in Textbook Town," *Progressive Education,* 31:133–140, 166–167; March, 1954.

Tenenbaum, Samuel. "The Teacher, the Middle Class, the Lower Class," *Phi Delta Kappan,* 45:86; November, 1963.

Tomlinson, Ethel. "Language Arts Skills Needed by Lower Class Children," *Elementary English,* 33:279–283; May, 1956.

Trueblood, Dennis L. "The Role of the Counselor in the Guidance of Negro Students," *Harvard Educational Review,* 30:252–269; Summer, 1960.

U.S. Department of Health, Education and Welfare, Office of Education, Elementary Schools Section. "The Elementary School in the City: Special Effort for the Disadvantaged Child," *School Life,* 45:26–29; June, 1963.

Utter, Lawrence W. "Helping Our Culturally Impoverished Children," *NEA Journal,* 52:28–30; November, 1963.

Vance, Barbara J. "Social Learning Theory and Guidance in Early Childhood," *Young Children*, 21: 30–42; October, 1965.

Voinovich, M. J. "Parent-Teacher Relationship Contributes to Pupil Success," *Ohio Schools*, 42:42; March, 1964.

Wolman, Thelma G. "A Preschool Program for Disadvantaged Children—The New Rochelle Story," *Young Children*, 21: 98–111; November, 1965.

Ware, Kay. "English Programs for the Culturally Different: Significant Aspects of the St. Louis Program," *Elementary English*, 40:611–614; October, 1963.

Whipple, Gertrude. "Multi-Cultural Primers for Today's Children," *Education Digest*, 29:26–29; February, 1964.

Whiteman, Martin. "Intelligence and Learning," *Merrill-Palmer Quarterly*, 10:297–309; July, 1964.

Wilkerson, Doxey A. "Bibliography on the Education of Socially Disadvantaged Children and Youth," *Journal of Negro Education*, 33:358–366; Summer, 1964.

———. "Prevailing and Needed Emphasis in Research on the Education of Disadvantaged Children and Youth," *Journal of Negro Education*, 33:346–357; Summer, 1964.

Willie, C. V. "Anti-Social Behavior Among Disadvantaged Youth: Some Observations on Prevention for Teachers," *Journal of Negro Education*, 33:175–181; Spring, 1964.

Witmer, Helen L. "Children and Poverty," *Children*, 2:207–213; November-December, 1964.

Wolf, Eleanor P., and Leo Wolf. "Sociological Perspective on the Education of Culturally Deprived Children," *School Review*, 70:373–387; Winter, 1962.

Wolfe, Deborah P. "Curriculum Adaptations for the Culturally Deprived," *Journal of Negro Education*, 31:139–151; Spring, 1962.

Wolgamot, Irene H. "Low-Income Groups," *Journal of Home Economics*, 56:27–39; January, 1964.

Wolman, Marianne. "Cultural Factors and Creativity," *Journal of Secondary Education*, 37:454–460; December, 1962.

Wood, Nancy. "Summer School Help for Migrant Workers' Children," *NEA Journal*, 51:18–19, May, 1962.

Wrenn, C. G. "Culturally Encapsulated Counselor," *Harvard Educational Review*, 32:444–449; Fall, 1962.

Wrightstone, Jacob W. "Discovering and Stimulating Culturally Deprived Talented Youth," *Teachers College Record*, 60:23–27; October, 1958.

Youmans, E. Grant. "Factors in Educational Attainment," *Rural Sociology*, 24:21–28; March, 1959.

Yourman, Julius. "The Case Against Group I.Q. Testing," *Phi Delta Kappan*, 46:108–110; November, 1964.

C. RESEARCH STUDIES

Abrahamson, Stephen. "School Rewards and Social Class Status," *Educational Research Bulletin*, 31:8–15; January, 1952.

Arnez, Nancy. "A Study of Attitudes of Negro Pupils Toward Their School," *Journal of Negro Education*, 32:289–293; Summer, 1963.

Battle, Esther S., and J. B. Rotter. "Children's Feeling of Personal Control as Related to Social Class and Ethnic Group," *Journal of Personality*, 31:482–490; 1963.

Bexton, William H., Woodburn Heron, and T. H. Scott. "Effects of Decreased Variation in the Sensory Environment," *Canadian Journal of Psychology*, 8:70–76; 1954.

Bledsoe, Joseph C. "An Investigation of Six Correlates of Student Withdrawal from High School," *Journal of Educational Research*, 53:3–6; September, 1959.

Boger, Jack H. "An Experimental Study of the Effects of Perceptual Training on Group I.Q. Scores of Elementary Pupils in Rural Ungraded Schools," *Journal of Educational Research*, 46:43–53; 1952.

Boyd, G. F. "The Levels of Aspirations of White and Negro Children in a Non-Segregated Elementary School," *Journal of Social Psychology*, 36:191–196; 1952.

Brazziel, William F. and Mary Terrell. "An Experiment in the Development of Readiness in a Culturally Disadvantaged Group of First Grade Children," *Journal of Negro Education*, 31:4–7; Winter, 1962.

Clark, Kenneth B., and Mamie P. Clark. "Emotional Factors in Racial Identification and Preference in Negro Children," *Journal of Negro Education*, 29:341–350; 1950.

Crandall, Virginia, W. Katkovsky, and Anne Preston. "A Conceptual Formulation of Some Research on Children's Achievement Development," *Child Development*, 31:787–797; 1960.

Davidson, Helen H., and Gerhard Lang. "Children's Perception of Their Teachers' Feelings Toward Them Related to Self-Perception, School Achievement, and Behavior," *Journal of Experimental Education*, 39:107–118; December, 1960.

Dennis, Wayne. "Causes of Retardation Among Institutional Children," *Journal of Genetic Psychology*, 96:47–59; 1960.

——, and Marsena G. Dennis. "Infant Development Under Conditions of Restricted Practice and Minimum Social Stimulation: A Preliminary Report," *Journal of Genetic Psychology*, 53:151–156; 1938.

——. "Infant Development Under Conditions of Restricted Practice and Minimum Social Stimulation," *Genetic Psychology Monographs*, 23:149–155, 1941.

——. "The Effect of Cradling Practice Upon the Onset of Walking in Hopi Children," *Journal of Genetic Psychology*, 56:77–86; 1940.

——. "The Effect of Restricted Practice Upon the Reaching, Sitting, and Standing of Two Infants," *Journal of Genetic Psychology*, 47:21–29, 1935.

Deutsch, Martin. "Minority Group and Class Status as Related to Social and Personality Factors in Scholastic Achievement," *Society for Applied Anthropology*, 1960, No. 2. Ithaca, N.Y.: Cornell University, 1960.

——. "Some Psycho-Social Aspects of Learning in the Disadvantaged," in *Mental Health and Educational Achievement*. Englewood Cliffs, N.J.: Prentice-Hall, Inc., 1964.

Duncan, C. P. "Transfer in Motor Learning as a Function of Degree of First-Task and Inter-Task Similarity," *Journal of Experimental Psychology*, 45:1–11; 1953.

Feldhusen, John F., and Herbert J. Klausmeier. "Anxiety, Intelligence, and Achievement in Children of Low, Average, and High Intelligence," *Child Development*, 33:403–409; 1962.

Forgays, Donald G. "Subject Characteristics and the Selective Influence of Enriched Experience in Early Life," symposium paper presented at a meeting of the American Psychological Association, Philadelphia, August, 1963.

Fowler, William. "Cognitive Stimulation, I.Q. Changes, and Cognitive Learning in Three-Year-Old Identical Twins and Triplets," *American Psychologist*, 16:373; 1961 (abstract).

————. "Teaching a Two-Year-Old to Read: An Experiment in Early Childhood Learning," *Genetic Psychology Monographs*, 66:181–283; 1962.

Frost, Joe L. "Effects of Enrichment Program on Personality Development of Disadvantaged Children," *Childhood Education*, 42:271–272; December, 1965.

————. "Welfare Recipiency Status and School Achievement of Rural Elementary School Children," *Association for Research Growth Relationships Journal*, 6: 13–22; November, 1964.

Gauron, E. F. and W. C. Becker. "The Effects of Early Sensory Deprivation on Adult Rat Behavior Under Competition Stress: An Attempt at Replication of a Study by Alexander Wolf," *Journal of Comparative Physiology*, 52:689–693, 1959.

Gill, Lois J. and Bernard Spilka. "Some Non-Intellectual Correlates of Academic Achievement Among Mexican-American Secondary School Students," *Journal of Educational Psychology*, 53:144–149; 1962.

Gist, Noel P., and William S. Bennett, Jr. "Aspirations of Negro and White Students," *Social Forces*, 42:40–48; October, 1963.

Goddard, H. H. *The Kallikak Family: A Study in the Heredity of Feeble-Mindedness.* New York: The Macmillan Co., 1912.

Goff, Regina M. "Some Educational Implications of the Influence of Rejection on Aspiration Levels of Minority Group Children," *Journal of Experimental Education*, 23:179–183; 1954.

Goldman, Jacquelin R. "The Effects of Handling and Shocking in Infancy upon Adult Behavior in the Albino Rat," *Journal of Genetic Psychology*, 104: 102; 1964.

Gordon, Edmund W. "Characteristics of Socially Disadvantaged Children," *Review of Educational Research*, 35: 377–388; December, 1965.

Gough, Harrison G. "The Relationship of Socio-Economic Status to Personality Inventory and Achievement Test Scores," *Journal of Educational Psychology*, 37:527–540; 1946.

Grann, Lloyd R., and Associates. "The Relationship Between Academic Achievement of Pupils and the Social Structure of the Classroom," *Rural Sociology*, 21:179–180; June, 1956.

Gray, Susan W., and Rupert A. Klaus. "An Experimental Preschool Program for Culturally Deprived Children," *Child Development*, 36: 887–898; December, 1965.

Grotberg, Edith H. "Learning Disabilities and Remediation in Disadvantaged Children," *Review of Educational Research*, 35: 413–425; December, 1965.

Haggard, Ernest A. "Social Status and Intelligence: An Experimental Study of Certain Cultural Determinants of Measured Intelligence," *Genetic Psychology Monographs*, 49:141–186; 1954

Hansen, Carl F. "The Scholastic Performances of Negro and White Pupils in the Integrated Public Schools of the District of Columbia," *Harvard Educational Review,* 30:216–236; Summer, 1960.

Hebb, Donald O. "The Effects of Early Experience on Problem-Solving at Maturity," *American Psychologist,* 2:306–307; 1947.

Hess, Robert D., and Virginia C. Shipman. "Early Experience and the Socialization of Cognitive Modes in Children," *Child Development,* 36: 869–886; December, 1965.

Hilgard, Josephine R. "Learning and Maturation in Pre-School Children," *Journal of Genetic Psychology,* 41:36–56; 1932.

John, Vera P., and Leo S. Goldstein. "The Social Context of Language Acquisition," *Merrill-Palmer Quarterly,* 10:265–275; July, 1964.

Justman, Joseph. "Academic Aptitude and Reading Test Scores of Disadvantaged Children Showing Varying Degrees of Mobility," *Journal of Educational Measurement,* 2: 151–155; December, 1965.

Kagan, Jerome, and others. "Personality and I.Q. Change," *Journal of Abnormal Social Psychology,* 56:261–266; 1958.

Karp, Joan M. and Irving Sigel. "Psychoeducational Appraisal of Disadvantaged Children," *Review of Educational Research,* 35: 401–412; December, 1965.

Katkovsky, Walter, Anne Preston, and Virginia J. Crandall. "Parents' Attitudes Toward Their Personal Achievements and Toward the Achievement Behaviors of Their Children," *Journal of Genetic Psychology,* 104:67–82; 1964.

Katz, Irwin. *Review of Evidence Relating to Effects of Desegregation on the Intellectual Performance of Negroes,* ONR Technical Report, No. 8. New York: New York University, Research Center for Human Relations, 1964.

Klineberg, Otto. "Negro-White Differences in Intelligence Test Performance: A New Look at an Old Problem," *American Psychologist,* 4:198–203; April, 1963.

Levinson, Boris M. "Subcultural Variations in Verbal and Performance Ability at the Elementary School Level," *Journal of Genetic Psychology,* 97:149–160; September, 1960.

McCandless, Boyd, and Alfred Castaneda. "Anxiety in Children, School Achievement, and Intelligence," *Child Development,* 27:379–382; 1956.

McCord, William. "Negro Versus White Intelligence: A Continuing Controversy," *Harvard Educational Review,* 28:120–135; Spring, 1958.

Melzack, Ronald, and T. H. Scott. "The Effects of Early Experience on the Response to Pain," *Journal of Comparative and Physiological Psychology,* 50:155–161; 1957.

———, and William R. Thompson. "Effects of Early Experience on Social Behavior," *Canadian Journal of Psychology,* 10:82–90; 1956.

Montague, D. O. "Arithmetic Concepts of Kindergarten Children in Contrasting Socio-Economic Areas," *Elementary School Journal,* 64:393–397; 1964.

Moriber, Leonard. *School Functioning of Pupils Born in Other Areas and in New York City,* Pamphet No. 168, May, 1961. New York: Board of Education of the City of New York, 1961.

National Education Association, Educational Research Service. *School Program for the Disadvantaged*. Washington: The Association, 1963.

Osborne, R. Travis. "Racial Differences in Mental Growth and School Achievement: A Longitudinal Study," *Psychological Reports*, 7:233–239; 1960.

Pasamanick, Benjamin, and Hilda Knoblock. "Early Language Behavior in Negro Children and the Testing of Intelligence," *Journal of Abnormal and Social Psychology*, 50:401–402; 1955.

———. "The Contribution of Some Organic Factors to School Retardation in Negro Children," *The Journal of Negro Education*, 27:4–9; 1958.

Piaget, Jean, and Bärbel Inhelder. "Diagnosis of Mental Operations and Theory of Intelligence," *American Journal of Mental Deficiency*, 51:401–406; 1947.

Raph, Jane Beasley. "Language Development in Socially Disadvantaged Children," *Review of Educational Research*, 35: 389–400; December, 1965.

Sackett, Gene P. "Effects of Rearing Conditions Upon the Behavior of Rhesus Monkeys (Macca Mulatta)," *Child Development*, 36: 855–868; December 1965.

Schreiber, Daniel. "The Dropout and Delinquent: Promising Practices Gleaned from a Year of Study," *Phi Delta Kappan*, 44: 215–221, February, 1963.

Schultz, Raymond E. "A Comparison of Negro Pupils Ranking High with Those Ranking Low in Educational Achievement," *Journal of Educational Sociology*, 31:265–270; March, 1958.

Semler, Ira J., and Ira Iscoe. "Comparative and Developmental Study of the Learning Abilities of Negro and White Children Under Four Conditions," *Journal of Educational Psychology*, 54:38–44; 1963.

Skeels, Harold M. "Effects of Adoption on Children from Institutions," *Children* 12:33–34; January-February, 1965.

Stallings, Frank H. "A Study of the Immediate Effects of Integration on Scholastic Achievement in the Louisville Public Schools," *Journal of Negro Education* 28:439–444; Fall, 1959.

Swift, Joan W. "Effects of Early Group Experiment: The Nursery School and Day Nursery," in M. L. Hoffman and L. W. Hoffman, *Review of Child Development Research*. New York: Russell Sage Foundation, 1964.

Thomas, Robert J. "An Empirical Study of High School Dropouts in Regard to Ten Possible Related Factors," *Journal of Educational Sociology*, 28:11–18 September, 1954.

Thompson, William R., and Woodburn Heron. "The Effects of Restricting Early Experience on the Problem-solving Capacity of Dogs," *Canadian Journal of Psychology*, 8:17–31; 1954.

Wakefield, Robert A. "An Investigation of the Family Backgrounds of Educable Mentally Retarded Children in Special Classes," *Exceptional Children*, 31:143–146; November, 1964.

Weiskrantz, Lawrence. "Sensory Deprivation and the Cat's Optic Nervous System," *Nature*, 181:1047–1050; April 12, 1958.

Wilkerson, Doxey A. "Programs and Practices in Compensatory Education for Disadvantaged Children," *Review of Educational Research*, 35: 426–440; December, 1965.

Wilson, Margaret, J. M. Warren, and Lynn Abbott. "Infantile Stimulation, Activity, and Learning by Cats," *Child Development*, 36: 843–853; December, 1965.

SOLANO COLLEGE
100 Whitney Avenue
Vallejo, California 94590

PB 0007724
547-06